P9-CCP-646

INSIDERS' GUIDE® TO

TWIN CITIES

SEVENTH EDITION

JAY GABLER

INSIDERS' GUIDE

GUILFORD, CONNECTICUT
AN IMPRINT OF GLOBE PEQUOT PRESS

To my cousin Sara Vargas, who took me to the 7th Street Entry for my first concert.

All the information in this guidebook is subject to change. We recommend that you call ahead to obtain current information before traveling.

To buy books in quantity for corporate use or incentives, call **(800) 962–0973** or e-mail **premiums@GlobePequot.com.**

INSIDERS' GUIDE ®

Editor: Amy Lyons
Project Editor: Heather M. Santiago
Text Design: Sheryl Kober
Maps: XNR Productions, Inc. © Morris Book Publishing, LLC

ISSN 1525-7460
ISBN 978-0-7627-5703-9

Printed in the United States of America
10 9 8 7 6 5 4 3 2 1

CONTENTS

CONTENTS

Directory of Maps

ABOUT THE AUTHOR

Jay Gabler is a writer, editor, and college teacher who grew up in St. Paul and Duluth and now lives in Minneapolis. He is associate editor of the *Twin Cities Daily Planet,* where he serves as arts editor and frequently writes reviews, features, and blog entries about local happenings. He also teaches at Rasmussen College. His previous books are *Reconstructing the University* (with David John Frank, Stanford University Press, 2006) and *Sociology for Dummies* (Wiley, 2010).

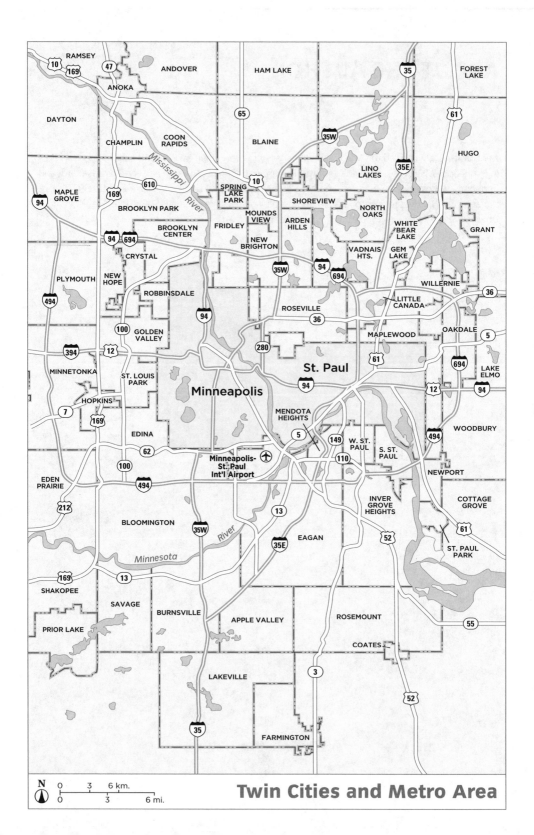

Twin Cities and Metro Area

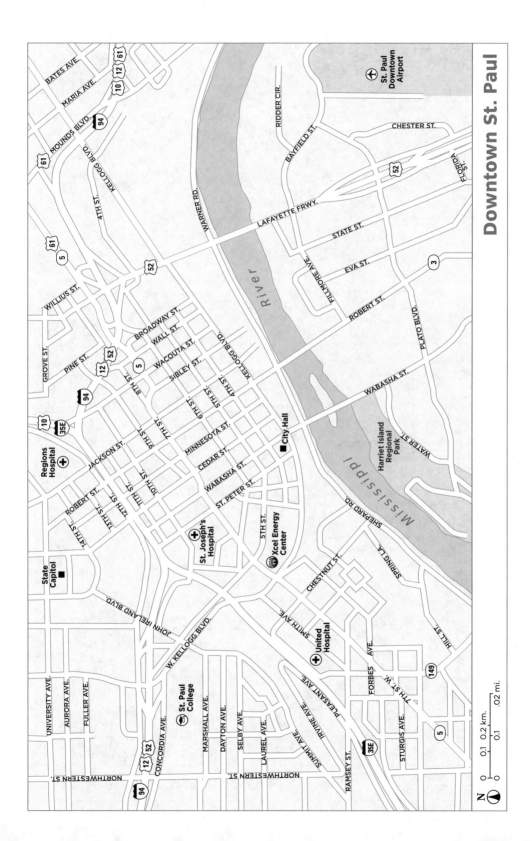

Downtown St. Paul

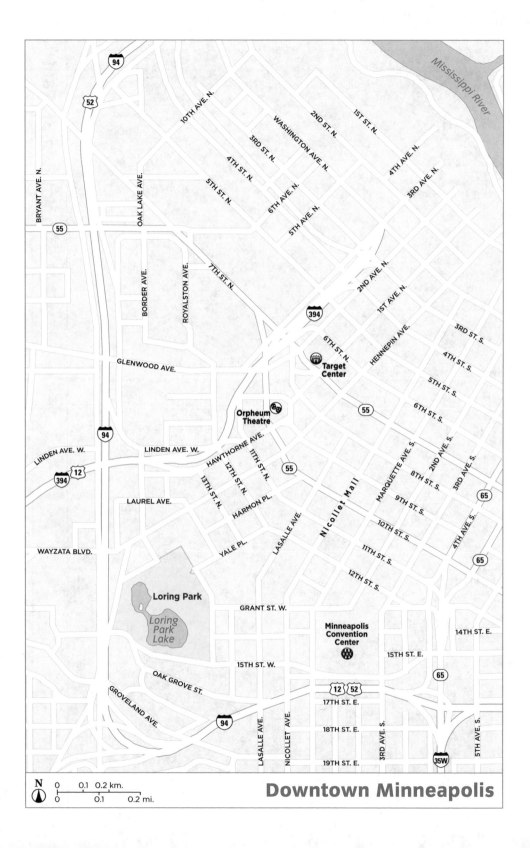

Downtown Minneapolis

Mississippi River

94
52
55

10TH AVE. N.
WASHINGTON AVE. N.
2ND ST. N.
1ST ST. N.
3RD ST. N.
4TH AVE. N.
4TH ST. N.
6TH AVE. N.
3RD AVE. N.
5TH ST. N.
5TH AVE. N.

BRYANT AVE. N.
OAK LAKE AVE.
BORDER AVE.
ROYALSTON AVE.
7TH ST. N.

2ND AVE. N.
394
1ST AVE. N.
3RD ST. S.
6TH ST. N.
HENNEPIN AVE.
4TH ST. S.
Target Center
5TH ST. S.
GLENWOOD AVE.
55
6TH ST. S.
Orpheum Theatre

LINDEN AVE. W.
LINDEN AVE. W.
HAWTHORNE AVE.
55
MARQUETTE AVE. S.
2ND AVE. S.
3RD AVE. S.
94
12TH ST. N.
11TH ST. N.
8TH ST. S.
65
394
12
13TH ST. N.
9TH ST. S.
LAUREL AVE.
HARMON PL.
Nicollet Mall
10TH ST. S.
4TH AVE. S.
WAYZATA BLVD.
LASALLE AVE.
11TH ST. S.
65
YALE PL.
12TH ST. S.

Loring Park
GRANT ST. W.
Minneapolis Convention Center
14TH ST. E.
Loring Park Lake
15TH ST. E.
15TH ST. W.
OAK GROVE ST.
65
12 52
GROVELAND AVE.
94
17TH ST. E.
LASALLE AVE.
NICOLLET AVE.
18TH ST. E.
3RD AVE. S.
5TH AVE. S.
19TH ST. E.
35W

N

0   0.1   0.2 km.
0   0.1   0.2 mi.

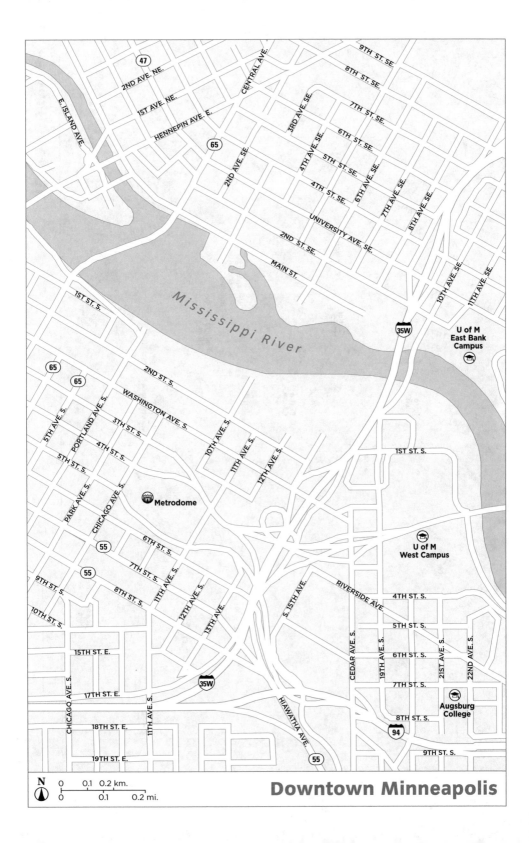

Downtown Minneapolis

N

0   0.1   0.2 km.

0   0.1   0.2 mi.

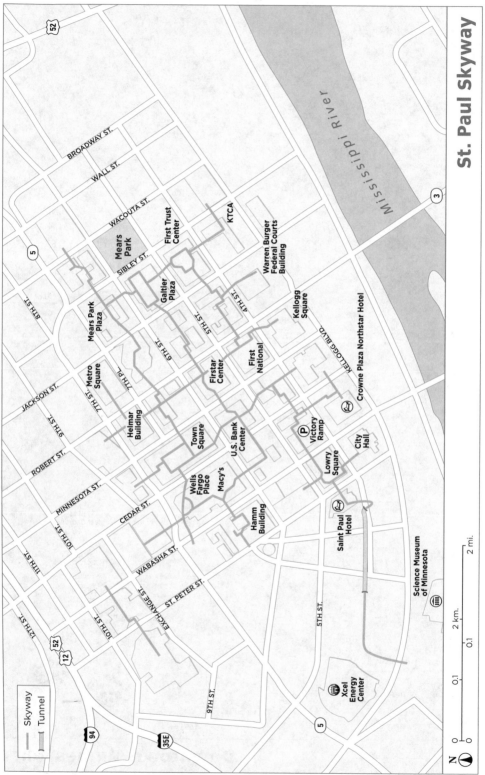

St. Paul Skyway

Legend:
— Skyway
▬ Tunnel

Labeled locations:
Mears Park
Mears Park Plaza
First Trust Center
KTCA
Galtier Plaza
Metro Square
Helmar Building
Town Square
Firstar Center
First National
Warren Burger Federal Courts Building
Kellogg Square
Wells Fargo Place
Macy's
U.S. Bank Center
Victory Ramp
Lowry Square
Hamm Building
City Hall
Saint Paul Hotel
Crowne Plaza Northstar Hotel
Xcel Energy Center
Science Museum of Minnesota

Streets:
BROADWAY ST.
WALL ST.
WACOUTA ST.
SIBLEY ST.
8TH ST.
7TH ST.
7TH PL.
6TH ST.
5TH ST.
4TH ST.
JACKSON ST.
ROBERT ST.
MINNESOTA ST.
CEDAR ST.
WABASHA ST.
ST. PETER ST.
EXCHANGE ST.
9TH ST.
10TH ST.
11TH ST.
12TH ST.
1ST ST.
9TH ST.
KELLOGG BLVD.
5TH ST.

Highways: 52, 5, 3, 94, 35E, 12

Mississippi River

N

Scale: 0   0.1   0.1
0   2 km.   2 mi.

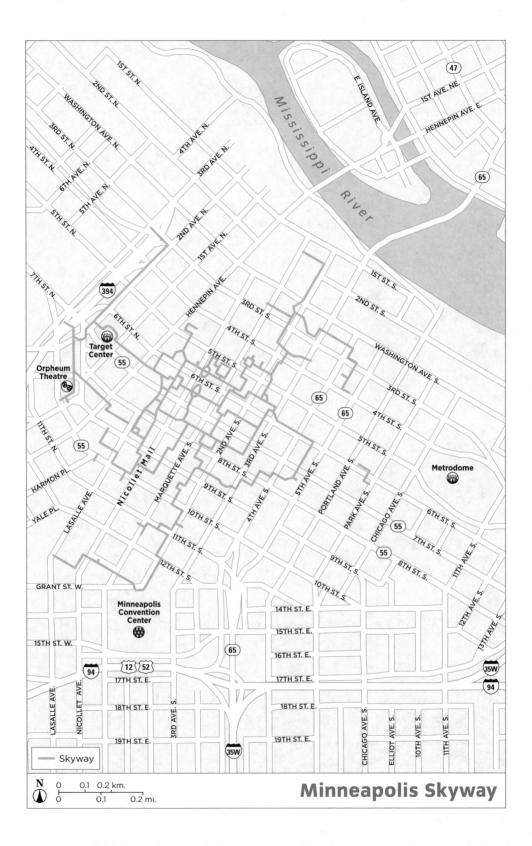

Minneapolis Skyway

Skyway

HOW TO USE THIS BOOK

For the most part, those who live in the Twin Cities don't consider themselves Twin Cities residents—in the Metro you're either from Minneapolis or St. Paul. While the two cities have much in common, differences in architecture, city layout, history, and industry set St. Paul and Minneapolis apart. Each could fill a separate guidebook by itself.

The Insiders' Guide to the Twin Cities is organized so that information can be accessed as quickly as possible. In addition to the comprehensive table of contents and index, each chapter includes multiple subheadings. Chapters are divided by city where appropriate for easier navigation through the Cities and suburbs. Other chapters are organized alphabetically by subject or chronologically by event. You'll also find interesting tips scattered throughout the text, flagged with the symbol. Look for the close-up features for an in-depth look at the many reasons the Twin Cities are special.

The book should be useful for anyone interested in the Twin Cities, but it's particularly aimed at someone moving to or visiting the Twin Cities for the first time, or someone visiting a given establishment for the first time. Not every establishment appears here—with the richness and density of the Twin Cities, that would be impossible. The attractions and establishments listed here are those that are most noteworthy, most frequented, and generally exceptional. Some of the establishments that don't appear here were omitted because the previous editions' authors and I found them unimpressive, some were omitted for reasons of time and space, and some may have opened or closed after the book went to press. (Restaurants, especially, are prone to open and close often and unpredictably.)

Moving to the Twin Cities or already live here? Be sure to check out the blue-tabbed pages at the back of the book, where you will find the **Living Here** appendix that offers sections on relocation, retirement, child care, education, health care, and media.

Although we encourage you to use this guidebook and are confident that you will find it useful in choosing places to your liking, we also encourage you to stop by that intriguing Ethiopian restaurant, visit that interesting shop selling bobblehead dolls or what have you, or buy a house in a neighborhood that "feels right," whether or not it is included in this book. This book is a diving board to get you into the pool; once there, you can swim wherever you like.

AREA OVERVIEW

Legend has it that the many lakes that cover the face of Minnesota are actually the footprints of Paul Bunyan and his mighty blue ox, Babe, created as they stomped around the countryside when Paul was just a boy. If this is true, then he must have been doing jumping jacks in the Twin Cities: St. Paul and Minneapolis alone have 22 lakes, with many more just outside their borders. Just about everywhere you go, you're bound to drive by, cross over, or end up at one of the metro area's lakes, not to mention the mighty Mississippi and Minnesota Rivers, which come together at the location (no coincidence) of the historic Fort Snelling.

Even with all their historic buildings, soaring bridges, and whimsical experiments in architecture, the most remarkable physical feature about the Twin Cities has always been their natural beauty. Where else can you find wildlife preserves, rich fossil beds, and fishing lakes, all within a short walk from either downtown?

This, of course, was not always so. Minneapolis was partially built on the lumber industry, and thousands and thousands of old-growth trees were leveled and shipped out of state, almost completely destroying the Big Woods, a maple, oak, and basswood forest that once covered most of southern Minnesota. The Mississippi River valley Native American populations were cut down along with the forests that had been their home for thousands of years, and many of their spiritual centers, including the ill-fated Spirit Island that once rose out of the Mississippi River below St. Anthony Falls, were either gutted or dynamited in the name of progress.

With the founding of the two cities in the mid-1800s, however, a new level of civility and sophistication came to the residents. Multiple parks boards were established to protect wildlife areas, and even more groomed areas were set aside for outdoor activities. Today Twin Citians have the luxury of being able to walk past wetlands full of migratory waterfowl and turtles on their way to downtown Minneapolis, or through thickly forested areas housing species of rare native animals and birds just minutes from downtown St. Paul. Kids who grow up in the Twin Cities get to share in pleasures usually reserved for children who grow up in the country, whether it be fishing in one of the many regularly stocked urban lakes, berry picking, or just enjoying being surrounded by trees, songbirds, and wildflowers in parks practically in their own backyards.

THE PERSONALITY OF THE CITIES

Minnesota has long suffered a reputation of being an American Siberia peopled with blond-haired, blue-eyed Scandinavian types. And while it's true that some parts of the state do have six-month cold seasons, often complete with snow for the entire six months, the Twin Cities enjoy relatively (yes, *relatively*) mild temperatures, partly due to our proximity to the swift-moving Mis-

sissippi River. Summers can top the scale at 100 degrees occasionally, and, conversely, winters can drop well below zero. (The only other place on earth with seasonal temperature extremes as wide as those in the Upper Midwest is—you got it—Siberia.) A good rule of thumb is to just be prepared for it to get cold in the winter and warm in the summer, and dress accordingly.

While most residents of the Twin Cities will go on and on about how much we love the changing of the seasons, to the point of ridiculing visitors who complain about "a little snow," as soon as any of us have enough money to take a vacation somewhere warm during the winter, we're gone. Our snowbird migrations—RV-driving senior citizens who winter in the South and summer in Minnesota—are legendary.

In all weather, but especially in the summer, anyone who can go outside, is outside. City parks are well-used here in the Twin Cities, from huge group picnics to locally organized volleyball and baseball games. Many neighborhood parks have a splash pool for kids, and at any given time during the summer, families can be seen splashing around in the ridiculously shallow waters. At night the streets of downtown Minneapolis and St. Paul are full of people either out for a late-night walk in the evening air or heading out on foot for a night on the town.

HOLLYWOOD AND THE TWIN CITIES

Minnesota has long been a favorite filming spot for moviemakers, especially those who need to shoot in snowy, cold areas with lots of open spaces. The Twin Cities are a logical spot to find actors and actresses to fill these scenes, as both Minneapolis and St. Paul have more than enough talent trained on the many professional and amateur theater stages in the area. Some of the films that have been shot in the Twin Cities metro area include *Airport, Beautiful Girls, Drop Dead Fred, Equinox, Fargo, Feeling Minnesota, Foolin' Around, Grumpy Old Men, Grumpier Old Men, Jingle All the Way, Mall Rats, The Mighty Ducks (I, II, and III), The Personals, A Prairie Home Companion, A Simple Plan, Twenty Bucks,* and *Untamed Heart.* Brothers Joel and Ethan Coen, film directors and producers of such films as *Raising Arizona, Blood Simple, Fargo, O Brother Where Art Thou,* and *No Country for Old Men,* are from here, as are *Twin Peaks* producer Mark Frost and the director of *The Sting,* George Roy Hill.

Television and big-picture actors and actresses who hail from the Twin Cities include Eddie Albert (*Roman Holiday, Green Acres*), Loni Anderson (*WKRP in Cincinnati*), Richard Dean Anderson (*General Hospital, MacGyver, Stargate SG-1*), James Arness (*Gunsmoke*), Julia Duffy (*Newhart, Designing Women*), Mike Farrell (*M*A*S*H, Providence*), Terry Gilliam (*Monty Python*), Peter Graves (*Mission: Impossible*), Tippi Hedren (*The Birds*), Josh Hartnett (*Pearl Harbor*), Charlie Korsmo (*Hook, Dick Tracy*), Dorothy Lyman (*All My Children, Mama's Family*), Kelly Lynch (*Drugstore Cowboy*), Mike Nelson (*Mystery Science Theater*), Kevin Sorbo (*Hercules, Andromeda*), Lea Thompson (*Back to the Future I, II, III; Howard the Duck, Caroline in the City*), Robert Vaughn (*The Man from U.N.C.L.E.*), and Vince Vaughn (*Into the Wild, The Break-Up*).

LITERATURE, MUSIC, THEATER, AND ART

There's nothing like a long Minnesota winter to make you want to curl up with a good book—or sit down and write one. Some best-selling authors from the Twin Cities area (of varying literary prowess) have included *Prairie Home Companion*'s Garrison Keillor, Sinclair Lewis, F. Scott Fitzgerald, Meridel Le Sueur, Harvey Mackay, Robert Bly, Tim O'Brien, Gordon Parks, and journalist Eric Severeid. *Peanuts,* by general consensus the greatest comic strip of all time, is set in a neighborhood inspired by creator Charles Schulz's St. Paul boyhood.

The Twin Cities music scene has long been known for nurturing creative geniuses including blues legends Koerner, Ray, and Glover; Bob Dylan (who hung out at the University of Minnesota); post-punk legends the Replacements; and Prince (who, with producers Jimmy Jam and Terry Lewis, was responsible for popularizing a sleek, urban "Minneapolis sound" in the 1980s). Most recently, the local music scene has produced Owl City, whose single "Fireflies" became a #1 national hit. The Twin Cities each also have a world-class classical ensemble: Minneapolis has the Minnesota Orchestra, and across the river there's the St. Paul Chamber Orchestra.

If you're a theater lover, outside of New York there may be no better place in the country to be than in the Twin Cities. In the 1960s Minneapolis's Guthrie Theater pioneered the model of the top-

⊙ Close-up

Twin Cities Timeline

1680: Father Louis Hennepin, after being held captive in a village of the Mille Lacs Dakotas, is the first European to see the Falls of St. Anthony.

1819: The United States establishes Fort St. Anthony (renamed Fort Snelling in 1825) to protect the confluence of the Minnesota and Mississippi Rivers.

1837: Governor Henry Dodge of Wisconsin signs a treaty at Fort Snelling with the Ojibwes, who agree to cede all their pinelands on the St. Croix River and its tributaries. A treaty is also signed at Washington, D.C., with representatives of the Dakotas for their lands east of the Mississippi. These treaties lead the way for extensive white settlements within the area of what would become Minnesota.

1838: Franklin Steele establishes a claim at the Falls of St. Anthony in what is today Minneapolis; Pierre "Pig's Eye" Parrant builds a shanty and settles on the present site of the city of St. Paul, then called Pig's Eye.

1841: The Chapel of St. Paul is built and consecrated, giving the name to the future capital of the state.

1848: On August 26, after the admission of Wisconsin to the Union, the Stillwater Convention adopts measures calling for a separate territory to be named Minnesota. On October 30, Henry Hastings Sibley is elected the delegate to Congress for the Minnesota Territory.

1855: On January 23 the first bridge to span the main channel of the Mississippi River anywhere along its length is opened between Minneapolis and St. Anthony.

1858: Minnesota becomes the 32nd state on May 11. At the time of its entry, Minnesota is the third-largest state in land area—only Texas and California are larger.

1861: On April 14 Governor Alexander Ramsey offers President Abraham Lincoln 1,000 men for the Civil War effort, making Minnesota the first state to offer troops to the Union. The first Minnesota regiment leaves Fort Snelling on June 22.

1862: The first railroad in Minnesota is opened between Minneapolis and St. Paul.

1881: Technological advances in flour milling made during the 1870s help turn Minneapolis into the flour milling capital of the world.

1883: The Northern Pacific Railroad completes its transcontinental route from Minnesota to the Pacific.

1884: The first iron ore is shipped from Minnesota, a product of the Soudan Mine on the Vermillion Range. Six years later iron is discovered on the Mesabi Range and shipped from there beginning in 1892.

1894: The town of Hinckley, Minnesota, about 80 miles north of St. Paul, and six neighboring communities are destroyed by an apocalyptic forest fire. More than 600 people lose their lives.

1914: Minneapolis becomes home to the Ninth District Federal Reserve Bank, one of 12 Federal Reserve Banks founded after Congress passed and President Woodrow Wilson signed the 1913 Federal Reserve Act.

1927: Charles Lindbergh, originally from Little Falls, Minnesota, becomes the first person to fly nonstop across the Atlantic Ocean alone.

1930: Minnesotan Frank B. Kellogg, serving as U.S. secretary of state, is awarded the Nobel Peace Prize for his work on the Kellogg-Briand Peace Pact, signed in Paris in 1928.

1944: The Democratic and Farmer-Labor Parties merge to form the Minnesota Democratic-Farmer-Labor Party (DFL).

1947: Engineering Research Associates Inc. designs the ATLAS—the beginning of Minnesota's computer industry.

1947: The NBA's Minneapolis Lakers, originally part of the National Basketball League, begin play. The Lakers, led by big man George Mikan, win several league championships in Minneapolis before moving to lakeless Los Angeles in 1960.

1948: The value of manufactured products exceeds cash farm receipts in the state for the first time.

1958: Prince Rogers Nelson, better known as the often purple and always funky musician Prince, is born in Minneapolis.

1965: Hubert H. Humphrey becomes the first Minnesotan to win election to national executive office when he is sworn in as Lyndon B. Johnson's vice president on January 20.

1968: Minnesota politicians play a central role in the 1968 presidential campaign, as both Vice President Humphrey and U.S. Senator Eugene McCarthy of Minnesota seek the Democratic nomination. Humphrey wins the nomination, but Richard Nixon wins the general election.

1969: Warren Burger of St. Paul becomes chief justice of the U.S. Supreme Court.

1970: Minnesotan Harry Blackmun is named to the U.S. Supreme Court.

1977: Walter Mondale becomes the second Minnesotan to win election to national executive office when he is sworn in as Jimmy Carter's vice president on January 20.

1977: Rosalie Wahl becomes the first woman to serve on the state supreme court.

1987: Led by Kirby Puckett, the Minnesota Twins win their first World Series.

1990: The Minnesota Supreme Court becomes the first state supreme court to have a majority of women seated as justices, following the appointment of Appeals Court Judge Sandra Gardebring.

1991: Casino gambling becomes legal in and around Minnesota's Indian reservations.

1991: The Minnesota Twins win their second world championship in five years.

1992: The Mall of America, the nation's largest shopping and entertainment complex, opens in Bloomington.

1993: Minnesota loses professional hockey when the Minnesota North Stars move to Dallas.

1993: Sharon Sayles Belton is elected mayor of Minneapolis, the first African-American woman to preside over a major American city.

continued on next page

Close-up (cont.)

1999: On January 3 Reform Party candidate Jesse Ventura, whose only previous political experience was as the mayor of the Minneapolis suburb of Brooklyn Park, is sworn in as Minnesota's governor.

1999: On March 10 the *St. Paul Pioneer Press* breaks the story of widespread academic misconduct involving players, coaches, and support staff of the University of Minnesota basketball team, including hundreds of term papers written for players by an academic tutor. After a nine-month investigation, the university fires men's basketball coach Clem Haskins. The NCAA later forces the university to forfeit all of its postseason games played between 1993 and 1998, including all of the games leading up to their 1997 trip to the Final Four, and to surrender 90 percent of the school's earnings from those postseason appearances. George Dohrmann, the *Pioneer Press* reporter who broke the original story, won the 1999 Pulitzer Prize for Beat Reporting.

2000: NHL hockey returns to Minnesota on September 29 when the Minnesota Wild play their first game before a sold-out crowd at the brand-new Xcel Energy Center in downtown St. Paul.

2002: On October 25, 11 days before the election, U.S. Senator Paul Wellstone of Minnesota, his wife, his daughter, three campaign workers, and two pilots die in a plane crash in northern Minnesota.

2004: The Twin Cities' first light-rail line, which runs between downtown Minneapolis and the Mall of America, opens on June 26.

2006: The Minnesota Fifth Congressional District, located in Minneapolis, elects Keith Ellison to the U.S. House of Representatives, making Minnesota the first state to send a Muslim to Congress. Ellison is sworn in with his hand on Thomas Jefferson's copy of the Koran.

2007: The bridge carrying I-35W over the Mississippi River in downtown Minneapolis collapses during the evening rush hour on August 1, dumping some 100 cars and trucks into the river. Thirteen people are killed.

2008: St. Paul hosts the Republican National Convention, at which John McCain and Sarah Palin are nominated to compete against Democrats Barack Obama and Joe Biden. The convention attracts national attention to the Twin Cities, but many locals are disturbed by severe security measures that see downtown St. Paul filled with police in riot gear.

quality regional repertory theater, and today the Twin Cities are home to a brilliant profusion of theater ranging from the solidly traditional to the wildly experimental.

If visual art is your bag, you'll be very happy here too—especially if your tastes run toward the contemporary. The Walker Art Center is a dynamo institution of contemporary art, and a frequent stop for culture vultures of all ages. The Minneapolis Institute of Arts houses an impressive, encyclopedic collection, and small galleries and studios dot the Cities, particularly the two downtowns and the neighborhoods of Northeast and Uptown Minneapolis.

GEOLOGY

The state of Minnesota is known throughout the world for its once-productive iron mines as well as its quarries of beautiful St. Peter sandstone and marble deposits. Of more scientific interest, some of the oldest exposed rock known in the world can be found in the Minnesota River valley, the Morton gneiss, which was formed approximately 3.6 billion years ago. The Morton gneiss and "younger" (1.7- to 1.8-billion-year-old) quarries of Minnesota granite and basalt have been prized as building materials throughout the world for years, as have St. Peter sandstone, marble, and fossil-rich kaolinite clay.

Millions of years ago the area now known as Minnesota lay submerged beneath shallow continental seas. During the Ordovician period (505 million to 438 million years ago), Minnesota was located 10 to 40 degrees south of the equator, making the area about as tropical as Hawaii is today. The waters were rich with primitive animal life, much of which can be seen today as layers in the fossil record at paleontology digs throughout the state. Large numbers of corals, trilobites, snails, mussel and clam shells, and ancestors of modern-day octopi and squid have been unearthed at sites such as Harriet Island/Lilydale Park and Shadow Falls in St. Paul and near Cannon Falls in Goodhue County.

Most of Minnesota is part of the Canadian Shield—a core of Precambrian rocks that contains the record of the history of the North American continent from about 3,600 million to 600 million years ago. Much of this ancient shield had been protected by the covering of the Ordovician seas, and later by layers of sediment and earth, but was again exposed by the eroding progress of glaciers over a mile thick that last covered the area more than 12,000 years ago— the same glaciers that eventually carved out the 15,000-plus lakes and rivers that pockmark the face of the state today.

THE ORIGINAL SETTLERS

Before European settlement, Dakota (Sioux) and Ojibwe (Chippewa) tribes populated the Twin Cities area, and before that the area was occupied by an amalgam of people known as the Woodland Indians (or Hopewell Indians), who left behind thousands of burial mounds throughout the Midwest, six of which can still be seen at Mounds Park in St. Paul. The Mississippian cultures of the Dakotas and Ojibwes replaced these American Indians circa AD 800 to 1000.

While the Ojibwes' origins were to the east and north, the Dakotas were western Plains Indians who at the time of European exploration occupied the Twin Cities area, western and southern Minnesota, and much of present-day North and South Dakota. The French referred to the Dakotas as Sioux, a meaningless abridgement of the Ojibwe term *Nadouessioux,* which meant "little viper" or "lesser enemy." The derogatory name stuck for centuries until recently, when the tribe began referring to itself by its original name. Both the Dakotas and Ojibwes were hunting societies, and their hunting techniques evolved by incorporating European tools, wares, and implements such as guns, hatchets, blankets, knives, and kettles. On a cultural level, the European introduction of glass beads and colored cloth and yarn to the Native peoples resulted in a revolution in American Indian artwork, producing the spectacular woven blankets and intricate beadwork that we associate with American Indian craftwork today.

The Twin Cities are home to the largest urban population of American Indians in the United States and are the birthplace of the American Indian Movement (AIM). AIM produces locally and nationally distributed literature that addresses Indian concerns on everything from legal issues to finding hospitals that practice Native American medicine.

St. Paul

Home to thousands of American Indians for centuries, the earliest known name for St. Paul is that given by the Indians: *Im-in-i-ja ska,* which translated into English means "White Rock," taken from the high limestone bluffs in the area. Fort Snelling (originally named Fort St. Anthony), the first European settlement in the area, was completed in 1825, and soon after, seeking the nearby protection of the fort, the community of St. Peter's (today known as Mendota) was established.

Soon the more privileged military officers and the residents of St. Peter's became disturbed at the lifestyle of the residents of the squatter

Twin Cities Vital Statistics

Founded: Minneapolis: 1856; **St. Paul:** 1819

Incorporated: Minneapolis: 1867; **St. Paul:** 1854

Size: Minneapolis: 54.9 square miles; St. Paul: 52.8 square miles

Elevation: 824 feet above sea level

Population: Minneapolis: 382,618; **St. Paul:** 287,151

Mayor: Minneapolis: R. T. Rybak; **St. Paul:** Chris Coleman

Governor: Tim Pawlenty

Airport: Minneapolis–St. Paul International Airport

Average temperatures:
    July: 72 degrees F
    January: 12 degrees F

Average yearly precipitation: 26.5 inches

Colleges and universities:
    Minneapolis: Augsburg College, Capella University, Dunwoody College of Technology, Minneapolis College of Art and Design, Minneapolis Community and Technical College, Northwestern Health Science University, the University of Minnesota–Twin Cities
    St. Paul: Bethel College and Seminary, the College of St. Catherine, Concordia University–St. Paul, Hamline University, Luther Seminary, Macalester College, McNally Smith College of Music, Metropolitan State University, William Mitchell College of Law, Northwestern College, St. Paul College, University of Minnesota–Twin Cities, University of St. Thomas

Daily newspapers: *Star Tribune, St. Paul Pioneer Press*

Radio stations: 48

Television stations: 9

Driving laws: Driver's license at age 16; maximum speed limit on interstate freeways varies from 55 mph to 70 mph; seat belts mandatory for driver and all passengers; child seats mandatory for children under age five or under 45 pounds; helmets mandatory for motorcycle riders.

camp, most of whom were refugees from the ill-fated Selkirk Colony in Manitoba. They were especially perturbed about the activities of a notorious and highly popular retired fur trapper whose talents had been turned to moonshining, Pierre "Pig's Eye" Parrant. The whiskey trade infuriated the straitlaced Major Lawrence Taliaferro, Fort Snelling's Indian agent, who issued a proclamation banishing the squatters from lands controlled by the fort. This forced them to move upriver to the northeast—just outside the fort's jurisdiction.

This site, then known as Fountain Cave, was located near what is now the southern part of St. Paul. A small monument today marks a spot on the riverbank near where the small group settled. Soon after they set up their new squatter camp, Major Taliaferro decided they were not quite far enough out of his sight and extended the jurisdiction of the fort to include the Fountain Cave site, sending his soldiers to burn the Fountain Cave encampment. The settlers were again forced to move farther up the river, this time settling on the north bank in what is now part of downtown St. Paul.

Institutions such as government and the Roman Catholic Church have been central to St. Paul's history since its earliest days. Since the Minnesota Territory was established in 1849, St. Paul has served as the capital. At about the same time, it also became a Catholic diocese established by Father Lucian Galtier, who had come to save the souls in the crassly named settlement of "Pig's Eye."

Industry and technology were paramount in the historical development of St. Paul. Minnesota Mining and Manufacturing Company (3M) is one of the Cities' most important companies. 3M's history began in 1902 in Two Harbors, a small town north of Duluth, as a manufacturer of sandpaper. The company relocated to St. Paul in 1909, where sandpaper is one of the most important 3M products today. 3M has always placed a premium on producing and developing diverse and innovative products, such as Scotch brand tape and Post-it Notes. As time has passed, 3M has grown into an international corporation but remains essentially a St. Paul company, even after relocating its headquarters to the adjoining suburb of Maplewood.

Minneapolis

The emergence of the other Twin City, Minneapolis, was far less colorful. In 1680 Father Louis Hennepin happened upon St. Anthony Falls, and 140 years later soldiers from nearby Fort Snelling constructed a sawmill and flour mill at the falls. Fort Snelling retained control of the current site of downtown Minneapolis until 1852, but the across-the-river town of St. Anthony was founded in 1849 as a milling and lumbering center. Minneapolis and St. Anthony were linked by a bridge in 1855, the first suspension bridge to span the Mississippi; today downtown Minneapolis's Hennepin Avenue Bridge sits on the site of the 1855 span. The town of Minneapolis formed in 1856 on the opposite bank of the Mississippi from St. Anthony. Minneapolis's name was formed from a derivative of *minnehaha*, which means "waterfall" in the Dakota language, and *polis*, the Greek suffix for "city." Literally speaking, Minneapolis means

"city of waters." The city of Minneapolis was incorporated in 1867, and in 1872 Minneapolis and St. Anthony were united to form one city.

Minneapolis was founded to mill Minnesota grain with the tremendous power-generating capabilities of St. Anthony Falls, and by the late 19th century, Minneapolis became nationally known as the Mill City. To businessmen in the area, the falls represented an unbridled source of energy for milling the vast Midwestern wheat crops, which rapidly expanded as Minnesota and the Upper Midwest were settled. The milling industry became increasingly decentralized as the largest and most successful Twin Cities milling companies gradually diversified into related industries.

i The Wabasha Street Caves used to be a St. Paul gangster hideout. Now they're a popular place to hold weddings and other events.

The Cities Together

Since the beginning of the 20th century, the Twin Cities economy has become increasingly diverse, depending less on a single industry—such as lumber, milling, or mining—and expanding into the technological, medical, retail, and agricultural fields.

Some companies' roots reach back to industry and manufacturing that began in the late 19th and early 20th centuries, as is the case with the 3M Corporation, while others quickly became important businesses because of technological innovation. Medtronic founder Earl Bakken began his company in a northeast Minneapolis garage in 1949, and it was the first of many medical supply companies that have made their home in the Twin Cities. The Twin Cities are also home to one of the nation's largest retailers, the Target Corporation.

Recent immigration is transforming the composition of the Twin Cities, much as it did in the late 19th and early 20th centuries. These new immigrant populations include Vietnamese, Laotians, Khmers (Cambodia), Hmong (Laos), East

Africans, Russians, Bosnians, and many other nationalities. With the exception of the Bosnians, Europeans are a relatively small component of the new immigration. The Twin Cities, especially St. Paul, have the largest Hmong population in the nation. (Several local Hmong actors appear in Clint Eastwood's movie *Gran Torino,* about a bitter veteran's relationship with a Hmong family.) The Hmong and other Southeast Asians have started more than 400 area businesses and have transformed St. Paul's Frogtown and Midway neighborhoods.

The new wave of immigration is just one parallel linking the Twin Cities past and present. Both Minneapolis and St. Paul are reviving important elements of their past on the Mississippi riverfront. Since the late 1980s Minneapolis has focused on regaining its greatest historical assets—the Mississippi River and the Mill District. Down the river in St. Paul, the renovated Harriet Island Regional Park celebrates its city's rich history.

THE SEVEN-COUNTY METRO AREA

Anoka County

Anoka County's history starts in 1849, when the Minnesota territorial legislature organized the counties of Washington, Ramsey, and Benton. What is now Anoka County was originally parts of both Ramsey and Benton Counties, with the Rum River dividing the two. As more settlers came to the area, the plot of land bordering the Rum River's shores was given the name Anoka. The name originated from a Dakota word meaning "on both sides."

Anoka County has grown from a largely rural area in 1857 to a present-day urban center. It is one of the largest and fastest-growing counties in the state. Anoka County, with its county seat in the city of Anoka, encompasses a 424-square-mile area, has a population of approximately 327,000, and is the fourth-largest county in Minnesota. Anoka County is also the third most

densely populated county in the state, following Ramsey and Hennepin Counties, and includes the cities of Andover, Anoka, Bethel, Blaine, Burns, Centerville, Circle Pines, Columbia Heights, Columbus, Coon Rapids, East Bethel, Fridley, Ham Lake, Hilltop, Lexington, Lino Lakes, Linwood, Oak Grove, Ramsey, St. Francis, and Spring Lake Park within its borders.

Carver County

With the signing of the Treaty of Traverse de Sioux in 1851, the formerly Dakota lands that soon became Carver County were opened for settlement by white pioneers. The county was named in honor of the 16th-century English explorer of the Upper Midwest, Jonathan Carver. The original county seat was in San Francisco Township, but in 1856 voters moved it to Chaska, where it remains today.

Today Carver County has a population of approximately 88,000, divided among the cities of Carver, Chanhassen, Chaska, Cologne, Hamburg, Mayer, New Germany, Norwood, Norwood–Young America, Victoria, Waconia, and Watertown.

Calling in the Metro Area

The Twin Cities metropolitan area has four area codes (612, 651, 763, and 952), but callers do not have to dial "1" before calling phone numbers in the other area codes. You can dial the seven-digit phone number for calls within your area code or the ten-digit number (area code plus phone number) for calls to areas outside your area code within the Metro. Your call will still go through if you dial "1" first, but you will be charged for a long-distance call.

Dakota County

Located minutes south of the Twin Cities, Dakota County offers the amenities of the metropolitan area with the charm and serenity of a small town. Approximately 388,000 people live within the county's limits, making it the third most populous county in the state. Yet one-half of its land remains undeveloped or rural.

The quality of life in Dakota County is high due to its excellent schools, its proximity to renowned health care facilities, and pleasant neighborhoods. Parks, fishing lakes, trail systems, and recreation areas are abundant, as well as the spacious grounds of the Minnesota Zoo, the second-largest zoo in the country. Dakota County cities include Apple Valley, Burnsville, Eagan, Farmington, Hastings, Inver Grove Heights, Lakeville, Lilydale, Mendota, Mendota Heights, Miesville, New Trier, Randolph, Rosemount, South St. Paul, Sunfish Lake, and West St. Paul.

Hennepin County

Hennepin County, incorporated in 1852, forms part of one of the nation's major metropolitan areas, with Minneapolis as its largest city and county seat.

More than 1,122,000 people live in the 557 square miles that make up Hennepin County, with the greatest percentage living in Minneapolis and the rest distributed among the cities of Bloomington, Brooklyn Center, Brooklyn Park, Champlin, Chanhassen,Corcoran, Crystal, Dayton, Deephaven, Eden Prairie, Edina, Excelsior, Golden Valley, Greenfield, Hamel, Hanover, Hopkins, Howard Lake, Independence, Long Lake, Loretto, Maple Grove, Maple Plain, Medicine Lake, Medina, Minnetonka, Minnetonka Beach, Minnetonka Mills, Minnetrista, Mound, Navarre, New Hope, Orono, Osseo, Plymouth, Richfield, Robbinsdale, Rockford, Rogers, St. Anthony, St. Bonifacius, St. Louis Park, Spring Park, Tonka Bay, Wayzata, Woodland, and Young America.

The largest employers with holdings in Hennepin County include the state government, the University of Minnesota, General Mills, Cargill, Target Corporation, and the U.S. Postal Service.

Ramsey County

Ramsey County, established in 1849, is home to Minnesota's state capital, the city of St. Paul. More than 493,000 people live in the 156 square miles that make up the county, which includes the cities of Arden Hills, Blaine, Falcon Heights, Gem Lake, Lauderdale, Little Canada, Maplewood, Mounds View, New Brighton, North Oaks, North St. Paul, Roseville, St. Anthony, St. Paul, Shoreview, Spring Lake Park, Vadnais Heights, and White Bear Lake.

Ramsey County is the site of many popular attractions, both man-made and natural, including Como Park Zoo and Conservatory, Indian Mounds Park, Harriet Island and Lilydale Parks, and the Alexander Ramsey House. St. Paul's suburbs are built around lakes and parks for summer and winter recreation alike.

Scott County

Scott County, established in 1853 and named after War of 1812 and Mexican-American War General Winfield Scott, is an area of 357 square miles located in the southwest corner of the Twin Cities metro area. Shakopee, the county seat, began in 1851 as a trading post near the Dakota village of Chief Shakopee (or Shakpay). Town sites were established along transportation routes provided by the Minnesota River and the numerous oxcart trails that crisscrossed the region. Years later the railroad was the choice of transport in Minnesota, and still later, highways developed along the oxcart trails and between communities.

Today urban sprawl and suburbanization are threatening this primarily rural county. Industry has taken hold, and transportation issues play a primary role in development decisions, just as they did in the past. Shakopee has become a popular tourist destination home to the amusement park Valleyfair, the dog-racing track Canterbury Downs, and the seasonal attraction Sever's Corn Maze.

The county has a population of approximately 124,000. Located within the county lines are the cities of Elko, Jordan, New Prague, Prior Lake, and Savage.

Washington County

Washington County is located on the eastern edge of the Metro. Incorporated in 1849, its 392 square miles now house more than 225,000 people divided among the cities of Afton, Bayport, Birchwood, Cottage Grove, Dellwood, Forest Lake, Hastings, Hugo, Lake Elmo, Lake St. Croix Beach, Lakeland, Lakeland Shores, Landfall, Marine on St. Croix, Newport, Oak Park Heights, Oakdale, Pine Springs, St. Mary's Point, St. Paul Park, Scandia, Stillwater, Willernie, and Woodbury. The county seat is located in Stillwater, along the St. Croix River.

Washington County has more than its share of beautiful natural areas. Located within county lines are Afton State Park, Lake Elmo Park Reserve, St. Croix Bluffs Regional Park, and Square Lake Park, as well as dozens of smaller protected wilderness areas. The county is bordered by the Lower St. Croix National Scenic Riverway. Stillwater is a favorite day-trip getaway for Twin Cities residents who love its history, its small-town feel, and its many antiques shops.

GETTING HERE, GETTING AROUND

In the beginning the Mississippi, Minnesota, and St. Croix Rivers all made the lumber industry possible in Minnesota, turning communities like Stillwater, St. Anthony, and Minneapolis into important centers of commerce and trade. The rivers were also important in transporting iron, granite, sandstone, and marble from Minnesota to the rest of the world, and for bringing military supplies and luxury items from the rest of the world to Minnesota. Trains later replaced boats as the preferred means of transporting raw materials, and commuter trains became Twin Cities residents' favorite means of personal transportation. The Great Northern Depot in St. Paul, built in 1914, connected passengers to nearby resort destinations like Minnehaha Park and White Bear Lake as well as to the East and West Coasts.

Electric streetcars made their debut in the Twin Cities in 1889, and by the 1920s Minneapolis and St. Paul were home to one of the largest streetcar systems in the world. More than 1,000 cars on 500 miles of track took commuters to work and back home again each day, and the system was so extensive that it was possible to take a streetcar from downtown Minneapolis all the way to Stillwater or Excelsior. As interstate highways were developed, the streetcar system was abandoned in the 1950s. (The only remaining stretch of rail is now a tourist attraction, with short rides in original streetcars, near Lake Calhoun in Minneapolis.) In 1954 street buses replaced the electric streetcars, and the electric tracks that crisscrossed the metro area were paved over to facilitate automobile use. The Twin Cities have recently begun to restore streetcar service in the modern-day guise of light-rail trains; Minneapolis launched a light-rail line from downtown Minneapolis to the airport and on to the Mall of America in 2004, and Metro Transit is now in the planning stages of a light-rail line between downtown Minneapolis and downtown St. Paul along University Avenue.

Today, in addition to light rail, the Twin Cities are home to one large international airport and six smaller ones and a bus line that runs 24 hours a day in the busy downtown areas. Truth be told, the Twin Cities are relatively hard to live in without a car: Those accustomed to the extensive subway systems and frequent bus service in cities like New York, Boston, and Chicago will find that, though individual neighborhoods in the Twin Cities are wonderful for walking, it's not very convenient to travel among them by public transit.

In part because of this fact, biking is another story: The Twin Cities are home to a large and avid population of bicyclists who are undeterred by all but the harshest winter weather. Bike lanes are increasingly to be found on streets across town, and the acclaimed Midtown Greenway allows bikers to cross Minneapolis without hitting a stoplight or dodging a car.

AIR TRAVEL

MINNEAPOLIS–ST. PAUL INTERNATIONAL AIRPORT

Charles A. Lindbergh Terminal
4300 Glumack Dr., St. Paul
(612) 726-5555

Hubert H. Humphrey Terminal
7150 Humphrey Dr., Minneapolis
(612) 726-5800
www.mspairport.com

Minneapolis–St. Paul International Airport (MSP) is a sprawling complex of two terminals serving 34 million people annually. The airport is located between Minneapolis and St. Paul on the southern side of the Metro, with relatively quick access to both downtowns and the rest of the Twin Cities region. With a steady stream of takeoffs and landings, it ranks as the busiest airport in the Upper Midwest. Among American cities, only Denver has an airport serving more nonstop destinations per capita.

Getting to the Airport

MSP encompasses two terminals—the Lindbergh Terminal and the Humphrey Terminal. The Lindbergh Terminal is accessible from MN 5 via the Lindbergh Terminal exit. The Humphrey Terminal is accessible from I-494 via the 34th Avenue South exit. You can also reach the Lindbergh Terminal by city bus, and both terminals by light rail (visit www.metrotransit.org for schedules and routes). Most commercial passenger airlines fly into Lindbergh, while Humphrey is the landing site for many charter airlines. Check your ticket carefully to determine your terminal before driving to the airport or instructing someone where to pick you up, although if you end up at the wrong terminal, you can hop on the light rail—free of charge between terminals—to quickly get back on track.

Design

If you haven't been through MSP for a few years, you probably won't recognize either of the terminals today. MSP and the six reliever airports

operated by the Metropolitan Airports Commission (MAC) are wrapping up a $3.1 billion reconstruction project known as MSP 2010, and things have come a long way since work began in 1996.

Despite the changes, it is not difficult to find your way around either the Lindbergh or Humphrey Terminal. The top level of the Lindbergh Terminal is for ticketing and departures. You can be dropped off at this level via the elevated roadway just outside the doors. The gate concourses at Lindbergh are lettered sequentially, A through G. Generally, if your concourse letter is A through E, you will veer right after passing through the security checkpoints in between the check-in counters; if your concourse letter is F or G, you will veer left. You can easily find your gate by observing the concourse number and gate (for example, E8 would be Gate 8 on Concourse E). The lower the number of the gate, the shorter your walk down the concourse. Note that Concourses A and B, designated for smaller commuter airlines, are at the end of Concourse C.

People-mover walkways carry passengers down Concourses C and G, the two longest at MSP, and across the Skyway Connector between Concourses C and G. An aboveground shuttle tram—which, incongruously, makes automated announcements with a British accent—also carries passengers the length of Concourse C, with several stops along the way, and an underground Hub Tram runs from Level T, two floors below the ticketing and departures concourse, to escalators leading to the Skyway Connector. This tram also carries passengers to the outer Blue and Red parking ramps and to the Transit Center, where you will find the rental car counters, city bus stop, and the light rail station.

At Lindbergh the baggage claim area is one floor below the ticketing and departures concourse. Electronic displays on this level indicate which of the 14 baggage carousels will deliver the luggage from your flight.

The much-smaller Humphrey Terminal will not make your feet as sore. Ticketing and departure counters, as well as the baggage claim area, are all located on the first floor of the terminal. The gates are one floor up and accessible via a short escalator ride. Taxis and shuttles to rental car agencies can be found on the commercial roadway on the first level of the parking ramp.

Domestic Airlines

AIRTRAN AIRWAYS
(800) 247-8726
www.airtran.com

ALASKA AIRLINES
(800) 426-0333
www.alaskaair.com

AMERICAN AIRLINES
(800) 433-7300
www.aa.com

CONTINENTAL AIRLINES
(800) 525-0280
www.continental.com

DELTA AIRLINES
(800) 221-1212
www.delta.com

FRONTIER AIRLINES
(800) 432-1359
www.frontierairlines.com

MIDWEST AIRLINES
(800) 452-2022
www.midwestairlines.com

NORTHWEST AIRLINES
(800) 225-2525
www.nwa.com

SOUTHWEST AIRLINES
(800) 435-9792
www.southwest.com

SUN COUNTRY AIRLINES
(800) 359-6786
www.suncountry.com

UNITED AIRLINES
(800) 241-6522
www.united.com

US AIRWAYS
(800) 428-4322
www.usairways.com

International Airlines

AIR CANADA
(888) 247-2262
www.aircanada.com

ICELANDAIR
(800) 223-5500
www.icelandair.com

Ground Transportation

You can get to or from the airport via a variety of means. For the Lindbergh Terminal: For car rentals, city buses, hotel shuttles, or light rail, take the Hub Tram on Level T to the Transit Center.

Once at the Transit Center, follow the signs on Level T to the escalators to reach the taxi station. Also follow the signs for car rental agencies, although the signage can be a little confusing; check around for a sign with your rental agency on it before getting on an escalator or walking out a door. At the Humphrey Terminal, you can find the rental car counters in the Ground Transport Center on the bottom floor of the parking ramp directly across from the terminal building. Car rental agencies that have locations at the airport (at both terminals) are **National Car Rental** (800-227-7368; www.nationalcar.com); **Budget Car & Truck Rental** (800-527-0700; www.budget .com); **Avis Rent A Car** (800-831-2847; www .avis.com); **Alamo** (800-327-9633; www.alamo .com); **Dollar Rent A Car** (800-800-4000; www .dollar.com); **Enterprise Rent-A-Car** (800-325-8007; www.enterprise.com); and **Hertz** (800-654-3131; www.hertz.com). Car rental agencies with off-airport locations are **Ace** (800-243-3443) and **Thrifty** (800-367-2277; www.thrifty.com). At the Lindbergh Terminal's Transit Center, you can catch a shuttle bus designated for your agency.

At the Humphrey Terminal, you must arrange pickup by using the call boards in the baggage claim area to contact your agency.

You can catch taxis at the Lindbergh Terminal in the Transit Center, one level up from the Tram Level. At the Humphrey Terminal, taxis queue up at the Ground Transport Center on the bottom floor of the parking ramp directly across from the terminal building. Let the attendant know if you have special needs, such as a cab that takes credit cards. For a list of taxi companies and their contact information, see the Taxis section later in this chapter.

City buses and the light-rail transit (LRT) are far and away the cheapest ways to get to and from the airport. If you're traveling light and in no big hurry, you can catch a city bus at the Transit Center (Humphrey Terminal passengers arriving by bus or riding a bus to their Twin Cities destination must take the LRT between terminals, which is free between the airport stops). As a faster option, if your destination or starting point happens to be along its path, the LRT stops at the Lindbergh Terminal's Transit Center and the Humphrey Terminal's Ground Transport Center on its way to and from the Mall of America and downtown Minneapolis. Contact **Metro Transit** at (612) 373-3333 or visit www.metrotransit.org for route and schedule information for buses or light rail. For more information on both, see the Public Transportation section later in this chapter.

Parking

The Lindbergh Terminal offers short-term, long-term, and valet parking in the four ramps surrounded by the terminal concourses. Follow the signs as you enter the terminal area. Short-term parking is designed for stays of less than two hours; long-term parking is designed for stays longer than two hours. You can access the terminal from any of the ramps via enclosed skyways, the Hub Tram (accessible from the Transit Center), or Level T.

The Humphrey Terminal offers short- and long-term parking in the ramp across the street from the terminal. Travelers can get to the terminal by walking across the street or using the enclosed skyway on the second level.

For off-airport parking, the following lots offer shuttle transportation to and from MSP every 5 to 10 minutes, 24 hours a day:

- **EZ Air Park** (651-777-7275; www.ezairpark .com); 2804 Lexington Ave., Eagan
- **Park 'N Fly** (952-883-3606; www.pnf.com); 3700 American Blvd. East, Bloomington
- **Park 'N Go** (952-854-3386; www.parkngo.net); 7901 International Dr., Bloomington
- **Team Parking** (651-690-1200; www.teampark ing.com); 1465 Davern St., St. Paul

For parking availability and information, call the MSP Parking Information Line at (877) 359-7275 or visit www.mspairport.com/parking/realtime .aspx.

Amenities

With the last big series of expansions made to MSP in the 1990s, the Lindbergh Terminal's waiting area went from being a midsize airport to a mall of shops and restaurant courts. The centerpiece of the terminal's lobby is Northstar Crossing, a collection of more than 100 retail shops and restaurants. (Northstar Crossing gained international infamy in 2007 when Larry Craig, a U.S. senator from Idaho, was apprehended in one of its bathrooms for lewd conduct. The ensuing scandal resulted in Craig's resignation from the Senate.) The area features Minnesota-themed shops and nationally known retailers. Throughout the terminals can be found a number of fast-food and sit-down restaurants as well as bars, coffee shops, and of course newsstands. For passengers with disabilities, all airlines operating out of MSP provide wheelchairs for the flight. For carts, wheelchairs, or medical transportation, airline passengers should contact their travel agent, ticketing agents, flight attendants, or gate agents. Travelers Assistance (TA) can also help with wheelchair requests. TA volunteers may be reached by calling (612) 726-5500. Wheelchairs are also available for checkout at the information booth on Level T and at security checkpoints.

If you lose something at either of the terminals, call Airport Lost and Found at (612) 726-5141. The Lost and Found Office is located in the Lindbergh Terminal on the Mezzanine Level, one floor above the ticketing area.

TRAIN TRAVEL

AMTRAK
Twin Cities Passenger Station
730 Transfer Rd., St. Paul
(651) 644-1127 or (800) 872-7245
www.amtrak.com
The Twin Cities share a train station in St. Paul's Midway neighborhood. To get to the station, take the Cretin Avenue/Vandalia Street exit from I-94 and turn north at the stoplights. Turn east (right) at University Avenue, and then turn north (left) at the next stoplight (Cleveland/Transfer Road). The station is about a block up on the right. You can also get to the station from downtown Minneapolis or St. Paul on Metro Transit bus route 16 along University Avenue. The station and ticket counter are open 6 a.m. to midnight daily.

BUS TRAVEL

GREYHOUND LINES
166 West University Ave., St. Paul
(651) 222-0507

950 Hawthorne Ave., Minneapolis
(612) 371-3325
www.greyhound.com
Greyhound is a Minnesota company, founded in Hibbing on northern Minnesota's Iron Range in 1914. St. Paul and Minneapolis each have a Greyhound station. St. Paul's station is just west of the State Capitol building on University Avenue and is open 6 a.m. to 8 p.m. daily. The downtown Minneapolis station is next to the Hawthorne Transportation Center, a few blocks west of Target Center (First Avenue becomes Hawthorne Avenue as it heads west), and is open 6 a.m. to 1 a.m. daily. Greyhound also picks up and drops off (but doesn't sell tickets) at the Amtrak Station, 730 Transfer Road, St. Paul (651-644-0616); at both the St. Paul and Minneapolis campuses of

the University of Minnesota; and at several locations in the Twin Cities suburbs.

Jefferson Lines serves both Greyhound terminals, the St. Paul Amtrak Station, the Lindbergh Terminal at Minneapolis–St. Paul International Airport, the University of Minnesota, and Anoka. Call (800) 451-5333 or visit www.jeffersonlines.com for more information.

MEGABUS
Stops at the intersection of 3rd Ave. South and University Ave.; and at the intersection of South 3rd St. and Chicago Ave.
(877) 462-6342
http://us.megabus.com
The Megabus is a relatively new arrival on the Twin Cities' mass-transit scene, but it's already infamous—mention "Megabus" at any gathering, and expect to see at least one person smile and roll his or her eyes. For a sliding price based on time of ticket purchase (the earlier you buy in advance of your trip, the cheaper your ticket is), the comfy double-decker Megabuses will shuttle you to Madison, Milwaukee, or Chicago. They're not the most reliable—nor do their bus stops have roofs, let alone vending machines—but the service is a welcome and increasingly popular alternative to Greyhound and other bus services.

CAR TRAVEL

Highways

Minneapolis–St. Paul has well-thought-out arterial and surrounding highways, and by and large traffic flows freely. However, be aware that some major highways become parking lots during the morning and evening rush hours.

The Twin Cities are ringed by the I-494/I-694 loop. I-494 starts at the interchange with I-94 in the eastern suburb of Woodbury; arcs south around South St. Paul; heads due west through Eagan, Bloomington, and Eden Prairie; and then swings north through the western suburbs to reunite with I-94 in the suburb of Maple Grove northwest of Minneapolis. I-694 also starts at the intersection with I-94 in Woodbury but heads north through Oakdale, swings west to the intersection with I-35E in Little Canada, and then meanders roughly northwest through the suburbs of New Brighton, Fridley, Brooklyn Center, Brooklyn Park, and Maple Grove, where it meets I-94 again.

The ragged rectangle made by the I-494/I-694 loop is sliced by two branches of I-35 heading north–south through the Metro.

I-35 splits into I-35W and I-35E in the southern suburb of Burnsville. I-35W heads due north through the western part of the Metro. Since the tragic 2007 collapse of the I-35W bridge across the Mississippi River near downtown Minneapolis, the fallen bridge has been replaced with a state-of-the-art and (as highway bridges go) good-looking new span. Eventually the artery wiggles northeast of downtown through the northern suburbs to merge with I-35E in Columbus Township and becomes I-35 again. I-35E heads northeast from Burnsville into downtown St. Paul and then shoots north to briefly merge with I-694 before stretching north again for its eventual reunion with I-35W. Due to neighborhood politics surrounding its construction, as it runs through the city of St. Paul, I-35E is technically a "parkway" with a 45 mph speed limit; locals jokingly refer to it as "the practice freeway."

I-94 and I-394 split the I-494/I-694 rectangle east–west. I-94 rolls into the eastern Metro from Wisconsin, passing through downtown St. Paul and downtown Minneapolis before abruptly swinging north, where it merges for a few miles with I-694 in Brooklyn Center before going it alone again in its long march westward. I-394 runs from the western suburbs to downtown Minneapolis. The newest of the Twin Cities freeways, I-394 includes separate carpool lanes (open during times of heavy congestion), as well as Minnesota's first pay-per-use highway. Solo drivers in a hurry can use the carpool lanes on I-394 (and a stretch of I-35W south of downtown) as long as they have a MnPASS account and a transponder, which can be electronically read by highway sensors; drivers are automatically charged a toll that varies based on traffic levels and on where they enter or exit the highway. (For more information

about MnPASS, contact the Minnesota Department of Transportation MnPASS Service Center at 866-397-4334 or www.mnpass.net.) Whether you choose to use the MnPASS, are driving with more than one person, or are willing to drive on the free noncarpool, non-MnPASS lanes, I-394 will take you from the western Metro right into the heart of downtown Minneapolis's Warehouse District and back again.

Several other federal and state highways cross-hatch the I-494/I-694 loop. US 169 arrives in the Metro from southwestern Minnesota in the suburb of Eden Prairie, on the southwestern edge of the Cities, and then shoots due north through the western suburbs, crossing I-694 in Maple Grove just east of the intersection of I-694 and I-494. US 169 and the roughly parallel MN 100 are the principal north–south routes in the western suburbs.

MN 62 is the major east–west route through the southern Metro north of I-494. MN 62, referred to locally as the Crosstown, runs from its intersection with US 169 in Minnetonka in the southwestern Metro to its intersection with MN 55, just north of the Minneapolis–St. Paul International Airport. The Crosstown looks convenient on a map, but the highway briefly merges with I-35W in Richfield, and the resulting bottleneck is considered one of the worst in the nation. Current construction along I-35W, which will one day separate the two highways and relieve the bottleneck, is slowing things down even more.

Other useful highways in the south-central Metro include MN 77, which runs from the southern suburb of Apple Valley to its intersection with the Crosstown in the Lake Nokomis area of south Minneapolis. This highway passes, among other things, the Minnesota Zoo, the Mall of America, and MSP airport. MN 55 stretches all the way from the town of Hastings, 20 miles southeast of St. Paul, to downtown Minneapolis, passing over the Minnesota River via the 4,119-foot concrete-arch Fort Snelling–Mendota Bridge and skirting Fort Snelling State Park, MSP airport, and Minnehaha Park before gliding through the commercial districts of south Minneapolis. Known as Hiawatha Avenue along its path inside Minneapolis, this road is the route of the Hiawatha light-rail transit

(LRT) leg from downtown Minneapolis to the airport. There are stoplights along parts of this route, but it can be a quick alternative to get downtown from the southeastern Metro.

The principal highways in the eastern Metro include MN 110, which starts at its intersection with I-494 just west of the intersection with US 52, then takes a short tour of the St. Paul suburbs of Inver Grove Heights, Sunfish Lake, West St. Paul, and Mendota Heights before intersecting with MN 55 just before the Fort Snelling–Mendota Bridge over the Minnesota River.

US 52 is perhaps more useful, arriving from southern Minnesota and intersecting I-494 in the southern St. Paul suburb of Inver Grove Heights. From there the highway conveniently heads through the suburbs of South St. Paul and West St. Paul right to downtown St. Paul, passing St. Paul Downtown Holman Field airport and crossing the Mississippi River in the process. The route into the city along US 52, particularly at night, provides some of the most spectacular views of the St. Paul skyline.

US 10 and 61 unite in Hastings and follow the Mississippi River to I-94 just east of downtown St. Paul, passing through the suburbs of Cottage Grove, St. Paul Park, and Newport in the process. From there, US 61 veers north at Arcade Street, following city streets until hitting the suburb of Maplewood and then spiking north through the suburbs of Mahtomedi, Gem Lake, White Bear Lake, and Hugo before ending just north of Forest Lake about 25 miles north of downtown St. Paul. US 61 roughly parallels I-35E in the northern suburbs, and the interstate is almost always a better choice except during heavy rush-hour traffic.

US 10 takes the easy route after intersecting I-94 by merging with the interstate in the westbound direction, then turning north and merging with I-35E for a few miles, and then merging with I-694 and heading northwest to the northern suburb of Arden Hills. From there US 10 briefly follows its own route northwest, then merges with I-35W in Mounds View for a few miles, finally going it alone through the suburbs of Blaine, Coon Rapids, Anoka, Ramsey, and Elk River before skipping out of the Metro.

MN 36 is another useful eastern highway, running from its intersection with I-35W in the northern suburb of Roseville through Little Canada, Maplewood, North St. Paul, and Oakdale all the way to Stillwater on the St. Croix River. MN 36 is the quickest outlet to the St. Croix Valley and a convenient artery leading to many shopping areas in the first-tier northern suburbs.

MN 280 provides an appreciated shortcut for motorists on I-94 on the western edges of St. Paul intent on reaching the northern suburbs and for commuters trying to reach downtown Minneapolis from the north. The highway runs from its intersection with I-94 just east of the Minneapolis city boundary due north through Lauderdale to intersect I-35W in Roseville after just a few miles. The highway provides access not only to the retail outlets of Roseville but also to the University of Minnesota–St. Paul Campus and Luther Seminary.

i Twin Citians are notorious for the speeds at which they enter city highways. They definitely try to merge onto the freeway already traveling at freeway speed—and they expect that you will accelerate rapidly, too.

Twin Cities Streets

Minneapolis and St. Paul are two distinctly governed municipalities, separated along much of their boundary by the Mississippi River. For this reason, Minneapolis and St. Paul share a few important streets, which include University and Como Avenues. However, several streets change their names when crossing the county line. Most notable, Larpenteur Avenue in St. Paul becomes East Hennepin Avenue in Minneapolis, and Marshall Avenue in St. Paul turns into Lake Street after crossing the Mississippi into Minneapolis. More confusing, both cities have streets that share names but are not connected to their counterparts across the river, including Minnehaha and Grand Avenues. These things happen when urban centers develop next to each other. Try to keep this in mind when navigating Twin Cities streets.

St. Paul Streets

Tradition and character often come before efficiency and transparency in St. Paul, and to the consternation of many Minneapolitans used to their numbered plan, St. Paul's street nomenclature is no exception. The St. Paul street plan really isn't that confounding—and in the downtown area, it is numbered—but things do get a little tricky where main thoroughfare Kellogg Boulevard takes a southeasterly bend to run along the Mississippi River. Kellogg connects the action at the southeastern end of the city (Xcel Energy Center, the Science Museum of Minnesota) with the artsy Lowertown district. The main streets unfolding away from the river, or northwest of Kellogg, are numbered beginning with 4th and reach 11th just before I-94 and I-35E rein in downtown St. Paul. These numbered streets are labeled "west" and "east" depending on which side of Wabasha Street they are. Wabasha is a main northwest–southeast thoroughfare, and it, along with Robert and Smith Streets, crosses the Mississippi River to what's called St. Paul's West Side (it's actually on the city's south side), which is the premier Twin Cities Latino neighborhood. Seventh Street (again, labeled east or west in relation to Wabasha) is the main northeast–southwest route. It and all the other major arteries named here are prone to congestion during rush hour or major Xcel Energy Center events, though St. Paul generally has less traffic than Minneapolis.

Another of St. Paul's main streets, Snelling Avenue (MN 51), starts on far western Seventh Street, northeast of MSP airport. It then runs north through the St. Paul neighborhood of Highland Park and through the university-riddled west side of the city, where it intersects major avenues such as Randolph, Grand, Summit, and University, as well as I-94, before continuing past the Minnesota State Fairgrounds into St. Paul's northern suburbs. Snelling is often busy, as is cross street University Avenue, which starts near the Minnesota State Capitol just north of downtown St. Paul, then parallels I-94 west on into Minneapolis.

East–west-running Grand and Summit Avenues are good to know, too. They begin on a bluff on the northwest side of downtown, just 1 block from each other—Summit is one of the country's premier surviving Victorian boulevards, and Grand is St. Paul's main shopping and dining street.

i Parking availability signs are conveniently located on downtown St. Paul streets. The signs post the number of available parking spots and are helpful in guiding drivers to lots with spaces open. You'll notice that in the Twin Cities, large parking structures are typically referred to as "parking ramps" rather than "parking garages"—so if someone says, "I'm parked in the ramp," that probably doesn't actually mean they're blocking traffic.

Minneapolis Streets

A key piece of advice for drivers new to downtown Minneapolis: Get your numbered avenues and streets straight. The streets run northwest–southeast, beginning with First Street along the Mississippi River. They're named north or south depending on which side of the main thoroughfare Hennepin Avenue they lie. Avenues, such as Hennepin, run northeast–southwest, and they have names more often than numbers. Downtown Minneapolis is bound by I-94, which runs east–west below Minneapolis before angling north–south along the city's west edge. Both Hennepin and Third Avenues have bridges across the Mississippi into St. Anthony and the hip Northeast neighborhood. The beautiful Stone Arch Bridge, like Nicollet Mall, is for people and bikes only. All of downtown is congested at rush hour and during events at the Metrodome (on the southeast side of downtown) or Target Center (on the northwest); the same will surely be true of baseball games at Target Field (confusingly, located very close to Target Center), which the Minnesota Twins moved into in spring 2010.

Things get easier both northeast and southwest of the city when the grid straightens out. At that point streets run plain-old north–south, and the avenues go, for the most part, east–west. Take Hennepin southwest out of downtown, for example, and you're headed to Loring Park, the Walker Art Center, and, once the street curves south, the Uptown shopping and dining district. Lake Street and Hennepin Avenue are at the heart of Uptown—follow Lake Street west a few blocks and you're at Lake Calhoun (one of this area's many lakes). Follow Lake Street east and you'll cross major north–south-running Lyndale Avenue, I-35W, Chicago Avenue, and Hiawatha Avenue (home to the LRT line) before eventually crossing the Mississippi into St. Paul.

Snow Emergency Information

Although the words "snow emergency" may sound ominous to the uninitiated, such events are declared so that the City of Minneapolis or St. Paul can get people to park their cars in the proper places to allow plows through. Declaration of an "emergency" does not (necessarily) mean that you will need to stock up on batteries or canned chipped beef. Both Minneapolis and St. Paul have extensive snow emergency ordinances, and though in most cases the two cities will declare a snow emergency simultaneously, the subsequent parking restrictions are very different—in Minneapolis, you have to pay attention to which side of the street you park on (odd or even house numbers), whereas in St. Paul what matters is whether you're on a north–south or an east–west street. In some situations, not complying with snow removal rules will result in the towing of your vehicle, a hefty fine, or both, so beware. Snow emergencies are announced through the local media, and if one happens you'll probably hear about it from multiple people—it seems like every Twin Cities resident regards him- or herself as the sole source of information regarding snow emergencies, and feels a responsibility to keep friends in the loop. Both cities are also on Twitter and Facebook, so you can follow those accounts, even if it seems absurd to become a "fan" of snow emergencies.

You can also check to see whether restrictions are in effect in Minneapolis by calling (612) 348-SNOW or visiting www.ci.minneapolis.mn

.us/snow/parking-info. For St. Paul call (651) 266-PLOW, or check the Web at www.stpaul.gov/depts/publicworks/snowplow.

It is your responsibility to know whether a snow emergency has been declared; pleading ignorance will not get you out of paying a fine or towing fees. The following is a list of guidelines and helpful hints for snow emergencies.

Minneapolis

When a Minneapolis snow emergency is declared before 6 p.m., the entire city enters a three-day cycle that dictates where you can park your car. On the first day of a snow emergency, from 9 p.m. to 8 a.m., the city allows no parking on either side of Snow Emergency Routes, which are marked with red signs along the side of the street or blue street-name signs (non–snow emergency routes have green or brown street-name signs). You can park on either side of any non–snow emergency route and on parkways. On the second day of the snow emergency, from 8 a.m. to 8 p.m., there is no parking on either side of parkways or on the even-numbered side of non–snow emergency routes; however, you can now park on plowed Snow Emergency Routes. Restrictions are then lifted for twelve hours, but don't sleep in! From 8 a.m. to 8 p.m. on the third day of the snow emergency, you cannot park on the odd-numbered side of non–snow emergency routes.

St. Paul

St. Paul divides its streets into "night plow" and "day plow" routes. The night plow routes are plowed between 9 p.m. and 6 a.m. on the night the snow emergency is declared. These routes are marked with Night Plow Route signs. All downtown streets are plowed the first night. Note that some north–south residential streets have signs reading NIGHT PLOW ROUTE THIS SIDE OF STREET. You can park on the nonsigned sides of these streets during the first night of a snow emergency. The snow is removed on day plow routes from 8 a.m. to 5 p.m. These routes, which are not marked with signs, include east–west residential streets and north–south residential streets without Night Plow Route signs.

Parking

The rates at downtown Minneapolis and St. Paul parking ramps and lots range widely based on location, time of day, the owner of the facility, and whether a sporting event or other major happening is occurring in the area. Generally you can expect to pay $4 to $7 minimum for the first hour at downtown lots in either city, but there's usually a maximum amount you'll pay—likely somewhere between $8 and $20.

To get the best price, look for surface lots near event sites or ramps/lots on the fringes of either city's downtown. For many ramps in downtown Minneapolis, parking charges can be avoided by patronizing stores and restaurants that participate in the "Do the Town" parking program, where a $20 purchase after 4 p.m. and all day on weekends will get you a parking validation. Patience is a virtue in Twin Cities parking—with prices varying so widely, you can sometimes save a bundle just by driving a block or two.

Both cities have many parking meters. Rates and enforcement times vary, so check the signs carefully and carry plenty of quarters. It's illegal to replug (put more money in the meter once it has expired) in both cities.

Keep in mind when parking in either downtown that you do not necessarily have to park right next to your destination when the winter winds blow and the temperatures plummet. In both downtown Minneapolis and downtown St. Paul, many buildings and parking ramps are connected through the Cities' respective skyway systems.

The skyway systems provide an added bonus in the summer, too—walking over the main pedestrian thoroughfares means you don't have to stop for traffic lights or crosswalks, or watch out for puddles or rogue automobiles.

Park-and-Ride Lots

Thousands of free parking spaces are available for city bus and LRT passengers at more than 100 Park-and-Ride lots throughout the Twin Cities metro area. For locations, call **Metro Transit** at (612) 373-3333, or visit the Web at www.metrotransit.org.

PUBLIC TRANSPORTATION

City Buses

METRO TRANSIT
(612) 373-3333
www.metrotransit.org
Metro Transit, the principal transportation provider in the Minneapolis and St. Paul area, is one of the country's largest transit systems. Each weekday, customers board Metro Transit buses and LRT trains an average of 240,000 times. Buses run between the Cities and the suburbs every day and evening—some downtown Minneapolis lines even run 24 hours a day. The system is made up of 118 routes served by a fleet of 821 buses, and Metro Transit has its own police department.

Adult rates for Metro Transit buses are $1.75 during non-rush-hour times and $2.25 for rush-hour times for local bus routes and $2.25 outside rush hour and $3 during rush hour for express routes. Rush hour is defined as 6 to 9 a.m. and 3 to 6:30 p.m., Mon through Fri (except holidays). Seniors over 65 and kids under 12 can ride at reduced fares during non-rush-hour times. Persons with disabilities can ride for 75 cents anytime.

Light Rail

METRO TRANSIT
(612) 373-3333
www.metrotransit.org
The Twin Cities' first light rail line, the **Hiawatha LRT,** opened in 2004. The line stretches 12 miles from downtown Minneapolis, past the Metrodome and near the University of Minnesota West Bank Campus, and then follows Hiawatha Avenue through south Minneapolis past Lake Street, tunnels under Minnehaha Park, resurfaces to pause at the Veterans' Administration Medical Center, and then moves on to Fort Snelling State Park. The line dives underground again via tunnels to the Lindbergh Terminal and emerges to stop at the Humphrey Terminal at MSP airport, then travels to the Mall of America in Bloomington.

The line features 17 stations, all individually designed to fit in with the surrounding neighborhoods. Train fares are $2 during rush hours and

$1.50 at other times—the same fares as local bus service. Rail riders must pay this fare before boarding trains and show proof of payment to transit police officers when asked. Ticket vending machines are available on rail platforms.

The Hiawatha LRT line was a source of great public debate for many years in the Twin Cities and in Minnesota state government—not surprising given the project's $715 million price tag. However, not long after the first south Minneapolis residents rode to the Mall of America, the first conventioneers boarded a train at the airport that dropped them off near their downtown Minneapolis hotels, and the first Metro commuters took advantage of the several park-and-ride lots for quick trips to their downtown jobs, the arguments were over. During the first 15 months of service, customers took 8.5 million rides—67 percent higher than projections, and Metro Transit is now planning future expansions of LRT lines. Most imminently, a Central Corridor line is set to connect the two cities' downtowns; condos on University Avenue, the Central Corridor's proposed route, are already advertising "LRT living."

Suburban Bus Systems

Several suburban areas have smaller bus systems serving outlying communities, with connections to the larger Metro Transit system in the Twin Cities. For more information on bus service in specific areas, contact the following organizations.

Northwestern suburbs

MAPLE GROVE TRANSIT
(763) 494-6005
www.ci.maple-grove.mn.us

NORTHSTAR COMMUTER COACH
(888) 528-8880
www.commutercoach.org
Northstar Commuter Coach connects the communities of Elk River and Coon Rapids with downtown Minneapolis.

PLYMOUTH METROLINK
(763) 509-5535
www2.ci.plymouth.mn.us

Southern suburbs

MINNESOTA VALLEY TRANSIT AUTHORITY
(952) 882-7500
www.mvta.com
The Minnesota Valley Transit Authority serves several suburbs just south of the Minnesota River, including Apple Valley, Burnsville, Eagan, Rosemount, and Savage.

Southwestern suburbs

SOUTHWEST METRO TRANSIT
(952) 949-2287
www.swtransit.org
SouthWest Metro Transit serves the communities of Eden Prairie, Chanhassen, and Chaska.

i Are you concerned about road conditions? Check out the Minnesota Department of Transportation Web site (www.dot.state.mn.us) or call (800) 657-3774.

Taxis

Unless you're in one of the downtowns—and probably even then—taking a taxi in the Twin Cities requires a bit of planning. You normally can't just snag one on the street; your best bet is to call a cab company and have it send a ride over to you.

The one exception to this rule is at the airport. Parked cabs waiting for fares line up at the taxi station at Lindbergh Terminal and at the curb in front of Humphrey Terminal.

The following taxi companies provide service in both the Twin Cities. Consult the Minneapolis or St. Paul Yellow Pages for further options, but understand that most companies don't have cabs in both cities.

GREEN & WHITE/SUBURBAN TAXI
Minneapolis Service: (612) 522-2222
St. Paul Service: (651) 222-2222

YELLOW CHECKER TAXI
Minneapolis Service: (763) 586-9999
St. Paul Service: (651) 777-1111

HISTORY

Like every metropolitan area in the Midwest, the Twin Cities were founded and developed as a gateway for the harvesting and processing of natural resources—in this case, notably lumber and grain. What's special about the Twin Cities is the way they've balanced continued economic and industrial development with a rich cultural life and the preservation of livable public spaces.

THE ORIGINS OF THE TWIN CITIES

Minneapolis is nicknamed the "City of Lakes" and the "Mill City." In stark contrast, St. Paul is the "Saintly City" and the "Capital City." But there are more similarities than differences between the cities—and, in fact, St. Paul's reputation as the relatively prudish half of the pair is a complete reversal from the Cities' early history, when St. Paul was about big-city high life and Minneapolis was about a conservative, Puritan work ethic. Human habitation of the Twin Cities area dates back at least 11,500 years to the Paleo-Indians, who hunted big game such as woolly mammoths, then abundant in Minnesota. The Woodland Indians left a rich fossil record: Their burial mounds were scattered throughout Minnesota when the state was settled. Indian Mounds Park, overlooking downtown St. Paul, has some of the area's finest examples of Hopewell and Dakota Indian mounds. The Mississippian cultures of the Dakotas and Ojibwes replaced these early peoples. Archaeologists posit that this occurred between A.D. 800 and 1000. The mounds and their human remains, tools, and other artifacts are protected as the historical record of the first known local residents.

In the past, the Ojibwes, or Ojibwas, were often referred to as the Chippewas and had origins in the area near Sault Ste. Marie, Michigan. The skilled hunters' territories expanded to include parts of the northern metropolitan Twin Cities. While the Ojibwes' origins were to the

east and north, the Dakotas were western Plains Indians, who at the time of European exploration occupied the Twin Cities, western and southern Minnesota, and much of present-day North Dakota and South Dakota. The French referred to the Dakotas as Sioux, a meaningless abridgement of the Ojibwe term *Nadouessioux*. The word translates as "little viper" or "lesser enemy." The derogatory name stuck for centuries, until recently when the tribe publicly assumed the proper, and more respectful, name Dakota. Both the Dakotas and Ojibwes were hunting societies, and they evolved tremendously by incorporating European tools, wares, and implements such as guns, hatchets, blankets, knives, and kettles. The contact and cultural exchange transformed the local American Indians and the Europeans. The Europeans rapidly pushed the less densely populated American Indians from their lands through treaties and warfare. Frequently internecine warfare occurred between the Dakotas, usually supported and supplied by the British, and the Ojibwes, supported by the French. However, the French *voyageurs* were the first Europeans to leave a mark on the area, even if they did not establish a permanent settlement.

The names of French explorers and traders are found on the streets, avenues, counties, and institutions in the Twin Cities. Father Louis Hennepin, a Belgian, explored French territories—including the area that became the Twin Cities—in 1680 and three years later wrote the then-best-selling book *Description of Louisiana*, in which he exaggerated the splendor of the area's natural wonders. During his visit he named the Falls of St. Anthony—which remain, as the only waterfall on the Mississippi River—after his patron saint. The town of St. Anthony, today a Minneapolis neighborhood, was located across the Mississippi River from the later birthplace of Minneapolis. In 1872 St. Anthony and Minneapolis merged. Hennepin's name is commemorated in Minneapolis's most famous thoroughfare, Hennepin Avenue, and the county of the same name. Fur trapping remained important in the area for well over a century, but a permanent settlement in the area did not occur until the United States won independence from England.

Fort Snelling was the first site permanently settled in Minnesota. The federal government established the fort to protect the then-northwestern edge of the United States. Lt. Col. Henry Leavenworth came to the present site of Fort Snelling in 1819, at the confluence of the Mississippi and Minnesota Rivers. Today the fort adjoins Minneapolis–St. Paul International Airport. Leavenworth didn't care for Minnesota winters, however, and he was reassigned to Florida in 1820. Command of the distant outpost went to Col. Josiah Snelling, and Snelling oversaw the construction of what was first known as Fort St. Anthony. The fort was completed in 1825 and was renamed in honor of its commander that same year. The fort sits on a cliff overlooking the rivers and remains one of the Twin Cities' grandest overlooks. When Fort Snelling was constructed, civilians began squatting in the area to serve the needs of soldiers and take advantage of the protection of the U.S. military.

The birth of St. Paul was a colorful page of Twin Cities history. Pierre "Pig's Eye" Parrant, a 60-year-old former *voyageur,* was the liquor bootlegger for the soldiers and citizens in and around Fort Snelling. Parrant's nickname was the result of his disfigured and blind eye; "Pig's Eye" was the original name given to St. Paul. Not surprisingly, the porcine name for the city did not last. In 1840 a young Catholic priest, Lucian Galtier, arrived in Pig's Eye, where he christened the Chapel of St. Paul. Afterward the city was generally referred to as St. Paul's Landing. Following the arrival of the

post office in 1846, the city's name was shortened to St. Paul.

Just up the Mississippi, the emergence of the other twin city, Minneapolis, was less colorful. The town of St. Anthony was founded in 1849 as a milling and lumbering center; settlers also inhabited the area that now comprises downtown Minneapolis in the 1840s, just across the Mississippi River from St. Anthony. The village of Minneapolis was not officially founded until 1856, four years after Congress rescinded 26,000 acres from Fort Snelling's control. This allowed squatters such as Col. John H. Stevens to claim and develop the land that would become downtown Minneapolis.

Minneapolis's name has interesting origins. It is an amalgam of words from two languages, the Dakota word *minne,* meaning "waters," and *polis,* the Greek word for "city." Minneapolis was founded on the west bank of the Mississippi River and St. Anthony on the east bank. In the 21st century it is difficult to believe that St. Anthony's importance early in its history eclipsed Minneapolis's, which had a relatively late start and was not chartered as a city until 1867. But as time marched on, Minneapolis's growth significantly outpaced St. Anthony's. In 1855 a suspension bridge was constructed to link the two communities. It was the first permanent bridge across the Mississippi River, and it created extensive commercial and civic ties between the rapidly expanding urban centers. The two cities merged in 1872, which established a much larger Minneapolis. The Twin Cities' growth had a significant impact on Minnesota, which became a territory in 1849 and the 32nd state in 1858.

i French explorers referred to the Minnesota River near what is now St. Paul as "Sans Pierre," meaning "without stones," because of its smooth bottom. English speakers misunderstood this to mean "St. Peter," and by the time Father Galtier arrived, the settlement once known as Pig's Eye was commonly known by that name. Galtier was more partial to St. Paul, and he decided that was close enough.

The Mill City

In the late 19th and early 20th centuries, Minneapolis became nationally prominent as the "Mill City." The emergence of milling came as the lumbering industry began to decline because of competition from the west. The ascendancy of milling created numerous allied industries and was important to the development of the diverse Minneapolis economy in the 20th century.

Milling began in Minneapolis and St. Anthony because of the proximity to St. Anthony Falls. Since the 19th century, industry and government programs have tamed much of the turbulence of the falls; in fact, to arrest the falls' natural upstream creep, engineers constructed a permanent location for the falls near what is now downtown Minneapolis. To businessmen in the area, the falls represented a source of energy for milling the vast wheat crops in the area, which rapidly expanded as Minnesota and the Upper Midwest were settled. As time progressed, each succeeding generation of mills became larger. This led to further consolidation, and industry leaders, internationally recognizable even today, emerged to dominate Minneapolis's market.

Innovations were instrumental in the development and dominance of General Mills. The corporation emerged gradually after a succession of mergers in Minneapolis's milling industry. Washburn-Crosby and Company is the major original component of General Mills. The star of the company skyrocketed following an important innovation, "new process flour," which originated in Paris but was brought to Washburn-Crosby and Company in 1871, where millers improved upon the method. The revolutionary new process flour involved milling spring wheat into white flour. No longer was winter wheat preferred. Quickly many Minneapolis mills acquired the revolutionary technology for producing new process flour. Many competitors acquired the information by dubious means. Washburn-Crosby and Company found tremendous success again in 1880, when they won the gold medal at the Millers' Exhibition in Cincinnati; thereafter the company marketed the Gold Medal brand of flour. The new technology catapulted Washburn-Crosby and Company and other Minneapolis mills to prominence as the nation's leading milling companies. By 1890 Minneapolis was the largest wheat market in the nation.

Minneapolis spawned many of the world's largest and most important mills, and they have had a profound impact on the Cities' development. Pillsbury is another Minnesota-based company, and it began milling on the Mississippi in Minneapolis. The world's largest agribusiness company—Cargill—also has origins in Minneapolis; today Cargill is headquartered in Minnetonka, a Minneapolis suburb. Milling's influence still deeply pervades Minneapolis culture. The city's minor-league baseball team between 1884 and 1960 was named the Millers. Moreover, the call letters of one of Minneapolis's radio and television stations is WCCO. The station takes its name from Washburn-Crosby and Company, an early owner of the station.

i The advertising slogan of the Washburn-Crosby Company was "Eventually—why not now?" The implication was that eventually you would realize that Washburn-Crosby's flour was better than any of its competitors', so you might as well start buying it sooner rather than later. The slogan became a national catchphrase; children across the country who told their parents they'd take out the trash eventually would find themselves rejoined with, "Eventually—why not now?"

The Capital City

St. Paul's history is encompassed in the view from the steps of the Cathedral of St. Paul on Summit Hill. Behind you is the spectacular cathedral, representing the Catholic Church; to your left is the State Capitol, representing the government; and to your right is the historic house of railroad baron James J. Hill, representing industry.

The institution of government has been central to St. Paul's history. Since the beginnings of the Minnesota Territory in 1849, St. Paul has served as the capital city, although it almost lost the capital to St. Peter (a south-central Minnesota city) in 1857. Joe Rolette, a territorial councilman, pocketed a bill passed by both houses of the legislature calling for relocating the territorial capital to St. Peter. Rolette hid with the bill for a week, but a copy of the bill was passed on to the governor, who signed it. Fortunately for St. Paul, the territorial governor was not reappointed. Later a federal district judge ruled that Minnesota Territory could not name another capital site. The capital remained in St. Paul.

The Roman Catholic Church is another important institution in the city's history. Catholicism has always found more adherents in St. Paul than in Minneapolis. The city includes large populations of Irish and German Catholics, and a small but significant number of Italian immigrants, while Minneapolis's immigration in the 19th century was dominated by Scandinavian and German Lutherans. St. Paul was established as a diocese by 1850, and in 1888 it was expanded to become the archdiocese of St. Paul. Today known as the archdiocese of St. Paul and Minneapolis, it remains headquartered in St. Paul. The Cathedral of St. Paul, which held its first mass in 1915, is one of the city's most prominent landmarks.

Industry and technology were paramount in the historical development of St. Paul. Minnesota Mining and Manufacturing Company (3M) is one of the Cities' most important companies. 3M's history began in Two Harbors, a small town northeast of Duluth, in 1902 as a manufacturer of sandpaper. The company relocated to St. Paul in 1909. Over time 3M has grown into an international corporation and remains essentially a St. Paul company, even after relocating its headquarters to the adjoining suburb of Maplewood.

Europeans Settle the Twin Cities

Minnesota immigration in the 19th and early 20th centuries for the most part mirrored patterns throughout the United States. However, there were exceptions specific to the state of Minnesota and the Twin Cities. The national perception of Minnesota is that of a state dominated by Scandinavians. This generalization is fairly accurate, if slightly exaggerated. German heritage is in fact the most common ethnic background among Minnesotans, followed closely by Norwegian, Swedish, and Irish ancestry.

Germans came to the state in greatest numbers from 1875 to 1900. Germans' contributions have been significant, especially in communities like New Ulm. In the south and west metropolitan area, there are numerous communities with German names and origins, such as New Germany, Hamburg, and Heidelberg.

Minnesota's second most-numerous group of immigrants were Norwegians, whose legacy is felt to this day. From 1875 until 1910 Norwegian immigrants came to Minnesota in the greatest numbers. O. E. Rolvaag was among this immigrant group. He wrote *Giants in the Earth* (1927), a classic novel about Norwegian immigrant farmers. His son, Karl Rolvaag, served as governor of Minnesota.

The Swedish are the third-largest ancestral group in Minnesota. The Swedes followed similar immigration patterns as the Norwegians, and the two quickly became largely indistinguishable to outsiders. The legacy of Scandinavians is manifest in the cities they founded and settled, for example, Scandia and Lindstrom. Moreover, public facilities bear the name of important past citizens of Scandinavian heritage. Olson Memorial Highway is named after governor Floyd B. Olson, who died suddenly in 1936 while running for the U.S. Senate.

Scandinavians dominated Minnesota politics during much of the state's history. Since Knute Nelson was elected governor in 1893, there have been 25 additional heads of state, and of this number only 6 were not of Scandinavian heritage. The Irish are also an essential component of Minnesota's ethnic heritage. The Irish were influential in the development of St. Paul, especially in the formation of the Catholic Church under the leadership of Archbishop John Ireland. Heavy Irish immigration began in the 1860s and ended about 1890. The ethnic group quickly integrated into the community and ascended to government positions.

Additional immigrant groups came to Minnesota and the Twin Cities. From 1820 to 1890 small groups of Swiss, Belgians, and Dutch settled in the area. Later, echoing national trends, southern, central, and eastern Europeans came to the Twin Cities. Compared with many other areas of the nation, they were smaller in number. However, they were a significant immigrant group from 1890 until 1920. Primarily Russians and various groups from the Austro-Hungarian Empire were included in this wave of immigrants. Unlike many other areas of the country, Italians and Greeks were a relatively insignificant immigrant group during this time in Minnesota. Since the 1960s Twin Cities immigrants have been predominantly non-European. Today the Twin Cities have the largest populations of Somali and Hmong settlers in the United States.

The Diverse Twin Cities' 20th-Century Economy

In the 20th century the Twin Cities diversified and developed an economy consistently among the strongest in the United States.

The milling industry became increasingly decentralized, as the largest and most successful Twin Cities milling companies gradually diversified into related industries. The decline of Minneapolis milling occurred fairly rapidly, and in the 1920s flour production was halved from the levels of the glory years before and immediately after the turn of the 20th century. Washburn-Crosby and Company changed its name to General Mills in 1928. The corporation had developed Wheaties breakfast cereal in 1924 and invented the fictional Betty Crocker, a globally recognized advertising character, in 1921. The name change represented the growing national focus of the company. General Mills moved into other food-related businesses, including numerous breakfast foods, dough mixes, and frozen foods.

Pillsbury followed a similar path, diversifying its food lines and businesses throughout the 20th century. The home of the Pillsbury Doughboy moved into prepared doughs as well as frozen and canned foods. The company entered the restaurant business in 1967, acquiring Burger King, and later became involved in additional restaurant ventures. Pillsbury was acquired by London-based Grand Metropolitan PLC (later known as Diageo PLC) in 1989 and became a subsidiary of General Mills in 2001.

As the traditional industries of the Twin Cities diversified, new high-tech businesses asserted themselves as an important component of the local economy. Some companies' roots reach back to industry and manufacturing that began in the late 19th and early 20th centuries, as is the case with the 3M Corporation, while others quickly became important businesses in the area because of technological innovation.

One such Twin Cities company is Medtronic Inc. Earl Bakken, a University of Minnesota graduate student, began his company in a northeast Minneapolis garage in 1949. Medtronic's first big success came with the development of an implantable pacemaker in 1960. Medtronic diversified into numerous medical technology fields and today is an internationally recognized corporation.

Honeywell is another important Twin Cities high-technology company. The origins of Honeywell date from a failed spring-powered thermostat company developed by A. M. Butz in 1885. Over time the fledgling company honed its technological devices. After success with its thermostat line, the company moved into heating, air-conditioning, and varied technological devices for industry and Cold War defense programs. Honeywell's military products became an important component of the company's revenues. As the Cold War came to an end, however, Honeywell ran into economic hard times.

The Twin Cities are also home to one of the nation's largest retailers, the Target Corporation. For most of its long history in the Twin Cities, Target was known as the Dayton Corporation, and later the Dayton Hudson Corporation. George Dayton opened the first Dayton's department store in downtown Minneapolis in 1902, and in 1962 the Dayton Corporation opened the first Target store in nearby Roseville. Dayton Hudson officially changed its name to the Target Corporation in 2000. The corporation is known for its local largesse, and

Close-up

Larry Millett, Author

"I always tell people the most interesting place in the world is the place where you grew up," says Larry Millett, author of the award-winning books *Lost Twin Cities* and *Twin Cities Then and Now,* as well as several Sherlock Holmes mysteries that take place in Minnesota. "I've been a fan of local history for a long time because I find it intriguing. I grew up in the Cities and went to school in downtown Minneapolis and saw firsthand the demolition of the Gateway District. My father's family goes way back in Minneapolis—my grandfather owned a bar on Washington Avenue, and his wife was the granddaughter of one of the early founders of the city. So I have deep roots in this area."

Millett, who worked as a reporter and editor at the *St. Paul Pioneer Press* for more than 30 years, has taken his love for architecture and history to write some of the most amazing and heartbreaking literary tours of the Twin Cities. Using photos kept on record at the Minnesota History Center for more than 150 years, Millett's books show in great detail how much the cities have both changed and stayed the same over the past century. *Lost Twin Cities* is composed completely of photographs and the histories of the many architectural wonders that were destroyed over the years—including the beautiful Gateway Park, which became a hangout for homeless people during the Depression—while *Twin Cities Then and Now* provides side-by-side pictures of Twin Cities neighborhoods and business districts at various points in time.

"The cities are not hugely distinct from each other architecturally, I think," says Millett about the Twin Cities today. "What happened historically is that there was a different set of architects for St. Paul and Minneapolis, so there were initial differences from the individual hands involved. But what's happened in St. Paul since is that it's probably got a better stock of historic buildings than Minneapolis, while Minneapolis probably has a better stock of newer buildings. St. Paul has been more fortunate in preserving its historic housing stock than Minneapolis, and there are reasons for that that have more to do with relative lack of development and change than any great historic sentiment, I think. Minneapolis since the turn of the century has been a more dynamic city, and the more dynamic a city is, the more quickly its architecture tends to change."

Millett's favorite buildings today? "I love St. Paul's city hall," he says. "I think it's one of our country's great art deco buildings, as is the county courthouse. The public library in St. Paul, and the Hill Reference Library, which is next door and is part of the same building but a different institution. Of course Landmark Center, the State Capitol, St. Paul Cathedral, the basics. In Minneapolis, I'm very fond of the IDS building, I think that's a nationally and internationally significant skyscraper, and the Norwest Tower (renamed the Wells Fargo Center) is very nice for its kind, too.

"It's amazing as a researcher to find out how many places aren't documented," finishes Millett. "There are places in both cities where basically there's no clue to how it looked 100 years ago because there are no pictures in the public collection. That's especially true of some of the residential neighborhoods. The downtowns of both cities are well documented, but once you get out to the residential districts, the documentation is much spottier. It all depends on how good a job the city's photographer did at the time. The Minnesota Historical Society has more than 190,000 images on their Web site (www.mnhs.org), so you can cruise through all those now. It's really phenomenal what they have, all the images of the Twin Cities in particular."

across the Twin Cities you'll find everything from art galleries to baseball fields named after the company. Other major retailers based in the Twin Cities include Best Buy and Dairy Queen.

As the 20th century came to a close, the Twin Cities saw significant corporate reorganization. Larger domestic and multinational corporations acquired several local firms. Several Twin Cities economists questioned the vitality of the area's economy, while many others felt the event was simply emblematic of global restructuring of the economy.

The Twin Cities Enter the New Millennium

The Twin Cities underwent a substantial transformation during the late 1990s. The economy is still a topic of conversation because of acquisitions and mergers of several blue-chip Twin Cities firms.

Corporations outside the Twin Cities acquired several area firms. In 1998 Norwest, a bank headquartered in the Twin Cities, was purchased by Wells Fargo of San Francisco. Honeywell merged with New Jersey–based Allied Signal in 1999 and then was bought by General Electric in 2001. Minneapolis-based ReliaStar, a financial products firm, was purchased by ING Group of the Netherlands in 2000.

Reflecting the strength of the local economy, there was a sharp increase in immigration over the past decade. The most recent Twin Cities immigrants are largely from Asia, Africa, and areas of the world that before the late 1970s were largely absent from area demographics. Many of the new immigrants came to the United States to escape political tumult, repression, and warfare. The first group to arrive were displaced Vietnamese, who were followed by numerous other Southeast Asian groups, which included Laotians, Khmers (Cambodia), and the Hmong (Laos). With the exception of Bosnians and Russians, Europeans are a relatively small component of the new arrivals.

The Hmong are a significant immigrant group in the Twin Cities. Since the late 1970s they have come from Laos, or relocated to the area from other American cities, to take advantage of the area's low unemployment and booming economy. Today more than 200,000 Hmong live in the United States. The Twin Cities, in particular St. Paul, have the largest Hmong population in the nation. The Hmong and other Southeast Asians have started hundreds of local businesses and have transformed St. Paul's Frogtown and Midway neighborhoods.

A more recent trend has seen East Africans settling in the Twin Cities. The first significant wave of African immigrants came from Ethiopia and Eritrea in the late 1980s and early 1990s. Today Ethiopian and Eritrean restaurant businesses are scattered throughout the Twin Cities, and many of the former immigrants now hold government positions.

An estimated 40,000 Somalis currently live in the United States, and approximately 20,000 reside in Minnesota. However, members of the Somali community feel the government numbers are low and believe there may be as many as 90,000 in Minnesota. The Somalis' presence is felt in the many small businesses owned and operated by the community.

The new wave of immigration is just one parallel linking the Twin Cities' past and present. Both Minneapolis and St. Paul are also reviving important elements of their past on the Mississippi riverfront.

Since the late 1980s, Minneapolis has focused on regaining its greatest historical assets—the Mississippi River and the Mill District. It began with the restoration of the James J. Hill Stone Arch Bridge—one of Minneapolis's most scenic vistas—and the Minneapolis riverfront is now home to the Mill City Museum, founded in 2003, and the new Guthrie Theater, opened in 2006. In addition, the Minneapolis Park and Recreation Board completed Mill Ruins Park in 2001.

Downriver in St. Paul the renovated Harriet Island Regional Park celebrates its city's rich history. During late summer 2000 more than 50,000 citizens attended the reopening of the park. The park represents the Cities' commitment to the riverfront.

ARCHITECTURE

The Twin Cities have different histories and perspectives on architecture. Both cities draw architectural inspiration from different sources, and it is reflected in their respective architecture.

St. Paul has always looked to the east, and in particular Boston, as a source for civic inspiration. The design of the city reflects this perspective and was in large part developed by transplanted old-stock New Englanders. The streets, like Boston's, were platted much narrower than those in Minneapolis. St. Paul views itself as a city of tradition and as the "Capital City." With a few exceptions, most notably Wells Fargo Place, St. Paul's architecture has concerned itself with human-scale structures of elegance.

St. Paul's rival across the river has taken a considerably different approach to architecture. Minneapolis has always embraced progress and modernity. This distinction between the cities has only been exacerbated as Minneapolis architecture has increasingly grown vertically.

TWIN CITIES ARCHITECTURE IN DETAIL

The Downtown Minneapolis Skyline

CAMPBELL MITHUN TOWER
222 South Ninth St., Minneapolis
(612) 342-2222
www.campbellmithuntower.com
Immense glass skyscrapers have transformed the look of downtown Minneapolis. Looking down Ninth Street, the chasm between the past and present is highly visible. On the corner of Marquette Avenue and Ninth is the 32-story Foshay Tower. Continuing down Ninth Street to Third Avenue South is the Campbell Mithun Tower. By no means is it one of the most well-known pieces of architecture in Minneapolis, yet the structure easily eclipses the once-giant Foshay Tower in sheer size. Rising 42 stories, the Campbell Mithun Tower is the fifth-tallest building in the city. Constructed in 1985, it was an early addition to the skyward growth of downtown.

CAPELLA TOWER
225 South Sixth St., Minneapolis
The Capella Tower is recognizable throughout Minneapolis by the crown that sits atop the large glass skyscraper. The 776-foot building is the second tallest in Minneapolis. It was completed in 1992 as First Bank Place; in 2008 it was renamed after primary tenant Capella University. The nationally respected firm of Pei, Cobb, Freed and Partners designed the 56-story building, which, despite its size and unusual architecture, receives far less attention than the Wells Fargo Center and the IDS Center. In the central trio of buildings topping the Minneapolis skyline, it adds a welcome touch of fanciful postmodern flair to the classic art deco look of the Wells Fargo Center and the cool modern look of the IDS Center.

DAIN RAUSCHER PLAZA
60 South Sixth St., Minneapolis
Dain Rauscher Plaza is one of the many large glass skyscrapers erected in downtown Minneapolis in the '90s. Like all of the recent additions to the Minneapolis skyline, it has a system of skyways, which connect it to the second and fourth levels of the Wells Fargo Center. At 539 feet and 40 stories, Dain Rauscher is the seventh-tallest building in Minneapolis.

THE FOSHAY TOWER
821 Marquette Ave. South, Minneapolis
(612) 359-3030

It is difficult to imagine that this obelisk once stood as the tallest skyscraper west of Chicago. The 448-foot building dominated the Minneapolis skyline and was the tallest building in the Twin Cities until the completion of the 792-foot IDS Center in 1973. Today the Foshay Tower is surrounded by modern glass-and-steel giants, which dwarf what is now the sixteenth-tallest building in the city.

The Foshay Tower draws its name from the financier behind its construction, Wilbur H. Foshay. A utilities magnate, Foshay became wealthy enough during the boom of the Roaring Twenties to construct a building modeled on the Washington Monument. The 32-story obelisk was topped with 10-foot-high letters that spelled out *Foshay*. The Foshay's dedication in 1929 was one of the most lavish in the city's history. The festivities included fireworks and a 75-piece brass band conducted by John Philip Sousa, which included his composition "Foshay Tower–Washington Memorial March." Unfortunately for Foshay, the good times were not to last. Shortly after the dedication the stock market crashed. Foshay's finances were decimated; in addition, he was convicted of fraud and sentenced to 15 years at Fort Leavenworth. Even the $20,000 check to Sousa bounced, and Sousa forbade the march to be played again until the debt was paid. (A group of Minneapolitans finally paid Foshay's debt in 1999, so Sousa's march can once again be heard.) President Franklin Delano Roosevelt pardoned Foshay after he had served three years.

Today the Foshay is one of the Twin Cities' memorable sights, with its lights illuminating the Minneapolis sky. And it does this despite its relatively diminutive stature alongside the many larger skyscrapers built in the wake of the '80s and '90s. The open-air observatory, the only outdoor observation deck in Minneapolis, offers a spectacular panoramic view of Minneapolis.

In 2008 the Foshay became the W Hotel, featuring luxury accommodations and decadent comestibles at venues including the Prohibition Bar built in Wilbur Foshay's former boardroom on the 27th floor.

HENNEPIN COUNTY GOVERNMENT CENTER
300 South Sixth St., Minneapolis
(612) 348-3000
The twin-tower exterior of the Hennepin County Government Center is unassuming enough, and offers no comfort to weary Twin Citians trudging up to contest parking tickets. However, the 24-story atrium provides a truly spectacular view, which grows as you ascend the 403-foot building. There is another interesting feature to the building—Sixth Street passes directly under the structure.

The building was completed in 1977, and it serves Hennepin County (Minneapolis and suburbs) well. In addition to the wonderful atrium, the building includes an immense water fountain.

IDS CENTER
80 South Eighth St., Minneapolis
(612) 376-8000
www.ids-center.com
The IDS Center supplanted the Foshay Tower as the tallest building in the Twin Cities when it opened in 1973—a position it has not relinquished. The IDS Center is arguably the most well-known building in the Twin Cities and is recognized as the centerpiece of the Minneapolis skyline. Seen from downtown Minneapolis and even the suburbs, the IDS Center looms large.

The IDS Center distinguishes itself in several other ways. The 57-story, 792-foot structure has more than 42,000 panes of glass as well as a 105-foot waterfall, which was added during the 1998 renovation. Designed by world-renowned architects Philip Johnson and John Burgee, the skyscraper has frequently attracted national attention.

The grandeur of the Crystal Court, named one of America's top 500 architectural landmarks by historian G. E. Kidder Smith, was featured in the *Mary Tyler Moore Show* and two motion pictures.

US BANK PLAZA
200 South Sixth St., Minneapolis
Minneapolis was known throughout the nation as the Mill City during the 19th and early 20th

centuries. As time has passed, the importance of milling has been de-emphasized, and the "City of Lakes" nickname has moved to the forefront. However, milling and its many allied services and industries remain a vital part of the area's dynamic economy.

The US Bank Plaza, which has two towers, was originally built as the Pillsbury headquarters. Pillsbury Center was completed in 1981. In 2001 Pillsbury was acquired by General Mills, which relocated the company to its suburban Golden Valley campus. US Bank took up the empty space in Pillsbury Center, and soon thereafter the building was renamed to reflect this change. US Bank Plaza is in the heart of downtown Minneapolis, where the 40-story and 22-story towers overlook the city with their immense neighbors. The beautiful atrium distinguishes it from other structures, with its eight stories of enclosed open space.

WELLS FARGO CENTER
90 South Seventh St., Minneapolis
(612) 344-1200
www.wellsfargocenter.com
The Wells Fargo Center sits at the heart of downtown and is perhaps Minneapolis's most recognizable building, with its golden-hued glow and art deco look. The third-tallest building in the Twin Cities, the Wells Fargo Center is 57 stories high, the same number of stories as the neighboring IDS Center, although it is 18 feet shorter. The building was completed in 1988 as the Norwest Center. The name changed when the Norwest and Wells Fargo banks merged in 1998.

The Wells Fargo Center was constructed in the ashes of tragedy. A Thanksgiving 1982 fire destroyed the Northwestern National Bank Building. The structure itself was not as important a piece of architecture to the community as the 157-foot "weatherball," which sat atop the building and changed color to reflect the weather forecast. Norwest set out to construct a replacement for its destroyed headquarters.

The Wells Fargo Center was completed in 1989. The Cesar Pelli–designed building features a 100-foot-high domed ceiling rotunda as well as a gorgeous lobby that hearkens back to the

1920s. The golden color of the building is created by the Kasota limestone used in its facade.

Minneapolis Architectural Landmarks
AMERICAN SWEDISH INSTITUTE
2600 Park Ave., Minneapolis
(612) 871-4907
www.americanswedishinst.org
A hundred years ago, Minneapolis's wealthy resided on Park Avenue The affluent relocated many years ago and left behind the elegant American Swedish Institute.

Completed in 1908, the palatial 33-room mansion was once a single-family residence. The châteauesque mansion was constructed for Swan and Christina Turnblad and their daughter, Lillian. The Turnblad family amassed their fortune through the *Svenska Amerikanska Posten,* a Swedish-language newspaper with a circulation of 40,000 at its zenith. In 1929 the Turnblads donated the mansion to the American Institute for Swedish Arts, Literature, and Science, which later changed its name to the American Swedish Institute. The rooms inside the mansion display interesting architectural details. For example, there is a rococo revival salon, a two-story fireplace in the Grand Hall made of carved mahogany, and 11 Swedish *kakelugnar* (porcelain stoves) in various rooms.

The institute is the oldest museum of Swedish-American history and culture in the United States. The American Swedish Institute shines on as one of the best reminders of the Park Avenue's architectural history.

BUTLER SQUARE
100 North Sixth St., Minneapolis
www.butlersquare.com
(612) 339-4343
Butler Square is perhaps the finest example of a renovated warehouse in Minneapolis. The building, formerly known as Butler Brothers Warehouse, is situated on the southwestern edge of the historic Warehouse District. The Warehouse District is filled with classic buildings that once housed Minneapolis's bustling industrial and shipping sector.

The Warehouse District, like much of the city, was neglected in the era following World War II as people flocked to the suburbs. Many businesses closed or left the warehouses for the suburbs, and much of the district sat dormant, a fate much better than that met by the neighboring Gateway District of downtown, which was largely torn down. The Warehouse District was spared the wrecking ball because the area was too far from downtown and was not considered financially lucrative. In the 1970s urban revitalization gradually began in the Warehouse District, and Butler Square was the first converted for modern use. Today the once-moribund section of Minneapolis is filled with converted warehouses that serve as office space, restaurants, bars, art galleries, and retail shops.

Butler Square's architecture is based on its past strengths combined with a superb renovation in 1973. The exterior is dark brick, and it distinguishes itself with a Moorish-style turret atop the building. The interior is where the building sets itself apart. The renovation maximized the building's open space. The original wood beams were cleaned and left exposed, and windows were installed to gaze out at the atrium. There are two large atriums from floor to ceiling, and sculptures such as George Segal's *Acrobats* accent the interior's striking beauty. After the success of Butler Square, many other renovations followed in the Warehouse District, but none have matched its architectural grandeur.

GUTHRIE THEATER
818 South Second St., Minneapolis
(612) 377-2224
www.guthrietheater.org
When the Guthrie's historic original home next to the Walker Art Center was torn down, local preservationists wept—but there's no disputing that the Guthrie's dramatic new riverside facility is a much more powerful base for what is arguably the nation's premier regional theater company. The building, which was designed by Jean Nouvel and opened in 2006, definitely makes a visual statement: it's big and it's blue. Inside, the Guthrie has three separate stages that can be (and often are) used simultaneously to host shows on different scales, as well as a gigantic skyway connecting the theater to its set-construction department across the street. Visitors will find a number of cozy spaces inside, with as many different views of downtown, the Mississippi, and the adjacent Gold Medal Park. Particularly notable is the "Endless Bridge," oddly named insofar as the cantilevered protrudance does actually end, and quite abruptly—with a fantastic view of St. Anthony Falls, the Stone Arch Bridge, and northeast Minneapolis.

HENNEPIN CENTER FOR THE ARTS
528 Hennepin Ave., Minneapolis
(612) 465-0230
www.mnshubert.org
An example of 19th-century Richardsonian romanesque architecture, the Hennepin Center for the Arts was completed in 1889 as a Masonic Temple. Like its neighbor the Lumber Exchange, it is an excellent example of the architecture that coexisted with the Hennepin Avenue Theater District until the mid-1940s. Thereafter it was neglected and the architecture modified. The onion dome on the top corner facing Fifth Street and Hennepin Avenue was lopped off. However, after years of neglect, parts of downtown were reborn. Today the Hennepin Center for the Arts thrives as a performance arts building. In 2007 the building became part of the Minnesota Shubert Performing Arts and Education Center.

LUMBER EXCHANGE BUILDING
425 Hennepin Ave., Minneapolis
In the late 19th century, downtown Minneapolis was lined with large stone structures like the Lumber Exchange Building. Completed in 1890, the 11-story building was one of Minneapolis's first "skyscrapers." Today downtown is dominated by immense glass, steel, and concrete buildings occupied by large corporations. The Lumber Exchange retains the character of the city when it first rose to prominence, and it exudes the ambience that once pervaded the city.

MINNEAPOLIS CENTRAL LIBRARY
300 Nicollet Mall, Minneapolis
(952) 847-8000
www.hclib.org

The best thing about the remarkable new Minneapolis Central Library—designed by Cesar Pelli and opened in 2006—is that it looks absolutely nothing like a library, yet functions as one very well indeed. The roof protrudes in a dramatic point under which you walk as you enter the bustling airport-like central atrium, which stairs and glass elevators climb as they convey patrons to the stacks, to a theater, and to conference rooms. What you don't see from the ground is the building's green roof, planted with grass and other growing things to increase the building's efficiency and add just a tiny bit of oxygen to the well-breathed air of downtown Minneapolis.

MINNEAPOLIS CITY HALL
350 South Fifth St., Minneapolis
(612) 673-3000

The Minneapolis City Hall was an extraordinarily expensive and time-consuming project that marked the city's arrival on the national scene. Constructed between 1888 and 1906, the city hall came at great financial costs but symbolically represented much more for the fledgling city. The city hall covers an entire city block and is distinguished by its 341-foot-high clock tower, which rings daily throughout downtown.

MINNEAPOLIS POST OFFICE
100 South First St., Minneapolis
(612) 349-4715

The Minneapolis Post Office is a colossal 2-block art moderne structure located in the heart of the birthplace of the city. The building was completed in 1933, and the architecture reflects its Works Progress Administration (WPA) origins.

The site of the post office was once the home of Col. John H. Stevens's white frame house, the first structure in Minneapolis. This important piece of architecture was relocated to Minnehaha Park in south Minneapolis, where it can be visited today.

The post office is an excellent example of the fine government structures built by the WPA. The interior is particularly stunning. The lobby includes plenty of fine stone, brass, and glass, which is immaculately maintained. The exterior is more subdued and is constructed of stone with large metal grilles over the two entrances. The post office exudes the confidence that was necessary during the darkest days of the Great Depression.

SHUBERT THEATER
Fifth St. and Hennepin Ave., Minneapolis
www.mnshubert.org

The 1910 Shubert Theater is one of the Twin Cities' most contentious pieces of architecture. The grand old theater sat vacant for years on the corner of Seventh Street and First Avenue, where it was once a part of Minneapolis's extensive Hennepin Avenue and Seventh Street theater district. But much had changed since the Shubert's construction, and the Shubert had fallen from glory.

Local leaders and business interests called for the theater's demolition, especially in light of its location on the lucrative, vacant, and until recently undeveloped Block E. The theater stood in the way of development on the highly sought piece of property. A plan for the theater's destruction was met by resistance from local arts organizations. Fortunately, the theater was spared; in 1999 it was moved 2 blocks away and placed beside the Hennepin Center for the Arts. The Shubert weighs an astounding 5,816,000 pounds or 2,908 tons, and its move set a world record for the largest structure relocated.

In 2007 the building became part of the Minnesota Shubert Performing Arts and Education Center; in 2009, ground was broken on a renovation that will restore and reopen the Shubert as the Cities' premier dance venue.

TARGET FIELD
1 Twins Way, Minneapolis
(612) 659-3400
http://minnesota.twins.mlb.com

Target Field, located on the west side of downtown Minneapolis, is the Twin Cities' newest major athletic field: As this guide went to press, the Minnesota Twins were just preparing to play their 2010 season opener on its carefully watched grass after spending nearly three decades on Astroturf in the Hubert H. Humphrey Metrodome. The lack of a roof (not even a retractable one) will be the first thing baseball fans notice about this new park, but it also happens to feature steeply raked seats designed to put spectators as close as possible to the action, as well as a massive scoreboard that will be the envy of the Major Leagues. People will surely find nits to pick when the field opens, but anticipation is high—and all signs are that the hype is justified.

WALKER ART CENTER
1750 Hennepin Ave., Minneapolis
(612) 375-7600
www.walkerart.org
You wouldn't expect one of the country's premier contemporary art centers to skimp on design quality when building a new wing, and indeed, the Walker went right to the top, hiring cutting-edge international architects Herzog and de Meuron to design the 2005 addition to its 1971 facility. There's no danger of missing the new Walker if you come anywhere near it: Herzog and de Meuron designed a massive silver-screened cube that perches high on Hennepin Avenue right at the point where Uptown becomes downtown. The addition reminds many of an ice cube, and the polar theme continues inside, where the tall, asymmetrical white corridors will make you feel like you're in Superman's ice palace. The galleries are more flexible than the original building's spaces, but the real gem of the new addition is the dark and beautiful McGuire Theater, which hosts performances by local, national, and international dance and theater groups. It's a cool place.

UNIVERSITY OF MINNESOTA—TWIN CITIES: MINNEAPOLIS CAMPUS CIVIL AND MINERAL ENGINEERING BUILDING
500 Pillsbury Dr. SE, Minneapolis
(612) 625-5522
Civil Engineering stands in stark contrast to the variations of classic architecture that dominate the campus. More than 95 percent of the building was constructed underground, and it extends 110 feet below the surface. Civil Engineering was planned during the OPEC oil embargo of 1974, when the building was simultaneously an architectural curiosity and a source for research into more efficient energy and land use. The Minnesota Legislature allocated funds for numerous experimental features in the structure, which was completed in 1983. Both active and passive solar heating are included for research purposes.

FREDERICK R. WEISMAN ART MUSEUM
333 East River Rd., Minneapolis
(612) 625-9494
www.weisman.umn.edu
The Frederick R. Weisman Art Museum is one of the Twin Cities' most controversial pieces of architecture. Detractors have called the structure an ugly, discombobulated homage to the Tin Man in *The Wizard of Oz*, while enthusiasts glow incessantly about Frank Gehry's internationally acclaimed style. However, one fact is for certain: Gehry created a museum that is not, in the words of former University of Minnesota president Nils Hasselmo, "another brick lump."

The museum features brushed stainless steel arranged in bold, undulating angles. Gehry links the museum to the more architecturally conservative buildings with terra-cotta bricks on the south and east sides. The interior of the museum includes extensive use of natural lighting sources, whether it is the skylights or large windows tastefully framing the view of downtown Minneapolis. The Weisman houses five galleries. Gehry designed an expansion of the museum (including a new gallery wing and a café), construction of which is now under way.

The Weisman Art Museum has housed the University of Minnesota's art collection since 1934, although the current building opened in 1993. The museum emphasizes art of recent vintage. The Weisman is definitely worth a visit for its fine galleries and strong programming as well as its astounding architecture. The Weisman is on the East Bank of campus, where Washington Avenue crosses over East River Parkway. Admis-

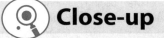 **Close-up**

Mill City Museum

Minneapolis is most commonly known to visitors as the City of Lakes. But the city's first nickname, "Mill City," was the nickname that elevated the city to national prominence. In recent years, the Minneapolis riverfront has undergone a renaissance as, piece by piece, elements of Minneapolis's past have been revived. The **Mill City Museum,** which opened in 2003, reclaimed that once-buried and nearly forgotten history.

The Mill City Museum is located in the heart of Minneapolis's historic milling district. Shortly after the town of Minneapolis was founded in 1856, small mills congregated on both the east bank (until 1872, St. Anthony) and the west bank of the Mississippi River near St. Anthony Falls. At this, the only waterfall on the Mississippi, the river provided an exceptional source of power for milling the increasingly limitless wheat of the Upper Midwest, and the number and size of the mills swelled. By 1890 Minneapolis had established itself as the nation's largest wheat market, and Washburn-Crosby and Company (the antecedent of General Mills) was among the Cities' leaders in the industry with its nationally recognized trademark, Gold Medal Flour.

To serve these needs, the company constructed the Washburn A Mill. Like its predecessor, the A Mill was plagued by fire, but none as deadly as the May 2, 1878, explosion, which killed 18. The mill was rebuilt and remained in operation until 1965; for many years thereafter, the A Mill was left dormant, during which time the structure was seriously damaged. Parts of the old mill were destroyed and enormous gaping holes were left, exposing the structure to Minneapolis's harsh weather. In 1991 another fire nearly destroyed the vacant building. This was the challenge for the Minneapolis architectural firm of Meyer, Scherer & Rockcastle Ltd., which designed the Mill City Museum to incorporate the ruins of the Washburn A Mill.

The Mill City Museum design retained many elements of the old mill: milling machinery, flour bins, rail corridor, engine house, and wheat house. While much of the mill has been restored, in some cases the architect has exploited scenic views created by fire damage, including a breathtaking view of St. Anthony Falls.

Architect Tom Meyer adapted this unique structure for the numerous attractions at the Mill City Museum. The museum emphasizes hands-on experiences, like those offered by the Minnesota Historical Society, and includes a waterpower laboratory and a test kitchen. The eight-story "Flour Tower" ride features regional history; during the holidays it serves as the venue for a unique and humorous theatrical presentation about Christmas at the mill. Another attraction is the open-air courtyard within the walls of the mill ruins, which in the summer hosts live music by popular artists.

The museum features several historical exhibits beyond milling, examining the influence of waterpower both in milling and in allied industries on the Mississippi River. The museum demonstrates the role of milling in the development of Minneapolis's dynamic economy and its impact on immigration patterns, railroad development, and agriculture.

The structure includes a bookstore, classrooms, and a restaurant. The mill also incorporates lofts on the top five floors, with spectacular views of downtown Minneapolis and St. Anthony Falls.

The Mill City Museum is located on the Minneapolis riverfront at 704 South Second St. near the intersection with Portland Avenue. For more information, you can contact the museum at (612) 341-7555 or visit the museum on the Web at www.millcitymuseum.org.

sion is free, although the parking garage will set you back a few bucks.

MCNAMARA ALUMNI CENTER
200 Oak St. SE, Minneapolis
(612) 624-7570
www.alumnicenter.umn.edu
The McNamara Alumni Center, completed in 2000, is an apt bridge between the alumni and present students and contains something for the admirers of both the school's august history and daring architecture. Detractors, however, refer to the domed 90-foot geode as "the Death Star"; its unusual striated look earned it a mention in the book *Weird Minnesota*.

The McNamara, a $45 million monument to the school's alumni, sits on the eastern edge of the campus 1 block south of the intersection of Oak Street SE and University Avenue SE. Until the 1980s the McNamara Alumni Center's lot was the site of Memorial Stadium. The stadium served as the home for the Minnesota Golden Gophers football team; when the university announced a few years ago that it would build a new outdoor stadium, some alumni grumbled that it should never have torn down the first one. Today the restored Memorial Stadium arch serves as the entrance to the Curtis L. and Arleen M. Carlson Heritage Gallery, where the University of Minnesota's alumni and faculty are honored with artifacts, images, and stories.

NORTHROP MEMORIAL AUDITORIUM
84 Church St. SE, Minneapolis
(651) 624-2345
http://northrop.umn.edu
Northrop Memorial Auditorium stands out elegantly on the north end of Northrop Mall, a long grassy area at the heart of the Minneapolis campus. The mall is lined with stunning architecture, and it was the dream of architect Cass Gilbert that the mall would stretch to the banks of the Mississippi River. Unfortunately, his dreams were thwarted when the Coffman Memorial Union was completed at the base of the Mall in 1940. Since then the union has stared across the mall at Northrop Memorial Auditorium, and Gilbert's plan has not been revived.

The neoclassical building is among the most beautiful and storied on campus. The large brick structure features a 10-column facade and was named after University of Minnesota president Cyrus Northrop (1884–1911). Completed in 1929, Northrop Memorial Auditorium serves as an auditorium and concert hall. And with more than 4,800 seats, the auditorium is one of the area's most beautiful venues. Today the auditorium hosts dance and jazz performances, as well as other special events.

TCF BANK STADIUM
2009 SE University Ave.
(612) 625-5000
http://stadium.gophersports.com
The Metrodome will always hold a special place in the hearts of Minnesota sports fans—and it still holds the Vikings pro football team, somewhat to their displeasure—but between Target Field and this new (2009) field for the Golden Gophers, Minnesotans are basking in the sunshine and the fresh air as beloved teams return to the great outdoors. The Gophers aren't just coming back outside with this stadium, they're coming back to campus, where energy is high on game days. "The Bank" is built in the style of classic college football stadiums, open on one side to fully engage its surroundings and allow a view of downtown Minneapolis. Game tickets aren't easy to come by, but it's worth planning ahead to take part in a great Minnesota tradition. (Starting with a planned stop by U2 in summer 2010, the stadium will also host concerts and other events.) Gooooooooooooo, Gophers!

WALTER LIBRARY
Pleasant Ave. SE, Minneapolis
(612) 624-3366
www.lib.umn.edu
Walter Library, which underwent a $63.4 million renovation between 1999 and 2002, is a building important in the history of the campus and the Twin Cities. Constructed in 1924, it was the university's third principal library. The recent renovation included restoring the staircase, lobby, and reading rooms to their original glory, and

creating spaces for the Digital Technology Center, the Science and Engineering Library, the Learning Resources Center, and the Minnesota Supercomputing Institute. The structure is built in the Roman Renaissance style, the dominant style of the campus's architectural epicenter, Northrop Mall. It has the most decorative facade on the mall, making use of red brick and limestone trim.

St. Paul's Architectural Treasures

BANDANA SQUARE
1021 East Bandana Blvd., St. Paul
During the past century the site of present-day Bandana Square has served several roles. The structure was constructed to serve as a train repair shop. As the railroad industry declined, the repair shop closed. After sitting vacant the huge building was renovated in the 1980s and reopened as a shopping mall. Unfortunately, the beautiful shopping center did not fare well, and Bandana Square is now used for office space. Bandana Square hosts a link to its past—the Twin Cities Model Railroad Club—where fans of architecture can revisit the old train garage in miniature surrounded by facades of the historic Twin Cities.

FIRST NATIONAL BANK BUILDING
332 Minnesota St., St. Paul
(651) 225-3666
www.firstnationalbankbuilding.info
What the Foshay Tower is to downtown Minneapolis, the First National Bank Building is to downtown St. Paul: a charming and historic skyscraper (built in 1931) that still makes a strong impression despite being surrounded by newer peers. Between the two, the First National Bank Building has the advantage of being in a town where construction has proceeded much more slowly, meaning that its iconic red-lit "1st" sign is still visible as you approach downtown St. Paul from any direction. Among this building's historic distinctions is that it is one terminal of the world's first skyway, built to connect the First National Bank Building with the adjacent Merchants Bank Building—its predecessor as St. Paul's tallest building.

FORT SNELLING
MN 5 and 55, St. Paul
(651) 726-1171
www.mnhs.org/fortsnelling
Completed in 1825, Fort Snelling was the first permanent white settlement in what would become Minnesota and was once the farthest west military post in the United States. As the surrounding area was developed, the fort's outer structures were torn down; though the fort was rebuilt in the 1960s and '70s, the only original structure to remain is the central Round Building, the oldest surviving building in Minnesota.

The restored fort features examples of 19th-century architecture that emphasize practical, defense-oriented designs over opulence. On the site are a hospital, a forge, and a garrison for defending the confluence of the Mississippi and Minnesota Rivers. Minnesota, like much of the Midwest, has a relatively brief history, and at Fort Snelling visitors can examine a restored version of the architecture of the first Minnesotans of European heritage.

GOVERNOR'S RESIDENCE
1006 Summit Ave., St. Paul
www.admin.state.mn.us/govres
The location of the governor's residence is ideal. Summit Avenue is the historic home of St. Paul's old wealth. The beautiful wide parkway is lined with trees and elegant Victorian homes and was the childhood home of F. Scott Fitzgerald and railroad baron James J. Hill.

William Channing Whitney, a prominent Twin Cities architect, designed the home in the English Tudor revival style; it was donated to the State of Minnesota in 1965 and has served as the governor's official residence ever since, though recent governors have generally preferred to remain in their own homes most of the time. The interior has been renovated several times. Tours are available.

JAMES J. HILL HOUSE
240 Summit Ave., St. Paul
www.mnhs.org/places/sites/jjhh
(651) 297-2555

The James J. Hill House was once one of the largest mansions in the Midwest, appropriately built for one of St. Paul's wealthiest and most powerful men. In the age of barons of industry, Hill was one of the area's most prominent citizens. Mansions like Hill's helped create the reputation Summit Avenue retains even today—as the street where St. Paul's old money resides.

Ironically, James J. Hill arrived via riverboat at age 17 from Ontario, Canada, in 1838. Hill was to play a central role in the development of another conveyance, the railroad, in the rapidly developing United States. He built a railroad empire, the Great Northern Railroad, from his adopted home of St. Paul.

Perhaps the most impressive aspect of the Hill House is its sheer size. The beautiful home was constructed with red sandstone and has many examples of skilled craftsmanship. The carved woodwork and stained glass are of the finest quality. There are 32 rooms, 13 bathrooms, and 22 fireplaces, which were a necessity for Minnesota's harsh winters when the house was constructed in 1891. Boasting 36,000 square feet of living space, it was a fitting residence for one of Minnesota's, and the nation's, greatest railroad tycoons.

LANDMARK CENTER
75 West Fifth St., St. Paul
www.landmarkcenter.org
(651) 292-3233
Landmark Center is one of many architectural gems in downtown St. Paul's cultural quarter, which includes the Ordway Center for the Performing Arts, the Children's Museum, and the Science Museum. Landmark Center was erected in 1906 as the Federal Courthouse, where St. Paul's famous gangsters were once prosecuted. Today Landmark Center serves as home to offices and small museums, but the architecture continues to convey the structure's history. The building's tower overlooks Rice Park, which is surrounded by several of St. Paul's most attractive pieces of architecture.

MARJORIE MCNEELY CONSERVATORY AT COMO PARK
www.comozooconservatory.org
1225 Estabrook Dr., St. Paul
(651) 487-8201
The Marjorie McNeely Conservatory at Como Park is the architectural centerpiece of this lovely St. Paul public park. The park was designed by one of St. Paul's most important landscape architects, Horace W. S. Cleveland, and a German immigrant, Frederick Nussbaumer. Later Nussbaumer drew up the plans for the conservatory, which was inspired by London's Crystal Palace in Hyde Park.

The conservatory features a palm dome in the center of this glass structure, and the building is split into several wings displaying seasonally blooming flora. The conservatory is expertly integrated into the landscape of the rolling hills, ravine, and gardens that surround the structure. The conservatory had a major facelift in 1993, and in 2006 was expanded with a lauded design that has its own character but complements the classic core structure. The combination of architecture and flowers make the conservatory a treat for Twin Citians throughout the year.

MINNESOTA STATE CAPITOL
75 Constitution Ave., St. Paul
www.mnhs.org/places/sites/msc
(651) 296-2881
The Minnesota State Capitol is one of the area's architectural landmarks for several reasons. The 223-foot unsupported marble dome is the largest in the world. The architectural splendor also includes statues, columns, arches, and murals.

Cass Gilbert won a capitol design competition in 1898. Gilbert designed several Twin Cities buildings and the plan for the University of Minnesota's Northrop Mall (which was significantly modified) before moving on to national prominence with designs such as the Woolworth Building in New York City. The capitol was completed in 1904, and the cost of the new structure was the subject of great controversy. The third state capitol, most Minnesotans would agree today, was worth the hefty price tag.

ORDWAY CENTER FOR THE PERFORMING ARTS

345 Washington St. North, St. Paul

(651) 282-3000

www.ordway.org

A quarter-century after the Ordway was built, people seem to be astonished by the fact that it doesn't look ugly yet! The Ordway occupies prime real estate along Rice Park, and it has some of the most distinguished architectural neighbors in town—good company that it very comfortably sits among. Behind its cascading glass facade is a lobby that seems to stretch forever in each direction once you're inside: right, left, up and up and up. Inside, the Ordway's main stage is modeled on a classic opera-house template, and indeed it's at its best when hosting productions by the Minnesota Opera or the Ordway's own top-notch productions of Broadway musicals. It's a fine home for the St. Paul Chamber Orchestra as well, but it will be even finer when the McKnight Theatre—the complex's undistinguished smaller hall—is replaced by a concert hall custom-built for orchestral music. (That project remained in the fund-raising stage as this guide went to press.)

ST. PAUL CITY HALL AND RAMSEY COUNTY COURTHOUSE

15 West Kellogg Blvd., St. Paul

www.stpaul.gov

(651) 266-8989

St. Paul City Hall and the Ramsey County Courthouse is an exemplary combination of neoclassical and art deco. The building's facade is an example of neoclassical style, while the art deco interior is where the building shines. Constructed during the Great Depression, St. Paul City Hall was built with the finest craftsmanship. When the nation's economy hit rock bottom, many of the nation's most talented artists and artisans were unemployed. Building costs plummeted, but the city decided to carry on with its original allocation for construction costs, and it got a lot of bang for its many bucks. The results are breathtaking, particularly in the lobby, which glitters with black marble walls and features a 36-foot-high rotat-

ing statue named *Visions of Peace*. The original 1931 structure was renovated in 1993, restoring its luster.

ST. PAUL HOTEL

350 Market St., St. Paul

(651) 292-9292

www.saintpaulhotel.com

The St. Paul Hotel is one of the city's grand old institutions, and it looks it. The elegant, asymmetrical building holds St. Paul's most elite hotel rooms and a historic bar that has been a popular stop for downtown denizens since the building's 1910 construction—including a now-notorious stint in the '30s as a hangout for the many gangsters who were made right at home by the corrupt Capital City cops.

ST. PAUL PUBLIC LIBRARY

90 West Fourth St., St. Paul

(651) 266-7000

www.sppl.org

Twin Cities libraries are distinguished by unusually fine architecture. The St. Paul Public Library is a case in point—especially the James J. Hill Reference Library Reading Room. The reading room is an exemplar of Beaux-Arts classicism, and the two-story reading room is surrounded by the book stacks and Ionic columns, with abundant finely crafted woodwork and granite floors. Large comfy tables and chairs entice visitors to enjoy the resources available or quietly absorb the architecture. Recently renovated, the library is one of downtown St. Paul's many beautiful public buildings.

SCIENCE MUSEUM OF MINNESOTA

120 Kellogg Blvd. West, St. Paul

(651) 221-9444

www.smm.org

Inside, the Science Museum gives curators and museumgoers exactly what they want: massive amounts of flexible exhibit space, as well as extensive classroom space and an Omnitheater dome that rotates back to reveal a flat IMAX screen. From the outside, it looks like exactly what it is: a series of big boxes. (The 1999 building is the fourth home of the museum, which was founded in 1907.) Say this for the museum: It fits all too well into a St. Paul skyline with plenty of other undistinguished boxes to keep it company. Say this also: It makes good use of its riverbluff location, with a huge glass wall and multiple balconies providing fine views of a charming stretch of the river and, beyond it, Harriet Island and West St. Paul.

UNION DEPOT
214 East Fourth St., St. Paul
The Union Depot was constructed between 1917 and 1923. At the time the railroad was a prominent means of transportation, and a serpentine labyrinth of tracks circled the depot. Since then the importance of the railroad has dwindled, but the depot remains—although it serves a different purpose. Today the Union Depot is an awe-inspiring architectural work that takes advantage of a high ceiling, balconies, and plenty of stone. Restaurants occupy the immense lobby where passengers once arrived and departed, and visitors may dine in one of St. Paul's most historic and architecturally attractive settings.

WELLS FARGO PLACE
30 East Seventh St., St. Paul
www.wellsfargoplace.com
(651) 229-2800
Completed in 1987, the 37-story Wells Fargo Place (formerly known as the Minnesota World Trade Center) sits high atop the St. Paul skyline as the city's tallest building. The architectural design of the building is similar to many of the colossal Minneapolis structures. The exterior has plenty of dark glass, which reflects light on sunny summer days.

HOUSES OF WORSHIP

Minneapolis

THE BASILICA OF SAINT MARY
88 North 17th St., Minneapolis
(612) 333-1381
www.mary.org

The Basilica of Saint Mary celebrated its first Mass on May 31, 1914, as a then-unique Catholic place for worship. It was the first basilica in America, an institution created to serve the needs of Minneapolis. While St. Paul held the first mass in its own breathtakingly beautiful cathedral in 1915, the other Twin City was allowed by the Vatican to construct the basilica. As with the Cathedral of St. Paul, Emmanuel L. Masqueray (1861–1917) was the architect for the Basilica of Saint Mary.

Masqueray unveiled his design in 1906. The colossal basilica features a 200-foot dome and an impressive nave. At the time of its construction, the 140-foot by 82-foot nave was considered the widest in the world. The stained-glass windows, designed by Thomas Gaytee, are another extraordinary feature of the basilica.

CHRIST CHURCH LUTHERAN
3244 34th Ave. South, Minneapolis
(612) 721-6611
www.christchurchluth.org
Built in a humble working-class neighborhood in south Minneapolis, Christ Church Lutheran is the last design of Finnish architect Eliel Saarinen.

Saarinen's great architectural pieces began with the railway station in Helsinki (1905–1914). He went on to design a series of central European railway stations. Later, Saarinen immigrated to the United States, where his work culminated with the Cranbrook School (circa 1925). He was selected for Christ Church Lutheran's design, which became his last architectural triumph, completed in 1949.

Christ Church Lutheran is on 34th Avenue South 2 blocks south of East Lake Street and 5 blocks east of Minnehaha Avenue.

HENNEPIN AVENUE UNITED METHODIST CHURCH
511 Groveland Ave., Minneapolis
(612) 871-5303
www.hennepinchurch.org
The Hennepin Avenue United Methodist Church is yet another impressive piece of architecture near Hennepin Avenue. Like the St. Mark's Episcopal Cathedral, it was designed by Hewitt and

Brown and is an example of English Gothic revival work. The octagonal base of the steeple and tall, slender spire set the church apart and position it among the Twin Cities' most spectacular architectural churches. The church is on Groveland Avenue 1 block east of Hennepin Avenue and 1 block south of Loring Park.

OUR LADY OF LOURDES CHURCH
One Lourdes Place, Minneapolis
(612) 379-2259
www.ourladyoflourdesmn.com
Not only is Our Lady of Lourdes the oldest standing church in Minneapolis, but it also has a simultaneously tumultuous and intriguing history. During each successive turn in the history of the church, at least minimal architectural alterations were made. Surprisingly, despite the cobbled nature of the church's construction, it is an awe-inspiring work and a landmark in historic St. Anthony.

Our Lady of Lourdes can be found at the intersection of Hennepin Avenue East and Lourdes Place, in the St. Anthony neighborhood across the Hennepin Avenue Bridge from downtown Minneapolis.

ST. MARK'S EPISCOPAL CATHEDRAL
519 Oak Grove St., Minneapolis
(612) 870-7800
www.ourcathedral.org
The Cathedral Church of St. Mark was designed by one of the Twin Cities' most renowned architectural firms in the early 20th century, Brown and Hewitt. Between 1904 and 1930 the firm created several outstanding pieces of architecture, including this church, completed in 1910. Edwin H. Hewitt was the primary designer of most of the firm's work, which was heavily influenced by the eclectic Beaux-Arts style. Emphasizing revivalism in architectural designs, Beaux-Arts works are symmetrical and balanced. The style was a popular foil for modernism.

As a member of the church, Hewitt set out to create a design appropriate to his faith. Denominationally, the church is Episcopalian; the design reflects this heritage. English Gothic revival domi-

nates the church's architectural style. The tower is inspired by the example found at Magdalen College at Oxford, albeit significantly scaled down.

Adding to the church's splendor is its location on the southern edge of Loring Park, which is one of Minneapolis's most beautiful parks. You can find the Cathedral Church of St. Mark at the intersection of Oak Grove Street and West 15th Street.

St. Paul
ASSUMPTION CHURCH
51 West Seventh St., St. Paul
(651) 224-7536
The Assumption Church was constructed between 1869 and 1874. Located in an area of downtown St. Paul where architectural change has occurred at a rapid pace, the church remains a distinctive and important piece of architecture.

As St. Paul developed, religious communities constructed churches to fulfill their spiritual needs. The ethnic heritage and denomination of the church often profoundly influenced the architecture of individual structures. This was certainly the case with the Assumption Church, which was formed to meet the needs of German Catholics. The Ludwigskirche in Munich, Germany, heavily influenced the German Romanesque revival design of the church. For materials, the church makes use of Minnesota limestone. Rising 210 feet, the twin towers are the most distinguishable features of the church and are a perennial landmark in the ephemeral architecture of downtown St. Paul.

Assumption Church is located at the intersection of West Seventh Street and St. Peter Street, 2 blocks northeast of the Xcel Energy Center.

CATHEDRAL OF ST. PAUL
239 Selby Ave., St. Paul
(651) 228-1766
www.cathedralsaintpaul.org
The Cathedral of St. Paul is one of the Twin Cities' most recognizable landmarks. The sheer size of the structure is daunting, and it stands like a sentinel atop Cathedral Hill, where it overlooks

downtown St. Paul, directly across the interstate from the Minnesota State Capitol. Capitol City residents are justly proud of the edifice, though famous son F. Scott Fitzgerald was unimpressed with its sturdy proportions. "A big white bulldog on its haunches," he called it.

The grand scale of the Cathedral of St. Paul reflects its source of inspiration. The cathedral, which was designed by Emmanuel L. Masqueray, was modeled after Saint Peter's Cathedral in Rome. Also instrumental in erecting the cathedral was Archbishop John Ireland, who envisioned and raised the money as a tribute to the faith of the archdiocese. The cathedral held its first mass in 1915, although the building wasn't completed and dedicated until 1958.

The features of the cathedral are breathtaking. The interior is baroque in design, makes use of Minnesota granite and travertine, and is decorated with stained glass and paintings, including several beautiful frescoes. The dome extends 175 feet above the cathedral and can be seen from great distances. Guided tours are held Monday, Wednesday, and Friday (except holidays) at 1 p.m., when visitors may enjoy the Cathedral of St. Paul's astounding beauty.

MOUNT ZION TEMPLE
1300 Summit Ave., St. Paul
(651) 698-3881
www.mzion.org
Founded in 1856 as the Mount Zion Hebrew Congregation, Mount Zion Temple was the first Jewish house of worship in the Twin Cities and is lauded by architects as one of the finest such buildings in the nation. The present building, the fourth to house the congregation, is located on elegant Summit Avenue. Eric Mendelsohn, an internationally renowned Bauhaus architect, designed the stylish, modern building, which was dedicated in 1954. Guided tours of the interior are offered regularly.

ST. CLEMENT'S EPISCOPAL CHURCH
901 Portland Ave., St. Paul
(651) 228-1164
www.stclements-stp.org

Many are surprised to hear that this attractive and quaint church was designed by Cass Gilbert, who later served as architect for the colossal Minnesota State Capitol. The structure makes fine use of material but on a much smaller scale. Intimacy is stressed. The church is constructed of slate, stone, and wood; conveys a sense of solace; and is scaled to parishioners' size. St. Clement's Episcopal Church was completed in 1894.

VIRGINIA STREET SWEDENBORGIAN
170 Virginia St., St. Paul
(651) 224-4553
www.virginiastchurch.org
This small gem by Cass Gilbert is easy to miss—in fact, most locals don't even know it exists. The stone exterior is like something out of a hidden village, and the interior provides an intimate venue for meetings of the Swedenborgian congregation (an obscure branch of Christianity that had numerous adherents among intellectuals and mystics when the church was built in 1886) as well as for readings sponsored by the nearby Common Good Books. Don't miss a chance to see Common Good Books owner Garrison Keillor perched on one of the chapel's thrones, in conversation with a visiting author sitting in the other.

West

COLONIAL CHURCH OF EDINA
6200 Colonial Way, Edina
(952) 925-2711
www.colonialchurch.org
The Colonial Church of Edina is a curiosity that stands in stark contrast to the first-tier suburban architecture in the neighborhoods just north of MN 62. The church was modeled on a New England colonial village. Architect Richard Hammel visited a church in Barnstable, Massachusetts, that was built by the Pilgrims in the 17th century. The Edina design, in keeping with the source architecture, is simple and subdued. The church is gray with white trim and features a bell tower at the center. The colonial village design includes space for a sanctuary, lounges, and additional rooms for church activities.

East

CHURCH OF ST. MICHAEL
611 South Third St., Stillwater
(651) 439-4400
www.stillwatercatholics.org
Catholic missionaries arrived in Stillwater in 1849, and the first Church of St. Michael was built in 1853. In 1873 the construction of the present Church of St. Michael began, and the building was completed in 1875. The yellow Kasota-stone church with its 190-foot spire sits atop a hill overlooking the city of Stillwater and the St. Croix River Valley. Over the years St. Michael's has been renovated several times to maintain its striking beauty. In a city filled with architectural treasures, the Church of St. Michael stands out as one of Stillwater's prettiest structures.

TWIN CITIES BRIDGES

With the Mississippi River winding through Minneapolis and St. Paul, the Twin Cities are blessed with many bridges, ranging from the historic Stone Arch Bridge to—almost adjacent to that span—the high-tech new I-35W bridge.

HENNEPIN AVENUE SUSPENSION BRIDGE
Main Street SE and Hennepin Avenue
Minneapolis
The original Hennepin Avenue Bridge was completed in 1855; it was the first permanent span across the Mississippi River and was necessary for the creation of the city of Minneapolis in 1872. The villages of St. Anthony (east bank) and Minneapolis (west bank) could not have merged into one city without it.

The current bridge is the fourth structure on the site. It is a larger, architecturally scaled-down version of the Disneyesque first two bridges that stood here between 1855 and 1891. On the current bridge, completed in 1990, two minimally ornamented, relatively short towers sit on either side of the Mississippi, anchoring the lopping cables that support the elegant bridge. It's notable internationally as the world's shortest cable-stayed suspension bridge, and locally for its view of the iconic Grain Belt Beer sign.

HIGH BRIDGE
Smith Ave., St. Paul
The High Bridge is a landmark that provides one of the best views of downtown St. Paul. The original High Bridge opened in 1889 to link St. Paul's West Seventh Street and the upper West Side. The span of the bridge was an astounding 2,770 feet, and it was constructed with more than one million pieces of iron. It was no small accomplishment for its era; however, the bridge deteriorated over the course of almost a century, and it was razed in 1985.

St. Paul completed construction of the current replica High Bridge in 1987. Once again, the 160-foot-high bridge had a steep 4 percent grade. In addition, the bridge consisted of 11 spans, the longest stretching 520 feet.

I-35W BRIDGE
The 2007 collapse of the bridge replaced by this span made international news: It was a major tragedy that took 13 lives, as well as a wake-up call to a country that wondered whether it had been paying enough attention to its aging infrastructure. Despite the fact that this new bridge was built at a breakneck pace, opening in September 2008, you can feel as safe crossing it as on any highway bridge in the world: It's been inspected more closely than a teenager's secret copy of *Playboy,* and it features the very latest in active stress-monitoring technology. It's even pretty good-looking: When the sleek span is blue-lit at night, it's clearly visible from any number of vantage points along the river, serving both as a monument to the fallen and as a beacon of hope for the future.

MENDOTA BRIDGE
MN 55, Mendota
The spectacular 4,119-foot Mendota Bridge carries MN 55 over the Minnesota River and Fort Snelling State Park to link southeast Minneapolis with the southern suburbs of St. Paul. When the original bridge was completed in 1926, it was the longest concrete arch bridge in the world, and it remains one of the longest bridges of any kind in the United States—only New York City's Verraz-

ano-Narrows Bridge, San Francisco's Golden Gate Bridge, and several highway trestle bridges in the Louisiana bayous are longer. The deck of the bridge was completely rebuilt in the early 1990s, a two-year project that closed the bridge entirely during construction. The Mendota Bridge is on the National Register of Historic Places.

STILLWATER LIFT BRIDGE
WI/MN 64 and Water Street, Stillwater

The Stillwater Lift Bridge is one of only two automotive lift bridges in Minnesota (the other is the Aerial Lift Bridge in Duluth), but its future is uncertain. The span linking Stillwater, Minnesota, to Houlton, Wisconsin, was constructed in 1931. The vertical-lift bridge rises to allow large vessels on the St. Croix River to pass under it. Despite the bridge's architectural significance, it has a questionable future because of the population growth in the western Wisconsin counties along the St. Croix. A 2007 Sierra Club lawsuit against the National Park Service (the current and potential future bridges span the St. Croix National Scenic Riverway) has halted planning on the replacement bridge, adding another chapter to one of Minnesota's longest-running environmental controversies.

i The Stone Arch Bridge is the best place in Minneapolis to view both Minneapolis's historic milling district architecture and the city's skyline.

STONE ARCH BRIDGE
Main St. SE and Fifth Ave., Minneapolis

The Stone Arch Bridge was constructed in 1883 for James J. Hill's Great Northern Railway. The bridge spanning the Mississippi took two years to complete. In 1978 the bridge was closed because of decreased train traffic. The bridge remained dormant until the State of Minnesota purchased it in 1992. The historic railroad bridge, the second oldest surviving bridge over the Mississippi, was renovated to serve pedestrians and bicyclists; the bridge reopened in 1994.

ACCOMMODATIONS

here are a few good rules to remember when trying to find hotel accommodations in the Twin Cities. First of all, winter rates for rooms are almost half that of spring and summer rates. Second, staying in St. Paul is cheaper than staying in Minneapolis, even though there are far fewer hotel options in St. Paul. Most hotels in the Cities have package plans that can knock up to a couple hundred dollars off the price of a room if you reserve a few months in advance and you plan to stay for two or more days. All major credit cards are accepted at the following establishments except where noted. Also, all the following hotels have both smoking and non-smoking rooms unless otherwise noted; however, none of the bed-and-breakfasts listed here allow smoking inside the rooms. All hotels in the metro area are required to have wheelchair-accessible ramps outside and inside the hotels.

If you visit the Twin Cities during the chilly winter months, try to find a hotel connected to either the Minneapolis or the St. Paul skyway system. These wonderful second-floor walkways are climate controlled and link most of the downtown businesses, so you don't have to step outside unless you want to. You can enter the skyway system through the parking garages in both cities, and posted maps let you know where you are at every junction.

Note: Accommodations are listed alphabetically under the headings Minneapolis, St. Paul, Neighboring Communities, and Bed-and-Breakfasts.

Price Code

The following rate information is based on the cost of a standard, double-occupancy room in spring-time (May–June), which is generally considered to be the peak tourist season in the Twin Cities.

$ . . . . Less than $100
$$ . . . . $101 to $150
$$$ . . . . $151 to $200
$$$$ . . . . $201 to $250
$$$$$ . . . .$251 and up

Minneapolis

BEST WESTERN NORMANDY INN $
405 South Eighth St., Minneapolis
(612) 370-1400
www.bestwesternnormandy.com
Conveniently located in the heart of downtown Minneapolis, this hotel is equally close (5 blocks) to the Metrodome and the Minneapolis Convention Center, 3 blocks from the light-rail line's Government Plaza Station, and across the street from an entrance to the skyway system. The hotel—which is familiar to downtown denizens for its cheesy French-chateau facade, complete with "distressed" panels meant to accentuate the *ye olde* effect—offers guests a complimentary continental breakfast; has an indoor pool, a Jacuzzi, and a fitness room; and serves milk and chocolate chip cookies every night. Every room has free wireless Internet.

CHAMBERS, THE LUXURY
ART HOTEL $$$$$
901 Hennepin Ave., Minneapolis
(612) 767-6900
www.chambersminneapolis.com
Opened in September 2006, Chambers is the Midwestern sister of New York's Chambers Hotel and has, in the estimation of at least one international magazine, eclipsed the original as the world's premier art hotel. The small, 60-room hotel is filled with a staggeringly valuable collection of contem-

porary art from the collection of the hotel's owner, Ralph Burnet; the first floor houses the Burnet Gallery, a public space for exhibits by cutting-edge contemporary artists. The rooms are modernistic and hip with big windows, plasma-screen TVs, glass-tiled bathrooms with rain showers, free wireless Internet access, 400-thread-count sheets, and art-bedecked walls. D'Amico Kitchen offers the creations of chef Richard D'Amico (for more information on eating at D'Amico Kitchen, see the Restaurants chapter), and the top floor hosts a glass-walled, balconied lounge. The hotel is located in the heart of the Hennepin Theater District and is a short walk from Target Center, the Block E Entertainment Complex, and Nicollet Mall.

COMFORT SUITES $$$
425 South Seventh St., Minneapolis
(612) 333-3111
www.comfortsuites.com
This newly renovated all-suite hotel in downtown Minneapolis 2 blocks from the Metrodome features an open atrium and access to the skyway system. Suite amenities include a separate bedroom, living area, and a fully equipped kitchen; hotel facilities include a gym, an indoor swimming pool, a restaurant with room service, and complimentary cooked-to-order breakfasts.

CROWNE PLAZA NORTHSTAR HOTEL $$
618 Second Ave. South, Minneapolis
(612) 338-2288
www.msp-northstar.crowneplaza.com
This hotel offers a comfortable stay for tourists and business travelers alike, with a year-round fitness center and a 24-hour business center. Each room includes an oversize desk with an ergonomic chair, individually controlled heating and air-conditioning, and high-speed Internet access. The hotel is in the middle of downtown Minneapolis and minutes from all the entertainment venues and shopping.

DAYS INN UNIVERSITY $
2407 University Ave. SE, Minneapolis
(612) 623-3999
www.daysinn.com

This friendly six-story hotel is located on the eastern edge of the Minnepolis campus of the University of Minnesota and is within walking distance of Dinkytown and all its stores and restaurants. The hotel offers guests a complimentary continental breakfast, free lot parking, and complimentary shuttle service to sites within 2 miles of the hotel. The hotel is a convenient choice if your plans include the Minneapolis university area.

THE GRAND HOTEL MINNEAPOLIS $$$$$
615 Second Ave. South, Minneapolis
(612) 288-8888
www.grandhotelminneapolis.com
Originally the home of the historic Minneapolis Athletic Club, the Grand Hotel Minneapolis remodeled and reopened as a hotel in 2000. Based on the AAA rating system, the hotel is the top luxury hotel in downtown Minneapolis. Although you will pay for the experience, you will be pampered from the moment you step in the door. The 140 rooms of the hotel feature such indulgences as Egyptian cotton sheets, silk bathrobes, Aveda bath products, leather-topped desks, marble bathrooms, and Tuscan furniture. The hotel is connected to the skyway system and is within easy walking distance of the luxurious Gaviidae Common shopping center (anchored by such stores as Neiman Marcus and Saks Fifth Avenue), the Minneapolis Convention Center, Nicollet Mall, and the Hennepin Theater District.

i Nicollet Mall is a prime location for hotels. For a cheaper rate that's still near the action and insulated from a Minnesota winter, look for a hotel that's a block or two off the mall and connected to the skyway.

GRAVES 601 HOTEL $$$$
601 First Ave., Minneapolis
(612) 677-1100 or (866) 523-1100
www.graves601hotel.com
Formerly Le Méridien, Graves 601 is across the street from the Target Center in the Block E entertainment and shopping complex and is connected to the skyway system. Since opening in 2003, this

swank hotel has gotten rave reviews from local and national publications—and travelers. Rooms have features such as glass-etched, handcrafted headboards; backlit photographs inspired by Twin Cities culture; huge plasma televisions; high-speed Internet access; and artistically designed bathrooms with rain shower features. In addition to an on-site health club, the hotel has a restaurant (Cosmos) and a street-level, futuristic lounge (Infinity).

HILTON MINNEAPOLIS $$$$$
1001 Marquette Ave., Minneapolis
(612) 376-1000
www.minneapolis.hilton.com
The Hilton Minneapolis is located next door to Orchestra Hall in the center of downtown and is connected to the skyway system. The 25-story brick hotel has 821 rooms, all featuring large windows and hand-carved oak trim. The hotel has an on-site health club (including a full gym, whirlpool, sauna, and swimming pool); 73,000 square feet of meeting space including the new Symphony Ballroom; wireless Internet access; and more. There's a coffee cart in the lobby as well as an on-site restaurant and bar (SkyWater).

HOLIDAY INN METRODOME $$
1500 Washington Ave. South
Minneapolis
(612) 333-4646 or (800) 448-DOME
www.metrodome.com
Located on the eastern edge of the downtown business district with the Minneapolis campus of the University of Minnesota on one side and the Metrodome on the other, the Holiday Inn Metrodome has one of the best hotel locations for sports fans in the Twin Cities. The 265-room hotel has an indoor pool, a whirlpool and sauna, a gym, and a restaurant (the Grill Room Restaurant and Lobby Bar) and offers guests shuttle transportation within a 3-mile radius.

HOTEL IVY $$$$$
201 South 11th St., Minneapolis
(612) 746-4600
www.starwoodhotels.com
"A historic landmark in the heart of downtown Minneapolis," reads its Web site, "the Hotel Ivy captivates with Ziggurat style." A 4,000-year-old Mesopotamian building style you were quizzed on in junior high may not immediately scream *luxury*, but apparently it did when the tower was built in 1930 as a local headquarters for adherents of Christian Science. Investors turned it into a 136-room luxury hotel in 2008. The Hotel Ivy offers the standard array of luxury features, notably including an in-house spa and Porter & Frye, a steakhouse that's one of the Twin Cities' best restaurants. (See Restaurant section for more.)

HYATT REGENCY HOTEL $$$
1300 Nicollet Mall, Minneapolis
(612) 370-1234
www.minneapolis.hyatt.com
This 24-story hotel is located right on the Nicollet Avenue pedestrian mall near Orchestra Hall, with direct access to the skyway system. The hotel has 533 guest rooms and suites, four restaurants, an indoor pool, a full-service athletic club, a business center, and a retail area that includes clothing stores, salons, gourmet coffee shops, and delis. The hotel features a bistro, Taxxi, the over-the-top sports bar Spike's Dugout (think giant world globes in basketball hoops), and neighbors Manny's Steakhouse and the city's finest "flown-in daily" seafood restaurant, the Oceannaire Seafood Room.

MARQUETTE HOTEL $$$
710 Marquette Ave., Minneapolis
(612) 333-4545
www.marquettehotel.com
Located in the heart of downtown Minneapolis, the Marquette has the distinct advantage of being part of the IDS Center complex, which is connected to the downtown skyway system. The rooms are large with great views of the downtown area from all sides. Amenities include Egyptian cotton sheets, luxury bath products, free wireless Internet access, a business center, and a 24-hour fitness center. The hotel has a restaurant, Basil's, which overlooks the Crystal Court of the IDS Center, and a bar, the MARQ VII Lounge. The Marquette also operates Windows on Minnesota, a banquet and meeting space on the 50th floor

of the IDS Center, which features 11-foot-high windows with spectacular views of the Metro.

MINNEAPOLIS MARRIOTT
CITY CENTER $$$$
30 South Seventh St., Minneapolis
(612) 349-4000
www.marriott.com
Connected to the skyway system, this hotel is conveniently located just off Nicollet Mall with its numerous shops and restaurants. The hotel also provides guests with a fitness center, a business center, the Lobby Bar, and an on-site restaurant—Northern Shores Grille, a casual dining establishment.

NICOLLET ISLAND INN $$$$
95 Merriam St., Minneapolis
(612) 331-1800
www.nicolletislandinn.com
The small, intimate Nicollet Island Inn sits in the middle of the Mississippi River on Nicollet Island across from downtown Minneapolis and is easily accessible from the Warehouse District via the Hennepin Avenue Bridge. The building that houses the inn was built in 1893 as the factory for the Island Door and Sash Company, a maker of window shades and blinds. Today the National Historic Building, which completed extensive renovations in 2007, includes 24 individually decorated guest rooms with fine linens, plasma screen TVs, Select Comfort Sleep Number beds, and gorgeous views of the downtown skyline and the river. The Nicollet Island Inn also has a romantic restaurant well known throughout the Cities for its wonderful brunch.

i If you choose not to stay at the Nicollet Island Inn, try it out for dinner or drinks. The inn's restaurant and bar are perfect for romantic evenings on the town.

RADISSON PLAZA
HOTEL MINNEAPOLIS $$$$$
35 South Seventh St., Minneapolis
(612) 339-4900
www.radisson.com/hotels/mpls_dt

This luxury hotel on Nicollet Mall is a short walk from the Hennepin Theater District and Target Center. The Radisson Plaza features a restaurant, a lounge, a 24-hour business center, and a health club. Through the connected skyway you can easily reach most of downtown Minneapolis's attractions and shopping areas. The comfortable rooms feature free high-speed Internet access, marble and granite bathrooms, and large desks.

RADISSON UNIVERSITY $$$
615 Washington Ave. SE
Minneapolis
(612) 379-8888
www.radisson.com
The Radisson University is set on the University of Minnesota–Minneapolis campus. A short walk from U of M sporting venues and Dinkytown—the main college-kid hangout—this is a great place to catch most of the sports action in town, college or otherwise. The hotel offers amenities including an on-site Applebee's (if, indeed, that counts as an "amenity"), a gift shop, a Starbucks, and a Great Clips salon. Guests receive free access to the university's Sports and Recreation Facility next to the hotel, complimentary shuttle service to any destination within 5 miles of the hotel on an appointment basis, and free high-speed wireless Internet access.

RESIDENCE INN MINNEAPOLIS DOWNTOWN
AT THE DEPOT $$
425 South Second St., Minneapolis
(612) 340-1300
www.thedepotminneapolis.com
This relatively inexpensive hotel is connected to the restored Historic Depot Complex in downtown Minneapolis near the riverfront and the new Guthrie Theater. The hotel, built in 2000 and last renovated in 2006, features an indoor water park and free deluxe continental breakfast, as well as suites with in-room kitchens, fold-away sofabeds, and high-speed Internet access. More basic rooms are also available. All rooms are nonsmoking.

W HOTEL MINNEAPOLIS $$$$$
821 Marquette Ave., Minneapolis
(612) 215-3700
www.starwoodhotels.com
The opening of the historic Foshay Tower as a luxury W Hotel in 2008 was a major event in the Twin Cities, a return to glory for the 1929 art deco landmark. The 230-room hotel offers plush accommodations and serves as a social hub for stylish and well-heeled (especially the latter) travelers and locals alike. Dining options include the decadent extravagance of Manny's Steakhouse and, with less table linen but equally big portions, Keys Café. There is a comfortable bar on the hotel's 1st floor and on the 27th floor, Wilbur Foshay's boardroom has been converted into the '30s-themed Prohibition Lounge. Numerous other amenities are at your fingertips—it is, after all, a luxury hotel.

St. Paul

BEST WESTERN BANDANA SQUARE $$
1010 Bandana Blvd. West, St. Paul
(651) 647-1637
www.bestwestern.com
Built inside the original shell of a Northern Pacific Railroad foundry repair shop, this beautiful yellow-brick hotel has 130-year-old train tracks running through its lobby. It's connected to Bandana Square, an office complex that is home to a cool model-train museum. Nearby are the Minnesota State Fairgrounds and Midway Stadium, a great open-air baseball field that is home to the St. Paul Saints, the Twin Cities' minor league baseball team. The hotel facilities include an indoor pool, kiddie pool, fitness room, and hot tub, and wireless high-speed Internet throughout. The centrally located hotel is about 5 miles away from downtown St. Paul and about 8 miles from downtown Minneapolis.

BEST WESTERN KELLY INN $$
161 St. Anthony Ave., St. Paul
(651) 227-8711
www.bestwesternstpaul.com
Hardly St. Paul's most luxurious hotel, but certainly its most visible, the Kelly Inn sits right next to I-94 only 2 blocks from the State Capitol with a great view of the Cathedral of St. Paul. It offers guests comfortable, moderately priced rooms near downtown. Amenities include an indoor swimming pool, hot tub, and fitness center, as well as high-speed Internet access and a full-service bar/restaurant (Sweetwater) that delivers to your room. Parking is free.

CROWNE PLAZA HOTEL ST. PAUL-RIVERFRONT $$
11 East Kellogg Blvd., St. Paul
(651) 292-1900
www.cpstpaul.com
Right across the street from the Mississippi River, the Crowne Plaza Hotel St. Paul-Riverfront is in the heart of downtown St. Paul. The hotel offers a restaurant, coffee and sandwich counter, and lounge. Other hotel amenities include a heated indoor pool, a fitness center, a business center, and free wireless Internet access. The hotel was renovated in 2006.

i Downtown St. Paul's pedestrian skyways are a nice way to walk around comfortably in wintertime. As in downtown Minneapolis, many shops and restaurants are on the skyway level or connected to the skyway.

EMBASSY SUITES ST. PAUL $$
175 East 10th St., St. Paul
(651) 224-5400
www.embassystpaul.com
The Embassy Suites St. Paul has 210 rooms, all two-room suites. Hotel amenities include a business center, swimming pool, fitness club, whirlpool, sauna, downtown shuttle service, full-service restaurant (Woolley's), and Irish sports bar (Cork's Pub), which features a nightly happy hour. The price of the room includes a cooked-to-order breakfast, and the tropical atrium belies the Northern Plains climate beyond the glass. The hotel is about 7 blocks from the heart of downtown.

HOLIDAY INN RIVERCENTRE $$
175 West Seventh St., St. Paul
(651) 225-1515
www.holiday-inn.com/stpaulmn
Located right across the street from the Xcel Energy Center, home of the Minnesota Wild NHL team, and the RiverCentre convention center, this hotel is within 4 blocks of the Science Museum of Minnesota, the Children's Museum, and the Ordway Center for the Performing Arts. It's also a short walk from the Minnesota State Capitol, the Minnesota History Center, and the Fitzgerald Theater. The hotel was completely renovated in 2005. Guest amenities include an indoor pool and fitness center. It's attached to a wonderful Irish pub and restaurant called the Liffey, which provides room service. The Liffey has great food and a rooftop patio with an incredible view of downtown St. Paul.

ST. PAUL HOTEL $$$
350 Market St., St. Paul
(651) 292-9292 or (800) 292-9292
www.stpaulhotel.com
Built in 1910 and located in the center of St. Paul on beautiful Rice Park, this premier luxury hotel is a member of the Historic Hotels of America and during the Depression was frequented by notorious gangsters. Fully restored to its original splendor (the most recent update was in 2005), the hotel offers guests a unique combination of turn-of-the-20th-century charm and modern convenience. The hotel is within walking distance of St. Paul's RiverCentre, the Ordway Center for the Performing Arts, the Science Museum of Minnesota, and Xcel Energy Center, as well as the Mississippi River walk, plus more business and shops via the climate-controlled skyway.

Neighboring Communities

AFTON HOUSE INN $$-$$$
3291 St. Croix Trail South, Afton
(651) 436-8883
www.aftonhouseinn.com
The Afton House Inn is located about 20 miles east of downtown St. Paul in the quaint town of Afton on the St. Croix River. Built in 1867, the

25-room hotel is on the National Register of Historic Places. The nicely furnished rooms include such amenities as gas fireplaces and Jacuzzis. The hotel also operates Afton Hudson Cruise Lines, with several boats that ply the St. Croix. The hotel has three restaurants—two fine-dining rooms plus the casual Catfish Saloon and Café, which has outdoor seating.

AMERISUITES $$-$$$
7800 International Dr., Bloomington
(952) 854-0700
www.amerisuites.com
This all-suite hotel is within a mile of the Mall of America and near Minneapolis–St. Paul (MSP) International Airport. The 128 rooms all have small kitchens and free high-speed Internet access. The hotel has an exercise room and indoor pool. Amerisuites operates a shuttle service to the airport and to the Mall of America. This is a good choice for travelers wishing to be near the airport or the mall.

FANTASUITE HOTEL $-$$$
250 North River Ridge Circle, Burnsville
(952) 890-9550
www.fantasuite.com
Cinderella? Arabian Nights? Jungle Safari? Log Cabin? Pharaoh's Chambers? Sherwood Forest? Space Odyssey? Under the Sea? A universe of fantasy environments is at your disposal at the FantaSuites. You may just be looking for something off the beaten path, but most couples seek the FantaSuites for amorous encounters. (To accommodate postcoital cigarettes, only 2 of the 28 fantasy suites are nonsmoking.) Beyond the fantasy environments, the accommodations at this Burnsville hotel are nothing to write home about (free in-room coffee! free local calls!), but there are 60 standard guest rooms for travelers who are on a budget—or whose secret fantasies involve beige bedspreads and floral prints.

THE LOWELL INN $$$
102 North Second St., Stillwater
(651) 439-1100
www.lowellinn.com

The elegant Lowell Inn in Stillwater (20 miles east of downtown St. Paul) harbors 21 individually decorated rooms featuring period antiques. Elmore Lowell established the Sawyer House on the land where the Lowell Inn now stands in 1848, the year Stillwater was incorporated as the Minnesota Territory's first city. The colonial inn standing today dates from 1927, and the interior brings to mind the regal atmosphere of southern plantation homes. The Lowell has 23 unique guest rooms and four distinct dining rooms. Guests can also relax in front of the colonial fireplace in the Front Parlor.

i When you get into the Twin Cities, pick up a copy of the free weekly newspaper, *City Pages,* for information on what's happening in the Twin Cities as well as for restaurant and event coupons.

MYSTIC LAKE CASINO HOTEL $$
2400 Mystic Lake Blvd., Prior Lake
(952) 445-9000 or (800) 262-7799
www.mysticlake.com
About 25 miles southwest of downtown Minneapolis, the 600-room Mystic Lake Casino Hotel rises next to the alcohol-free casino of the same name. The hotel features such amenities as an Olympic-size pool with water slide, 18-hole golf course, fitness center, and the largest casino in the Upper Midwest, with some 4,000 slot machines and 100 blackjack tables. Major celebrities regularly headline at the Mystic Showroom, and guests can partake in the massive buffet. The hotel is near Canterbury Park, which features betting on live horse racing during the summer months and a card room year-round.

RADISSON BY MALL OF AMERICA $$$$
1700 East American Blvd., Bloomington
(952) 854-8700
www.waterparkofamerica.com
Conveniently close to MSP airport and the Mall of America, the Bloomington Radisson is an excellent (though pricey) choice for families whose younger members have a lot of energy. Why? Because it contains the Water Park of America,

the largest indoor waterpark in the United States. The lodge has 403 rooms, some of which have views of the water park. Guests can enjoy such amenities as bunk beds for the kids, refrigerators and microwaves, and shuttle service to area attractions. The lodge has three restaurants (Split Rock Grille, Sleepy Eye Cafe, and Camp Many Point) and a lounge (Split Rock Bar).

RADISSON HOTEL &
CONFERENCE CENTER $$$
3131 Campus Dr., Plymouth
(763) 559-6600
www.radisson.com
The Radisson Plymouth in the western Metro is located near I-494 and MN 55 in a parklike setting overlooking a 25-acre marshland preserve. All guest rooms include a minibar, two telephones, free high-speed Internet, and a lighted work desk. Hotel facilities include a full-service fitness center, an indoor pool, two restaurants, and a lounge.

SOFITEL MINNEAPOLIS $$$
5601 West 78th St., Bloomington
(952) 835-1900
www.sofitel.com
The French-style Sofitel is located at the intersection of I-494 and MN 100 on the Bloomington Strip. The hotel is about 10 minutes from the Mall of America and 15 minutes from MSP airport. The 282-room hotel also hosts two French restaurants—Chez Colette, in particular, is worthy of destination dining (see the Restaurants chapter for more information). Other amenities include a business center, wireless Internet access, and comfortable guest rooms. The entire hotel is non-smoking and was completely renovated in 2006.

Bed-and-Breakfasts

COVINGTON INN BED AND
BREAKFAST $$$
100 Yacht Club Rd. West, St. Paul
(651) 292-1411
www.covingtoninn.com
The only floating bed-and-breakfast in the Twin Cities, the Covington Inn is a renovated tugboat

first launched in 1946 and now moored in the Mississippi River across from downtown St. Paul. Open year-round, the B&B has four comfortable rooms, all with fireplaces and private baths. The inn's common areas are trimmed in bronze, brass, and mahogany, and many salvaged fixtures suggest what it must have been like when the tug *Covington* pushed barges up and down the river. You can sit out on the deck and watch the mighty river flow by gleaming downtown St. Paul.

WALES HOUSE $
1115 SE Fifth St., Minneapolis
(612) 331-3931
www.waleshouse.com
Since opening to the public in 1994, this 10-bedroom bed-and-breakfast has been providing the charm of a home for faculty, staff, and other visitors to the University of Minnesota for extremely reasonable rates. Hundreds of visitors from more than 68 countries have stayed in this antiques-furnished turn-of-the-20th-century home. The living rooms, which are open to guests, include a four-season porch, large front parlor, fireplace room, lounge, dining room, and kitchen. Outside, guests can use the front patio. Amenities include free continental breakfast, free wireless high-speed Internet access, a furnished guest kitchen, on-site laundry, and a cleaning service. The bed-and-breakfast is nonsmoking throughout.

WILLIAM SAUNTRY MANSION $$$–$$$$
626 North Fourth St., Stillwater
(651) 430-2653 or (800) 828-2653
www.sauntrymansion.com
Lumber baron William Sauntry had his 25-room Victorian mansion built in the booming sawmill town of Stillwater on the St. Croix River in 1881. Today this B&B, listed on the National Register of Historic Places, has six guest rooms, all with fireplaces, private baths, and double whirlpool tubs. The ornate house features wood floors, original chandeliers, stained-glass windows, and Victorian furnishings. The William Sauntry Mansion is close to downtown Stillwater, with its quaint antiques stores, lovely cafes, and antiquarian bookshops.

RESTAURANTS

With thousands of restaurants in the metropolitan area, the Twin Cities boast one of the most diverse and tastiest dining scenes in the country. Once considered the land of the smorgasbord or simple meat-and-potato fare, the Twin Cities today offer a vast array of culinary choices.

The chapter has been organized alphabetically by cuisine, followed by listings for sweets and treats and coffeehouses and teashops. In general each cuisine section is divided into regions: Minneapolis, St. Paul, and the suburbs north, south, east, and west. Also listed for most restaurants are which meals are served, days of the week the restaurant is open, and reservation policies. If the listing does not say otherwise, you can assume that the restaurant accepts all major credit cards. These policies frequently change, so call the restaurant if you have any questions. Both St. Paul and Minneapolis ban smoking in all restaurants and bars.

Price Code

The following price code is based on one adult dinner entrée, without beverage, gratuity, or tax.

$	Less than $10
$$	$11 to $20
$$$	$21 to $30
$$$$	$31 and up

Afghani
St. Paul

KHYBER PASS CAFÉ $$
1571 Grand Ave., St. Paul
(651) 690-0505
www.khyberpasscafe.com
Khyber Pass Café has served delicious Afghani cuisine since 1985. When entering the restaurant, the diner is immediately struck by its personality, charm, and aesthetic sense. The restaurant has a comfortable, clean, and cobbled-together feel, which integrates potted plants and Afghani crafts with numerous tasteful paintings.

The menu comprises well-executed entrées. The possibilities include chicken, lamb, beef, and vegetarian dishes. The korma-e-murgh, boneless chicken in curry sauce with potatoes and peas, is one savory option. Another interesting choice is

kof a-chalau, which is made of meatballs, onions, and spices. The restaurant is open for lunch Monday through Friday and for dinner Monday through Saturday.

South

DA AFGHAN RESTAURANT $$
929 West 80th St., Bloomington
(952) 888-5824
www.daafghan.com
Da Afghan serves Southwest Asian and Middle Eastern specialties, including spring lamb chops, kabeli palow with chicken or lamb, mantou, and many kinds of kebab. The beautiful restaurant is decorated with Afghani artifacts and Afghani rugs on the tabletops. Beer and wine are served. Da Afghan is open for dinner Tuesday through Sunday and for lunch on Thursday and Friday (for lunch, Da Afghan offers a buffet).

American
Minneapolis

ACADIA CAFE $
329 Cedar Ave. South, Minneapolis
(612) 874-8702
www.acadiacafe.com
Despite its prime location in the heart of the Cedar-Riverside neighborhood, for years this space

seemed cursed: A string of restaurants opened and closed until the Acadia took residence after rising rents forced it out of its longtime home at Franklin and Nicollet. It's now a hopping spot with a well-curated beer selection and a solid live music calendar. Besides booze and coffee, Acadia makes fresh soups, sandwiches, store-made bread, yogurt parfaits, and homemade Belgian waffles with fruit and whipped cream that are worth waking up early for. Worth noting is that the Acadia's one of the surprisingly few local establishments with both beer and Wi-Fi.

AL'S BREAKFAST $
413 14th Ave. SE, Minneapolis
(612) 331-9991
This tiny hole-in-the wall near the University of Minnesota has been serving customers since the 1940s. It has been called the "narrowest restaurant in the Twin Cities," and when visiting this counter-seating-only diner, you'll quickly see why. College students and folks from the neighborhood have been known to line up around the block waiting for the place to open or to get a seat. Eggs, hash browns, and pancakes are served, as well as exotic omelets, many of which are named after Al's patrons or employees. Al's is open for breakfast and lunch (serving dishes off the breakfast menu) daily. Al's is a Twin Cities institution, and if you don't mind the wait or the grease, get your day started at Al's. Al's has no Web site, accepts no credit cards, and in various other ways declines to acknowledge that the world has much changed since World War II. That's why people love it.

ASTER CAFE $
125 Main St. SE, Minneapolis
(612) 379-3138
Located across the Mississippi River from downtown Minneapolis, this little cafe is the perfect place to stop by for lunch or to grab a cup of coffee or a beer in the evening. The menu includes premade sandwiches and homemade soups, cookies, focaccia bread pizzas, and dessert bars. The dining area inside is large and opens up into the art gallery next door, and there's also a beautiful fenced-in outside patio that's nice for summer lounging. The cafe often books acoustic music but entertainment is also provided by people wandering in to play the piano set up in the corner. The cafe keeps about a dozen board and card games on hand for patrons who want to hang out past lunch—and there's a bowl full of dog biscuits under the counter for hounds accompanying patrons. The Aster Cafe is open daily.

BAD WAITRESS $–$$
2 East 26th St., Minneapolis
(612) 872-7575
The menus at the Bad Waitress make clear that its name is both a tribute to the stereotype of the surly diner plate-tosser and to the Michael Jackson sense of the word "bad." Both senses are completely ironic, because there isn't even traditional table service at the Bad Waitress: You place your order at the counter and it's simply brought out to you. For a late-night diner with a swank retro atmosphere and a great selection of microbrews, the Bad Waitress isn't nearly as crowded as you'd expect. The high style is the best reason to patronize the Bad Waitress, but the food is pretty decent too—and as you'd expect at an establishment run by the same people who own the Spyhouse Coffee Shop, the coffee is exceptional.

BANK $$–$$$
88 South 6th St.
(The Westin Minneapolis), Minneapolis
(612) 656-3255
www.bankmpls.com
BANK, inside the new Westin Minneapolis, serves up modern American food in a gorgeous art deco seating area (the restaurant space once housed the Farmers and Mechanics Bank). Chef Todd Stein's menu is nontraditional yet familiar, including such things as wild duck, steamed mussels, steaks, and leg of lamb. The restaurant is open for not only lunch and dinner, but also breakfast, and a morning stop at BANK is worth it. Omelets, frittatas, lobster Benedict, and French toast are some of the items you are likely to see on the menu. Be prepared to spend a little more for breakfast than you might be used to, as most

of BANK's breakfasts rise above $10. BANK is open daily for all three meals

THE BROTHERS DELI $
50 South Sixth St. (skyway level)
Minneapolis
(612) 341-8007
www.thebrothersdeli.com
The Brothers Deli offers authentic New York–style deli fare in downtown Minneapolis. This small deli, located on a busy second-floor skyway route, serves mouthwatering delicacies composed of only the best breads, meats, toppings, and condiments. The deli has cold sandwiches, grilled sandwiches, all-vegetable sandwiches, kosher sandwiches, and even grilled-cheese sandwiches, all at pretty cheap prices for downtown Minneapolis. The deli also serves breakfast, including some very inexpensive scrambles. The deli is open weekdays for breakfast and lunch.

i Restaurateur Kim Bartmann has created three of Minneapolis's best-loved establishments: the Bryant-Lake Bowl (yes, it's a restaurant—and also a theater), Barbette, and the Red Stag Supperclub. Each restaurant is unique, but they all have a comfortably informal, cozy feel. If you have time, you won't regret making a hat trick of the three of them.

BRYANT-LAKE BOWL (BLB) $–$$
810 West Lake St., Minneapolis
(612) 825-3737
www.bryantlakebowl.com
A bowling alley? Well, yes, but the Bryant-Lake Bowl in Uptown breaks every stereotype of bowling-alley eats. The inside of the restaurant is vintage 1940s, with beautiful woodwork and closely placed tables for intimate eating. Famous for its delicious breakfasts, including bison hash, several BLB scrambles (eggs scrambled with a choice of ingredients), and Amy's Breakfast Burrito, the BLB serves lunch and dinner as well. Diners favor such specialties as the turkey, avocado, and bacon sandwich; grilled ahi tuna sandwich; and

basmati rice and vegetables (with tofu or chicken optional). The BLB has a full bar, with many microbrews on tap. In addition to the 1950s-era bowling lanes, where you get to relearn the lost art of scoring your game by hand, the BLB is attached to a cabaret theater, where you can also order from the full menu. (See the Arts chapter for more information on the Bryant-Lake Bowl Theater.) The Bryant-Lake Bowl is open 8 a.m. to 2 a.m. daily.

THE BULLDOG $–$$
2549 Lyndale Ave. South, Minneapolis
(612) 872-8893

401 East Hennepin Ave., Minneapolis
(612) 378-BULL

237 East Sixth St., St. Paul
(651) 221-0750
www.thebulldogmpls.com
Each of the three Bulldog locations is about beer—and, secondarily, the food that goes best with beer. Each Bulldog has a smashing selection of domestic and international brews on tap, with quite a few more stowed in the cooler. (Belgian fans especially should take note.) The food options center on hot dogs and burgers, but what hot dogs and burgers! Dogs are available in several styles, with special offers featuring pairs of hot dogs and pints for either couples or hungry singles. Snacks are also taken seriously at the Bulldog: In a town that loves its tater tots, the Bulldog's are among the best.

CHINO LATINO $$–$$$
2916 Hennepin Ave. South, Minneapolis
(612) 824-7878
www.chinolatino.com
A popular spot for the ogle-and-be-ogled dinner crowd at Lake and Hennepin. The foods of Thailand, Mexico, Jamaica, Polynesia, and Korea are represented on Chino Latino's true melting pot of a menu. Chino Latino's menu changes daily, and the foods here run the gamut of these countries' spiciest cuisines, including five-spice duck, taco plates, and peppery steamed mussels. The restaurant also serves a variety of sakes

and tequilas to accompany your meal—and just about the biggest banana split in the state to finish it off. The global menu is perfectly matched with the wild, complicated decor, with its cushioned orange-vinyl wall, a satay bar, giant round booths, semi-unisex bathrooms (shared sinks), and an open kitchen. There's a sexy, dimly lit lounge just off the bar that party promoter Dan Vargas calls "my favorite room without windows." Chino Latino is open daily for dinner.

CORNER TABLE $$–$$$
4257 Nicollet Ave., Minneapolis
(612) 823-0011
www.cornertablerestaurant.com
"Food-driven, not chef-driven" is the philosophy of this restaurant, which is at the forefront of the strong local movement to make dining out both delicious and environmentally responsible. Chef Scott Pampuch is one of the most respected cooks in Minnesota, and he's created a contemporary American menu with an Italian flair, heavy on grass-fed meats and sustainably harvested fish. For starters, try the "nosh plate" sampler; don't think that just because it's a fancy restaurant you ought to avoid the savory burger; and be sure to save room for a slice of one of Corner Table's amazing cakes.

FRENCH MEADOW BAKERY & CAFE $
2610 Lyndale Ave. South, Minneapolis
(612) 870-7855
www.frenchmeadow.com
There's no disputing the quality of the food at this trendy eatery in the Wedge neighborhood. It sells organic sourdough breads, coffees, elaborate cakes, and several kinds of quiches. French Meadow uses no oil, no preservatives, and no yeast in producing chewy and flavorful organic loaves in flavors ranging from multigrain to hemp to rye with sunflower seeds. Step to the counter to order up a French Meadow sandwich and you can request any of those breads with a tasty topping of hummus, roasted eggplant, rosemary chicken salad, whitefish, or smoked turkey. With a comfortable country decor that includes simple tables and chairs, dried grapevines winding up the walls, and

enough antiques to keep you intrigued but not overwhelmed, French Meadow is the perfect place to get a cup of coffee and a sandwich for lunch. French Meadow is open daily for breakfast, lunch, and dinner, and has an extensive to-go menu.

HARD TIMES CAFE $–$$
1821 Cedar Ave. South, Minneapolis
(612) 341-9261
www.hardtimes.com
The Hard Times isn't named to be cute, like the Bad Waitress, or like the national Hard Times Cafe chain (with which this gritty spot has absolutely nothing to do)—most of the regular patrons of the Hard Times have had and/or are having some genuinely hard times. The cafe is cooperatively run, and a decidedly DIY spirit dominates: you place your order, they call your name, you grab your order, you bus your own dishes. It's no greasy spoon—the breakfast-heavy menu offers many tasty options—but don't wear your fancy pants. The tables and the patrons are both apt to wobble, but the Cedar-Riverside neighborhood is fierce in its devotion to this very local institution.

HELL'S KITCHEN $–$$
89 South Ninth St., Minneapolis
(612) 332-4700
www.hellskitcheninc.com
This breakfast, brunch (on weekends), and lunch spot features wonderfully inventive dishes such as eggs Benedict with bison flank steak and tangerine jalapeño hollandaise sauce, wild-rice porridge, and walleye hash. Despite higher prices than most other breakfast places in the Twin Cities, Hell's Kitchen serves food that is a cut above the rest. Be sure to order some toast with the restaurant's justly lauded custom-made peanut butter. Duluth-bound breakfasters can drop by Hell's Kitchen's second outlet (310 Lake Ave. South; 218-727-1620) in Canal Park a couple of blocks from the Duluth Lift Bridge.

JAX CAFÉ $$$–$$$$
1928 University Ave. NE, Minneapolis
(612) 789-7297
www.jaxcafe.com

Jax has been a strange combination of kitsch and elegance since it opened in 1933 (right after Prohibition ended), with a long wooden bar accented by a stained-glass window depicting the seven dwarfs, and a trout stream in back. The menu includes shrimp cocktail, crab cakes, gigantic aged steaks, lobster, lamb chops, and salmon. In spring and summer request a place on the outside patio. Jax is open daily for lunch and dinner.

JOE'S GARAGE $$
1610 Harmon Place, Minneapolis
(612) 904-1163
www.joes-garage.com
Joe's integrates the culinary flavors of the world with traditional American fare, including several interesting takes on the burger. The menu includes the Greek lamb burger, a Mediterranean spin on a traditional burger, with feta, black olive pesto, tomato, and spinach. Other offerings include the spicy Asian pork burger and the classic beef burger. Pasta and risotto are also prominently featured on the menu. Joe's is open for lunch and dinner Monday through Saturday, and for brunch and dinner Sunday. In warm weather you can enjoy the rooftop deck with a view of Loring Park.

KINGS WINE BAR $$
4555 Grand Ave., Minneapolis
(612) 354-7928
www.kingsmpls.com
Located 15 blocks south of Lake Street, Kings is well off the beaten path—which is one of the things its regulars love about it, though there's lots to love. Kings opened in 2009 in a cozy and stylish renovated corner space in Minneapolis's Kingfield neighborhood, with a well-chosen wine list and a strong menu. It was quickly adopted as a favored retreat for writers and musicians— prominent music critic Jim Walsh tends bar, and HowWasTheShow.com editor David De Young curates the restaurant's soundtrack of exclusively local music—which helped word of its virtues spread quickly. To see Kings in all its glory as a classy but unpretentious social hub, time your visit to coincide with one of the new-music listening parties it regularly hosts.

THE MALT SHOP $–$$
809 West 50th St., Minneapolis
(612) 824-1352
www.themaltshoprestaurant.com
The Malt Shop serves gourmet burgers and sandwiches as well as shakes and malts. Besides the standard cheeseburgers and Reubens, there are items like the Malibu chicken, a sautéed chicken breast with Swiss cheese, bacon, and avocado. Most important are the malts and shakes, available in almost 40 flavors. They range from strawberry and chocolate to black cherry and cookies 'n' cream.

MARKET BAR-B-QUE $$
1414 Nicollet Ave., Minneapolis
(612) 872-1111

15320 Wayzata Blvd., Wayzata
(952) 475-1770
www.marketbbq.com
Established in 1946 (although not always at this location), Market Bar-B-Que's been a Twin Cities family tradition for years. The menu includes fabulous, lean spareribs and beef tips, barbecue beef sandwiches, and an amazing "dessert trough" including key lime pie and grasshopper ice cream pie. The extensive wine list is printed on the side of giant empty wine bottles set on the tables. The decor is simple and comfortable, with large carved wooden booths and tables and black-and-white photographs of celebrities who have dined at Market, including Jay Leno and Willie Mays. Each table is equipped with a small jukebox that carries popular music selections from the '50s to the present. Both locations are open for lunch and dinner daily.

MATT'S BAR $
3500 Cedar Ave. South, Minneapolis
(612) 722-7072
www.mattsbar.com
For most of its hyperloyal Minneapolis patrons, the only real choice at Matt's is whether to have chopped onions on your Jucy Lucy. The pitcher of 3-2 Premium and the sandwich itself are regarded as absolutely mandatory, and you

may need to be explicit with your server if you want (gasp!) anything else. Matt's Bar is famous for its Jucy Lucy, a burger with cheese sealed inside—and yes, that is the correct spelling of the south Minneapolis super-cheeseburger. By general consensus Matt's makes the best Jucy Lucy, although a couple of south Minneapolis bars disagree on where it was first created in the Twin Cities. Jucy Lucy novices beware; the burger, when removed from the grill, is filled with steaming hot cheese; get a side order of fries to sop it up. For the record, the menu does include additional burger selections and sandwiches.

MODERN CAFE $-$$
337 13th Ave. NE, Minneapolis
(612) 378-9882
www.moderncafeminneapolis.com
The Modern, a vintage restaurant with a diner-like vibe, serves pot roast with carrots, pork sandwiches on apple bread, omelets, and giant malts and milk shakes. If you have a hankering for grilled cheese, have one here: they're made with Asiago cheese, Dijon mustard, and caramelized onions to create the yummiest variation on this old standby you'll probably ever need (there may be better ones out there, but when they're this good, why bother?). To mix it up a bit, the cafe also makes walleye egg rolls, penne with goat cheese and crimini mushrooms, tomato risotto with capers and lemon zest, and heavenly chocolate crème brûlée. The Modern serves lunch and dinner Tuesday through Friday, and adds breakfast Saturday and Sunday. (Tip for the cash-conscious: Last night's pot roast, just as delicious the next morning, can be had at a bargain price as part of a breakfast hash.) Closed Monday.

PSYCHO SUZI'S MOTOR LOUNGE $$
2519 Marshall St. NE, Minneapolis
(612) 788-9069
www.psychosuzis.com
Psycho Suzi's is the Twin Cities' preeminent tiki lounge, which lends it a cachet that allows it to be regularly packed with customers despite prices somewhat higher than its passable food might otherwise command . . . but when you

need to drink out of a steaming volcano bowl, you need to drink out of a steaming volcano bowl, and you know just where to go. Summer is high season at Suzi's, with tiki torches (natch) illuminating a patio buzzing with the buzz of the buzzed. Suzi's deliberately lowbrow appetizers, such as sliced pickles rolled in cream cheese and cold cuts, will allow you to taste some traditional Minnesota backyard BBQ fare if you don't happen to be invited to a Maple Grove cookout while you're in town.

RED STAG SUPPERCLUB $$-$$$
509 First Ave. NE, Minneapolis
(612) 767-766
www.redstagsupperclub.com
The Red Stag is the newest jewel in the small but beloved empire of restaurateurs (and sisters) Kim and Kari Bartmann, who also run Barbette and the Bryant-Lake Bowl. When the Red Stag opened in 2007, it made history as Minnesota's first fully LEED-certified restaurant. Just because the toilets have variable-volume flush mechanisms doesn't mean the joint is uptight, though: It's as warm and cozy as its sister establishments, and hosts a range of fun events, live music, and dance nights. Chef Brian Hauke offers a superlative menu of contemporary American fare with tasty meat entreés and many vegetarian options as well.

SAPOR CAFE AND BAR $$
428 Washington Ave. North
Minneapolis
(612) 375-1971
www.saporcafe.com
Diners in search of a sophisticated and eclectic fusion cuisine will love the Sapor Cafe. Entrées meld together high-quality, seemingly disparate ingredients to create piquant culinary delights. The menu changes seasonally and emphasizes local, organic ingredients. Dinners include a miso-baked salmon and a pork chop in jerk spices. The restaurant features a comfortable bar, which is frequented by a hip crowd. Sapor is open Monday through Friday for lunch, and Monday through Saturday for dinner. Closed Sunday.

SEWARD CAFE $
2129 East Franklin Ave., Minneapolis
(612) 332-1011
www.sewardcafempls.net
Minneapolis's riverside Seward neighborhood has the reputation of being progressive in the granola-and-Birkenstocks sense of that word, and the Seward Cafe is one of the emblematic reasons why. The cooperatively run diner is a favorite of artistically inclined families who bleed blue (Democratic blue, not aristocratic blue), but you don't have to be a Nader voter to appreciate the delicious "earth breakfast" and the warm, funky atmosphere. Behind the counter there's a closet conspicuously labeled "Makeout Room," for reasons that even the staff don't know (or have conveniently chosen to forget).

TED COOK'S 19TH HOLE BAR-B-QUE $–$$
2814 East 38th St., Minneapolis
(612) 721-2023
www.tedcooks19tholebbq.com
Ted Cook's is a small takeout-only restaurant in south Minneapolis that serves some of the best barbecue in the Twin Cities. One of the restaurant's secrets is that they cook their barbecue over a cherrywood fire. All aspects of the meats, sides, and desserts are carefully executed, and the end result is outstanding. The meats include pork ribs, beef ribs, and barbecue chicken and beef. The tender meat is accompanied by the rich and tasty barbecue sauce, which can be ordered mild or spicy. Prices are very reasonable at Ted Cook's and even cheaper with lunch sandwich combinations. Hungry night owls are wise to show up for takeout shortly before the restaurant closes: The portions become humongous when the kitchen begins to shut down. Ted Cook's is open for lunch and dinner Tuesday through Saturday. Closed Monday.

VERA'S CAFE $
2901 Lyndale Ave. South, Minneapolis
(612) 822-3871
Open until midnight seven nights a week, Vera's is a popular late-night dining establishment in the Lyn-Lake neighborhood, serving homemade soups, huge sandwiches, six kinds of scrambled eggs, and European coffees. During the summer months the gated patio is a beautiful place to take in lunch or to hang out after a movie. Inside, Vera's is outfitted with antique-looking tables, ice-cream-parlor chairs, and velvet and mohair couches. Vera's is open daily for breakfast, lunch, and dinner.

St. Paul

ACME DELI $
1552 Saint Clair Ave., St. Paul
(651) 698-8191
www.acmedeli.com
"A couple o' tables," reads the sign outside Acme Deli, and it doesn't lie: Don't count on finding a place to sit inside. The seating is limited for a good reason, though: Acme's owners have wisely chosen to devote their storefront space largely to housing a big sandwich-making space, with a mouthwatering variety of stuffings from which to assemble your feast. Faculty at the nearby colleges love to have Acme cater their symposia, and you can get in the spirit by taking your Saran Wrapped sandwich to the bucolic grounds of St. Kate's or Macalester for a picnic lunch.

BLUE DOOR PUB $
1811 Selby Ave., St. Paul
(651) 493-1865
www.thebdp.com
This establishment's door was blue before it became the Blue Door Pub in 2008: The Selby Avenue storefront was Puerta Azul, a beloved but under-patronized Puerto Rican restaurant. As the Blue Door, the establishment sees lines out the door for its "blucy lucy" cheese-stuffed burgers. As the only beer-and-burgers pub (aside from the legendary O'Gara's, up the street) in a neighborhood packed with hungry families and college students, the Blue Door has a built-in clientele that keeps it consistently hopping, so shoot for an off-hour stop if you don't care to wait for a table.

CECIL'S RESTAURANT, DELICATESSEN & BAKERY $
651 South Cleveland Ave., St. Paul
(651) 698-6276
www.cecilsdeli.com

Cecil's, established in 1949, is where the Twin Cities' expat New York Jews find solace. The front of the building is a huge deli with fresh meats, cheeses, breads, and baked goods; in the back is a modest restaurant. The menu contains almost every hot and cold sandwich imaginable, including several kosher selections. All of Cecil's food can be ordered for takeout. Cecil's Restaurant is open for lunch and dinner daily, and the delicatessen is also open seven days a week.

i In summer, take a little time to check out Vera's Garden along the Midtown Greenway biking trail next to the cafe. Patrons of Vera's banded together to plant trimmings from their home gardens, and a spectacular array of flowers and other plants adorns the hillside.

CHEEKY MONKEY DELI $–$$
525 Selby Ave., St. Paul
(651) 224-6066
www.cheekymonkeydeli.com

The Cheeky Monkey opened in 2009, adding a spacious and classy yet casual option to an already-hopping stretch of Selby Avenue. The Cheeky Monkey's culinary style is perhaps best described as "high deli wine bar," with a soup-and-sandwich menu that includes ingredients like cumin pork, arugula, tarragon, hummus, gardinera, and cheeses you've never even *heard* of. But this is still St. Paul, and the Cheeky Monkey knows how to deliver the bottom-line comfort food: The grilled peanut-butter-and-Nutella sandwich will make you feel like you've gained a new lease on life. Happily for people who would just as soon pass on the worn-and-wobbly tables at Cecil's or Acme, the atmosphere at the Cheeky Monkey is much more like a pub than like a deli, with burgundy wood paneling, comfortably spacious booths, and even a fireplace.

DAY BY DAY CAFE $
477 West Seventh St., St. Paul
(651) 227-0654
www.daybyday.com

Day by Day is a lovely spot just west of downtown St. Paul; its name refers to the fact that it was founded by a recovering alcoholic and employs others who are kicking dangerous addictions. The restaurant meanders through several rooms of multiple storefronts on busy West Seventh Street, and the plants, bookshelves, and tables at odd angles will make visitors feel right at home. Breakfast (served all day) highlights include homemade buckwheat cakes, the earth breakfast (two eggs scrambled with hash browns and onions and covered with melted cheese), and the breakfast burrito. For lunch and dinner the restaurant features a guacamole burger, triple-decker clubhouse sandwich, and stir-fried sesame chicken or tofu. Each menu has unique handmade cover art. Day by Day is open for early dinner Monday through Friday, and is open for breakfast and lunch seven days a week. On weekdays and Saturday, the cafe opens at 6 a.m., making it popular with people (especially insomniacs) who work downtown.

FABULOUS FERN'S BAR & GRILL $$
400 Selby Ave., St. Paul
(651) 225-9414
www.fabulousferns.com

Love it or hate it, Fabulous Fern's is the lowest common denominator among the many dining establishments on St. Paul's Cathedral Hill: You've got your burgers, you've got your beer, you've got your darts, and you've got your free popcorn. Restaurant specialties include wild rice and chicken salad with cranberry vinaigrette dressing, the Cajun meat loaf sandwich, Fern's pot roast, and pecan-crusted walleye. Popular with sports fans who flock to Fabulous Fern's to watch the bar's 4 plasma TVs and 10 regular TVs, the place really gets hopping during Vikings games. Fern's is open for lunch and dinner seven days a week and serves their full menu until midnight every day.

FOREPAUGH'S $$–$$$
276 South Exchange St., St. Paul
(651) 224-5606
www.forepaughs.com
Set in a Victorian mansion and named for Joe Lybrandt Forepaugh, the dry-goods merchant who built the house in 1870, Forepaugh's is an elegant oasis in St. Paul's historic Irvine Park neighborhood. Soft light in nine cozy dining rooms offers the warmth of a turn-of-the-20th-century parlor, lace curtains and all. Forepaugh's main courses include duck, lamb, veal, steak, and seafood. Forepaugh's offers a shuttle ride to and from the Ordway Center in downtown St. Paul, very helpful if your evening includes a concert or show or if you plan to attend a Wild game at the Xcel Energy Center next to the Ordway. Ask about the shuttle when you make your reservations, which are recommended. The restaurant is open for lunch weekdays, for dinner Monday through Saturday, and for brunch and dinner on Sunday.

i Forepaugh's is a delicious upscale restaurant housed in a gorgeous Victorian mansion that's said to be haunted. Ask the waitstaff for details—if you dare.

HICKORY HUT $
647 University Ave. West, St. Paul
(651) 224-9464
The Hickory Hut serves up great barbecue in a fast-food and take-out environment. Don't go for the decor ("hickory" describes the flavor, not the woodwork), but go for the tangy, meaty wings, barbecue beef sandwiches, and ribs; for the catfish, shrimp, and at least a dozen side dishes; for the large, inexpensive portions; and for the superb barbecue sauce. This is some seriously tasty food.

THE LEXINGTON $$–$$$
1096 Grand Ave., St. Paul
(651) 222-5878
www.the-lexington.com
The Lexington—known locally as "the Lex"—is the kind of place old-school St. Paul Catholic families take their dressed-up kids out to eat for a "fancy" meal with their godparents after Confirmation. Its style is almost a parody of colonial class, with "a collection of pediments, pilasters, cornices, arches, keystones, and shutters pasted like oversized Post-it notes to the smooth brick walls" (in the words of architecture critic Larry Millett), but after three-quarters of a century, the sense of community and neighborhood history at the Lex are no joke. Still, if you're looking for objectively fine dining rather than "fine dining," for the price there are better bets elsewhere.

MICKEY'S DINER $
36 West Seventh St., St. Paul
(651) 222-5633
Mickey's is on the National Register of Historic Places and has been featured in several Hollywood movies, but don't think that means it's full of tourists and hipsters: The burly hostesses aren't afraid to throw people out for getting fresh, and you may just see them do so. Mickey's serves up real ice-cream malts, eggs any way you like 'em, burgers and fries, Mulligan stew, and pancakes 24 hours a day. Set in a '30s-era dining car with a chrome and Formica interior, the diner has been family owned and operated since 1939.

MUFFULETTA CAFÉ $$
2260 Como Ave., St. Paul
(651) 644-9116
www.muffuletta.com
Located in the charming, London-like St. Anthony Park neighborhood near the University of Minnesota's St. Paul campus, Muffuletta serves an eclectic menu in a colorful, casual-yet-classy atmosphere. The restaurant changes its menu daily, but you can expect to find such things as pork tenderloin, duck, gnocchi, and steaks, all prepared with great attention to detail and an eye toward succulence. Muffuletta also offers a prix fixe menu that changes weekly, with an appetizer, main course, and dessert for one price. Muffuletta serves beer and wine, including a fabulous wine list courtesy of the sommelier on staff. The restaurant is open for lunch and dinner Monday through Saturday and brunch only on Sunday.

PORKY'S $

1890 University Ave. West, St. Paul
(651) 644-1790

In the early 21st century, there are few drive-in restaurants, but Porky's, founded in 1953, bucks the trend. And the pickup window is open regardless of Twin Cities weather. The restaurant is a modified drive-in where you have the option of ordering at the pickup window or at a counter inside the restaurant. Diners may enjoy their food in their car under the large awning or, when weather permits, on the half-dozen picnic tables provided by the restaurant. Porky's menu is filled with drive-in favorites such as hamburgers, cheeseburgers, fried chicken, chicken wings, pork sandwiches, catfish, shakes, fries, and much more. Especially in the summer, you're apt to see some vintage automobiles at Porky's, en route to or from classic-car shows at the State Fairgrounds. (Some nights the vintage-auto eye candy is so thick that people actually lay down blankets and set up folding chairs on University Avenue, as though a parade were going by.) Porky's is open seven days a week for lunch and dinner.

ST. PAUL GRILL $$$$

350 Market St., St. Paul
(651) 224-7455
www.stpaulgrill.com

Located in the four-star St. Paul Hotel, the St. Paul Grill overlooks elegant Rice Park, one of downtown St. Paul's loveliest blocks. The St. Paul Grill serves upscale food and spirits. The menu includes steaks, lobster, halibut, lamb chops, and much more. The food is first-rate, but you'll pay for your delight: Several entrées top $30 and the Surf & Turf tops an eye-popping $60. The restaurant features an excellent wine list, which, like the cuisine, has received countless local and national awards. The St. Paul Grill is also famous for its extensive list of cognacs, Armagnacs, single-malt scotches, and Irish whiskies, and the bartenders are also well known for their Bloody Marys. The bar is a lovely place to stop for a drink before or after events at the nearby Ordway Center for the Performing Arts. Reservations are highly recommended. The St. Paul Grill is open for lunch and dinner Monday through Saturday, and for brunch and dinner on Sunday.

TAVERN ON GRAND $$–$$$

656 Grand Ave., St. Paul
(651) 228-9030
www.tavernongrand.com

Tavern on Grand is a Minnesota classic, serving up plates of walleye fillets to the masses. Sure, you can also come here for sirloin, lasagna, and slow-roasted ribs, but you're unlikely to order walleye in Memphis, so get with the program and order up a plate of the exalted fish with all the trimmings. (True, almost none of the walleye served in Minnesota restaurants actually comes from Minnesota…but when it's this good, why nitpick?) The restaurant has a north-woodsy feel like a lakefront lodge, complete with built-in fish tank, and the walleye is simply spectacular. Options abound, including a choice of a grilled or deep-fried (with "secret batter") one- or two-fillet dinner, the walleye basket, the walleye sandwich, and the Lakeshore Special, which includes a fillet and an eight-ounce steak. You can also add a flaky fillet to any meal as a side order, if spaghetti, meatballs, and walleye are your thing. The waitstaff won't bat an eye. The Tavern on Grand is open daily for lunch and dinner.

W. A. FROST AND COMPANY $$$

374 Selby Ave., St. Paul
(651) 224-5715
www.wafrost.com

W. A. Frost is located in the Cathedral Hill neighborhood of St. Paul in the elegant 19th-century Dacotah Building. The menu is brief but well executed and includes ahi tuna, duck, walleye, filet mignon, and more. Of particular note is the house-smoked gravlox, salmon cured in sugar, salt, and dill (the dill distinguishes gravlox from regular lox). The restaurant also serves some unusual and delightful cheeses paired with wines and sherries. Also of note is the extensive loose-tea list, courtesy of St. Paul's Tea Source. If you're in the Twin Cities in summer, try to get a table on the leafy patio, which time and again is voted the best outdoor dining experience in the Twin

Cities. It's refreshing and comfortable during the day, and cozy and romantic after the sun sets. W. A. Frost is open Monday through Saturday for lunch and dinner, and Sunday for brunch and dinner. Reservations are highly recommended.

East

CHICKADEE COTTAGE RESTAURANT $-$$
9900 Valley Creek Rd., Woodbury
(651) 345-5155
www.chickadeecottagecafe.com
The Chickadee Cottage Restaurant offers an extensive menu of American and European-influenced favorites. The cottage theme pervades the restaurant, with each room having a particular cottage motif (e.g., rustic lodge or rural getaway). Chickadee's breakfast menu is enormous and includes many fresh-baked goods as well as pancakes, waffles, eggs, omelets, and much more. The lunch and dinner menus also provide plenty to choose from, including meat loaf sandwiches, scallops and shrimp, vegetable lasagna, and smoky apple pork chops. The restaurant is family friendly: Children are provided with crayons and a menu that includes pancakes or scrambled eggs for breakfast and grilled cheese or peanut butter and jelly sandwiches for dinner. Chickadee Cottage Restaurant is open Tuesday through Sunday for breakfast, lunch, and dinner.

THE LOWELL INN $$-$$$
102 North Second St., Stillwater
(651) 439-1100
www.lowellinn.com
The Lowell Inn is widely known for its Swiss cheese fondue, served in the Stillwater inn's Matterhorn Room. But at the Lowell the Swiss cheese fondue is just the starter of a four-course meal (with optional wine accompaniment) featuring beef tenderloin, duck breast, or jumbo prawns with Minnesota wild rice pilaf. Desserts include grapes Devonshire and Grand Marnier chocolate fondue for two. The whole shebang is delivered tableside for a set price. For those looking to choose individual dishes rather than a multicourse extravaganza, the Lowell's George

Washington Room offers such entrées as duck breast, filet mignon, and lobster tail. (For more information on the Lowell Inn's guest rooms, see the Accommodations chapter.)

West

PARK TAVERN $-$$
3401 Louisiana Ave. South, St. Louis Park
(952) 929-6810
www.parktavern.net
Bar and bowling alley food is generally not highly regarded for its taste. The Park Tavern is an exception. The appetizers are tasty and edible, with or without suds, and include nachos, quesadillas, and chicken strips. Also featured are top-notch burgers and sandwiches such as the French dip au jus and the prime melt sandwich, which features prime rib topped with sautéed onions and cheese. Salads are another option for less ravenous diners. The Park Tavern serves lunch and dinner Monday through Friday, and breakfast, lunch, and dinner on weekends.

Cajun/Southern

DIXIE'S ON GRAND $-$$
695 Grand Ave., St. Paul
(651) 222-7345
www.dixiesongrand.com
There are only a few Cajun and southern restaurants in the North Star State. Cajun- and southern-cooking purists may balk at Dixie's menu since it includes such foods as calamari, Cuban black bean soup, and fusion foods like the Cajun burger. However, the menu also includes Cajun and southern staples such as jambalaya, blackened catfish, shrimp and crawfish étouffée, and Carolina crab cakes. The ribs are another specialty at Dixie's and are available in baby back and country-style pork. Dixie's has an extensive wine list as well as a large selection of domestic and imported beers, and later in the evening, the bar can get pretty hopping (or pretty crowded and loud, depending on your sensibilities). Every other Friday, oddly, the Tropical Zone Orchestra sets up at Dixie's for one of the Twin Cities' hottest salsa-dancing events. On Sunday the restaurant hosts a champagne brunch, which

includes red beans and rice, corn bread, country ham, barbecue chicken, and much more. The entire menu is available for take-out. Reservations for dinner are recommended, especially on weekend evenings. Dixie's is open for lunch and dinner daily.

Cambodian

CHENG HENG $
448 University Ave. West, St. Paul
(651) 222-5577
Definitely a diamond in the rough, Cheng Heng is one of the most amazing deals (and best-kept secrets) in town. Cheng Heng looks, to the casual observer, like just one more uninviting sign in a line of strip malls. But this is the only place in town where you can get a pile of beautifully steamed mussels in black bean sauce for under $10, and that's about the most expensive selection on the menu. The couple who run the place take hospitality to new levels, positioning fans to cool down your table when it's hot out and fussing over you as though you were their house guest and not just another restaurant customer. This has long been a favorite place to take relatives for special occasions or wow out-of-town friends when they come to visit. Cheng Heng is open daily for breakfast, lunch, and dinner.

Caribbean

Minneapolis

HARRY SINGH'S ORIGINAL CARIBBEAN RESTAURANT $–$$
2653 Nicollet Ave., Minneapolis
(612) 729-6181
www.harrysinghs.com
Great prices and tasty West Indies cuisine distinguish Harry Singh's. The restaurant specializes in roti, a crepe-like Caribbean flatbread with your choice of more than a dozen curries. You can get roti with such ingredients as potatoes, chickpeas, cardamom seeds, curried beef, and jerk chicken. The servings are enormous here, often enough for two hungry diners. Harry Singh's is open for lunch and dinner Tuesday through Saturday.

St. Paul

WEST INDIES SOUL CAFE $
625 University Ave., St. Paul
(651) 665-0115
West Indies Soul began serving the Twin Cities at annual neighborhood festivals. The savory tastes of the Caribbean created a demand for catering and later a restaurant to serve jerk chicken, curry chicken and goat, fried plantains, and roti (Caribbean breads filled with meats). Though not a fast-food restaurant, the order-in and take-out counter-style dining facilitates quick service. The restaurant serves homemade drinks of carrot punch, ginger beer, and lemonade but does not serve alcohol. West Indies Soul is open for lunch and dinner Tuesday through Saturday.

East

SAN PEDRO CAFE $$
426 Second St., Hudson, WI
(715) 386-4003
www.sanpedrocafe.com
The San Pedro Cafe offers Mediterranean and tropical cuisine and atmosphere in scenic Hudson, Wisconsin. The menu overflows with flavor. There are sandwiches, wraps, pastas, salads, seafood, jerk chicken, and Neapolitan pizzas. The restaurant is located in a wonderful restored building in downtown Hudson and is often packed with customers. The San Pedro Cafe is open for lunch and dinner Monday through Friday, and for all three meals on weekends.

Chinese

Minneapolis

1ST WOK $–$$
3236 West Lake St., Minneapolis
(612) 922-8883

415 East 78th St., Bloomington
(952) 881-2413
1st Wok features an extensive menu of Hunan- and Szechuan-style Chinese food. Fine renditions of sesame chicken, kung pao chicken, lo mein, and pepper steak are served, as well as numerous seafood items. The restaurant features specialties such as sesame shrimp, Double Wonder, and

princess chicken and shrimp. Daily lunch specials are a steal and include an entrée plus soup and fried rice. Vegetarian items include bean curd selections (kung pao bean curd and spicy bean curd Szechuan-style). 1st Wok is open daily for lunch and dinner.

> **i** Watch for the annual Taste of Lake Street event at Minneapolis's Midtown Global Market for a chance to experience a wide sample of ethnic food offerings under one roof.

HONG KONG NOODLES RESTAURANT $–$$
901 Washington Ave. SE, Minneapolis
(612) 379-9472
Several excellent Chinese restaurants are in the vicinity of the University of Minnesota—this is arguably one of the best. The restaurant is rather small and seats no more than 50 people in an often-packed room. But it is the food that garners the restaurant accolades from its regular patrons and critics alike. With almost 300 menu items, Hong Kong Noodles offers plenty to choose from, but noodles are the restaurant's specialty. The menu is divided into extensive soup, chicken, beef, fried rice, hot pot, seafood, pork, and vegetable choices. A few standouts are the Singapore-style rice noodles, seafood lo mein, and beef brisket fun. Hong Kong Noodles is open for lunch and is open for dinner late daily, which is relatively uncommon in the Twin Cities.

RAINBOW CHINESE RESTAURANT & BAR $–$$
2739 Nicollet Ave., Minneapolis
(612) 870-7084
www.rainbowrestaurant.com
Rainbow Chinese's menu features exciting examples of Chinese cuisine prepared with fresh ingredients. Rainbow's signature dishes include Szechuan wontons, honey walnut shrimp and Singapore chow mai fun, and fried walleye pike with black bean sauce. There are many other options, including vegetarian entrées. Alcohol is available with meals and at the lovely bar, where

diners can feel free to bask in the comely decor of the restaurant, which is superbly decorated in greens and yellows. Try Rainbow's custom-made ginger ale, which will knock your socks off! Reservations are accepted only for groups of four or more. The restaurant serves lunch and dinner daily.

SHUANG CHENG RESTAURANT $–$$
1320 Fourth St. SE, Minneapolis
(612) 378-0208
On weekends Shuang Cheng, which is located in Dinkytown near the U, draws huge crowds, mainly for the delicious seafood prepared with a tantalizing Chinese flair. The menu includes shrimp, crab, scallops, oysters, clams, lobster, squid, and four walleye dishes. Chicken, beef, pork, and vegetarian options are available. Daily specials are posted on a whiteboard and erased when the item sells out. Shuang Cheng is open Monday through Saturday for lunch and dinner, and Sunday for dinner only.

St. Paul

LITTLE SZECHUAN $–$$
422 University Ave. West, St. Paul
(651) 222-1333
www.littleszechuan.com
Little Szechuan has many of the "Chinese" favorites most Americans enjoy (kung pao chicken, beef strips with garlic sauce, etc.) but also has many items more common to actual restaurants in China. Such succulent creations as tea-smoked duck and eel strips with spicy sauce will get your attention, to say the least. Little Szechuan is open daily for lunch and dinner.

North

WILLOWGATE $
1885 West Perimeter Dr., Roseville
(651) 628-0990
www.willowgateonline.com
Willowgate's menu is extensive and features several hundred Chinese and Vietnamese items. At lunch there are combination meals for under $5, including several seafood items. The curry shrimp and chicken fried rice are two favorites. Each is

accompanied by a choice of two chicken wings or cheese wontons. Dinner offers larger combination plates as well as traditional Chinese fare, such as lo mein, egg foo young, fried rice, and seafood. Willowgate serves beer and wine, and lunch and dinner are served daily.

West

YANGTZE CHINESE RESTAURANT $$
5625 Wayzata Blvd., St. Louis Park
(952) 541-9469
www.yangtze.us
The Yangtze Restaurant serves Hunan, Szechuan, Cantonese, and Mandarin Chinese dishes. Specials of the house include duck, Szechuan-style leg of lamb, and tangerine beef. The extensive menu also includes everything from lobster to eggplant in a garlic sauce, moo shu pork, several versions of lo mein and chow mein, two preparations including fresh Maine lobster, and much more. Yangtze Restaurant is open daily for lunch and dinner and features an excellent dim sum over the weekend lunch hours.

Cuban

VICTOR'S 1959 CAFE $
3756 Grand Ave. South, Minneapolis
(612) 827-8948
www.victors1959cafe.com
Serving Cuban and American breakfast and lunch cuisine, this tiny restaurant is packed with photographs and memorabilia of both Cuba and Fidel Castro. The yellow, graffiti-covered walls give a Caribbean feel to the restaurant, as does the Cuban music in the background. The menu includes eggs Havana, mango waffles, ranchero Cubano, the Bay of Pigs pork sandwich, both sweet plantains and fried green plantains, and Cuban coffee. Under no circumstances should you fail to order the fried yucca. The restaurant is a popular neighborhood stop, and with fewer than ten tables inside, the wait to get seated can be an hour or so. Victor's serves breakfast and lunch Tuesday through Sunday and dinner Tuesday through Saturday.

Eastern European

KRAMARCZUK SAUSAGE COMPANY $
215 Hennepin Ave. East, Minneapolis
(612) 379-3018
www.kramarczuk.com
Specializing in the cuisine of Ukraine and some other countries in that neck of the steppe, the casual Kramarczuk Sausage Company serves delicious, cheap eats in their cafeteria-style restaurant across the river from downtown Minneapolis. Specialties include *varenyky* (dumplings stuffed with meat, cheese and potato, or sauerkraut), *holubets* (cabbage rolls stuffed with rice and meat and topped with tomato sauce), *szegedin* goulash (meat, sauerkraut, and onions in a paprika sauce), and several selections of sausages. Soups include borscht and sausage vegetable, and Kramarczuk serves beer and wine. The restaurant also has an on-site deli and market. Live accordion music livens things up on Saturday night. Kramarczuk is open for breakfast and lunch Monday through Saturday, and for lunch on Sunday; the market and deli are open daily for sausages (and many other items) to take home and grill.

Ethiopian

Minneapolis

BLUE NILE $–$$
2027 Franklin Ave. East, Minneapolis
(612) 338-3000
Blue Nile was one of the first Ethiopian restaurants in the area. The restaurant, in Minneapolis's Seward neighborhood, is in a huge complex including a voluminous dining room, bar, and dance floor. Blue Nile's menu items include *maraka hoolaa* (lamb flavored with ginger root and other exotic spices), a shish kebab combo, and several vegetarian options, to name a few. For an overview of the culinary treats offered at the Blue Nile, try the gosa-gosa C, which is a sampler of two of the menu's vegetarian entrées and *maraka* (Ethiopian stewed meat dishes). Blue Nile is open for dinner daily; on Tuesday and Wednesday nights the restaurant hosts the Poet's Groove, the top spoken-word open-mic night in town.

St. Paul

QUEEN OF SHEBA CAFÉ & RESTAURANT $–$$
2447 West Seventh St., St. Paul
(651) 690-0068

Queen of Sheba serves primarily Ethiopian food—stewed beef, chicken, and vegetables spiced and served with *injera* (delicious, spongy pieces of flatbread). It's a strange mixture of elegant and casual, as the restaurant is beautifully decorated with hand-embroidered tablecloths and framed needlepoints, but all the food is prepared to be eaten with your hands alone, although if you ask, they'll gladly bring you silverware. A counter at one side of the restaurant serves Ethiopian coffee. The restaurant is open for lunch and dinner daily.

French

Minneapolis

BARBETTE $$
1600 West Lake St., Minneapolis
(612) 827-5710
www.barbette.com

Barbette is a little snooty, and that's part of the fun. From the cafe-style sidewalk tables to the insides of the famous pommes frittes, Barbette is a loving re-creation of a Parisian bistro. Chef Sarah Master offers a delectable range of savory dining options and a range of tasty appetizers to savor—whether during a romantic late-night date or just by yourself. Barbette's open secret is its reasonable price point: The restaurant justifiably likes to quote *Star Tribune* food critic Rick Nelson's observation that the food tastes much more expensive than it actually is. The restaurant also hosts a series of top-notch local performers for free Monday-night shows, where they seem happy to be drowned out by the amiable conversation at the busy bistro.

LA BELLE VIE $$$$
510 Groveland Ave., Minneapolis
(612) 874-6440

La Belle Vie is by general consensus the finest restaurant in Minnesota. As the crown jewel of the several restaurants overseen by top chef Tim McKee—winner of the 2009 James Beard Award for best chef in the Midwest—La Belle Vie offers French cuisine that will make your heart stop. Foie gras, sautéed scallops, duck breast, goat cheese, and—wait for it—truffle poached rabbit are among the options you might see on the menu at La Belle Vie. It's decidedly an indulgence—you don't really want to think about what you're paying for each bite—but for local foodies, this is the alpha and the omega.

VINCENT $$$
1100 Nicollet Mall, Minneapolis
(612) 630-1189
www.vincentrestaurant.com

Vincent, named for head chef and owner Vincent Francoual (not one for false modesty), is a lovely spot for casual fine dining. Beautiful oak woodwork, high ceilings, and large windows overlooking Nicollet Mall and Orchestra Hall provide the upscale atmosphere for the restaurant's French-American specialties. The menu changes every two months, but some past dishes include "porchetta" of suckling pig, rosemary-scented chevre cheese ravioli, and roasted Hawaiian barracuda. Vincent is open for lunch Monday through Friday and dinner Monday through Saturday; reservations are recommended, particularly on weekends.

South

LA FOUGASSE $$$
Sofitel Minneapolis Hotel,
5601 West 78th St., Bloomington
(952) 835-1900
www.lafougasseminneapolis.com

This hotel restaurant serves a wide variety of elegant French dishes, including onion and caramelized fennel soup, bouillabaisse marseillaise, and a lovely collection of scrumptious desserts. The restaurant also features several Spanish dishes (including paella and empanadas) and two prix fixe tasting menus. Warm saffron, deep red, and azure blue give the restaurant a relaxing Mediterranean look. Reservations are almost always required, as the place fills up quickly with hotel guests. La Fougasse is open Monday through

Saturday for lunch and dinner, and Sunday for brunch and dinner.

German
Minneapolis

BLACK FOREST INN $$
1 East 26th St., Minneapolis
(612) 872-0812
www.blackforestinnmpls.com
For more than 40 years, the Black Forest has served as a sturdy reminder to Eat Street gourmands that "ethnic food" doesn't just mean Vietnamese pho. The restaurant has a lovely, shaded courtyard—with fish pond, no less—open in the summertime. Another asset at the restaurant is the large bar stocked with imported German, Austrian, Czech, Belgian, English, Irish, and domestic beers (or, as the Black Forest's billboards put it, "what you Americans call 'beer'"), including several excellent pilsners and two weissbiers on tap. The hearty suds go great with the robust German food, including such specialties as wiener schnitzel (breaded veal cutlets), sauerbraten (marinated beef), *hasenpfeffer* (braised rabbit), and *kaseller rippchen* (smoked and boiled pork chop), as well as sauerkraut and spaetzle (German dumplings). Dessert is outstanding, too, especially the decadent Black Forest torte and the equally rich sacher torte. The restaurant is open for breakfast, lunch, and dinner daily.

St. Paul

GLOCKENSPIEL $–$$
605 West Seventh St., St. Paul
(651) 292-9421
www.glockenspielrestaurant.com
The Glockenspiel's location, a Czech and Slovak fraternal hall, is one of the restaurant's greatest assets. On entering the restaurant, you see a huge bar stocked with German beers. The dining area is a classy continuation of the bar and is decked out in plenty of blue against a large mural in the long, narrow, spacious dining area.

German specialties fill the large menu, including *schweinhaxe* (pork hocks), *Eisbach pfeffersteak* (a German version of sirloin steak), and *schwein-rippchen* (pork spare ribs). And for those with a smaller appetite, there are *kleine speise* (lighter fare) such as bratwurst, weisswurst, *käsespätzle* (German dumplings with cheese), and *leberkäse* (German pork loaf). Stop in for the Friday Night Fish Fry, an all-you-can-eat affair available for lunch or dinner. Finally, for dessert the restaurant features tortes, cakes, and other German delights. Glockenspiel is open for lunch and dinner daily.

East

GASTHAUS BAVARIAN HUNTER $–$$
8390 Lofton Ave. North, Stillwater
(651) 439-7128
www.gasthausbavarianhunter.com
Gasthaus has specialized in the cuisine of southern Germany since 1966, and the extensive menu offers something for everyone. The restaurant has the largest variety of schnitzels (cutlets) in the Twin Cities. Also featured are sausages, sauerbraten (a tangy beef), and, for large appetites, a couple of Bavarian combination platters. Surprisingly, the meaty restaurant has two *kein fleisch* (no meat) meals—vegetable rouladen and vegetable casserole. And don't forget to wash the meal down with a German beer, especially since the restaurant does not stock domestic brews. For diners' entertainment, polka music is performed on Friday and Sunday as well as for the many German events. The Gasthaus Bavarian Hunter is open daily for lunch and dinner.

THE WINZER STUBE $$
516 Second St., Hudson, WI
(715) 381-5092
www.winzerstube.net
One of the area's best German restaurants is located in Hudson, Wisconsin, 25 miles east of downtown St. Paul. The menu features several excellent dishes. One savory item is the *roulade mit speck und gurke*. The flavorful beef rollups and smoky bacon are wrapped around a tasty pickle. Also outstanding is the *jägerschnitzel*. The fine pork cutlet is the restaurant's biggest seller and comes accompanied by spaetzle (homemade noodles) and *rotkraut* (red cabbage). The *schwein-haxe* (pork hocks) is a popular daily special that occasionally sells out during lunch. For smaller

appetites there are soups and sausage platters (bratwurst, weisswurst, bauern mettwurst, and knackwurst) on the menu. The restaurant has a children's menu (for the "little lederhosens") and outstanding dessert options such as Black Forest cake, apple strudel, and chocolate torte.

Greek

Minneapolis

GARDENS OF SALONICA NEW GREEK CAFE AND DELI $-$$
19 Fifth St. NE, Minneapolis
(612) 378-0611
www.gardensofsalonica.com
Anna and Lazaros Christoforide's sunny restaurant serves fresh bread with delightful dips, like their zingy *skordalia* (potatoes, lemon juice, and garlic) and *tyro* (feta cheese blended with roasted peppers, garlic, and herbs); chicken souvlaki and lamb-and-beef gyro sandwiches; and fancier dishes like rice-stuffed squid baked in red wine sauce and the fresh artichoke-and-braised-lamb dish that's a spring special. The house specialty, popular for lunch or dessert, is *boughatsa:* phyllo pastries that come in sweet and savory varieties. Located in a turn-of-the-20th-century storefront on an obscure side street, this family-owned Greek cafe and deli draws patrons from all over the Metro. Gardens of Salonica is open for lunch and dinner Tuesday through Saturday.

IT'S GREEK TO ME $$
626 West Lake St., Minneapolis
(612) 825-9922
This restaurant is casual and welcoming, with high pressed-tin ceilings, freshly painted wall murals, and terra-cotta-like tiled floors. It's also inexpensive, considering that a dinner-size portion of anything costs around $10 and will usually leave you enough for tomorrow's lunch. The menu offers nearly two dozen appetizers to precede classic Greek specialties such as souvlaki and spanakopita, fried smelt, octopus, chicken gyros, and flaming cheese. Every night the place bustles with couples, small families, and intimate clusters of friends devouring spicy-hot feta

cheese spread, roast leg of lamb, or vegetarian dolmades. The restaurant is open Tuesday through Sunday for lunch and dinner.

St. Paul

ACROPOL INN RESTAURANT $
748 Grand Ave., St. Paul
(651) 298-0151
The Acropol Inn is one of the Twin Cities' oldest Greek restaurants. The Apostolou family opened the restaurant in 1975 to serve gyros and other Greek specialties. The restaurant serves all the traditional Greek standards—moussaka (meat and eggplant), *dolmades* (grape leaves stuffed with rice and meat), and pasticcio (a Greek version of lasagna). Wash the Greek cuisine down with a cold beer or glass of wine. The Acropol Inn Restaurant is open Monday through Saturday for lunch and dinner.

CHRISTOS GREEK RESTAURANT $$
214 East Fourth St., St. Paul
(651) 224-6000

2632 Nicollet Ave., Minneapolis
(612) 871-2111

15600 Hwy. 7, Minnetonka
(952) 912-1000
www.christos.com
Christos serves all your Greek favorites from three Twin Cities locations. The St. Paul restaurant is one of the most beautiful and historical dining spots in the area, the Union Depot Place. Christos is situated in the middle of the immense former Union Depot, atop a riser, and is surrounded by columns and plenty of big windows and marble. It's hard for a restaurant to fail with such grandeur and beauty.

All three locations feature tasty versions of Greek cuisine. The menu includes gyros, *dolmades,* spanakopita, moussaka, and many other traditional Greek dishes. The prices are reasonable, especially for lunch, when the St. Paul location serves a buffet Monday through Friday. The buffet offers a relatively inexpensive introduction for Greek food novices as well as connoisseurs. All three Christos restaurants are open for lunch and dinner daily.

West

SANTORINI $$$
13000 Technology Dr., Eden Prairie
(952) 546-6722

Greek cuisine and American specialties dominate the menu at Santorini, which moved in 2008 from its St. Louis Park location to a new space in Eden Prairie. For lunch and dinner there are numerous choices. Sandwiches ranging from a traditional burger to Moroccan chicken, which features a unique pepper spread, onions, and cucumbers, are served along with pastas and more elaborate entrées. Shrimp, steaks, lamb chops, and much more are available as well as Greek combination platters. Santorini is open daily for lunch and dinner.

Indian

Minneapolis

GANDHI MAHAL $$
3009 27th Ave. South, Minneapolis
(612) 729-5222
www.gandhimahal.com

Gandhi Mahal is dedicated to the spirit of Mohandas Gandhi, and the proprietors' goal is to "bring the peace by pleasing the palate." Whether they're achieving the former, they're definitely good at the latter. Many Minneapolitans cite this restaurant—a world unto itself just off the intersection of Lake Street and Minnehaha Avenue—as their favorite spot to get a tikka masala fix.

NAMASTE CAFÉ $$
2512 Hennepin Ave., Minneapolis
(612) 827-2496
www.namastechai.com

Namaste Café and the Duplex restaurant sit in adjacent houses on Hennepin, with banners advertising their respective merits: best first-date spot for the Duplex, best chai tea for Namaste. In fact, Namaste wouldn't be a bad spot for a first date either—or a second, or a third. The cuisine is a Nepalese/Indian fusion, with unusually fresh and flavorful offerings. In the summer you can dine on the porch and watch Uptown life go by as you sip your iced chai.

OM $$
401 North First Ave., Minneapolis
(612) 338-1510
www.omminneapolis.com

Minneapolis's newest Indian restaurant is this swank Warehouse District establishment founded by local celebrity chef Raghavan Iyer (author of best-selling cookbook *660 Curries*). The food is excellent, but the atmosphere—complementing Iyer's daring and contemporary approach to cooking—is another big draw. The restaurant is increasingly programming live music and other events, starting with a monthly Mumbai Saturday Night event featuring Indian musicians, henna tattoos, and street food such as you might find on the streets of India's entertainment capital.

St. Paul

INDIA HOUSE $$
758 Grand Ave., St. Paul
(651) 293-9124
www.indiahousesaintpaul.com

India House manages to feel warm and cozy despite being a spacious establishment with big picture windows looking out on Grand Avenue. Don't be fooled by the richly decorated space and the fancy address: India House offers a reasonably priced menu of tasty Indian cuisine, including a daily lunch buffet.

North

INDIA PALACE $–$$
2570 Cleveland Ave. North, Roseville
(651) 631-1222

8362 Tamarack Village, Woodbury
(651) 731-6300
www.indiapalacemn.com

India Palace creates some of the area's best cuisine at its two locations. Featured menu items include tandoori specialties, curries, and vindaloos. Also available is the lunch buffet, where seven days a week diners may enjoy the flavors of India. In addition, the restaurant offers takeout as well as an extensive beer and wine list. Both locations are open daily for lunch and dinner.

South

TANDOOR RESTAURANT $–$$
8062 Morgan Circle, Bloomington
(952) 885-9060
www.tandoormn.com

True to its name, the specialty of Tandoor Restaurant is the meats, seafood, and other foods cooked in the tandoor, a clay oven heated to high heat using charcoal. Favorites include tandoori chicken, tandoori naan bread, lamb rogan nosh, and chicken makhani, as well as various curry dishes. The restaurant features an all-you-can-eat lunch buffet. Tandoor Restaurant is open Monday through Saturday for lunch and dinner.

East

TASTE OF INDIA $–$$
1745 Cope Ave. East, Maplewood
(651) 773-5477
www.tasteofindiamn.com

This Taste of India has different ownership than the St. Louis Park location and a different menu. The restaurant features an extensive list of mainly north Indian dishes. Curries and tandoori specialties dominate the menu. The menu also has many vegetarian options. The restaurant offers a daily lunch buffet and a selection of beers, wines, and Indian drinks such as *lassi* (yogurt drink) and Indian tea. Taste of India serves lunch and dinner daily.

West

TASTE OF INDIA $–$$
5617 Wayzata Blvd., St. Louis Park
(952) 541-4865

The Taste of India in St. Louis Park, similar in spirit to the Maplewood restaurant of the same name, offers an extensive menu of excellently prepared curries and tandoori (clay-oven) specialties. The restaurant specializes in north Indian cuisine, with treats from throughout the subcontinent thrown in to enthrall the taste buds. The tandoori items are especially tasty. Indian specialty drinks (mango milk shakes, mango *lassi* yogurt drink, etc.) as well as wines and beers, both imported and domestic, are offered. The restaurant features a daily lunch buffet with a particularly large

spread. Taste of India is open daily for lunch and dinner.

Irish

THE LOCAL $–$$
931 Nicollet Mall, Minneapolis
(612) 904-1000
www.the-local.com

Food is served in a lovely dining room draped with velvet curtains and a charming bar, which is amply stocked with Irish and domestic beers. The menu includes reasonably priced sandwiches and entrées. Among the sandwiches offered are the pot roast beef, chicken breast, and an Irish specialty, corned beef (topped with Swiss cheese). For lighter appetites, diners may choose from a half-dozen salads. Entrées include salmon, sirloin steak, fish and chips, and lamb steak. Reservations are recommended. The Local is open Monday through Friday for lunch and dinner, and Saturday and Sunday for brunch and dinner. At night the restaurant turns into a hot spot for locals looking for a hopping downtown bar without the bump-and-grind scene to be found at venues like Drink and the Imperial Room. When the flirting gets hot and heavy, you and your partner can retire to the broom closet that's been redecorated and christened "the Kissing Room."

Italian
Minneapolis

AL VENTO $$$–$$$
5001 34th Ave. South, Minneapolis
(612) 724-3009
www.alventorestaurant.com

Al Vento is a trattoria serving southern Italian specialties prepared with simplicity and authenticity. This is one of the rare Italian restaurants serving dishes from the south of Italy, and the menu ingredients include plenty of tomatoes and, in many cases, the wonderful spice fennel. But this isn't a restaurant of spaghetti and meatballs (although a version with veal meatballs is often on the menu); much more experimentation is worth a try here, with some examples of recent dishes including gnocchi, bucatini, steak, pizza, and halibut. (The menu changes regularly.) Al Vento is open for lunch Monday through Friday, brunch on Sunday, and dinner Sunday through Saturday.

BRODERS' CUCINA ITALIANA $
2308 West 50th St., Minneapolis
(612) 925-3113
www.broders.com
Back in the early 1950s, Tom and Molly Broder founded this amazing neighborhood deli that served handmade pastas, imported olive oils, olives, cheese, meats, and other high-quality imported and homemade ingredients. Since then they've added spicy pizzas sold by the slice, sandwiches, take-out homemade pasta sauces, and deli treats from grilled asparagus to homemade cannolis to the menu. And they don't skimp on anything. The deli serves a full range of desserts, including triple-chocolate cheesecake and tiramisu. The restaurant is open for lunch and dinner daily.

BRODERS' PASTA BAR $$
5000 Penn Ave. South, Minneapolis
(612) 925-9202
www.broders.com
Made by hand by the excellent chefs at Broders', the different styles of pasta served here are all amazingly tender and rich, complemented by sauces and toppings that range from steamed green lip mussels to broiled fish and fresh herbs. It's about as far away from ordinary spaghetti as you can get, and for a price that's more than reasonable, especially for the quality of the food Broders' serves. The one drawback is the no-reservation policy, and mere minutes after the doors open for dinner, the place is packed. But the restaurant does allow you to call an hour ahead of time to put your name on the waiting list, something you'll want to take advantage of. In summer guests can sip drinks on the modest outdoor patio while waiting for a seat, but in winter latecomers will more than likely be left out in the cold. Broders' is open for dinner daily.

CAMPIELLO $$$
6411 City West Pkwy., Eden Prairie
(952) 941-6868
www.campiello.damico.com
Campiello is a great place to impress a date. The smart lighting makes everyone look fabulous, and the stunning presentations make everyone look like a big spender without breaking the bank. Campiello is high class without being snobby, as are the waitstaff. Bond in his tuxedo might feel a little overdressed, but everyone else, from the blue jeaned to the all in black, fits right in. On the menu the crackly thin-crusted pizzas make for stunning appetizers, the salads are solid, and the entrées (especially the pastas and the rotisserie meats) are absolutely top drawer. The Eden Prairie location is open for lunch and dinner Monday through Friday, and dinner only on weekends.

D'AMICO KITCHEN $$–$$$
901 Hennepin Ave., Minneapolis
(612) 767-6960
www.chambersminneapolis.com
D'Amico Kitchen is the restaurant at the Chambers art hotel, a contemporary Italian restaurant designed by local dining baron Richard D'Amico. The menu is a little more casual than the setting, highlighting two dozen antipasti "small plates." Dining in the subterranean lounge, you'll almost forget you're right in the middle of the Theater District action. Almost.

FAT LORENZO'S $
5600 Cedar Ave. South, Minneapolis
(612) 822-2040
www.fatlorenzos.com
A southside neighborhood institution, Fat Lorenzo's tables are covered with white butcher paper for customers to doodle on with supplied crayons while they wait for their pizzas to show up. The menu features New York–style pizza and Italian specialties such as lasagna, baked rigatoni, spaghetti, and chicken cacciatore. Hot and cold hoagies (including meatball, turkey, and roast beef) round off the menu nicely. Fat Lorenzo's is open daily for lunch and dinner.

IL GATTO $$
3001 Hennepin Ave., Minneapolis
(612) 822-1688
www.ilgattominneapolis.com

Il Gatto is the Parasole chain's 2009 revamping of the restaurant formerly known as Figlio—a two-decade institution in one of the best restaurant spaces in the Cities, at the corner of Lake and Hennepin, but one that was showing its age. Accessible haute cuisine is the goal of Il Gatto, which features contemporary Italian food including sausages and meatballs made on the premises. Try one of the handspun pizzas, accompanied by one of the many reasonably priced selections on the excellent wine list.

GALACTIC PIZZA $
2917 South Lyndale Ave., Minneapolis
(612) 824-9100
www.galacticpizza.com

Galactic Pizza is quintessential Lyndale Avenue: cheap but tasty pizza and beer served in a funky storefront that feels more like a coffee shop than a pizzeria. Galactic Pizza is best known for its unmissable delivery people, who ride tiny little motorized vehicles and wear superhero outfits, but it's also a favorite neighborhood destination featuring open-mic nights and other entertainment. Check out their spicy Mexicali pizza, which one local refers to as "a fiesta in your mouth."

PANE VINO DOLCE $$-$$$
819 West 50th St., Minneapolis
(612) 825-3201

Pane Vino Dolce offers fine Italian cuisine in a small, busy dining room. The menu includes small pizzas, risotto, ravioli, and seafood. All are prepared with fresh ingredients, and great attention is paid to presentation. Daily specials are offered. The restaurant is open daily for dinner. Pane Vino Dolce does not accept credit cards.

PIZZA LUCÉ $-$$
119 North Fourth St., Minneapolis
(612) 333-7359

3200 Lyndale Ave. South, Minneapolis
(612) 827-5978

2200 East Franklin Ave., Minneapolis
(612) 332-2535

1183 Selby Ave., St. Paul
(651) 288-0186
www.pizzaluce.com

Pizza Lucé specializes in, well, pizza, and they're pretty good at it. Including the classic taste of the Lucé, which is made of Italian sausage, onions, garlic, and extra cheese, there are many gourmet pizza choices, such as the barbecue chicken and the luau (Canadian bacon, pineapple, green onions, and mozzarella). And if the large selection of gourmet pizzas doesn't meet your needs, then build your own. The menu of more than 50 fresh ingredients includes meats, seafood, vegetables, and eight cheeses. In addition to pizza, the restaurant serves hoagies, spaghetti, lasagna, mostaccioli, and several vegetarian and vegan dishes. The Lyndale location serves beer and wine; the downtown, East Franklin, and St. Paul locations have full bars. All restaurants are open daily for lunch and dinner and stay open late, making Pizza Lucé a gourmet alternative to the Green Mill.

ZELO $$$-$$$$
831 Nicollet Mall, Minneapolis
(612) 333-7000
www.zelomn.com

This splashy restaurant is doing everything right to please couples in search of a memorable date, combining impeccable service with an accessible menu and a nicely focused wine list. Daily fish specials are the highlight, such as flaky walleye Milanese with a golden crown of Italian bread crumbs or a lusciously rare grilled ahi tuna moistened with Chinese mustard vinaigrette and served with green wasabi mashed potatoes. Steaks, veal chops, and lemon-herb chicken round out the entrées, while commendable pizzas and pastas present more economical options. The most popular dessert is their incredible tiramisu layered with mascarpone. Zelo is open for lunch and dinner Monday through Saturday, and dinner only on Sunday.

St. Paul

CARBONE'S ON RANDOLPH   **$–$$**
1698 Randolph Ave., St. Paul
(651) 771-3320
www.carbonesonrandolph.com
Carbone is one of the biggest names in Minnesota pizza, but it would take Mario Puzo to chronicle the family's complicated history. Though it was founded by a member of the same family that created the franchised chain you'll find across the Twin Cities, this Carbone's is independently run and, except for the selections in the jukebox and the inflation-adusted pricing, looks, feels, and—most important—tastes almost precisely the same as it did when it opened in 1962. A Carbone's pie is notably heavy on the cheese, with a thin, floppy crust that exists as a boundary and not much else. If you want to know just what it was like for baseball greats Paul Molitor and Joe Mauer to relax and chow down after games when they were students at the nearby Cretin-Derham Hall high school, grab a booth, a pitcher of root beer, and a pepperoni pizza at Carbone's.

CARMELO'S   **$$**
238 South Snelling Ave., St. Paul
(651) 699-2448
Carmelo's is a small, intimate Italian restaurant in St. Paul's Mac-Groveland neighborhood. The busy, family-run restaurant is a nice choice for a romantic evening, with a hand-picked selection of wines and beers to complement such made-from-scratch dishes as chicken carmelo, seafood canneloni, and spinach and cheese ravioli. If you can't find a parking place out front, park in the lot next to Sweeney Cleaners at the intersection of Snelling and St. Clair Avenues just south of the restaurant. Reservations are highly recommended for dinner, especially on the weekend. The restaurant is open for lunch Tuesday through Friday and dinner Monday through Saturday.

COSSETTA ITALIAN MARKET & PIZZERIA   **$**
211 West Seventh St., St. Paul
(651) 222-3476
Cossetta's is one of the busiest lunch spots in St. Paul. It draws throngs of patrons because of the fine pizzas and pastas prepared for eating in or takeout. The delicious chewy thick crust of Cossetta's Chicago-style pizza is topped with a piquant marinara sauce, tasty mozzarella, and fresh ingredients. Huge pieces of pizza are ready to eat at the counter. Another counter offers lasagna, sausage and peppers, chicken marsala, sausage calabrase, chicken cacciatore, and more a la carte items. Ample seating is provided on two floors, where recordings by Italian-American singers such as Tony Bennett and Frank Sinatra are played over the sound system. A wine list is available. Michael and Irene Cossetta opened the adjoining market in 1911, where the now-sprawling market and restaurant began. Today Cossetta's does booming business for lunch and dinner daily.

DAVANNI'S PIZZA & HOT HOAGIES   **$**
41 Cleveland Ave. South, St. Paul
(651) 690-4848
20 additional Twin Cities locations
www.davannis.com
Since 1975 Davanni's has been well known for its pizzas and hot hoagies. Diners have an option of three crust types: traditional, thin, and Chicago deep-dish. The deep-dish is especially tasty. The thick, light crust is topped with a tangy tomato sauce, and the toppings and cheese are always fresh. Diners can also choose one of 16 hoagies, including salami, turkey, roast beef, meatball, pizza, and tuna. The calzones here are also worth a try. If you'd rather eat at home, delivery is always an option at Davanni's. There are 21 Davanni's spread across the metro area; the original location at Grand and Cleveland has been a St. Paul institution for years. The restaurant frequently sponsors fund-raising days for local youth teams, and on any given night you're likely to have to squeeze your way in between little kids in T-ball shirts and teenagers in Cretin-Derham letter jackets.

GREEN MILL   **$–$$**
1342 West Grand Ave., St. Paul
15 additional Twin Cities locations
(651) 690-0539

The Green Mill quickly earned a reputation as having some of the best pizza in the area when it opened at this location in 1976; since then the proprietors have opened dozens of franchises and expanded the scope of the menu to include pasta, calzones, sandwiches, fish, fowl, and much more. The pizza remains the standout and the restaurant's best value. The Green Mill offers flat, deep-dish, pescara, and numerous specialty pizzas. Many night owls regard the Green Mill's late-night happy hour as being the most underrated boozing bargain in the Cities; try a Bloody Mary, which includes a skewer of such large hunks of meat and cheese that it's practically an appetizer balanced on a glass.

LUCI ANCORA $$–$$$
2060 Randolph Ave., St. Paul
(651) 698-6889
www.ristoranteluci.com
Luci Ancora has been influenced by the trend toward minimalist preparation and organic ingredients. The menu is brief, but all dishes are well executed. Each evening a four-course *prezzo fiso* (fixed price) meal is offered, which includes antipasto, soup or salad, pasta, and fish. In addition, wine and delicious desserts are offered. Call ahead for reservations. Luci Ancora is open for lunch and dinner Tuesday through Friday and for dinner only on Saturday, Sunday, and Monday.

PAISANO'S PIZZA & HOT HOAGIES $
619 Selby Ave., St. Paul
(651) 224-3350
www.pizza651.com
Paisano's deep-dish pizza is sold by the slice as well as in large, medium, and "solo" sizes. There are several specialty pizzas to choose from, and diners can also choose any of the 24 offered ingredients to build a pizza to their liking. In addition, there are eight varieties of cold and hot hoagies. For the health conscious, house, classic Caesar, and Mediterranean salads are available. Paisano's is open seven days a week for lunch and dinner.

PAZZALUNA URBAN TRATTORIA AND BAR $$$
360 St. Peter St., St. Paul
(651) 223-7000
www.pazzaluna.com
Pazzaluna serves upscale regional Italian cuisine in downtown St. Paul. Specialties of the house include risotto alla Milanese, gnocchi (the house specialty), and filleto di manzo al pepe. A full bar features many Italian wines and several varieties of grappa, as well as single-malt scotches and numerous cordials. Reservations are recommended, and valet parking is available for bar and restaurant patrons. Pazzaluna is open for dinner nightly.

PUNCH NEAPOLITAN PIZZA $$
704 Cleveland Ave. South, St. Paul
(651) 696-1066
Six other locations across the Twin Cities
www.punchpizza.com
Yet another major pizza chain that started in St. Paul and has spread across the Cities, Punch takes its plate-size Neapolitan pizzas very seriously. Since the restaurant opened its first location, here, in 1996, it has been a member of the Associazione Vera Pizza Napoletana, an Italian organization that regulates pizza purity. Since Punch's inception, owner John Soranno has adhered to the organization's guidelines requiring only the highest quality ingredients and methods. The result is outstanding pizza. All pizzas are thin crusted and vary only in their high-quality toppings, such as the Puttanesca, which includes anchovies, capers, olives, onions, and oregano. With more than 20 pizzas, the choices are almost endless. Calzones and salads are other options on the menu. A wine list is also provided. Punch is open Tuesday through Saturday for dinner.

i Groups of 6 to 10 people can reserve the Chef's Table at Pazzaluna, which includes a five-course menu and an evening with the chef.

RED'S SAVOY PIZZA $
421 East Seventh St., St. Paul
(651) 227-1437
Five other locations across the Twin Cities

The original Red's Savoy Pizza, just east of downtown St. Paul, became a subject of snickering in 2006 when then-U.S.-Senator Norm Coleman's 81-year-old father was caught in flagrante with a female "friend" in a car in its parking lot. But long before then, Red's was well known in St. Paul for its delicious pizzas heaped with what feels like about a pound of ingredients per square inch. There are now several other locations—including a new Minneapolis shop in Uptown, replacing the dilapidated yet beloved Golooney's—but the nature of the pie varies much more among locations than is the case with other pizza chains, so the new spots are truly no substitute for the original. Red's is open daily for lunch and dinner.

RISTORANTE LUCI $$–$$$
470 Cleveland Ave. South, St. Paul
(651) 699-8258
www.ristoranteluci.com
Ristorante Luci serves spectacular classical Italian cuisine in a modestly decorated location. The restaurant is owned by the Smith family, Al and Lucille, who also own Luci Ancora, kitty-corner across Cleveland and Randolph from Ristorante Luci. Ristorante Luci specializes in pastas and seafood, which are prepared to perfection. This is one of the reasons the neighborhood restaurant is a perennial favorite. Another is the wine list and the excellent desserts. Reservations are recommended for dinner, especially on weekends. Ristorante Luci is open for dinner Tuesday through Saturday.

South

I NONNI $$
981 Sibley Memorial Hwy., Lilydale
(651) 905-1081
Focusing on the cuisine of central Italy, I Nonni is an elegant, romantic restaurant only minutes from downtown St. Paul via I-35E South. Freshly made pastas, ingredients such as rabbit, and fresh seafood distinguish the menu, and the spectacular wine list with more than 400 options will have something for every taste and wallet size. The post-dinner menu includes 14 varieties of grappa and other wines and spirits, along with cheeses

and impeccable desserts. This is a great place to take a date you wish to impress or to pamper yourself. The restaurant is connected to an Italian market and wine shop. I Nonni is open for lunch and dinner Monday through Saturday.

West
VESCIO'S $–$$
4001 County Rd. 25, St. Louis Park
(952) 920-0733

406 14th Ave. SE, Minneapolis
(612) 378-1747
www.vescioscucina.com
Vescio's serves ravioli, rigatoni, tortellini, fettuccine, and spaghetti as well as sandwiches. The sandwiches are Italian-inspired creations that include the Big Boy Italiano (various meats and cheeses on French loaf) and the sweet fried pepper sandwich. And don't forget Vescio's pizza. The pizzas are available in small and large and include one notable specialty: Sid's Special Pizza is topped with sausage, mushrooms, pepperoni, sweet fried peppers, extra cheese, and special seasoning and is named after longtime *Minneapolis Star Tribune* sports columnist Sid Hartman, who frequents the restaurant. Vescio's Cucina in St. Louis Park is open daily for lunch and dinner. Vescio's Originalé in Minneapolis is open Tuesday through Sunday for lunch and dinner.

Japanese
Minneapolis
FUJI YA JAPANESE RESTAURANT $$–$$$
600 West Lake St., Minneapolis
(612) 871-4055

465 North Wabasha St., St. Paul
(651) 310-0111
www.fujiyasushi.com
Fuji Ya is located in the Lyn-Lake neighborhood of south Minneapolis. It is the fourth location in the long history of the restaurant, which first opened its doors in downtown Minneapolis in 1959. A new St. Paul location opened in 2005. Fuji Ya offers a wide array of Japanese food in all price ranges. For lunch, the restaurant's noodle soups as well as more expensive items are available,

and there is also a sushi bar to satisfy lovers of the Japanese delicacy. Dinner specialties include shrimp tempura, sukiyaki, and chicken teriyaki. Fuji Ya has an extensive list of beers and wines. In Minneapolis, Fuji Ya serves dinner Tuesday through Sunday. The St. Paul location is open for lunch and dinner Monday through Friday, and dinner only on Saturday. Reservations are recommended.

KIKUGAWA $$–$$$
43 Main St. SE, Minneapolis
(612) 378-3006
www.kikugawa-restaurant.com
The best seats in the house are in the Kikugawa atrium, from which restaurant patrons can look out over the Mississippi and beyond to the Minneapolis skyline. Inside, the lighting is romantically dim, reflecting off the large gold-leaf fans decorating the walls. The sukiyaki (a simmered beef dish) is the best in town, and the restaurant also offers a large selection of sushi and pickled vegetable appetizers. To drink, there are Japanese beers and flavored sakes to choose from. At night (if you're lucky) drinking businessmen and big-spending hipsters take turns at the karaoke machine, belting out hits from the '60s on up. Kikugawa is open for lunch and dinner daily.

KOYI SUSHI $–$$
122 North Fourth St., Minneapolis
(612) 375-9811
www.koyisushi.com
Koyi Sushi serves fresh sushi at some of the best prices in town, with some very tasty renditions. Some of the more popular choices include the Dynamite Roll (spicy salmon and yellowtail), the Dragon Roll (cooked tuna, masago, and spicy mayo topped with unagi and avocado), and the Marilyn Monroll (grilled chicken, asparagus, and avocado). Koyi offers sushi a la carte (two pieces per serving), as well as small and large rolls. Non-sushi offerings include *kalbee* (marinated and grilled beef ribs served with Korean vegetables) and seafood tempura. The restaurant is open daily for dinner and for lunch Monday through Friday.

MIDORI'S FLOATING WORLD CAFÉ $$
2629 East Lake St., Minneapolis
(612) 721-3011
www.floatingworldcafe.com
First and foremost, Midori's is cute. If settling into Midori's charming dining room surrounded by bamboo plants and children's laminated drawings of fish doesn't warm your soul, you may want to check to see whether it's actually there. The food is great, too: a nice, reasonably priced selection of sushi and other Japanese delicacies. Try any of the bento boxes with a transparent mug of art tea—tea made from flowers that open and float upward before your eyes. Bliss.

SEVEN SUSHI ULTRALOUNGE
AND SKYBAR $$–$$$
700 Hennepin Ave., Minneapolis
(612) 238-7770
www.7mpls.com
Ladies, teetering on your strappiest heels? Men, gone a little overboard on the Drakkar Noir? You'll be safe at Seven, the Theater District's sleekest spot to see, be seen, and—oh yeah—eat. Seven is not the place to bring guests to impress them with the Twin Cities' culinary wonders, but if you're looking for a rooftop deck where you can bask in the glow of the blinking Orpheum sign while you sip sake from the skybar and whisper sweet nothings on an expansive private couch, Seven is your best bet. It's not just a lounge, it's an *ultralounge*.

SUSHI TANGO $$
3001 Hennepin Ave., Minneapolis
(612) 822-7787
www.sushitango.com
Sushi Tango's logo is a crazed anime boy with spiked hair, but that image doesn't necessarily represent its atmosphere. It's a chill and happily uncrowded spot that emphasizes the social side of Japanese dining, with highly sharable appetizers and drink selections including a tasty sake Bloody Mary. A place like this takes happy hour seriously, and there are two of them every day—with a full eight hours of happy hour each weekend day. (The "weekend," of course, includes Thursday—this is Uptown, after all.)

St. Paul

SAKURA RESTAURANT AND
SUSHI BAR $$–$$$
350 St. Peter St., St. Paul
(651) 224-0185
www.sakurastpaul.com

Sakura's menu is divided into tempura, teriyaki, donburi, noodles, salads, and of course, sushi. Sushi is the most important menu item—although there are many other standouts. The sushi bar is prominently placed at the center of a large open room. With more than 30 types of fresh sushi, connoisseurs have plenty of choices. The sushi bar offers California rolls, salmon egg, shrimp, crab, albacore tuna, scallop, sea eel, and many additional options; all are beautifully presented. The restaurant has a relaxed atmosphere and a friendly waitstaff. Reservations are recommended for dinner. Sakura is open daily for both lunch and dinner.

TANPOPO NOODLE SHOP $
308 Prince St., St. Paul
(651) 209-6527
www.tanpoporestaurant.com

There are numerous Vietnamese noodle shops in the Twin Cities but few Japanese restaurants specializing in the fine delicacy. The act of making noodles is elevated to an art at Tanpopo. The menu changes seasonally, and the restaurant concentrates on a concise, inexpensive, well-executed menu for lunch and dinner composed of various udon (wheat flour noodles) and soba (buckwheat flour noodles) as well as teishoku (set meals). The Nabeyaki Udon is one superb selection, which includes shrimp tempura, chicken, mushrooms, vegetables, and fish cake. The noodle shop is a beautiful renovated warehouse space in St. Paul's lower arts district. Tanpopo is open for lunch Tuesday through Saturday and dinner Monday through Saturday.

Korean

St. Paul

MIRROR OF KOREA $–$$
761 Snelling Ave. North, St. Paul
(651) 647-9004
www.mirrorofkorea.com

Mirror of Korea's large menu belies the humbly decorated restaurant. Soups, stir-fries, and stews fill out the menu. One excellent dish is the chop chae, a traditional Korean dish of beef, vegetables, and rice noodles. There are also more exotic dishes, like the yook hwae (raw beef). The restaurant also offers Korean lunch specials. Mirror of Korea is open for lunch and dinner daily, except on Tuesday when the restaurant is closed.

SHILLA KOREAN RESTAURANT $–$$
694 Snelling Ave. North, St. Paul
(651) 645-0006

Shilla Korean Restaurant is much larger than its neighbor, Mirror of Korea, just up the street, but both share many of the same menu items. The restaurant is a combination of '70s decor accented with Korean motifs and serves as the meeting place for many activities in the local Korean community. The menu is extensive. A few standout dishes are bi bim bop (vegetable salad with a boiled egg) and man do (pork and vegetable dumplings). Takeout is also available. Shilla is open Tuesday through Sunday for lunch and dinner and does not accept reservations.

SOLE CAFE $–$$
684 Snelling Ave. North, St. Paul
(651) 644-2068

In an area with two additional Korean restaurants within walking distance, this restaurant is certainly the most authentic and arguably the best. The Sole Cafe is a friendly mom-and-pop operation. Unlike those of its neighboring Korean restaurants, the menu is not extensive. It is, however, remarkably well executed. The menu includes traditional Korean favorites, such as bulgogi (the spicy Korean version of barbecue), kim chi soup, and chop chae (beef, vegetables, and noodles), as well as less familiar items for American diners. Soups and seafood are also prominent menu items. Sole Cafe is closed Wednesday but open Thursday through Tuesday for lunch and dinner.

South

HOBAN $
1989 Silver Bell Rd., Eagan
(651) 688-3447
http://hobanrestaurant.com
Hoban is a casual, small restaurant specializing in favorites such as *bi bim bop* (steamed vegetables over rice) and *kalbee* (thinly sliced marinated beef ribs that are grilled). The restaurant serves beer and wine and is open for lunch and dinner Tuesday through Sunday. The restaurant accepts Visa and MasterCard only.

Kurdish

BABANI'S KURDISH RESTAURANT $
544 St. Peter St., St. Paul
(651) 602-9964
www.babani.com
Babani's Kurdish is the first restaurant of its kind in the United States. The beautiful building on the outskirts of downtown St. Paul is decorated with Kurdish designs on rugs, pictures, and green curtains. The restaurant provides an excellent opportunity to learn about Kurdish culture and cuisine. The servers are attentive and eager to answer questions regarding Kurdish food, which includes heavy influences of Middle Eastern, Indian, and Mediterranean cuisine. Chicken *tawa*, a sautéed chicken in lemon with vegetables over rice, is an excellent choice. The *biryani* (rice with almonds, raisins, vegetables, and spices) is also excellent and quite similar to the Indian dish of the same name. Babani's serves lunch Monday through Friday and is open for dinner seven days a week.

Latin American

BRASA ROTISSERIE $$
600 East Hennepin Ave., Minneapolis
(612) 379-3030

777 Grand Ave., St. Paul
(651) 224-1302
www.brasa.us
Brasa's distinctive Caribbean-American menu, created by chef Tamara Murphy, puts it among the Twin Cities' top names in dining. The restaurant calls its fare "comfort food," but this isn't your mother's comfort food—even if your family is Caribbean. The pulled chicken, roasted pork, and (yep) grits are carefully sourced and lovingly prepared; both locations offer stylish in-house dining rooms as well as take-out options.

CONGA LATIN BISTRO $$–$$$
501 East Hennepin Ave., Minneapolis
(612) 331-3360
www.congabistro.com
You won't have any trouble spotting Conga: Its neon sign featuring an animated pair of hands beating on (natch) a conga drum is a northeast Minneapolis landmark. The owners of Conga, the Thunstrom family, are also responsible for the perennially popular south Minneapolis Latin restaurant El Meson. The nuevo Latino menu features a couple of paellas, the popular Spanish rice and seafood dish, as well as a wide selection of chicken, pork, beef, and seafood items. Other choices include the seafood casserole and Jamaican chicken. The beer and wine list is extensive, and there is ample opportunity for dancing. Conga is open for lunch Monday through Friday and for dinner daily.

> **i** Are you looking for a unique ethnic meal? Try Babani's Kurdish Restaurant in St. Paul. It is the first restaurant in the nation to serve Kurdish food.

MACHU PICCHU $$–$$$
2940 Lyndale Ave. South, Minneapolis
(612) 822-2125
www.machupicchurestaurante.com
Machu Picchu is a Peruvian restaurant that specializes in Latin seafood. Located in the heart of the Lyn-Lake neighborhood, an area overflowing with stores, theaters, and coffee shops, the restaurant attracts a hip crowd looking for an exotic dining experience. Machu Picchu is open for dinner Tuesday through Saturday.

Mexican

Minneapolis

BARRIO TEQUILA BAR $$
925 Nicollet Mall, Minneapolis
(612) 333-9953

235 East 6th St., St. Paul
(651) 222-3250
www.barriotequila.com

Barrio is indeed a tequila bar, and both locations offer some of the Twin Cities' most distinctive drink menus, featuring specialty tequilas and margaritas that will put you in orbit. Barrio isn't a one-trick pony, though: Its menu was created by top chef Tim McKee, and it puts a deliciously new spin on Mexican favorites like tacos (potato-chorizo, for example), sopes (goat cheese!), and steak (it comes with chile-lime-tequila butter). Guacamole? Of course—custom-made. Andale, for reals.

CHIAPAS RESTAURANT $
2416 Central Ave. NE, Minneapolis
(612) 789-2971

Chiapas Restaurant serves authentic Mexican food in northeast Minneapolis. Silverio Perez, who also owns the Pancho Villa restaurant on Eat Street, operates this 50-seat eatery. The restaurant specialties include chile relleno, enchiladas, and fajitas. Also featured are several vegetarian items. Chiapas is open daily for late breakfast, lunch, and dinner.

CHINO LATINO $$$
2916 Hennepin Ave. South, Minneapolis
(612) 824-7878
www.chinolatino.com

Chino Latino is a chic hangout with a menu influenced by the food of Asia and Latin barrios. The food is often delicious and sometimes, well, interesting, such as an item that caught the eyes of local animal lovers: guinea pig. Chino Latino is open for dinner (and stays open past midnight) daily.

LITTLE TIJUANA $
17 East 26th St., Minneapolis
(612) 872-0578

Open until 3 a.m. daily, "Little T's" is the bar-rush capital of the Eat Street environs. The tattooed servers brace themselves like linebackers for the happily drunk 2 a.m. crowd, who arrive to chow on enchiladas and draw obscene pictures on the butcher-paper tablecloths with the provided crayons. The restaurant doesn't serve alcohol, which is definitely a good thing. Are there any special reasons to go to Little T's *before* the show? Not really, though the fried ice cream's darn good at any hour.

ME GUSTA MEXICAN CUISINE $–$$
1507 East Lake St., Minneapolis
(612) 724-6007

For decades Me Gusta Mexican Cuisine has satisfied Twin Citians' needs for authentic Mexican cuisine. Today there are numerous authentic Mexican restaurants in the area, but not that long ago Me Gusta was an oasis in a sea of bland, tasteless pseudo-Mexican eateries. Like the rest of the menu, the chips are fresh and the salsa is spicy. Then satisfy your thirst with Mexican beer, wine, or Jarritos, a sweet Mexican soda. The menu includes several burrito, fajita, and enchilada dinners and, for more adventurous diners, *nopales asados* (grilled cactus), the chile relleno, or the enchiladas en mole. Me Gusta is open daily for lunch and dinner.

PANCHO VILLA RESTAURANT $
2539 Nicollet Ave., Minneapolis
(612) 871-7014
www.panchovillasgrill.com

In Minneapolis the words "Pancho Villa" are most often heard in combination with one or both of the words "margarita" and "birthday." Bring six friends to Pancho Villa on your birthday, and you can drink for free all night while wearing the birthday sombrero. On 200-plus other days of the year (that is, the weekdays), you can enjoy two-for-one margaritas all day long. The food is also tasty and surprisingly authentic, but as for the atmosphere, all that can be said is … two-for-one margaritas!

PEPITOS MEXI-GO DELI $
4820 Chicago Ave. South, Minneapolis
(612) 822-2104

4624 Nicollet Ave. South, Minneapolis
(612) 825-6311
www.pepitosrestaurant.com
These two Mexican restaurants carry an amazing selection of Mexican foods at reasonable prices, including vegetarian enchiladas and tacos, Azteca sandwiches served on teleta-style Mexican bread, huge nacho plates, and quesadillas made with homemade tortillas, all of which are excellent when topped with one of the six fresh-made salsas offered at the salad table. Pepitos is open daily for lunch and dinner.

St. Paul
CAPITOL VIEW CAFÉ $
637 Smith Ave. South, St. Paul
(651) 290-0218
www.capitalviewcafe.com
The Capitol View is not a "Mexican restaurant" per se, but it's run by Mexican-Americans and its diner fare has a novel south-of-the-border twist. Named for the view of the State Capitol that can be had by stepping out onto Smith Avenue and looking down its precipitous incline, this spacious and friendly restaurant is a neighborhood favorite. Top pick on a menu of generous length and generous portions: the Cajun Benedict, featuring andouille sausage.

EL BURRITO MERCADO—
EL CAFE RESTAURANT $
175 Cesar Chavez St., St. Paul
(651) 227-2192
www.elburritomercado.com
St. Paul's District del Sol neighborhood on the city's West Side is a historically diverse area and one of the first Latino settlements in the Twin Cities. In this enclave there is a large Mexican grocery, a bakery, and the cafeteria-style restaurant, El Cafe in El Burrito Mercado. Tucked in the back of the complex, El Cafe does astounding business by serving excellent Mexican food at reasonable prices. Get in line and make a selection from the menu, which features tortas, quesadillas, tamales, tacos, and burritos. After a shorter wait than at many fast-food restaurants, take a seat and enjoy a fine Mexican meal. El Cafe also serves breakfast, and don't forget to visit the bakery and grocery.

LA CUCARACHA $$
36 South Dale St., St. Paul
(651) 221-9682
www.lacucaracharestaurante.com
One of the first Mexican restaurants in St. Paul, and the only Mexican restaurant in its tony Summit Hill neighborhood, the family-run La Cucaracha is a beloved St. Paul institution—but also one that's beloved more as an institution than for its cuisine, which does not compare favorably to that at many of its newer competitors. Still, a stop at La Cucaracha at some point is a St. Paul must.

Middle Eastern
Minneapolis
CASPIAN BISTRO & MARKETPLACE $$
2418 University Ave. SE, Minneapolis
(612) 623-1113
Since 1986 the Caspian Bistro has served the nearby University of Minnesota with scrumptious Persian foods including kebabs, including beef, chicken, and lamb versions accompanied by basmati rice and salad. The menu also includes Middle Eastern treats such as gyros and lamb shank. The small adjoining market offers Middle Eastern delicacies and staples. The restaurant is open for lunch and dinner Tuesday through Saturday. The restaurant accepts Visa, MasterCard, and Discover.

FALAFEL KING $
701 West Lake St., Minneapolis
(612) 824-7887

121 South Eighth St. (TCF Tower), Minneapolis
(612) 339-5560

8405 Lyndale Ave. South, Minneapolis
(952) 888-3008
www.falafelking.com
Falafel King provides Middle Eastern foods in a casual atmosphere. From the counter, diners

may select from numerous appetizers, salads, sandwiches, combinations, and dinner entrées. Middle Eastern favorites such as kebabs, hummus, and falafel are served. The restaurant also serves omelets, and Greek and Middle Eastern–style breakfasts. Falafel King is open daily and offers lunch and dinner buffets. The downtown Minneapolis location is takeout or delivery only.

HOLY LAND BAKERY, GROCERY & DELI $
2513 Central Ave. NE, Minneapolis
(612) 781-2627

Holy Land Midtown
920 East Lake St. (Global Market), Minneapolis
(612) 870-6104
www.holylandbrand.com

Holy Land is not only one of the best specialty markets in the area, it also serves enormous portions of outstanding Middle Eastern cuisine on disposable plates. The choices include kebabs, falafel, hummus, spinach pie, shawarma (gyro), and much more. The menu offers large pita sandwiches and much larger dinners, which generally include a salad and rice or hummus paired with one of several meats (*shawarma,* kebabs, combinations, etc.) and a basket of fresh pita. Select a self-service drink, and there will be plenty of leftovers for less than $10. On request the deli offers halal meals to meet the dietary needs of Muslims. Holy Land does not serve alcohol. Both Holy Land locations are open daily for lunch and dinner.

JERUSALEM'S $–$$
1518 Nicollet Ave. South, Minneapolis
(612) 871-8883

Jerusalem's, a perennial feature on local best-of restaurant lists, dishes up the flavors and ambience of the Middle East in a surprisingly intimate atmosphere. The restaurant is topped by a mosquelike onion dome, and stepping inside the otherwise unassuming building on Nicollet Avenue will transport you to another world filled with exotic spices, sights, and sounds. Jerusalem's serves a pan–Middle Eastern menu. Lovers of hummus, *kibbe* (bulgur, beef, onion, and pine nuts), and stuffed grape leaves will find

plenty of satisfying choices. Desserts are simple but tasty, including baklava and krima. Do not leave the table without a demitasse of Turkish coffee; the restaurant serves a just-sweet-enough version with a floating cardamom seed that is perhaps the best this side of Ankara. If your schedule allows, come to Jerusalem's on a Friday or Saturday night, when belly dancers wiggle on stage and through the dining room, although be sure to call ahead for reservations; the small restaurant is often packed on those nights. The sword dance, in particular, is a crowd pleaser. Jerusalem's is open daily for lunch and dinner.

TRIESTE CAFE $
10 South Fifth St., Minneapolis
(612) 333-4658

Trieste Cafe is an international eatery with flair. The menu includes hot hoagies, subs, gyros, hummus, falafels, spanakopita, salads, and more. The Trieste Cafe occupies a small, cramped space on the ground floor of the historic Lumber Exchange building and is open from breakfast until 6 p.m. on weekdays.

North
EL BUSTAN $–$$
4757 Central Ave. NE, Columbia Heights
(763) 502-8888

This Columbia Heights restaurant features halal foods (in accordance with Islamic dietary laws), no alcohol, and hookah, a traditional water pipe. The menu is an extensive survey of Middle Eastern standards and includes delicious hummus, kebabs, and shrimp *sayyadiya*. The latter dish is a spicy combination of shrimp in tomato sauce served over a bed of rice. El Bustan is open daily.

Moroccan
BARBARY FIG
720 Grand Ave., St. Paul
(651) 290-2085

Like many businesses on St. Paul's buzzing Grand Avenue, Barbary Fig operates out of a house. But chef Brahim Hadj-Moussa is doing wonderful things with the foods of north Africa in his cozy restaurant. The menu includes Morrocan-, Tunisian-, and Mediterranean-influenced specialties with savory ingredients such as figs, couscous, phyllo dough, cinnamon, pears, and apricots. Barbary Fig's *tangine* (a Moroccan stew) is a menu standout. Desserts here are also fantastic. The restaurant is open for lunch Monday and Wednesday through Saturday, and for dinner Wednesday through Monday.

Nepali and Tibetan

EVEREST ON GRAND
1278 Grand Ave., St. Paul
(651) 696-1666
www.everestongrand.com
Everest on Grand serves Nepali and Tibetan dishes in a cozy space on Grand Avenue. The restaurant specializes in Tibetan *momos,* tasty steamed dumplings mixed with vegetables, pork and turkey, or yak. Nepali specialties include a variety of vegetarian and meat or fish (chicken, goat, lamb, cod, or shrimp) curries and *daal-bhatt,* traditional Nepali combination meals. During the week the restaurant features a lunch buffet, allowing patrons to sample many of the kitchen's Himalayan dishes at a set price. Both locations are open daily for lunch and dinner.

Pan-Asian

AZIA $$-$$$
2550 Nicollet Ave., Minneapolis
(612) 813-1200
www.aziarestaurant.com
Vietnamese immigrant Thom Pham is one of the Twin Cities' most visible restaurateurs, and Azia is his (quite successful) experiment in creating a restaurant that's both a social hub and a culinary adventure. The cuisine is an eclectic mix of elements from across Southeast Asia, with distinctly Minnesotan elements (for example, walleye) thrown in wherever he sees fit. The restaurant's prime Eat Street location and stylish vibe guarantee a lot of traffic, and Pham fans the flames with DJs seven nights a week. While some are more grudging in their support than others, just about everyone agrees that Azia serves its purpose with flair.

> **i** In 2008 Azia's flamboyant proprietor, Thom Pham, tried a now-infamous experiment in "naked sushi"—sushi served on a model's prone, nude body—at his restaurant Temple. The stunt made headlines but couldn't save Temple, which Pham closed soon thereafter.

GINGER HOP $-$$
201 East Hennepin Ave., Minneapolis
(612) 746-0305
www.gingerhop.com
The new restaurant Ginger Hop is all atmosphere, say some locals, but it's a hell of an atmosphere: Held over from Times Café, the previous restaurant in its near-Northeast space, Ginger Hop's ambiguously regal charm lies somewhere between *Casablanca* and *Julius Caesar.* The Pan-Asian menu is nothing special, but it will satisfy your craving for curry while you sip your IPA. Watch for downstairs cocktail bar Honey, an up-and-coming night spot.

20.21 $$$$
Walker Art Center
1750 Hennepin Ave., Minneapolis
(612) 253-3410
www.wolfgangpuck.com
Founded in 2005, this Wolfgang Puck establishment serves spectacularly good Pan-Asian cuisine with a panoramic view of Loring Park, the Basilica of St. Mary, and downtown Minneapolis from its second-floor perch in the new wing of the Walker Art Center. (The name of the restaurant is taken from the Walker's emphasis on 20th- and 21st-century art.) The menu features local ingredients in season and has influences from many Asian cultures, including Chinese, Indian, Japanese, Thai, and Korean. Such dishes as miso-sake glazed black cod and grilled Mongolian lamb chops will make you feel wonderful inside, perhaps even good enough to stomach the hefty check your waitperson will bring. Desserts are also memorable here, especially when complemented with one of 20.21's many ports, single-malt scotches, cognacs, or martinis. The restaurant is open Tuesday through Saturday for lunch and dinner, and Sunday for brunch and dinner.

Puerto Rican

CAFE LURCAT
1624 Harmon Place, Minneapolis
(612) 486-5500
www.cafelurcat.com

Cafe Lurcat, just north of Loring Park in the fabulous space once occupied by the legendary Loring Cafe, features what the restaurant describes as regional New American cuisine. What that means in practice is fresh ingredients in dishes including such things as sea bass, pot roast, lamb shank, and oysters on the half shell. Vegetables and side dishes, including roasted cauliflower, butternut squash, and potato puree, are ordered separately. The desserts are heavenly. Cafe Lurcat is open daily for dinner.

CRAFTSMAN $$$
4300 East Lake St., Minneapolis
(612) 722-0175
www.craftsmanrestaraunt.com

Serving what Craftsman calls "regionally inspired New American cuisine," this restaurant near the Mississippi River on East Lake Street is a great choice for a semi-casual tour of the tastiest things the Midwest has to offer. The restaurant uses organic produce, meat, and fish, the majority of which is produced locally by independent farmers. Recent notable entrées include pan-roasted rainbow trout wrapped with pancetta and served with kohlrabi puree and sautéed chard, grilled grass-fed beef steak with fries and béarnaise sauce, and potato gnocchi with green and yellow beans and crème fraiche. Craftsman also serves pizzas and burgers with Midwestern flair (one recent pizza included green bean pesto) and lovely desserts, including a crème brûlée of the day. Wash it down with one of the wines on the somewhat short wine list, a beer from the much longer beer list, or a Minnesota Pickle Martini, the latter made with pickle juice, Minnesota-made vodka, olive juice, and mini-pickles.

RESTAURANT ALMA $$$–$$$$
528 University Ave. SE, Minneapolis
(612) 379-4909
www.restaurantalma.com

Chef Alex Roberts, a veteran of such restaurant kitchens as New York City's Bouley and Union Square Cafe, serves up incredible New American–style dishes emphasizing seasonal, local ingredients. The menu changes often but may feature such delights as salmon tartare, beef-ricotta ravioli, and braised lamb with spicy lamb sausage. Don't leave without having dessert; whatever you choose, you won't be disappointed. Reservations are highly recommended, especially on weekends. Restaurant Alma is open for dinner daily.

SPOONRIVER $$–$$$
750 South Second St., Minneapolis
(612) 436-2236
www.spoonriver.com

The new Guthrie Theater and the Mill City Museum have unleashed a renaissance in the downtown riverfront areas of Minneapolis. Opening right across the street from the Guthrie, Spoonriver is an upscale second establishment for Minneapolis restaurateur Brenda Langton, who also owns Cafe Brenda. As at Cafe Brenda, Spoonriver features local, organic ingredients including grass-fed beef, wild mushrooms, and Lake Superior herring. (Unlike Cafe Brenda, Spoonriver serves free-range animal dishes.) The narrow restaurant with orange and green color scheme positively exudes culinary wholesomeness: If a Jamba Juice somehow morphed into a fine restaurant, it might look like this. Open for lunch Tuesday through Friday from 11:30 a.m. to 2 p.m.; brunch Saturday from 8 a.m. (or 10 a.m. in winter) to 2 p.m. and Sunday from 10 a.m. to 2 p.m.; and dinner Tuesday through Thursday from 5:30 to 10 p.m., Friday and Saturday from 5:30 to 11 p.m., and Sunday from 5 to 10 p.m.

St. Paul

HEARTLAND: A CONTEMPORARY
MIDWESTERN RESTAURANT $$$–$$$$
1806 St. Clair Ave., St. Paul
(651) 699-3536
www.heartlandrestaurant.com

Hidden behind a plain storefront in the heart of St. Paul's residential Mac-Groveland neighborhood, Heartland is a special place, serving dishes with ingredients from the Midwest and south-central Canada. Whenever possible, the chefs purchase organic or naturally raised foods from small family farmers. The menu changes nightly and includes two fixed-price full meals, as well as many a la carte items. Examples of dishes the restaurant has served include a sherried-rabbit consommé with pork-rabbit meatballs and locally picked wild king bolete mushrooms; wild-leek-crusted lake cisco with cherry-tomato relish, baby Pontiac onions, and Wisconsin crayfish cream; and a Yorkshire pork chop with braised Michihili cabbage, spiced watermelon reduction, and roasted local apples. The extensive wine list allows diners to choose the perfect complement to their meal. The Arts and Crafts–style dining room and food preparation area on the dining room floor, as well as the Heartland's elegant wine bar, all add up to one of the nicest dining experiences in the Twin Cities.

Seafood

Minneapolis

ANCHOR FISH & CHIPS $
302 13th Ave. NE, Minneapolis
(612) 676-1300
www.theanchorfishandchips.com
The Anchor dropped in northeast Minneapolis in 2009, to over-the-top ecstatic reviews. It remains to be seen whether the crowds are there to stay or they'll fade with the buzz, but for now expect to wait for a table—and to be well fed once you score one. The Anchor serves true British-style fish and chips, with a solid selection of beers to enjoy before and after your deliciously greasy meal.

COSMOS $$$–$$$$
610 First Ave. North (Graves 601 Hotel),
Minneapolis
(612) 312-1168
www.cosmosrestaurant.com
Cosmos can be loosely categorized as a seafood restaurant, but the modernistic restaurant with attentive service and a AAA Four Diamond rating goes well beyond such simplistic branding. The restaurant, which is in the middle of the Henne-

pin Theater District in the Graves 601 Hotel, features a multiple-course tasting menu, available paired with wine or alone, that changes weekly. Recent dinner entrées include wild rice–crusted ahi tuna with rock shrimp, lemon sunchoke puree, and root vegetable remoulade; vanilla butter poached lobster with sweet onion risotto and red curry reduction; and a grilled Colorado lamb chop with cabbage-wrapped lamb confit, rosemary demi, and Verjus grape compote. For dessert, you're unlikely to go wrong with the heavenly chocolate fig tart. The restaurant, in a hotel, is open daily for breakfast, lunch, and dinner. Cosmos is also open on holidays with special menus. Eating at one of the earlier meals can save some money while still giving you access to Cosmos's first-class dishes.

OCEANAIRE SEAFOOD ROOM $$$$
1300 Nicollet Mall (Hyatt Regency
Hotel), Minneapolis
(612) 333-2277
www.theoceanaire.com
The fish here is all fresh, flown in daily from both coasts, and, depending on the catch of the day, the restaurant serves meals like black bass in black butter; a zesty cioppino boasting an immense catch of mussels, clams, shrimp, and fish; yellowfin tuna with wild mushrooms and rich red-wine sauce; Chilean sea bass; and a fantastic oyster bar. The menu changes daily, according to what's available, and the fish fresh on any given day are identified at the top of the menu. The Oceanaire is open for dinner daily.

SEA CHANGE $$–$$$
818 South Second St., Minneapolis
(612) 225-6499
www.seachangempls.com
When Cue, the Guthrie Theater's initial attempt at hosting a destination restaurant in its riverfront home, fumbled, the Guthrie called on understudy Tim McKee to work his magic. McKee's vision: a seafood restaurant that emphasizes creative cuisine and sustainable practices. You can't taste the sustainability, but the food is smashing: The scallops and shrimp at Sea Change have more

flavor in every bite than the average restaurant offering has in an entire meal. During the summer outdoor seating offers a fantastic view of the Stone Arch Bridge and St. Anthony Falls.

SEAFOOD PALACE
CHINESE RESTAURANT $–$$
2523 Nicollet Ave. South, Minneapolis
(612) 874-7721
www.seafoodpalacemn.com
The Seafood Palace Chinese's menu begins with extremely reasonable lunch specials, then moves on to the dinner specialties, which include shrimp, scallops, mussels, lobster, and crab as well as traditional Chinese favorites like fried crispy duck, sweet-and-sour pork, and vegetarian dishes such as bean curd with brown sauce and mushrooms with Chinese cabbage. The restaurant is open daily for lunch and dinner.

SEA SALT EATERY $–$$
4825 Minnehaha Ave., Minneapolis
(612) 721-8990
http://seasalteatery.wordpress.com
This casual restaurant, located in a park pavilion right next to Minnehaha Falls, serves up cheap and tasty seafood. Specialties include several types of fish tacos, po'boys, and oysters, the latter broiled, fried, raw, or served up as part of an Oil Pan, along with shrimp and libations. You order at the counter and the food is brought to your table, either inside the small restaurant or on the patio under the shade of the park's tree canopy. The Sea Salt Eatery can be packed on weekend evenings; get there early, eat lunch instead of dinner, eat during the week, or bring a thick book. Open daily.

STELLA'S FISH CAFÉ $$$
1402 West Lake St., Minneapolis
(612) 824-8862
www.stellasfishcafe.com
Stella's is right in the middle of the strike zone for Uptown partiers, but there usually aren't people peeing on the indoor stairs of the multistory restaurant—that only happens on New Year's. Stella's offers one of the Twin Cities' biggest sea-

food menus, emphasizing the luxurious end of the continuum with oysters and lobster galore. The restaurant is also notable for what its proprietors justifiably plug as "the city's most spectacular rooftop deck." It's no wonder frighteningly tanned cougars flock to that deck: Sipping one of Stella's stellar mint juleps on a summer evening while watching the sun set over Minneapolis is an experience that can make anyone feel young again.

THE TIN FISH $
3000 East Calhoun Pkwy., Minneapolis
(612) 823-5840
www.thetinfish.net
Tin Fish is a national chain, but you wouldn't know it from the friendly feel of this favorite spot on Lake Calhoun. Place your order at the counter, and take your food (and beer) over to a picnic table to watch the sailboats while you munch. The fish tacos are favorites, as are the ultracrunchy deep-fried chips with salsa.

St. Paul
MAC'S FISH & CHIPS $
1330 Larpenteur Ave. West, St. Paul
(651) 489-5299
www.macsfishandchips.com
Mac's is tiny, none too fancy, and takeout oriented, but for fish and chips that would make a Londoner proud, it is a must-visit restaurant in the Twin Cities. Mac's specializes in haddock fillets, and the lightly breaded, deep-fried fish pieces seem as light as clouds and taste otherworldly. You can get the best deal if you buy a basket, which includes haddock, shrimp, chicken strips, or a combination thereof, along with fries, coleslaw, bread, and a beverage. You can also buy the haddock fillets and shrimp by the piece, chicken strips in six-strip servings, half and full orders of fries, and plenty of slaw, allowing you to customize the size of your meal. Mac's harbors a few tables in its dining room, but it is best to call ahead and pick up your order, heading back to your hotel or home with a basket or two of fish and chips for a low-key, inexpensive, filling feast. Mac's is open daily for lunch and dinner.

Southwestern

Minneapolis

BAR ABILENE   **$–$$**
1300 Lagoon Ave., Minneapolis
(612) 825-2525
www.barabilene.com
The flavors of the Southwest are available in the Twin Cities at Bar Abilene. Located in the Uptown neighborhood of Minneapolis, the restaurant does brisk business among young professionals; on weekend nights its dance floor turns into a shameless meat market. For starters the menu features Texas tapas that include potato–pepper jack flautas, barbecue chicken quesadillas, and tortilla soup. Dinner is divided into burgers and southwestern specialties. The restaurant features entrées such as savory jalapeño skewered shrimp, and several types of tacos, ranging from peanut-pasilla glazed chicken to crab. Bar Abilene is open daily for dinner and on Saturday and Sunday for lunch.

Spanish

Minneapolis

EL MESON   **$–$$**
3450 Lyndale Ave. South, Minneapolis
(612) 822-8062
www.elmesonbistro.net
El Meson features Spanish and Caribbean cuisine in a relaxed, comfortable atmosphere. A few popular dishes include the arroz con mariscos (rice with seafood) and the paellas (a Spanish rice and seafood dish). In addition, the restaurant serves various chicken and pork dishes with savory rice and beans. For lunch the restaurant offers an ever-popular buffet of home-style Latin favorites. The restaurant has repeatedly received kudos for its delicious, nutritious cuisine. El Meson serves beer and wine. The restaurant is open Monday through Saturday for lunch and dinner, and Sunday for dinner only.

SOLERA   **$$–$$$**
900 Hennepin Ave., Minneapolis
(612) 338-0062
www.solera-restaurant.com

Chef Tim McKee's triumph with Solera is to create a dining destination with an atmosphere so rich you'd never think it was a place that puts the food first. A tower of stylish Spanish ambience on Hennepin, Solera has a surreal Dalí-esque buzz that begins before (and may end after) your sangria buzz. The menu is spicy and adventurous, with a tasty selection of tapas (small plates) to peruse: sobrasada, olives, croquetas, chorizo, and, of course, escargot. Solera is a top nightlife spot; it's host to one of the Cities' hottest New Year's Eve parties and hosts many private events for tasteful and well-heeled partiers.

Sri Lankan

SRI LANKA RESTAURANT   **$$–$$$**
3226 West Lake St., Minneapolis
(612) 926-0110
This lovely restaurant specializes in the bounty of tastes from Sri Lanka, where fresh fruits, vegetables, meats, and spices are combined to make exciting dishes. A warning to those who are inexperienced with Sri Lankan cuisine: Spice is very important. However, the cooks will spice the dishes to meet diners' tastes. Seafood and vegetarian items are prominent on the menu. The restaurant serves a brunch on Friday, Saturday, and Sunday. The brunch is one of the best in the area and features salads, meats, vegetables, and desserts. The range of flavors and combinations of tastes are astounding. Sri Lanka Restaurant is open daily for dinner; reservations are recommended.

Steakhouses

Minneapolis

FOGO DE CHÃO   **$$$–$$$$**
645 Hennepin Ave. (City Center)
Minneapolis
(612) 338-1344
www.fogodechao.com
Fogo de Chão is part of a much welcome trend of Brazilian churrascarias (steakhouses) that are popping up around the country. Here, "gauchos" complete with red kerchiefs, cowboy boots, and swords (for cutting the meat) roam the dining

room with multiple skewers of fire-roasted steak in several distinct cuts, as well as ribs, leg of lamb, chicken, and linguica (spicy pork sausages). And (burp) it's all-you-can-eat. The central location near Nicollet Mall, the Hennepin Theater District, and the Target Center is about as convenient as it gets; women in strappy heels and tiny dresses are so omnipresent at the restaurant that some locals refer to them as "Fogos" when they see them walking down Hennepin. Fogo de Chão is open Monday through Friday for lunch and dinner, and Saturday and Sunday for dinner only.

MANNY'S STEAKHOUSE $$$$
825 Marquette Ave., Minneapolis
(612) 339-9900
www.mannyssteakhouse.com
With the bad rap cholesterol gets these days, it's hard not to feel a little bit naughty eating here: a longtime Nicollet Mall institution, Manny's moved to the Foshay as part of the historic building's conversion to the W Hotel. This bustling, Manhattan-style steakhouse serves obscenely huge and gloriously tender steaks, lobster, salmon, and chops—and that's about it besides the great wine list and a couple of desserts. Be prepared to either share dinner with a companion or get a doggy bag to go, because there's almost no way for one person to eat a whole dinner entrée here.

MURRAY'S $$$-$$$$
26 South Sixth St., Minneapolis
(612) 339-0909
www.murraysrestaurant.com
The New York strip sirloin is a tradition for Twin Cities upscale dining. Either the porterhouse or the ribeye will also make you shimmy with exultation. Other menu items are offered, but the many regulars come in droves for the steaks and the charming and elegant dining room. Reservations are a necessity. Even then, diners must compete with the regulars for a good table. Murray's serves lunch Monday through Friday and dinner every day of the week.

PORTER & FRYE $$$-$$$$
1115 Second Ave. South, Minneapolis
(612) 353-3500
www.porterandfrye.com
Located at the base of the Ivy Tower, the swanky steakhouse Porter & Frye serves rich food to a (mostly) rich clientele. Chef Joan Ida takes no prisoners in selecting the finest cuts of beef and preparing them in an utterly succulent fashion. She's not afraid to throw you for a bit of a loop: pairing walleye with lobster risotto, giving you a side of mac & cheese with your veal chop. For an especially memorable experience (and $95 a head), you can reserve a spot at the Chef's Table, where you'll get a behind-the-scenes glimpse at the kitchen action and will be personally served a unique meal crafted by Ida and her staff.

St. Paul

MANCINI'S CHAR HOUSE $$-$$$
531 Seventh St. West, St. Paul
(651) 224-7345
www.mancinis.com
It's no coincidence that Mancini's calls itself a "char house" rather than a "steakhouse": You'll find no prissy grass-fed beef or sustainable ahi tuna at this St. Paul institution, where dinner is a banquet and red meat is *red meat*. Generations of St. Paul families have made their way to Mancini's for grown-ups' nights out, and happily it hasn't been significantly renovated for several presidential administrations. Order a steak with baked potato or a lobster with baked potato: You won't be disappointed, because really, what were you expecting? Before or after dinner, enjoy an *aperitif* in the mirrored lounge, a not-so-little piece of Vegas on West Seventh.

THE STRIP CLUB $$-$$$
378 Maria Ave., St. Paul
(651) 793-6247
www.domeats.com
Note the URL above, because the Strip Club is the least Googleable restaurant in Minnesota. You're not likely to stumble across it, either, unless you're a resident of its West Side neighborhood in St. Paul. Chef J. D. Fratzke founded the Strip

Club under the assumption that people would go a little out of the way to find it, and he's been proved very right: It's one of the top *what-you've-never-been-oh-wow-you've-got-to-go* restaurants in the Twin Cities. As the name indicates, meats are first and foremost at the Strip Club, with tasty and colorfully named (Thai Me Up; Tuscan Titellation; Whip Me, Beet Me) sauces to accompany your prime cut cooked just as you like it. (And as you like it isn't well-done…right? Right?!)

Thai

Minneapolis

AMAZING THAILAND $$
3024 Hennepin Ave., Minneapolis
(612) 822-5588
What's most amazing, noted restaurant critic Jeremy Iggers when this spot opened, is that Uptown Minneapolis can support so many Thai restaurants. But the neighborhood's demand for pad thai is insatiable, and among the local options, Amazing Thailand is a gem hidden in plain sight just off the intersection of Lake and Hennepin. The decor is rich—with a small, pleasant patio area in the summer—and the food is more than decent. When shopping leaves you peckish, put your feet up and hit the happy hour at Amazing Thailand.

CHIANG MAI THAI $$
3001 Hennepin Ave., Minneapolis
(612) 827-1607
www.chiangmaithai.com
Chiang Mai Thai is the Thai restaurant in Calhoun Square, the mall in the heart of Uptown. Accordingly, it has a built-in clientele, but it would likely attract crowds wherever it was: its food has won it the honor of Best Thai Restaurant in *City Pages'* annual awards for four years in a row. Besides the Pad See Yew and Pad Prig King, Chiang Mai Thai has a particularly deadly drink list.

THE KING AND I THAI $$
1346 Lasalle Ave., Minneapolis
(612) 332-6928
www.kingandithai.com

The King and I is tucked away in a basement off Loring Park, but don't be put off by the mysterious and seemingly sketchy location: It's one of the Twin Cities' best and most beloved Thai restaurants. It's a favorite date spot, and its late-night happy hour makes it a destination for midnight drinkers of all nationalities. Those who just can't get their Thai food spicy enough appreciate the King and I's famous "ring of fire": a trio of spice options served on the side so you can choose your own degree of pain.

ROAT OSHA $$
2650 Hennepin Ave., Minneapolis
(612) 377-4418
When the überugly building that was formerly home to Sawatdee was bulldozed in 2008, local gossip had it being replaced by everything from a yoga center to a mosque. When the dust cleared, it turned out to be…another Thai restaurant! Authenticity is not a priority at Roat Osha—its menu offers the same selection of pan-fried noodles and cream cheese wontons you'll find at most other Thai-merican restaurants in town, but what the hell, there's no other Thai restaurant for at least 50 feet in any direction, so Uptown has embraced Roat Osha as the sports bar of Thai restaurants. The best thing about Roat Osha is its spacious seating area, with various distinctive rooms and nooks in which to nosh.

TRUE THAI $$
2627 East Franklin Ave., Minneapolis
(612) 375-9942
www.truethairestaurant.com
A Seward outpost nowhere near Eat Street or Uptown, True Thai is the black sheep of Minneapolis Thai restaurants—and if you ask many discerning diners, the best of the lot. It's well worth seeking out True Thai for its authentic cuisine and decor, and at lunchtime the restaurant offers a tasty and affordable buffet that has more vegetarian options than you might expect.

TUM RUP THAI $$
1221 West Lake St., Minneapolis
(612) 824-1378
www.tumrupthai.com

Tum Rup Thai is the sleekest among the many Thai restaurants in Uptown Minneapolis, a perfect spot for a first date followed by bowling across the street at the BLB. There's not a thing on the menu that disappoints, and while you're waiting to be seated (without a reservation, especially on weekend nights, you may well have to wait), you can hang out at the bar and watch Lake Street go by. A bit pricier than the average Thai joint, Tum Rup Thai is worth it.

St. Paul

PAD THAI GRAND CAFE $–$$
1681 Grand Ave., St. Paul
(651) 690-1393

The food at the Pad Thai Grand Cafe—a spacious but still oft-crowded restaurant at the western end of Grand Avenue—includes spring rolls with a tangy spicy fish sauce, pad thai, drunken noodles, and pra ram rong song (stir-fried meat with vegetables in a peanut sauce). The menu includes seafood and vegetarian options as well as a wine list. The service is friendly, and the chef will spice dishes according to patrons' desired heat level. Pad Thai is open Monday through Saturday for lunch and dinner and Sunday for dinner only.

TASTE OF THAILAND $
1671 Selby Ave., St. Paul
(651) 644-3997

1753 Old Hudson Rd., St. Paul
(651) 774-6905

527 South Seventh St., Minneapolis
(612) 333-0082

7890 University Ave. NE, Fridley
(763) 571-1188

7705 West 147th St., Apple Valley
(952) 431-4144

The original location of Taste of Thailand, on a very slowly gentrifying stretch of Selby Avenue west of Snelling Avenue in St. Paul, won't wow you with its intimate atmosphere or with its speedy service. But it makes up for lack of ambience with its extensive menu of wonderful Thai dishes. The restaurant has all the classics, including oh-so-light spring rolls, fiery miang kham, the house specialty tom yum soup, and the ever-popular pad thai. Other notable dishes include pad goong, pad med mamnang himaphane, and gaeng ped pla. If it's summertime, wash it all down with a glass of Thai lemonade. All Taste of Thailand locations are open daily for lunch (there's a lunch buffet Monday through Friday) and dinner.

North

ROYAL ORCHID $–$$
2401 Fairview Ave., Roseville
(651) 639-9999
www.thebestthaifood.com

Royal Orchid serves delicious Thai dishes in a pleasantly purple restaurant. Instead of cooking with cliché tastes and using shortcuts, the Royal Orchid marries complex spices, vegetables, and meats. Particularly notable are the masmon curry, pad thai, Moslem salad, pineapple fried rice, and tri-flavored fish. Also available are many dishes with beef, chicken, pork, tofu, scallops, and shrimp, which all can be prepared with eight different sauce choices, from garlic to saffron curry, satay, and mock ginger chili with green beans. Royal Orchid is open for lunch and dinner Monday through Saturday.

Turkish

BLACK SEA $–$$
737 Snelling Ave. North, St. Paul
(651) 917-8832

The first Turkish restaurant in Minnesota (opened in 2001) is arguably one of the best. The menu is filled with authentic Turkish delights such as döner (gyros), köfte (meatball kebabs), shish kebabs, and several vegetarian entrées, including falafels. The seasonal cold cucumber soup and the falafel salad are also worthy of your consideration, as is the yogurt drink—though if you're new to the establishment, the proprietors will make you try a sip before giving you a whole glass. And don't pass up the thick Turkish coffee, which is particularly tasty here. Turkish teas are also available. The restaurant does not serve alcohol. Black Sea is open for lunch and dinner Monday through Saturday.

Vegetarian and Vegan

BIRCHWOOD CAFE $
3311 East 25th St., Minneapolis
(612) 722-4474
www.birchwoodcafe.com
Although not completely vegetarian, Birchwood often wins accolades for their largely vegetarian menu. Formerly a dairy and grocery store, Birchwood has an old-fashioned stay-a-spell sense of welcome that makes it Seward's informal community center. You can set yourself down in the 1950s-era dining room or at one of the tables on the outdoor patio in summer. Birchwood serves sandwiches on fresh country bread, rustic pizzas, daily changing entrées such as enchiladas and curries, soups, and half a dozen salads. Known for its fresh organic ingredients and extensive vegetarian and vegan dishes, the Birchwood menu also includes nonvegetarian items. Service is semicafeteria style; you get your salads, desserts, and beverages (including wine and beer) at the counter, and hot or custom-made items are brought to your birchwood-topped table. The cafe is open for breakfast, lunch, and dinner Monday through Saturday, and for breakfast and lunch on Sunday. Birchwood accepts Visa and MasterCard only.

ECOPOLITAN $$–$$$
2409 Lyndale Ave. South, Minneapolis
(612) 874-7336
www.ecopolitan.com
Ecopolitan's menu is 100 percent organic, vegan, and raw, the only such restaurant in the Twin Cities. But it's not just the food that is good for you and the environment; Ecopolitan uses biodegradable cleaning products, generates solar/wind power on site, and used nontoxic materials to finish the restaurant and attached store. Vegans (and others) can enjoy collard greens burritos, pizzas, and several salads, among several other menu items. The restaurant and store also has (are you surprised?) an attached Oxygen Bar.

ST. MARTIN'S TABLE $
2001 Riverside Ave., Minneapolis
(612) 339-3920
www.communityofstmartin.org
This small vegetarian restaurant run by the Community of St. Martin will convert even the most agnostic palates with its menu (which changes daily) of fresh-baked breads, ingenious sandwiches, savory soups, and fair-trade coffee. The restaurant uses organic produce, non–bovine growth hormone milk, and purified water in its dishes and is committed to serving simple, nutritious food that sustains our natural resources and supports growers. St. Martin's waitstaff are all volunteers, and they donate their tips to local, national, and international charities. St. Martin's Table is open for lunch only Monday through Saturday. The restaurant does not serve alcohol. You dine well, and all for a higher purpose.

Vietnamese
Minneapolis
THE LOTUS RESTAURANT $
313 Oak St. SE, Minneapolis
(612) 331-1781

113 West Grant St., Minneapolis
(612) 870-1218

3037 Hennepin Ave. South, Minneapolis
(612) 825-2263
Each Lotus location has its own unique character. The menus include favorites such as Vietnamese beef salad, curried chicken Vietnamese-style, spring rolls, and egg rolls. Lunch specials are also offered; the mustard chicken is particularly good and includes chicken and onions in a spicy mustard sauce. The Lotus Restaurant is closed Monday but provides a casual environment for lunch and dinner the rest of the week.

LUCKY DRAGON
RIVERSIDE RESTAURANT $–$$
1827 Riverside Ave., Minneapolis
(612) 375-1690
Lucky Dragon's menu includes soups, combination meals, noodles, stir-fried entrées, and

numerous Vietnamese and Chinese specialties. Vegetarian items are available, and the entire menu contains no MSG. There is a large lunch and dinner buffet Monday through Friday. The egg rolls, hot-and-spicy chicken, and beef in black bean sauce are exceptional and usually available with the buffet. Lucky Dragon is open daily for lunch and dinner.

PHO 79 $
2529 Nicollet Ave., Minneapolis
(612) 871-4602
www.pho79mpls.com
At the heart of Eat Street, Pho 79 may be the best-known of that strip's many pho houses. The decor is, to put it generously, unpretentious, but the soup is, to put it mildly, delicious. Served with heaps of bean sprouts and other fixings, this is pho to remember (and, at several bucks a bowl, to afford). Try the duck pho, but be prepared: You'll get what seems like about half a duck floating in your bowl of broth, with delicious meat hanging off its bones. You'll have a little prep work to do, but it's worth it.

QUANG RESTAURANT $–$$
2719 Nicollet Ave. South, Minneapolis
(612) 870-4739
The hip Quang Restaurant serves fine renditions of Vietnamese favorites. Popular items include caramelized lemongrass chicken, grilled pork chops, and the seafood noodle soups. In addition to fine versions of egg rolls and spring rolls, the menu features such dishes as grilled sugarcane shrimp (*banh hoi choi*). The restaurant does not serve alcohol. Quang Restaurant is closed Tuesday and open for lunch and dinner the rest of the week.

St. Paul
SAIGON RESTAURANT & BAKERY $
601 University Ave. West, St. Paul
(651) 225-8751
Saigon Restaurant is the best and most affordable authentic Vietnamese restaurant in the Twin Cities. The specialties are *pho* and *banh mi*. Pho, the national dish of Vietnam, is a huge bowl of soup. It includes vegetables, noodles, and a choice of meats from roast pork to several delicious seafood combinations. Banh mi is a savory Vietnamese sandwich composed of pâté, cilantro, cucumber, Vietnamese mayo, and any of a number of meats combined on a fresh baguette. There is a deli counter where banh mi and baked goods are available for takeout, all at incredibly low prices. The restaurant and bakery are open Tuesday through Sunday for lunch and dinner.

VINA HIGHLAND $
756 Cleveland Ave. South, St. Paul
(651) 698-8408

VINA VIETNAMESE RESTAURANT
6401 Nicollet Ave., Richfield
(612) 866-5034

VINA PLUS
1821 University Ave., St. Paul
(612) 644-1384
http://vinaplusrestaurant.tripod.com
The casual Vina serves delicious, inexpensive dishes. The menu is filled with Vietnamese favorites such as curry shrimp, egg roll salad, and hot-and-spicy chicken. The hot-and-spicy chicken is an excellent rendition of the Vietnamese favorite and is composed of chicken with onions, lemongrass, and red peppers. All items are spiced to order and contain no MSG. For lunch, Vina features more inexpensive combination meals, where Chinese menu items are an important part. Vina is open seven days a week for lunch and dinner. Vina accepts Visa and MasterCard.

South
KIMSON VIETNAMESE CUISINE $
8654 Lyndale Ave. South
Bloomington
(952) 885-0230
With more than 200 items, Kimson's menu provides plenty of pork, chicken, beef, tofu, seafood, and vegetarian selections. The restaurant offers many Vietnamese favorites, including hot-and-spicy chicken, sautéed beef over fried potatoes, curry chicken, and egg rolls. The menu includes

many vegetarian dishes. There are nearly a dozen tofu entrées, which range from chow mein and sweet and sour to ginger bean curd. Kimson is open daily for lunch and dinner.

KINHDO RESTAURANT $
2755 Hennepin Ave. South, Minneapolis
(612) 870-1295

2709 Winnetka Ave. North, New Hope
(763) 544-8440
Kinhdo Restaurant has two unique Twin Cities locations, but both serve excellent renditions of Vietnamese cuisine as well as a few favorite Chinese dishes. The menu features exceptional values on Vietnamese favorites. The menu also features such Chinese items as chow mein, egg foo young, and a great version of sweet-and-sour chicken. Egg rolls, though, are the signature items—other restaurants have all but given up trying to compete with Kinhdo's delicious deep-fried cylinders for egg roll honors on local best-of lists. Both Kinhdo restaurants are open daily for lunch and dinner.

Sweets and Treats
Minneapolis
A BAKER'S WIFE PASTRY SHOP $
4200 28th Ave., Minneapolis
(612) 729-6898
Many a Minneapolitan is addicted to the sweet eats to be had at A Baker's Wife: danishes, croissants, turnovers, tea cakes, cheesecake, caramel rolls, brownies, blondies, and doughnuts for the win. "Do you serve anything low-fat?" reads a sign in the store, a sign that also provides its own answer: "Yeah, water!"

CUPCAKE $
3338 University Ave. SE, Minneapolis
(612) 378-4818
www.cupcake.com
Cupcake's specialty is—you get three guesses, and two don't count. The cupcakes at Cupcake come in four price tiers: simple (Betty Crocker, I Love Lucy), gourmet (Mad Cow, Cup o Mud), premium (Global Warming, Tres Leche), and alcoholic party

cakes (Chocolate Covered Cherry, Pina Colada with cocktail flag). When you just want a bite, there's the baby line (Baby Hilton, Baby Betty).

DAIRY QUEEN $
7700 Normandale Blvd., Minneapolis
(952) 830-0330
Dozens of additional locations across the Twin Cities
www.dairyqueen.com
Minneapolis is Dairy Queen's hometown: The world headquarters of the international chain are located here. Unsurprisingly, there are many DQ restaurants in the Twin Cities, including both year-round indoor establishments and small window-service venues that are closed during the winter months. Any DQ will hook you up with a superthick Blizzard or a soft-serve cone, but if you want to be on the cutting edge, visit this south Minneapolis location, which is located just a block from the corporate headquarters and often serves as a proving ground for new concepts in frozen treats and savory snacks.

FRANCE 44 WINES & SPIRITS $
4351 France Ave. South, Minneapolis
(612) 925-3252
www.france44.com
Wines and spirits are in the shop's name—and indeed there are alcoholic treats galore within its walls—but France 44 belongs in this section for its superfine selection of gourmet cheeses. Brie, Swiss, Roquefort, Gouda…and beer, too! Pretty much anything savory that you'd regard as a "treat" you'll find in either the wine shop or the cheese shop at France 44. Sister establishment the St. Paul Cheese Shop opened in 2009 at the corner of Snelling and Grand; both shops do brisk lunchtime business with their deli sandwiches.

ISLES BUN & COFFEE COMPANY $
1424 West 28th St., Minneapolis
(612) 870-4466
This bakery and coffeehouse at the corner of West 28th Street and Hennepin Avenue South in the heart of Uptown does a brisk business. What people are coming for are the big, fresh

cinnamon rolls. You can see the bakers at work at this small establishment, so the rolls' freshness is never in doubt. The hefty monsters taste particularly good with an extra dollop of icing from the pot set out for just that purpose. (If you're on a budget, the day-old dollar buns are among the best deals in town.) There's limited seating inside and only a few sidewalk tables, so you'll probably want to get your bun to go. For the slightly less decadent-minded, the bakery offers other baked goods—including a vegan scone of the day, cakes, muffins, brownies, biscotti, and dog treats—as well as plenty of java.

MEL-O-GLAZE BAKERY AND DONUT SHOP $
4800 28th Ave., Minneapolis
(612) 729-9316
www.meloglaze.com
The Mel-o-Glaze Bakery smells so good, it adds to the property value of every house within a quarter-mile of its southeast Minneapolis location. First off, you're going to need to try a doughnut, then move on to the cake. Then have a cup of coffee for fortification, then cap it off with a cookie. You won't need to eat again for days, but when your appetite returns, you may find your car mysteriously making its way back to Minnehaha and 28th.

SALTY TART $
920 East Lake St., Minneapolis
(612) 874-9206
www.saltytart.com
Salty tart? Gross! Right? Wrong. Pastry chef Michelle Gayer has a national reputation for working magic on the palate, and she's been enlisted to create desserts for top local restaurants including La Belle Vie and Solera. Cordon Bleu? She didn't just *go* there, she *taught* there. So when she tries to sell you a goat cheese tart, you really ought to let her.

SEBASTIAN JOE'S $
1007 Franklin Avenue West, Minneapolis
(612) 870-0065

4321 Upton Ave. South, Minneapolis
(612) 926-7916
www.sebastianjoesicecream.com
When Italian immigrant Sebastiano Pellizer arrived in the Twin Cities in the 1930s, he was almost immediately rechristened Joe by his employer, a construction-crew chief. The moniker stuck, and in 1984 when his grandchildren Mike and Todd founded this ice-cream shop, Sebastiano gave them permission to use his name. The ice-cream list tops 80 flavors (15 daily) and includes both new spins and old favorites, such as basil strawberry, chocolate, fresh strawberry, vanilla made from ground vanilla beans, ginger cream, and cayenne pepper–laced Chocolate Coyote.

St. Paul
CAFE LATTE $
850 Grand Ave., St. Paul
(651) 224-5687
www.cafelatte.com
Cafe Latte is ground zero for pure decadence. The establishment is renowned for its decadent turtle cake—dark chocolate cake layers separated by and topped with buttery caramel and pecans—as well as the tart key lime pies, raspberry marzipan, and thick scones served with crème fraîche, jams, and fresh fruit. Also of particular note is the exceptionally moist tres leches cake, with three cake layers each soaked in a different type of milk and fresh raspberries circling the cake's top. Yum. A few desserts are available as individual servings, but the restaurant primarily makes full cakes for parties and events. Cafe Latte is open daily.

CANDYLAND $
435 Wabasha St. North, St. Paul
(651) 292-1191

811 Lasalle Court, Minneapolis
(612) 332-3220

Dayton Radisson Arcade, Minneapolis
(612) 332-7752
www.candylandstore.com
Did somebody say *popcorn?!* Candyland's gotcher popcorn, and you can get your fix in either of the Twin Cities' downtowns—as well as by mail, if you live out of town or don't want to tempt yourself

with the dazzling variety of candy-coated options. Candyland also stocks a range of specialty and vintage candies: brittle, bark, jawbreakers, jelly beans. Most candy stores are a pure sugar rush, but at Candyland salt and sugar run neck-and-neck. What will win? Everything but your waistline.

DAIRY SALES ROOM STORE $
Andrew Boss Meat Science Building
University of Minnesota
1354 Eckles Ave., St. Paul
(612) 624-7776

If your timing is right, you can find some of the best ice cream and cheeses in the Twin Cities in this little-known and rarely open outlet on the University of Minnesota's St. Paul Campus. Open only 3 to 5 p.m. Wednesday, the store sees customers line up early to get their hands on dairy products produced by university students and researchers. Don't worry, no failed experiments make it to the sales floor, and if you're willing to make the effort to find the store, you will be treated to rich (12 percent fat!) and creamy ice cream in a variety of flavors and a range of cheeses, the weekly selection depending on what is available from the university's work and the time of year. The store may (or may not) have on hand such favorites as Gopher Gold ice cream (French vanilla and raspberry), aged cheddar, and Nuworld, a spreadable variety of blue cheese that is all white. Quantities available for sale are always limited: Arrive early for the best selection.

GRAND OLE CREAMERY $
750 Grand Ave., St. Paul
(651) 293-1655
Two additional Twin Cities locations
www.grandolecreamery.com

The Grand Ole Creamery has been creating some of the area's most imaginative and delicious ice-cream flavors in its parlor since 1984. And the flavors, including Irish coffee eggnog and chocolate malt banana, aren't just interesting experiments in flavor, they're also very, very good. The store serves up to 32 flavors from a master list of more than 100, and customers can satisfy their chocolate, strawberry, or vanilla cravings or

try the black walnut, cinnamon, or sweet cream. At the bottom of each ice-cream cone is a malted milk ball carefully placed so that the ice cream doesn't leak out onto your shirt. The store also makes thick, rich malts and shakes, banana splits, and sundaes. During the dog days of summer, folks line up out the door to indulge in this stuff. Grand Ole Creamery is open daily.

IZZY'S ICE CREAM CAFE $
2034 Marshall Ave., St. Paul
(651) 603-1458
www.izzysicecream.com

Izzy's immediately became a local favorite when it opened in 2000, but it gained national fame in 2006 when Food Network host Bobby Flay, having been informed that the little St. Paul spot had the best ice cream in America, arrived unannounced to challenge founder Jeff Sommers to a televised ice-cream-making competition—which Sommers won handily. Izzy's serves an amazing variety of homemade ice cream, including blueberry cheesecake, green tea, Mexican chocolate fiesta, mango, ginger, hot brown sugar, Guinness, crème de menthe, pineapple, Oreo cookie, and coffee, the latter flecked with coffee grounds. Each dish or cone comes with the establishment's trademark "izzy"—a small scoop of any flavor you'd like added to the top. Izzy's also offers malts, shakes, floats, sundaes, and egg creams, and to ease your environmental conscience, about a third of the shop's power comes from solar panels on its roof. Izzy's is open daily.

i The south side of Marshall Avenue just east of Cleveland Avenue has become known as St. Paul's "Treat Street" for its string of small establishments serving tasty snacks: Izzy's Ice Cream, Legacy Chocolates, Sweets Bakeshop, My Living Room Café, and—just around the corner on Cleveland—Trotter's Café.

JUST TRUFFLES $
1326 Grand Ave., St. Paul
(651) 690-0075
www.justtruffles.com

Like its name says, this store carries nothing but truffles: thick, rich, gigantic homemade chocolate truffles kept in a refrigerated glass case until purchase. They are available in dozens of flavors, including Kahlua, raspberry, maple nut, amaretto, and pecan turtle. The edible chocolate boxes are a special and delicious way to send the truffles as a gift. Just Truffles is open Monday through Saturday.

REGINA'S CANDY SHOP $
2073 St. Clair Ave., St. Paul
(651) 698-8603

1905 South Robert St. (Southview Square)
West St. Paul
(651) 455-8864
www.reginascandies.com
Founded in 1926 by a young Greek craftsman and his bride, Regina (pronounced Ruh-GEE-nuh, with a hard G), and passed on to their children and grandchildren, Regina's uses old-world craftsmanship in making its amazing (and amazingly inexpensive) caramels, chocolates, toffees, and more than 20 flavors of dark chocolate truffles.

SWEETS BAKESHOP $
2042 Marshall Ave., St. Paul
(651) 340-7138
www.sweetsbakeshop.com
Just opened in 2009, Sweets is one of the newest establishments to appear on the "Treat Street" stretch of Marshall Avenue. Sweets is a unique collaboration between artist Ly Lo and pastry chef Krista Steinbach; possibly Minnesota's only pastry chef who's also a war veteran, Steinbach was deployed in Iraq with the National Guard. The shop offers baked goods that are beautiful to look at—but not so beautiful that you will have any qualms about popping them into your mouth. Try the cupcakes topped with big heaps of rich buttercream frosting.

TASTE OF SCANDINAVIA CATERING AND BAKERY $
2900 Rice St., Little Canada
(651) 482-8876

845 Village Center Dr., North Oaks
(651) 482-8285

401 West 98th St., Bloomington
(952) 358-7490
www.tasteofscandinavia.com
This charming European bakery has luscious desserts spinning inside a glass case—the Scandinavian strawberry torte layers yellow sponge cake with chocolate mousse, fresh banana slices, and raspberry preserves and is covered in strawberries and peaks of cream. Sweets from elegantly decorated layer cakes to muffins and cookies to Finnish cinnamon pulla can also be found. On late afternoons the bakery offers many half-price deals, so stop in late and indulge yourself. All four locations are open daily.

WUOLLET BAKERY $
2447 Hennepin Ave., Minneapolis
(612) 381-9400

1080 Grand Ave., St. Paul
(651) 292-9035
Four additional Twin Cities locations
www.wuollet.com
Wuollet is a family-run bakery, watched over by two brothers, their uncle, and a cousin. In the hands of Wuollet's cake artists, traditional white-on-white wedding cakes can ascend to seven tiers covered in white chocolate ropes, orchids, and other adornments, while soufflé cakes featuring genoise (egg-rich sponge cake) disappear under drifts of Bavarian cream. A sweets table covered in profiteroles, fancy French pastries, cheesecake, and trifle is a reception addition that uses Wuollet's skills to their tastiest advantage. The shop also sells delicious doughnuts and princess tortes layered in Bavarian cream and raspberry preserves. All six Wuollet bakeries are open Monday through Saturday.

Coffeehouses and Teashops

Minneapolis
ANODYNE $
4301 Nicollet Ave., Minneapolis
(612) 824-4300
www.anodynecoffeehouse.com

Anodyne seeks to meld modern design and progressive values with the cozy community feel of a neighborhood coffee shop, and it has a fierce following in its Kingsfield neighborhood. Beans? Roasted locally. Food? Sourced locally. Muffins? Baked in-house. Even its tea is blended in Minneapolis. Anodyne has a notably ambitious menu for a coffee shop, with artichoke melts and quiche among its daily offerings.

THE BEAT COFFEEHOUSE $
1414 West 28th St., Minneapolis
(612) 710-3992
www.thebeatcoffee.com
The Beat is a unique hybrid of coffeehouse and music club; it books both local and national acts for evening gigs in its back room, formerly a comedy club that hosted the likes of Steve Martin and Jay Leno. It's no First Avenue, but its coffee is sure a lot better—it's roasted by local company Bull Run and brewed exclusively by French press. It's a great place to hear bands, and it's a particular favorite of up-and-coming bands whose members (and/or fans) aren't 21 yet. By day it's a spacious and friendly spot that manages to feel off the beaten track despite being located right in the heart of the Uptown action.

BLUE MOON COFFEE CAFE $
3822 East Lake St., Minneapolis
(612) 721-9230
www.drinkbluemoon.com
Everything about the Blue Moon breathes comfort and relaxation. The soothing purple and blue color scheme and sparkling strings of white and colored Christmas lights make the cafe the perfect place for a calming evening of quiet revitalization. There are many coffee drinks on the menu and a choice of eight kinds of coffee, 16 types of tea, homemade biscotti, pastries, sandwiches, and a big ice-cream cooler that carries Häagen-Dazs bars and other treats. Blue Moon is open daily.

BOB'S JAVA HUT $
2651 Lyndale Ave. South, Minneapolis
(612) 871-4485
www.bobs33.com

This funky little coffee shop stays open late in the summer months and closes earlier depending on how many customers linger in the winter. The shop's theme is vintage motorcycles, and at any given time you're likely to see a few choppers parked at the curb. The menu is predominantly coffee drinks and juice, with a few baked goods for the morning and lunch crowds. The house specialty is Kool-Aid. On warm days and nights, the large storefront window rolls back to let fresh air and conversation from the outside patio in. Bob's is open daily.

CAFFETTO $
708 West 22nd St., Minneapolis
(612) 872-0911
www.myspace.com/caffetto
Caffetto has a reputation as a hookup spot for singles, and it's no wonder: The close-packed, irregular seating pretty much forces you to get social. Once you do warm up, there are booths for cuddling—sometimes to the disgust of other patrons, they are indeed used for such—and a dark basement featuring a ping-pong table and a pinball machine starring an oversexed robot. (Seriously.) The coffee's good, too, if you care about that.

COMMON ROOTS $
2558 South Lyndale Ave., Minneapolis
(612) 871-2360
www.commonrootscafe.com
Common Roots faces off against the C.C. Club at the corner of 26th and Lyndale, playing the roles of angel and devil on Uptown denizens' shoulders. Common Roots is the angel, a brightly colored and sunlit spot serving wholesome food, mediocre but fair trade coffee, and even a few microbrews. Consistent with its forward-thinking philosophy, Common Roots offers its back room for nonprofits to hold meetings—and then after closing time, everyone heads over to the C.C. Club to pay the devil his due.

JAVA JACK'S $
818 West 46th St., Minneapolis
(612) 825-2183
www.javajacks.com

Java Jack's is geographically located midway between Uptown and Edina, and its atmosphere and clientele are representative of the lifestyle fence upon which it sits: There's a little bit of shopping-mall burnish and a little bit of indie funkiness, the latter especially to be found in the subterranean lounge. The baked goods are tasty, but the coffee is skippable.

LA SOCIÉTÉ DU THÉ $
2708 Lyndale Ave. South, Minneapolis
(612) 871-5148
www.la-societe-du-the.com
This well-stocked, comfortable teahouse offers more than 100 varieties of specialty and whole-leaf teas sold in three-ounce portions, ranging in price from $4.50 to more than $20. The helpful staff gives careful instructions about heating water, steeping time, and the story behind each particular type of tea, all of which are preserved in airtight canisters. You can also enjoy tea by the cup or the pot in the teahouse. La Société du Thé is open Monday through Saturday.

MUDDY WATERS $
2401 Lyndale Ave. South, Minneapolis
(612) 872-2232
"I didn't know that people in Boise were gonna ask me about the Muddy Waters coffee shop," rapper Slug said about his favorite south Minneapolis hangout when his local act Atmosphere became nationally famous. This long-established coffeehouse, furnished like a college student's first apartment, caters specifically to the quirky hipster crowd, with menu items like Pop-Tarts and Spaghetti O's. Saturday-morning cartoons are often featured on the TV screens. Muddy Waters is open daily.

SPYHOUSE COFFEE SHOP $
2451 Nicollet Ave., Minneapolis
(612) 871-3177

2404 Hennepin Ave., Minneapolis
(612) 377-2278
What the Beat Coffeehouse is to rock clubs, the original Spyhouse on Nicollet is to art galleries.

Located just a block from the Minneapolis College of Art and Design, the Spyhouse displays top-notch original art alongside its staple decorative elements, which are stylishly retro and a little kitschy. That Spyhouse also serves as a living room for many Minneapolis creative types, who hang out there to work, socialize, and get the scoop on what's new. (If a flyer for an art show or theater event is dropped anywhere in the Twin Cities, it's dropped at the Spyhouse.) The "new" Spyhouse over on Hennepin serves the same powerful drinks—try the Spychaser, a cocoa-laced depth charge that's the coffee equivalent of a Long Island Iced Tea—but has a decidedly less laid-back atmosphere.

URBAN BEAN $
3255 Bryant Ave. South, Minneapolis
(612) 824-6611
The Urban Bean doesn't display art on its walls—the shop itself is a work of art. Designed in a modern, minimalist style but saturated with red and aquamarine rather than boring white, the Urban Bean is an independent coffee shop with a design theme that's more coherent and better developed than you'll find at any chain shop—there's even a branded merchandise line featuring iterations of the shop's raccoon-face logo. The social atmosphere is largely work-oriented: Voices ricochet right off the bare walls, so a non-whispered conversation at one end of the shop can earn you a dirty look from someone sitting clear across the room. When you stop looking at your cup and actually drink the coffee, you'll find yourself pleased with that, too.

WILDE ROAST CAFE $
518 East Hennepin Ave., Minneapolis
(612) 331-4544
www.wilderoastcafe.com
Precisely as its name suggests, Wilde Roast is a magnet for Minneapolitans who are droll, literate, gay, and decadent. If any of those words describe you—and especially if more than one of them do—you'll want to invite yourself to Wilde Roast. Besides coffee, the extremely comfortable spot has a fine wine list and a food menu that is with-

out peer among local establishments that could conceivably be called coffee shops. Specialty pizzas, mixed-green salads, strata and frittata, desserts made from scratch: It's food to die for, but if you truly want to follow Oscar's example, you'll wait to expire until you've delivered some highly quotable last words.

St. Paul

BEAN FACTORY $
1518 Randolph Ave., St. Paul
(651) 699-7788
www.jsbeanfactory.com

The Bean Factory clientele are so social, it's almost awkward—no, actually, it *is* awkward. Sit down anywhere at the Bean Factory and you could well find yourself party to a conversation about your neighbor's divorce, international politics, or an ingrown toenail. As the name suggests, the Bean Factory roasts its own; while the relatively low volume of sales means that your beans won't be as fresh as they are at the nearby Dunn Bros., the Bean Factory lets you try before you buy. You can ask the barista to custom-drip a cup of any of the Bean Factory's offerings—including, for a little more, the expensive Blue Mountain and Kona varieties—for you right there on the spot. The Bean Factory is also notable for its extra-spicy Mexican mocha, made with chile powder.

DUNN BROS. COFFEE $
1569 Grand Ave., St. Paul
(651) 698-0618
Over 40 locations across the Twin Cities
www.dunnbrosgrand.com
www.dunnbros.com

Dunn Bros., founded at this Grand Avenue storefront in 1987, has grown into the largest Minnesota-owned coffee chain. (Caribou was founded in Minnesota but was later sold to out-of-state investors.) As with many other Dunn Bros. locations, all the coffee is roasted on the spot, just a few feet from where it's brewed and served. Because the shop does such brisk business (it's one of the few coffee shops in the Twin Cities where you can't count on finding an open table), you're probably drinking coffee made from beans

roasted just a day or two ago. The espresso, and roasted beans for purchase, may well be the Cities' best. There's also regular live music at this location, which is open daily.

GINKGO COFFEEHOUSE $
721 Snelling Ave. North, St. Paul
(651) 645-2647
www.ginkgocoffee.com

By day, Ginkgo is a friendly java joint with mismatched furniture, potted plants, and a few outdoor tables in summer. A couple of nights a week, however, the atmosphere changes, and this coffeehouse on the edge of St. Paul's Hamline University campus becomes a dimly lit, cozy, acoustic music venue. Ginkgo is open daily.

KOPPLIN'S COFFEE $
490 South Hamline Ave., St. Paul
(651) 698-0457
www.kopplinscoffee.com

Though you wouldn't suspect the fact based on its address—its neighbors are stolid establishments like the Copper Dome diner, the Nook bar, and Ran-Ham Lanes—Kopplin's is Minnesota's mecca for coffee geeks. Andrew Kopplin, its young proprietor, is the metro area's sole owner of a Clover, a machine whose brewing abilities are legend in the specialty coffee field. Kopplin's prices are noticeably higher than at most local coffee shops, but there's only one place in Minnesota that's on *Bon Appétit*'s list of America's top ten boutique coffee shops, and this is it.

LORI'S COFFEE HOUSE $
1441 Cleveland Ave. North, St. Paul
(651) 647-9007

Lori's is a nice little corner coffeehouse across the street from the St. Paul campus of the University of Minnesota. Lori's makes wonderful homemade soups on site and throws a couple of huge slices of also-homemade bread in for free. There's coffee and espresso, cookies, muffins, a good selection of bottled juices to pick from, and fresh-squeezed orange juice. Lots of college kids hang out here, and there's definitely room for them—

the inside is spacious and airy, and summertime loungers opt to sit outside.

MADHATTER COFFEE CAFE $
943 Seventh St. West, St. Paul
(651) 227-2511

The Madhatter, it's said in St. Paul, is like Harry Potter's Platform 9 3/4: You can find it only if you've been there before. It's owned by Dave Thune, who represents its district in the St. Paul City Council. (A man of many talents, he also plays in a rock band.) It specializes in tea, coffee, and homemade baked goods. Its hours are limited and eccentric—Saturday mornings are your best bet—but when you get in, you'll find a gallery and framing shop as bonus attractions.

TEA GARDEN $
1692 Grand Ave., St. Paul
(651) 690-3495
Four additional locations across the Twin Cities
www.teagardeninc.com

The Tea Garden is the Twin Cities' premier purveyor of bubble tea, the Japanese favorite with tapioca pearls loaded into cups of hot or cold tea. Each of the Tea Garden's five locations is a magical land of sweet tea, upbeat indie rock, and remarkably happy-looking patrons. On weekend nights, when DJs take to the turntables, the Tea Gardens are favorite hangouts for local teens.

TEA SOURCE $
752 Cleveland Ave. South, St. Paul
(651) 690-9822

2908 Pentagon Dr. NE, St. Anthony
(612) 788-4842
www.teasource.com

Owner Bill Waddington personally selects the fine teas he sells to customers of all tastes. Although Tea Source sells loose teas in two- to four-ounce bags, you can also stop in either store and enjoy a cup or pot of your favorite tea. With dozens of options among black, green, oolong, tisanes (herbal teas), and blends, you can pick out a few ounces of your favorite or an adventurous alternative to take home. A detailed guide available in the store helps make sense of the inventory, and Tea Source offers similar information in its catalog and online. Tea Source is open daily.

TROTTER'S CAFÉ AND BAKERY $
232 North Cleveland Ave., St. Paul
(651) 645-8950

Part coffee shop, part bar, part restaurant, all wholesomeness. Trotter's baked goods—many of which are organic, vegan, or both—are the best reason to patronize the establishment, but it's also a favorite meeting place and hangout for its Merriam Park neighbors. Some patrons are taken aback by the venue's prices (those responsibly farmed ingredients don't come cheap) and DIY ethic, but it was ahead of its time for the up-and-coming intersection of Marshall and Cleveland and has become a local landmark with a very loyal clientele.

North

THE CORNER COFFEE HOUSE $
87 West County Rd. C, Little Canada
(651) 482-1114

One of the few true coffeehouses in the suburbs, the Corner Coffee House is a big, friendly-looking, yellow two-story house with a large back patio, several cozy rooms inside for neighborhood get-togethers, and lots of lot parking. The menu includes a couple dozen coffee and espresso drinks, huge fresh-fruit smoothies topped with whipped cream, breakfast pastries, and Italian desserts. Art and knickknacks are for sale, most of which are made by local artists, and live musicians stop by to play weekend afternoons and evenings. There's even a drive-through window in back for a quick pickup.

NIGHTLIFE

A casual drive through the Twin Cities might lead you to think that Minnesotans have a serious drinking problem. There are hundreds of little drinking holes throughout the region, sometimes spaced less than a city block apart. The truth is that Minnesotans just like to be together, especially in the winter.

If your idea of a night on the town is catching a good live band, you're in luck—nearly all the bars and coffee shops in the Twin Cities metro area offer at least one night of live music every week. There are clubs that cater to just about every musical taste you can imagine.

ALTERNATIVE MUSIC AND ROCK CLUBS

Minneapolis

THE CABOOZE
917 Cedar Ave., Minneapolis
(612) 338-6425
www.cabooze.com
Since 1974 the Cabooze has opened its doors to nationally recognized touring rock, folk, and instrumental acts as well as many local bands. The Cabooze features musical acts Wednesday through Saturday. It has a large dance floor for those who don't feel like just standing around, as well as the largest bar in the Twin Cities.

CLUB 3 DEGREES
113 North Fifth St., Minneapolis
(612) 781-8488
www.club3degrees.com
Kind of a rarity in the Twin Cities, Club 3 Degrees is an alcohol-free, smoke-free nightclub for audiences of all ages (until 11 p.m., when the club allows only those 18 and over). The club mostly books politically correct punk bands and Christian rock, but the occasional acoustic act makes its way in now and again.

CLUB UNDERGROUND
355 Monroe St. NE, Minneapolis
(612) 627-9123
www.clubunderground.us

If you're an adult, Club Underground is about as close as you're going to get to partying in your friends' basements while their parents are away. Unpretentious—to say the least—Club Underground gets the job done, and gets it done *loudly*. Microbrew aficionados and fans of gentle acoustic strumming can look elsewhere, because Club Underground is about drinking Bud and rocking out. It's also home to (on Sunday) a weekly comedy show and (on Monday) pub trivia in the least "pub"-like venue in town.

FINE LINE MUSIC CAFE
318 First Ave. North, Minneapolis
(612) 338-8100
www.finelinemusic.com
Offering a blend of folk music, adult rock, and funk, including many local bands with dreams of making it big, the Fine Line is an intimate, comfortable club on good nights and extremely packed and uncomfortable on bad nights. A small menu with American basics such as salads, steak, and pasta is available on nights featuring national touring acts.

FIRST AVENUE/SEVENTH STREET ENTRY
701 First Ave. North, Minneapolis
(612) 338-8388
www.first-avenue.com
Yes, this is that place from *Purple Rain*. Not only did local legend Prince film parts of his movie at First Avenue, he also spent his fair share of time here

when the cameras weren't rolling, both on stage and in the crowd. The world-famous First Avenue has been a popular hangout for bands, musicians, and club goers since Joe Cocker took the stage on opening night in 1970. Since then the club has featured top-40, alternative, and classic rock acts and has opened its floors to crowds dancing to techno, house music, salsa, hip-hop, reggae, and likely any other type of music you can think of. The real beauty of First Avenue is the layout. No matter where you stand in the club, whether on the massive dance floor or upstairs at the bar, you always get a decent view of the stage.

Set in a side room, with its own separate entrance on Seventh Street, the Entry is the more intimate venue. The stage setting is great here, too, and though the room gets packed quickly, on good nights this is about as close to having a major-label act play in your living room as you can get. The dress code is informal, and the bar offers some of the cheapest tap beer you'll find at a live-music venue.

400 BAR
400 Cedar Ave. South, Minneapolis
(612) 332-2903
www.400bar.com
The owners' former association with Soul Asylum helped bring people into the club when the band was big, but it's the club's reputation as a good venue to play that brings the bands in now. Everything from alternative rock to folk to blues acts (and everything in between) from all over the world make this club a regular stop on their tours.

GROUND ZERO/THE FRONT
15 Northeast Fourth St., Minneapolis
(612) 378-5115
Ground Zero offers diverse theme nights three times a week. One of the club's most popular dance nights is "Bondage a go-go," where every Thursday and Saturday dancers perform relatively tame S&M; some patrons dress in corresponding attire.

Besides the large dance floor, Ground Zero has a smaller, cozier lounge room, the Front.

Theme nights include Funky Friday, with old-school soul, disco, and R&B; and Astro Lounge, with disco, hip-hop, house, and whatever the DJ feels like playing.

HEXAGON BAR
2600 27th Ave. South, Minneapolis
(612) 722-3454
The Hex is in the middle of nowhere (in other words, it's not downtown, Uptown, Northeast, or on the West Bank), and some nights it feels like the neighborhood bar no one's discovered; other nights it's so packed that it feels like no one's discovered any other neighborhoods. There's lots of space to pack, too: One half of the venue has tables and a stage for music, while the other half has pool tables. The bar hosts a strong lineup of local indie-rock bands, and on the first Saturday of every month it hosts a now-legendary Surf Night, where the Dick Dales of the 21st century swing their axes with a vengeance.

KITTY CAT KLUB
315 14th Ave. SE, Minneapolis
(612) 331-9800
www.kittycatklub.net
No, the Kitty Cat Klub is *not* too good to be true—it just feels like it. A sprawling, funky venue furnished in a style that might be best described as through-the-looking-glass Victorian, the KCK serves drinks at surprisingly decent prices. A favorite spot for couples looking to cuddle in one of its many deep couches and for groups of people of all ages who feel too old for, say, the Library, the KCK hosts an impressive and growing lineup of music both acoustic and electric, as well as dance nights with DJs. (The dance floor is small, which just means you have to get friendly all the faster.) The stage doesn't offer the greatest view lines in town, but the ambience is warm enough that no one seems to mind.

LEE'S LIQUOR LOUNGE
101 Glenwood Ave., Minneapolis
(612) 338-9491
www.leesliquorlounge.com

Lee's hosts live music almost every night, and covers generally run $5 or less for the local and touring acts. The sight lines are good, and the bar is clean and comfortable, despite its slightly rough-around-the-edges roadhouse feel. This is the type of place where you're equally comfortable tossing back a few beers while bobbing your head or doing your thing on the dance floor. And who doesn't benefit from rockin' music, wood paneling, and taxidermy every once in a while?

MAYSLACKS POLKA LOUNGE
1428 Northeast Fourth St., Minneapolis
(612) 789-9862
www.mayslacksbar.com
This place can be the best bang for your buck so far as seeing live music. The cover is rarely more than $3, and bands usually play for a good two or three hours—and for the low cover, you can see anything from a brand-new band made up of neighborhood kids to a major label act. The downside is that there are rarely opening bands for acts, so by the time the headliners are finished playing, they're sometimes panting, out of breath, and usually very drunk. The sound system is better than you might expect from a neighborhood bar. The beer's moderately priced, too, and on football/soccer/hockey/bartender's-in-a-good-mood nights, the lounge has some really great specials.

> **i** If you're looking to sing your heart out, make your way to northeast Minneapolis—where you can bar-crawl from the You Otter Stop Inn to the Vegas Lounge to the Moose on Monroe, all stops along what is known as "the Minneapolis Karaoke Corridor."

TERMINAL BAR
409 Hennepin Ave. East, Minneapolis
(612) 623-4545
Most of the patrons of this bar are people from the neighborhood who like to stop by after work for a beer and college kids coming to see local bands perform on the small stage in the back.

The draft beer is a little high priced, but there's a popcorn machine always full of popcorn, and if you ask nicely, you can always sample the bar favorite, a hard-boiled egg on a Ritz cracker with a little mustard. The cover charge, if there is one, is usually very cheap.

TRIPLE ROCK SOCIAL CLUB
629 Cedar Ave. South, Minneapolis
(612) 333-7499
www.triplerocksocialclub.com
The Triple Rock Social Club is the punk rock bar and restaurant of the Twin Cities. It is owned by Erik Funk, a member of legendary local punk band Dillinger 4. The jukebox is particularly interesting—filled with a surprisingly eclectic range of music, from punk to R&B to metal—patrons' selections never cease to amaze and create an interesting atmosphere. Also of note is the wide selection of beers on tap, a dozen at last count. The Triple Rock's menu contains sandwiches, salads, burgers, and one of the Twin Cities' largest selections of vegetarian and vegan items.

WHISKEY JUNCTION
901 Cedar Ave., Minneapolis
(612) 338-9550
www.whiskeyjunction.com
With lots of local music and beer and food specials, Whiskey Junction, just down the street from the Cabooze, attracts a slightly grungy crowd, including plenty of students from the nearby University of Minnesota and Augsburg College. Two bars keep thirsty patrons busy, and the Whiskey has several pool tables and TVs, often flickering with various sporting events (the bar is the base for the unofficial Cleveland Browns Fan Club, making a brave statement in Vikings country). Whiskey Junction has an excellent selection of tap beers, including the local favorite, Summit, as well as rarer finds on tap, such as Beamish Stout, Boddington Cream Ale, Fullers India Pale Ale, and Paulaner Hefe Weizen. The bar also serves bar food, such as burgers, pizza, sandwiches, hot wings, and salads.

THE WHOLE MUSIC CAFE
Coffman Memorial Union
300 Washington Ave. SE
Minneapolis
(612) 625-2272
www.coffman.umn.edu/whole

The Whole, originally called the Gopher Hole, occupies the basement of Coffman Union on the University of Minnesota–Minneapolis campus. The 40-year-old venue has a venerable history, including early days as a coffeehouse featuring folky songsters and poets and later as a haven for new wave, punk, and indie-rock bands and their devoted student (mostly) fans. When Coffman Union underwent a $71 million renovation, improvements to the Whole included such coveted features as bathrooms and a rocking sound system. But the architects wisely left the gritty, down-in-the-cellar atmosphere much as it always has been, a nod to the tradition of this little underground club in the heart of the university.

St. Paul

BIG V'S SALOON
1567 University Ave. West, St. Paul
(651) 645-8472

Big V's Saloon features live music from local and national indie bands every weekend and some weekdays, and karaoke on Sunday and Tuesday. The decor of the bar is fabulous—the walls feature an old menu from the 1940s, while the bar itself is a classy antique curved wooden affair with a mirrored backdrop. The placing of the stage is a little inconvenient, tucked back where only patrons in the back room can actually see the stage, but considering that the saloon doesn't usually have a cover charge of more than a few dollars, not many people complain.

STATION 4
201 East Fourth St., St. Paul
(651) 298-0173
www.station-4.com

Station 4 features local rock and some national touring bands. The club is divided into two parts, one with a long bar with lots of dartboards and the other for the music. There is a large stage and lots of seating for the young bar crowd, who on weekends fill the club. Station 4 always runs shuttles to Wild hockey games and other big events at Xcel Energy Center. The bar includes separate areas for all ages and for 21+.

TURF CLUB
1601 University Ave., St. Paul
(651) 647-0486
www.turfclub.net

Billing itself as the "Best Remnant of the '40s," St. Paul's Turf Club combines upscale sophistication with the feel of an old-fashioned cowboy bar. Local, domestic, and imported beers are on tap, and the club features an elegant, curved wooden bar for customers to perch at, as well as booths and tables throughout the establishment. Long having a reputation for giving local original bands a much-needed performance outlet, the Turf Club is one of the hippest hangouts in the Twin Cities, with music almost every night for ridiculously low cover charges. The Turf Club clientele is refreshingly free of the "beautiful people" crowd found at many downtown Minneapolis dance clubs, and the music here ranges from foot-stomping country to ska. Downstairs is a second bar known as the Clown Lounge, which features local and guest jazz musicians. The lounge retains an intimate, basement-rec-room feel, with wood paneling and taxidermied fish. It's definitely worth checking out if you're around on an evening this downstairs bar is open. It provides a good aural break if the music upstairs doesn't turn out to be your thing.

North

THE ROCK NIGHTCLUB
2029 Woodlynn Ave., Maplewood
(651) 770-7822
www.therocknightclub.com

It's not like it's particularly hard to find a suburban bar where you can listen to hair metal and play pool, but the Rock is in a class of its own, attracting the kind of national acts (2 Live Crew, David Lee Roth, Molly Hatchet, Nashville Pussy) whose most devoted listeners are aging frat boys. The Rock's Web site insists it's "the metro's premier live music venue," and if the most-played songs on your iTunes are by Vanilla Ice and Warrant, you're not going to argue.

West

MEDINA ENTERTAINMENT CENTER
500 Hwy. 55, Hamel
(763) 478-6661
www.medinaentertainment.com
About 5 miles west of I-494 in the western suburb of Hamel, the Medina Entertainment Center hosts local bands like the disco kings Boogie Wonderland and the White Sidewalls, a 1950s and 1960s cover band. In addition to live music, the Medina often has poker events.

COMEDY CLUBS

Minneapolis

ACME COMEDY COMPANY
708 North First St., Minneapolis
(612) 338-6393
www.acmecomedycompany.com
Acme hosts local and national comedians in its Warehouse District space inside the Itasca Building. The club has shows nightly except Sunday, with free open mic on Monday. The on-site restaurant serves pasta, steaks, and ribs, and you have the choice of buying a ticket for the comedy show alone, for $15, or a dinner and show special for $27.

COMEDYSPORTZ
3001 Hennepin Ave. South (Calhoun Square), Minneapolis
(612) 870-1230
www.comedysportztc.com
Part of the national ComedySportz chain, this club sets up refereed comedy teams that compete for the biggest laughs and the most points for their unscripted, improvisational performances. Audience members are encouraged to heckle the teams as well as throw out suggestions for comedy themes. But make sure your suggestions

are clean, or the referee could call the "Brown Bag Foul" on you and you'll end up wearing a paper bag over your head. Shows are every Thursday at 8 p.m. and every Friday and Saturday at 8 and 10:30 p.m.

DANCE CLUBS

Minneapolis

BAR FLY
711 Hennepin Ave., Minneapolis
(612) 333-6100
www.barflyminneapolis.com
BarFly (tagline: "More quaint than a club. More liberal than a lounge.") sits in the old Skyway Theater on busy Hennepin Avenue downtown. DJs spin for the beautiful people dancing and bellying up to moodily lit bars. This club is open Wednesday through Sunday.

COWBOY SLIM'S
1320 West Lake St., Minneapolis
(612) 353-5156
www.cowboyslims.com
You can imagine the founders of Cowboy Slim's looking east down Lake Street and seeing the Country Bar and Grill, then looking west and seeing Bar Abilene, and nodding their heads knowingly, thinking, "Yes…yes! Combine the two! Brilliant!" Thus, Uptown has a new haven for urban cowboys looking to get their drink on and watch cowgirls ride a mechanical bull—and, of course, for cowgirls seeking a bull to ride. No more need be said.

THE DRINK
26 Fifth St. North, Minneapolis
(612) 659-9000

1400 Lagoon St., Minneapolis
(612) 824-3333
www.drinkmpls.com
First-time Minneapolis visitors probably think it's some kind of performance-art piece when they see a guy standing on the corner of Lake and Hennepin handing out tokens and yelling, "Free drink at the Drink!" Nope, there's actually a venue

called Drink—in fact, there are three. One's in downtown Minneapolis, one's in Uptown, and the third is in Iowa. The Drink advertises itself as "the original fun bar," and once you've visited a Drink, you'll appreciate how no one really had any fun at a bar until Drink came along with its novel combination of loud music and beer. If you're looking for a place to shake your tailfeathers and have them appreciatively ogled, tell the cabbie to take you to the Drink—any Drink.

EL NUEVO RODEO
2709 East Lake St., Minneapolis
(612) 728-0101
www.elnuevorodeo.com
Boasting three hardwood dance floors, two bars, and highly danceable Latin music, El Nuevo Rodeo is one of the biggest dance clubs in the Cities. The club features live Latin music several nights a week, especially on weekends, and a DJ playing very sexy Latin tunes the rest of the time. At 20,000 square feet, El Nuevo Rodeo is large, but it rarely feels empty when the music is playing. The club is on East Lake Street a couple of blocks west of the Lake Street/Midtown Station of the Hiawatha Light-Rail Transit line.

EPIC NIGHTCLUB
110 North Fifth St., Minneapolis
(612) 332-3742
www.epicmpls.com
Since the implosion (financially, not physically) of Myth, Epic is left as the Twin Cities' last club standing for those seeking big-name DJs in cavernous rooms with VIPs sitting in balconies throwing sushi down into the general-admission crowd just because they can. Hip-hop and, rarely, rock/pop acts also play Epic sometimes, but by and large it's a place to pop your pill, drink your drink, and get good 'n' sweaty. Theme parties are a specialty; subscribe to the venue's e-mail newsletter for updates.

ESCAPE ULTRA LOUNGE
600 Hennepin Ave. South, Minneapolis
(612) 333-8855
www.escapeultralounge.com

This 12,000-square-foot 18-plus club is right above the Hard Rock Cafe in the heart of Minneapolis's entertainment district on Hennepin Avenue (there is also a club entrance on First Avenue). A "fashionable" dress code is enforced here, where plasma screens, leather couches, and serious uplighting make for a hip, high-tech mood. Two VIP rooms up the swank factor. Escape is open from 5 p.m. to 2:30 a.m. seven days a week and features drink specials and a range of music including hip-hop, latin, R&B, rock, and dance hall.

THE IMPERIAL ROOM
417 North First Ave., Minneapolis
(612) 376-7676
www.imperialroom.com
You could call the Imperial Room a bar—you could even call it a restaurant. But at its best (such as it is), it's a dance club. On Friday nights the floor fills with people who have escaped their cubicles and really, really don't want to think about work…unless "thinking about work" means thinking about that cute guy who just started in marketing.

SPIN
10 South Fifth St., Minneapolis
(612) 333-5055
www.spinmn.com
In Minneapolis's hip Warehouse District, this place is designed for people to see and be seen—and to dance. The sound and the lighting are state-of-the-art amazing, and the ambience can't be beat. There are 40-foot ceilings, a 20-foot water wall, blasts of fog, and the bathrooms—you must visit the bathrooms, where plasma screens perch above the urinals and the stall doors are clear glass that turn opaque when they are closed. Spin's annual November Studio 54 party is totally hot and totally 1970s. The club is open Thursday through Sunday from 9 p.m. to 2 a.m. Watch for nightly specials, and be aware that the dress code is enforced.

WILD ONION
788 Grand Ave., St. Paul
(651) 291-2525
www.wild-onion.net

The Wild Onion is St. Paul's attempt to show Minneapolis that the bigger city doesn't have a monopoly on sweaty booze-fueled grinding—and it's a very convincing attempt at that. By day, the Wild Onion is a mundane purveyor of beer and wings; at night, it comes alive with awkward dance moves the likes of which you haven't seen since the last time your foot fell asleep.

FOLK, IRISH, AND ACOUSTIC MUSIC

Minneapolis

CEDAR CULTURAL CENTER
416 Cedar Ave. South, Minneapolis
(612) 338-2674
www.thecedar.org
The Cedar Cultural Center is a great place to see musicians perform. The auditorium is designed specifically for listening to music, with beautiful hardwood floors, a large raised stage in the front, excellent acoustics, and a soundman who actually pays attention to musicians' cues. Exciting acts perform at this venue, from traditional Irish bands to folk duos to world-famous acoustic soloists such as Pierre Bensusan and Didier Malherbe. The Cedar is also the home of the annual Nordic Roots festival, a three-day event that features elemental, contemporary, and experimental groups from the Nordic countries. The refreshment bar is worth noting, too—this establishment includes cheap, good beer on tap, wine, homemade cookies, and Indian samosas on the menu. Dress light if you're heading to the Cedar in summertime—when the venue's sold out, it can get mighty sticky in there.

KIERAN'S IRISH PUB & RESTAURANT
600 Hennepin Ave. (Block E), Minneapolis
(612) 339-4499
www.kierans.com
One of the few Irish bars in Minneapolis, Kieran's has a full bar and an excellent menu that includes traditional Irish foods like lamb stew and pot roast with Guinness gravy. The bar usually has live Irish and folk music playing on two different stages

Friday and Saturday nights and infrequently during the week, with the occasional open-mic night and scheduled poetry readings on the smaller stage. During the summer, Kieran's sets up an outside bar and lots of tables for clients, with the occasional live band set up outside to serenade both patrons and random passersby. (Note: Kieran's was moving into its new location, above, just as this guide went to press.)

Care for a Drink?

"Bar time" in Minnesota is 2 a.m. although many bars close earlier. Some bars and restaurants stay open later but do not continue to serve alcohol. Liquor stores in the Twin Cities can be open from 8 a.m. to 8 p.m. Monday through Thursday and until 10 p.m. Friday and Saturday, as well as on July 3 and New Year's Eve. Liquor stores are closed on Sunday, although some convenience stores and grocery stores sell 3.2 beer on Sunday.

O'DONOVAN'S IRISH PUB
700 First Ave. North, Minneapolis
(612) 317-8896
www.odonovans.com
O'Donovan's is a nice addition to the small Twin Cities Irish pub scene. Unlike the Dubliner Pub or Kieran's Irish Pub, O'Donovan's authenticity to all that is Irish is mostly left to the beautiful decor. The pub was actually built in Ireland and shipped to the Twin Cities in pieces. O'Donovan's draws a young, collegiate crowd, who enjoy the pub's live music selection, which often includes top-40 hits. Location is a prime asset for O'Donovan's—the Target Center and First Avenue/Seventh Street Entry are directly across the street.

St. Paul

THE DUBLINER PUB
2162 University Ave. West, St. Paul
(651) 646-5551

The Dubliner Pub is an old-style Irish themed bar for its working-class industrial location. The cozy, box-shaped pub is painted green and has a beautiful long bar, where Irish, English, and domestic beers are on tap. There is also a small stage for Irish music on the weekends as well as darts and free popcorn.

HALF TIME REC
1013 Front Ave., St. Paul
(651) 488-8245
www.halftimerec.com

The Half Time Rec is an authentic neighborhood Irish bar that attracts large crowds on the weekends for its live Irish music, numerous ales and stouts on tap, and boccie court in the basement. It features a long, U-shaped bar and an adjoining room with a stage for music Tuesday through Saturday (the show is free Tuesday through Thursday). At the Half Time Rec, patrons vociferously have fun. They frequently sing along with the music or get up and dance to the jig-inspiring Irish music. The Half Time Rec is a few miles from the major thoroughfares, but it is well worth the effort.

GAY BARS

Minneapolis

THE MINNEAPOLIS EAGLE
515 Washington Ave. South, Minneapolis
(612) 338-4214
www.minneapoliseagle.com

If there's such a thing as an "authentic" gay bar, the Eagle is it. No bachelorettes with suckers, no bored straights looking for something off the beaten path, just gay men and women (mostly the former) looking to party. The attached Bolt is a straight-up (so to speak) hookup spot, especially on underwear nights and leather nights.

GAY NINETIES THEATRE CAFE & BAR
408 Hennepin Ave., Minneapolis
(612) 333-7755
www.gay90s.com

The state's largest gay club, the Gay Nineties features a six-night-a-week (none on Monday) drag show at the La Femme Show Lounge on the second floor. The club has a dedicated straight following as well, who come for the strong mixed drinks and the excellent dance music with no cover charge—Friday and Saturday nights are packed, and there's nearly always a line to get inside. The club has nine different bars on the premises, two discos, a supper club, male strippers, and a game room.

JETSET BAR
115 First St. North, Minneapolis
(612) 339-3933
www.jetsetbar.com

Jetset is the Twin Cities' most stylish gay bar—indeed, it's one of the area's most stylish bars of any description. When you step into Jetset you may feel as though you've passed through a wormhole into Manhattan: the couches are sparse and low, the walls are tall and white, the drink shelf behind the bar is well-stocked and underlit. It's notably straight-friendly, so you have absolutely no excuse not to make your way there for a martini (or, if you absolutely *must,* a beer).

THE SALOON
830 Hennepin Ave., Minneapolis
(612) 332-0835
www.saloonmn.com

The Saloon is one of the most popular bars and dance clubs for Twin Cities gay men, featuring a large, dark dance floor with plenty of loud music and a large bar in the back for socializing and imbibing. The Saloon has various themes for the days of the week, including Hard Mondays (hard rock, industrial, and Goth music) and Boys Night Out on Thursday (18+ are allowed in), as well as DJs on the weekends.

JAZZ, BLUES, AND R&B

Minneapolis

BUNKER'S MUSIC BAR & GRILL
761 Washington Ave. North, Minneapolis
(612) 338-8188
www.bunkersmusic.com
A popular lunch spot serving soups and sandwiches during the day, this neighborhood bar turns into a blues and rock club at night. The acts booked range from alternative rock bands to blues, R&B, and jazz acts. The cover charge is pretty low—usually under $6—and there are also pool tables and video games.

THE DAKOTA BAR & GRILL
1010 Nicollet Ave., Minneapolis
(612) 332-1010
www.dakotacooks.com
At least once a week, a national headlining jazz act comes through town to play at this club, and while the ticket prices are high (usually around $30) for the area, jazz fans will definitely get their money's worth. The cuisine served is elegant and as stylish as the music: Caribbean-seasoned prime rib of pork, Hawaiian line-caught snapper, and Tabasco-molasses glazed New York strip steak. There's an extensive wine list, a full bar, and a happy hour Monday through Friday from 4 to 6 p.m. Lighter fare is served in the jazz club.

FAMOUS DAVE'S BBQ & BLUES
3001 Hennepin Ave. South
(Calhoun Square), Minneapolis
(612) 822-9900
www.famousdaves.com
Not only does Famous Dave's have some of the best barbecue ribs and fried catfish in the Twin Cities (especially for a chain restaurant), the Uptown branch also books some of the rawest blues in the area. The music is free, and the drinks are reasonably priced.

St. Paul

ARTISTS' QUARTER
408 St. Peter St., St. Paul
(651) 292-1359
www.artistsquarter.com
The Artists' Quarter's acoustics are great in its small basement space, the stage is big enough to hold a full piano and an accompanying band, and the bar serves cheap tap beer as well as wine and liquor. Primarily a haven for local jazz artists but occasionally featuring a national act, the club is a great place to stop by late at night to unwind—the bartenders are friendly, the cover charge is usually under $5 during the week, and most of the bands that play here are a lot of fun.

LOUNGES, PUBS, AND BARS

Minneapolis

BEV'S WINE BAR
250 Third Ave. North, Minneapolis
(612) 337-0102
Bev's is ultraromantic, so dimly lit you may have a hard time reading the exceptional wine list. High ceilings, dark wood, and big windows looking out on the Warehouse District make this one of the Twin Cities' most appealing spots for a quiet drink—especially if you're a wine connoisseur. The wine list isn't particularly long, but it's very well chosen. You won't go wrong.

BRIT'S PUB & EATING ESTABLISHMENT
1110 Nicollet Mall, Minneapolis
(612) 332-3908
www.britspub.com
This upscale downtown bar is almost always packed on weekends. The main room is lavishly furnished with mock-Georgian lounges and armchairs as well as beautiful wooden bar stools set next to tables and wall outcroppings to set your beer on throughout the room. During summer Brit's opens its rooftop patio for outdoor libations surrounded by Minneapolis's skyscrapers. You can also watch lawn bowlers practicing their avocation on the rooftop grassy field, the

only elevated lawn bowling field in the country. When there is open lawn bowling on the weekends, you can attempt to roll your "bowl" as close as possible to the "jack"—for a small fee. Groups can reserve the green—for a much larger fee—several afternoons and evenings during the week. Brit's is located on Nicollet Mall (buses only) across from Orchestra Hall.

CHATTERBOX PUB
2229 East 35th St., Minneapolis
(612) 728-9871

4501 France Ave. South, Minneapolis
(612) 920-3221

800 Cleveland Ave. South, St. Paul
(651) 699-1154
www.chatterboxpub.net
This bar's big claim to fame is the huge collection of Atari, Nintendo, and Sega Genesis video games available for customers. The bar also makes available vintage board games such as Connect 4 and Yahtzee. If you're hungry in addition to wanting to play games and drink intoxicating beverages, the Chatterbox serves breakfast (St. Paul location only), lunch, several full entrée dinners, burgers, and pizza. Of special note on the menu: baked macaroni and cheese with your choice of ingredients, pizza-style. It's deadly good.

CLUBHOUSE JÄGER
923 Washington Ave. North, Minneapolis
(612) 332-2686
www.myspace.com/clubhousejager
Sitting alone at the far west end of Washington Avenue, Club Jäger isn't a likely candidate for any bar crawls, but when you find it you feel like you've found the prize in the box of Cracker Jack. It's richly decorated in high Bavarian style, but it's less kitschy than, say, the Black Forest. You'll want to pull up an armchair and stay awhile, especially on winter nights when the (gas) fireplace is crackling and the friendly waitstaff are happy to keep you supplied with a steady stream of suds. The bar is also a notable nightlife destination, especially to beat the midweek blahs. Jägercon—the Twin Cities' smallest, most frequent, and friendli-

est sci-fi convention—takes place each Tuesday night and Transmission—DJ Jake Rudh's dance party—happens on Wednesday.

DONNY DIRK'S ZOMBIE DEN
2027 North Second St., Minneapolis
(612) 588-9700
Apparently deciding that with Psycho Suzi holding the torch for traditional tiki, a South Seas theme was insufficient, the proprietors of Donnie Dirk's Zombie Den threw in a zombie theme as well. Given that the Twin Cities are home to an annual Zombie Pub Crawl that attracts thousands, founding a year-round zombie bar made sense, and it's paying off in a regular clientele who enjoy the stiff (pun intended) drinks.

GLUEK'S RESTAURANT & BAR
16 North Sixth St., Minneapolis
(612) 338-6621
www.glueks.com
Gluek's is Minneapolis's original brewpub. Since 1902 Gluek's has served Minneapolis with its tasty beer. Located in the historic Warehouse District, Gluek's draws huge crowds with its brew, other domestic and foreign beers, and liquors. Gluek's is across the street from the Target Center, home of the Minnesota Timberwolves and Minnesota Lynx, and within walking distance of the shops of downtown Minneapolis.

GRUMPY'S
1111 Washington Ave. South, Minneapolis
(612) 340-9738

2200 Fourth St. NE, Minneapolis
(612) 789-7429

2801 Snelling Ave. North, Roseville
(651) 379-1180
www.grumpys-bar.com
The downtown Grumpy's is a Washington Avenue landmark, a big bar serving platters of tater tots that seem to take up about half the table (and that's just the *half* order). It's a favorite destination for pregaming Metrodome events—which there will be many fewer of now that the Twins are moving to Target Field and the

Gophers have gone back to campus, but that just leaves more room for the bar's loyal regulars. Except for sharing ownership and a name, the northeast Grumpy's and the Roseville Grumpy's don't have too much in common with the original—though they both have their own followings, and the northeast location has become the kind of "neighborhood joint" that people from other neighborhoods seek out.

ℹ️ At Grumpy's Northeast, Monday nights are devoted to Minnesota music: Local music critics take turns DJing sets of all-local music while bartender Tony Zaccardi (bassist in the band Romantica) serves Minnesota beers at half-price.

THE HERKIMER PUB & BREWERY
2922 Lyndale Ave. South, Minneapolis
(612) 821-0101
www.theherkimer.com
The Herkimer Pub & Brewery offers a large selection of freshly made beers. Despite its location in the trendy Lyn-Lake neighborhood, the beers made in-house cost less than a bottle of domestic. Each day there are different "Today's Brews" written on a chalkboard, including light lagers and heavier dunkels (German for dark). The Herkimer also serves food and appetizers (burgers, sandwiches, fish and chips, etc.) until midnight.

THE INDEPENDENT
3001 Hennepin Ave., Minneapolis
(612) 378-1905
www.theindependent-uptown.com
The Independent is kind of the default bar at Lake and Hennepin: rarely packed, rarely dead, good (but not great) beer selection, good (but not great) cocktail menu, decent atmosphere . . . If you spend much time in Uptown, chances are that before too long you'll find yourself in a group of people looking for a spot to go when one person says, "How about the Independent?" And you'll all shrug and go to the Independent. (Note: It's not a dance club, and people have been kicked out for trying to turn it into one—so stir your booty, don't shake it.)

THE LIBRARY
1301 Fourth St. SE, Minneapolis
(612) 604-1900
With brilliant irony, the busiest bar on the University of Minnesota campus is a multilevel monster called the Library. (From the outside, it even looks kind of like a library—though it sure doesn't sound like one.) If you're a U of M student looking for a crowded bar, you're probably on your way there right now, memorizing the name and address on your fake ID. If you're not a U of M student looking for a crowded bar . . . move along, there's nothing to see here.

LIQUOR LYLE'S BAR AND RESTAURANT
2021 Hennepin Ave. South, Minneapolis
(612) 870-8183
www.liquorlyles.com
On the edge of Uptown, one would think that Liquor Lyle's, as most area residents call this establishment, would tend toward a hipster crowd. But this neighborhood watering hole attracts everyone from construction workers to artists to its somewhat smudgy, dated-yet-colorful ambience. The booths have vinyl seats, the men's restrooms have trough urinals, and the bouncer is big and hairy; but if you want to share a pitcher of beer and a basket of deep-fried cheese curds with a friend on a day when you haven't taken a shower, Lyle's is hard to beat. Just stay away from the Bloody Marys.

MACKENZIE
918 Hennepin Ave., Minneapolis
(612) 333-7268
www.mackenziepub.com
MacKenzie specializes in Scottish beers and liquors but also has a large selection of American libations, all at reasonable prices. The inside of the bar features Scottish decor and theater posters on lots of beautiful exposed brick. Located next to the historic Orpheum Theatre and within walking distance of several others, MacKenzie is a great stop before or after Hennepin Avenue theater events. The bar has five TVs and shows NFL games whenever one is broadcast.

MAC'S INDUSTRIAL SPORTS BAR
312 Central Ave. SE, Minneapolis
(612) 379-3379
www.macsindustrial.com

Mac's advertises itself as "redefining the dynamic of Northeast," but really it would redefine the dynamic of *any* neighborhood to open a bar that includes both the words "industrial" and "sports" in its name. Mac's is noted for its unusually nosh-worthy bar food and for its daily happy hour—which on Saturdays from 7 to 11 p.m. turns into the best happy hour in town, with all taps (including a wide range of microbrews) just two bucks each.

MARIO'S KELLER BAR
2300 University Ave. NE, Minneapolis
(612) 781-3860
www.gasthofzg.com

Mario's Keller Bar occupies the large and comfortable basement of the Gasthof zur Gemütlichkeit Restaurant. A festive atmosphere overtakes the club, especially on weekends, when fraternity members pack the dance floor and consume massive quantities of beer, which comes as no surprise, considering the excellent selection of German beers on tap and available by the glass, pint, or enormous glass boot. Connoisseurs of German beers will enjoy the bar's selection, which runs a bit pricey, while many others will revel in the raucous German beer-hall atmosphere.

NYE'S POLONAISE ROOM
112 East Hennepin Ave., Minneapolis
(612) 379-2021
www.nyespolonaise.com

A few years ago *Esquire* named Nye's the best bar in America, and if success hasn't quite gone to Nye's head, it's certainly gone to its prices—Nye's is not cheap, whether you're drinking at the bar or eating the mediocre Polish food in the dining room. Still, *Esquire* was on to something: Nye's is a permanent blast from the past, with shag carpeting, garish fixtures, and sit-around-the-piano karaoke in the dining room and loud bands (on Friday and Saturday nights, the World's Most

Dangerous Polka Band) in the bar. There's no place like Nye's, so you might as well give in and enjoy it.

THE RIVERVIEW WINE BAR AND CAFÉ
3745–3753 42nd Ave. South, Minneapolis
(612) 729-4200
www.theriverview.net

In the heart of Minneapolis's Longellow neighborhood, you've got your uppers and your downers conveniently conjoined: A single door separates the Riverview Café (coffee) from the Riverview Wine Bar (wine)—and yes, you can bring your espresso across to the wine bar, though not vice versa. Either or both make for great stops before or after a screening at the adjacent Riverview Theater; the wine bar is a close second to Bev's for the Twin Cities' most romantic and atmospheric wine bar.

The Summit Brewing Company

The **Summit Brewing Company** (901 Montreal Circle, 651-265-7800; www.summitbrewing.com) of St. Paul brews some solid microbrews, and most Twin Cities bars and restaurants have at least one Summit beer on tap. The brewery makes Extra Pale Ale, Pilsener, India Pale Ale, ESB, and Porter year-round and seasonal varieties such as Maibock and Winter Ale. The brewery offers tours Tuesday, Thursday, and Saturday at 1 p.m. (tours are free, but reservations are required on Saturday).

WHITEY'S WORLD FAMOUS SALOON
400 Hennepin Ave. East, Minneapolis
(612) 623-9478

Whitey's is a neighborhood bar that has weekend specials on Jägermeister shots and about half a dozen domestic and locally brewed beers on tap. The interior is beautiful—the bar is an elegant, curved length of carved wood surrounded by high-backed stools, and in summertime patrons can sit inside the bar or at the tables set outside on the fenced-in patio.

St. Paul

GREAT WATERS BREWING COMPANY
426 St. Peter St., St. Paul
(651) 224-2739
www.greatwatersbc.com
Great Waters Brewing Company serves flavorful microbrews from its location inside downtown St. Paul's Hamm Building. The brewpub's beers include cask-conditioned ales, served at cellar temperature of 52 degrees F and "hand pulled" from casks in the basement, and pushed beers, which are served at 38 degrees F, similar to other tap beers in the United States. Beers include the Saint Peter Pale Ale, Flying Circus Big Hop Ale, the Knights Who Say "Nee" ESB, and the "Jumby," the latter brewed with wildflower honey, ginger root, and orange peel. Great Waters also brews its own root beer and has an outdoor patio and full menu, featuring several pastas, grilled duck breast, jambalaya, and a top-notch London broil.

GROVELAND TAP
1834 St. Clair Ave., St. Paul
(651) 699-5058
www.grovelandtap.com
The Groveland Tap is an old-school bar in a neighborhood that's defined by old schools. The glossy logo is the only sign of gentrification at the Groveland Tap, where, as it's been for years, you can safely expect to find a decent burger, a bottle of beer, and a bunch of people sitting around relaxing and watching the game. If you live in the neighborhood, you're probably a regular. If you don't live in the neighborhood, it's good to keep in mind for when you need an uncrowded spot to kick back before or after a movie at the Grandview or Highland. Other than that, it's not really a destination bar—though if it were, the fried pickle spears would be what made it one.

HAPPY GNOME
498 Selby Ave., St. Paul
(651) 287-2018
www.thehappygnome.com
Ask a Minneapolitan to name one St. Paul bar, and chances are he or she will name the Happy Gnome. It's a memorable place, built from a former fire station. Inside it's cozy but spacious, and the deck seating out back is some of the best in the Cities. The food is decent but overpriced, while the beer list is far better than decent: there are dozens of varieties on tap, and the knowledgable staff rotate them regularly. Tell the bartender what you usually order and ask him or her to suggest a different beer to try; you won't be disappointed.

MUDDY PIG
162 North Dale St., St. Paul
(651) 254-1030
www.muddypig.com
The Muddy Pig is the middleman in the great triumverate of Selby/Dale bars—it's not as sceney as the Happy Gnome, nor as neighborhood-y as Sweeney's, and it's physically located right between them. It's a nice spot to grab a fine beer (its tap selection, while not as extensive as the Happy Gnome's, is nonetheless top-notch) and a meal as well—its food is better than the Gnome's, and less expensive. Smokers, and drinkers seeking fresh air, will get social real quick: The Muddy Pig's outdoor seating is arrayed along a thin sliver of real estate.

O'GARA'S BAR & GRILL
164 Snelling Ave. North, St. Paul
(651) 644-3333
www.ogaras.com
O'Gara's is at the boozy, beating heart of St. Paul's Union Park neighborhood. This is the St. Paul that *Peanuts* creator Charles Schulz knew: When he was a boy, his father's barbershop was just around the corner from O'Gara's, in a space on Selby that is now part of the expanded bar. When Schulz's mother fell ill, the family moved to one of the apartments just above the shop, where they lived for a number of years. You'll always

find a happy crowd of locals at O'Gara's, and on St. Patrick's Day, good luck squeezing in the door. The adjoining O'Gara's Garage hosts local bands, mostly straightahead blues-rockers.

SWEENEY'S SALOON
96 North Dale St., St. Paul
(651) 221-9157
www.sweeneyssaloon.com
Sweeney's is a local pub with beautiful woodwork and a popular patio bar open during the summer; try to score a spot near the fireplace so you don't have to move when the night gets chilly. With many excellent beers on tap, lots of booths, and a pub-food menu, Sweeney's attracts young, cute singles and attached (or not) 30-somethings looking for a pint or a pitcher.

MOVIE THEATERS

Minneapolis

ASIAN MEDIA ACCESS
2418 Plymouth Ave. North, Minneapolis
(612) 376-7715
www.amamedia.org
Asian Media Access specializes in the best of Asian cinema from the present and the past. Lacking a theater of its own, the organization rents two local theaters (Riverview and Oak Street) on a regular basis for screenings. Asian Media Access provides action-packed Hong Kong cinema, contemporary Japanese film, Chinese comedies, and more. Be sure to call or check the Web site for details about upcoming events.

BELL AUDITORIUM
U of M Campus, 10 Church St., Minneapolis
(612) 331-3134
www.mnfilmarts.org
Formerly home to the University Film Society, the Bell Auditorium has long been home to offbeat films. Since its inception, the Bell Auditorium has hosted directors and film scholars of the likes of Robert Altman, Jean-Luc Godard, and Roberto Rosellini. Of late, the infrequent screenings at the Bell Auditorium have tended to be of

documentary films; don't miss a chance to see a show in this swank salmon-colored art deco gem. The nonprofit Minnesota Film Arts promotes an appreciation for the art of filmmaking through screenings both at Bell Auditorim and at Oak Street Cinema, and through events such as the Minneapolis–St. Paul International Film Festival.

KERASOTES BLOCK E STADIUM 15
Block E, 600 Hennepin Ave., Minneapolis
(612) 338-5900
www.kerasotes.com
The only cinema downtown, the Block E 15 inside the Block E shopping and entertainment complex shows first-run movies in full digital sound with stadium seating.

LAGOON CINEMA
1320 Lagoon Ave., Minneapolis
(612) 825-6006
www.landmarktheatres.com
Lagoon Cinema is part of Landmark's national art theater chain. Arty, indie, and a few foreign hits are often held over at the Lagoon after playing at its sister theater a couple blocks away, the Uptown. The Lagoon screens smaller-budget films for a longer duration and others that would not otherwise have been shown. The five theaters in this multiplex are roomy and comfortable, with excellent sound and large movie screens.

OAK STREET CINEMA
309 SE Oak St., Minneapolis
(612) 331-3134
www.mnfilmarts.org
Oak Street Cinema is the only Twin Cities theater dedicated to classic film revivals. Occasionally new films from famous directors or student films are shown, but beyond that, Oak Street Cinema sticks to reviving cinema's illustrious as well as forgotten past. Schedules have included great films of the 1970s, the French New Wave, and the films of directors such as Tarkovsky, Bergman, Mel Brooks, Bunuel, and a host of others. Thematic scheduling such as the best of vampire films or silent films is common. Oak Street Cinema is one of the Twin Cities' great artistic treasures. The Oak

🔍 Close-up

The Trylon Microcinema

What's a "microcinema"? In the case of the **Trylon,** it's a 50-seat theater equipped with a screen spanning 20 feet from corner to corner. The Trylon departs from stadium megatheaters in another way: instead of traditional flip-down movie seats, it's filled with rocking chairs. Three or four nights a week, it shows classics from the cinematic repertory to audiences of a few dozen extremely satisfied film buffs.

The Trylon is also one of the Twin Cities' newest movie theaters, opened in 2009 by Take-Up Productions, an all-volunteer organization dedicated to ensuring that local filmgoers have more to choose from than Dwayne Johnson comedies and CGI blockbusters. Take-Up was founded in 2006 by Barry Kryshka and several associates, most of whom had worked alongside Kryshka at the Oak Street Cinema in its halcyon days of the 1990s, when it was showing four or five films a week.

Kryshka is a transplant to the Twin Cities: He grew up in Queens, New York, in the 1980s. "I was within walking distance of six different theaters," he remembers. "The Trylon is named after a theater on Queens Boulevard, which is itself named after a pavilion in the 1939 New York World's Fair. That was a golden age of cinema, so it just seemed right."

Besides the twin 35mm projectors required to show aging multireel prints, the Trylon also has a 1080p video projector. It shares a space with the shop Kryshka runs as a day job, selling and maintaining A/V equipment. Take-Up also partners with theaters like the Heights for especially popular series, such as one showcasing the films of Cary Grant, and using the Trylon for cult classics. When I spoke with him, Kryshka was planning a series of films about newspapers, one devoted to Jack Nicholson, and one featuring the films of Steven Spielberg.

With home theaters becoming increasingly elaborate, formats like Blu-ray upping the ante on picture and sound quality, and services like Netflix putting the entirety of film history in every mailbox, why open a small movie theater devoted to old movies? "People have been predicting the death of repertory cinema since the debut of broadcast radio," says Kryshka. "What they underestimate is the social component of moviegoing. You can buy liquor in a store and go sit in your basement, but that doesn't mean bars are going to go out of business."

Street has recently served as a venue for Minnesota Film Arts, a nonprofit organization that seeks to foster an appreciation for the art of filmmaking through screenings, but that organization is moving most of its screenings to St. Anthony Main; after a long battle with developers, the Oak Street is slated for destruction.

PARKWAY THEATER
4814 Chicago Ave. South, Minneapolis
(612) 822-3030
www.theparkwaytheater.com
One of the few single-screen theaters surviving in the Twin Cities, this south Minneapolis theater has a knack for consistently showing the best of second-run indie and mainstream films. Despite the Parkway's less than spectacular ambience, this old mom-and-pop theater more than makes up for it in value. Ticket prices are low, and concession prices are a steal. If you are curious about what is playing at the Parkway, give the theater a call; the message on the answering machine is always homey and interesting.

RIVERVIEW THEATER
3800 42nd Ave. South, Minneapolis
(612) 729-7369
www.riverviewtheater.com
The Riverview Theater presents second-run movies in one of the Cities' most beautiful theaters. The Riverview is a fine example of art deco architecture and furnishings. The lobby is of particular distinc-

tion—appearing today very much as it did 50 years ago—decorated with art deco lamps and sofas.

Films screened at the Riverview are usually popular second-run films. There are occasional deviations. *The Wizard of Oz* and other cinema classics have been shown at this Minneapolis gem. Prices for tickets are a bargain ($3 for most evening shows; $2 for matinees), and concessions are much cheaper than at the suburban multiplexes, especially if you purchase a combo.

ST. ANTHONY MAIN THEATRE
115 SE Main St., Minneapolis
(612) 331-4723

This theater is in Minneapolis's beautiful St. Anthony area. It is also within walking distance of Nicollet Island and the Stone Arch Bridge and across the river from downtown Minneapolis. St. Anthony Main Theatre has much more charm than your average suburban multiplex. The individual theaters and seating are comfortable and the concessions comparable to other theaters in town. Go for a walk and enjoy the grandeur and the sights of downtown and St. Anthony, then stop by the theater for a movie.

SUBURBAN WORLD THEATRE
3022 Hennepin Ave. South, Minneapolis
(612) 822-9000
www.suburbanworldtheatre.com

The historic Suburban World Theater was renovated into a one-screen cinema and restaurant. The menu includes the usual burgers and pizza as well as wraps, salads, tapas, and sandwiches, plus wine and beer—all served during shows.

The Suburban World first opened in 1927 as the Granada Theatre. It was and is an example of Spanish-Moorish architecture, adorned with stucco facades of balconies, plants, and statues. The combination of the food and the architecture makes this an interesting place to see a revival or second-run film. The theater also hosts special television sports events, concerts, and live performances. Be sure to look up—that's right, there's a sky of glittering stars above your head when you're sitting in the Suburban World.

TRYLON MICROCINEMA
3258 Minnehaha Ave., Minneapolis
(612) 424-5468
www.take-up.org

The Trylon, operated by nonprofit film society Take-Up Productions, opened in 2009 as one of the coolest ideas anyone in the Twin Cities has had in a while: Keep the space small and the overhead low, and you have a sustainable venue for showing classic films. The Trylon is now the most consistently programmed revival "house" (actually, it's more like a room) in the Cities, with thoughtfully chosen series highlighting great filmmakers and beloved genres. The seating? Rocking chairs! Cool.

UPTOWN THEATRE
2906 Hennepin Ave. South
Minneapolis
(612) 825-6006

The Uptown Theatre features art and indie cinema debuts. Films frequently are screened exclusively at the Uptown, owned by Landmark Theatres before moving a block away to Landmark's Lagoon Cinema and farther afield to suburban theaters.

The Uptown's towering marquee is the symbolic heart of its eponymous neighborhood—though unfortunately, the top of the tower no longer boasts a spotlight as it originally did. The programmers have fun with the marquee and with the lineup: On Saturday nights the Uptown hosts midnight movie screenings, often with local bands "opening" for the films. The cavernous interior space boasts restored art deco murals (maidens pouring water among the city's lakes, in case you couldn't tell) as well as the Twin Cities' only remaining movie theater balcony.

St. Paul

GRANDVIEW THEATER
1830 Grand Ave., St. Paul
(651) 698-3344

Two neighborhood theaters showing first-run movies survive in St. Paul, and the Grandview, opened in 1933, lives on at its Grand Avenue location near Macalester College and the University of St. Thomas. The theater has two screens, a large theater downstairs and a smaller room upstairs (originally the theater's balcony). Designed in the art moderne style, the classic theater—today part of the Mann Theatres chain—is a neighborhood treasure.

HIGHLAND THEATER
760 Cleveland Ave. South, St. Paul
(651) 698-3085
This 1938 art deco theater in St. Paul's Highland Park neighborhood shows first-run movies (like the Grandview, the Highland is owned by the Mann Theatres chain). Competition from suburban megacomplexes has hit many one- and two-screen cinemas in the Cities hard over the years. The Highland is a holdover from another era.

The Suburbs

AMC ROSEDALE 14
850 Rosedale Center, Roseville
(888) 262-4386
www.amcentertainment.com/rosedale
From the ashes of the little-mourned Har Mar and Pavilion Place theaters in Roseville has risen the AMC Rosedale 14, an emporium of stadium-style theaters that includes the Twin Cities' smallest IMAX screen. IMAX buffs like to point out that it's not a "true" IMAX theater, but a digital IMAX system. Whatever.

i When the AMC Rosedale 14 first opened in 2007, it was not-so-subtly pointed out to its proprietors that they'd made a minor miscalculation given that their theater was located in the coldest of the continental United States: They'd located the box office windows outdoors. Renovations quickly ensued, moving the box office indoors.

HEIGHTS THEATRE
3951 Central Ave. NE, Columbia Heights
(763) 788-9079
www.heightstheater.com

Once a dilapidated theater, the Heights was transformed into one of the most beautiful theaters in the Twin Cities when the inside and outside were painted, comfortable new seats installed, and a vintage theater organ put in place. The organ allows silent film classics to be scored for the audience's pleasure.

Besides occasional silent film revivals, the Heights books second-run and classic films as well as special events such as Tromafest, a festival dedicated to the kitschy horror of Troma Studios For adventurous film lovers, the Heights is one of the most interesting movie theaters in the Twin Cities.

REGAL BROOKLYN CENTER STADIUM 20
6420 Camden Ave. North Minneapolis
(763) 560-6300
www.regalcinemas.com
The gigantic Brooklyn Center Stadium 20 theater megaplex offers stadium seating, high-back adjustable chairs, digital sound in all of its theaters, and, obviously, many film choices. Despite its size, Regal feels more comfortable due to its design, which includes larger individual theaters decorated with murals. The complex includes a cafe stocked with coffees and ice creams and a video arcade.

SHOWPLACE 16 THEATRES
5567 Bishop Ave., Inver Grove Heights
(651) 453-1916
www.kerasotes.com
One of the first mammoth megaplexes in the Twin Cities, Showplace 16 Theatres offers some of the largest movie screens in the area and comfortable stadium seating. Until the new Rosedale 14 was constructed, the Showplace 16 was the destination of exotic excursions into the suburbs undertaken by city slickers looking for stadium seating.

THEATRES AT MALL OF AMERICA
401 South Ave., Mall of America,
60 East Broadway, Bloomington
(952) 851-0074
Originally part of the AMC chain, the Mall of America theaters are now run independently and have recently been spiffed up—including the conver-

sion of one screen into a luxurious VIP theater with drinks (yes, alcoholic drinks) available. The theaters often host premieres and other events.

SPORTS BARS

Minneapolis

BIG TEN RESTAURANT & BAR
606 Washington Ave. SE, Minneapolis
(612) 378-0467

1106 Main St., Hopkins
(952) 930-0369

1045 Frontage Rd., Owatonna
(507) 451-2090
www.big10restaurant.com

The Big Ten Restaurant & Bar is a University of Minnesota institution, known both for good subs and for covering Minnesota Golden Gophers athletics. The Washington Avenue restaurant and bar is filled with memorabilia from Gophers sports; included are numerous autographed photos of triumphs in football, basketball, and hockey. For atmosphere alone, this is the place to catch a Gophers game, not to mention the beer and the excellent bar food.

DUBS PUB & GRILL
412 14th Ave. SE, Minneapolis
(612) 331-4111

Over the years this has been the site of numerous restaurants, bars, and grills. All have served as a principal watering hole for the student population of the University of Minnesota. Dubs is a popular place to watch Minnesota Golden Gophers basketball, football, and hockey games. The big-screen television and the cheap burgers and subs are also big draws.

WILLIAM'S UPTOWN PUB & PEANUT BAR
2911 Hennepin Ave. South, Minneapolis
(612) 823-6271

If you are looking for variety in domestic and imported beers, William's is the place. This Uptown establishment boasts more than 300 different bottled beers from around the world, including Russia, Thailand, Africa, Finland, and

Greece. An additional 70+ beers are on tap. William's offers plenty of daily specials on domestic beers and appetizers. William's is divided into a pub on the first floor and a more casual peanut bar in the basement. Things get raucous down there on weekend nights as the peanut shells pile up and the beers drain down—fights and make-out sessions often break out spontaneously, and sometimes it's hard to tell the difference.

St. Paul

BILLY'S ON GRAND
857 Grand Ave., St. Paul
(651) 292-1316
www.billysongrand.com

For the backward-baseball-cap crowd, Billy's is *the* bar on Grand. Billy's has, so to speak, it all: 29 TVs, bar food, cheap(ish) pitchers of Miller Lite, free popcorn, video trivia, and a patio for smoking. Its big booths can accommodate big groups of big people. If all that and a prime location isn't sufficient recommendation for you to patronize a bar, you'd best look elsewhere.

TIFFANY SPORTS LOUNGE
2051 Ford Pkwy., St. Paul
(651) 690-4747
www.tiffanysportslounge.com

The swank neon martini hanging out front may lead you to believe Tiff's (aka "Stiff's") is a retro lounge along the lines of the Monte Carlo or Mancini's, but no: It's a "sports lounge," which in this case means that the interior is so bland, the average hotel bar looks like Nye's by comparison. Still, it's what there is in Highland Village for serious drinking without the family-game-night atmosphere of the Chatterbox, and it's where clerks meet to trade bad-customer stories.

TOM REID'S HOCKEY CITY PUB
258 West Seventh St., St. Paul
(651) 292-9916

Hockey returned to Minnesota in 2000 at the Xcel Energy Center; in its wake, many new bars and restaurants have sprung up. And who better to open a pub than Tom Reid, a former NHL player with the

Minnesota North Stars (now the Dallas Stars) and current Minnesota Wild broadcaster? Not only does the pub broadcast the game on television screens, but it also hosts a radio pregame show on KFAN.

The Suburbs

BIFF'S SPORTS BAR & GRILL
7777 NE MN 65,
Spring Lake Park
(763) 784-9446
Biff's provides inexpensive pool, darts, food, and sports viewing for the northern suburbs. Televisions range in size from big to bigger screens at Biffs, where you can watch all your Vikings game-day action. There are more than 25 pool tables, where suburbanites play in organized pool leagues and enjoy the many beer specials.

BILLIARD STREET CAFÉ/TWO STOOGES BAR & GRILL
7178 University Ave. NE, Fridley
(763) 574-1399
www.billiardstreet.com
Since 1988 Billiard Street Café has served as a pool hall with a cafe and a proshop, and in 2005 it added the Two Stooges Bar & Grill. It is inconspicuously located in a strip mall; despite this, it is one of Minnesota's largest billiard clubs, with more than 40 pool tables. In-house nine-ball leagues make the Billiard Street Café busy, and it is sometimes difficult to reserve a table on weekday evenings, although they are usually available after a wait. The late night/early morning hours also provide ample opportunity for billiards.

JOE SENSER'S SPORTS GRILL & BAR
2350 Cleveland Ave., Roseville
(651) 631-1781

4217 American Blvd. West, Bloomington
(952) 835-1191

3010 Eagandale Place, Eagan
(651) 687-9333

16605 County Rd. 24, Plymouth
(763) 559-1990
www.sensers.com

Joe Senser's Sports Grill & Bar is a popular spot for Minnesota Vikings fans. All four locations feature big-screen, high-definition TVs encircling the bar, as well as numerous smaller monitors. Joe Senser, a former Minnesota Viking, is the local legend/owner and also participates in a Vikings postgame show, Vikings Unsensored (on sports radio station KFAN), after each game. In addition, Senser's features college football and basketball, as well as professional basketball, baseball, and hockey. Offering a wide selection of beers, Senser's also has plenty of food to accompany the suds.

PARK TAVERN
3401 Louisiana Ave., St. Louis Park
(952) 929-6810
www.parktavern.com
The Park Tavern is one of the Twin Cities' premier sports bars. Twin Citians come in hordes to watch sports on the big-screen televisions and enjoy the kitchen's excellent food. Many other sports bars treat the food as secondary, but the Park Tavern excels, with delicious burgers and sandwiches. Plus it has some of the best beer specials in town during Vikings games.

G. B. LEIGHTON'S PICKLE PARK
7820 University Ave. NE, Fridley
(763) 786-1515
www.gbleightonspicklepark.com
Pickle Park is the mammoth establishment owned by local roots-rocker G. B. Leighton, and Leighton knows how to give his unpretentious fans what they want in a bar. A huge guitar is mounted on the bar's ceiling, and the St. Paul Chamber Orchestra would comfortably fit on the stage. The portions? Also big. The menu makes a game attempt to convince you through theming (fried breaded onions are "guitar strings") that it's unique, but of course it's not: It's bar food, pure and simple. Rock on!

SHOPPING

Whatever "shopping trip" means to you, you're sure to find satisfaction shopping in the Twin Cities. There are tiny neighborhood shops, heady metropolitan areas, and suburban malls that carry everything from sports to celebrity memorabilia; specialty grocery complexes that sell novelty items and foods from around the world; and stores that carry everything you'd ever need to have a successful and beautiful wedding, professional social event, or child's themed birthday party. Here is a taste of what the Twin Cities have to offer the antiques buff.

ANTIQUES SHOPS

Minneapolis

CITY SALVAGE AND ANTIQUES
507 First Ave. NE, Minneapolis
(612) 627-9107
http://citysalvage.com
Mantels, archways, buffets, stained glass, and other high-end items salvaged from pre-1950s buildings fill this architectural-salvage store. The changing inventory has at times included Charlie the Tuna lamps, a full pub complete with booths, and church pews. Owner John Eckley has more than two decades' experience in architectural salvage.

St. Paul

MALL OF ST. PAUL
1817 Selby Ave., St. Paul
(651) 647-6163
www.mallofstpaul.com
A decade ago it looked like the Selby-Fairview area was set to explode into gentrified glory, with the several nearby antiques shops as its main attraction. That hasn't quite happened; except for the opening of the wildly popular Blue Door Pub, the intersection looks pretty much the same now as it did then. In the middle of things is this big two-story shop, where antiques of various vintages are sold on consignment. There are great finds to be had here, if you're willing to take your time and explore.

WESCOTT STATION ANTIQUES
226 West Seventh St., St. Paul
(651) 227-2469
Wescott Station Antiques is a family-run business offering seven rooms full of antique furniture, glassware, lamps, and more. Thousands of antiques and collectibles line the walls of this tightly packed store, making a visit here as much a treasure hunt as it is a shopping spree.

West

BATTLEFIELD MILITARY ANTIQUES
3915 West County Hwy. 93, St. Anthony
(952) 920-3820
www.battlefieldstore.com
Battlefield Military Antiques is absolutely packed with war memorabilia, including rows and rows of books, magazines, and unopened boxes of model soldiers, frontiersmen, warplanes, and boats. The books, new and used, cover every era of combat from Hadrian's Wall to Vietnam, in incredible levels of both technical and strategic detail. What catches the eye first, though, are the neatly racked and displayed antiques: a clothing store's worth of old uniforms, helmets worn by both good guys and bad guys, blue and green caps topping the shelves in perfect rows, ribbons, and medals. Collectors will also appreciate the selection of limited-edition G.I. Joes.

BOOKSTORES

Minneapolis

AMAZON BOOKSTORE COOPERATIVE
4755 Chicago Ave. South, Minneapolis
(612) 821-9630
www.truecolorsbookstore.com
Amazon opened in the late 1960s, making it the oldest independent feminist bookstore in the country. The bookstore in south Minneapolis stocks some 10,000 fiction and nonfiction titles as well as gifts, music, and art all by, for, and about women. The bookstore, which specializes in titles from small feminist presses, is a worker cooperative, and the friendly staff will steer you to titles of interest.

B. H. BIERMAIER'S BOOKS
809 Fourth St. SE, Minneapolis
(612) 378-0129
Bill Biermaier has been selling used books from his Minneapolis location for a quarter century and is proud of his success in locating hard-to-find copies of out-of-print or obscure books. Arts, literature, and children's books dominate the store's collection in sheer number, but Biermaier's is a good source for just about any genre of book, including rare and collectors' editions. With ceiling-high stacks and books spilling out into the aisles, this place practically begs you to browse for hours. Finding a specific book can become a daylong challenge, but if you need to get out in a hurry, Bill can find it for you awfully quick.

BIG BRAIN COMICS
1027 Washington Ave. South
Minneapolis
(612) 338-4390
www.bigbraincomics.com
This small, well-stocked comic book store focuses more on unusual and underground comic books and magazines than the superhero type that Marvel and DC put out. There are lots of imported comics in the stacks, as well as American independent and collectible comic books. The staff are friendly and enthusiastic, and look precisely the way you'd expect comic store employees to look.

BOOK HOUSE IN DINKYTOWN
429 14th Ave. SE, Minneapolis
(612) 331-1430
www.bookhouseindinkytown.com
The Book House has been a mainstay of the U of M's Dinkytown area for more than 30 years, carrying used hardcover and softcover books. With more than 150,000 volumes in stock, this store has bookshelves that run from floor to ceiling and has excellent fiction, drama, and poetry sections, not to mention rows and rows of foreign language material and an entire basement level dedicated to scholarly works. Book House buys tons of used books, so it's worth checking back regularly to see what's new in stock.

BIRCHBARK BOOKS
2115 West 21st St., Minneapolis
(612) 374-4023
www.birchbarkbooks.com
St. Paul has Garrison Keillor's Common Good Books, and Minneapolis has Birchbark, the shop owned by Louise Erdrich. Erdrich is a Native woman, and her store offers an array of books and crafts that particularly celebrate—you got it—Native women. Given that Erdrich is often called Minnesota's greatest living writer (sorry, Garrison), the shop is a must for bookworms both visiting and local.

BOOKSMART
2914 Hennepin Ave. South, Minneapolis
(612) 823-5612
BookSmart is the place to go to buy cheap used books, with a huge selection of mysteries and a great biography section. Turnover is quick, so if you see something you want in stock, you'd better buy it or someone else will.

CUMMINGS BOOKS
417 14th Ave. SE, Minneapolis
(612) 331-1424
www.cummingsbooks.com

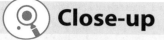 **Close-up**

Nicollet Mall

Nicollet Mall is downtown Minneapolis's main shopping artery. The 12-block stretch of stores, restaurants, and hotels between Washington Avenue and Grant Street hums year-round. This is a pedestrian mall—no cars allowed, although Metro buses can drive on the mall. It's all about people here.

In spring people, after being cooped up all winter, descend from their offices in the Minneapolis skyscrapers and exit the skyways to savor the season on Nicollet Mall. In summer they stroll along the mall, pick up dinner ingredients or flower bouquets at the bustling farmers' market, and eat on streetside patios. In winter it's true that a lot of the action stays indoors, but you can count on the **Holidazzle Parades** to draw people back out. On cold, snowy days, well-insulated spectators line Nicollet Mall up to an hour before the nightly twinkle-lit parades begin, which are held from just after Thanksgiving until Christmas. After each parade, the spectators turn into holiday shoppers flitting in and out of businesses along the parade's mall route.

There's a two-story **Target** here (the discount store's headquarters are on the mall, too) and name-brand stores await in the stretch's shopping centers: **Neiman Marcus, Macy's, Saks,** and lots of smaller stores you'd find in any major shopping center. There are a few independent stores here, too—though if that's what you're primarily seeking, you're better off walking a few blocks to the **Warehouse District,** where storefront rents are cheaper and independents thrive.

In the past few years, city promoters gave the mall a nickname: **Restaurant Row.** It's easy to see why. One of the coolest things about the mall is that the dining options run the gamut from fancy fusion to basic deli to Irish pub food. As soon as Nicollet crosses Grant Street, on its southwestern end, it changes from Restaurant Row to Eat Street, well established and known for its range of ethnic restaurants.

Activities, too, draw people to Nicollet Mall, and those go beyond the street performers and the biweekly farmers' market. **Peavey Plaza,** next to Orchestra Hall, has lots of free concerts throughout the summer and a Rockefeller Centeresque ice-skating rink in the winter. Macy's continued the traditions of its predecessor, Dayton's, Minnesota's old-school department store born on Nicollet Mall. These include a spectacular garden show every spring and a storybook holiday show each winter, both free, and both Twin Cities family traditions. Branch out just a block or two from the mall and you've got the clubs of the Warehouse District, the theaters of Hennepin Avenue, the events of Target Center, and more.

This is a used bookstore for book lovers. The variety of books includes literary criticism, special interest, and Canadian history. If you can't find what you're looking for, the friendly staff can help.

DREAMHAVEN BOOKS & COMICS
2301 East 38th St., Minneapolis
(612) 823-6161
www.dreamhavenbooks.com
DreamHaven is a dream destination for fans of comic books, Japanese anime, kung fu movies, and everything pop-cultural, from Dr. Who to

Asterix. After many years in a prominent Lake Street space, DreamHaven recently moved to a more intimate (and cheaper) storefront in the Powderhorn neighborhood.

MAGERS & QUINN
3038 Hennepin Ave., Minneapolis
(612) 822-4611
www.magersandquinn.com
A couple of decades ago, the Twin Cities were the envy of the country for their independent bookstore scene, with titans like the Hungry Mind and

Odegard Books stocking their shelves generously and intelligently, and bringing everyone who was anyone to read their work. That time is sadly past (the Hungry Mind and Odegard, among others, are now closed), but Magers & Quinn stands as the best reminder of what those days were like. The Twin Cities' biggest and best independent bookstore, Magers & Quinn is a hub of literary activity in the heart of the Uptown action. It sponsors more events and readings than any other store in town, and partners with bars and theaters to promote multiple public book clubs. Enjoy it while it lasts: The proprietors just had to lay off their full-time event planner (David Unowsky, former owner of the Hungry Mind), and recent history suggests that even the best independent bookstores can be surprisingly fragile.

MAGUS BOOKS & HERBS
1309 Fourth St. SE, Minneapolis
(612) 379-7669 or (800) 99-MAGUS
www.magusbooks.com
Magus Books sells new books on Wicca, magic, tarot, astrology, alchemy, Buddhism, Taoism, midwifery, UFOs, Bibles, and aphrodisiacs, to name a few subjects. The bookstore also sells herbs, candles, incense, scented oils, jewelry, and meditation and New Age tapes and CDs.

ONCE UPON A CRIME
604 West 26th St., Minneapolis
(612) 870-3785
www.onceuponacrimebooks.com
One of two independent bookstores in Minneapolis devoted to crime and mystery novels (Uncle Edgar's is the other), Once Upon a Crime is a true family business: Not only are its owners married, they were married *in the store*. The underground Uptown store is packed with books representing every corner of the criminal mind, and it hosts a constant parade of writers who read from their work, as well as a book club and other events.

PAPERBACK EXCHANGE
2227 West 50th St., Minneapolis
(612) 929-8801
www.paperbackexchange.com

Paperback Exchange carries more than 300,000 used paperback books covering pretty much any subject, from pulp mystery to criticism, depending on what's in their current, quick-turnover stock. You can get a better discount on your book purchase if you bring in paperback books to trade. The store also rents hardcover books for nominal charges, many of which are brand-new and not yet available at local libraries.

For (appropriately) unknown reasons, Minnesota is a hub of crime fiction. Besides being home to two bookstores devoted to crime and mystery, the state has produced more than its share of top authors in the crime/thriller genre. Among them are John Sandford, William Kent Krueger, Julie Kramer, and Ellen Hart, one of the country's top writers of gay mysteries.

PRESENT MOMENT BOOKS & HERBS
3546 Grand Ave. South, Minneapolis
(612) 824-3157
www.presentmoment.com
A major purveyor of herbs and homeopathic remedies, Present Moment also offers more than 36,000 new and used book titles. Whether your New Age and wellness needs run to *Cooking with Herbs* or *The Spirit of Place: A Workbook for Sacred Alignment*, you'll find it at Present Moment. Their specialties include books on alternative health, world religions, New Age, Wicca, and yoga, as well as women's studies and environmental issues.

UNCLE EDGAR'S MYSTERY BOOKSTORE/
UNCLE HUGO'S SCIENCE FICTION
BOOKSTORE
2864 Chicago Ave. South, Minneapolis
(612) 824-6347 or (612) 824-9984
www.unclehugo.com
Specialization is the name of the game for many independent booksellers in these days of giant chain bookstores, but Uncle Edgar's/Uncle Hugo's was at it long before the trend began in the late 1980s. Uncle Hugo's opened in 1974, and Uncle Edgar's opened in 1980. The two shops

merged into one location in south Minneapolis in 1984. With a huge selection of their respective genres, both new and used, they sponsor many author readings every month. Check the Web site for information about upcoming events.

St. Paul

COMMON GOOD BOOKS
165 Western Ave. North, St. Paul
(651) 225-8989
www.commongoodbooks.com
Garrison Keillor has done a lot for Minnesota, and the love the public radio icon has for St. Paul is evident at his bookstore, Common Good Books, in the city's Cathedral Hill neighborhood. Until the late 1990s and early 2000s, St. Paul was home to such legendary bookstores as the Hungry Mind (later known as Ruminator Books) and Odegard's, but such independents closed their doors one by one. Keillor, a prolific author as well as host of radio's *Prairie Home Companion*, opened Common Good Books in November 2006. The 2,200-square-foot store is in the cellar beneath Nina's Coffee Cafe and has plenty of choices, whether you are in the mood for "classic American literature or quality trash," as the store says. Local authors are given emphasis, but the store has all the big-name authors as well. Common Good Books is a delightful bookstore, ideal for leisurely browsing.

MIDWAY USED & RARE BOOKS
1579 University Ave. West, St. Paul
(651) 644–7605
www.midwaybook.com
Midway Books has three stories of used and rare books, including huge pulp fiction and small-press poetry sections. The Web site offers some of the store's stock online, but far more titles are available in their store in St. Paul's Midway neighborhood. In addition to books, the store has a wide selection of vintage comics and magazines.

PLAY BY PLAY BOOKS
(651) 330-2219
www.playbyplaybooks.com
The Twin Cities' newest independent bookstore is devoted to the topic of theater, and it's been warmly received by the large local theater community. Unfortunately, it's without a home as this guide goes to press: After only two months of selling books and hosting events, its building was sold and the nascent enterprise was unceremoniously booted from its new space. Owner Kelly Schaub promises to reopen, though, in a bigger and better space—watch the store's Web site for details.

THE RED BALLOON BOOKSHOP
891 Grand Ave., St. Paul
(651) 224-8320
www.redballoonbookshop.com
This spacious bookstore, specializing in educational and fun books for kids, is located in a beautiful converted Victorian house on St. Paul's Grand Avenue. The store carries books, audiobooks, DVDs, and selected toys for young people from birth to junior high age. The bookstore offers nonprofit discounts, takes mail and phone orders, and hosts in-store events featuring children's book authors and educators.

SIXTH CHAMBER USED BOOKS
1332 Grand Ave., St. Paul
(651) 690-9463
www.sixthchamber.com
Sixth Chamber Used Books is a well-organized and spacious used book store featuring hardcover and paperback editions in most major categories. Especially notable is the used science fiction and fantasy section, which takes up several ceiling-to-floor shelves in the back of the store.

CLOTHING STORES

Minneapolis

HUBERT WHITE
747 Nicollet Mall, IDS Crystal Court,
Minneapolis
(612) 339-9200 or (800) 776-3920
www.hubertwhite.com
Hubert White carries brand-name, high-end men's contemporary, casual, and formal wear, including Gran Sasso, Bobby Jones, Scott Barber, Canali, Oxxford, Tallia, and Burberry. The professional staff is helpful in both assisting with selecting purchases and arranging alterations at the last minute.

LAVA LOUNGE
3037 Lyndale Ave. South, Minneapolis
(612) 824-5631
www.lavalounge.com
Lava Lounge's inventory makes it a one-stop shop for club clothes. Beyond the staples—shiny, leathered, glittery, synthetic clothes—it also carries an impressive array of cuffs, handbags, and eyewear, with brand names like Miss Sixty, Betty Blush, and Merc stocked for all seasons. Lava Lounge's annual patio sale occurs during the Lyn-Lake Festival in August, when prices on the store's wares are significantly dropped.

NATE'S CLOTHING COMPANY
27 North Fourth St., Minneapolis
(612) 333-1401
A fixture in the Minneapolis Warehouse District since 1916, Nate's carries a staggering collection of worsted wool, nubby tweed, and linen suits and shirts. The store carries suits and sportcoats from designers like Bill Blass and Ralph Lauren, and Nate's expert staff can find something sharp and classy for even hard-to-size guys. The store's sales are legendary, so sign up for Nate's mailings for the inside scoop on sale dates.

TOP SHELF CLOTHIERS & CONSULTANTS
3040 Lyndale Ave. South, Minneapolis
(612) 824-2800
www.topshelfinc.com

Located inside a turn-of-the-20th-century former home, Top Shelf is divided into many small, friendly rooms that are perfect for the personalized business of creating custom clothing. A formal dining room now acts as the library for a collection of the finest offerings of suit, sportcoat, pant, and topcoat materials from the woolen mills of England, Italy, Spain, and the United States. Well-known fabric lines such as Zegna, Loro Piana, Roger La Viale, Scabal, Reda, Barberis, Cerruti, Holland, Sherry, and many others are available for custom designs, including shirts.

VSTATE CLOTHING
3001 Hennepin Ave., Minneapolis
(612) 823-4699
www.vstateclothing.com
VState, a Calhoun Square fixture about to open a larger space in the wake of the mall's renovation, caters to men and women looking to be outfitted at the affordable but still trendy end of the boutique-clothing spectrum. The store offers several sales and special events each year; become a Facebook fan to receive invitations.

St. Paul

C'EST FOU SHOWROOM
1128 Grand Ave., St. Paul
(651) 602-9133
This French boutique–style retail store carries one-of-a-kind and custom-made clothes as well as elegant shoes and eclectic and glamorous jewelry and accessories. The store offers free alterations on all clothes purchased here, with an emphasis on creating a flattering fit for customers. The store displays and sells a rotating stock of artwork and jewelry created by local artists.

COAT OF MANY COLORS
1666 Grand Ave., St. Paul
(651) 690-5255
This Grand Avenue store specializes in natural fabric women's clothing in a wide range of sizes, as well as jewelry and gifts from around the world. Most of the jewelry is handmade, focusing on sterling silver set with semiprecious stones,

bone, seeds, and metals. Coat of Many Colors is a socially and environmentally conscious store that returns 20 percent of its profits to Third World development projects.

GRAND JETE
975 Grand Ave., St. Paul
(651) 227-0331
www.grandjete.com

Grand Jete is a retail store carrying dancewear for children and adults, including dance tights, leotards, and skirts, and ballet, pointe, tap, and jazz shoes in a full range of sizes. The store staff is especially helpful in assisting customers in the selection and proper fit of pointe shoes.

West

WHYMSY
3360 Galleria, Edina
(952) 924-4176

Whymsy is a retailer of creative attire and accessories for women, including distinctive one-of-a-kind and limited-edition items. The store is full of brand-name lines of upscale, coordinated women's clothing and accessories, with a focus on elegant casual and special occasion attire for the nontraditional woman.

FARMERS' MARKETS

ALDRICH ARENA FARMERS' MARKET
1850 White Bear Ave., Maplewood
(651) 227-8101
www.stpaulfarmersmarket.com
8 a.m. to noon Wed, May through Nov.

AT THE FARM
8880 East MN 5, Waconia
(952) 442-4816
www.atthefarmwaconia.com
10 a.m. to 4:30 p.m. daily, Memorial Day through Halloween.

AXDAHL'S GARDEN FARM/GREENHOUSE
7452 Manning Ave., Stillwater
(651) 439-2460
www.axdahlfarms.com

Call for hours. Open mid-April to Oct and during the Christmas season.

BROOKLYN PARK FARMERS' MARKET
5200 85th Ave., Brooklyn Park
(763) 493-8154
www.brooklynpark.org
Hours are 3 to 7 p.m. Wed, late June to mid-Oct.

BURNSVILLE FARMERS' MARKET
Diamondhead Senior Campus, 200 West Burnsville Pkwy., Burnsville (Saturday)
Mary, Mother of the Church,
(952) 227–8101
www.stpaulfarmersmarket.com
Hours are 7 a.m. to noon Sat (June to Oct).

CAL'S MARKET AND GARDEN CENTER
6403 Egan Dr., Savage
(952) 447-5215
www.calsmarketandgardencenter.com
Hours are noon to 6 p.m. Tues through Fri, 10 a.m. to 4 p.m. Sat, year-round.

CITY OF WHITE BEAR LAKE FARMERS' MARKET
Downtown White Bear Lake
(651) 429-8526
8 a.m. to noon Fri, late June to late Oct.

EXCELSIOR FARMERS' MARKET
Downtown Excelsior
(952) 474-5330
2 to 6 p.m. Thurs, May to Oct.

FALCON HEIGHTS FARMERS' MARKET
2025 Larpenteur Ave., Falcon Heights
(651) 227-8101
www.stpaulfarmer`smarket.com
8 a.m. to 12:30 p.m., Tues, May to Oct.

HMONGTOWN MARKETPLACE
217 Como Ave., St. Paul
(651) 487-3700
8 a.m. to 8 p.m. every day, year-round.

HOPKINS FARMERS' MARKET
16 Ninth Ave. South, Hopkins
(763) 557-1335
www.hopkinsmn.com
7:30 a.m. to noon Sat, mid-June to Oct.

JORDAN RANCH
6400 Upper Afton Rd., Woodbury
(651) 738-3422
Call for hours.

MARKETFEST
4701 MN 61, White Bear Lake
(651) 429-8537
www.marketfest.org
6 to 9 p.m. Thurs, mid-June to the end of July.

MILL CITY FARMERS' MARKET
702 Second St. South, Minneapolis
(612) 341-7580
www.millcityfarmersmarket.org
8 a.m. to 1 p.m. Sat, mid-May to mid-Oct.

MINNEAPOLIS FARMERS' MARKET
312 Lyndale Ave. North, Minneapolis
(612) 333-1737
www.mplsfarmersmarket.com
Hours vary by season.

MINNEAPOLIS FARMERS' MARKET ON NICOLLET MALL
Nicollet Mall between 5th and 12th St., Minneapolis
(612) 333-1737
www.mplsfarmersmarket.com
6 a.m. to 6 p.m. Thurs, May through Nov.

PAHL'S MARKET
6885 West 160th St., Apple Valley
(952) 431-4345
www.pahls.com
9 a.m. to 5 p.m. Mon through Fri, year-round.

PETERSON PRODUCE
8910 MN 12, Delano
(763) 972-2052
http://goodnessgrowspetersonproduce.com
9 a.m. to 7 p.m. daily, May to Oct.

RICHFIELD FARMERS' MARKET
6335 Portland Ave. South, Richfield
(612) 861-9385
www.richfieldfarmersmarket.org
7 a.m. to noon Sat, May to Oct.

ST. THOMAS FARMERS' MARKET
1079 Summit Ave., St. Paul
(651) 227-8101
www.stpaulfarmersmarket.com
1:15 to 5 p.m. Fri, May to Oct.

SEVENTH PLACE MALL FARMERS' MARKET
Seventh and Wabasha Streets, St. Paul
(651) 227-8101
www.stpaulfarmersmarket.com
10 a.m. to 1:30 p.m. Tues and Thurs, mid-June to mid-Oct.

i Farmers' markets and roadside produce spring up just about everywhere during summer and early fall. Check for official summer opening dates and business hours, as they're subject to change and dependent on growing seasons.

ST. PAUL DOWNTOWN FARMERS' MARKET
Fifth and Wall Streets, St. Paul
(651) 227-8101
www.stpaulfarmersmarket.com
6 a.m. to 1 p.m. Sat, 8 a.m. to 1 p.m. Sun, April to Nov (call for winter hours).

WOODBURY FARMERS' MARKET
Central Park/YMCA lot on Radio Dr. Woodbury
(651) 227-8101
www.stpaulfarmersmarket.com
8 a.m. to 1 p.m. Sun, June to Oct.

FLOWER AND GARDEN SHOPS

Minneapolis

BROWN & GREENE
4400 Beard Ave. South, Minneapolis
(612) 928-3778
www.bgfloral.net

Brown & Greene floral designer Lyn Williams has been creating beautiful, nontraditional arrangements from her historic neighborhood store since 1989. Her designs are centered around customers' color choices and feature unusual flower combinations, like gerberas and black calla lilies with roses and other more conventional flowers.

INDULGE & BLOOM
651 Nicollet Mall, Gaviidae Common
Minneapolis
(612) 343-0000 (option 1)

3054 Excelsior Blvd., Minneapolis
(612) 343-0000 (option 2)

2315 18th Ave. NE, Minneapolis
(612) 343-0000 (option 3)
www.indulgeandbloom.com

Indulge & Bloom carries beautiful, unusual flowers and plants from all over the world, including Ecuadorian roses, orchids, and topiaries. Wedding arrangements are their specialty. The store also features home-decor items, Waterford crystal, bath-and-body products, garden-related items, ornaments, books, cards, truffles, and children's gifts.

ROGER BECK FLORIST
1100 East Franklin Ave., Minneapolis
(612) 871-7080
www.rogerbeckflorist.com

Roger Beck does brisk business creating floral arrangements for events, but he also maintains a big, well-stocked retail showroom at Franklin and 11th, complete with a walk-in cooler where you can lose yourself among the big blossoms. The shop carries an assortment of gifts and personal care items (soaps, lotions, etc.) as well.

St. Paul
LAUREL STREET FLOWERS
488 Hamline Ave. South, St. Paul
(651) 221-9700
www.laurelstreetflowers.com

This shop's guiding style leans to English and French provincial, and typical arrangements include fresh blooms such as tulips and lilies of the valley in spring and summer to boutonnieres

shaped as miniature Christmas wreaths for winter weddings. Owner and designer Paula Flom uses a European hand-tie method in her bouquets instead of plastic holders, and her creations often include such unusual choices as mixed fruits in dark colors dripping from centerpieces and viney garlands hanging from chandeliers.

MARTHA'S GARDENS
2484 University Ave. West, St. Paul
(651) 696-2993
www.marthasfloralstudio.com

Those topiaries and whimsical banners flying along an otherwise plain block of University Avenue mark the charming studio of Martha Gabler Lunde, one of the Twin Cities' top specialty florists. The studio doesn't have regular public hours—most of Lunde's business is by delivery—so call ahead to ensure that someone will be there when you arrive, but a visit to the studio is the best way to appreciate Lunde's special style. The studio hosts performances of live music and other public events throughout the year; subscribe to the studio e-mail list to get the heads-up.

STEMS & VINES
917 Grand Ave., St. Paul
(651) 228-1450

401 Robert St. North, St. Paul
(651) 224-9641

386 West Bernard St., West St. Paul
(651) 451-9539
www.stemsandvines.com

Stems & Vines designs flower bouquets and events around personalities instead of colors and styles. The store's designers are booked well in advance; it's recommended that reservations be made no later than nine months prior to your event date. Stems & Vines is a sponsor of the Twin Cities Bridal Association and holds exhibitions at every bridal and floral event in town.

GROCERY CO-OPS

The Twin Cities feature one of the highest concentrations of independent food cooperatives in the United States, with stores throughout the Cities and in the suburbs.

Co-ops are member (customer) owned and governed, and most specialize in natural, local, and organic foods; environmentally sensitive products; sustainable goods; and bulk whole foods. Some offer membership, which entitles shoppers to discounted prices and a role in the governance of the co-op, and some require members to volunteer a certain number of hours monthly to keep the co-op running.

Minneapolis

EASTSIDE FOOD CO-OP
2551 Central Ave., Minneapolis
(612) 788-0950
www.eastsidefood.coop

LINDEN HILLS CO-OP
2813 West 43rd St., Minneapolis
(612) 922-1159
www.lindenhills.coop

SEWARD CO-OP GROCERY & DELI
2823 East Franklin Ave., Minneapolis
(612) 338-2465
www.seward.coop

THE WEDGE
2105 Lyndale Ave. South, Minneapolis
(612) 871-3993
www.wedge.coop

St. Paul

MISSISSIPPI MARKET NATURAL FOODS CO-OP
1500 West Seventh St., St. Paul
(651) 690-0507

622 Selby Ave., St. Paul
(651) 310-9499
www.msmarket.coop

South

VALLEY NATURAL FOODS
13750 County Rd. 11, Burnsville
(952) 891-1212
www.valleynaturalfoods.com

East

RIVER MARKET COMMUNITY CO-OP
221 North Main St., Stillwater
(651) 439-0366
www.rivermarket.coop

West

LAKEWINDS NATURAL FOODS
17501 Minnetonka Blvd., Minnetonka
(952) 473-0292

1917 Second Ave. South, Anoka
(763) 427-4340

435 Pond Promenade, Chanhassen
(952) 697-3366
www.lakewinds.coop

HOMEBREWING AND WINEMAKING SUPPLIES

St. Paul

NORTHERN BREWER
1150 Grand Ave., St. Paul
(651) 291-8849
www.northernbrewer.com
Northern Brewer is the place to go to get everything you need to brew your own beer. All of the equipment you need is here, including carboys, bottling buckets, thermometers, brew kettles and fermentation locks. You can buy things individually or get everything you need in a starter kit. As for the beer ingredient kits, the St. Paul Porter, German Alt, and India Pale Ale are particularly notable. The store also carries many specialty kits, such as Dark Cherry Stout and Peach Wheat, as well as traditional American lagers. If you know what you're doing already, you can buy individual ingredients—including hops, malt extracts, grain malts, and yeast—to craft your own unique brew. Northern Brewer is open daily.

West

MIDWEST HOMEBREWING AND WINEMAKING SUPPLIES

3440 Beltline Blvd., St. Louis Park
(952) 925-9835 or (888) 449-2739
www.midwestsupplies.com

Midwest Homebrewing and Winemaking Supplies can get you started making your own beer, but the store also carries everything you need to make your own wine. The store features several "clone" kits designed to make beer that tastes like high-quality commercial brands, including local favorite Summit Pale Ale, as well as Foster's Lager, Watney's Cream Stout, and Redhook ESB. If your tastes lean more toward reds and whites, Midwest has various winemaking equipment kits, as well as wine kits for many popular varieties, including Cabernet Sauvignon, Merlot, Pinot Grigio, and Chardonnay. You can also buy ingredients to make fruit wines, ranging from apple to plum. Midwest is open daily.

MUSIC STORES

CHEAPO DISCS

170 89th Ave. NE, Blaine
(763) 574-2308

80 Snelling Ave. North, St. Paul
(651) 644-8981

1300 West Lake St., Minneapolis
(612) 827-8238
www.cheapodiscs.com

Cheapo is the Twin Cities' largest seller of new and used CDs. The first store opened decades ago as Cheapo Records but eventually was forced to be a little less choosy regarding format. After much shuffling of inventory, Cheapo's vinyl stock settled in the basement of the Minneapolis store and in a satellite location across the street from the St. Paul location. Cheapo stocks a large selection of local music; while it can't compete with the Electric Fetus for pure cachet, its generous stock and smart selection make it a popular destination.

ELECTRIC FETUS

2000 Fourth Ave. South, Minneapolis
(612) 870-9300
www.efetus.com

The Electric Fetus is the holy land for the Twin Cities' biggest music buffs; some of the biggest names in local music were employed at this big store on I-35W while they paid their dues. Not only does the Fetus have an excellent selection, they frequently host free in-store performances by some of the hottest national acts to pass through town; follow efetusmpls on Twitter for updates on these shows. The store stocks a groovy array of clothes and gift items, and it's a painless spot to grab tickets to shows at First Avenue and its associated venues without paying the onerous Ticketmaster fees. You'll smell like incense for a week after visiting the Fetus, but it's totally worth it.

EXTREME NOISE RECORDS

407 West Lake St., Minneapolis
(612) 824-0100
www.extremenoise.com

Extreme Noise Records is a co-op specializing in punk rock records and CDs. The store sells its merchandise at lower prices because of the all-volunteer staff and offers many punk titles not available at other Twin Cities music stores. Whether you are looking for classic Buzz-cocks, the Ramones, the Germs, or GG Allin, or more recent punk stars such as local boys Dillinger 4, Extreme Noise usually will have it. Punk records and CDs are available from throughout the world. The store also features zines, books, and videos about the punk rock lifestyle.

FIFTH ELEMENT

2411 Hennepin Ave., Minneapolis
(612) 377-0044
www.fifthelementonline.com

Fifth Element is home base for Rhymesayers, a top national hip-hop label whose roster is especially strong in Twin Cities artists: Atmosphere, Brother Ali, Eyedea & Abilities, P.O.S., I Self Devine, Toki Wright. Fifth Element is a record store, a merchandise mart, a performing space, and an all-around hangout for Rhymesayers artists and their fans; hip-hop records from other labels are for sale as well.

LANDFILL BOOKS & MUSIC
1222 University Ave. West, St. Paul
(612) 644-8612

With vinyl making a comeback, the high end of the market is bursting with heavy high-fidelity platters; Landfill represents for the low end, selling buck-a-pop LPs by artists (say, Jermaine Jackson) whose cult followings have yet to find them. If you're a music fan on a budget—or if you're really serious about looking for that "warm" sound you can only get from a genuinely beat-up record—Landfill is your go-to spot.

LANDSPEED/ROADRUNNER RECORDS
4304 Nicollet Ave. South, Minneapolis
(612) 822-0613
www.landspeedrecords.com

Landspeed/Roadrunner Records specializes in new and used vinyl records in all genres of music, including hard-to-find titles. The largest selection can be found in the rock area; however, the store also features jazz, punk, and world music. The store also stocks a limited number of new and used CDs, particularly strong in world music.

TREEHOUSE RECORDS
2557 South Lyndale Ave., Minneapolis
(612) 872-7400
http://treehouserecords.blogspot.com

Treehouse advertises itself as "the last record store on earth." While the rest of this section demonstrates that's not quite true (yet), the slogan says something about owner Mark Trehus's commitment to the old-school record store values of community, diversity, and funkiness. As Oar Folkjokeopus, the store was one of the hot spots of the punk-pop era that produced the Replacements and Hüsker Dü; today it remains a favorite spot for music fans looking for hard-rocking hard copies.

ODDS 'N' ENDS

Minneapolis

COLECCIÓN Y ELEGANCIA
1515 East Lake St.,
Mercado Central, Minneapolis
(612) 728-5416

Colección y Elegancia, a small store tucked into Mercado Central, carries beautiful music boxes, snow globes, porcelain figurines, and other objets d'art. The prices are reasonable for the quality of work, and inventory moves quickly.

GOLDEN LEAF, LTD.
3032 Hennepin Ave. South, Minneapolis
(612) 824-1867

Golden Leaf carries premium cigars from the leading companies in the industry. The walk-in humidor contains more than 250 brands of the freshest and best-priced cigars in Minnesota. Other products for sale include accessories, humidors, pipes, tobacco, newspapers, lighters, and other smoking accessories. The former Calhoun Square store is now located across Hennepin Avenue from the mall.

INGEBRETSEN SCANDINAVIAN GIFTS & FOODS
1601 East Lake St., Minneapolis
(612) 729-9333
www.ingebretsens.com

Ingebretsen carries Norwegian pewter, Scandinavian crystal (Hadeland, iittala, Nybro), dinnerware from Porsgrund, candles and holders, housewares, linens, Norwegian sweaters, wood carvings, and rosemaling and other folk art. The jewelry case holds beautiful pieces wrought in silver, pewter, bronze, leather, porcelain, enamel, and wood. At the needlework shop next door, you can find fabrics, kits, books, and supplies for Danish counted cross-stitch, Hardanger embroidery, Norwegian Klostersøm needlepoint, lace making, and Norwegian knitting. The select food section includes such Scandinavian delights as lutefisk and lefse, Swedish meatballs and sausage, herring, cheeses, lingonberries, chocolate, and flatbread.

KITCHEN WINDOW

3001 Hennepin Ave. South, Calhoun Square, Minneapolis

(612) 824-4417 or (888) 824-4417

www.kitchenwindow.com

Kitchen Window is filled with such brands as All Clad, Calphalon, and Le Creuset cookware; Wusthof Trident, Chef's Choice, and Lamson cutlery; Rosle kitchen tools; and Cuisinart, Kitchen Aid, Krups, and Panasonic small appliances. Kitchen Window features espresso machines and coffeemakers, teamakers, mugs, carafes, and press pots. It also carries items for ethnic cooking that range from lefse griddles and krumkake irons to pasta makers, tortilla presses, sushi mats, and gadgets of all kinds. Kitchen Window also holds cooking classes in its swank test kitchen.

i Bibelot means "small decorative object," and you'll discover a lot of these at eclectic Bibelot stores found all around the Twin Cities. This is a good place to purchase a last-minute gift for just about anyone. Check www.bibelotshops.com for the Bibelot closest to you.

PATINA

2057 Ford Pkwy., St. Paul

(651) 695-9955

Five other locations across the Twin Cities.

www.patinastores.com

Patina offers stylish and relatively inexpensive gift options—many under $25. This is the type of place where you can find a present in nearly any price range for nearly anyone—and lose track of time doing so. There's lots to look at: contemporary photo frames, bed-tent tops for kids, trendy jewelry, designer stationary, leather passport cases, trout staplers, Band-Aids that look like bacon, and a cheeseboard shaped like France.

TWIN CITIES GREEN

2405 Hennepin Ave. South, Minneapolis

(612) 374-4581

www.twincitiesgreen.com

Twin Cities Green is an eco-friendly boutique, most notable for its products made from creatively reused items like license plates (lampshades), bike tires (wallets), and paperback book covers (postcards). As headquarters for Do It Green! Twin Cities, the store also houses an information resource and environmental action center.

St. Paul

AX MAN SURPLUS

1639 University Ave. West, St. Paul

(651) 646-8653

1021 East Moore Lake Dr., Fridley

(763) 572-3730

8100 Minnetonka Blvd., St. Louis Park

(952) 935-2210

6600 Bass Lake Rd., Crystal

(763) 536-7786

www.ax-man.com

Ax Man has everything you want that you never thought you wanted at more than reasonable prices, including iron lungs, ancient airplane models, antiquated TI-80 computer keyboards, beads, buttons, Pogs, snail shells, seashells, remote control wiring, police tape, public address horns, maps, huge bags of shredded money, rock videos, test tubes, copper cable, bar magnets, refrigerator magnets, transformers, all sizes of electrical motors, music box innards, marbles, bicycle tires, and doll heads. The stock is constantly changing, and some truly strange things wind up for sale, including school bus fenders and fake cheese.

THE BEAD MONKEY

867 Grand Ave., Victoria Crossing Mall, St. Paul

(651) 222-7729

3717 West 50th St., Minneapolis

(952) 929-4032

www.thebeadmonkey.com

With two Twin Cities locations, the Bead Monkey is the place to go to buy pipes of inexpensive glass beads, charms, jewelry-making supplies, beading needles and wire, and semiprecious stones. If you are interested in beading but aren't sure how to go about a project, the knowledgeable staff can either help you on the spot or refer you to one of the many beading classes for all ages.

COOKS OF CROCUS HILL
877 Grand Ave., St. Paul
(651) 228-1333
www.cooksofcrocushill.com
The gold standard for Twin Cities cooking stores, Cooks is full of top-quality kitchen accessories from pans to pulverizers. Even the most experienced cook is apt to find something new at Cooks, and both amateur and experienced cooks can improve their skills at the popular classes held in the kitchen upstairs from the retail shop. None of this product, or knowledge, comes cheap . . . but it does last.

GARDEN OF EDEN
867 Grand Ave., St. Paul
(651) 293-1300
www.gardenofedenstores.com
This luxury bath shop carries soaps, oils, perfumes, bath candles, and aromatherapy items. Soaps include handmade bars of glycerin with ribbons of flowers and herbs in them to novelty bars with "Satan Be Gone" emblazoned across the package. While most of the items here are aimed at women, the shop also carries aftershave and other men's products.

IRISH ON GRAND
1124 Grand Ave., St. Paul
(651) 222-5151 or (888) IRISH-55
www.irishongrand.com
Irish on Grand caters to St. Paul's many Irishmen and -women who want their ethnic heritage reflected in all their consumer goods: clothing, music, books, food, teas, crystal, china, artwork, and more. The store carries beautiful Irish-made woolen capes and throws, sweaters, mittens, scarves, and hats, as well as fine silver and gold jewelry.

LEGACY ART & GIFTS
1209 Grand Ave., St. Paul
(651) 221-9094

Legacy Art & Gifts carries items created by local artists showcased in a fabulous converted Victorian house. The shop features pottery, etchings, handblown glass, watercolors, textiles, wood boxes, one-of-a-kind jewelry, and more.

ST. PATRICK'S GUILD
1554 Randolph Ave., St. Paul
(651) 652-9767 or (800) 652-9767
www.stpatricksguild.com
St. Patrick's Guild, established in 1949, is a huge Catholic-themed store that carries religious books, rosaries, medallions dedicated to different saints, holy water bottles, religious figurines, children's Bibles, and concrete garden statues. (It's also a good place to pick up a last-minute priest costume for Halloween—but don't tell them we sent you.)

STOGIES ON GRAND
961 Grand Ave., St. Paul
(651) 222-8700
www.stogiesongrand.com
Stogies on Grand is a premier tobacconist that also offers a comfortable smoking lounge, complete with big-screen TV, newspapers, and board games, for those who want to immediately try out the cigars and tobacco they just purchased. Stogies carries more than 300 premium cigars in their large walk-in humidor and a wide selection of pipes, tobacco, humidors, lighters, cutters, and other tobacco-related accessories.

TEN THOUSAND VILLAGES
867 Grand Ave., St. Paul
(651) 225-1043
www.tenthousandvillages.com
Ten Thousand Villages, located in Victoria Crossing West shopping mall, is a nonprofit shop featuring handcrafted jewelry, gifts, clothing, and home furnishings from around the world, with many pieces contributed by artists in developing nations. The profits from purchases made at Ten Thousand Villages go directly back to the artists of these nations in an effort to provide them with a fair living income for their work.

TWIN CITIES MAGIC & COSTUME
250 East Seventh St., St. Paul
(651) 227-7888
www.twincitiesmagic.com
There is really no place like Twin Cities Magic & Costume. The store has just about everything you need to embark on your career as a magician or for those days you need to be disguised as a gorilla, Little Bo Peep, or Dracula. Costumes, theatrical supplies, and special effects equipment are for sale and rent, including fog machines, strobe lights, explosive paper and powders, wigs, hats, boas, fake mustaches and teeth, tiaras, and more.

West

AMPERSAND
3445 Galleria, Edina
(952) 920-2118
www.ampersandstores.com
Ampersand carries everything you might possibly need for a party, whether it be a very formal affair or a casual lawn party. Ampersand has boxed invitations for every event under the sun, including birthdays, weddings, showers, anniversaries, barbecues, and cocktail parties, as well as silver olive forks, Italian pottery, designer cork tops, hand-painted dishware, flatware, elegant crystal punchbowls, and a huge selection of candles.

GABBERTS FURNITURE & DESIGN STUDIO
3501 Galleria, Edina
(952) 927-1500
www.gabberts.com
Gabberts has earned acclaim for its fine home furnishings that suit every lifestyle and span the spectrum of design from traditional to casual to contemporary. Tell a Twin Citian (especially one over the age of 50) that your leather chair came from Gabberts, and watch their eyes grow wide with admiration. The stock changes with the seasons and times and is always amazing— hand-painted desks, tables, and chairs with farm motifs or ocean scenes, or primary-color furniture that looks like adult versions of a kid's playset. Gabberts also carries lush, soft leather couches, beautiful lamps, chandeliers, and pretty much

anything else you need to make your home glow with luxury.

GENERAL STORE OF MINNETONKA
14401 Hwy. 7, Minnetonka
(952) 935-7131
www.generalstoreofminnetonka.com
With more than 20,000 square feet of retail space and an inventory that ranges from a Me-ow Me-ow Cat Bowl to a Loon Whirly-Gig, you're bound to find something you just have to have or the perfect gift at the General Store of Minnetonka. Items tailored to men, women, children, and even pets crowd the huge floor space, with particular attention paid to the whimsical and the downright weird. The store also has the General Store Cafe, with a menu that changes daily but includes salads, deli sandwiches, homemade soups, and desserts such as chocolate chip cookies and bread pudding.

QUE SERA
3580 Galleria, Edina
(952) 924-6390
This eclectic store, identified in front by a detailed chipped-tile mosaic, carries vintage-inspired home furnishings, lighting, beautiful costume jewelry, and knickknacks of all sorts. Que Sera offers custom upholstery and slipcovered sofas and chairs incorporating vintage fabrics, hand-painted furniture, custom iron and wood beds, custom bedding, hand-blown glass chandeliers, table lamps, candles, mirrors, frames, and more.

SPECIALTY GROCERS

Minneapolis

HOLY LAND BAKERY, GROCERY AND DELI
2513 Central Ave. NE, Minneapolis
(612) 781-2627

920 East Lake St., Midtown Global Market, Minneapolis
(612) 870-6104
www.holylandbrand.com
This Mediterranean deli and grocery store sells everything you need to make your own lamb kebabs, hummus, spinach pie, and falafel,

although chances are you probably won't be able to make them quite as well as the Holy Land deli counter does. The store stocks items such as pita (made fresh in the bakery every day), meats, gigantic bags of basmati rice, roasted and dried chickpeas, at least six types of feta cheese, black and green olives, specialty coffees, and a wide selection of Middle Eastern cookies, candies, and specialty chocolates.

MIDTOWN GLOBAL MARKET
920 East Lake St., Minneapolis
(612) 872-4041
www.midtownglobalmarket.com
Opened in 2006 in an attempt to give Minneapolis a multiethnic urban market like Pike Place in Seattle or Quincy Market in Boston, the Midtown Global Market is a colorful and tasty collection of Hispanic, Arabic, Hmong, African American, Scandinavian, and Tibetan, among others, markets, shops, and casual eateries in the heart of south Minneapolis. There is no other place in the Twin Cities where you can eat jerk chicken, buy hand-sewn Hmong wall hangings, and learn to salsa in quick succession. The marketplace is also a particularly good spot to find unusual gifts (tree-trunk sculpture and stretchy, frilly, tubetop-like shirts, for example) and to shop for spices and foods from Latin America, the Middle East, Southeast Asia, and elsewhere.

SHUANG HUR ORIENTAL MARKET
2710 Nicollet Ave. South, Minneapolis
(612) 872-8606

654 University Ave. West, St. Paul
(651) 253-0456
Shuang Hur carries thousands of products from China, Taiwan, and Thailand. The full-service grocery store has a large fresh-produce section with melons, bean sprouts, and crates of aged duck eggs; freezers full of egg roll and spring roll wraps and desserts; and a Chinese BBQ deli that carries whole roasted pigs and BBQ duck and chicken meat. In the dry goods sections are rows and rows of dried mushrooms, noodles, soups, spices, rice, and shrimp crackers.

SURDYK'S
303 East Hennepin Ave., Minneapolis
(612) 379-3232
www.surdyks.com
This Minneapolis shop is a wine connoisseur's dream come true—if you're actually going to sample all the wines available for taste-testing on weekends, you'd better have someone else do the driving. Surdyk's carries a wide selection of wines and other spirits, plus a gourmet cheese shop that makes this the place to consider when planning cocktail or dinner parties. Cigar smokers will appreciate the large humidor, which was a part of the store long before puffing cigars became trendy.

St. Paul
EL BURRITO MERCADO
175 Cesar Chavez St., St. Paul
(651) 227-2192
www.elburritomercado.com
El Burrito Mercado is an all-purpose Mexican and Latin grocery store located in the District del Sol neighborhood on St. Paul's West Side. The immense store features a bakery where you can purchase fresh pastries, fruit turnovers, breads, and cookies; a meat counter that carries fresh seafood, shredded pork, chicken, and beef, as well as gigantic fried pork rinds; a restaurant that whips up tacos, quesadillas, and burritos as quick as most fast-food restaurants, except the ingredients here are fresh, spicy, and good for you; and a full-service grocery carrying everything from Mexican coffees and candies to fresh, homemade corn chips and statues of tiny, sombrero-wearing skeletons playing guitars.

SPIROS MEDITERRANEAN MARKET
2264 University Ave. West, St. Paul
(651) 645-4607
This wonderful deli and grocery carries Greek staples such as frozen beef and lamb for gyros, tzatziki (cucumber) sauce, and a good selection of cheeses. The grocery section has Mediterranean candies, coffees, beans, pastas, fruit preserves, nuts, flour, jars of olives, pickled squid, and

anchovy paste. The deli counter has delicious baklava, as well as hummus and Greek salad, and makes gyros and other sandwiches fresh to order. In the freezer section are trays of moussaka and frozen spinach pies made fresh in the store.

SPORTS AND RECREATION OUTFITTERS

Minneapolis

ALTERNATIVE BIKE & BOARD SHOP
3013 Lyndale Ave. South, Minneapolis
(612) 374-3635
www.altbikeboard.com
Alternative Bike & Board Shop carries all the respected bicycle, skateboard, and snowboard brands like Burton, Clicker, Nitro, and K2. It also carries clothing, accessories, and gear and has a knowledgeable staff that can help set you up with anything you need to get out on the road or on the slopes. The store also offers bike repairs.

ERIK'S BIKE SHOP
1312 Fourth St. SE, Minneapolis
(612) 617-8002
11 additional Twin Cities locations
www.eriksbikeshop.com
This chain of local shops offers an excellent selection of equipment and a knowledgeable staff. Cyclists will find an extensive assortment of mountain, road, touring, and BMX bikes from such companies as Cannondale, Specialized, and Haro, as well as accessories, including car racks, helmets, parts, and apparel. Winter sports enthusiasts will be pleased by Erik's selection of snowboards, clothing, and boots. Erik's also has a full-service bike shop for quickie to major repairs.

THE HUB BIKE CO-OP
301 Cedar Ave. South, Minneapolis
(612) 238-3593

3020 Minnehaha Ave. South, Minneapolis
(612) 729-0437
www.thehubbikecoop.org

A disproportionate number of bicyclists are also idealists, especially in Minnesota, and the Hub manages its two shops with a socially responsible cooperative model in which the stores are worker-owned and worker-managed. New bikes and components are sold at the Cedar-Riverside shop, while used bikes are matched with new owners down at the Minnehaha shop. Not just a gimmick for buyers with a conscience, the Hub has a wide selection of makes and models to suit bikers from recreational to dead-serious.

FREEWHEEL BIKE
1812 South Sixth St., Minneapolis
(612) 339-2219
www.freewheelbike.com
Freewheel Bike carries mountain, road, and tandem bikes from Trek, Fisher, LeMond, Schwinn, Univega, Bontrager, Klein, and Santana, but its best feature is arguably the Public Shop, where, for under $10 an hour you can use the store's racks and tools to fix your bike—if you get in over your head, the staff is on hand to offer assistance. Freewheel also hosts maintenance classes jointly with the University of Minnesota's Open U, rents bikes, and sponsors riding groups and teams.

MIDWEST MOUNTAINEERING
309 Cedar Ave. South, Minneapolis
(612) 339-3433
www.midwestmtn.com
Midwest Mountaineering takes up nearly an entire block of Cedar Avenue on the University of Minnesota's West Bank and is one of the most complete retail stores for brand-name outdoor adventure gear (including a giant outdoors-related book section) and one of the few outfitters to rent kayaks, canoes, and other paddling gear. The store's bouldering cave allows novices and seasoned climbers to try out equipment or practice their skills. Once you sign a waiver, you're free to hit the walls. The store's staff is extremely helpful and can direct you to some of the better climbing, rafting, or hiking opportunities in the region.

St. Paul

FINN-SISU
1841 University Ave. West, St. Paul
(651) 645-2443 or (888) FINN-SISU
www.finnsisu.com
This tiny Midway shop stocks recreational, racing, and skate cross-country skis, as well as equipment and supplies by all the top makers. The staff is very good at matching people with just the right gear. The store is also conveniently located near Como Park, giving you a chance to try out your new toys mere minutes after leaving the store.

i Thrifty Outfitters (612-339-6290 or 800-866-3162), located upstairs inside the Midwest Mountaineering store, sells new and used outdoors equipment, clothing, and boots at steep discounts. Thrifty Outfitters also repairs outdoors equipment, from tents to backpacking stoves.

JOE'S SPORTING GOODS
33 Country Rd. B, St. Paul
(651) 209-7800 or (888) 463-6563
www.joessportinggoods.com
Joe's carries a solid selection of top-of-the-line fishing equipment, from rods, reels, and flies to clothes, boots, and hats, as well as a complete array of hunting, camping, and gear for snow sports, such as downhill and cross-country skiing, and snowboarding.

VINTAGE CLOTHES AND THRIFT STORES

Minneapolis

BLACKLIST VINTAGE
2 East 27th St., Minneapolis
(612) 872-8552
www.blacklistvintage.com
Proprietors Jennifer Mumm and Vanessa Messersmith (wife of singer-songwriter Jeremy Messersmith) run one of the sharpest vintage shops in the Twin Cities, where men and women can choose from the best of the past when assembling their out-on-the-town looks. In addition to the "redistribution" of retro trends, the shop also offers free games on a tabletop Ms. Pac-Man machine. What more can you ask?

EVERYDAY PEOPLE CLOTHING EXCHANGE
323 14th Ave. SE, Minneapolis
(612) 623-9095

2912 Hennepin Ave. South, Minneapolis
(612) 824-3112
www.everydaypeopleclothing.com
This vintage and resale store, with locations in Dinkytown and Uptown, carries an eclectic (and sometimes hilarious) collection of disco clothes, old band T-shirts, go-go boots, comfortably broken-in Levis, and studded leather and plastic belts.

RAGSTOCK
1433 West Lake St., Minneapolis
(612) 823-6690
Eight additional Minnesota locations
www.ragstock.com
Ragstock is the Target of vintage stores: It's the big chain that stocks seemingly everything. Hats? Walls of 'em. Belts? Racks and racks. Shirts? And shirts and shirts and shirts. It makes for good shopping when you're shooting for a specific look, but it's also a spot to pick up everyday wear. The remaindered-books rule applies, though: In general, this is stuff where the supply exceeds demand. Often there's a reason for that.

TATTERS
2928 Lyndale Ave. South, Minneapolis
(612) 823-5285
Originally called Tatters and Platters, a retailer selling apparel and vinyl records, Tatters has been a Twin Cities retro-alternative clothing establishment for many years. Tatters offers freshly laundered used and vintage clothing that spans decades, carrying seasoned motorcycle and letter jackets, Hawaiian and bowling shirts, party dresses from the 1940s onward, and lots and lots of Levis. It also stocks new apparel ranging from partywear to T-shirts and underwear.

St. Paul

LULA
1587 Selby Ave., St. Paul
(651) 644-4110

Lula boasts beautiful vintage clothes and accessories, including especially large and eclectic collections of women's dresses, men's shirts, and coats and jackets. The reasonably priced clothing moves quickly, and it's largely from the 1980s and earlier. The owner has been known to load up dressing rooms with all sorts of possibilities you may have overlooked. Trust this woman. She's totally into selling you vintage clothes that make you look and feel incredible.

JERABEK'S NEW BOHEMIAN
63 West Winifred St., St. Paul
(651) 228-1245
www.jerabeks.com

If you're looking for vintage clothes or housewares, try Jerabek's New Bohemian, a coffee shop tucked into St. Paul's West Side that's been around for 100 years. Not only is Jerabek's famous for its homemade pastries, it doubles as a vintage shop.

UNIQUE THRIFT STORE
1657 Rice St., St. Paul
(651) 489-5083
Two additional Twin Cities locations

All three Unique Thrift Store locations are the place to go to get beautiful, barely worn summer dresses, business suits, boots and shoes, ice skates, in-line skates, leather jackets, winter coats, and kids' stuff at unbelievable prices. You can pretty much buy a fashionable, brand-name wardrobe for your son or daughter for a whole growing season, including shoes and a coat, for under $50; prices on adult clothes and shoes are just as reasonable.

ATTRACTIONS

There is never a reason to be bored in the Twin Cities. The metro area is host to amusement parks, a bevy of hands-on historical exhibits, one of the largest zoos and one of the best free zoos in the country, and lots of interesting spots to just hang out for the day. In winter, flocks of teenagers and adults head to the Mall of America to spend the day walking among the tropical canopies of wild orchid displays that fill Como Park's spectacular Marjorie McNeely Conservatory. In summer there's no excuse for staying inside on the weekend—bike trails await and if you'd prefer to get wet without getting muddy, several water parks beckon.

Price Code

The following price code is based on the cost for general admission for one adult. Most sites offer considerably discounted tickets for children and seniors, and some allow discounts or even free entry for employees, members of the military, and certain organizations.

$. . . . . .Less than $5
$$ . . . .$6 to $15
$$$ . . . . $16 to $30
$$$$ . . . .$31 and up

Amusement and Water Parks

NICKELODEON UNIVERSE   **$$$**
Mall of America, 5000 Center Court,
Bloomington
(952) 883-8800
www.nickelodeonuniverse.com
Located at the center of Mall of America, this seven-acre indoor theme park—the largest indoor theme park in the country—offers more than 25 rides and attractions. Strolling through the park is free, but its many attractions will cost cold cash or, more often, points from tickets available at booths or automated machines. The theme park was Knott's Camp Snoopy when the mall first opened in 1992; Knott's pulled out after disagreements over budgeting and promotion, and after a short stint as the generically themed Park at MOA, SpongeBob dropped in to save

the day. Among the effects of the Nickelodeon revamp was to up the excitement level, with rides like the Rock Bottom Plunge and the Fairly Odd-Coaster supplying about as much thrill as you can reasonably expect underneath a roof. There are plenty of options for younger kids as well, and a family willing to approach or break the $100 mark for a day of big fun can, indeed, have it.

VALLEYFAIR AMUSEMENT PARK   **$$$$**
1 Valleyfair Dr., Shakopee
(952) 445-6500
www.valleyfair.com
With more than 75 rides and attractions, Valleyfair is the Upper Midwest's largest theme park. While it doesn't have thrill rides as extreme as you'll find at the likes of Six Flags, Valleyfair has a large variety of clean and well-maintained rides upon which you can enjoy unlimited trips once you pay the entry fee (it varies from year to year, but is likely to be around $30 in 2010). You can enjoy a relaxing inner tube ride down a gently sloping canal; bumper cars and electric car tracks; exciting water rides like the Flume, which sends passenger boats off a 50-foot drop at the end of the ride; and the Excalibur, a high-speed wooden roller coaster with a 105-foot drop and lots of quick twists and turns. The Steel Venom impulse coaster plummets at speeds up to 68 mph, corkscrewing you straight toward the ground before veering to a horizontal ride just before impact. For those with no fear of heights, the 275-foot

Power Tower will take you high in the air and then, well, drop you. There are lots of rides for the really little guys, too, from bumble bee–shaped electric cars to a multilevel foam-ball factory to an antique carousel. An IMAX theater is an added attraction to the park and a great place to hide out during sudden late-summer showers. The amusement park is open mid-May through September, reopening on weekends (with limited attractions and added ghouls) for a period of "Valleyscare" in October.

Valleyfair also has Whitewater Country, a three-and-a-half-acre waterpark with multiple water slides, raft rides, and such attractions as Raging Rapids, Splash Station, and Giggle Run. The waterpark is open late May through late August, and has different hours than the amusement park. Call ahead for more information.

The separate Challenge Park (which has separate fees and different hours than the amusement park) will get the adrenaline and competitive juices flowing with such rides as RipCord (which lifts you up in the air 180 feet and spins you, then drops you, simulating flying and freefall), Adventure Golf, Go-Karts, and Bumper Boats.

i Get half-price tickets to Valleyfair by buying Starlight admission after 5 p.m. Check the park's hours of operation on the day you wish to go, as Valleyfair is only open until 6 p.m. on some days early and late in the season (although until midnight on weekends during the heart of the summer).

WATER PARK OF AMERICA $$$
1700 East American Blvd., Bloomington
(952) 698-8888
www.waterparkofamerica.com
Adjacent to the Mall of America, the Water Park of America offers the only surfing simulator in Minnesota, a wave pool, a ten-story raft ride, swimming pools, and more. Arrive early during warm summer weekends as the waterpark often fills to capacity. The waterpark is open seasonally and hours vary (call ahead for details). The waterpark complex includes a game arcade with many different prizes for winners, a hotel (see the listing in the Accommodations chapter for more information on the hotel), a spa, and two restaurants.

Animals and Plants

**COMO ZOO/MARJORIE MCNEELY
CONSERVATORY AT COMO PARK**   FREE
1225 Estabrook Dr., St. Paul
(651) 487-8200
www.comozooconservatory.org
This year-round zoo offers intimate exhibits housing reticulated giraffes, black-footed penguins, snow leopards, yellow-rumped caciques, blue-eyed black lemurs, gray wolves, and more. One of only four free metropolitan-area zoos in the country, Como Zoo has been an institution in St. Paul for more than a century. The first Siberian tigers successfully bred in captivity were born here in 1958, and the big cat display is still one of the best features of the zoo, including a breeding pair of lions that has had several healthy pairs of cubs over the past decade.

Located right next door to the zoo is the Marjorie McNeely Conservatory at Como Park, the region's largest botanical garden. The Victorian-style, glass-domed conservatory features hundreds of plants from throughout the world and is divided into eight sections featuring palms, ferns, tropical food plants, bonsai trees, seasonal flowers, orchids, Japanese landscapes, and butterfly-friendly plants. In summer a side door opens into the Como Ordway Memorial Japanese Garden, a sansui (mountain and water) design created by St. Paul's sister city, Nagasaki, Japan, for the park.

The antique wooden Cafesjian's Carousel is beautifully restored, and the brightly painted and mirrored wooden animals are available to ride throughout the summer for a nominal charge. The nearby Como Town is an amusement park for little ones, and the Putt'er There minigolf course is one of the best in the Cities.

Both the Como Zoo and the Marjorie McNeely Conservatory at Como Park are open year-round. The zoo and conservatory in Como Park can be found about halfway between I-94 and MN 36 off of Lexington Avenue. Call ahead or visit the Web site for further directions.

MINNESOTA LANDSCAPE
ARBORETUM $$
3675 Arboretum Dr., Chaska
(952) 443-1400
www.arboretum.umn.edu
Minnesota is a fertile place—and not just because of all the German Catholics. The diversity of flora that thrives in the cool northern climate is simply astonishing, and one of the best places to go to get a feel for the woodsy, prickly, shady, pretty, and pungent side of the Twin Cities is the Minnesota Landscape Arboretum. Minnesota's largest public garden, the arboretum is maintained by the University of Minnesota. But it is not the outdoor equivalent of a musty plant textbook, although an industrious sort could probably research one here. From the Three-Mile Drive and its sampler of trees, flowering plants, grasses, and shrubs to the new Maze Garden, the arboretum is an intriguing and fun place at which both adults and kids will find much to love.

The arboretum is open daily (except for Thanksgiving and Christmas Day) at varying hours depending on the season and the day of the week; call for details. To get to the Minnesota Landscape Arboretum, follow MN 5 west from I-494 in the southwest part of the Metro. After approximately 10 miles, you'll reach the intersection with MN 41. Continue straight ahead on Highway 5 and follow the directional signs to the arboretum.

MINNESOTA ZOO $$
13000 Zoo Blvd., Apple Valley
(952) 431-9200 or (800) 366-7811
www.mnzoo.org
Located in the southeastern suburb of Apple Valley and housing approximately 500 species of animals from five continents, the Minnesota Zoo and its IMAX theater see a million visitors per year. The zoo's 500 acres include an indoor Tropics Trail, populated by gibbons, tapirs, tree kangaroos, hissing cockroaches, and endangered red pandas. The newly redesigned Minnesota Trail, also an indoor walk, is home to gray wolves, porcupines, great horned owls, river otters, and other Minnesota residents. At Discovery Bay, dolphins

officially perform for audiences every afternoon and unofficially any time enough people gather around their huge, glass-walled tank; a walk-through aquarium has sharks, fish, and deep-sea plants; and there is a hands-on area where kids (and adults) can pet different kinds of sharks, rays, and starfish. Outside the main exhibit building, you can find ducks and swans, a prairie dog town, wild horses, camels, tigers, and many, many other animals. Domesticated animals like pigs and chickens get their day in the sun at the Wells Fargo Family Farm exhibit. It's worth the extra few dollars to ride the Monorail around the zoo, as it is the least strenuous way to see many animals requiring room to roam, including endangered and extremely rare Mexican wolves, musk oxen, and Siberian tigers.

The zoo also features the 600-seat Great Clips IMAX theater (it's no surprise that a discount hair-care chain would sponsor a venue where you sit in the dark) and the Weesner Family Amphitheater, which hosts concerts all summer long.

To reach the zoo, follow I-35E south from I-494 in the southeast Metro, exit at MN 77, and follow the signs.

UNDERWATER ADVENTURES
AQUARIUM $$–$$$
Mall of America, 120 East Broadway
Bloomington
(952) 883-0202 or (888) 348-3824
www.underwaterworld.com
Underwater Adventures is a huge (1.2 million gallons) walk-through aquarium located under the Mall of America. The facility features more than 4,500 different sea creatures from around the world in eight displays. For a one-time admission charge, visitors can walk through a 300-foot glass-walled tunnel that leads them through the middle of the three freshwater exhibits: Touch of the Wild Woods, Fisherman's Hollow, and the Wild Amazon, and five ocean exhibits: Shark Cove, Rainbow Reef, Seacrits of Hollywood, Circle of Life, and Starfish Beach, where you can touch harmless sharks and stingrays (if you dare it, you may be given an I TOUCHED A SHARK sticker for bragging purposes).

Casinos and Racetracks

CANTERBURY PARK RACETRACK AND CARD CLUB
1100 Canterbury Rd., Shakopee
(952) 445-7223
www.canterburypark.com
Canterbury Park, located about 25 miles south of both downtown St. Paul and Minneapolis, hosts live horse racing with on-site pari-mutuel betting early May through the beginning of September. In addition, the Canterbury Park Race Book offers year-round on-site betting on simulcast horse races around the country. Canterbury also has a Card Club, including the Poker Room, with 34 tables featuring such games as Texas hold 'em, seven-card stud, and Omaha hi-lo, and the Casino Games Room, with games like blackjack, Caribbean stud, and Let It Ride, as well as additional poker games. The entire facility is smoke free. To reach the race-track and card club, follow I-494 in the southwest Metro and exit at US 169 South. Follow US 169 to Canterbury Road and turn right (north).

MYSTIC LAKE CASINO
2400 Mystic Lake Blvd., Prior Lake
(952) 445-9000 or (800) 262-7799
www.mysticlake.com
Besides its trademark high-stakes bingo, Mystic Lake Casino has nearly 4,000 slots and 100 blackjack tables as well as restaurants, including a huge buffet. The gaming facility offers concerts by big middlebrow draws (Alan Jackson, Tony Bennett, and Kenny G), a hotel, and free daily shuttles across the Twin Cities. It is operated by the Shakopee Mdewakanton Sioux Community. The casino is smoke and alcohol free. Mystic Lake Casino is about 6 miles south of Canterbury Park and about 30 miles from either downtown St. Paul or downtown Minneapolis. It is the closest full casino to the Twin Cities.

i Down in History motorcoach tours (651-292-1220), led by costumed actors, are a fun way to get oriented to the Twin Cities and learn a little in the process. The St. Paul Gangster, Historic Cave, No Blarney, and Uff Dah! Tours are among your choices.

TREASURE ISLAND RESORT AND CASINO
Off MN 61, Welch
(800) 222-7077
www.treasureislandcasino.com
Located 45 minutes southeast of St. Paul near the Mississippi River town of Red Wing, tropical-themed Treasure Island features 2,500 slots, 44 blackjack tables, 10 poker tables, bingo, video poker, video keno, and video roulette. The casino has smoking and nonsmoking gambling areas and does not serve alcoholic drinks. Guests can take a cruise down the scenic Mississippi River aboard the *Spirit of the Water,* the casino's 150-passenger yacht. The Indigo Bay Showroom features live comedy and music; recent shows featured Rodney Carrington and Wanda Sykes. You can delay your drive back to the Cities by booking a room in the casino's 250-room tropi-cal-themed resort or by parking your Airstream at the casino's 95-pad RV park.

Should you get hungry, there are plenty of great places to eat at Treasure Island, including the Tradewinds all-you-can-eat buffet, Java's Restaurant for meals ranging from steak to seafood, and several other options serving sandwiches, coffee and pastries, and burgers.

Guided Excursions

THE HITCHING COMPANY $$$–$$$$
(612) 338-7777
www.thehitchingcompany.com
Romantic horse-drawn carriage tours of down-town Minneapolis cover, depending on the tour, such sites as the Stone Arch Bridge, the new Guthrie Theater, the Mississippi riverfront, the Warehouse District, Loring Park, the Basilica of St. Mary, Nicollet Mall, and more. Tours range from 15 minutes to an hour, and the carriages seat up to six, less romantic but great fun for families. Operating year-round (The Hitching Company provides blankets when the mercury drops), the carriage can pick you up at numerous spots in downtown Minneapolis. Call ahead for reservations.

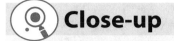

Close-up

Rice Park

There aren't many urban green spaces in the country as pleasant and perfectly situated as St. Paul's **Rice Park.** It is one preserved block carved out of St. Paul's core, surrounded by cobble-stone streets and towering buildings and replete with benches and trees. One of St. Paul's old-est parks, the square was donated to the city in 1849, the same year St. Paul was incorporated as a town and nine years before Minnesota became a state. The man who donated the park, Henry Mower Rice, was first a fur trader, and then a businessman and one of the town's first cheerleaders. If only Henry knew what his gift would become.

Benches around the huge circular fountain at Rice Park's center make nice spots to eat lunch or listen to a concert in the square. There's a statue of F. Scott Fitzgerald, who wrote and published *This Side of Paradise* (1920) while living on Summit Avenue, the grand St. Paul street full of Victorian mansions. It also contains bronze sculptures of the *Peanuts* characters invented by St. Paul boy Charles Schulz, built with money raised by several years of selling fiberglass versions (many of which are still to be seen around town). During the Winter Car-nival each year, Rice Park holds the festival's ice-sculpting contest. Massive frosty sculptures glow amid trees dressed in twinkling white lights for as long as the weather allows.

But the park is defined as much by what's around it as what's in it. On the north side, along Fifth Street, sits the **Landmark Center,** built in 1902. It has huge stone towers, the tallest of which holds a clock. Landmark Towers was originally the federal courthouse and post office for the Upper Midwest, during which time it saw the trials of many big-name gangsters. Take a peek inside. Now a National Historic Landmark, the building holds lots of offices of nonprofit organizations and is open for tours. The atrium is amazing, and some of the courtrooms and judges' chambers have been restored to their original grandeur.

Along the park's south side, the stately marble Italian Renaissance revival rectangle that is the **St. Paul Central Library** inspires awe from its spot on Fourth Street. It cost $1.5 million (and that's in 1917 dollars) to construct. It's still a library today, and thankfully, it recently benefited from a $15.9 million restoration. The St. Paul Central Library is also on the National Register of Historic Places. Inside, it's all handsome stone and wood, and there's even a nice little coffee shop and store to visit.

On the park's west side, along Market Street, is one of the premier accommodations in all of the state, the **St. Paul Hotel.** It was the luxurious brainchild of St. Paul businessman Lucius Pond Ordway, designed to wow back in 1910 with a grand ballroom, a fine dining room, and guestrooms with scenic views. This is the kind of hotel with a doorman in a top hat, afternoon teas by the fire, and huge arrangements of fresh flowers everywhere. The hotel's St. Paul Grill is still known around the Cities as a premier dining spot, the ballroom still hosts events, and the view is still—well, try to get a room overlooking Rice Park.

Directly across from the St. Paul Hotel, on Washington Street, is the **Ordway Center for the Performing Arts,** which opened in 1985. Sally Ordway Irving, Lucius's granddaughter, is behind this theatrical gem. By far Rice Park's newest structure, its creators met the archi-tectural challenge of fitting in with the neighbors. The Ordway is a fine example of modern architecture that exists in harmony with vintage surroundings—the low-lying building's soar-ing glass-walled lobby gives audiences a reason to linger over a spectacular view.

Despite all this history and elegance, Rice Park is a wonderfully and comfortably low-key spot. It gets nice and quiet here, especially at night after the Ordway show has let out and the fancy St. Paul Grill diners have finished and the carriage that waits outside the hotel has gone home. You can practically feel the city's breath in this park, its heart. Depending on the angle, Rice Park could be now or 65 years ago, but it's unquestionably St. Paul, with its best foot forward.

PADELFORD PACKET BOAT
COMPANY INC. $$-$$$$
Harriet Island Regional Park, St. Paul
(651) 227-1100
www.riverrides.com
Hop on one of five riverboats leaving from Harriet Island in St. Paul for a Mississippi River excursion. These paddleboat river tours offer an excellent way to experience the river up close.

Padelford Packet Boat Company offers two narrated daily public excursions seven days a week in June, July, and August and at 2 p.m. every Saturday and Sunday in May and September. Elegant evening dinner cruises depart Fridays, June through September. A Sunday brunch cruise, a lunch cruise, a showboat cruise, a birding cruise, a fall color cruise, private charters, and more are also available.

SEGWAY MAGICAL HISTORY TOUR $$$$
Saint Anthony Main, 125 Main St. SE,
Minneapolis
(952) 888-9200
www.humanonastick.com
One of the funnier-looking ways to tour the historic sites of the Minneapolis riverfront is aboard a Segway, a perfectly balanced scooter-like device that travels up to 10 mph. After some brief training on how to drive a Segway, a guide-led convoy departs Saint Anthony Main and tours such sites as the Stone Arch Bridge, Saint Anthony Falls, Mill Ruins Park, the Hennepin Avenue Bridge, and Nicollet Island. The 5-mile tour includes a loaner helmet, free admission to and refreshments at the Mill City Museum, and discounts at area restaurants.

Historical Attractions
ALEXANDER RAMSEY HOUSE $-$$
265 South Exchange St., St. Paul
(651) 296-8760
www.mnhs.org/ramseyhouse
Completed in 1872, this is one of the country's best-preserved Victorian homes. The Ramsey House is one of the most detailed and intimate historical sites in the Twin Cities. The only owners

were the Ramsey family, and so the history stayed in the house. More than 90 percent of the furnishings are original, which is rare for historical sites.

Costumed guides lead visitors on a tour of the impressive home of Alexander and Anna Ramsey. Alexander Ramsey was Minnesota's first territorial governor and the second state governor, and he held many other prominent positions in public life.

The Ramsey House features original furniture, crystal chandeliers, carved walnut woodwork, and marble fireplaces. The costumed interpreters play out vignettes showing life in the late 1800s. Free fresh-baked cookies are handed out by the "servants." There are special events and tours throughout the year, particularly during holidays. Tours run year-round on Friday and Saturday between 10 a.m. and 3 p.m., with expanded hours during summer and the holiday season.

AMERICAN SWEDISH INSTITUTE $-$$
2600 Park Ave., Minneapolis
(612) 871-4907
www.americanswedishinst.org
Set in a spectacular 33-room turn-of-the-20th-century mansion that looks more like a castle than a former residence, the American Swedish Institute is the largest and oldest museum of Swedish culture, arts, and history in the country. Completed in 1908, the châteauesque structure is all ornately carved Indiana limestone on the outside. The inside is a marvel of hand-carved wood, with intricate designs lining the walls, and each sculpted plaster ceiling is a work of art. There's also a *kakelugnar* in each of eleven rooms, which is basically a colorful, porcelain-wrapped Swedish fireplace. While taking in the decor, expect also to be taken with tales of immigrants who left Scandinavia to settle in Minnesota, which bears similar scenery, albeit sans mountains and fjords. The museum is a rich resource for local history as well as a showcase for artwork by Swedish and Swedish-American artists and artisans. There are concerts and theater performances in the upper rooms and lectures and other events in the modernized lower level. (It's a special treat to visit when the mansion is decked

out at Christmastime.) There are also fiddling and dancing groups that come through to entertain visitors, special festivals with music and food, and Swedish language classes for kids and adults.

Tours of the institute are available Tuesday through Sunday.

THE ARD GODFREY HOUSE   **FREE**
50 University Ave. NE, Minneapolis
(612) 813-5300
(tours are arranged through the Woman's Club of Minneapolis)
www.womansclub.org
Built in 1848, the Ard Godfrey House was the family residence for the millwright who helped build the first dam and sawmills to put the waterpower of the Falls of St. Anthony to use. The oldest wood frame house in Minneapolis, this Greek revival structure was restored and refurbished by the Woman's Club of Minneapolis as a gift to city residents.

The Godfrey House was reopened to the public in 1979. Today the house is available for guided tours Saturday, and Sunday June through September and for private tours by appointment year-round.

FORT SNELLING   **$–$$**
MN 5 and MN 55, St. Paul
(612) 726-1171
www.mnhs.org/fortsnelling
First established in 1819 as a military encampment, Fort Snelling was built on a bluff overlooking the Mississippi and Minnesota Rivers in 1825. The fort was once the westernmost U.S. outpost in the mostly unexplored wilds of the Northwest Territory (encompassing eastern Minnesota and many of the future states of the Upper Midwest) and was the center of frontier commerce and government on the upper Mississippi. At the time, an outpost on the confluence of the Minnesota and Mississippi Rivers meant control of river traffic throughout the region; British fur traders, American outlaws, and warring American Indian nations could be held in check. Today themed tours provide insight into what life was like at the fort, with costumed guides reenacting scenes

from military, civilian, and Native American life of the 1800s. Not only are these some of the oldest surviving buildings in the state, but both Twin Cities trace their pedigrees to the fort. Soldiers from the fort built the first sawmill at St. Anthony Falls, and the first residents of St. Paul were moved there after being sheltered as immigrants.

This reconstruction of the first permanent settlement in Minnesota is open May through October and is staffed by costumed guides portraying fort life in 1827. Events at the fort include demonstrations, historical skits, practice military drills, watching or joining in with residents of the 1820s military post as they prepare the harvest for storage and winter use, and book readings and lectures from Minnesota authors and historians. Contact the fort directly to hear about special events year-round.

GIBBS MUSEUM OF PIONEER
AND DAKOTAH LIFE   **$–$$**
2097 West Larpenteur Ave.
Falcon Heights
(651) 646-8629
www.rchs.com/gbbsfm2.htm
Near the farm fields that make up the northern border of the University of Minnesota's agriculturally focused St. Paul campus, you'll find this quaint little barn and farmhouse, which date from 1854. They're preserved in their original state (additions to the original cabin were constructed in 1867 and 1873) as an educational opportunity for those who would like to step back in time. On summer weekends expect to see people in period dress doing farm chores like churning butter on the porch. Interpreters share the process and results of their extensive archaeology of this site, displaying excavated artifacts and explaining their historic significance to the public. The Gibbs Museum's medicine and vegetable gardens are especially interesting, with many native plants that no longer exist naturally in the area but were especially important to the Dakotah (Dakota) people and pioneer settlers.

The Gibbs Museum is open early May through late October.

HENRY SIBLEY HOUSE HISTORIC SITE $
1357 Sibley Memorial Hwy., Mendota
(651) 452-1596
www.mnhs.org/sibleyhouse
Henry Hastings Sibley, an American Fur Company regional manager and Minnesota's first governor, lived in a limestone home amid a trading post in the riverside hamlet of Mendota. Today visitors can walk through three of the structures in one of Minnesota's oldest European-American settlements, including the home of Sibley and his neighbor, Jean Baptiste Faribault. Sibley's restored house is full of fur trade stuff and the trappings of frontier gentility—pelts, muskets, and loads of blue china. The guides' stories of Sibley and company are vivid snapshots of the difficulties faced by these tough frontiersmen living in a wild world.

Plan ahead: The house is only open six days a year (the first and third Saturdays of June, July, and August).

JOHN H. STEVENS HOUSE $
4801 Minnehaha Ave. South, Minneapolis
(612) 722-2220
www.johnhstevenshouse.org
The John H. Stevens House, built in 1849 and originally located in the present-day riverfront spot of the Minneapolis Post Office, is the first permanent settler's home in Minneapolis. The home of Col. John H. Stevens and his family served as the social and civic hub of the new city. People met here to discuss a name for the city and to organize local schools and government. It was here that John Stevens drew up the original territorial boundaries for Hennepin County. The first county elections were held here in 1852.

The house is in south Minneapolis's Minnehaha Park on Minnehaha Avenue just south of East Minnehaha Parkway. It is across the street from the 50th Street Light-Rail Transit station.

MILL CITY MUSEUM $–$$
704 South Second St., Minneapolis
(612) 341-7555
www.millcitymuseum.org
Minneapolis was once known as the "Flour Capital of the World," and much of that rich heritage is on display at the Mill City Museum, which opened in 2003 on the city's riverfront. The museum is constructed around the ruins of the Washburn A Mill, originally constructed in 1874. The first mill exploded and burned to the ground on May 2, 1878, killing 18. The mill was rebuilt and reopened in 1880, and during its busiest years, the Washburn A ground enough flour every day to make 12 million loaves of bread. The mill continued to grind flour until 1965, but a 1991 fire severely damaged the abandoned mill. The Mill City Museum incorporates the stabilized limestone ruins of the mill into its design and includes many of the old mill's features, including milling machinery, flour bins, the engine house, and more. The museum also features a waterpower laboratory and an eight-story "Flour Power" ride that carries riders through Minneapolis's flour-milling history. In the museum's Baking Lab, visitors can grind wheat and bake bread. There is also an entertaining film, "Minneapolis in 19 Minutes Flat," which features local radio personality Kevin Kling.

The museum can be found just north of the Metrodome in downtown Minneapolis along the Mississippi River. The museum is open Tuesday through Sunday.

MINNESOTA STATE CAPITOL FREE
75 Rev. Dr. Martin Luther King Jr. Blvd.,
St. Paul
(651) 296-2881
www.mnhs.org/statecapitol
Soaring domes, monumental arches, columns, statues, and symbolic murals dominate the scene for visitors today as they did when the Minnesota State Capitol was completed in 1905. The first two capitols, one destroyed by fire and one outgrown, were in downtown St. Paul. The current structure is the stark, white capitol topped by a magnificent marble dome and the four golden horses—the Quadriga—that are usually what people remember after their visit to this masterpiece of Italian Renaissance architecture.

Today the State Senate, House of Representatives, and Supreme Court have been restored to their original appearances, as has the Rathskellar Cafe, now open to the public during the legislative session. Guided tours of the capitol leave every hour; self-guided tour brochures are available at the front entrance. (Groups of ten or more, please call ahead for reservations.) The State House and Senate are easily accessible to visitors, and if your timing's right, you can hear important issues being decided. The tours showcase amply captioned oil portraits of Minnesota governors around the rotunda, and go on to give insight to the history of the building, including information on the Civil War, and on architect Cass Gilbert's role in selecting art and furnishings for the building. The capitol is open daily year-round.

WABASHA STREET CAVES $-$$$
215 South Wabasha St., St. Paul
(651) 224-1191
www.wabashastreetcaves.com
Burrowed into the sandstone bluffs that line the Mississippi River on St. Paul's West Side (across the river from downtown), this is the site of the late Castle Royal nightclub, which was a speakeasy during the days of Prohibition and, before that, a mushroom farm. There's a lot of St. Paul history here, especially for those interested in the city's incarnation as a gangster mecca. Considering that the city of St. Paul was built around a cave (Pig's Eye Parrant's cavern and tavern), a cave is an appropriate dwelling for a night out. Dancers come to the caves on Swing Night, held every Thursday as well as select Fridays and featuring live big bands. The Historic Cave Tour covers the history of the Wabasha Street Caves, while the St. Paul Gangster Tour stops at several sites outside the caves where infamous crimes took place. Each October motorcoach tours depart from the caves to deliver St. Paul's haunted history. The caves are open year-round (see Web site for tour times and reservations).

Indoor Recreation

HUBERT H. HUMPHREY METRODOME
900 South Fifth St., Minneapolis
(612) 332-0386
www.msfc.com

This multipurpose facility, home of the Minnesota Vikings, features events year-round. First-time visitors to the Metrodome are awed by its interior volume; regular fans sometimes feel they're watching theater, not sports. The Metrodome is big enough to host motocross events and monster-truck rallies as well as football games, occasional rock concerts, and in-line skaters.

During many evenings November through March, when there's no previously scheduled event, the Metrodome turns into the Rollerdome—hordes of skaters take over its half-mile concourses, taking advantage of the tremendous workout the field provides.

Parking for Rollerdome and the Metrodome is free in the Metrodome lot, which you can enter at the intersection of South 5th Street and 11th Avenue. Enter the Dome at Gate D. No cameras, recording devices, or outside cans, bottles, coolers, or containers are allowed at the Metrodome or Rollerdome, but concessions are available inside on weekends in case you get peckish.

MALL OF AMERICA
60 East Broadway, Bloomington
(952) 883-8800
www.mallofamerica.com
This gigantic mall says only one thing about the state of American shopping: Fantasy moves product. And at this cement-and-plastic Bloomington behemoth, there's a lot of product to move. The largest shopping and entertainment complex in the United States, the megamall—at 4.2 million square feet—is the size of seven Yankee Stadiums and home to more than 520 stores, 50 restaurants, a 14-screen movie theater, an indoor amusement park, and an aquarium. To make your shopping experience more pleasurable, the mall rents strollers, wheelchairs, shopping carts, and lockers. In case you change your mind about shopping and decide to get married instead, there's a wedding chapel conveniently located inside the mall.

Museums

THE BAKKEN LIBRARY AND MUSEUM $–$$
3537 Zenith Ave. South, Minneapolis
(612) 926-3878
www.thebakken.org
Established in 1976 by Earl E. Bakken, inventor of the first transistorized cardiac pacemaker and cofounder of Medtronic, a Twin Cities company on the cutting edge of electrocardio technology, this Tudor-style mansion houses an incredible collection of rare books, manuscripts, and scientific thingamajigs that are all related to the role electricity plays in life.

The Bakken Museum is open Tuesday through Saturday; the museum's research library, with 11,000 rare books and 2,500 scientific instruments, is open Monday through Friday. The museum and library are on the west side of south Minneapolis's Lake Calhoun on Zenith Avenue South just north of West 36th Street.

BELL MUSEUM OF NATURAL HISTORY $
University of Minnesota
10 Church St. SE, Minneapolis
(612) 624-7083
www.bellmuseum.org
The Bell preserves an impressive collection of stuffed creatures displayed in simulated natural environments, with background murals painted by landscape artist Francis L. Jaques. The exhibits are primarily Northland animals and confined to North America, with emphasis on Minnesota wildlife including porcupines, bears, moose, and ground squirrels. There is also a temporary exhibit hall that features artwork, animal remains, and fossils from around the world, changing approximately every two months.

The Bell Museum is closed Monday and major holidays. Admission is free every Sunday and to Bell members, University of Minnesota faculty, and U of M students. The museum is on the northern side of the university's Minneapolis Campus at the intersection of Church Street SE and SE University Avenue.

HENNEPIN HISTORY MUSEUM $
2303 Third Ave. South, Minneapolis
(612) 870-1329
http://hennepinhistory.org
Founded by the Hennepin County Territorial Pioneers Association in 1858, the Hennepin History Museum has long been dedicated to preserving the history of Hennepin County. Today the Hennepin History Museum serves as a gateway to historical resources. Housed in the George H. Christian mansion, designed by Hewitt and Brown, the museum offers a series of rotating exhibits focusing on everything from toys to technology. Past exhibits have highlighted Ojibwe and Dakota cultures, toys, quilt making, the creations of local artists, medical instruments, and historic wedding dresses. City Kids' Gallery is one place where touching the artifacts is not only allowed but encouraged.

The Hennepin History Museum is open varying hours. The museum is on Third Avenue South a block and a half south of West Franklin Avenue.

MINNESOTA AIR GUARD MUSEUM $
Air National Guard Base
Off MN 62 and MN 55
Minneapolis–St. Paul International Airport
(612) 713-2523
www.mnangmuseum.org
This small but historically important museum displays vintage aircraft and memorabilia of the Minnesota Air National Guard. The memorabilia—airplane pictures, portraits, helmets, patches—is crowded into a couple of cramped rooms in a hangar. The museum's focus is on local flyboys, but 22 cool old planes are on display on the tarmac outside, including fighter jets, transports, and the terrifying black A-12, the CIA's favorite superfast spy plane.

Because the museum is located on an active military base, visitors must arrive by vehicle (rather than light-rail transit) and must show a photo ID. Its hours vary by season and by staffing. The museum is in a corner of the National Guard Base, and it is best to check the Web site, call ahead, or ask at the guard station for directions.

MINNESOTA CHILDREN'S MUSEUM   **$$**
10 West Seventh St., St. Paul
(651) 225-6000
www.mcm.org
Einstein said that "play was the highest form of research," and if you have children, you will appreciate the diversion this museum can offer your kids. Traveling exhibits have included items on Peter Rabbit and Mister Rogers, while permanent exhibits are interactive and give children a chance to crawl through simulated ant colonies, create paper from gooey slop, or take the stage in a TV studio. This is an especially popular place for graduate students to take their kids, as it keeps the youngsters entertained while letting education-minded parents comfortably take a study break. Recommended for children six months to 10 years of age and for parents looking to entertain their brood during the winter.

The Minnesota Children's Museum is open Tuesday through Sunday, closed Monday and major holidays. The museum is at the intersection of West Seventh and Wabasha Streets in downtown St. Paul.

i An admittance stamp at the Minnesota Children's Museum lets you come and go from the building all day, so you can sneak out and get a decent lunch and still come back and play for no extra charge.

THE MINNESOTA HISTORY CENTER   **$-$$**
345 West Kellogg Blvd., St. Paul
(612) 726-1171
www.mnhs.org/historycenter
The Minnesota History Center definitely looks the part: It's a massive edifice constructed from Minnesota-quarried Rockville granite and Winona limestone. Exhibits touch on all aspects of Minnesota history. Encounter early settlers in "Tales of the Territory" or learn the facts about our storied weather in "Weather Permitting." The Minnesota History Center has a gigantic library of Minnesota-related books and historic photographs, as well as information on family genealogy; visitors are allowed to pore through the collection for free.

The museum also presents a lecture series and book readings from local historians and authors. The Minnesota History Center museum is open Tuesday through Sunday year-round and on Mondays during the summer and on Monday holidays; the research library is open Tuesday through Saturday year-round.

The center sits at the corner of Kellogg Boulevard West and John Ireland Boulevard in downtown St. Paul.

MINNESOTA TRANSPORTATION
MUSEUM   **$-$$$**
Various locations
(651) 288-0263
www.mtmuseum.org
Discover the history of transportation at this museum's exhibit sites. Among other things, visitors may ride diesel-powered trains in Osceola, Wisconsin, or view locomotive restoration up close at Jackson Street Roundhouse in St. Paul.

Minnesota Transportation Museum's Osceola and St. Croix Valley Railway's trains start at the Osceola, Wisconsin, depot (715-755-3570) about an hour northeast of the Twin Cities. There are two available trips: one to Marine on St. Croix, Minnesota, and one to Dresser, Wisconsin. Trains run weekends and holidays, April through October. In addition, the railway operates special events all season long.

The Jackson Street Roundhouse, located at 193 East Pennsylvania Avenue in St. Paul (651-228-0263), is the first railroad maintenance shop in Minnesota of the oldest known railroad in St. Paul—not bad for a city whose history has been dominated by railroading. Here, train lovers can climb aboard train cars of varying eras and styles and learn the state's railroad history through vintage posters and railroad maps. There's a gift shop, a working turntable (used to turn the locomotives), a kids' play area, and a working repair shop.

The museum also maintains several historic train depots around the state and in Wisconsin. The 1875 Milwaukee Road Depot at Minnehaha Park in south Minneapolis is one such station, open Sunday and holidays between Memorial

Day and Labor Day. Although no longer in operation, the station was known as "The Princess," where overheated Twin Citians once disembarked to enjoy the cool waters of Minnehaha Creek in summertime.

i The Science Museum of Minnesota sits beside its parking ramp, which is easiest to reach from Chestnut Street several stories below Kellogg Boulevard West. From Kellogg, turn west on Eagle Street and then turn left on Chestnut.

SCIENCE MUSEUM OF MINNESOTA $$
120 West Kellogg Blvd., St. Paul
(651) 221-9444
www.smm.org
With eight indoor acres of both permanent and temporary exhibits that include an extensive collection of dinosaur, mammal, insect, and fish fossils, plus a set of T. rex jaws you can operate, there's lots of interaction at this museum. In the Cell Lab, kids don lab coats and check out what their cheek cells look like under the microscope. In the Mississippi River Gallery, kids pretend to drive a real tugboat as they look out over the river. The nine-hole minigolf course is actually a lesson in river science, and the prairie maze is made from native Minnesota plants and grasses.

The Science Museum has traveling exhibits and a curved-screen Omnitheater that—oh, snap!—converts to a flat-screen IMAX theater. (Yes, that makes it America's only convertible Omnitheater.) Both the traveling exhibits and the Omnitheater have admission fees that can be purchased separately or as a package with admission to the museum.

The Science Museum of Minnesota is located at the intersection of Kellogg Boulevard West and Washington Street, just east of the Xcel Energy Center in downtown St. Paul.

TWIN CITY MODEL RAILROAD MUSEUM $
Bandana Square, 1021 Bandana Blvd. East, St. Paul
(651) 647-9628
www.tcmrm.org
Since 1939 this museum has featured the role played by railroads in the history and development of Minnesota. An extensive collection of railroad artifacts and art is available, including a changing photo exhibit in the museum focusing on a different historic train or train line each month.

The centerpiece of the museum is the scale-model railroad of the re-creation of the Twin Cities pre-1950. Up to six trains at once glide through the depots and tunnels of the incredibly detailed model, while miniature streetcars seen running back and forth over the Third Avenue Bridge model are sometimes brought out to run on the tracks as well. The museum is closed Monday.

You can find the museum in Bandana Square on Energy Park Drive halfway between Lexington Avenue and Snelling Avenue in the Midway area of St. Paul.

KIDSTUFF

From science- and nature-oriented attractions to water parks and bumper cars, your kids won't get bored in the Twin Cities. Luckily, even most museums and art events are fully prepared to receive and entertain children.

As for dining options, you're welcome to bring your kids into plenty of Twin Cities establishments—bars that double as restaurants in the daytime welcome underage patrons (accompanied by adults) until just before happy hour. The restaurants in this chapter try to make children feel comfortable, from the menu to service to decor. Most are also easy on the wallet.

Price Code

The following price code is based on the cost for general admission for one adult. Most sites offer discounted tickets for children and seniors, and some allow discounts or even free entry for members of their respective organizations.

$	Less than $5
$$	$6 to $15
$$$	$16 to $30
$$$$	$31 and up

Amusement and Water Parks

CASCADE BAY $$
1360 Civic Center Dr., Eagan
(651) 675-5577
www.cascadebay.com
Seven-acre Cascade Bay in the St. Paul suburb of Eagan is the largest outdoor municipal water park in the Midwest. Its lazy river, multiple slides, sand beach, and more are extremely popular with just about any kid. Guests under 42 inches tall and those older than 62 get in at a reduced price.

COMO TOWN $$$
1301 Midway Pkwy., St. Paul
(651) 487-2121
www.comotown.com
Como Town is a small-but-nice amusement park, with 17 attractions geared toward kids ages 2 to 12, who can fight pretend fires with a personal truck and water cannon, navigate ministreets by kiddie car, and climb, swing, and bounce their way through a mega–jungle gym called Hodge Podge Park. A couple of rides have some height and speed, too. Admission to the park is free, then you buy rides with one to four 75-cent tickets. You can buy ticket packages that will help get the price down if you're planning on hitting a bunch of the rides.

GRAND RIOS $$–$$$
6900 Lakeland Ave. North, Brooklyn Park
(763) 566-8855
www.grandrios.com
Grand Rios is located inside the Grand Rios Hotel in the Minneapolis suburb of Brooklyn Park. At 45,000 square feet, it's one of the biggest indoor water parks in this neck of the woods. Grand Rios is a Caribbean-themed affair with water basketball, spas, a lazy river, a 500-gallon dumping bucket, and multiple tube slide, one of which dumps into Hurricane Plunge. Check the Water Park Calendar on the Web site, as the prices fluctuate dramatically depending on what day and at what time you'd like to visit.

NICKELODEON UNIVERSE $$$
Mall of America, 5000 Center Court
Bloomington
(952) 883-8600
www.nickelodeonuniverse.com

Located at the center of the Mall of America, Nickelodeon Universe, the largest indoor amusement park in America, has more than 25 rides and attractions for kids and adults alike. Admission to the park is free; you purchase points or a wristband for rides. If you'd like to sneak some kid-free shopping in, drop the little ones off at Kids Quest in Nickelodeon Universe. The child care facility charges by the hour, and there's plenty for kids to do here, including read books, sing karaoke, and play nonviolent video games.

VALLEYFAIR $$$$
1 Valleyfair Dr., Shakopee
(952) 445-6500
www.valleyfair.com
With more than 75 rides and attractions, Valleyfair is the Upper Midwest's largest theme park, with something to offer the littlest kid or the bravest adult. Take an inner tube down a gently sloping canal for a relaxing, meditative ride on Ripple Rapids, or take a boat off a 50-foot drop on the Flume. The park is packed with twists, turns, flips, and freefalls, from the classic wooden High Roller to the Xtreme Swing, like your typical playground version on steroids, new in 2006. There are also many rides for the really little ones, too, from bumble bee–shaped electric cars to a multilevel foam-ball factory to an antique carousel. If it's hot out, don't miss Whitewater Country, a three-and-a-half-acre waterpark with multiple water slides, raft rides, and attractions with names like Raging Rapids, Splash Station, and Giggle.

> **i** Twin Cities parents love Toddler Tuesday at the Mall of America for its great deals, including free meals and activities.

WATER PARK AT THE DEPOT $$$
225 Third Ave. South, Minneapolis
(612) 758-7818
www.thedepotminneapolis.com
With 15,000 square feet, this locomotive-themed water park includes a three-story waterslide, multiple pools, and a slide/train that sprays water. It's pretty pricey for its size (or lack thereof), but it's connected to hotels that offer package deals and it's downtown, near many other attractions.

WATER PARK OF AMERICA $$$
1700 East American Blvd.
Bloomington
(952) 698-8888
www.waterparkofamerica.com
Adjacent to the Mall of America, the Water Park of America offers the only surfing simulator in Minnesota, a wave pool, a ten-story raft ride, swimming pools, and more. Arrive early during warm summer weekends, as the water park often fills to capacity. The water park is open seasonally and hours vary (call ahead for details). The water park complex includes a game arcade with many different prizes for winners.

Animal Adventures

COMO ZOO FREE
1225 Estabrook Dr., St. Paul
(651) 487-8200
www.comozooconservatory.org
One of only four free metropolitan-area zoos in the country, Como Zoo has been an institution in St. Paul for more than a century. The zoo offers intimate exhibits housing reticulated giraffes, black-footed penguins, snow leopards, yellow-rumped caciques, blue-eyed black lemurs, gray wolves, and more. There is a great primate display, with about a dozen ring-tailed and brown lemurs, spider monkeys, a couple of breeding pairs of tamarins, orangutans, and gorillas. There are bears, giraffes, zebras, buffalo, and the ever-popular Sparky the Sea Lion show, held Memorial Day through Labor Day. (The show's been an institution for so long that the zoo's on Sparky VI.)

But it doesn't stop at the animals. There's also an antique wooden carousel, Cafesjian's Carousel, for kids and adults to ride in a building near the entrance of the zoo, and in summer check out the amusement park Como Town. In late October the zoo opens in the evening for its annual "Zoo Boo," where kids come in their Halloween costumes and are given candy and gifts by more than 300 volunteers.

MINNESOTA ZOO $$
13000 Zoo Blvd., Apple Valley
(952) 431-9200 or (800) 366-7811
www.mnzoo.com

Located in the southeastern suburb of Apple Valley and housing some 500 animal species from five continents, the Minnesota Zoo and its IMAX theater see a million visitors per year.

The zoo also features the 600-seat Great Clips IMAX theater and the Weesner Family Amphitheater, which hosts concerts all summer long.

To reach the zoo, follow I-35E south from I-494 in the southeast Metro, exit at MN 77, and follow the signs.

UNDERWATER ADVENTURES
AQUARIUM $$–$$$
Mall of America, 120 East Broadway
Bloomington
(952) 883-0202 or (888) 348-3824
www.underwaterworld.com

Underwater Adventures is a huge (1.2 million gallons) walk-through aquarium featuring more than 4,500 different sea creatures from around the world in eight exhibits. For a one-time admission charge, visitors can walk through a glass tunnel that leads them underneath the three freshwater exhibits: Touch of the Wild Woods, Fisherman's Hollow, and the Wild Amazon, and five ocean exhibits: Shark Cove, Rainbow Reef, Seacrits of Hollywood (with famous fish like Nemo), Starfish Beach, and Circle of Life, where children can touch harmless sharks and stingrays.

Berry Pickin'

Driving out to the country to pick fresh strawberries, blueberries, or apples is a Minnesota-childhood staple. For a small per-bucket fee, the following farms let visitors pick as much fruit as they can carry home, and there are often bonus attractions such as petting zoos, wagon rides, and gift shops. For apples, we suggest you stop by Aamodt's Apple Farm, 6428 Manning Ave. North, Stillwater (651-439-3127; www.aamodtsapplefarm .com); or the Afton Apple Orchards, 14421 South 90th St., Hastings (651-436-8385; www.aftonapple .com). For strawberries and blueberries, try either the Bauer Berry Farm, 10830 French Lake Rd., Champlin (763-421-4384; www.bauerberry.com); or Covered Bridge Farm, 18655 Forest Blvd. North, Forest Lake (651-464-0735). For a comprehensive list of basically anything grown in the state that you can buy directly from farms, contact Minnesota Grown (www.minnesotagrown.com).

Arts and Culture

THE CHILDREN'S THEATRE COMPANY $$$
2400 Third Ave. South, Minneapolis
(612) 874-0400
www.childrenstheatre.org

Since 1965 the Tony Award–winning Children's Theatre Company and its cast of incredibly talented children and professional adult actors have been putting on performances at its two-stage theater in south Minneapolis. Most of the performances are based on children's stories and fairy tales, such as *Alexander and the Terrible, Horrible, No Good, Very Bad Day* by Judith Viorst, but there's a healthy dose of impressive original works as well.

> **i** The Twin Cities have arguably the nation's best youth theater scene. If your kids can't find a play they like in the Twin Cities, then theater is definitely not for them.

IN THE HEART OF THE BEAST PUPPET AND
MASK THEATRE $$
1500 East Lake St., Minneapolis
(612) 721-2535
www.hobt.org

Unusual masks and large, fantastical puppets teach themes of natural and cultural understanding here. Outside of regular original performances and the much-lauded MayDay parade, Heart of the Beast offers kids' performances every Saturday morning for $3, with a $2 discount if you're from the neighborhood.

MINNEAPOLIS SCULPTURE GARDEN   FREE
725 Vineland Place, Minneapolis
(612) 375-7577
www.walkerart.org
Located across the street from the Walker Art Center, this beautiful collection of large sculptures made by local and internationally known artists is a great place to take kids because it's outside, it's interesting, and it's free. The Minneapolis Sculpture Garden features one of the most photographed spots in Minnesota: the gigantic *Spoonbridge and Cherry* by Claes Oldenburg and Coosje van Bruggen, conveniently placed for pictures of the sculpture against the Minneapolis skyline. In all, more than 40 works of art spread out on the lawns of the sculpture garden. Right across another street is Loring Park, with restrooms, a wading pool, a playground, and lots of sunny spots for a relaxing summer picnic.

MINNESOTA CENTER FOR BOOK ARTS $$
1011 Washington Ave. South, Suite 100
Minneapolis
(612) 215-2520
www.mnbookarts.org
The Minnesota Center for Book Arts, the largest independent book arts facility in the nation, offers classes to children, teens, families, and adults on making paper, binding books, and working in a printing-press studio. Kids can take their literary creations to the next level by making a beautiful cover out of found objects and binding their books using traditional methods, or they can create their own newspapers in the letterpress studio using both modern and antiquated letterpress equipment.

STAGES THEATRE COMPANY $$
1111 Main St., Hopkins
(952) 979-1123
In a metro area with a wealth of options for children's theater, Stages stands as a sturdy option in the first-ring western suburb of Hopkins. Especially if your travels or living arrangements have you in the vicinity of their space, Stages's offerings are worth taking a look at. Like other children's theater companies, Stages also offers

classes; in recent years Stages students have had the chance to work with top theater artists including the innovative Jon Ferguson, who oversees theater programming at the Southern.

STEPPINGSTONE THEATRE $$
55 Victoria St. North, St. Paul
(651) 225-9265
www.steppingstonetheatre.org
After years wedged uncomfortably into Landmark Center, in 2007 SteppingStone moved into a grand new space just off Summit Avenue: a sizable venue for performances, with subterranean space for classes. SteppingStone offers theater for kids, by kids: grown-ups are rarely to be seen on the Stepping Stone stage, which gives the average SteppingStone production the feel of a really well-done school musical. Appropriately, their annual holiday offering is *The Best Christmas Pageant Ever*.

YOUTH PERFORMANCE COMPANY $$
3338 University Ave. SE, Minneapolis
(612) 623-9080
www.youthperformanceco.com
Though the Youth Performance Company (YPC) works with kids of all ages, it's especially strong as a venue for teens, who take an active role in creating stage productions and films for an audience of their peers. While YPC can tell a fairy tale well when it wants to, it also takes on tough social issues including race, sex, and family turmoil. It's theater to talk about.

Museums and Historical Attractions

THE BAKKEN LIBRARY AND MUSEUM $–$$
3537 Zenith Ave. South, Minneapolis
(612) 926-3878
www.thebakken.org
It starts in the lobby, where kids dive into the shocker machine, thought a cure-all in the 1920s, while parents read about the museum's founder, Earl E. Bakken, inventor of the first portable pacemaker. The rest of the electricity-related thingamajigs throughout this Tudor-style mansion are often hands-on—adults tend to hog the

theremin, that instrument that makes B-movie UFO sounds, and kids really like the crack and spark that comes from cranking out 60,000 volts. Nine informational exhibits include the popular "Frankenstein: Mary Shelley's Dream." Recommended for ages six and above.

BELL MUSEUM OF NATURAL HISTORY $
University of Minnesota, 10 Church St. SE, Minneapolis
(612) 624-7083
www.bellmuseum.org
The Bell Museum is designed to preserve the past, protect the future, and bring people closer to nature. Taxidermied animals may creep you out, but how else is your kid going to get the chance to pet a Kodiak bear? The Touch and See Room lets children handle history, such as a 10,000-year-old woolly mammoth tusk; various fossils, bones, and rocks; and live animals including lizards and turtles. The museum has two floors of diorama-style exhibits featuring North American mammals and birds, with an emphasis on Minnesota wildlife, including a bald eagle, moose, and squirrels. There's also a rain-forest plant exhibit and a hall for traveling exhibits and artwork. The museum hosts many classes and activities for children.

FORT SNELLING $-$$
MN 5 and MN 55, St. Paul
(612) 726-1171
www.mnhs.org/fortsnelling
Established on a bluff overlooking the Mississippi and Minnesota Rivers in 1819, Fort Snelling was once the last American outpost in the mostly unexplored wilds of the north and was the center of frontier commerce and government on the upper Mississippi. Themed tours provide insight into what life was like at the fort, with costumed guides reenacting scenes from military, civilian, and American Indian life of the 1800s. Kids can join in the fun by taking up a musket and pretending to be a soldier, scraping hides with fur traders, or "working" in the laundry or kitchen of the fort. Programming includes day camps and kids' activities.

THE JACKSON STREET ROUNDHOUSE $
193 East Pennsylvania Ave., St. Paul
(651) 228-0263
www.mtmuseum.org
It's all about trains here at the first railroad maintenance shop in Minnesota, part of the Minnesota Transportation Museum. Climb aboard train cars of varying eras and styles. Learn the state's railroad history through vintage posters and railroad maps. There's a gift shop, a kids' play area, and a working shop, too, where locomotives are restored. Choo-choo-loving youngsters will love it here.

MILL CITY MUSEUM $$
704 South Second St., Minneapolis
(612) 341-7555
www.millcitymuseum.org
Lots of hands-on, kid-friendly exhibits here make Minneapolis's flour-milling saga intriguing for both child and adult. Seeing the building itself is worth the trip. A fire nearly destroyed the mill, and the museum was built around the ruins.

MINNESOTA CHILDREN'S MUSEUM $$
10 West Seventh St., St. Paul
(651) 225-6000
www.mcm.org
The great thing about this museum, which is geared toward children six months to 10 years, is that all the exhibits are hands-on. While in the World Works Gallery, kids can operate a crane to pick up blocks, build a house foundation out of rubber masonry, or learn how to make art out of recycled newspaper. The Earth World Gallery has a giant anthill (populated by giant ant statues and nests) that kids can crawl through, pulley-operated clouds that can be moved across the ceiling by remote control, and a beaver dam and a giant hollow log that kids can climb in and out of.

For toddlers ages six months to four years, there's a wonderful playroom, the Habitot, that's set up like a nature preserve, with a giant "pond" playpen filled with plush lily pads and frog, turtle, and fish puppets at one end and a padded crawl-through cave filled with more stuffed animals and puppets at the other end. Changing rooms are connected to the exhibit, too, so parents don't have to rush to the other end of the building to take care of emergencies. Performances and activities take place in the second-floor atrium at scheduled intervals throughout the day.

THE MINNESOTA HISTORY CENTER $$
345 Kellogg Blvd. West, St. Paul
(651) 259-3000 or (800) 657-3773
www.mnhs.org/historycenter
A few of the permanent exhibits at the Minnesota History Center are particularly kid friendly—though kids will probably be most excited at the prospect of running wildly down the museum's long, wide hallways.

SCIENCE MUSEUM OF MINNESOTA $$
120 West Kellogg Blvd., St. Paul
(651) 221-9444 or (800) 221-9444
www.smm.org
Cool fossils and dinosaur skeletons, including a set of T. rex jaws you can operate, are at the heart of the Science Museum of Minnesota. But there's lots more interaction among the eight indoor acres of permanent and temporary exhibits. In the Cell Lab, kids don lab coats and check out what their cheek cells look like under the microscope. In the Mississippi River Gallery, kids pretend to drive a real tugboat as they look out over the river.

There are river views everywhere, from the museum's patios and soaring glass windows and from the new outdoor exhibits—the nine-hole minigolf course (summertime only) is actually a lesson in river science, and the prairie maze is made from native Minnesota plants and grasses. There's an Omnitheater, too, as well as kids' and family classes with activities such as fossil hunting, robot building, and experimenting with dry ice.

i In both Minneapolis and St. Paul, there's a park in nearly every neighborhood for you to stop and let the kids get out and stretch their legs.

TWIN CITY MODEL RAILROAD MUSEUM $
Bandana Square, 1021 Bandana Blvd. East, St. Paul
(651) 647-9628
www.tcmrm.org
A great treat for children and adults alike, this museum will particularly impress anyone even slightly interested in history, railroads, or miniatures. In existence in one form or another since 1939, the Model Railroad Club has been educating and entertaining the public with model locomotives, building its incredible panoramic sets to scale to complete the illusion. The museum is set inside a former passenger-train repair shop that houses a wonderful scale model of the Twin Cities and the surrounding communities, including parts of the Mississippi River and the old Mill District in Minneapolis prior to 1950, when trains were still the main means of transporting goods throughout the country. Up to six trains run at once through the model, disappearing into tunnels and climbing through the tree-filled landscapes with their tiny headlights blazing. The exhibit changes monthly—miniature streetcars run back and forth over the Third Avenue Bridge model, or steam engines like the *Milwaukee Hiawatha* pull passenger cars in and out of the 1914 Great Northern passenger depot. In the winter, the museum stays open a little later on Saturday to show off the special "Night Trains" exhibit, where all the lights are turned off in the museum and the lights on the trains and miniature buildings become the only source of illumination in the room.

Parks (Favorites of Little Insiders)
CENTENNIAL LAKES PARK $
7499 France Ave. South, Edina
(952) 832-6790
www.ci.edina.mn.us/content/facilities/centennial_lakes
Centennial Lakes is really more like an amusement park than a conventional city park—the precisely landscaped 10-acre park has a pond stocked with sunfish (yes, you can catch them), paddleboats, and model boats from the Edina

Model Yacht Club; a miniature golf course that actually looks like a tiny little golf course (complete with course-side condos); croquet; a maze; and more. In winter there's skating and other snowy fun. If you're in the mood for a little commercial entertainment, there's also an adjacent Chuck E. Cheese.

i The Greater Minneapolis Convention and Visitor's Association has a Web site for visitors with children. See www .minneapolis-kids.com for information about discounts, family-friendly hotels, and kid-approved sights.

HARRIET ISLAND REGIONAL PARK   FREE
West of Wabasha and Water Streets,
St. Paul
(651) 292-7010
www.stpaul.gov
In the shadow of St. Paul sits the largest urban river park in North America. Seems there's always an event going on at Harriet Island, such as the summer children's concert series and the Taste of Minnesota, the state's popular annual Independence Day celebration (both of which are free, by the way). The Padelford Packet Boat Company launches riverboat tours from here. And you'll find, among other things, a riverboat-themed playground, the floating River Boat Grill, and big, wide steps that head right down into the Mississippi.

HYLAND PLAY AREA
10145 Bush Lake Rd., Bloomington
(763) 694-7687
www.threeriversparks.org
This play area is legend among Twin Cities children, who refer to it as "Chutes and Ladders" for its extra-long slides—up to 50 feet long. If your kids can't get the monkeying around out of their system at this giant maze of climbing structures, you actually will need to follow through with that threat to donate them to the zoo.

LAKE CALHOUN
3000 Calhoun Pkwy., Minneapolis
(612) 230-6400
www.minneapolisparks.org
Lake Calhoun is part of Minneapolis's inner-city chain of lakes, which are immensely popular year-round, especially with families. This particular lake has a little bit of everything, including sandy beaches, a fishing dock, picnic areas, walking and biking paths, and a tot lot. You can rent canoes, kayaks, and paddleboats at the Lake Calhoun Pavilion on the east side of the lake. The waterside pavilion houses a restaurant called Tin Fish, with all kinds of seafood, snacks, and kid-friendly items such as hot dogs, grilled cheese, fish and chips, and root-beer floats. While you're walking around the lake, be on the lookout for the treehole home of "Mr. Little Guy," for whom you can leave notes and return to find tiny little responses.

Restaurants That Like Kids (and vice versa)

AMERICAN GIRL BISTRO
5160 Center Court, Mall of America,
Bloomington
(877) 247-5223
www.americangirl.com
When you're running around with kids, you have to think about whether a dining establishment is kid-friendly . . . but if they're doll owners, what the kids need to worry about is whether the place is doll-friendly. There's no more doll-friendly diner in town than the American Girl Bistro, where little girls and the dolls who love them can dine in what will seem to them like sumptuous splendor. (Boys are also welcome, but the venue notes that "helping girls celebrate girlhood is what we do best.") Needless to say, the bistro also does birthday parties. Girl's birthday, doll's birthday . . . whatever.

CONVENTION GRILL & FOUNTAIN
3912 Sunnyside Rd., Edina
(952) 920-6881

The Convention Grill & Fountain is an authentic diner that's thankfully light on kitsch as well as on the pocketbook. Choose a booth seat or one at the stainless-steel counter overlooking the double-wide grill. The jukebox plays as servers zip around with vanilla Cokes, hamburgers, skin-on fries, and malts served as they should be—with a long spoon and the overflow in the metal cup each malt was made in.

CUPCAKE
3338 University Ave. SE, Minneapolis
(612) 378-4818

It's all about the cupcakes. The cafe/coffeehouse rotates randomly through about 50 tried-and-true cupcake recipes, and you'll find up to 12 varieties offered on any given day. One kid favorite is the Betty Crocker, if solely for its swirly pink frosting and pretty pastel sprinkles, but look for Boston Crème, Red Velvet, Lemon Sunshine, S'More, and Coco Loco as well. The menu holds soups, sandwiches, pizzas, PB&J, and egg salad, too.

i As any parent knows, kids are much less daring eaters than adults, and sometimes (maybe even usually) they'd choose McDonald's over any other dining option. The Twin Cities have plenty of those, as well as kid-pleasing chains like Old Country Buffet and Dairy Queen.

GALACTIC PIZZA
2917 Lyndale Ave. South, Minneapolis
(612) 824-9100
www.galacticpizza.com

Superheroes deliver the pizza from Galactic. Generic superheroes, not Spidey or Superman, but spandex and capes are involved. Delivery service, by electric vehicle, is limited to southwest Minneapolis, though it does extend to downtown Minneapolis during lunch. Travelers can order pizza delivered to their hotels. Or they can opt to eat on-site (where, note, you will not be served by superheroes). The clean, multicolored storefront has brightly colored, child-height tables outdoors, retro Formica kitchen tables inside, and some toys older kids might like, including pick-

up sticks, dominoes, and chess. Galactic is more kid friendly than kid oriented, though, and the nighttime crowd is primarily adult. The restaurant theme is social responsibility—you'll see a lot of words like hormone-free, recycled, and organic on the menu. The pizza can be plain or exotic, meaty or vegan, whatever you want. (The Paul Bunyan, with bison sausage, morel mushrooms, and wild rice, is surprisingly delicious.)

JAVA TRAIN $
1341 Pascal Ave. North, St. Paul
(651) 646-9179
www.javatraincafe.com

You'll have to seek out the Java Train: Hidden in a residential neighborhood near the State Fairgrounds, it's not something you're just going to stumble across unless you live close by. It's worth the hunt, though, especially for families with kids. There are spacious play areas indoor and out, a complete kids' menu, and candy machines for cheap treats. The venue also sponsors family events including cooking classes, Easter egg hunts, and more. Grown-ups will enjoy the tasty, vegetarian-friendly food and—of course—the java.

POP! A NEIGHBORHOOD RESTAURANT
2859 Johnson Ave. NE, Minneapolis
(612) 788-0455

6 West Sixth St., St. Paul
(651) 228-1002
www.poprestaurant.com

Pop! possesses hard-to-find qualities in a restaurant: a casually upscale atmosphere that welcomes children, gourmet food at reasonable prices, and a drink menu that holds both a solid wine list and an even bigger selection of pop, the preferred word for sweet, carbonated beverages here in Minnesota. The name also refers to the 1960s art movement, which informs the venue's decor. There's more than a hint of Latin America in the menu, where tamales and empanadas exist alongside pasta and burgers, and where smoked jalapeño mayo and avocado find their way onto the chicken sandwich. Try to save room for dessert.

(The recently opened second location, in St. Paul, is technically known as Pop!! See the difference?)

SPACE ALIENS GRILL & BAR
9967 Ulysses St. NE, Blaine
(763) 780-2383
www.spacealiens.com
Space Aliens advertises itself as "a franchise of galactic proportions"—which is a bit of an exaggeration given that the six restaurants are located only in Minnesota and North Dakota, but nonetheless, it's a pretty flippin' big deal if you're eight years old. Selling pizza and burgers to families sitting among statues of aliens under a giant space dome and then sending them off to play arcade games, Space Aliens is essentially a Chuck E. Cheese—but with its theme being aliens instead of giant mice. Win.

SNUFFY'S MALT SHOP
244 Cleveland Ave. South, St. Paul
(651) 690-1846

1125 Larpenteur Ave. West, St. Paul
(651) 488-0241

17519 Minnetonka Blvd., Minnetonka
(952) 475-1850

4502 Valley View Rd., Edina
(952) 920-0949
Ask a St. Paul family where their kids like to go out to eat, and it's a safe bet the first answer will be Snuffy's. There's nothing too unusual about this small chain's original and best-loved location on Cleveland Avenue—no play equipment, no crazy theme, no arcade games except for a single candy crane. It's simply very welcoming, and it's where everyone goes after baseball games and school plays; it's like the Cheers of the Mac-Groveland grade school set. Burgers? Check. Fries? Check. Malts? Read the sign. At Snuffy's, they've got the goods.

We All Scream For . . .
GRAND OLE CREAMERY
750 Grand Ave., St. Paul
(651) 293-1655
www.grandolecreamery.com

Do not be deterred by the line snaking out the door, spilling out onto the sidewalks of Grand Avenue. This ice cream is worth the wait. The waffle cones are made fresh daily and plugged with a malted milk ball to prevent sticky hands and ice-cream-smeared shirts. There are 200 flavors, and the 31 available on any given day tend toward the seasonal—strawberry kiwi sorbet in the summer, German chocolate and pumpkin apple strudel in the fall, and choices like egg nog and Winter Wonderland (loaded with peppermint candy) in the winter.

IZZY'S ICE CREAM CAFE
2034 Marshall Ave., St. Paul
(651) 603-1458
www.izzysicecream.com
Izzy's is a local favorite not only for its kid friendliness but also for its namesake feature: An "izzy" is the extra one-ounce scoop of ice cream that tops your single- or double-scoop cone here. With 31 of Izzy's 100-plus artisan options spread out before you, it's hard enough to choose a flavor, let alone decide which izzy would be the best complement. Kids go gaga over the bubble gum and the blue cotton candy flavors. The one-ounce izzy cone is a nice size for young children.

Shopping Kid-Style
CHOO CHOO BOB'S TRAIN STORE
2050 Marshall Ave., St. Paul
(651) 646-5252
www.choochoobobs.com
Sit at any of the coffee shops or bakeries on Marshall and Cleveland on a Saturday morning and you'll see a parade of kids walking past with their parents and, often, grandparents. They're on their way to story time at Choo Choo Bob's, a store dedicated to model trains. Toy trains are associated with the 1940s more than with the 2010s, but Choo Choo Bob's isn't an antiques shop: It's a place where kids of all ages can find trains to play with and tracks to put them on. Story time with "Engineer Paul" is always popular; check the store's Web site for Paul's upcoming appearances.

CREATIVE KIDSTUFF
4313 Upton Ave. South, Minneapolis
(612) 927-0653
Five additional Twin Cities locations
www.creativekidstuff.com
This neat little local toyshop chain offers educational and creative toys for both kids and parents to salivate over. Hands-on is the motto here. Lots of toys have been removed from their packaging and scattered about the store for kids to try out. There are three big sales a year—a storewide event in June and clearance sales in July and after Christmas. Creative Kidstuff holds in-store kids' events throughout the year, too.

KIDDYWAMPUS
4400 Excelsior Blvd., St. Louis Park
(952) 926-7871
www.kiddywampus.com
Opened in 2006, this unusual toy store carries things to monkey with from all over the world (not just China) and has a built-in play area. Products include an Alien Pizza-Making Kit (with green crust and purple pizza sauce), an Insect Color Paint and Draw Kit (not for use on real bugs), and a Balloon-Powered Boat (perfect for bath time). Kiddywampus actively courts parents looking for a birthday party venue and will host such gatherings, and the store also offers Abrakadoodle art classes for kids as young as 20 months.

PACIFIER
310 East Hennepin Ave., Minneapolis
(612) 623-8123
www.pacifieronline.com
Pacifier stocks an offbeat and artistic collection of clothes, wooden toys, diaper bags, gifts, and much more for the baby of the family and the baby's parents. The store features clothing from Global Mamas, high-quality handmade dresses and onesies made by Ghanan women who are guaranteed a fair wage for their work.

THE RED BALLOON BOOKSHOP
891 Grand Ave., St. Paul
(651) 224-8320
www.redballoonbookshop.com
Located in a house on St. Paul's cozy Grand Avenue, the Red Balloon has been turning kids on to books since 1984. The selection is comprehensive, with classics past and future, and the staff obviously loves what they do—they're ready with suggestions if you need ideas. There's nearly always an event scheduled, whether it be a story hour or an author reading or lecture.

WILD RUMPUS BOOKS FOR YOUNG READERS
2720 West 43rd St., Minneapolis
(612) 920-5005
www.wildrumpusbooks.com
The front door of this 2,000-square-foot bookstore hints at what's to come. It actually holds a door within a door, giving kids an entrance that's their own size rather than the same old adult-height doorway. This place is definitely designed for kids. The name, plucked from Maurice Sendak's *Where the Wild Things Are,* fits. Animals are everywhere—chickens, cats, birds, ferrets, tarantulas, geckos, fish, and even a rat, whose cage is appropriately placed in the floor of the scary books reading shack. You'll find old and new favorites as well as books from smaller presses that you simply can't find at your local chain bookstore—one of many refreshing ways this bookshop differentiates itself from the big guys.

ANNUAL EVENTS

Festivals abound year-round in the Twin Cities. In the winter elaborate festivities like the Holidazzle Parade and the St. Paul Winter Carnival stave off cabin fever. With the coming of spring, just about anything can kick off a festival, from an abundance of wildflowers blooming to charitable functions and building restoration projects. Entire city blocks are roped off for block parties in the summer, and the streets are filled with cars decorated with seashells, ribbons, sculptures, and big painted flowers. Just about every tiny town in the state holds at least one spring and summer festival, complete with parades, concession and merchandise kiosks, and live music.

The following calendar lists only events that have been around for a while and that we expect will continue to be around.

JANUARY

ST. PAUL WINTER CARNIVAL
Various locations around St. Paul
Last week of January through first week of February
(651) 223-4700
www.winter-carnival.com
The St. Paul Winter Carnival is by far the coolest celebration in the Midwest and one of the oldest winter festivals in the country. More than 50 events—including amazing snow and ice-sculpture exhibits, live music, and sporting events such as a 5K run and half marathon, and softball on ice—are a part of this annual festival, with the crowning events being the King Boreas Grande Day Parade and the more decadent evening Vulcan Victory Torchlight Parade.

FEBRUARY

MIDWEST KIDS FEST
RiverCentre/Touchstone Energy Place
175 Kellogg Blvd., St. Paul
www.midwestkidsfest.com
Kids Fest is Minnesota's longest-running children's event, with multiple stages of live entertainment, dozens of free activities and games for kids of all ages, and Minnesota's largest inflatable playground (featuring a superslide, Velcro wall,

maze, sports challenges, and much more), all guaranteed to keep your kids busy for at least a day, maybe two. The Saturday and Sunday festival features celebrity visits from national childrens' artists (usually of Nickelodeon fame). In addition, there's the perennial favorite, the petting zoo, a rain-forest stage filled with exotic creatures, and pony rides.

TWIN CITIES FOOD & WINE EXPERIENCE
Minneapolis Convention Center,
1301 Second Ave. South, Minneapolis
A mid-February weekend
(612) 371-5800
www.foodwineshow.com
Although tickets for this annual event get into the pricey range (over $50), you are likely to get your money's worth even if you don't come hungry. About 300 Twin Cities restaurants; local, national, and international wineries; and other exhibitors serve up their gourmet specialties to the masses. Additional events (at an additional charge) include wine seminars and wine lunches at restaurants throughout the Metro.

MARCH

ST. PATRICK'S DAY PARADE
Downtown St. Paul
(651) 292-3225

St. Paul's annual St. Patrick's Day Parade picks up at Fourth and Wacouta Streets and heads west all the way down Fourth Street, ending at Rice Park. The parade features Irish music and performers, and food, drink, and merchandise kiosks are set up along the parade route for the remainder of the day.

The parade is all part of St. Paul's annual Irish Celebration, paying homage to the many Irish immigrants who settled in the city. Entertainment, crafts, Irish foods, and beer (Irish and otherwise) are all part of the festivities, centered around Landmark Center in downtown St. Paul.

APRIL

MINNEAPOLIS–ST. PAUL INTERNATIONAL FILM FESTIVAL
Various locations
Three weeks in April
(612) 331-3134
www.mspfilmfest.org
In 20-plus years, Minnesota Film Arts' Minneapolis–St. Paul International Film Festival has gone from a weekend-long event to the present high-water mark where about 150 flicks from more than 60 nations are screened during three full weeks in April. The festival's participating theaters include the Oak Street Cinema, Bell Auditorium, Riverview Theater, Crown Theatres Block E, and other Twin Cities film houses.

IRONMAN BICYCLE RIDE
Lakeville High School, Lakeville
Last Sunday of April
(651) 251-1495
www.ironmanbikeride.org
An annual event for more than 40 years, the Ironman Bike Ride takes 5,000 participating bicyclists through 30-mile, 62-mile, or 100-mile scenic tours through the Minnesota countryside.

MAY

FESTIVAL OF NATIONS
175 Kellogg Blvd. West, RiverCentre, St. Paul
(651) 647-0191
www.festivalofnations.com

Founded in 1932 and held generally in late April or early May, the Festival of Nations has been an event of the people who helped create it for their pleasure and the ethnic values they treasured. Its underlying philosophy has been that as Americans of all backgrounds—native citizens and naturalized citizens alike—share experiences, their differences become less significant and barriers to understanding are removed. Today Minnesota's largest multicultural event showcases more than 100 ethnic groups through food, dance performances, cultural exhibits, folk art demonstrations, an international bazaar, and more.

CINCO DE MAYO FIESTA
District del Sol, St. Paul
First week in May
(651) 222-6347
www.districtdelsol.com
The Cinco de Mayo Fiesta lights up the District del Sol on the west side of St. Paul, across the Robert Street Bridge from downtown (for visitors, the "west" side of St. Paul is actually south of downtown). More than 100,000 people fill the streets of the Hispanic neighborhood to take in Mexican entertainment and food and to watch the Cinco de Mayo Parade.

IN THE HEART OF THE BEAST MAYDAY PARADE
Powderhorn Park, 3400 15th Ave. South, Minneapolis
First Sunday of May
(612) 721-2535
www.hobt.org
For more than 30 years, In the Heart of the Beast Puppet and Mask Theatre's annual MayDay Parade has been as true a sign of spring returning to the Twin Cities as robins choosing their mates. The brilliantly colored ensemble of friendly and scary creatures on stilts, children dressed as flowers, and other magical images travels along Minneapolis's downtown Bloomington Avenue and ends in a colorful pageant in Powderhorn Park, where puppets sail across the pond in boats. This funky celebration of spring will fill an entire day with dance, music, fun, and food all along the parade route.

JUNE

ALIVE AFTER FIVE CONCERT SERIES
Peavey Plaza, 11th Street and Nicollet Mall, Minneapolis
(612) 338-3807
Unwind after the workday with good food and music on the mall throughout June. Local and touring bands can be seen at the plaza for free, and drink and food kiosks are set up close to the stage.

BASTILLE DAY BLOCK PARTY
Barbette, 1600 West Lake St., Minneapolis
A Sunday in June
(612) 827-5710
www.bastilledayblockparty.com
Barbette's French ambience spills out into Lake Street each June for a block party that features not only favorite musicians but also burlesque performers, circus acts, theater troupes, skateboarders, and roller girls. Watch your toes—and your head—as you raise a glass to the spirit of '89.

GRAND OLD DAY
Grand Avenue, St. Paul
First Sunday of June
(651) 699-0029
www.grandave.com
More than 200,000 people show up for this granddaddy of Twin Cities celebrations with everything from a Strongest Man and Woman on Grand contest to local bands performing on multiple stages. Lots of food vendors and merchant kiosks, and various family attractions are featured during the event, as well as the 10 a.m. Kiddie Parade followed at 10:30 by the Grand Old Day parade.

The festival engulfs 30 city blocks and is packed with more than 150 outdoor vendors offering every delicacy imaginable, from Cokes, pizza, and corn dogs to gyros, egg rolls, and Jamaican beef.

EDINA ART FAIR
50th and France, Edina
First weekend in June
(952) 922-1524
www.50thandfrance.com

More than 400 local, regional, and national artists whose works include clothing, dolls, woodcarving, and more are featured at this annual festival.

MILL CITY MUSEUM SUMMER MUSIC
704 South Second St., Minneapolis
Throughout summer
(612) 341-7555
www.millcitymuseum.org
The Mill City Museum makes use of its courtyard to host favorite local acts like Jeremy Messersmith, Roma di Luna, and Caroline Smith and the Goodnight Sleeps.

RED HOT ART FESTIVAL
Stevens Square Park, Second Ave. and 18th St., Minneapolis
First weekend in June
(612) 874-2840
www.redhotart.org
Works by local emerging artists are showcased at this event, along with food, music, and other entertainment.

ROCK THE GARDEN
Walker Art Center, 1750 Hennepin Ave., Minneapolis
A Saturday in June
(612) 375-7600
www.walkerart.org
This annual birthday party for the Minneapolis Sculpture Garden is not actually held in the garden—it's on the grassy hill where the Guthrie used to be, just across the street. The Walker partners with 89.3 The Current for this event, which features a daylong lineup of local and national bands in one of the most anticipated shows of the year. Watch the Walker's news channels for the springtime announcement of the lineup, and move quickly when tickets go on sale—they don't last long.

ST. ANTHONY MAIN SUMMER MUSIC SERIES
219 SE Main St., Minneapolis
www.saintanthonymain.com/musiccalender.shtml
(note misspelling in URL—no one's perfect!)

Throughout the summer, weekends, and July 4, you can catch live music for free on the stage outside Tuggs Tavern, located right across the street from the Mississippi River.

ST. ANTHONY PARK ARTS FESTIVAL
Como Ave., St. Anthony Park Neighborhood, St. Paul
First Saturday of June
www.stanthonyparkartsfestival.org
More than 100 Midwestern artists showcase their goods annually in one of St. Paul's prettiest neighborhoods, with food and music available all along Como Avenue from Carter to Luther Seminary. You can find spectacular deals on truly unusual items at this juried art show.

TATER DAZE
Downtown Brooklyn Park
A weekend in June
(763) 493-8013
www.brooklynpark.org/taterdaze
Tater Daze celebrates Brooklyn Park's potato-growing heritage. The weekend festival kicks off with a parade on the first night and is followed by a host of events, including live music and lots of family activities.

ART ON THE LAKE
Downtown Excelsior
A weekend in June
(952) 474-6461
www.excelsiorartonthelake.com
For more than 20 years, Excelsior's juried Art on the Lake has showcased the work of local and national artists through art competitions, demonstrations, and other related activities. Food, live music, and other entertainment are almost as important a part of this festival as the art itself.

FATHER HENNEPIN FESTIVAL
Downtown Champlin
Second weekend in June
(763) 421-2820
www.fatherhennepinfestival.com

This is a family-oriented festival, featuring fireworks, powerboats, personal watercraft races, and amusement park rides.

SOUTH ST. PAUL KAPOSIA DAYS
Various locations, South St. Paul
(651) 451-2266
www.kaposiadays.org
This family-oriented festival includes a street dance, a treasure hunt, a grand parade, children's activities, a flea market and craft sale, royalty pageants, bingo, water war games, fireworks, a Kiss the Pig contest, and athletic tournaments.

ST. LOUIS PARKTACULAR
Various locations, St. Louis Park
(952) 924-2550
www.parktacular.org
St. Louis Park's annual community celebration features a carnival, live music, a parade, food vendors, a silent auction, and an art fair.

STONE ARCH FESTIVAL OF THE ARTS
Mississippi Riverfront, Old St. Anthony Main, Minneapolis
Father's Day weekend
www.stonearchfestival.com
More than 250 artists, along with vendors, bands, and street performers, congregate along the riverfront, making this a fun festival to either take Dad to for the afternoon or to shop for a present for him. The festival also features free dance, theater, and music performances; kids' art projects; free cooking demonstrations; and an Art Car show.

MIDSOMMAR CELEBRATION
American Swedish Institute, 2600 Park Ave. South, Minneapolis
Mid-June
(612) 871-4907
www.americanswedishinst.org
Celebrate Midsommar in the Swedish tradition with music, folk dance, and food. Join the museum's costumed guides and performers in this traditional festival that celebrates everything good about summer.

MIDSOMMAR DAG
20880 Olinda Trail, Scandia
Third Saturday in June
(651) 433-5053
www.gammelgardenmuseum.org/mid sommar.shtm
Midsommar Dag kicks off the festival season in the picturesque town of Scandia, located east of the Twin Cities a few miles north of Marine on St. Croix. Sponsored by the Gammelgården Museum, the festival is a bright affair of parades, traditional Scandinavian dancing and costumes, and lots of food.

BUCKHORN DAYS
Long Lake
A weekend at the end of June
www.longlake-orono.org
This weekend-long festival in the western suburb of Long Lake features live music, dancing, carnival games, fishing contests, "mad scientist" exhibits, and concession stands.

EARLE BROWN DAYS FESTIVAL
Downtown Brooklyn Center
Last week of June
(763) 569-3400
www.cityofbrooklyncenter.org/ earlebrowndays
This annual festival honoring civic leader and activist Earle Brown, features a parade, fireworks, arts and crafts fair, ice-cream social, live music and entertainment, and special events aimed at kids and teens, including a kids' fishing contest and lots of games.

MINNETONKA SUMMER FESTIVAL
Various locations, Minnetonka
Last Saturday in June
(952) 939-8200
www.eminnetonka.com
This citywide festival includes family-oriented activities for all ages: live entertainment, rides, games, food vendors, and fireworks.

MSRA'S BACK TO THE '50S WEEKEND
Minnesota State Fairgrounds, St. Paul
End of June
(651) 641-1992
www.msra.com
Every year, the Minnesota Street Rod Association (MSRA) heads to the state fairgrounds to show off its members' street rods, classic cars, and custom cars. More than 11,000 show cars can be seen at the event, which also features food and merchandise kiosks, commercial exhibits, and live music.

TWIN CITIES GLBT PRIDE FESTIVAL
Various locations, Minneapolis
Two weeks at the end of June
(612) 305-6990
www.tcpride.org
The largest annual gay/lesbian/bi/transsexual pride festival in the Upper Midwest includes a parade, music, food, and more. An estimated 400,000 people show up for the festival over the course of two weeks.

UPTOWN PRIDE BLOCK PARTY
Bryant-Lake Bowl
810 West Lake St., Minneapolis
A Friday in June
(612) 825-3737
www.uptownprideblockparty.com
The name of this annual block party thrown by the Bryant-Lake Bowl has a dual meaning: It's about having pride in both the Uptown neighborhood and in the Twin Cities' loud and proud GLBT population. (Its timing coincides with the larger Twin Cities Pride celebration.) You don't have to be an Uptown resident and/or gay, however, to enjoy the bands, drag performers, and breakdancers who parade across the stage over the course of an überfun evening.

JULY

ARTERY
Soap Factory, 518 Second St. SE, Minneapolis
24 hours in late July
(612) 623-9176
www.artery24.com

Artery is a marathon of performance art that runs 24 hours straight, with each artist having 30 minutes to an hour to perform. What started as a curiosity in 2008 has become an increasingly visible showcase for performers both established and new to strut their stuff. Admission is free, so you can come and go as you please over the course of the day.

BASILICA BLOCK PARTY
Corner of Hennepin Ave. and 17th St.
Basilica of Saint Mary, Minneapolis
Beginning of July
www.basilicablockparty.org
Proceeds from this annual outdoor festival go to restore the historic Basilica of Saint Mary, which in turn offers outreach and charitable programs to poor and impoverished people throughout the state. More than 20,000 people of all ages and denominations come to this event, which features big-name bands, food, and drink.

TASTE OF MINNESOTA
Harriet Island Regional Park, St. Paul
Five days ending July 4
(651) 772-9980
www.tasteofmn.com
This huge event offers food prepared by more than 40 of the Twin Cities' best restaurants, and dozens of national and regional performers. Each night concludes with fireworks.

TEN-SECOND FILM FESTIVAL
Soap Factory, 518 South Second St.,
Minneapolis
July 4
(612) 623-9176
www.soapfactory.org
Yes, you read that right—ten seconds. That's how long each entry in the Ten-Second Film Festival is; a further stipulation is that the films not be recorded on conventional video cameras. This is where cell-phone videographers shine, with often hilarious and sometimes strangely touching results. The films are projected on the wall of the Soap Factory immediately following the 4th of July fireworks, with beer and hot dogs available to enjoy while you watch.

EDEN PRAIRIE'S FOURTH OF JULY "HOME TOWN" CELEBRATION
Round Lake, 7550 Constitution Ave.
July 4
(952) 949-8450
www.edenprairie.org
This celebration finishes with spectacular fireworks at the Eden Prairie Center. Daytime activities at Round Lake Park include a kiddie parade, youth baseball tournament, live music, games, and concession stands.

MINNEAPOLIS RIVERFRONT FOURTH OF JULY CELEBRATION
Old St. Anthony Main, Minneapolis Riverfront
July 4
(612) 230-6400
www.mplsredwhiteboom.com
This is one of the best Fourth of July fireworks displays in the Twin Cities, with music and self-guided tours of the area's Mississippi River bridges. The best seat in the house is anywhere on Nicollet Island, where the fireworks seem to explode directly overhead.

PAN-O-PROG
Downtown Lakeville
First week of July
(952) 469-2020
www.panoprog.org
Since 1967 Lakeville has celebrated its Panorama of Progress festival, now called Pan-o-Prog, which features family entertainment including races, picnics, pet shows, dances, a scholarship pageant, Fourth of July fireworks, and a parade.

ANOKA RIVERFEST & CRAFT FAIR
Historic Downtown Anoka
Second Saturday of July
(763) 421-7130
www.anokariverfest.com

This all-day riverfront festival includes a craft/artisan fair, historical society events, live music, youth activities, and, of course, lots of food.

SOMMERFEST
Minnesota Orchestra
Peavey Plaza, downtown Minneapolis
Mid-July to early August
(612) 371-5656 or (800) 292-4141
www.minnesotaorchestra.org

The Minnesota Orchestra's annual Sommerfest features a series of concerts on Peavey Plaza (corner of South 12th Street and Nicollet Mall) adjacent to Orchestra Hall. The festival opens with Macy's Day of Music, a 24-hour, free music marathon with dozens of bands, singers, and ensembles playing from noon one day to noon the next. Numerous concerts follow, some played by the Minnesota Orchestra but also with many guest artists performing everything from opera to Zydeco.

SUMMER MUSIC AND MOVIES
Loring Park, 1382 Willow St., Minneapolis
(612) 375-7622
www.walkerart.org

Every Monday night from mid-July through August, free live music is followed by a movie in downtown Minneapolis's Loring Park. This is a collaboration between the Walker Art Center and the Minneapolis Park and Recreation Board.

SUBWAY BLOCK PARTY
Nicollet Mall between Third and Fourth Streets, Minneapolis
Second weekend in July
(612) 338-0634
www.aquatennial.com

Part of the Minneapolis Aquatennial Celebration, this free outdoor concert always features big-name bands and big crowds.

MINNEAPOLIS AQUATENNIAL
Various locations around Minneapolis
Third full week of July
(612) 338-0634
www.aquatennial.com

Royalty pageants, parades, milk carton boat races, and other events are featured in this citywide celebration nicknamed the 10 Best Days of Summer. The Aquatennial has the Torchlight Parade, a huge fireworks show, sand castle competitions, a triathlon, programs for juniors and seniors, and tons of family-oriented activities. One of the highlights of the celebration, the milk carton boat races, invites participants of all ages to create full-size boats out of hundreds of sealed milk cartons and race on Lake Calhoun.

i In 1978 millionaire and philanthropist Percy Ross rode in the Minneapolis Aquatennial's Torchlight Parade and threw $16,500 worth of silver into the crowd. This would get Percy in big trouble today—throwing objects from parade floats is now illegal in Minneapolis.

LUMBERJACK DAYS
Lowell Park, Stillwater
Second to last weekend of July
(651) 430-2306
www.lumberjackdays.com

This huge, weekend-long event features live concerts from local and regional artists, tons of concession stands, Minnesota's fastest 10-mile and 5K runs, kids' events, a huge parade, and Minnesota's biggest fireworks display—all located in historic downtown Stillwater. Wine tasting, ice-cream socials, lumberjack exhibits, logrolling and pie-baking contests are just a few of the events that you can expect to be torn between, not to mention the annual Treasure Hunt.

AUGUST

UPTOWN ART FAIR
Lake St. and Hennepin Ave. South, Minneapolis
First full weekend of August
(612) 823-4581
www.uptownminneapolis.com

The Uptown Art Fair is the largest art fair in Minneapolis, featuring work from hundreds of local and national artists as well as food and live music.

Painting, photography, sculpture, jewelry, ceramics, and fiber are on display and for sale at the event.

LORING PARK ART FESTIVAL
Loring Park, Oak Grove St. and Hennepin Ave. South, Minneapolis
First full weekend in August
(612) 203-9911
www.loringparkartfestival.com
Held at the same time as the Uptown Art Fair and Powderhorn Art Fair, the Loring Park Art Festival features more than 130 artists showing (and selling) their work on the grassy lawn surrounding Loring Lake. The juried show includes all manner of media, and the festival also has food booths, musicians wandering through the crowds, and stage performances.

POWDERHORN ART FAIR
Powderhorn Park, 3400 15th Ave. South
Minneapolis
First weekend of August
(612) 729-0111
www.powderhornartfair.org
The popular Powderhorn Art Fair, which runs concurrently with the Uptown Art Fair and the Loring Park Art Festival, is a winning attraction for crafts-fair fans. The weekend-long festival—originally billed as an alternative to the "big one down the street"—has developed a flavor of its own, exposing an eclectic variety of both artwork and artists to the public. Free bus service connects it with the Uptown Art Fair and Loring Park Art Festival.

MINNESOTA FRINGE FESTIVAL
Various venues in Minneapolis
First two weeks of August
(612) 872-1212
www.fringefestival.org
This annual celebration of offbeat live stage performances and visual art has hundreds of shows in multiple venues throughout the Twin Cities. The venues range from well-known theaters, such as the Southern and the Bryant-Lake Bowl, to "bring-your-own" venues, such as swimming pools and condos. Musicals, puppetry, dance, theater,

spoken word, and performance art are just some of the events during the festival. All performances are 60 minutes or less, and all are selected for inclusion in the festival by a lottery system rather than a juried competition, making this America's largest unjuried fringe festival and making it a real adventure to attend. Sometimes you'll see amazing things, sometimes you'll see complete trash—the uncertainty is part of the fun.

OLD TIME HARVEST FESTIVAL
Fairview Lane, across from the Scott County
Fairgrounds, Jordan
First weekend of August
www.scottcarverthreshers.org
This family-oriented festival has a vintage tractor show, a flea market, an antiques auction, and an antique car show, as well as demonstrations of threshing, sawing, spinning, and quilting. There's even a vintage farm equipment parade each afternoon.

MINNESOTA IRISH FAIR
Harriet Island, St. Paul
Second weekend of August
(952) 474-7411
www.irishfair.com
From bagpipes to bodhrans, corned beef to ceilis, this free three-day celebration of Irish culture features Irish music, dance, theater, exhibits, sports, a marketplace, genealogy information, and a special children's area.

MINNESOTA STATE FAIR
State Fairgrounds, 1265 Snelling Ave. North,
St. Paul
12 days ending on Labor Day
(651) 288-4400
www.mnstatefair.org
The State Fair is ground zero for what many Minnesotans consider the quintessential spirit of their state. More than 1.6 million people attend the Minnesota State Fair—usually drawing crowds of over one hundred thousand a day. The fair has big-name entertainment, exhibits, competitions, food, demonstrations, horse shows, auto races, a huge midway carnival, and lots of food on a

stick. There's also a bust of the festival's princess sculpted in butter, farm animal shows and competitions, a huge garden show, a vintage tractor display on Machinery Hill, and juried arts and crafts from state elementary, high school, and college students.

PIZZA LUCÉ BLOCK PARTY
Pizza Lucé, 3200 Lyndale Ave. South, Minneapolis
A Saturday in August
(612) 827-5978
www.luceblockparty.com
Pizza Lucé knows what music people who love Pizza Lucé love, and each summer the pizza chain fills a stage with a parade of indie-rock bands for a daylong celebration of local music and local pizza. Is there beer? Need you ask?

WOODBURY DAYS
Ojibway Park, Woodbury
Last weekend of August
www.woodburydays.com
Woodbury Days is a community event with lots of activities for the whole family, including carnival rides, games, food, the Woodbury Days Annual Bike Ride, inflatable slides, water fights, a petting zoo, the Rod & Custom Car Club Car Show, fireworks displays, a daily parade, and live music.

STIFTUNGSFEST
Downtown Norwood Young America
Last full weekend of August
(952) 467-1812
www.stiftungsfest.org
Stiftungsfest, founded in 1861, is the oldest festival in Minnesota. There's something for everyone at this celebration of German heritage and culture: German choirs, dancers, polka bands, arts, crafts, ethnic foods, and beverages.

MINNESOTA RENAISSANCE FESTIVAL
3 miles south of Shakopee on MN 169
Mid-August through the end of September
(952) 445-7361 or (800) 966-8215
www.renaissancefest.com/mrf

Huzzah! Jump back in time to experience life in the 16th century, or at least the fun parts of it. Food, fun, sword fights, games, comedy, dancers, singers, music, multiple stages of continuous entertainment, and royalty are regular staples of this annual event, which is open weekends in mid-August and through the end of September, as well as on Labor Day. The food choices are extensive, with some of the more notable including turkey drumsticks, Rice Krispie Kabobs, and Bangers & Mash. Wash it all down with a tankard of mead. The site of the Minnesota Renaissance Festival is a bustling, permanently standing replica of a 16th-century village filled with hundreds of costumed villagers, period buildings, and a huge marketplace. Dress in character to make the most of the experience. (Note, though, that the RenFest is not cheap: Besides the admission charge, most of the attractions and vendors inside charge additional fees.)

RED STAG BLOCK PARTY
Red Stag Supperclub, 509 First Ave. NE, Minneapolis
A Saturday in August
(612) 767-7766
www.redstagblockparty.com
The Red Stag clears its parking lot each August for one of the biggest among the numerous free block parties sponsored by local eateries. The party draws a big crowd to see big acts like Mark Mallman and Roma di Luna, with DJs spinning a hopping afterparty inside the Stag itself.

SEPTEMBER

EXCELSIOR APPLE DAY
Downtown Excelsior
First Saturday after Labor Day
(952) 474-5233
www.ci.excelsior.mn.us
Excelsior Apple Day is a main street festival with antiques, crafts, apples, produce, entertainment, food, and the children's Red Wagon and Doll Buggy Parade.

SUNBONNET DAY
Riley-Jacques Barn, 9096 Riley Lake Rd.
Eden Prairie
Second Sunday in September
(952) 949-8450

Each September, Eden Prairie steps back in time on Sunbonnet Day, with old-fashioned wagon rides, pony rides, a farmers' market, and games of Pennies in the Hay.

JOHNNY APPLESEED BASH
Utley Park, 50th St. West and Woodale Ave.,
Edina
Third weekend of September
(952) 920-0595
www.ststephens.com/stst/the_bash

This annual benefit for St. Stephen's Episcopal Church takes place in Utley Park. Food, live entertainment, a silent auction, a petting zoo, and pony rides are just a few of the things you can expect at this community-oriented festival.

LONE OAK DAYS
Historic Holz Farm, 4665 Manor Dr., Eagan
End of September
(651) 675-5500
www.eaganmn.com

Hayrides, farming demos, games, and self-guided tours of 1940s-era farm life at Holz Farm highlight Eagan's heritage festival.

HARVEST FESTIVAL
Gibbs Museum of Pioneer and Dakota Life
2097 Larpenteur Ave. West, Falcon Heights
Late September or early October
(651) 646-8629
www.rchs.com/gbbsfm2.htm

At this annual event with food, music, and square dancing, guests can participate in crop gathering, kitchen duty, and other farm activities. The festival also features craft demonstrations.

OCTOBER

TWIN CITIES MARATHON
Minneapolis and St. Paul
First weekend of October
(763) 287-3888
www.twincitiesmarathon.org

The Twin Cities Marathon's unique scenery and aesthetics have earned it the distinction as the most beautiful urban marathon in America. It's also ranked as one of the nation's top marathons, period. The 26.2-mile course begins near the Metrodome in Minneapolis and finishes at the State Capitol on John Ireland Boulevard in St. Paul. The course is easy to navigate, mostly asphalt, and very scenic with mile after mile of parkways, lakes, rivers, and tree-lined boulevards. Prospective runners should register early for the race, as this race attracts contestants from around the world. Good viewing spots include the Lake Harriet Rose Garden, Minnehaha Falls, and along Summit Avenue.

ANOKA HALLOWEEN
Downtown Anoka
Mid-October through Halloween
(763) 421-7130
www.anokahalloween.com

Anoka celebrates almost 90 years as the self-styled "Halloween Capital of the World" with three parades and many other activities for young and old alike. The celebration begins with a football game dubbed "the Pumpkin Bowl." Other events include cemetery tours, a house-decoration contest, ghost stories, costume contests, a haunted house, and a 5K Grey Ghost Run.

ZOMBIE PUB CRAWL
Starting in Gold Medal Park, Minneapolis
A Saturday in October
www.zombiepubcrawl.com

Not even the organizers of this monstrous annual event are quite sure how the Twin Cities came to be such a mecca for the undead, but since its founding in 2005, the Zombie Pub Crawl has turned into the biggest itinerant-drinking event in the metro area. In 2009 nearly 6,000 local zombie buffs trooped across the West Bank in search of blood, brains, and beer. DIY costumes are highly encouraged, and if you need a little help getting sufficiently gory, you can show up early so the zombifiers on hand can suck the life out of you.

NOVEMBER/DECEMBER

AUTUMN FESTIVAL: AN ARTS AND CRAFTS AFFAIR
Canterbury Park, 1100 Canterbury Rd., Shakopee
November
(952) 445-7223
The largest crafts show in the Upper Midwest, the Autumn Festival draws more than 500 vendors from all over the country.

VICTORIAN CHRISTMAS AT THE HISTORIC COURTHOUSE
101 West Pine St., Stillwater
Weekend before Thanksgiving
(651) 275-7075
www.co.washington.mn.us
Fine handmade crafts by local artists are displayed at the elegantly decorated Stillwater courthouse. The building, beautifully decorated in Victorian style, resounds with laughter and music, while vendors in costume offer their wares to the public. Volunteers in period clothing offer jail tours, an exhibit, an old-fashioned tearoom, and music of the season.

i If you call ahead of time (612-616-7669), you can volunteer to march in the Holidazzle. Organizers offer a variety of costumes to volunteers, from elfin outfits to Old St. Nick himself. Call early for the best costumes and your preferred date. And don't forget the long underwear.

HOLIDAZZLE
Nicollet Mall, Minneapolis
Friday after Thanksgiving through December 23
(612) 376-SNOW
www.holidazzle.com
Costumed children, adults, and festooned floats covered with one million colored lights make up the Holidazzle. These free, 30-minute night parades head down Nicollet Mall from 12th to 5th Streets, beginning at 6:30 p.m. Wednesday through Sunday. Fairy tale–themed floats, marching bands, celebrity grand marshals, and, of course, Santa in his sleigh can be seen in the parade.

OLD-FASHIONED HOLIDAY BAZAAR
Landmark Center, 75 West Fifth St., St. Paul
A weekend in November or December
(651) 292-3230
www.landmarkcenter.org
Stroll through a marketplace of more than 80 exhibits featuring beautiful and unique gift items, all handcrafted by the area's finest artisans. Participating in this annual event is considered an important tradition by many, who get their holiday shopping done here.

THE ARTS

The Greater Twin Cities have been dubbed a "cultural Eden on the prairie," where people widely support more than 100 theater companies and classical music ensembles. Sir Tyrone Guthrie pumped up the theatrical boom back in 1963, enrolling large-scale local assistance to establish the classical repertory company named after him. The Twin Cities are now regarded as a top regional center of American theater, and at any given time there are dozens of professionally produced shows playing across the metro area.

Minneapolis and St. Paul are also serious museum towns, with a number of important collections housed in several world-famous buildings. Many, many more little galleries spread throughout the metro area take up any slack the major museums might have missed, displaying everything from concrete anatomy molds to metal mechanical sculptures.

More than 100 performing arts groups and organizations flourish in the Twin Cities area, ranging from tiny neighborhood-based production companies to full-fledged touring troupes.

No matter what your artistic passions are, you are likely to have them stoked and satisfied in Minneapolis–St. Paul.

ALL ABOUT BOOKS

OPEN BOOK
1011 Washington Ave. South, Minneapolis
(612) 215-2650
www.openbookmn.org
The first literary arts complex of its kind in the nation, this renovated historic building opened in 2000. Visitors can watch the book printing and binding process from beginning to end, explore the exhibitions gallery, or simply stretch out on the sofa in the literary commons with a good book from the center's library. Other amenities include occasional live performances, literary readings, writing workshops, family reading space, and a cafe. Located in the building is the Minnesota Center for Book Arts, the largest independent book arts facility in the nation; the Loft, which offers classes on writing and publishing; a performance space for visiting authors and lecturers; and Milkweed Editions, a nationally known nonprofit literary publisher. Open Book is fun to just walk around in, as so much of the original structure was preserved exposed in the restoration process, including pieces of the original wallpaper, staircases that go nowhere, and ancient bakery and factory signs painted on the brickwork itself.

ART GALLERIES

ART OF THIS
3506 Nicollet Ave., Minneapolis
(612) 721-4105
www.artofthis.net
This small storefront space packs a big punch: It's the Twin Cities' premier independent gallery for cutting-edge installations of visual art, performance art, and everything in between. At Art of This, it's sometimes hard to see the boundaries between art, performance, and party—which is exactly how its proprietors like it. Art events ranging in length from a single evening to several weeks rotate through this space: Keep a close eye on the gallery's Web site or, better yet, subscribe to its e-mail newsletter to keep track of all the activity.

AZ GALLERY
Northern Warehouse Building, 308 Prince St., St. Paul
(651) 224-3757
www.theazgallery.org
This prominent Lowertown St. Paul gallery holds opening receptions on the first Friday of each month, hosting artwork premieres of two featured artists plus a group exhibit. The 2,000-square-foot gallery also puts on performing arts events throughout the year.

CIRCA GALLERY
210 North First St., Minneapolis
(612) 332-2386
www.circagallery.org
CIRCA Gallery's mission is to provide awareness and appreciation of contemporary styles, media, and expressions. The gallery represents 40 regional and national artists, with an exhibition rotation approximately every five weeks.

GROVELAND GALLERY
25 Groveland Terrace, Minneapolis
(612) 377-7800
www.grovelandgallery.com
Groveland Gallery represents the work of nearly 50 regional artists and specializes in contemporary representational painting and drawing. Established in 1973, this elegant gallery is located in a restored 1890s mansion and carriage house on the edge of downtown Minneapolis. On the premises is a second gallery, the Annex, which features work by emerging local artists. Exhibitions in both galleries change every six weeks.

INSIDE OUT GALLERY
Interact Center for the Visual and Performing Arts, 212 Third Ave. North, Suite 140, Minneapolis
(612) 339-5145
www.interactcenter.com
Interact is a studio for actors and artists with physical and mental disabilities. The organization's Inside Out gallery has four exhibitions each year that are open to the public. Interact's theater company, supported by professional actors as teachers and peers, produces two major shows per year.

INTERMEDIA ARTS
2822 Lyndale Ave. South, Minneapolis
(612) 871-4444
www.intermediaarts.org
The graffiti on Intermedia's facade isn't just a nice concession to local taggers—giving them the space is part of the gallery's mission. More than perhaps any other gallery in town, Intermedia is dedicated to being a neighborhood space, with shows often focusing on the work of artists from the semibohemian streets of Lyn-Lake. As a result, Intermedia's exhibits lack the gloss and commercial appeal of other galleries' shows, but they do offer a compelling artistic window into the soul of a community.

> Almost every arts venue in town offers a discount to students with a valid student ID.

KATHERINE E. NASH GALLERY
Regis Center for Art, 405 21st Ave. South, Minneapolis
(612) 624-7530
www.nash.umn.edu
The mission of the Katherine E. Nash Gallery is to create an accessible environment for University of Minnesota faculty and students to exhibit their work, as well as to show art in various media by regional, national, and international artists.

MPLS PHOTO CENTER
2400 North 2nd St., Minneapolis
(612) 643-3511
www.mplsphotocenter.com
With the closing of the Minnesota Center for Photography, the Mpls Photo Center has become the metro area's central meeting point for photographers serious about their craft. Besides hosting rotating exhibits of local photogs' work, the center holds many classes and events, including a monthly open workshop with Minnesota photography legend Tom Arndt.

NORTHERN CLAY CENTER
2424 East Franklin Ave., Minneapolis
(612) 339-8007
www.northernclaycenter.org

Northern Clay Center's mission is the advancement of the ceramic arts. Ongoing programs include classes and workshops for children and adults at all levels of proficiency, more than 10 exhibitions a year of functional and sculptural work by regional and national clay artists, studio facilities and grants for artists, and a sales gallery representing many of the top ceramic artists across the region and country.

PINK HOBO
507 East Hennepin Ave., Minneapolis
(612) 216-3924
www.pinkhobo.com

"Please don't leave a mean note," pleads the Web site of the Pink Hobo gallery, a venue that opens to the public at least once for each exhibit—and maybe no more than that, spelling frustration for some local gallerygoers. Though it's run on a shoestring, Pink Hobo has won an ardent following of arthound fans for its fun shows devoted to things like Barack Obama commemorative paper plates. As this guide went to press, Pink Hobo was joining forces with boutique store ROBOTlove and PUNY, a local animation studio whose work can be seen on Nickelodeon and elsewhere—this development will likely mean longer hours, and fewer mean notes.

ROGUE BUDDHA
357 13th Ave. NE, Minneapolis
(612) 331-3889
www.roguebuddha.com

Rogue Buddha is at the pumping heart of the 13th Avenue arts scene, playing host to not only exhibits of alternately whimsical and grotesque painting and sculpture but also to some of the indie-oriented art world's biggest see-be-seen-and-drink-PBR parties. Every third Thursday, Rogue Buddha hosts an experimental music series (to be precise, the gallery refers to them as "experimental music happenings") called iQuit.

THE SOAP FACTORY
518 Second St. SE, Minneapolis
(612) 623-9176
www.soapfactory.org

The Soap Factory has become notorious for the ultrascary Haunted Basement experience it offers in October, but it's much more than that: It's an exciting, and expanding, nonprofit arts organization that supports emerging artists, raises the public's understanding and appreciation of their artistic expressions, and fosters strength and vitality within the arts, cultural, and education communities of the Twin Cities. The gallery is particularly supportive of experimentation in the visual arts. Each year, the Soap Factory presents several large-scale visual exhibitions featuring a wide range of media from local, national, and international emerging artists as well as performance art, film, video, and spoken-word events.

SOO VISUAL ARTS CENTER (SooVAC)
2640 South Lyndale Ave., Minneapolis
(612) 871-2263
www.soovac.org

The SooVAC hosts exhibits by some of Minnesota's most beloved contemporary artists—Erin Currie, Jennifer Davis, Sean Tubridy—as well as by national artists like Plasticgod. "Cute" is a word appropriate to describe work at the SooVAC much more often than at most galleries, but when it comes to art, just because something is eye candy doesn't mean it's not also nutritious. The Soo Too shop is one of the best spots in town to buy lovely, quirky prints and gift items made by local artists.

VERN CARVER & BEARD ART GALLERIES
2817 Hennepin Ave., Minneapolis
(612) 339-3449
www.verncarverbeard.com

Vern Carver & Beard is the oldest gallery in the Twin Cities. Founded in 1886, the gallery features fine original art by regional artists of past and present, antique prints, and art glass (stained glass, blown glass, etc). The gallery also provides custom framing for prints and paintings.

WEINSTEIN GALLERY
908 West 46th St., Minneapolis
(612) 822-1722
www.weinstein-gallery.com

The Weinstein Gallery, located on a quiet corner in south Minneapolis, is the Cadillac of serious art galleries in the Twin Cities: Here you can get up close and personal with the work of world-renowned artists like Man Ray, Chuck Close, Robert Mapplethorpe, August Sander, and Minnesota photographer Alec Soth. The gallery shows work in all media, but it's especially strong in photography.

ART MUSEUMS

FREDERICK R. WEISMAN ART MUSEUM
333 East River Pkwy., Minneapolis
(612) 625-9494
www.weisman.umn.edu

The Weisman is impossible to miss—it's the huge silver structure on the east side of the Washington Avenue Bridge. On the outside the museum faces the Mississippi River with an undulating, dramatic facade covered in stainless steel, especially beautiful at sunset. In comparison the interior is surprisingly conservative, and the modestly scaled and wonderfully lit galleries inside are so attractive that the *New York Times* called them "possibly the five best rooms for viewing art in the world."

The mostly 20th-century permanent collection contains the world's largest assemblage of works by Marsden Hartley and Alfred Maurer as well as paintings and prints by Georgia O'Keeffe, Arthur Dove, and Robert Motherwell, among others. The entrance is dominated by Roy Lichtenstein's World's Fair Mural. Be sure to take in the river view from the tiny balcony, located one floor above the galleries.

A teaching museum for the university and the community, this sculptural stainless-steel and brick landmark building designed by architect Frank Gehry provides a multidisciplinary approach to the arts through programs and a changing schedule of exhibitions. Gehry designed an expansion of the museum (including a new gallery wing and a cafe), which was 2009.

Admission is free, although the parking garage will set you back a few bucks.

THE MINNEAPOLIS INSTITUTE OF ARTS
2400 Third Ave. South, Minneapolis
(612) 870-3131 or (888) MIA-ARTS
www.artsmia.org

The Minneapolis Institute of Arts, one of the outstanding art museums in the country, features art and artifacts from around the world, from ancient sculptures to photography and film. Housed in a 1915 Beaux-Arts marble building designed by McKim, Mead, and White near downtown Minneapolis, the museum contains a world-class collection of nearly 100,000 objects representing artistic traditions and treasures spanning 5,000 years. Unlike many big-city art museums, which have the tendency to overwhelm casual visitors, the MIA can be easily explored in a few hours—and, unlike many big-city museums, no admission fee is charged.

MUSEUM OF RUSSIAN ART
5500 Stevens Ave. South, Minneapolis
(612) 821-9045
www.tmora.org

The Museum of Russian Art is the only museum in North America exclusively dedicated to Russian art, but even many locals haven't heard of it. The museum, a building in the Spanish revival style that was incongruously appropriated by the museum in 2005, is perched high above I-35W, where almost since its inception it's suffered through the construction meant to detangle that interstate and the Crosstown Highway. It's worth picking your way through the orange cones to see the museum's fine collection of historic treasures and contemporary works, with special exhibits highlighting everything from nesting dolls to landscape paintings to traditional textiles. A regular series of musical performances spotlights—what else?—the Russian classics.

SCHUBERT CLUB MUSEUM OF MUSICAL INSTRUMENTS
Landmark Center, 75 West Fifth St., St. Paul
(651) 292-3267
www.schubert.org

Considering how small this museum is, its collection of keyboards, phonographs, and musical instruments is amazingly complete. Owned and operated by the Schubert Club, this museum is a popular stomping ground for music aficionados of all types, local and otherwise.

WALKER ART CENTER/MINNEAPOLIS SCULPTURE GARDEN/COWLES CONSERVATORY
1750 Hennepin Ave., Minneapolis
(612) 375-7600
www.walkerart.org

For years the Walker's been the foremost modern art museum in the state. The displays include a permanent collection of 20th-century American and international art, including works from Willem de Kooning, Andy Warhol, Sol LeWitt, and Dan Flavin; the Walker also sponsors vanguard music, dance, theater, film, and video events throughout the year, as well as innovative education programs and visionary new media initiatives. Artists and filmmakers from around the globe have lectured and performed at the Walker. The popular After Hours parties offer cocktails, live music, and previews of new shows.

Located right across the street is the Minneapolis Sculpture Garden's beautiful collection of large sculptures made by local and internationally known artists. The 11-acre garden holds more than 40 sculptures, including works by Richard Serra, Dan Graham, George Segal, Jenny Holzer, and David Nash, set among tree-lined courtyards. The garden is one of the most-visited sites in Minneapolis, for good reason—the works of art combined with the ever-changing landscape make it a year-round delight.

DANCE

JAMES SEWELL BALLET
528 Hennepin Ave., Suite 205, Minneapolis
(612) 672-0480
www.jsballet.org

Founded in New York City in 1990 by James Sewell, the James Sewell Ballet relocated to Minnesota in 1993. The ballet specializes in original contemporary ballet, and the beautiful performances run the gamut from classical choreography to improvisation of entire movements. In the Twin Cities, the James Sewell Ballet performs at the O'Shaughnessy on St. Catherine University's campus in St. Paul.

RAGAMALA MUSIC AND DANCE THEATER
711 West Lake St., Suite 309, Minneapolis
(612) 824-1968
www.ragamala.net

Ragamala presents original works of dance, music, and poetry based on the ancient classical dance of southern India, Bharatanatyam. The cross-cultural performances of the company have developed a strong reputation for innovation, and the company's school offers classes from introductory to advanced levels. Ragamala performs at the O'Shaughnessy on St. Catherine University's Campus in St. Paul and at the Southern Theater in Minneapolis.

ZENON DANCE COMPANY
528 Hennepin Ave., Suite 400, Minneapolis
(612) 338-1101
www.zenondance.org

Zenon commissions original works of modern and jazz dance from emerging choreographers in Minnesota as well as established masters. The high-energy performances of the company appeal to communities not regularly reached by dance troupes. Zenon performs regularly at venues across the Twin Cities, and operates a school teaching modern, jazz, hip-hop, tap, breakdancing, and yoga.

MUSIC ENSEMBLES AND COMPANIES

GREATER TWIN CITIES YOUTH SYMPHONIES (GTCYS)
528 Hennepin Ave., Suite 404, Minneapolis
(612) 870-7611
www.gtcys.org
GTCYS boasts six youth orchestras and a student body with 600-plus members. While pursuing its mission of educating future musicians, it presents fall, winter, and spring concerts and the Young Soloists' Concerto Showcase. GTCYS sponsors a summer orchestra program as well.

MINNESOTA CHORALE
528 Hennepin Ave., Suite 211, Minneapolis
(612) 333-4866
www.mnchorale.org
Under the artistic direction of Kathy Saltzman Romey, the Minnesota Chorale has become the state's preeminent symphonic chorus and ranks among the best in the nation. At around 150 voices, the chorale is the principal chorus for the Minnesota Orchestra and the St. Paul Chamber Orchestra. Its nationally recognized Bridges series seeks to build musical and social bridges through artistic collaboration.

THE MINNESOTA OPERA
620 North First St., Minneapolis
(612) 333-2700
www.mnopera.org
The Minnesota Opera, founded in 1963, stages performances at the Ordway Center for the Performing Arts in St. Paul from November through May. An anchor tenant at the Ordway, the Minnesota Opera also offers classes at its Minnesota Opera Center in the Minneapolis Warehouse District. Walk-ins are welcome.

THE MINNESOTA ORCHESTRA
1111 Nicollet Mall, Minneapolis
(612) 371-5656 or (800) 292-4141
www.minnesotaorchestra.org
The Minnesota Orchestra—founded in 1903 as the Minneapolis Symphony Orchestra—has long been one of America's top orchestras. The orchestra performs nearly 200 concerts each year ranging from classical to pops. Performances are scheduled in Minneapolis's Orchestra Hall. The orchestra's award-winning concert broadcasts, produced by Minnesota Public Radio and distributed by American Public Media to more than 120 radio stations nationwide, reach approximately 200,000 people each week.

THE MINNESOTA YOUTH SYMPHONIES
790 Cleveland Ave. South, Suite 203, St. Paul
(651) 699-5811
www.mnyouthsymphonies.org
The Minnesota Youth Symphonies are open to students from elementary school through high school. Co-music directors Claudette and Manny Laureano oversee four advanced orchestras. The MYS presents major concerts at Orchestra Hall in Minneapolis. Auditions are held at the end of August of each year.

THE ST. PAUL CHAMBER ORCHESTRA
408 St. Peter St., St. Paul
(651) 292-3248
www.thespco.org
As the only full-time professional chamber orchestra in the United States, the SPCO presents more than 150 concerts annually and reaches millions more through radio broadcasts and regional, national, and international touring. The chamber orchestra performs at St. Paul's Ordway Center for the Performing Arts, Minneapolis's Ted Mann Concert Hall, and at other locations throughout the Twin Cities.

THE SCHUBERT CLUB
Landmark Center, 75 West Fifth St., St. Paul
(651) 292-3267
www.schubert.org
The Schubert Club is Minnesota's oldest arts organization, presenting world-renowned artists and local and regional musicians to Twin Cities audiences through various grants and private funding. The Schubert Club Museum of Musical Instru-

ments is located in Landmark Center as well. The club's saddlelike Heilmaier Memorial Bandstand, built in 2002 on Raspberry Island in the Mississippi River, has been hailed as one of the most beautiful structures built in Minnesota in recent memory.

VOCALESSENCE
1900 Nicollet Ave., Minneapolis
(612) 547-1451
www.vocalessence.org
VocalEssence is one of America's premier choral arts organizations. The chorus offers innovative programming under the direction of founder Philip Brunelle.

THEATERS AND PERFORMANCE SPACES

In addition to the following theater troupes and venues, various local, regional, national, and international shows are regularly staged at **St. Paul's Roy Wilkins Auditorium** (175 West Kellogg Blvd., St. Paul, (651-265-4800, www.theroy.com) and **Xcel Energy Center** (199 West Kellogg Blvd., St. Paul, 651-989-5151, www.xcelenergycenter .com), as well as Minneapolis's **Northrop Auditorium** on the University of Minnesota Campus (84 SE Church St., Minneapolis, 612-624-2345, www1. umn.edu/umato) and **Target Center** (600 First Ave. North, Minneapolis, 612-673-0900, www .targetcenter.com).

Minneapolis
BEDLAM THEATRE
1501 South Sixth St., Minneapolis
(612) 341-1038
www.bedlamtheatre.org
Bedlam is aptly named—and its many devoted patrons love it for exactly that quality. Just about anything goes in Bedlam's West Bank space, a multistory playhouse full of funky furniture, bikes dangling from the ceiling, and indie-spirited theater people galore. Bedlam is a theater company producing its own shows, a venue hosting productions by a range of small companies, a fully functional restaurant and bar, a meeting place, and even a dance club. During the Fringe Festival

Bedlam serves as "Fringe Central," a gathering place for participants and playgoers to hang out and catch up. On any given night at Bedlam you're likely to find some event or another taking place, but whether or not you're there for a show, it's a good place to stop by for a beer—especially in the summer, when you can hang out on the rooftop deck with its fantastic view of downtown Minneapolis. *La vie bohème* at its best.

BRAVE NEW WORKSHOP
2605 Hennepin Ave. South, Minneapolis
(612) 332-6620
www.bravenewworkshop.org
The country's longest-running satirical comedy theater, founded by Dudley Riggs in 1958 (and, amazingly, still directed by Riggs today), features original comedy shows and late-night improvisation—sometimes for just a dollar. The Brave New Workshop is known for its satirical takes on pop-culture icons and news-dominating factoids of the moment, creating shows like *Happiness for Dummies: An Idiot's Guide to the Soul* and B*rett Favre's Christmas Spectacular: The Immaculate Interception.* The company also offers classes on improvisation, acting, and writing.

BRYANT-LAKE BOWL THEATER
810 West Lake St., Minneapolis
(612) 825-3737
www.bryantlakebowl.com
The Bryant-Lake Bowl Theater has become a mainstay of local performance acts, bringing live music (including opera), dance, comedy, and theater to an intimate stage tucked behind the bowling alley. On any given night you may wander in and find the tiny performance area packed in support of local talent. No matter where you decide to sit, make sure to take advantage of the extensive beer and wine lists.

CAPRI THEATER
2027 West Broadway, Minneapolis
(612) 643-2048
www.capritheater.org
Located in north Minneapolis, the Capri Theater is the Apollo of the Twin Cities, showcasing the

rich musical and theatrical talent of Minnesota's black community. On any given night at the Capri, you might encounter a silky-voiced singer like Thomasina Petrus, a classic big-band jazz performance, or drumming and dancing in the African tradition. After a recent renovation, the Capri—run by the Plymouth Christian Youth Center—finally looks as good as the performers who grace its stage.

CEDAR CULTURAL CENTER
416 Cedar Ave. South, Minneapolis
(612) 338-2674
www.thecedar.org

The Cedar offers an eclectic selection of folk, blues, jazz, indie rock, and world music. The Cedar is also host to the annual Global Roots Festival, which brings performers from around the world to the Cedar-Riverside neighborhood.

THE CHILDREN'S THEATRE COMPANY
2400 Third Ave. South, Minneapolis
(612) 874-0400
www.childrenstheatre.org

The Tony Award–winning Children's Theatre Company (CTC), which the *New York Times* has called the country's top theater company for children, produces an annual season featuring hundreds of mainstage performances and a touring production. Since 1965 the CTC and its cast of incredibly talented actors and actresses, young and old, have been performing at the 746-seat facility adjoining the Minneapolis Institute of Arts—recently remodeled to include a second stage. Most of the performances are based on children's stories and fairy tales, such as *A Year with Frog and Toad*. There's a healthy dose of impressive original works as well, such as *Korczak's Children*, a story about the Holocaust through children's eyes, and *The Monkey King*, based on a 500-year-old Chinese story about a trickster on a quest with pious monks to recover sacred scrolls.

GUTHRIE THEATER
818 South Second St., Minneapolis
(612) 377-2224
www.guthrietheater.org

Anyone who knows American theater knows the Guthrie, the Minneapolis theater founded in the early 1960s by legendary director Sir Tyrone Guthrie. The company's metier has always been intriguing interpretations of classic drama. The largest nonprofit theater between New York and San Francisco, the Guthrie is renowned for its productions of classic, comedic, and contemporary plays.

In June 2006 the Guthrie moved into a new riverside building designed by French architect Jean Nouvel. With three stages, the restaurant Sea Change (see the Restaurants chapter for more information), and a lounge, the new facility is more than three times as big as the Guthrie's former home; it supplements the Wurtele Thrust Stage (a near-exact replica of the Guthrie's original theater) with a large proscenium stage and a black-box theater for smaller-scale work. The dark blue building along the Minneapolis riverfront features the Endless Bridge, a cantilevered appendage sticking out 178 feet from the main building toward the Mississippi River. Whether you're in town for a weekend or a decade, be sure to visit the Guthrie—even if you don't see a show (and FYI, rush tickets are available at $20 before most performances). It's worth a stop for the architecture and the view.

i An etiquette guide on the Guthrie's Web site nicely captures the Twin Cities attitude toward theatergoing. The Guthrie makes clear that it's okay to dress comfortably—what's not okay is standing up and walking out during curtain call. Much more important than whether you wear jeans or dress pants is whether you force the cast members to look at the seat of those pants while the performers are on stage hoping to receive your appreciation.

HENNEPIN THEATRE DISTRICT
800 LaSalle Ave., Minneapolis
(612) 373-5600
www.hennepintheatretrust.org

Downtown Minneapolis's Hennepin Theatre District comprises three historic theater venues and one smaller stage all within a short walk of each other. The district's theaters include the Orpheum (910 Hennepin Ave.), the State (805 Hennepin Ave.), and the Pantages (710 Hennepin Ave.), as well as the Hennepin Stages (824 Hennepin Ave.). The larger theaters host touring Broadway shows, major music acts, stand-up comedy, and an array of other miscellaneous entertainment; the Hennepin Stages typically hosts small-scale locally themed comedies with long runs. The Web site of the Hennepin Theatre Trust—the nonprofit organization that runs the four venues—has information about upcoming shows.

i Monthly tours of the Hennepin Theatre District depart from the State Theatre Box Office at 805 Hennepin Avenue. The tour includes a backstage look at one of the historic theaters. Tickets are $5 and can be purchased through the Hennepin Theatre Trust's Web site at www.hennepintheatretrust.org.

IN THE HEART OF THE BEAST PUPPET AND MASK THEATRE
1500 East Lake St., Minneapolis
(612) 721-2535
www.hobt.org
In the Heart of the Beast's unique theater production is marked by elaborate costuming; stories are told through puppets or actors hidden behind gigantic masks, giving performances a mystical and magical quality. The theater company uses the ancient traditions of puppet and mask theater to explore issues, events, and values of contemporary society. Though some performances are adaptations of children's stories, all shows are a wonder for eyes of any age. Puppets are hand-hewn by those involved with the shows, and the traveling company stages shows both regionally and nationally.

JUNGLE THEATER
2951 Lyndale Ave. South, Minneapolis
(612) 338-8371
www.jungletheater.com

The Jungle Theater, founded in 1991, stages world-class productions of serious (and not-so-serious) plays in its hushed and elegant LynLake space, perhaps the single best place to see theater anywhere in the Twin Cities. See anything that has the name of associate director Joel Sass on it (and that's just about everything at the Jungle); you won't be disappointed. If you're going to buy season tickets to one theater company in the Twin Cities, seriously consider making it the Jungle: For the quality of the work you'll see, its $100 Tuesday-night package is a bargain.

THE LAB THEATER
700 First St. North, Minneapolis
(612) 333-7977
www.thelabtheater.org
The Lab was built in 1988 under the auspices of the Guthrie Theater, which wanted a space to host emerging companies and try new work. The idea worked so well that the Guthrie built a lab theater into its grand new 2006 home—at which point it had no further need for the original Lab. The space is just now reemerging as a theatrical venue, with artistic director Mary Kelley Leer inviting dance groups, musical performers, and of course theater companies to make use of the big warehouselike space.

MCGUIRE THEATER—WALKER ART CENTER
1750 Hennepin Ave., Minneapolis
(612) 375-7600
www.walkerart.org
The McGuire is located inside the Walker Art Center, which programs its performances, but it deserves its own listing for two reasons. First of all, there's the space itself, which is one of the best places in the Twin Cities to see dance, music, and theater. A black-walled venue designed by Herzog & de Meuron as part of the Walker's new wing, it's a hushed space that puts the focus squarely on the performers. Second, there's the talent that appears on that stage. The Walker sends performing arts curator Philip Bither on excursions around the globe to find the most interesting, provocative, and talented companies to bring to Minneapolis. At only about $20—for

members, less—tickets to performances at the McGuire Theater are among the best entertainment bargains in the Twin Cities.

MINNEAPOLIS THEATRE GARAGE
711 West Franklin Ave., Minneapolis
Where's the phone number? There is no phone. Where's the Web site? Nope, none of that neither. The Minneapolis Theatre Garage is strictly a venue for various theater companies who rent it for their own productions. It looks and feels like exactly what it is: a former garage converted to a theater—excuse me, a *theatre*. If you're a fan of Fringe-y independent theater, you'll find yourself crossing its modest threshold often.

MIXED BLOOD THEATRE
1501 South Fourth St., Minneapolis
(612) 338-6131
www.mixedblood.com
Mixed Blood is a professional theater company whose mission is to expose and promote the Twin Cities' cultural melting pot. Founded in 1976 by Jack Reuler to provide voice and venue for actors of color, Mixed Blood has branched out into the working world to tackle hot topics like race, culture, gender, sexual orientation, and disability. The main stage is housed in a turn-of-the-20th-century brick firehouse, while the touring company itself performs in schools and organizations throughout the region.

MU PERFORMING ARTS
2700 NE Winter St., Suite 4, Minneapolis
(612) 824-4804
www.muperformingarts.org
Mu Performing Arts includes both Theater Mu, an Asian-American theater company, and Mu Daiko, a Japanese taiko drumming group. Dedicated to staging performances that showcase Asian and Asian-American plays, Theater Mu hosts three productions annually, while Mu Daiko stages one production. Mu Performing Arts also performs in outreach programs throughout the Twin Cities. The organization sponsors several Artist Development Festivals to support, encourage, and give experience to young directors, playwrights, and

taiko students. Mu Performing Arts also offers taiko drumming classes.

MUSIC BOX THEATRE
1411 Nicollet Ave., Minneapolis
(612) 871-1414
www.musicboxtheatre.org
The Music Box is a fantastic little space, seating 440 people in an auditorium with a thrust stage that makes it a superb venue for acoustic music and small-scale theater. The 1920 structure has a fascinating history, including stints as a movie theater and a church. Most recently, it was home for over a dozen years to the comedy show *Triple Espresso*. That show closed in 2009 and the venue reopened for music and theater rentals amid much fanfare, but that promise may be fading. As this guide went to press, the venue had no scheduled shows except for a weekly worship service and an encore run of...*Triple Espresso*.

During its years as a church, the Music Box Theatre was for a time home to the ministry of Jim and Tammy Faye Bakker, who were married there in 1961. (They went on to international fame as heads of the PTL ministry, which collapsed in 1987 amid financial and sexual scandal.) The hand-painted murals of the Holy Land and the sign welcoming youngsters to the Bakkers' "Navigators Club" are still extant in the Music Box basement.

OLD ARIZONA
2821 Nicollet Ave., Minneapolis
(612) 871-0050
www.oldarizona.com
A desert-southwest-themed theater would seem a little odd anywhere in Minnesota, so the eclectic Eat Street stretch of Nicollet Avenue is probably as suitable a place as any for Old Arizona. There's a flexible theater space, a cafe, a "Chocolate Lounge," a wine shop, a dance studio, and a rehearsal loft in this incongruous complex run by a nonprofit organization that also runs enrichment programs for youth. Because...well, why not?

OPEN EYE FIGURE THEATRE
508 East 24th St., Minneapolis
(612) 874-6338
www.openeyetheatre.org
Michael Sommers and Susan Haas, the married couple who run Open Eye Figure Theatre, had already made a national name for their company's dark and innovative blend of puppetry and live action when they opened this storefront space in 2006. Though it's in the middle of Minneapolis, the Phillips neighborhood theater isn't near any other venues—when you try to explain to locals exactly where it is, you'll see them squint their eyes and scratch their heads. The rich and intimate space is worth finding, though, especially when it's hosting one of the company's own magical performances.

ORCHESTRA HALL
1111 Nicollet Mall, Minneapolis
(952) 371-5600
www.minnesotaorchestra.org
The Minneapolis counterpart to St. Paul's Ordway, Orchestra Hall is the place to go to hear the Minnesota Orchestra. The auditorium, which seats 2,400, has a large main floor with three balconies symmetrically girding it. Whatever you think about the venue's aesthetics (the desert-red interior is not for everyone), you can't argue with its excellent acoustics. The hall lobby opens to Peavey Plaza, which holds the orchestra's popular outdoor summer music festival.

PATRICK'S CABARET
3010 Minnehaha Ave., Minneapolis
(612) 724-6273
www.patrickscabaret.org
Bawdy cabarets are all the rage in Minneapolis now, but they're nothing new for Patrick's, which for a quarter-century has hosted an incredibly eclectic mix of acts that are notably GLBT-inclusive. Patrick's is like a year-round Fringe Festival: The only thing you know for sure is that you don't know what you're going to get.

PILLSBURY HOUSE THEATRE
3501 Chicago Ave. South, Minneapolis
(612) 825-0459
www.pillsburyhousetheatre.org
Pillsbury House Theatre, a very nice little space, is located in a south Minneapolis community center; accordingly, its home company has a mission. That mission? "To create challenging theatre to inspire choice, change, and connection." Pillsbury House productions aren't just after-school specials, though; they feature some of the area's top artists working on ambitious shows about (very) real life. The theater also hosts local companies who mount mainstream—and not-so-mainstream—shows there.

THE PLAYWRIGHTS' CENTER
2301 East Franklin Ave., Minneapolis
(612) 332-7481
www.pwcenter.org
This former church converted into theater space stands in the middle of the Seward neighborhood on Franklin Avenue. If people know about it, it's because they read the name in another theater's playbill—usually because the Playwrights' Center supported the performance through a fellowship, residency, commission, or other funding. Plays supported by the center have been featured at the Guthrie and other local theaters, as well as on national and international stages. Behind the scenes this membership organization helps actors and writers workshop their creative ideas. It also hosts performances in its own black-box space.

RARIG CENTER
University of Minnesota Campus,
330 21st Ave. South, Minneapolis
(612) 624-6699
www.theatre.umn.edu
The Rarig Center, located on the West Bank of the University of Minnesota's Minneapolis campus, hosts University Theatre and Xperimental Theater productions throughout the year in four theaters: a proscenium, a thrust, an arena, and a black box. The Mainstage shows are usually the more popular ones, and the smaller theater spaces offer

experimental shows. The X Theater productions are directed and performed exclusively by undergraduate U of M students. At University Theatre, student and professional actors, designers, and directors write and direct musicals, comedies, and dramas. The Minnesota Centennial Showboat offers performances each summer aboard a sternwheeler riverboat anchored at Harriet Island in St. Paul.

RED EYE THEATER
15 West 14th St., Minneapolis
(612) 870-0309
www.redeyetheater.org
The Red Eye, converted from a former car dealership, is squeezed so tightly into its space at the southern edge of downtown that its lobby is in two parts—one on either side of the theater— but that can be taken for the foot-in-the-door the theater allows emerging playmakers. The theater's annual festival of works in progress is typical of its commitment to supporting new work in a community that's positively bursting with it.

RITZ THEATER
345 13th Ave. NE, Minneapolis
(612) 623-7660
www.ritzdolls.com
The Ritz is the landmark venue standing amid the restaurants and galleries in the northeast Minneapolis arts district, and it's home to an eclectic array of shows. It's favored particularly for dance, and it's home to the Ballet of the Dolls, an irreverent company best known for its naughty *Nutcracker*. If you've lived in Minneapolis for a while, you've learned to be delighted when a show you want to see goes up at the Ritz: the parking's easy, the sight lines are good, and the post- or preshow comestibles at the neighboring establishments are simply superb.

SOUTHERN THEATER
1420 Washington Ave. South, Minneapolis
(612) 340-1725
www.southerntheater.org
Though it's home to theater and music performances, the Southern has increasingly become a venue for dance due to its recently rebuilt stage floor and its commitment to smart programming. Many local dance companies perform here, and everything from flamenco to classical Indian dance to modern dance can be seen in this venue. Exposed-brick walls enclose the auditorium, lending a comfortable warehouselike feel to the performance experience.

i The site MinnesotaPlaylist.com does for the local theater scene what RottenTomatoes.com does for movies: It collects reviews from both professional critics and ordinary audience members so you can see what people are saying about a show before you buy tickets.

THEATRE IN THE ROUND
245 Cedar Ave., Minneapolis
(612) 333-2919
www.theatreintheround.org
Theatre in the Round, the oldest community theater in the Twin Cities, performs drama and comedy on a unique arena stage designed by the late Ralph Rapson, Minnesota's premier modern architect. Audience members surround the actors, who are unpaid volunteers performing largely traditional scripts both classic and new. The quality is high for community theater, and sometimes the company produces real gems— but it can also lay goose eggs, so you might want to check the reviews before planning a trip.

St. Paul
THE FITZGERALD THEATER
10 East Exchange St., St. Paul
(651) 290-1221
http://fitzgeraldtheater.publicradio.org
Opened in 1910 as the Schubert Theater and long known as the World Theater, this comfortable classic structure was renamed in 1994 after St. Paul's famous literary figure and social gadfly, F. Scott Fitzgerald. The man behind the restoration and renaming of the theater is its well-known tenant, Garrison Keillor, host of *A*

Prairie Home Companion radio show. As St. Paul's oldest surviving theater space, now restored to its former elegance, the Fitzgerald Theater presents its shows in a two-balcony, 1,000-seat hall with excellent acoustics and sight lines. The theater's many pleasant features make it popular with touring acts that could probably sell out much larger venues. The theater schedules classical, jazz, folk, country, and pop music events as well as film screenings and theater productions.

GREMLIN THEATRE
2400 University Ave., St. Paul
(651) 228-7008
www.gremlin-theatre.org
Gremlin Theatre is in St. Paul, but just barely: It's on the stretch of University east of the University of Minnesota campus. After years as an itinerent but acclaimed company, Gremlin procured this storefront space in 2009—a space that's already played host to several lauded shows by Gremlin's home company and by visiting companies.

ORDWAY CENTER FOR THE PERFORMING ARTS
345 Washington St., St. Paul
(651) 282-3000
www.ordway.org
The Ordway is an elegantly modern complex fronting Rice Park that's widely acknowledged as a worthy neighbor to the likes of Landmark Center, the St. Paul Hotel, and the St. Paul Central Library. Its expansive main hall is the closest thing to a classic opera house you'll find in the Twin Cities, and appropriately it serves as home to the Minnesota Opera as well as the St. Paul Chamber Orchestra. Additionally, the Ordway hosts touring performers and produces its own Broadway musicals, which are pricey to see (many tickets cost over $100) but of correspondingly high quality. The complex also houses the McKnight Theatre, a smaller space for crowd-pleasing shows like *The Full Monty* and *Sister's Christmas Catechism*. Plans are afoot to convert the McKnight Theatre into a new space specially designed to showcase the sound of the SPCO and other chamber music ensembles.

PARK SQUARE THEATRE
20 West Seventh Place, St. Paul
(651) 291-7005
www.parksquaretheatre.org
Located in the heart of downtown St. Paul in the center of Park Square—a block-long brick street that's for pedestrians only—Park Square Theatre is St. Paul's premier company producing traditional theater. Though it often suffers by comparison to the Guthrie and the Jungle across the river, Park Square has found success by enlisting top actors to enact classic scripts—including modern classics. How can you go wrong?

PENUMBRA THEATRE
270 North Kent St., St. Paul
(651) 224-3180
www.penumbratheatre.org
As the only professional African-American theater company in Minnesota, the Penumbra has a large following and a great reputation. Founded by artistic director Lou Bellamy with the mission of creating artistically exceptional productions that address the African-American experience, the troupe has a rich history of excellence that has included two-time Pulitzer Prize–winning playwright August Wilson, who got his start at Penumbra.

STEPPINGSTONE THEATRE
55 Victoria St. North, St. Paul
(651) 225-9265
www.steppingstonetheatre.org
The grand scale of this converted church—which opened as a theater in 2007—is out of all proportion to the children who make up the casts of SteppingStone shows, but it's a fine venue for them, with specially built classrooms and rehearsal space in the basement. SteppingStone also occasionally hosts productions by visiting companies, when its own li'l stars are ready to take a break from the spotlight.

West

CHANHASSEN DINNER THEATRES
501 West 78th St., Chanhassen
(952) 934-1524 or (800) 362-3515
www.chanhassentheatres.com
It says something about the quality of the local theater scene that not only do the Twin Cities have the pioneering Guthrie Theater, the country's largest nonjuried fringe festival, and the nation's top company producing work for children, the area's also home to arguably the top dinner theater in the country: the Chanhassen, which has been called "the Cadillac of dinner theaters." If you like to sit at a table and eat steak while you watch shows, you're not going to do much better than the Chanhassen's mainstage musicals. The smaller productions at the venue's other stages are a little more variable in quality, but the Chanhassen is a pillar of the local theater scene and a spot that's spelled pure class for generations of suburbanites. (Unfortunately, in this economic climate there are no sure things, and the Chanhassen has recently changed ownership as it struggles to stay alive. Visit while you can, in case your chances to do so suddenly disappear.)

OLD LOG THEATER
5185 Meadville St., Excelsior
(952) 474-5951
www.oldlog.com
At the Old Log Theater on the shore of Lake Minnetonka, you'll find American and British comedies with all of the slamming doors, mistaken identities, and double-entendres inherent in the genre. The Old Log is not for you if you're looking for Beckett or O'Neill, but it's a venerable institution that's keeping the Borscht Belt spirit alive; Don Stolz, who's 92 years old as this book goes to press, has introduced shows at the Old Log for decades and is currently the oldest active member of the national Actors' Equity Association.

PLYMOUTH PLAYHOUSE
2705 Annapolis Lane North, Plymouth
(763) 553-1600
www.plymouthplayhouse.com

The Plymouth specializes in dinner-theater productions long on laughs and music. *Nunsense, Pump Boys and Dinettes,* and revues featuring the Twin Cities' own Lovely Liebowitz Sisters have had extended runs here. Their popular long-running production, *How to Talk Minnesotan,* was adapted for the stage by the book's author, Howard Mohr. More recently, *Church Basement Ladies* poked similar fun at the stereotypical Minnesota church matrons.

STAGES THEATRE COMPANY
1111 Main St., Hopkins
(952) 979-1111
www.stagestheatre.org
Stages produces a full season of plays for young audiences. Housed in the Hopkins Center for the Arts, it offers acting, singing, and directing classes for youth ages 5 through 18. The theater often hosts plays featuring well-known kid-favorites such as Charlie Brown and Winnie the Pooh.

North

BURNSVILLE PERFORMING ARTS CENTER
12600 Nicollet Ave., Burnsville
(952) 895-4685
www.burnsvillepac.com
The Twin Cities were tightening belts in the financial recession of 2009 when they were surprised to find this spectacular, expansive new center sprouting up in Burnsville. Thousand-seat proscenium stage? Yep! Black-box lab theater? You betcha—with a resident theater company for children, to boot! Whether the venue will be used to its full potential anytime soon remains to be seen, but for now it's a very comfortable spot to catch touring musical artists and theatrical productions, as well as performances by local theater companies.

YELLOW TREE THEATRE
320 5th Ave. SE, Osseo
(763) 493-8733
www.yellowtreetheatre.com
The Yellow Tree Theatre is a dream. Specifically, it's the dream of founders Jason Peterson and

Jessica Lind, who decided to found a classic small-town theater in the Twin Cities exurb of Osseo. "Classic" might not be the first word that comes to mind when you pull up to the theater's front door in a strip mall, but inside the venue is very charming—and the slung-fabric lawn chairs make for the most comfortable theater seating in the Twin Cities. Peterson and Lind mound their own plays (many of which they write, direct, and act in) as well as host visiting companies and music acts.

South

BLOOMINGTON CENTER FOR THE PER-FORMING ARTS
107 East Chestnut St., Bloomington
(309) 434-2787
www.cityblm.org/bcd
When the Canadian Brass come to Bloomington, you know where they're gonna go—and the mayor will be waiting for them with the key to the city. The Bloomington Center for the Performing Arts hosts a flurry of comfort-food theatrical and musical productions like *Mama's Night Out* (where it's Mom's turn to suck at a bottle), *Seussical, The Wizard of Oz,* and *The Rat Pack Is Back.* Want to go out on the town without going *too* far out? This is totally your spot.

PARKS AND RECREATION

Twin Citians have the luxury of being able to walk past wetlands full of migratory waterfowl and turtles on their way to downtown Minneapolis, or through thickly forested areas housing species of native animals and birds just minutes outside St. Paul. Kids who grow up in the Twin Cities share in pleasures usually reserved for children in the country, whether it be fishing in one of the many regularly stocked urban lakes, berry picking, or just being surrounded by trees, songbirds, and wildflowers. Even in the dead of winter, you'll find people outside cross-country skiing, snowshoeing, or ice fishing in the many city and suburban parks around the Cities. Take a trip to any of the following, and you'll soon see why Minnesotans prize their wilderness areas.

PARKS

Minneapolis

BOOM ISLAND
Plymouth Avenue and NE Eighth Street, Minneapolis
(612) 230-6400
www.minneapolisparks.org
Boom Island Park is a jewel of the Minneapolis parks system. The island is a part of the Minneapolis Riverfront District, a series of parks that stretch from Plymouth Avenue to I-35W. Situated above historic Main Street, Nicollet Island, and the St. Anthony Lock and Dam, Boom Island is a popular destination for picnicking, tossing a Frisbee, sightseeing on a riverboat, launching one's own boat, or simply relaxing by the river on the plaza overlooks.

The boat launch is on the north side of the main parking area in a small, protected channel about 300 feet away from the water's edge and the dock area to the boat slips. Several sets of stairs and a wheelchair-accessible ramp go to the boat slip dock area, and a lovely promenade/plaza is just downriver of the boat dock. This area provides a nice view of the river as well as a stunning view of downtown Minneapolis. Another small plaza area with wood decking adjacent to the boat dock affords visitors an opportunity to view the comings and goings of both the riverboats and the private boats being launched nearby.

Boom Island is home to St. Anthony Falls' miniature "lighthouse," which sits on a prominent point overlooking the boat dock and river, although it is no longer operational.

LORING PARK
1382 Willow St., Minneapolis
(612) 230-6400
www.minneapolisparks.org
Modeled after New York's Central Park, although about 800 acres smaller than the real thing, Loring Park is an urban park with just about everything. There's a large, beautiful pond (Loring Pond) often with mallards, wood ducks, and Canada geese on and around the water; lush, green rolling hills; and, in summer, free live music and movies in the outdoor amphitheater several nights of the week. There's also a concession cart selling snacks and ice cream parked near the amphitheater most nights. The park is well maintained, with lots of paved trails that take you around the pond and the stunning fountain and bronze sculpture of Norway's esteemed violinist Ole Bull.

A short walk across the street takes you to either the Basilica of Saint Mary or the internationally acclaimed Walker Art Center and its sculpture garden, depending on which way you point your feet.

MILL RUINS PARK
704 South Second St., Minneapolis
(612) 230-6400
www.minneapolisparks.org
Mill Ruins Park on the Mississippi River is next to the Mill City Museum, the historic Crosby A Mill now preserved to celebrate the history of the flour mills that built the city of Minneapolis. The park overlooks the locks and St. Anthony Falls, and visitors can watch the barge traffic making its way through the locks and on down the Mississippi. The park connects to the Stone Arch Bridge, a pedestrian and bicycle pathway across the river, and to the bike trail system winding up and down the Mississippi and throughout the Twin Cities.

i First-time offenders getting a parking ticket at Minneapolis parks in lots with blue Patron Pass signs can purchase a cheaper annual Patron Pass parking permit in lieu of paying the fine. Check the fine print on your ticket to make sure the citation was issued while parking in a Patron Pass area. You'll have to pay the fine if you're a repeat offender. Call the Minneapolis Park and Recreation Board (612-230-6400) for more information.

MINNEAPOLIS CHAIN OF LAKES/RICE CREEK REGIONAL PARKS
Cedar Lake
25th Street West and Cedar Lake Parkway

Lake Calhoun
Calhoun Parkway and Lake Street

Lake Harriet
4135 Lake Harriet Pkwy. East

Lake Nokomis
Minnehaha Parkway East and Cedar Ave.

Lake of the Isles
25th Street West and Lake of the Isles Parkway East
(612) 230-6400
www.minneapolisparks.org
About 2,500 acres of parkland surround Minneapolis's Chain of Lakes, which includes Lake Harriet, Lake Calhoun, Lake of the Isles, Cedar Lake, and Lake Nokomis. The lakes are connected by Rice and Minnehaha Creeks, which makes canoeing through much of the parkland a fun trip that involves little or no docking to get from lake to lake. Both boat and shore fishing are popular in the Chain of Lakes, and many fishing piers and easily accessed shore fishing sites can be found throughout the parks.

Thomas Sadler Roberts Bird Sanctuary, located on the north shore of Lake Harriet, consists of 13 acres of unapologetically wild land that attracts more than 200 bird species each year. The sanctuary is named for Thomas Roberts, the late Minneapolis physician and University of Minnesota ornithology professor who in 1932 wrote what remains the definitive work on local avian culture, Birds of Minnesota. Created by the Minneapolis Park Board in 1936 as Lyndale Park Bird Sanctuary, its name was changed after Roberts's death to honor the man who led so many field trips here.

MINNEHAHA FALLS AND PARK
4801 Minnehaha Ave. South, Minneapolis
(612) 230-6400
www.minneapolisparks.org
This historic, heavily used, and recently refurbished 193-acre regional park gives visitors little wonder where Henry Wadsworth Longfellow got the inspiration to write his epic poem *Song of Hiawatha*, which was inspired by accounts the poet had read about Minnehaha Falls, though he never actually visited them. On-site tributes to Longfellow include a scale replica of the poet's Cambridge, Massachusetts, house and a fine sculpture of the brave Hiawatha holding Minnehaha in his arms.

The impressive falls are the primary destination point for most park visitors, with several wonderful overlooks and steps that take you to the base of the falls. From the bottom, you can pick up the Minnehaha Trail and follow it and the river to the Lower Glen area of Minnehaha Park. There you'll find a wide, open field, old stone bridges that cross the water at regular intervals, limestone cliffs, and areas of restored prairie and undeveloped wetlands. Throughout the park are statues, plaques dedicated to historic events, and historic buildings, including the historic Minnehaha Depot, built in 1875 to serve as a recreational gateway for visitors to the falls and as a departure point for soldiers from nearby Fort Snelling, and the Col. John H. Stevens House, which is open to visitors Memorial Day weekend through mid-September.

i Though Minnehaha Park is beautiful in summer, it's a real treat to go there in winter and see the powerful waterfall frozen solid. Most of the park trails are closed then, but you can still walk down to see the falls.

NICOLLET ISLAND PARK
40 Power St. (off Historic Main Street at East Hennepin Avenue), Minneapolis
(612) 230-6400
www.minneapolisparks.org
In summertime this little island located in the middle of the Mississippi River is a haven for native wildlife of all sorts, including the occasional deer. In winter the park is converted into a giant ice-skating rink. Year-round the park is a beautiful place for an afternoon or evening stroll—at night the lights of downtown Minneapolis reflect off the Mississippi River, giving one the feeling of being downtown yet still walking through a quaint, small town. Horse-and-carriage rides are available from the nearby Nicollet Inn, and fireworks displays can be seen from the park's rolling green hills on New Year's Eve, the Fourth of July, and during the Aquatennial celebration.

ST. ANTHONY FALLS HERITAGE TRAIL
Main Street, Minneapolis
(612) 767-8000
www.minneapolis-riverfront.com
This amazing stretch of land is often overlooked because the entrance is tucked behind the giant Pillsbury flour mill, next to Minneapolis's historic Main Street retail area directly across the Mississippi River from downtown.

The Heritage Trail is a highly accessible asphalt multiuse trail (bike, hike, jog, and skate) that takes visitors on a 1.8-mile loop, connecting them to most of the historic and natural features of early Minneapolis, including vistas of the tree-lined banks of the Mississippi River as well as many ruined brick arches from the days of the bustling milling industry.

THEODORE WIRTH PARK
1339 Theodore Wirth Pkwy., Minneapolis
(612) 230-6400
www.minneapolisparks.org
Theodore Wirth Park, or just Wirth Park, as it's usually called, is a huge chunk of land extending from Minneapolis at Glenwood Avenue to Lowry Avenue and from Vincent Avenue into Golden Valley. This beautiful 500-acre park surrounds Wirth Lake, which has a swimming beach as well as a boat launch. There's also an archery range, a playground, tennis courts, the Theodore Wirth Golf Course, and the Eloise Butler Wildflower Garden.

This is a particularly popular park in winter. Behind Theodore Wirth Park's great sledding hill (on the golf course's 10th fairway) is the lighted snow-tubing hill, which isn't too steep and has a tow rope. Cold, hungry snow tubers will appreciate the nearby Swiss Chalet, which has a fireplace and serves fast-food fare such as burgers and fries. Both a skate-skiing course and an intermediate traditional trail start from the chalet. From the top of the skiing hill, downtown Minneapolis's skyscrapers glittering in the afternoon sun may startle you with their closeness. This is known as one of the prettiest places in the Cities for nighttime skiing.

Named for schoolteacher Eloise Butler, who is buried in the bird sanctuary, the 15-acre Eloise Butler Wildflower Garden and Bird Sanctuary is a favorite spot for urbanites to escape the realities of city life and walk among the brilliant, carefully tended wildflower plots.

St. Paul

BATTLE CREEK REGIONAL PARK
2300 Upper Afton Rd. East, St. Paul
(651) 748-2500
www.co.ramsey.mn.us/parks
Battle Creek Regional Park, consisting of 1,840 acres in the southeast corner of St. Paul and southern Maplewood, provides a large natural area in a highly developed urban environment. The park's extensive areas of woods, wetlands, and grasslands provide habitat for many species of wildlife, including deer, foxes, herons, egrets, and hawks. In summer, the park offers biking and hiking trails. Winter visitors can tour the park on groomed cross-country trails. A large picnic pavilion accommodates groups of up to 500 people, and smaller picnic shelters are also available. In summer the park has a weekly concert series that showcases everything from local alternative acts to acoustic jazz combos.

COMO PARK
1360 North Lexington Pkwy., St. Paul
(651) 266-6400
www.stpaul.gov
This 450-acre urban park is one of the most visited sites in the Twin Cities, offering large picnicking areas, a conservatory, a zoo, a Japanese garden, a small amusement park with pony rides, and summer concerts and plays. There's also an 18-hole golf course that turns into a cross-country ski area in the winter; seasonal equipment rentals and refreshments are available at Como Lakeside Pavilion.

In the middle of a tough Minnesota winter, there's no palliative like a visit to the lush, green-filled Marjorie McNeely Conservatory at Como Park, which houses such exotic plants as 125-year-old palm trees and papaya trees. Outside, the teahouse in the Como Ordway Memorial Japanese Garden offers a traditional chanoyu tea ceremony several times throughout the summer. Look for the beautiful goldfish pond stocked with giant, colorful fish. (See the Attractions chapter for information on Como's zoo and conservatory.)

The historic Cafesjian's Carousel can be found just south of the conservatory. The carousel and its beautiful antique horses are available to the public during the summer, and a ride on the carousel is a great way to end a day at the park.

HIDDEN FALLS PARK
East Mississippi River Boulevard, St. Paul
(651) 266-6400
www.stpaul.gov/depts/parks
Hidden Falls Park dates from 1887, when the area was identified as one of four major park sites for the city of St. Paul. The park got its name from the small, spring-fed waterfall hidden deep inside the park. Today hiking and biking trails run along shady, wooded bottomlands next to the river and along the marshes of the lake before connecting to the trails along Mississippi River Boulevard. The park features a well-developed picnic area with pavilion and modern toilet facilities, a boat launch ramp, and picnic sites. Panfish can be caught in the Mississippi River. In October outsize ghoulish puppets and fire-spewing monsters take over the park for the annual BareBones Halloween Show.

The hiking/biking trail, which converts to a cross-country ski trail in the winter, takes users along the Mississippi River, where the flora and fauna of river life can be observed up close. Songbirds migrate and nest nearby, and deer and rabbits can be seen in the thick wooded areas around the park. At points along the trail, historic Fort Snelling can be seen on the high bluffs across the river.

FORT SNELLING STATE PARK
101 Snelling Lake Rd., St. Paul
(612) 725-2724
www.dnr.state.mn.us
For hundreds of years before Europeans arrived, generations of Dakotas lived in villages along the Mississippi and Minnesota Rivers that meet in what's now Fort Snelling State Park. The river confluence was believed to be the place of origin and center of the earth by the bands of Mde-wa-kan-ton-wan Dakotas, the "Dwellers by Mystic

Lake." By the late 1600s Europeans had visited the area. In the 1820s Fort Snelling was built on the bluff above the two rivers to control the exploration, trade, and settlement on these waterways.

Established as a state park in 1962, the 3,400-acre Fort Snelling State Park is located in the Mississippi River Sandplains Landscape Region at the confluence of the two great rivers. Most of the park is on the Minnesota River floodplain and is thickly wooded with large cottonwood, silver maple, ash, and willow trees along the braided channels of the Minnesota River. Picnic sites, a beach, and river and lake fishing invite visitors to enjoy the recreational opportunities offered by this historic and beautiful park nestled in the shadow of city freeways and airport flyways. The swimming beach is a popular summertime attraction, and the park offers miles of hiking, biking, and cross-country skiing trails, including a trail that leads up to historic Fort Snelling on the bluff above the confluence.

The Pike Island Interpretive Center hosts exhibits concerning historic Fort Snelling and the region in general. Golf equipment and canoes are available for rent in the park, and naturalist programs ranging from bird-watching tours to nature and snowshoe hikes are offered year-round.

INDIAN MOUNDS PARK
Earl Street and Mounds Boulevard, St. Paul
(651) 266-6400
www.stpaul.gov
Enshrining six 2,000-year-old Hopewell Indian burial mounds, Mounds Park occupies what was the choicest residential land in St. Paul in the 1860s, when this park was set aside. Today the bluffs of the park give visitors one of the best "aerial" views of the Twin Cities, with the Minneapolis skyline on the left, the St. Paul skyline on the right, and the Mississippi River below. The mounds are surrounded by metal rail fences but are easily seen and approached—the remains have long since been removed, but the mounds are still standing as a sacred memorial. Visitors are not permitted to climb on the mounds. A brass plaque describing the site stands near the

brick pavilion. The park is also the site of the first visit by Europeans to the Twin Cities area; Father Louis Hennepin and two other Frenchmen were brought here in 1680.

The park is actively used by families, groups, skateboarders, cyclists, hikers, and others. It is a well-worn park with old restrooms and access routes developed before accessibility regulations were in place, but there are plenty of picnic areas and play spaces for people of all ages and accessible parking spaces at many points in the park.

LILYDALE PARK/HARRIET ISLAND PARK/ CHEROKEE PARK
South side of Mississippi River at Wabasha, St. Paul
(651) 266-6400
www.stpaul.gov
The river-oriented Lilydale and Harriet Island Parks include the natural area of the Lilydale portion below the river bluffs and Harriet Island itself. Harriet Island, situated on the Mississippi River across from downtown St. Paul, was one of the first recreational sites in the city. Named for pioneer schoolteacher Harriet Bishop, the park was a true island separated from the mainland by a channel of water until 1950, when the channel was filled. At the top of the bluffs is Cherokee Park, which has picnic grounds and good spots overlooking Harriet Island, the Mississippi, and downtown St. Paul's skyline.

Harriet Island has long been a playground for St. Paul citizens who come alone or with friends and family to fish, launch their boats, cruise on a historic riverboat, picnic, take walks, and simply enjoy nature. The park has landscaped river edges, beautiful flower gardens that attract native and migratory songbirds, and a marina from which park visitors can board several large paddleboats to tour the waterways.

Lilydale, formerly a residential community, extends to the west of Harriet Island and is now an undeveloped floodplain. It used to be the site of former Twin City Brick Co.'s mining operations, until the company exposed extensive fossil beds, making the area well known among professional and amateur paleontologists, who are sometimes allowed to accompany professionals on guided digs at the park. A connected pond and about 200 acres of marsh and woodlands provide habitat for varied flora and fauna.

MEARS PARK
366 Sibley St., St. Paul
Located near Galtier Plaza in the distinctive Lowertown neighborhood of St. Paul, Mears Park serves as the neighborhood's village commons. The park is a popular lunchtime and evening gathering spot and is filled with trees, flowers, benches, sculpture, and even a rippling creek. Summertime brings outdoor concerts, performances, events, and festivals. In winter the park's many trees are covered with hundreds of thousands of twinkling lights.

PHALEN PARK
Off Wheelock Parkway and East Larpenteur Ave., St. Paul
(651) 266-6400
www.stpaul.gov
Founded in 1899, Phalen Park surrounds the quiet residential area around Phalen and Round Lakes in northeast St. Paul, with 3.2 miles of paved trails, an amphitheater, a beach, an 18-hole golf course, and a picnic shelter and pavilion. The park is named for Edward Phelan (whose name was spelled various ways), the earliest settler of the land around Phalen Creek. The park's trails connect to the Gateway State Trail, a paved biking and walking trail stretching from downtown St. Paul to Pioneer Park, north of Stillwater.

RICE PARK
140 Washington St., St. Paul
In the shadow of Landmark Center, the Ordway Center for the Performing Arts, the St. Paul Public Library, and the St. Paul Hotel, St. Paul's Rice Park is a restful yet active square of greenery and monuments. Young trees provide a little shade during the day, but the park is at its best for summer concerts and as the ice sculpture hub of the annual St. Paul Winter Carnival.

SHADOW FALLS
Near Mississippi River Boulevard and Exeter Place, St. Paul
For generations, neighborhood families (by day) and St. Thomas students (by night) have been hiking down into this little gorge to climb on, around, and behind the hidden 30-foot waterfall flowing into the nearby Mississippi River. The falls gave the nearby residential neighborhood its name, and the gentle hike makes for a nice excursion just off the beaten path. (Warning; Watch out for the broken beer bottles.)

WESTERN SCULPTURE PARK
Off Marion Avenue between I-94 and University Avenue, St. Paul
www.publicartstpaul.org/western.html
The Avis of Twin Cities sculpture parks. Hidden in plain sight, this funky little urban park features pieces sporting up-with-people inspirational quotes, a giant megaphone facing the nearby State Capitol, and at its center a spectacular Mark DiSuvero steelwork. Check the Web site before or after your visit to keep score: Labels for the pieces are often missing or weirdly hidden.

North
BALD EAGLE–OTTER LAKES REGIONAL PARK
5800 Hugo Rd., White Bear Township
(651) 748-2500
www.co.ramsey.mn.us/parks
Bald Eagle–Otter Lakes Regional Park, comprising 884 acres, is located in White Bear Township in the northeast corner of Ramsey County. The park features extensive woods, wetlands, and grasslands. The park is home to many species of wildlife, including red foxes, deer, woodcocks, herons, turtles, minks, beavers, osprey, otters, and muskrats. More than 3 miles of paved and woodchip-covered hiking trails offer visitors the opportunity to experience nature up close. Fishing— both when the park's lakes are liquid and when they are frozen—is popular here.

The Tamarack Nature Center offers a variety of programs, including bird-watching tours, syrup making, guided summer hikes, and winter snowshoe walks. Inside the nature center itself are mounted displays of many animals native to the area.

ℹ️ Rice Park and Mears Park in downtown St. Paul are picturesque strollworthy urban pockets, especially in winter, when they're decorated with myriad white lights.

COON RAPIDS DAM REGIONAL PARK
10360 West River Rd., Brooklyn Park
(763) 694-7790
www.threeriversparkdistrict.org/parks/
coon-rapids-dam.aspx
Situated on the banks of the Mississippi River, the 610-acre Coon Rapids Dam Regional Park offers visitors the chance to see our nation's greatest river up close. The centerpiece of this large park is the refurbished Coon Rapids Dam, which spans the Mississippi River. A wide dam walkway, usable by pedestrians, bicyclists, and in-line skaters, allows visitors a unique opportunity to walk across a working dam, with a scenic view of the riverway above and below the dam.

The stunning Native Prairie Restoration Area is on the nearby banks of the river, just past the visitor center entrance and extending to the picnic plaza. The park has two well-developed and conveniently linked and accessible asphalt bike/hike trails—all part of the extensive Mississippi River Trail Corridor that leads users south into Anoka Regional Park and eventually connects users with the Minneapolis Parkway Trail System at Boom Island and the Heritage Trail at historic Main Street in Minneapolis.

CROW-HASSAN PARK RESERVE
12595 Park Dr., Hanover
(763) 694-7860
www.threeriversparkdistrict.org/parks/
crow-hassan-park.aspx
It's hard to imagine an endless sea of grass flowing from Minnesota to the Rocky Mountains now that trees, crops, houses, and billboards muddy the view. But one of the best places in the Twin Cities to catch a glimpse of that sweeping landscape is Crow-Hassan Park Reserve, where 600 acres of old farm fields have been transformed back into prairie.

For pet owners, more than 40 acres are open for dogs to run off leash; a special permit is required and is available from Three Rivers Park District Headquarters for $30 per year or $5 per day. This is also a popular park for horseback riders, with more than 10 miles of trail dedicated for just this purpose. In winter cross-country skiing and snowmobiling bring crowds of enthusiasts. The beauty of Crow-Hassan, though, is that in between the rolling hills, the deep prairie grass, and the thick tree cover, you can be as completely alone as you want to be, even if the park is at peak season.

ELM CREEK PARK RESERVE
12400 James Dean Pkwy., Maple Grove
(763) 694-7894
www.threeriversparkdistrict.org/parks/
elm-creek-park.aspx
The Elm Creek Park Reserve, located northwest of Osseo, is a beautiful and varied park and nature reserve. A swimming beach, creative play area, and a concession stand with volleyball, horseshoe, and bike rentals are located on the premises, and horse trails, cross-country ski trails, hiking trails, and bicycle paths interlace the park.

The Eastman Nature Center includes displays giving a concise overview of the reserve's habitat. From here hikers can go on self-guided tours ranging from wildflower walks to a trip through turtle country. If the displays don't move you into the woods, the enthusiastic naturalists and creative courses (on tagging monarch butterflies, for example) offered will. On late afternoon weekend days in January and February, Eastman packs them in to view the white-tailed deer that come to feed.

FRANCONIA SCULPTURE PARK
29836 St. Croix Trail, Franconia
(651) 257-6668
www.franconia.org
For years Franconia had an almost mythic status: an outpost among the central Minnesota corn-

fields where towering creatures and garbage-can towers held silent domain over a land you seemed to have all to yourself. A few years ago the park moved a short distance to a location better suited to educational programs and other activities, and since then it's enjoyed a rising profile. There are classes for kids and residencies for sculptors, who can be seen in, as it were, their natural environment assembling their oft-massive creations. If your favorite piece at the Minneapolis Sculpture Garden is *Spoonbridge and Cherry* rather than Charles Ginnever's abstract *Nautilus,* Franconia is for you: The work here is weird, wild, and gleefully postmodern.

LAKE MARIA STATE PARK
11411 Clementa Ave. NW, Monticello
(763) 878-2325
www.dnr.state.mn.us/state_parks
Lake Maria State Park includes a native stand of maple, oak, and basswood, remnants of the Big Woods that once covered much of south-central Minnesota. The park offers hiking, backpacking, horseback riding, and cross-country ski trails. Backpack sites are located on remote lakes and ponds throughout the park. Log camper cabins, also located near lakes and ponds, provide bunk beds for six people and a table and benches.

The park maintains more than 20 miles of summer hiking trails, 16 miles of groomed cross-country ski trails, and 3 miles of winter hiking trails. Snowshoeing is permitted anywhere in the park except on groomed ski trails, and snowshoes can be rented at the visitor center. Boat and canoe rentals are available through the visitor center in summer. You can also make campsite and cabin reservations at the visitor center or on the park's Web site.

LONG LAKE REGIONAL PARK
1500 Old Hwy. 8, New Brighton
(651) 748-2500
www.co.ramsey.mn.us/parks
The 218 acres of Long Lake Regional Park include frontage on Long Lake and cattail marshes, oak woods, and restored prairie around Rush Lake. The park features a 3-mile hiking and biking trail,

a beautiful swimming beach, and a large picnic area near the swimming beach. After a dip in Long Lake, make tracks to the beach house for snacks, restrooms, changing rooms, and showers. A large picnic pavilion is complete with kitchen and public restrooms, and the group picnic area features a game field, a volleyball court, hiking/biking trails, and a wheelchair-accessible play area. On the south end of Long Lake, you can launch your boat and park your trailer—or just fish off the pier. The pier has a parking area, restrooms, a clean water source, and seated angler stations.

RIVERFRONT REGIONAL PARK/ ISLANDS OF PEACE
5100 East River Rd., Fridley
(763) 757-3920
www.anokacountyparks.com
This Anoka County park's biking, hiking, and ungroomed cross-country skiing trails offer nice views of the Mississippi River all along the trails. Canoes can be rented from the park, and fishing is permitted from the shore and the river. If you're lucky enough to hook some lunch, grills and picnic shelters are also available.

The Islands of Peace segment of the park, located north of I-694, has been developed by the Foundation for Islands of Peace. A reception center has a fireplace, restrooms, a library, a lounge, and meeting rooms. A walk bridge and paved trail link the center to Chase's Island facilities, which include paved trails, shelter, river viewing, and picnic facilities—all with wheelchair access. The 57-acre Durnam Island segment, located in the Mississippi River west of Chase's Island, has accessible nature trails and a boat shuttle service.

WILD RIVER STATE PARK
39797 Park Trail, Center City
(651) 583-2125
www.dnr.state.mn.us/state_parks/wild_river
Wild River State Park's name is derived from the fact that the St. Croix River was one of the original eight rivers protected by the U.S. Congress through the Wild and Scenic Rivers Act of 1968.

The park has 18 miles of shoreline along the St. Croix.

Wild River State Park attracts people who enjoy camping, hiking, horseback riding, canoeing, interpretive programs, self-guided trails, and cross-country skiing. Day visitors can enjoy a leisurely paddle down the St. Croix River from the Sunrise River access to the southern park river access. The park provides opportunities for drive-in camping, group camping, backpack camping, and canoe camping. (Winter camping is also available here.) Visitors who want modern amenities can reserve the guesthouse, which provides a living room, dining room, kitchen, and fireplace. The park also has two camping cabins, with bunk beds, a table, and benches. An all-season trail center is a great spot to relax after hiking, riding horses, biking, or cross-country skiing on the park's trail system. A visitor center with exhibits and environmental education programs is open year-round.

South

CAPONI ART PARK
1220 Diffley Rd., Eagan
(651) 454-9412
www.caponiartpark.org
Caponi Art Park is named for Anthony Caponi, a sculptor who served as chair of the Macalester College art department for decades. The hilly, forested lakeside land that now constitutes the Eagan art park started as Caponi's private land; since the 1940s he's both added sculptures to it and sculpted the land itself with tools ranging from shovels to bulldozers. Thus, it's not just a sculpture park but truly an art park—a space uniquely created by a single artist. It opened to the public in 1992 and is now run jointly with the Eagan parks department; in his late 80s, Caponi continues to live and work in a house on the land. It's obviously a must-see for art buffs, but the park has attractions for everyone, with an active programming schedule that includes children's activities, visits by spoken-word poets, and theatrical performances.

> **i** Put off by the cost and commercialism of the Renaissance Festival? In September Caponi Art Park hosts a Medieval Fair enacted by members of the Society for Creative Anachronism; admission is just a few dollars, by requested donation. Watch www.caponiartpark.org for details.

CLEARY LAKE REGIONAL PARK
18106 Texas Ave., Prior Lake
(763) 694-7777
www.threeriversparkdistrict.org
The 1,045-acre Cleary Lake Regional Park, southwest of Burnsville, is a popular year-round recreation spot in the southern metro area. A distinctive three-season pavilion, available by reservation, is great for large group gatherings, while golfers find challenge in the par 3, nine-hole golf course and driving range. Water sports available include swimming, boating, and fishing in Cleary Lake. Winter activities include cross-country skiing on groomed trails and snowshoeing anywhere in the park except the ski trails. Boats, bicycles, in-line skates, and cross-country skis are available for rent at the visitor center; reservation picnic areas and campsites are also available.

HYLAND LAKE PARK RESERVE
10145 Bush Lake Rd., Bloomington
(763) 694-7687
www.threeriversparkdistrict.org
The 1,000 acres of parklands at Hyland Lake Park Reserve, which include prairie lands, deciduous woods, and Normandale, Hyland, and Bush Lakes, have more than 9 miles of trails for hiking, an additional 8.5 paved miles for bicycling, and, in winter, 8 miles of groomed trail for cross-country skiing. The first cross-country ski trail in the Twin Cities was cut here, near the old Bush Lake ski jump in the winter of 1965–66. Hyland Lake Park Reserve is now one of the finest and most popular cross-country facilities in the area.

On the lakes there's a boat landing with a rental/storage facility for canoes, rowboats, and paddleboats, as well as a large fishing pier for shore fishing. Bush Lake has a clean swimming beach with picnic shelters nearby. Skis, bicycles, paddleboats, and seasonal recreation equipment can be rented at the visitor center for reasonable rates.

The Richardson Nature Center, located inside the park, is home to deer, pheasants, and wild songbirds. Richardson's spacious center focuses especially on raptors and raptor recovery, with programs on eagles, owls, hawks, and falcons. You can see ospreys banded and meet live owls, hawks, and kestrels.

LEBANON HILLS REGIONAL PARK
860 Cliff Rd., Eagan
(651) 554-6530
www.co.dakota.mn.us/parks
Less than 30 minutes from both downtown Minneapolis and St. Paul, this Dakota County park covers more than 2,000 acres of lakes, marshes, beaches, and trails. Open year-round, the park is divided into east and west sections connected by an immense network of trails. Nearly every outdoor activity is available—swimming in Schultz Lake (one of the few local beaches with lifeguards present), RV and tent camping, hiking, picnicking, horseback riding, mountain biking, and cross-country skiing. Fishing and all nonmotorized boats are allowed on Jensen Lake, and in winter ice fishing is allowed on the lake as well.

Lebanon Hills is a popular destination for winter sports enthusiasts. The park has two great ski areas: the 2-mile skate-ski offers long, tough uphills and fast, winding downhills (not recommended for beginners), and several other park trails are tracked for classic cross-country skiing. The trail system was originally laid out for hiking and horse paths, so some downhill corners can be awkward for skiers. Cross-country ski and snowmobile trails snake through the park's wooded, hilly terrain, and hot cocoa and snacks are available at the warming house at Schulze Lake.

MINNESOTA VALLEY NATIONAL WILDLIFE REFUGE AND RECREATION AREA
3815 American Blvd., Bloomington
(952) 854-5915
www.fws.gov/midwest/MinnesotaValley

Only minutes from the Twin Cities and the airport, the Minnesota Valley National Wildlife Refuge is dedicated to preserving the wildlife of Minnesota River habitats. This archipelago of river-valley land parcels functions as a federally managed nature preserve, particularly for waterfowl and migrating birds using the Minnesota River flyway. All told, 14,000 acres are at your disposal, including the Minnesota Valley Trail, which links Fort Snelling State Park and units of the Minnesota Valley National Wildlife Refuge to waysides and other public lands. The area is ideal for hiking, biking, cross-country skiing, mountain biking, canoeing, snowshoeing, camping, and snowmobiling. Wildlife observation and birdwatching are also popular activities year-round. The landscapes are just as diverse as the trail system and include wetlands, floodplain forest, remnants of farmlands settled in the late 1800s, and blufftop oak savanna.

In the state-managed Minnesota Valley Recreation Area, you can see the only remaining building from the town of St. Lawrence, visit the Jabs Farm Homestead, or ride your bike across a 1900s railroad bridge. The interpretive center in the recreation area contains engaging displays of Minnesota River Valley human history and natural history. Naturalists offer field trips to the woodcock dancing grounds in spring and to the heron rookery in winter via cross-country skis. The wildlife refuge occupies about half of the larger Minnesota Valley Recreation Area, which stretches 75 miles from historic Fort Snelling to Le Sueur.

MURPHY-HANREHAN PARK RESERVE
15501 Murphy Lake Rd., Savage
(763) 694-7777
www.threeriversparkdistrict.org
Murphy-Hanrehan Park Reserve is a largely undeveloped park. The park's hilly terrain attracts mountain bikers, horseback riders, and endurance hikers in summer and cross-country skiers and snowmobilers in winter. Boaters with oars, paddles, or electric-trolling motors can launch into Murphy Lake from the boat launch off County Road 75; the lake has been stocked with everything from bullheads to walleye.

East

AFTON STATE PARK
6959 Peller Ave. South, Hastings
(651) 436-5391
www.dnr.state.mn.us/state_parks
Five miles south of the town of Afton, Afton State Park is a 1,695-acre wilderness area set along the St. Croix National Scenic Riverway. The park is located in a landscape of rolling glacial moraines and rocky bluffs, surrounded by thick hardwood and pine forests, with protected remnants of original prairie being restored by park management. Throughout the park visitors get picture-perfect glimpses of the slow-moving St. Croix River.

Afton State Park has more than 20 miles of paved and groomed trails for horseback riding and hiking in spring and summer. In winter many of these trails are left open for cross-country skiers and snowshoers to explore. Many activities are offered throughout the year by volunteers who lead snowshoe hikes, demonstrate bird-banding practices, and teach visitors how to identify many of the birds that visit the park. There are also several primitive camping sites with nearby access to hiking trails—reservations are needed from April to November but not from November to April. Bird-watching, swimming, sledding, and fishing are other popular activities at Afton State Park.

i A $50 season pass is required to cross-country ski in most of the parks in the Three Rivers Park District. Call the park district at (763) 559-9000 or visit their Web site (www.threeriversparkdistrict.org) for more information.

COTTAGE GROVE RAVINE REGIONAL PARK
9940 Point Douglas Rd., Cottage Grove
(651) 430-8240
www.co.washington.mn.us
This handsome 506-acre park stays pretty quiet except when the high school teams are practicing. The park name refers to the nearby town (organized in May 1858) and the wooded ravine that was formed in glacial times and may once have been a channel of the St. Croix River. The park is home to native Minnesota wildlife, including the pileated woodpecker. These spectacular birds have a flaming red crest and can reach 16 inches in height. If a loud jackhammering sound breaks the silence, you'll know they are close by.

In winter this is a great park for the experienced cross-country skier, with almost 150 feet in elevation change and some great downhill runs through heavily wooded, dramatic ravines. It is also a popular spot for ski skaters.

A fishing pier on the eastern side of Ravine Lake, which is stocked with walleye and bluegill, beckons the angler.

INTERSTATE STATE PARK/GLACIAL-POTHOLE TRAIL
On MN 8 in Taylors Falls
(651) 465-5711
www.dnr.state.mn.us/state_parks
Carved by glacial meltwater, Interstate State Park follows the cliffs and bluffs bordering the beautiful St. Croix River. Established in 1895 when Minnesota and Wisconsin created separate parks across the river from each other, this was the first example of an interstate park collaboration in the country.

The main attraction of the park, besides the St. Croix, are the unusual basalt formations and potholes and the greenstone cliffs that were formed before there was any complex life on Earth. There is much to do at Interstate State Park. Cliff climbing, kayaking, canoeing, camping, hiking, picnicking, and playing volleyball (equipment is available in the park office) all forestall boredom. For daredevils, cliff diving into the St. Croix is also a popular—and very unofficial (in fact, illegal)—activity.

The park has a 22-acre campground with 37 drive-in sites (including some without electricity) located near the Glacial-Pothole Trail that fills up quickly in the summer months—reservations are highly encouraged. You can also camp here in the winter, although you'll have to break out the snowshoes or cross-country skis to get to the campground: The park does not plow the campground roads in winter. Canoes can be rented at the nearby boat dock and can be reserved by calling the park.

LAKE ELMO PARK RESERVE
1515 Keats Ave., Lake Elmo
(651) 430-8370
www.co.washington.mn.us
The Lake Elmo Park Reserve is 2,165 acres of forest, wetlands, and prairie restoration lands. Eighty percent of the parkland is set aside for preservation and protection, and because of this, Lake Elmo is home to a huge variety of native animals, birds, reptiles, and fish. People come to Lake Elmo year-round for both shore and boat fishing, canoeing, hiking, swimming, and cross-country skiing. There are also three campgrounds with a total of 103 campsites, restroom facilities, lighted picnic shelters with electricity, hand pumps for water, and a two-acre swim pond that's regularly maintained by the park.

ST. CROIX BLUFFS REGIONAL PARK
10191 St. Croix Trail South, Hastings
(651) 430-8240
www.co.washington.mn.us
Five miles south of Afton, this 579-acre park is made up of rolling hills, blufftop hardwood forests, and nearly a mile of scenic St. Croix River shoreline. Woodlands and ravines cut through tight bluffs to the riverbank, making great bird-watching areas for everything from eagles to wild turkeys. Swimming is not allowed in the St. Croix, but boating, fishing, and ice fishing are. The park features a fishing pier and a boat launch, as well as trails for hiking and cross-country skiing. The park has a large campground suitable for both tent and RV campers.

ST. CROIX NATIONAL SCENIC RIVERWAY
401 North Hamilton St., St. Croix Falls, WI
(715) 483-2274
www.nps.gov/sacn
The St. Croix River stretches more than 150 miles and partially forms the boundary between Minnesota and Wisconsin. It is the only river in the world that's protected along its entire length. Beginning near Gordon, Wisconsin, the Upper

St. Croix flows southerly to St. Croix Falls. The Lower St. Croix flows from St. Croix Falls dam to Prescott, Wisconsin, where it joins the Mississippi River. The Lower St. Croix is deeper, wider, and slower moving than the Upper St. Croix, making it a great place to fish, canoe, water-ski, and swim. Hot air balloon rides are available year-round. Winter activities include ice fishing, downhill and cross-country skiing, tubing, snowmobiling, and sledding. Nearby Lake St. Croix is formed by a dam on the Mississippi River and is popular for water recreation.

SPRING LAKE PARK RESERVE
13690 Pine Bend Trail, Rosemount
(952) 891-7000
www.co.dakota.mn.us/parks
This lovely park is criss-crossed with scenic hiking or skiing trails that wind through the woods and along the bluffs high above the Mississippi River. Spring Lake Park Reserve provides a scenic and peaceful setting for nature lovers to appreciate, as well as a model airplane flying field and a challenging archery trail. A youth campground with a heated lodge and an outdoor classroom is available to youth groups. The park also has 66 garden plots available for seasonal rental on a first-come, first-served basis.

i Three Rivers Park District's 25-foot climbing wall regularly moves to different parks in the park system—contact Three Rivers (763-694-7722; www.three riversparkdistrict.com) to find out its current location.

SQUARE LAKE COUNTY PARK
15450 Square Lake Trail North, Stillwater
(651) 430-8370
www.co.washington.mn.us
The 27-acre Square Lake County Park is known for having one of the clearest lakes in Minnesota, making it a popular spot for scuba divers, swimmers, and anglers alike. The lake is regularly stocked with trout and has a 950-foot clean sand beach, a concession stand where food and fishing supplies can be purchased, and restrooms

with showers. The park also has a boat launch, a fishing pier, and a picnic area.

WILLIAM O'BRIEN STATE PARK
16821 O'Brien Trail North, Marine on St. Croix
(651) 433-0500
www.dnr.state.mn.us/state_parks
A great "getaway" park only 45 minutes from the Twin Cities, the 1,520 acres of William O'Brien State Park provide a beautiful setting along the banks of the St. Croix River. The park is named for a pioneer lumberman in the St. Croix River Valley, and its human-made lake is named for O'Brien's daughter, Alice, who donated an additional 180 acres to the park in 1945.

O'Brien is an extremely popular camping spot, and in the summer the first-come, first-served campsites fill up quickly, especially on weekends; campsite reservations are strongly encouraged. Hiking/skiing trails offer quiet exploration of the park's rolling, wooded hills. For anglers, the channels of the St. Croix have northerns, walleye, bass, and trout. Ideal for canoeing, the river is also a migratory pathway that offers visitors an exciting diversity of sights and sounds. Canoes can be rented from the park for an outing on the St. Croix or on Lake Alice. Swimming in the river isn't allowed, but Lake Alice has a sandy beach and shallow water close to shore. On clear days you can see Taylors Falls from one overlook, and, although the park is heavily used, the 12 miles of hiking/skiing trails are rarely crowded. Snowshoeing is permitted anywhere in the park except on groomed ski trails. The park also has a warming house for huddling in after playing in the snow.

West

BAKER PARK RESERVE
2301 County Rd. 19, Maple Plain
(763) 694-7860
www.threeriversparkdistrict.org
Located on Lake Independence in central Hennepin County, Baker Park Reserve's 2,700 acres offer a 210-site campground, golfing at the Baker National Golf Course, swimming and boating in Lake Independence, and a playground for kids. The

kids' playground area is truly spectacular, almost fortresslike. Kids scramble over ramps, platforms, and paths made of recycled rubber mats that protect against minor falls and bumps and bruises.

In winter a sledding hill, a cozy warming chalet, and snowmobile, mountain biking, and groomed cross-country ski trails are opened. In summer paved hiking and biking trails wind through one of the remnants of a Big Woods forest. Boats, bikes, snowshoes, and skis are available for rent at the park's visitor center.

BAYLOR REGIONAL PARK
10775 County Rd. 33
Norwood Young America
(952) 467-4200
www.co.carver.mn.us/parks
Baylor Regional Park is located in the extreme southwest corner of the Twin Cities metro area, so far removed from the bright lights of the downtowns that it's a favorite observation point for junior astronomy clubs and amateur stargazers. Perched on the shoulder of Eagle Lake and surrounded by farmers' fields, Baylor preserves a rich mix of native habitats, from the large grove of mature maple trees that are tapped in early spring each year for maple syrup, to the floating boardwalk that carries visitors over wetland marshes to get a glimpse of turtles, waterfowl, and wildflowers.

The park offers a 50-site tent and RV campground with shower facilities, as well as a swimming beach and bathhouse on Eagle Lake, two large picnic shelters, tennis courts, and 4 miles of hiking trails. A community room in the park barn is available for group use with reservations in advance. In winter the hiking trails turn into neatly groomed cross-country ski trails, and a warming house is available for outdoor enthusiasts from 8 a.m. to sunset daily.

BRYANT LAKE REGIONAL PARK
6800 Rowland Rd., Eden Prairie
(763) 694-7764
www.threeriversparkdistrict.org
Bryant Lake Regional Park is located in Eden Prairie south of MN 62 and west of Shady Oak

Road on Rowland Road and has a three-season concession plaza, three-season pavilion, a paved boat launch, a fishing pier, a swimming beach, boat rentals, and 3 miles of turf and paved hiking/biking trails. The 170-acre park also provides habitat for deer, waterfowl, and songbirds; fishing, boating, swimming, and ice fishing are popular activities here. The park is set in a vista of rolling hills that block out the surrounding city lights and sounds, making it a perfect spot for an urban escape.

CARVER PARK RESERVE
7025 Victoria Dr., Victoria
(763) 694-7650
www.threeriversparkdistrict.org
Carver Park Reserve is one of the crown jewels of the Three Rivers Park District, with 3,500 acres and lakeshore frontage on six major lakes. One of the most popular places in the reserve is the Lowry Nature Center, which offers programs that focus on Carver's abundant natural resources, ranging from fall bird migration and waterfowl watches to the springtime activity of maple-syrup making and summertime stargazing, as well as tracking mink, voles, and foxes and building snowcaves. The park itself is home to deer, foxes, owls, hawks, and many other animals that can be seen from roads and trails. Wetland animals can be seen from the more than 1,700 feet of boardwalk that takes you through tamarack marshes. Park facilities include a boat launch and a campground at Lake Auburn. Four of the park's lakes are open for canoeing, fishing, and ice fishing, and the park has miles of trails for hiking, horseback riding, cross-country skiing, snowmobiling, and snowshoeing. On winter weekends the park turns a wood-heated barn into a warming house, with snack counters and restroom facilities conveniently located nearby. Cross-country skis, Norwegian kick sleds, and bicycles can be seasonally rented from the park.

FRENCH REGIONAL PARK
12605 Rockford Rd., Plymouth
(763) 694-7750
www.threeriversparkdistrict.org

French Regional Park, usually shortened to "French Park" by locals, was named for the first superintendent of the Hennepin County park system, Clifton E. French. Located on 310 acres on Medicine Lake, French Regional Park features many water-based activities. A self-guided canoe trail through the backwaters of the beautiful lake provides intimate views of wetland wildlife. Rental canoes, paddleboats, rowboats, and kayaks are available at the visitor center, and you can also rent a slip or wintertime lift storage to park your sailboat (under 20 feet only). Monthly outdoor education programs feature such activities as maple syruping, bird-watching, and guided hikes to beaver lodges. The open landscape of rolling glacial hills is broken along the lake and lagoons with second-growth forest. This is not a place to come for wintertime solitude. The park's central location attracts more than 20,000 skiers—half at night—during a good season.

The visitor center rents other equipment, from cross-country skis to volleyballs. A creative play area is available, and a shuttle tram runs throughout the summer season between the visitor center and the swimming beach. French Park's playground is usually humming with childhood energy, and the park features several miles of biking, hiking, and cross-country skiing trails. In winter, a lighted sledding hill makes for nighttime excitement.

i Dogs are permitted on Regional Trail corridors and on designated turf trails in all parks. Pets must be on a leash no more than 6 feet long, and owners must clean up after pets and dispose of pet droppings in a sanitary manner.

LAKE MINNETONKA REGIONAL PARK
4610 County Rd. 44, Minnestrista
(763) 694-7754
www.threeriversparkdistrict.org
This 292-acre park features picnic areas, a visitor center, a fishing pier, a boat launch, a unique 1.75-acre upland swimming pond with chlorinated water, and a wheelchair-accessible swimming ramp that extends into the pond. The

The Big Deal about the Big Woods

The **Big Woods** was a forest that once occupied 3,030 square miles in south-central Minnesota. The forest was composed of maple, basswood, white and red elm, red oak, tamarack, and red cedar on the banks of numerous lakes. The trees were so thick that sunlight couldn't penetrate to the forest floor in some places. French explorers who came to the area called the forest "Bois Grand," or "Bois Fort," which was later amended by English settlers to "Big Woods." Today farms, towns, suburbs, and industry have replaced much of the Big Woods. Fortunately, the 1,590 acres located in Lake Maria State Park at the northern edge of what was once the Big Woods retain a remnant of the grandness of these original forests.

Lake Minnewashta Park contains remnants of the Big Woods that once covered this area. Some of the oak trees here are so old that they're more than 12 feet in circumference. An ambitious reforestation project that included the planting of 25,000 new hardwoods was completed a few years ago but will realistically take many years to re-create the leafy canopy that once covered the park.

This park is tucked away and is visited mostly by locals, and at times you probably have a better chance of seeing deer than people while visiting. Lake Minnewashta is a popular fishing lake, allowing powerboats, canoes, and sailboats in summer and ice fishing in winter. The park also has a fishing pier and 5 miles of hiking/skiing trails.

LAKE REBECCA PARK RESERVE
9831 Rebecca Park Trail, Rockford
(763) 694-7860
www.threeriversparkdistrict.org
From canoeing on the Crow River to boat and ice fishing on Lake Rebecca, this 2,200-acre park offers outdoor activities in settings that suggest you are much farther away from the metropolitan area than you actually are. Lake Rebecca Park Reserve's gently rolling landscape, with numerous wetland areas, provides a haven for wildlife, including deer, beavers, and waterfowl. This reserve is also one of the sites for the trumpeter swan restoration program; you can often see the swans from the park's trails. The park has trails for mountain biking, road biking, hiking, cross-country skiing, dog walking, and horse riding. Boats are available for rent from the park's visitor center, and nonmotorized boat launching is permitted. Reservation picnic areas and group campsites are available. The park also features a fishing pier and swimming area.

NOERENBERG MEMORIAL GARDENS
2865 Northshore Dr., Wayzata
(763) 559-6700
www.threeriversparkdistrict.org
In 1972 the last surviving child of Frederick and Johanna Noerenberg—heirs to the Grain Belt

visitor center, which was formerly a private residence, contains meeting rooms, a reception area, exhibits concerning the area around Lake Minnetonka, and a garden containing a huge variety of native medicinal and herbal plants.

The park has a nice fishing pier, with two seated angler stations. There's a concession stand next to the changing rooms/bathrooms by the picnic area with accessible tables where folks can purchase goodies while enjoying the water. The beach is well maintained, with large umbrellas located around the water for families to use to keep themselves cool on the hottest summer days.

LAKE MINNEWASHTA REGIONAL PARK
6900 Ches Mar Dr., Chanhassen
(952) 474-0180
www.co.carver.mn.us/parks

brewery fortune—bequeathed the family lake-side estate to Hennepin County. The bequest stipulated that the 73 acres of flower beds, shade trees, and ornamental grasses be opened to the public.

Today the park features beautifully sculpted flower gardens that include unusual annuals and perennials, an assortment of grasses, and a large daylily collection. The park is a beautiful spot to stroll through and enjoy the flowers—however, part of the bequest of the Noerenberg family states that no picnics or boating activities are to be permitted on the premises, so light hiking and sightseeing covers the range of what park visitors can do here. The gardens are a very popular spot for weddings.

SUMMER RECREATION

In short, the best way to describe what to do in the Twin Cities during the summer is "Go outside." In this chapter we list not only where to go to play but also the local associations responsible for organizing many of the outdoor recreational events. We also list some of the more reasonable places to rent gear, from bicycles to canoes to scuba equipment. Whether you're looking for something for the whole family to do or seeking a quiet, beautiful spot to escape from city traffic and shopping malls, you're sure to find it in the Twin Cities.

Biking

Minnesota has more miles of paved trails than anywhere else in the country. Mountain biking trails wind their way through forests and along cross-country ski trails in the off-season. Lakes, creeks, waterfalls, bluffs, rivers—you can bike near them all without ever having to leave the metro area.

Inside the Cities proper, there are numerous paved bike trails to choose from. In Minneapolis the **Grand Rounds Parkway** follows the perimeter of the Chain of Lakes and encircles the city. Considered the crown jewel of metropolitan biking, this 50-mile scenic and urban trail traces the shorelines of Lake Nokomis, Lake Hiawatha,

Shingle Creek, Bassett Creek, Minnehaha Creek, and the Mississippi River.

Minneapolis is also home to the **Midtown Greenway** bike trail, which runs 5.7 miles from Chowen Avenue South just west of Lake Calhoun all the way to the Mississippi River. The trail connects to the Grand Rounds Parkway trails in the Uptown neighborhood in the west and the West River Parkway Trail section of the Grand Rounds in the east. You can also cross the Mississippi at Ford Avenue, Lake Street, Franklin Avenue, or Washington Avenue to connect with the East River Parkway Trail in St. Paul.

Commuters in the western suburbs can make use of the **Cedar Lake Trail,** which runs 3.6 miles from the intersection of 12th Street and 2nd Avenue in downtown Minneapolis to MN 100 near Cedar Lake Road South. The Cedar Lake Extension Trail continues west another 4.3 miles to Hopkins.

The other three trails are located in St. Paul. **Como Park's** 1.7-mile bike trail circles Como Lake and heads toward the Como Park Zoo and Conservatory area. **Hidden Falls/Crosby Farm's** 6.7-mile bike path follows the shady, wooded bottomlands along the banks of the Mississippi and is an especially pleasant ride to take during the dog days of summer. **Phalen Park's** 3.2-mile bike trail circles Lake Phalen and its beautiful swimming beach, a layout that makes it oh-so-convenient to stop riding and go in for a dip. St. Paul's **East River Parkway Trail** traces along the east bank of the Mississippi from downtown St. Paul all the way to the University of Minnesota's Minneapolis Campus.

The Cities also have extensive bike lanes along major thoroughfares, and the bike lanes and trails in the Twin Cities link to recreational trails stretching far into the suburbs, including the **Gateway Trail** from St. Paul to Stillwater, the **Bruce Vento Regional Trail** from St. Paul to Maplewood, and the **Southwest LRT Trail** from Minneapolis to Victoria, among others.

Parks in the metro area with paved biking trails include Anoka County Riverfront, Baker Park Preserve, Bryant Lake, Bunker Hills, Burlington-Northern Regional Trail, Carver Park Preserve,

Central Mississippi Riverfront, Cleary Lake, Coon Rapids Dam, Elm Creek Park Reserve, Fish Lake, French, Hyland-Bush-Anderson Lakes, Lake Elmo Park Reserve, Lake Minnetonka Regional Park, Lake Rebecca Park Reserve, Lebanon Hills, Lilydale/Harriet Island, Long Lake Regional Park, Minnehaha Parkway, Mississippi Gorge, Murphy-Hanrehan Park Reserve, North Hennepin Trail Corridor, Rice Creek–West Regional Trail, Rum River Central, Snail Lake, Southwest Regional LRT Trail, Theodore Wirth, and the Wirth-Memorial Parkway (see the Parks chapter for details about many of these parks). For more information about biking in the Twin Cities, call the Minnesota Safety Council at (651) 291-9150 or the Minnesota Office of Tourism at (888-TOURISM), or visit the latter's Web page at www.exploreminnesota.com.

There are several good places in the metro area to rent bicycles and get geared up. In Minneapolis you can rent bicycles at reasonable prices from **Calhoun Rental** (612-827-8231) at 1622 West Lake St. or from **Campus Bikes** (612-331-3442) at 213 SE Oak St.

Several in-town organizations hold annual bike-riding marathons worth checking out. One example: the **Minnesota Chapter of the Multiple Sclerosis Society** (612-335-7900; www.mssociety.org) holds three separate MS Bike Tours in the Cities each summer to raise funds for multiple sclerosis research and treatment.

The **Minnesota Cycling Federation** (www.mcf.net) comprises bicycle racing clubs in the Upper Midwest, whose purpose is the education and promotion of bicycle racing skills and safety and the promotion of races for bicycle racers. The federation provides cycling enthusiasts with the most current information about area race calendars, race results, MCF member clubs, the NCS Velodrome, and the Youth Cycling League.

Camping

Camping sites in the metro area are scarce and quickly snatched up, so it's a good idea to reserve a site at least two weeks in advance. To make camping reservations, call the campgrounds directly. For a free copy of the *Minne-sota Alliance of Campground Operators' Minnesota Campgrounds and RV Parks,* call the Minnesota Department of Tourism (888-TOURISM; www.exploreminnesota.com).

Baker Park Reserve (763-694-7662; www.threeriversparkdistrict.org) Campground is on Lake Independence, 20 miles west of Minneapolis on County Road 19, between US 12 and MN 55. There are 210 sites, including 98 with electricity. Each has a picnic table and fire ring and can accommodate two tents or one tent and one RV, with a maximum of six people per campsite. There are showers and flush toilets (wheelchair accessible) and an RV dump station. Daily fee: $17 per site, more for sites with electricity depending on exactly how much electricity you want.

Lake Auburn Campground is in **Carver Park Reserve** (952-443-2911; www.threeriverspark-district.org), near Victoria on County Road 11 between MN 5 and MN 7. Each site at Lake Auburn has a picnic table and fire ring and can accommodate two tents or one tent and one RV, with a maximum of six people per campsite. There are 55 sites plus 2 hike-in sites. This is rustic camping—there are pit latrines (wheelchair accessible), a hand pump, no showers, and no electricity. There is an RV dump station (for a fee). Daily fee: $11 per site.

The Clearly Lake Campground is in **Cleary Lake Regional Park** (763-694-7777; www.three riversparkdistrict.org), near Prior Lake on County Road 27 (Texas Avenue) just south of County Road 21. Red Pine has five sites with fire rings and picnic tables and can accommodate tent camping only. There are pit latrines (wheelchair accessible), a water pump nearby, no showers, and no electricity. Daily fee: $11 per site.

There are beautiful state parks with campsites within an hour's drive or so of the Twin Cities. Among the most popular are William O'Brien (651-433-0500), northwest near Marine-on-St. Croix; Interstate (651-465-5711), northwest near Taylors Falls; and Afton (651-436-5391), southwest near Hastings. Check out the parks online at www.dnr.state.mn.us/state_parks or contact the DNR reservations center (866-85PARKS, www.stayatmnparks.com). You'll need a day permit ($5) or an annual permit ($25), available at the parks, for your vehicle. Fees range from $11 to $18 per night, depending on the remoteness of the site and the amenities.

Canoeing and Kayaking

The benefits of canoeing and kayaking are many. Not only are they great ways to stay in shape, but they're also a pleasant way to get close to nature without noisy motors or worrying about getting hung up on waters too shallow for outboard motors. In the Cities several parks are perfect for canoes and kayaks. Lake Calhoun in Minneapolis is a popular canoeing and kayaking lake surrounded by swimming beaches and fishing piers. The lake has a great view of the downtown Minneapolis skyline and is absolutely spectacular at sunset. Connected to Lake Calhoun is Lake of the Isles, an especially beautiful place to take a canoe or kayak, with narrow waterways overhung with old stone bridges, wide areas full of friendly ducks and geese, and a small forested island in the middle of the lake. A city-run building on the Lake Calhoun grounds rents canoes and sailboats to park visitors.

i Most parks and campgrounds sell gift cards, which are thoughtful ideas for the outdoorsy types on your shopping list.

Adjacent and connected to Lake Calhoun, is Lake Harriet, a wide-open lake heavily used by canoes, kayaks, sailboats, pedal boats, and motorboats alike. The lake has several public swimming beaches and a refreshment stand on its northwestern shores—the perfect place to stop after a heavy workout on the water.

Other metro area parks that have waterways suitable for canoeing and kayaking include Anoka County Riverfront, Baker Park Preserve, Bald Eagle–Otter Lakes, Bryant Lake, Carver Park Preserve, Cleary Lake, Como, Coon Rapids Dam, Crow-Hassan, Fish Lake, French, Hidden Falls-Crosby Farm, Hyland-Bush-Anderson Lakes, Lake Byllesby, Lake Elmo Park Reserve, Lake George, Lake Minnewashta, Lake Rebecca Park Reserve, Lebanon Hills, Lilydale/Harriet Island, Long Lake Regional Park, Martin-Island-Linwood Lakes, Minneapolis Chain of Lakes, Nokomis Hiawatha, Phalen-Keller, Rice Creek/Chain of Lakes, Rice Creek–West Regional Trail, Rum River Central, Snail Lake, and Theodore Wirth (see the Parks chapter for more parks information). Canoeing is also popular in Interstate State Park in Taylors Falls and on other sections of the Lower St. Croix National Scenic Riverway east of the Metro.

The **Minneapolis Rowing Club** (612-729-1541; www.mplsrowing.org) has participated in regattas around the country almost every year since its founding in 1877. The club sponsors classes on rowing for youths of all ages as well as beginning adult rowers.

To rent canoes in the Cities, try **Wheel Fun Rentals** (877-273-2453; www.wheelfunrentals .com) at 3000 Calhoun Pkwy. East, or specific parks in the **Three Rivers Park District** (763-559-9000; www.threeriversparks.org). There are also many canoe rental places along the St. Croix River, particularly in Taylors Falls and Stillwater. Visit www.dnr.state.mn.us/canoeing for a complete list.

Some of the best canoeing in the world is available three to four hours north of the Twin Cities in the **Boundary Waters Canoe Area Wilderness** (BWCAW), a protected area in the Superior National Forest with thousands of lakes linked by streams and canoe portages. You can enter the Boundary Waters only with a permit for your specific entry point. It is best to plan well in advance for a trip to the Boundary Waters, as the most popular entry points are scooped up quickly when permits become available the previous winter. Some are available only through a lottery system, which means you may not get your preferred entry point even if you're the first to get your registration in; plan alternate routes to improve your chances. For more information about the Boundary Waters, permits, routes, and more visit www.bwca.cc. Detailed maps and books on the BWCAW can be found at REI stores (see www.rei.com for locations), as well as at **Midwest Mountaineering** (612-339-3433; www .midwestmtn.com) in Minneapolis.

Car Shows

For more than 30 years, the **Minnesota Street Rod Association** (MSRA; www.msra.com) has been sponsoring car shows in and around the Twin Cities area. More than 13,000 enthusiasts belong to the MSRA, a fact that's never more apparent than when the association's annual Back to the '50s show comes to town in June and the streets of St. Paul are filled with beautifully restored vintage hot rods.

ℹ️ **Friends of the Boundary Waters Wilderness** (612-332-9630; www .friends-bwca.org), based in Minneapolis, is a nonprofit membership organization dedicated to helping protect, preserve, and restore the wilderness character of the BWCA. Check out their Web site or give them a call for more information about how you can help.

Disc Golf

A combination of Frisbee and golf, disc golf is available throughout the metro. The rapidly growing sport involves throwing a special golf disc down a fairway with the aim of dropping it in a basket on a pole on the "green."

In St. Paul, the **Highland Park Disc Golf Course** (651-632-5111) has eight holes on what is considered a challenging course over rolling terrain. Across the Ford Bridge in Minneapolis, disc golfers can play a new layout at **Minnehaha Falls** (612-230-6400).

There are numerous courses in the Twin Cities suburbs, including at Bryant Lake Regional Park in Eden Prairie, Hyland Ski and Snowboard Area in Bloomington, Alimagnet Lake Park in Apple Valley, Oakwood Park in Cottage Grove, Lakewood Hills Park in White Bear Lake, Acorn Park in Roseville, Bassett Creek Park in Crystal, Central Park in Brooklyn Park, Plymouth Creek in Plymouth, and Rosland Park in Edina. To find out more and to locate courses near you, visit the Professional Disc Golfers Association Web site at www.pdga.com or the Minnesota Frisbee Association at www.mfaonline.org.

Fishing

Many of the 1,000-plus lakes in the Twin Cities metro area have either been stocked with fish by the Department of Natural Resources or are naturally just great fishing holes. For more information about licensing requirements and where to drop your line, see the Hunting and Fishing chapter.

Football

Cities Sports Connection (CSC; 612-929-9009; www.cscsports.com) offers coed and men's outdoor and indoor touch football leagues for all skill levels. CSC touch football leagues are offered year-round. CSC is open to all adults 18 or older—no membership or nonmember fees are charged to participate in CSC leagues.

Golf

With hundreds of acres of flat, open plains and gently rolling hills, Minnesota is naturally home to some exceptional golf courses. The Twin Cities region alone has more than 175 courses. Telephone reservations are highly recommended for all of the golf courses listed here. For more information about these courses and others in the metropolitan area, including amenities, tee fees, course features, and more, visit www.golf minnesota.com.

Hiking

Just about every park in the Twin Cities metro area has at least one hiking trail that wanders in and out of forests, follows rivers and streams, passes close by natural waterfalls, or winds along the banks of the Mississippi River. Area parks with easy to moderate paved and turf hiking trails abound (see Parks chapter for the parks listings).

For more experienced hikers, **Fort Snelling State Park** in St. Paul (612-725-2389), at 101 Snelling Lake Rd., has 18 miles of turf hiking trails that wind through the park's nature preserve, and **Minnesota Valley State Recreational Area** in Jordan (952-492-6400), at 19825 Park Blvd., has 47 miles of turf and paved hiking trails to explore.

If you're interested in meeting other hikers, **Friends of the Mississippi River** (651-222-2193; www.fmr.org) organizes bird-watching tours and wildflower hikes at different spots along the Mississippi River. For women who don't like hiking in the backwoods of Minnesota alone, the Department of Natural Resources' **Becoming an Outdoors-Woman in Minnesota** (651-296-6157) organizes group hikes for women as well as other solo and group gender-specific outdoors experiences ranging from canoeing to big-game hunting.

Horseback Riding

Many of the parks in the metro area allow horses to share paved and dirt paths with cyclists and pedestrians. The trick is finding a place to rent horses. Tourists and residents alike can rent horses or arrange for guided rides at many locations throughout the metro area suburbs for an average of $15 an hour.

North of the Twin Cities, horses can be rented at **Brass Ring Stables,** 9105 Northwest Norris Lake Rd., Elk River (763-441-7987); **Bunker Park Stables,** 550 Bunker Lake Blvd., Andover (763-757-9445; www.bunkerparkstable.com); and **Roselawn Stables,** 24069 Rum River Blvd. NW, St. Francis (763-753-5517).

In the eastern suburbs, horses can be rented at the **Diamond T Riding Stable,** 4889 Pilot Knob Rd., Eagan (651-454-1464); **Rockin' R Ranch,** 8540 Kimbro Ave. North, Stillwater (651-439-6878); and the **Windy Ridge Ranch,** 2700 Manning Ave. South, Woodbury (651-436-6557; www.windyridgeranch.com).

South of the Twin Cities and just outside Carver, horses can be rented at **River Valley Ranch,** 16480 Jonathan Carver Pkwy. (952-361-3361; rivervalleyhorseranch.com).

Parks in the metro area with specified horse paths are Baker Park Preserve, Carver Park Preserve, Crow-Hassan, Elm Creek Park Reserve, Lake Rebecca Park Reserve, and Murphy-Hanrehan Park Reserve (see the Parks chapter for more information).

> **i** The Minnesota Department of Natural Resources requires horse riders to carry a DNR Horse Pass to use state trails, state forests, or state parks. In the metro area, this would apply to riding in such places as Afton, Wild River, and St. Croix state parks; along the Gateway State Trail; on the Luce Line State Trail; and in the Minnesota Valley State Recreation Area. Other areas may also require the permit. For more information, contact the DNR (651-296-6157 or 888-646-6367; www.dnr.state.mn .us/horseback_riding).

Hot Air Ballooning

Minnesota Ballooning (800-585-5555) and **Aamodts Balloons** (651-351-0101; www .aamodtsballoons.com) in Stillwater offer balloon adventures from champagne rides to daylong trips. Call companies for specific takeoff times and sites. To learn how to pilot one of these big colorful beasts by yourself, **Wiederkehr Balloon Academy** in Lakeland (651-436-8172) offers classes in balloon navigation.

In-Line Skating

Both cities have plenty of paved paths open to in-line skaters. Some of the parks that allow in-line skates to share paved walking paths are Lilydale/Harriet Island, Minneapolis Chain of Lakes, Hiawatha, and Theodore Wirth (see the Parks chapter for listings). Two other particularly nice places to skate are along Lake Calhoun and Lake of the Isles; both the trails follow the lakeshore all the way and are wide enough that you don't have to worry about knocking pedestrians over or being hung up behind them for too long. There are also extended paved trails along both banks of the Mississippi in southwestern Minneapolis and southeastern St. Paul, and the newly completed Midtown Greenway is great for skating through south Minneapolis between Uptown and the Mississippi River.

Skate parks have their place here, too, and the most impressive one is in the western suburb of Golden Valley. **Third Lair Skatepark** (763-79-SKATE; www.3rdlair.com), 850 Florida Ave., has indoor and outdoor parks plus a really good skate shop. The **Tri-City Skate Park** at the Southdale YMCA (952-835-2567; www.ymcatwincities .org), at 7355 York Ave. South in Edina, has a skate park, too—the first all-concrete, in-ground, continuous-bowl skate park in the upper Midwest. You can sign up for summer skateboarding classes, too.

For more information about in-line skating events around town, contact the **Minnesota In-line Skate Club** (612- 827-3205; www.skatemin-nesota.com). This club has trail information and organizes weekly skates.

Kickball

Cities Sports Connection (CSC; 612-929-9009; www.cscsports.com) organizes coed kickball leagues for players ages 18 and over. Teams consist of players with lower to average and decent skill proficiency and game knowledge, with a focus on sportsmanship, having fun, and getting a good workout. No membership or nonmember fees are charged to participate in CSC leagues, and teams play events all over the metro area. CSC provides paid officials for all league action and free T-shirts for participants.

Miniature Golf

The Twin Cities are not a minigolf mecca, but fun courses are to be found—especially if you're willing to do a little driving. For that vintage vibe, try **Putt'er There** at St. Paul's Como Park (651-488-0277; www.putterthere.com) or the fantasy-themed **Lilli Putt** (get it?) in Coon Rapids (763-755-1450; www.lilliputtminigolf.com). If you want an authentic golf experience except for the ball never leaving the ground, try the course at Centennial Lakes, which actually looks like a tiny golf course (952-833-9580; www.ci.edina.mn .us). Putt-putt enthusiasts were delighted at the return of minigolf to the megamall, where the

space originally occupied by a minigolf course went through a couple of odd alternate uses including a cereal-themed playland. Now it's back to minigolf—excuse me, "adventure golf"—under the moniker **Moose Mountain** (952-883-8777; www.mallofamerica.com).

Nature Interpretation and Bird-Watching

Many of the metro area parks have ongoing wildlife conservation projects open to the public, which are a great way to get an up close look at Minnesota's wildlife. Bald eagles, hawks, egrets, deer, porcupines, and the occasional skunk are just a few of the animals you might see, especially in outlying parks. Raccoons and Canada geese are plentiful along the banks of the Mississippi River. Some of the metro area parks that have specific areas set aside for nature interpretation include Bald Eagle-Otter Lakes, Baylor, Bunker Hills, Carver Park Preserve, Como, Coon Rapids Dam, Elm Creek Park Reserve, French, Harriet Island, Hidden Falls-Crosby Farm, Lake Minnetonka Regional Park, Lebanon Hills,

Minneapolis Chain of Lakes, Noerenberg, Memorial Park, Rice Creek/Chain of Lakes, Springbrook Nature Center, Theodore Wirth, and Wood Lake Nature Center (see the Parks chapter).

Part of the **Minnesota River Valley Birding Trail** (651-739-9332; www.birdingtrail.org) lies in the southern Twin Cities, and many parks have bird-watching hikes. Check with **Three Rivers Park District** (763-559-9000; www.three riversparks.org), St. Paul Parks and Recreation (651-292-7010; www.stpaul.gov), and the **Minneapolis Park and Recreation Board** (612-230-6400, www.minneapolisparks.org) seasonally for more information.

Paintball

You have your choice of outdoor or indoor paintball arenas at **Adventure Zone** in Burnsville (952-890-7981; www.theadventurezone.com) at 13700 Nicollet Ave. South, and at **Splatball Inc.** (612-378-0385; www.splatball.org), at 2412

University Ave. SE in Minneapolis. The biggest outdoor paintball center is **Splat Tag** (651-488-7700 or 866-775-2882; www.splattag.com), at 835 County Rd. E, Hudson, Wisconsin. The park is open to groups of six or more (up to 24 participants per group), although walk-ons are sometimes okay, especially on weekends. See the Web site for more information and for detailed directions to Splat Tag's "battle courses."

Sailing and Sailboarding

Many lakes in the metro area are perfect for sailing and sailboarding alike, including Lake Harriet in Minneapolis, White Bear Lake in White Bear Lake, Keller Lake in St. Paul, Lake Minnetonka in Minnetonka, Medicine Lake in Plymouth, and Lake Nokomis in Minneapolis.

Parks in the metro area that allow sailboats and sailboards in their lakes are many (see the Parks chapter).

The **Minneapolis Park and Recreation Board** (612-230-6400) offers sailing classes and events throughout the summer, as does **Lake Calhoun Yacht Club and Sailing School** in Minneapolis (612-927-8552; www.lakecalhoun.org), at 3010 East Calhoun Pkwy.; and **Scuba Center** (612-925-4818; www.scubacenter.com), at 5015 Penn Ave. South in Minneapolis and 1571 Century Point in Eagan (651-681-8434).

Scuba Diving

Yes, there is scuba diving in Minnesota. Divers from around the world come to Minnesota to dry-suit dive in the frigid waters of Lake Superior, where hundreds of shipwrecks, including the famous Edmund Fitzgerald, can be found miles off the coast, and underwater life found only in this region can be studied up close. If you feel like exploring the bottom of a less cold and much less deep lake, pretty much any lake that has a swimming beach is fine for diving and snorkeling. Classes on scuba diving, scuba certification, and gear rental are provided by **Scuba Center** (612-925-4818; www.scubacenter.com), at 5015 Penn Ave. South, Minneapolis, and at 1571 Century Point, Eagan (651-681-8434). **FantaSea Scuba &**

Travel (952-890-3483; www.fantaseadivers.com), at 3429 East MN 13 in Burnsville, offers both classes and certification and arranges international scuba adventure packages.

Skydiving

The **Minnesota Skydivers Club** (612-597-5052; www.mnskydive.com) offers static line and tandem airplane jumps as well as free-fall jumps to those who have satisfactorily completed five static line jumps. Ground training is provided for beginning jumpers, with instruction given by jumpmasters and instructors who have been certified by the U.S. Parachute Association. **Skydive Twin Cities** (715-684-3416 or 800-SKYDIVE; www.skydivetwincities.com), based 30 minutes from the Twin Cities in Baldwin, Wisconsin, also offers ground training and tandem jumping for first-time parachuters. More experienced jumpers have additional options that progress in the skills used as you complete each training level.

Soccer

Cities Sports Connection (612-929-9009; www.cscsports.com) offers coed outdoor and indoor soccer leagues at various skill levels. CSC soccer leagues are offered outdoors in spring (May–July), summer (June–August), and fall (September–December). CSC also runs two indoor leagues, one in late fall (October–January) and the other in winter (January–March). CSC is open to all adults 18 or older; no membership or nonmember fees are charged to participate in CSC leagues.

Softball

Cities Sports Connection (612-929-9009; www.cscsports.com) organizes coed softball leagues at all skill levels. CSC softball leagues are offered in the spring (April–June) and summer (June–August). CSC is open to all adults 18 or older; no membership or nonmember fees are charged to participate in CSC leagues.

If you're looking to form your own softball team, the **Amateur Softball Association** (763-263-9993; www.asasoftball.com) can help.

Another option is to contact the **U.S. Slow-pitch Softball Association** (763-571-1305; www.mnusssa.com), which can help you put together a slow-pitch softball team. The association will send you the information you need or at least get you in touch with your local park and recreation department.

Running

Twin Cities Marathon Inc. (763-287-3888; www.mtcmarathon.org) is a nonprofit corporation that organizes and directs the annual Twin Cities Marathon, TC 10 Mile, and Saturday events as a community service for the Minneapolis–St. Paul area. The Twin Cities Marathon is often referred to as the most beautiful urban marathon in America and runs alongside the Mississippi River and through many metro area parks.

The **Minnesota Distance Running Association** (MDRA; 952-927-0983; www.runmdra.org) promotes running, stages many races and fun runs, and serves as a resource for runners in Minnesota. For a $25 membership fee, members of MDRA receive a subscription to the organization's magazine, *RunMinnesota,* the *Running Minnesota Annual* with details about running events throughout Minnesota, and the chance to participate (for free) in the many training runs the association sponsors year-round to help runners get in shape for distance runs.

Swimming

Summertime is beach weather, and all together there are more miles of swimming beaches in Minnesota than in California and Florida combined. There are more than 1,000 lakes throughout the seven counties in the Twin Cities metro area alone. In Minneapolis swimmers are welcome at Lake Calhoun, Lake Harriet, Cedar Lake, Lake Hiawatha, and Lake Nokomis. In St. Paul, swimmers can take to the water at Lake Phalen and Josephine Lake. White Bear Lake in White Bear has five public areas set aside for swimming, and in Minnetonka the 1,500-acre Lake Minnetonka is surrounded by swimming beaches and boat launches. Plymouth's Medicine Lake

has two public beaches with lifeguards and has an on-site outfitter that rents small boats and canoes. There are a number of parks in the metro area with swimming beaches (see the Parks chapter for more information).

If you want to take a quick dip in a pool, nearly every neighborhood park in the Twin Cities has a free wading pool for kids and adults to splash around in, while several parks have full-size pools for public use. In Minneapolis full-size public swimming pools can be found at **North Commons Water Park** (612-370-4945), at 1701 Golden Valley Rd. and **Webber Pool** (612-370-4915), at 4400 Dupont Ave. North. In St. Paul full-size public swimming pools can be found at **Como Pool** (651-489-2811), in Como Park at Como Avenue and Lexington Parkway; Highland **Aquatic Center** (651-695-3773), at 1840 Edgcumbe Rd.; and **Oxford Pool** (651-642-0650), at North Lexington Parkway and Iglehart Avenue.

> **i** One popular 5K race for runners (and walkers) of all levels is named after a beer. September's James Page Blubber Run has a halfway stop at a bar and ends at a party on Peavey Plaza in downtown Minneapolis. For more information, see www.blubberrun.net.

Volleyball

Cities Sports Connection (612-929-9009; www.cscsports.com) offers indoor and outdoor (sand and grass) coed volleyball leagues at all skill levels. CSC volleyball leagues are offered indoors in the fall (September–December), winter (January–March), and spring (March–May). CSC leagues move outdoors for early summer on sand (May–July) and on grass (May–July), and for late summer (July–September, sand). CSC is open to all adults 18 or older; no membership or nonmember fees are charged to participate in CSC leagues.

WINTER RECREATION

Provided you dress for conditions, there's no real weather-related reason to settle in for months of boring inactivity; winter, in a sense, is a state of mind.

Winter Car Safety

The American Red Cross and other organizations sometimes sell winter car safety kits that include a flashlight and batteries, a snack food item, flagging tape, a candle, matches, a pencil and notepad for messages, a guide for safe winter travel, and other roadside necessities. But you don't have to wait for these occasional special offers—you can compile your own emergency car kit. For tips on how to make one, contact Minnesota's Division of Homeland Security and Emergency Management (651-201-7400; www.hsem.state.mn.us) or the Minnesota Safety Council (651-291-9150; www.mnsafetycouncil.org).

Ballroom and Square Dancing

What better way to chase away the winter blues and meet new people than dancing? Several clubs in the Twin Cities area bring like-minded dance partners together, including the **Twin Cities Rebels Swing Dance Club** (952-941-0906; www.tcrebels.com), which has regular West Coast Swing classes and dances all over the Metro area, and the **Twin Town Twirlers Square Dancing Club** (651-488-7389), which holds weekly dances on Mondays and offers square dancing classes at various times of the year. To find out about a variety of dance classes and events, contact the Minnesota Chapter of the **U.S. Amateur Ballroom Dancers Association** (651-483-5467, www.usabda-mn.org).

Bowling

A great winter sport, bowling gets you out of the house and in someplace warm and friendly. Leagues and tournaments take place in bowling centers throughout the metro area. Stop in at your local lanes to inquire.

If you just want to bowl a couple of games with friends, there are dozens of bowling alleys to choose from. The **Brunswick Zone Eden Prairie** (952-941-0445; www.brunswickbowling.com), located at 12200 Singletree Lane in Eden Prairie, has 40 lanes and is open until midnight Sunday through Wednesday and 2 a.m. Thursday through Saturday. This is the original Twin Cities home of Cosmic Bowling, during which the lights fade to black, pins glow, fog machines blow, and laser lights keep time to dance music. There are also pool tables, video games, and dartboards, as well as the largest bar in Eden Prairie.

Memory Lanes (612-721-6211; www.memorylanesmpls.com), at 2520 26th Ave. South in Minneapolis, is where cosmic hipsters come to toss glow-in-the-dark bowling balls and drink reasonably priced fancy mixed drinks. Things get quite interesting on Punk Bowl Mondays and during Thursday-night Electrobowl (featuring electronica and other dance-club mix tunes), the latter fueled by College ID Night with cheap drinks for students in the hours up to and during the beginning of Electrobowl. Memory Lanes also has a full-service kitchen and 14 TVs in the bar—a hot spot on Sunday during football season thanks to its NFL package in high-definition format.

Park Tavern in St. Louis Park (952-929-6810; www.parktavern.net), located at 3401 Louisiana Ave., is another hot bowling spot. Every Friday and Saturday beginning at 10 p.m., the Park Tavern holds Cosmic Rock and Bowl (for ages 21 and over) with black lights, lots of music, and a flat fee for shoes and unlimited bowling. Be sure to show up early to reserve a lane on these nights, because the 20 in-house lanes are booked fast.

Bryant-Lake Bowl (612-825-3737; www.bryantlakebowl.com), 810 West Lake St. in Minneapolis, is a throwback to bowling alleys of the past. The 1950s-era lanes in this small bowling alley provide loads of atmosphere, and the Bryant-Lake Bowl does not have electronic scoring, so you get to practice scoring by hand. Bowling is cheap here, but the lanes are first-come, first-served, and no reservations are accepted. Expect to wait on busy nights, although the numerous microbrews on tap will make the wait enjoyable.

Boxing

Boxing is no longer a sport confined to men alone, and boxing rings have sprung up at health clubs all over the metro area, while those that have been long established have found new participants and audiences of both genders. In St. Paul, **Brunette's Boxing Gym** (651-779-6248), at 1135 Arcade St., is the oldest boxing gym in the metro. It hosts boxing competitions and offers personal training for men and women of all ages and skill levels, from beginner to professional. **Uppercut Boxing Gym** (612-822-1964; www.uppercutgym.com), at 1324 Quincy St. NE in Minneapolis, provides boxing training for all fitness levels, amateur to professional.

Broomball

Similar to hockey, except using brooms instead of sticks and an actual ball instead of a puck, broomball is a popular sport. The **Minneapolis Park and Recreation Board** (612-230-6400; www.minneapolisparks.org) organizes broomball teams for competitions and informal meets. **Cities Sports Connection** (612-929-9009; www.cscsports.com), offers coed and men's outdoor broomball leagues of all skill levels each winter (December–February).

Cross-Country Skiing

Nearly every park in the metro area has well-groomed ski trails, taking skiers through everything from heavily wooded tracked forest paths to gently sloping open spaces with incredible views of frozen waterfalls, lakes, and streams. On top of that, nearly every golf course in the metro area doubles as a cross-country ski park as soon

as there's sufficient snow to do so. In the Cities, St. Paul's **Como Park**, at 1431 North Lexington Pkwy., has a 5K trail that loops around the park. Also in St. Paul are **Fort Snelling State Park** (612-725-2389), which is located at 101 Snelling Lake Road and offers 12 miles of groomed trails for cross-country and skate-ski use; **Hidden Falls/Crosby Regional Park** (612-632-5111), at Crosby Farm Road and Shepard Road, which has 13.9K of trails for ski use; **Highland Nine Hole Golf Course** at 1797 Edgcumbe Rd., which has a 5K groomed track for experienced skiers and a 3K loop across the street for beginners; and **Phalen Golf Course** at 1615 Phalen Dr., which has 10K of groomed track for cross-country skiers. For more information on these and other St. Paul trails, call **St. Paul Parks and Recreation** at (651) 266-6400.

Metro area parks with groomed trails for cross-country skiers include Baker Park Preserve, Carver Park Preserve, Cleary Lake, Coon Rapids Dam, Cottage Grove Ravine, Elm Creek Park Reserve, French, Hyland-Bush-Anderson Lakes, Lake Minnewashta, Lebanon Hills, Murphy-Hanrehan Park Reserve, and Theodore Wirth, Wirth-Memorial Parkway. (See the Parks chapter for more park information.)

Cross-country ski gear can be rented or purchased in Minneapolis at **Midwest Mountaineering** at 309 Cedar Ave. South (612-339-3433). In St. Paul ski gear can be rented or purchased at either **Finn-Sisu** at 1841 University Ave. West (651-645-2443) or **Joe's Sporting Goods** at 33 East County Rd. B in Little Canada (651-209-7800).

Curling

Resembling a combination of ice hockey and shuffleboard, curling has gone from a popular sport confined mostly to Canada and the United Kingdom to an Olympic event and a well-loved, albeit still relatively obscure, winter sport. The **St. Paul Curling Club** (651-224-7408; www.stpaulcurlingclub.org), the largest member-owned curling club in the country, organizes curling matches and practices at its home at 476 Selby Ave. in St. Paul.

i Even most locals won't believe you when you tell them there's a bar in the St. Paul Curling Club—but there is. On nights when curling is taking place, you can walk up, order a pitcher of beer, and grab a table overlooking the ice. By the time you finish the pitcher, the sport may begin to make sense.

Dogsledding and Skijoring Trails

Dogsledding and skijoring—the latter in which a skier is pulled along by a horse or a vehicle—are permitted on designated trails in some metro area parks. With the exception of the multiuse trail at **Baker Park Reserve,** a special-use permit and a Park Patron permit are required for both activities; call the **Three Rivers Park District** reservations office at (763) 559-6700 for further information, permits, and maps.

Sections of snowmobile trails at Crow-Hassan Park Reserve and Elm Creek Park Reserve are open for skijoring and dogsledding on weekdays during the day and weekends and holidays from 5 a.m. to 10 a.m. **Crow-Hassan Park Reserve,** located west of Rogers on Sylvan Lake Road, has 5.5 miles of trail designated for dogsledding/skijoring use; **Elm Creek Park Reserve,** located northwest of Osseo on County Road 81, has 11 miles of trail designated for dogsledding/skijoring use; the North Hennepin Trail Corridor, connecting the Coon Rapids Dam Regional Park in Brooklyn Park to Elm Creek Park Reserve in Maple Grove, has 6 miles of trail designated for dogsledding/skijoring use. These trails are usually packed, so be prepared for lots of company.

Murphy-Hanrehan Park Reserve, located near Prior Lake on County Road 75, has 3 miles of trail designated for dogsledding and horseriding—no snowmobiles are allowed. The trail is open all week during daylight hours and is not usually heavily used.

Baker Park Reserve, located 20 miles west of downtown Minneapolis on County Road 19, has 4 miles of trails set aside for dogsledding, skijoring, mountain biking, and snowshoeing.

Downhill Skiing and Snowboarding

In the immediate Twin Cities metro area, there aren't a lot of options for downhill skiing or extreme snowboarding. But let's face it—we're on a glacial plain, and mountains don't really figure into our natural geography. For real downhill skiing, you have to make the three- to four-hour trek up to Duluth and the North Shore, where you'll find the **Giants Ridge Golf & Ski Resort** (800-688-7669; www.giantsridge.com), in the town of Biwabik off County Road 138; **Spirit Mountain** (218-628-2891 or 800-642-6377; www.spiritmt.com), at 9500 Spirit Mountain Place in Duluth; and **Lutsen Mountains** (218-663-7281; www.lutsen.com) found between Duluth and the Canadian border on Ski Road Hill near Lutsen. All three ski areas are also resorts, and discounts are offered seasonally on rooms and lift tickets for those who purchase a combination of both—advance reservations are highly recommended.

Closer to home—but not as tall or as steep as the North Shore slopes—are **Buck Hill** in Burnsville (952-435-7174; www.buckhill.com) located at 15400 Buck Hill Rd.; **Hyland Ski Area & Snowboard Area** in Bloomington (763-694-7800; www.hylandski.com), at 8800 Chalet Rd.; **Afton Alps** (651-436-5245 or 800-328-1328; www.aftonalps.com), located near Afton off County Road 20; **Welch Village Ski and Snowboard Area** (651-258-4567; www.welchvillage.com), located in Welch on MN 61 and County Road 7; and **Wild Mountain Ski and Snowboard** (651-465-6315 or 800-447-4958; www.wildmountain.com), located off MN 8 near Taylors Falls at 37200 Wild Mountain Rd.

Fencing

The **Twin Cities Fencing Club** (651-225-1990; www.twincitiesfencing.com) is one of the top fencing clubs in the country. Head coach Roberto Sobalvarro has coached U.S. National Teams at the World Championships, World Cup competitions, and the U.S. Olympic Festival. The club serves fencers of all ages and all levels of experience, from beginner to national champion. Kid, teen, and adult classes, as well as training and practice nights, will get you dodging, parrying, and thrusting in no time.

Health Clubs

The Twin Cities proper have many gyms and health clubs to choose from, many of which offer free child care and youth programs such as swimming lessons and martial arts. **Lifetime Fitness** (www.lifetimefitness.com) has dozens of locations across the Twin Cities. The facilities include Cybex, Nautilus, Gravitron, and ski machines as well as stair-climbers. Aerobics, dance, and karate classes are offered, as are massage, tanning beds, personal training, nutrition seminars, and free child care.

The **YMCA** (www.ymcatwincities.org) locations across the Twin Cities from Elk River to Hastings, including locations in both downtowns. In addition, there are YWCA locations in both cities, including in downtown Minneapolis (612-332-0501, www.ywca-minneapolis.org) at 1130 Nicollet Mall and in St. Paul (651-225-3741, www.ywcaofstpaul.org) at 375 Selby Ave. in the Cathedral Hill neighborhood. Another notable location is the **Midtown YWCA** (612-215-4333, www.ywca-minneapolis.org) at 2121 East Lake St. near the Hiawatha Light Rail Station. This beautiful facility is the largest YWCA in the country. Equipment, facilities, and classes vary by location.

Los Campeones Fitness & Body Building, 2721 Franklin Ave. East in Minneapolis (612-333-8181), features free weights and cable machines, treadmills and other cardio machines, a juice bar, and an on-site pro shop offering items including vitamin supplements. Special student and couple rates are available. The **Sweatshop Health Club** in St. Paul (651-646-8418; www.sweatshopfitness.com), located at 167 Snelling Ave. North, offers personal weight-training programs, kickboxing, spinning, and Pilates mat and reformer classes and has a child care facility on the premises.

Hockey

Kids in Minnesota start playing hockey about as soon as they can walk, and both boys and girls participate in the sport with equal fervor. Every winter, parks in the Twin Cities metro area are flooded to make ice-skating rinks for skaters and hockey players, and formal and informal hockey teams are formed among children and adults alike. During hockey season, large amounts of television time are blocked off on more than one station to bring live coverage of local high school and college hockey playoffs.

Traditionally St. Paul has been a much more dedicated hockey town than Minneapolis, and it shows. St. Paul has the Minnesota Wild's Xcel Energy Center arena and is home to groomed ice hockey rinks (some indoor, some outdoor), including **Conway Recreation Center Rink** (651-501-6343) at 2090 Conway Ave., **Edgcumbe Recreation Center Rink** (651-695-3711) at 320 South Griggs, **Griggs Recreation Center Rink** (651-298-5755) at 1188 Hubbard Avenue, **Langford Recreation Center Rink** (651-298-5765) at 30 Langford Park, and **Linwood Recreation Center Rink** (651-298-5660) at 860 St. Clair Ave. For more indoor and outdoor locations and information, contact *St. Paul Parks and Recreation* at (651-266-6400) or www.stpaul.gov/depts/parks.

But if you find yourself in Minneapolis and want to take to the ice, there are options. You can lace up your hockey skates at the **Palace Ice Garden** (612-370-4846) at 600 Kenwood Pkwy. and the **Northeast Ice Arena** (612-370-3920) at 1306 Central Ave. NE. For more information on these as well as outdoor rinks across the city, contact the **Minneapolis Park and Recreation Board** (612-230-6400, www.minneapolisparks.com).

There are dozens of suburban ice rinks as well.

Ice Fishing

Ice fishing entails setting up camp on top of a frozen lake, cutting a hole in the ice, and waiting for some sluggish fish to come along and snap up your bait. There are lots of fancy variations on this, including bringing portable houses, space heaters, and televisions out onto the ice with you, but this is basically the blueprint to every ice fishing trip. Pretty much every lake in the metropolitan area is a potential ice fishing bonanza, although some are more fruitful than others. Also remember the standard that ice be at least 6 inches thick to support a person and a foot thick to support a vehicle, and keep in mind ice thickness may vary on a given body of water. For more information, see the chapter on Hunting and Fishing.

Ice-Skating

Just about every park in the Twin Cities metro area, if not every park in Minnesota, has a picturesque area that gets flooded every winter and turned into a free neighborhood ice-skating rink. One great example is the **Wells Fargo Winter-Skate** (651-291-5608; www.capitalcitypartnership .com) on Landmark Plaza at St. Peter and Fifth Streets in downtown St. Paul from late November to late February, depending on conditions. **Rice Park**'s white lights twinkle nearby as you skate in the shadow of the massive old courthouse that is now Landmark Center. There is no fee to use the rink, skate rental is $2 (or free if you produce your Wells Fargo credit or check card), and there's a warming tent with hot chocolate and snacks.

Minneapolis skating rinks include **Lake Harriet** (612-230-6475) at 1300 42nd Street East; **Bryn Mawr Park** (612-370-4833) at 601 Morgan Ave. South; and **Longfellow Park** (612-370-4957) at 3435 36th Ave. South, (612-370-4957) **The Depot Ice Rink** (612-758-7873, www.thedepot minneapolis.com/rink.htm) in the refurbished 1899 Milwaukee Road Train Station is one of the most beautiful, with its floor-to-ceiling windows and turn-of-the-20th-century atmosphere. Skate rentals are available.

For more information on Minneapolis rinks, contact the **Minneapolis Park and Recreation Board** at (612) 230-6400 or www.minneapolis parks.com.

Rock Climbing

While there aren't any mountains in the Twin Cities, there are many bluffs in the region and several organizations that can put together mountaineering excursions for solo or group climbers. A few gyms and retail stores offer indoor climbing walls for varying skill levels.

St. Paul Rinks

In St. Paul you can find well-groomed skate rinks (some indoor, some outdoor) at:

Conway Recreation Center Rink
2090 Conway Ave.
(651) 501-6343

Eastview Recreation Center Rink
1675 East Fifth Street
(651) 772-7845

Edgcumbe Ice Skating Rink
320 South Griggs
(651) 690-4904

Griggs Recreation Center Rink
1188 Hubbard Ave.
(651) 298-5755

Hazel Park Recreation Center Rink
945 North Hazel Ave.
(651) 501-6350

Langford Recreation Center Rink
30 Langford Park
(651) 298-5765

Linwood Recreation Center Rink
860 St. Clair Ave.
(651) 298-5660

North Dale Recreation Center Rink
1410 North St. Albans
(651) 298-5812

Northwest Como Recreation Center Rink
1550 North Hamline
(651) 298-5813

There are many more options. Contact St. Paul Parks and Recreation for information at (651) 266–6400 or www.stpaul.gov/depts/parks/ specialservices.

REI (952-884-4315; www.rei.com), located at 750 West American Blvd. in Bloomington, has information on REI's annual trips to such destinations as the Summit Challenge in Nepal and the Kilimanjaro Climb. Staff can also direct you to local climbing spots. REI is a complete gear shop and can hook you up with anything you need to prep yourself for any level of climb. The Bloomington store has an indoor climbing wall available free to members (for a one-time fee of $20) and for $10 to nonmembers. (Note there are no climbing walls at REI's Roseville and Maple Grove stores.)

Midwest Mountaineering (612-339-3433, www.midwestmtn.com), located at 309 Cedar Ave. South in Minneapolis, is another great gear shop with clinics and information about local climbing spots for all levels of climbers. The store has erected an on-site climbing cave that's free and open to the public during store hours.

Other indoor climbing options include **Vertical Endeavors** (651-776-1430, www.vertical endeavors.com), at 855 Phalen Blvd. in St. Paul, has practice climbing options for all skill levels as well as on-site climbing instructors. The gym currently has more than 18,000 square feet of climbing space. It also holds clinics and organizes trips.

For outdoor climbing, you can head to **Interstate State Park** (651-465-5711) near Taylors Falls an hour northeast of the Twin Cities and climb 30–70-foot bluffs along the St. Croix River. There are also good climbing areas along the Mississippi River near Red Wing, an hour southeast of the Twin Cities, and fantastic wintertime ice climbing at Duluth and on the North Shore of Lake Superior, two to four hours north of the Cities. St. Paul offers ice climbing in some of the city's parks, particularly at Lilydale Regional Park along the Mississippi River. Ice climbing in St. Paul parks requires a permit; contact **St. Paul Parks and Recreation** (651-632-5111, www.stpaul .gov/depts/parks/userguide/iceclimbing.html) for more information.

Sledding/Tobogganing

There aren't really rules regarding or areas set aside for sledding or tobogganing—most Twin Cities metro parks have great sledding hills. Use your common sense and don't pick a hill that bottoms out at a busy street, and don't try to take your sled on a ski or snowboard slope. **Como Park** in particular has great areas built up especially for sledding/tobogganing—call (651) 632-5111 for more information.

Snowmobiling

An incredible sense of freedom comes with riding a snowmobile, and Minnesota has 18,000 miles of public and private snowmobile trails that cross wide-open frozen lakes and follow paths cut through thick Minnesota forests. If you follow a few common sense rules, this is a great way to see the outdoors in Minnesota. You can download a copy of the *Snowmobiler's Safety Laws, Rules & Regulations* from the **Department of Natural Resources** Web page at www.dnr.state.mn.us/snowmobiling, or call the DNR at (651) 296-6157 for a copy by mail. Maximum speed in Minnesota for snowmobiles is 50 mph. All resident snowmobiles must be registered with the DNR.

You are allowed to ride snowmobiles anywhere within the seven-county metro area on your own land (although you'd better be on good terms with your neighbors if you try it in the Cities), on land that has signs posted saying snowmobiles are allowed, and on land where you have written or spoken consent from the owner or lessee. Parks within the metro area that have trails specifically groomed for snowmobiles include Baker Park Preserve, Carver Park Preserve, Cleary Lake, Crow-Hassan, Elm Creek Park Reserve, Lake Rebecca Park Reserve, Lake Theodore, Lebanon Hills, Minnetonka Regional Park, and Murphy-Hanrehan Park Reserve (see the Parks and Recreation chapter for complete park listings). For additional information on trails and about snowmobiling events, call the **Minnesota United Snowmobilers Association** at (763) 577-0185 or visit www.mnsnowmobiler.org.

ℹ️ A Snowmobile State Trail Sticker is required for all snowmobiles being operated on state trails. For more information, contact the Minnesota Department of Natural Resources at (800) MINNDNR or www.dnr.state.mn.us/licenses/snowmobile/trailpermit.html.

Snowshoeing

Snowshoeing is an ideal means of transportation after a fresh snowfall. The wide, flat paddles make it possible to walk safely over the top of snowdrifts. Once you've mastered walking in snowshoes, you will practically glide over the soft snow.

The following parks have areas and trails set aside for snowshoers: Baker Park Preserve, Carver Park Preserve, Coon Rapids Dam, Crow-Hassan, Elm Creek Park Reserve, French, and Murphy-Hanrehan. Individual parks hold events like full-moon and naturalist-led hikes. Call ahead or check out the activities listed with **Three Rivers Park District** (763-694-7750; www.threeriversparkdistrict.org), **St. Paul Parks and Recreation** (651-266-6400; www.stpaul.gov), or **Minneapolis Park and Recreation Board** (612-230-6400; www.minneapolisparks.com).

Snow Tubing

Snow tubing sounds like an amateur version of tobogganing, but for sheer thrill—if that's what you're looking for—bouncing down an icy hill on your belly at ridiculous speed is right up there with skydiving, ski jumping, and tightrope walking. Some of the places that have designed and built special hills for snow tubing are **Eko Backen** (651-433-2422; www.ekobacken.com), at 22570

Manning Trail in Scandia; **Green Acres** (651-770-6060; www.greenacresrec.com), at 8989 55th St. North in Lake Elmo; **Trapp Farm Park** (651-675-5511; www.cityofeagan.com), at 841 Wilderness Run Rd. in Eagan; **Valleywood Golf Course and Park** (952-953-2323), at 4851 125th St. West in Apple Valley; and **Theodore Wirth Park** (612-230-6400), at 1339 Theodore Wirth Pkwy. in Minneapolis. Inner tubes can be rented at all of the aforementioned facilities for a nominal fee.

ℹ️ If venturing onto frozen lakes, watch for thin-ice warning signs, brightly colored buoys, or anything else that seems out of place. Minnesotans are intensely aware of the dangers of thin ice, and if nobody else is playing on a frozen public lake, it's a good idea to steer clear of it yourself.

Yoga

Depending on how you approach it and what you want to get out of it, yoga is a religion, an exercise routine, or a great way to forget about frigid outdoor temperatures. There are many different types—Hatha, Vinyasa, Ashtanga, and more. Find your style in Uptown Minneapolis at **One Yoga Studio** (612-872-6347; www.one-yoga.com), 2100 B Lyndale Ave. South; in northeast Minneapolis at **YogaLab** (612-868-6864; www.yogalabmpls.com), 681 17th Ave. NE; in St. Paul at **Yoga Center** (651-644-7141; www.stpaulyogacenter.com) 1162 Selby Ave.; or at Eagan's **Yoga Soul Center** (651-452-5789; www.yogasoul-center.com), located at 1121 Town Centre Dr.

HUNTING AND FISHING

In 1973, Minnesota Governor Wendell Anderson appeared on the cover of *Time* magazine for the magazine's feature on "The Good Life in Minnesota." The pose chosen to epitomize that "good life"? Standing on a dock, grinning from ear to ear with a fish raised triumphantly before him.

Hunting and fishing are at the heart of Minnesota's identity, and indeed there are many, many Minnesotans who spend serious time huddled in deer stands or perched in fishing boats. There are hundreds of hunting and fishing resorts all over the state, many of which can sell you your hunting or fishing licenses right on the premises, as well as bait, ammunition, and rod and boat rentals. **Hospitality Minnesota** (651-778-2400; www.hospitalitymn.com) and the **Minnesota Office of Tourism** (888-TOURISM; www.exploreminnesota .com) issue an annual booklet that lists resorts in detail and will mail you a free copy if you call or contact them through either Web site.

Hunters and anglers are encouraged to be ethical, safe, and responsible. Minnesota's Department of Natural Resources (DNR) has been working since 1931 to make sure that there will always be game and fish for future generations, and strict fines and imprisonment are some of the penalties imposed on poachers and careless hunters who disregard the laws. The DNR offers many valuable resources to hunters and anglers, including information booklets on the best places to go hunting and fishing, a regularly updated Web site (www.dnr.state.mn.us) with specific information about breeding and stocking programs for game animals and fish, the convenience of applying for hunting and fishing licenses over the telephone or on the DNR's Web site, regulations, and information about hunting seasons for specific game and for specific types of hunting.

HUNTING

Hunting is a heavily regulated sport in Minnesota, requiring specific licensing dependent on game targeted, whether you're hunting with firearms or bow and arrow, the area you plan to hunt in, and the age of the hunter. If you purchase a small-game license but do not specify that you plan to hunt migratory birds (waterfowl, woodcock, snipe, rails, etc.), you are not allowed to hunt those birds; you must reapply for the same license and specify that you do plan to hunt migratory birds. Deer and other big game licenses are awarded on a lottery basis depending on how many animals the Minnesota DNR considers expendable.

Trespassing laws are rigidly enforced, and if you're caught hunting on private property or on land that is not zoned for hunting, you'll be fined. (Fines vary by county.) Exceptions to the trespassing laws include entering private land on foot and without a weapon to retrieve a wounded animal that was lawfully shot or to retrieve a hunting dog. If a landowner does not allow you onto his or her land to retrieve a wounded animal, you must leave the private property immediately without the game animal.

Hunting dogs are not allowed to chase down, wound, or kill big-game animals, and at times may legally be killed (by anyone!) if they are seen to do so.

For current licensing rates for game hunting, call the **Minnesota DNR** at (651) 296-6157 or (888) 646-6367, or check out the Web site at www.dnr.state.mn.us. Most licenses, both hunting and fishing, can be picked up at almost any bait shop or convenience store near the popular hunting areas, but the DNR can immediately issue small-game licenses electronically if you apply through the DNR's Web site. Hunters are encouraged to apply for all licenses early, as the number of licenses issued is dependent on game availability.

Animal poaching is considered a serious crime in Minnesota. **Turn In Poachers** (TIP) Inc. is a nonprofit organization founded by hunters and concerned citizens to stop poaching in Minnesota. TIP offers cash awards for information leading to a poacher's arrest; all tipsters remain anonymous. For more information call the toll-free **TIP hotline** at (800) 652-9093.

The following listings are only general rules that apply to hunting and trapping game in Minnesota. Most parks and wildlife preserves have specific rules and restrictions regarding hunting and trapping, and it's important to check with both the DNR and with the specific park/preserve in question before going out.

Big Game

When hunting big game (deer, moose, bear, etc., as dictated by law) in Minnesota, the minimum caliber of rifle, shotgun, muzzleloader, or hand-gun that can be used is at least .23 caliber, and only single-projectile ammunition can be used. It's illegal to harvest big game with a bow and arrow while in possession of a firearm, with the exception of hunting bear, where possession of a firearm while in possession of archery equipment is allowed. Bows must be appropriate for big-game hunting, and crossbows are not allowed for either big- or small-game hunting, except by special permit given only to disabled hunters. Big game may be hunted only from one-half hour before sunrise to one-half hour after sunset.

Bear

Bear hunting is legal in much of northern and north-central Minnesota. Residents and nonresi-dents can obtain bear hunting licenses, which are usually made available by mid-March, from the DNR. Thousands of bear hunting permits are issued annually, with numbers adjusting annually depending on the bear population.

Deer

Open season for deer hunting generally begins in early November and lasts through early December. Archery season for deer traditionally begins in mid-September. Muzzleloader season typically begins in late November. Minnesota also offers an All-Season deer hunting license that allows a hunter to hunt in the archery, firearm, and muzzleloader seasons. Call the DNR for specific dates, as they vary from year to year. Any deer harvested by a hunter must be tagged according to DNR specifications. Brochures on proper tagging procedures are available at any of the 1,800 licensing stations across Minnesota or from the **DNR Information and License Center** (www.dnr.state.mn.us, 888-665-4236).

A limited number of Special Area Permits are issued each year to hunters in places where the number of hunters must be limited to control the harvest or for public safety. Permits are awarded by a lottery system dependent on a head count and estimation of expendable deer available. Hunters who receive Special Area Permits may also hunt deer outside that Special Area if they apply to do so and have it specifically punched on their hunting license. Laws can change significantly from year to year. For the most current deer hunting regulations, contact the **Minnesota DNR** at (888) 646-6367 or look online at www.dnr.state.mn.us.

Elk

Minnesota has a tiny population of elk primarily near the town of Grygla in the northwestern part of the state. During years when elk hunting is permitted, the season is open only to residents of Minnesota, and hunters must apply in parties of two. Elk hunting permits are not issued every year; contact the DNR to find out more about whether there will be a hunt and for more information about applying for permits. Permits are issued by random drawing, and the hunt is a once-in-a-lifetime event.

Moose

Minnesota's annual moose hunt is open only to Minnesota residents and each hunter is allowed to take down only one moose in his or her lifetime. Moose licenses are awarded annually on a lottery basis determined by actual animal populations. Some years no moose permits are issued. Generally the moose hunting season runs from late September to mid-October. Contact the DNR for more specifics.

Small Game, Waterfowl, and Migratory Birds

It's no accident that Minnesota has an abundance of wildlife in its parklands, wildlife preserves, and even in the Twin Cities. Careful monitoring of habitats and hunter/game interaction by Minnesota conservation officers has been an important facet of state government for more than a century, with the goal of creating safe hunting opportunities for residents and visitors while preserving as much of the native Minnesota wildlife as possible. Limits on migratory birds and many species of small game are strictly enforced.

Beaver, Mink, Muskrat, and Otter

It is unlawful to trap any furbearing animals within any state-owned game refuge without first obtaining a permit from the appropriate wildlife manager. Most of the state parks and state wildlife refuges allow trapping of furbearing small game as long as you get prior permission and have a small-game hunting license.

Foxes, Raccoons, Squirrels, Rabbits

A small-game hunting license is required, unless you are hunting on your own land.

Migratory Waterfowl

A State Migratory Waterfowl Stamp (State Duck Stamp), purchased from the DNR for a nominal fee, is required for hunting geese, ducks, and mergansers. All hunters—resident and nonresident—between the ages of 18 and 65 are required to have a valid State Duck Stamp in their possession while hunting migratory waterfowl, with the exception of those taking down waterfowl on their own property or who are in the U.S. Armed Forces and are stationed outside Minnesota with official military leave papers on their person.

Waterfowl hunting seasons and bag limits are set in late summer, and season dates are announced in early September. Contact the DNR for more information.

A special permit is also required for hunting Canada geese in season. During early September and late December, the entire state is open to hunting geese. Daily bag limits range from two to five geese per hunter, depending on the DNR-specified hunting zone, and shooting hours last from one-half hour before sunrise to sunset every day. Possession limits are double the daily bag limits. Migratory waterfowl must be transported in an undressed condition (with head and wings attached) at all times until delivery to either the hunter's home or to a commercial processing facility.

It is unlawful to take geese, ducks, mergansers, coots, or moorhens with lead shot or while having any lead shot in your possession. Only nontoxic shot approved by the U.S. Fish and Wildlife Service may be used. These nontoxic shot restrictions are responsible for preventing lead poisoning of more than 400,000 wild ducks nationwide each year.

i Parts of Beltrami, Lake of the Woods, Koochiching, Roseau, and St. Louis Counties are Ojibwe territories and are closed to nonband hunters and anglers except by special permission from the tribal council. Consult the DNR regarding specific contact information and how to acquire permission.

Wild Turkey

Spring and fall (check with the DNR for specific dates) are open for hunting wild turkey in Minnesota. Generally application deadlines for Wild Turkey Stamps are five or six months before the season begins. Although a small-game license is not necessary for taking wild turkey, you must purchase a Wild Turkey Stamp from the DNR to legally hunt the birds. Bag limit is one bird of either sex in the fall season per hunter and one male bird per hunter in spring.

Only fine shot size number 4 and smaller may be used to hunt turkey, and nothing smaller than a 20 gauge shotgun can be carried on turkey hunts. Bows must have a pull of no less than 40 pounds, and arrows must be sharp, have at least two metal cutting edges, and be at least 7/8 inch in diameter. Poison- or explosive-tipped arrows may not be used to hunt any game animal or bird in Minnesota. Hunting dogs and electronic tracking devices are not allowed on turkey hunts. Every hunter who takes a wild turkey must personally present the bird for registration at one of the 1,800 registration stations throughout Minnesota; the feathers, head, and feet must remain on the bird until it is officially registered.

Protected Animals

There is no open season for hunting bobwhite quail, prairie chickens, cranes, swans, hawks, owls, eagles, herons, bitterns, cormorants, loons, grebes, or any other species of birds except specified game or unprotected birds. Crows may be taken without a license in season (September 1 through February 28) or at any time when they are doing or are about to do damage. There is also no open season for hunting caribou, pronghorn, gray wolf, wolverine, cougar, or spotted skunk ("civet cat").

Unprotected Species

Minnesota residents are not required to have a license to hunt unprotected species. Weasels, coyotes, gophers, porcupines, striped skunks, and all other mammals for which there are no closed seasons or are not under protected status may be hunted year-round. They may be taken in any manner, except with the aid of artificial lights or by using a motor vehicle to chase, run over, or kill the animal. Poisons may not be used except in accordance with restrictions stated by the Minnesota Department of Agriculture.

House sparrows, starlings, common pigeons, chukar partridge, quail other than bobwhite quail, mute swans, and monk parakeets are all unprotected and may be hunted year-round.

No person may take a wild animal with a firearm or by archery from a motorized vehicle except a disabled person with an appropriate permit on a stationary vehicle. Also, it's against the law to transport an uncased firearm or shoot from any motorized vehicle in Minnesota.

FISHING

In the Land of 10,000 Lakes, it's no surprise that fishing is one of the most popular summer recreational activities. To meet the demand of thousands of dedicated anglers, the Minnesota DNR runs fisheries all over the state that are in charge of keeping some of the most popular lakes and fishing holes well stocked with walleye, pike, muskellunge, trout, bass, catfish, crappie, bluegill, and, in Lake Superior, salmon. Fishing licenses are available at any of the 1,800 licensing agents located at convenience stores, bait shops, and sports outfitters across the state. The DNR also issues fishing licenses electronically over the telephone (call 888-MNLicense for more information) and through its Web site at www.dnr.state.mn.us.

Regulations for fishing areas change per year according to species populations, so it's a good idea to call the DNR to request a current fishing guide or to ask about a specific fishing spot before heading out. The DNR's Web site regularly posts updated fishing information and regulation changes, if any.

Kids under age 16 do not need a license to fish in Minnesota when accompanied by an adult with a fishing license. Once you turn 16, you need a license—until you turn 90, after which you no longer require one.

Common Catches in the Twin Cities Area
Northern Pike
Although walleye is the most popular fish in Minnesota, the most widely spread game fish in the state is the northern pike. With its abundance of marshes and shallow streams, Minnesota has as

much as or more northern pike habitat than any other state.

Pike are a fun sport fish for all levels of angler, as they are fearless, toothy creatures and will snap at just about any bait you use. This makes catch-and-release tactics especially practical, as northern pike can be lured with harmless artificials as easily as live bait and tend to release their grip on artificials a lot easier than they do tasty organic bait.

Northern pike season generally runs mid-May through mid-February of the following year. Contact the DNR for specific season dates. A possession limit of three is in effect, and only one pike longer than 30 inches can be taken each day.

Northern pike are best caught in cool waters, so winter, early spring, and late fall are the best times to pursue these fish.

Bass

Bass are some of the scrappiest, most wildly gymnastic fish in Minnesota's waters and can fight an angler after being hooked for several hours before either wearing out or breaking free. Because of their aggressive reaction to being hooked, catch-and-release fishing is often not viable; these fish literally throw themselves into the air and against boats and rocks trying to escape, sometimes ripping hooks completely out of their bodies while doing so. Both smallmouth and largemouth bass are very strong for their size, and anglers should expect a good fight no matter what size the catch.

Largemouth and smallmouth bass season generally runs mid-May through mid-February of the following year; the dates change year to year and depend on what part of the state you intend to fish and which fish you are after. Contact the DNR for specific season dates. A six-fish possession limit of combined smallmouth and largemouth bass is in effect.

In the Metro, largemouth bass can be found in most Twin Cities–area lakes. Smallmouth bass are primarily found in the Mississippi River and its tributaries, and in some lakes in the outlying suburbs.

Catfish and Bullheads

Catfish and their close cousin, the bullhead, are incredibly hardy fish that can live on just about anything. Both fish, especially bullheads, are often stocked in urban ponds and lakes that have low oxygen levels due to high concentrations of algae or detritus, where they can be fished for fun by kids and those with limited mobility. Minnesota has two native catfish species, channel and flathead, and three species of bullheads—black, brown, and yellow. Found throughout the state, the fish prefer fertile waters but respond well to stocking programs that put them in waters other than where their populations would naturally occur. During winter catfish and bullheads seek deep waters where boulders or logs provide refuge from currents, and they sink into a torpor so deep that silt often collects on their bodies.

Catfish are plentiful throughout the Metro and are not usually stocked in lakes or streams unless they're put there to control other fish populations; some are also stocked in inner-city ponds to give kids and those with limited mobility a chance to enjoy the sport of fishing.

Currently the season for both bullhead and catfish is year-round. The DNR sets possession limits of 100 bullhead and 5 catfish. Contact the DNR for more information.

> **i** Minnesota actually has 11,842 lakes of 10 or more acres and thousands of smaller bodies of water to angle in, adding up to significantly more than the 10,000 the state's motto proclaims.

Crayfish

Licensed anglers and children under age 16 may take home up to 25 pounds of crayfish for personal use during crayfish season, as determined by the DNR. Crayfish cannot be sold as bait or for aquarium use, but you can use them for bait in the same body of water in which you caught the crayfish. Some areas—including the St. Croix National Scenic Riverway and Voyageurs National Park—do not allow fishing with live crayfish, even if caught there.

Muskie and Tiger Muskie

The muskellunge is one of the largest and most elusive fish in Minnesota and is also one of the most prized trophy fish sought by sport anglers.

Closely related to the northern pike, muskies can grow to more than 40 inches long and weigh 30 pounds or more. Light-colored with dark bars running up and down their bodies, muskies can be silver, green, or brown, with large, strong, tooth-lined jaws for grasping prey.

As with northern pike, stocking lakes and waterways with muskies is unnecessary. They prefer larger fish as prey, so introducing them to a fishing lake only guarantees the eventual annihilation of the already-existing bass and trout populations. Muskies are also very particular about their environment, requiring well-oxygenated, cool water (60 degrees and cooler) that's clear enough for these sight-feeding fish.

Because muskies are perceived as trophy fish only, and because large muskies are scarce and usually very old, Minnesota imposes a possession limit of one muskie per licensed angler, with a minimum length of 40 inches on most lakes, but 48 inches on some, including some lakes in the metropolitan area. See the DNR fishing regulations online for the latest updates on size limits. The muskie season generally runs early June through mid-February of the following year. Contact the DNR for specific season dates.

Tiger muskie, a sterile hybrid of the northern pike and the muskellunge, has characteristics of both parents. Tiger muskies have distinct bars that run along their light-colored bodies similar to the bars on a full muskie, fins and tail lobes rounded like a northern pike's, and cheekscale patterns that fall somewhere between those of both fish. The hybrid grows slightly faster than either pure-strain parent and can exceed 30 pounds in less than 10 years. Because of their quick maturation rate and because they are sterile, tiger muskie are often stocked in heavily fished lakes and streams throughout Minnesota, including some Metro area lakes.

i For information on which fish species are in Metro-area lakes, visit the DNR's Fish in the Neighborhood program on the Web at www.dnr.state.mn.us/fishing/fin/7_county.html.

Panfish

Panfish are not actually any particular species of fish but a blanket term referring to any number of small food fishes, especially those caught with hook and line and generally not available on the market. Minnesota has quite a few good-tasting panfish, and it's common practice to take home a few of them to eat to make up for all the undersize trophy fish you caught and had to let go.

Crappies and bluegills—two of the most well-known and populous panfish in the Twin Cities—are probably caught for eating more often than any other fish in Minnesota. Crappies are easy to catch and produce sweet-tasting fillets, and they travel in schools, which make them even easier to find and catch. Bluegills are Minnesota's biggest and most popular panfish, found in about 65 percent of Minnesota's lakes and slow streams, including the backwaters of the Mississippi and most lakes in the Metro. Though they occasionally exceed a pound, an 8-inch bluegill is considered a big fish.

Black and white crappies are among Minnesota's most popular panfish. Black crappies are much more widely distributed than white crappies and can be found in most lakes in the Twin Cities area. The two fish are very similar in appearance—in fact, the only real difference in appearance is that the black crappies are a slightly darker gray color than white crappies. Both fish rarely grow to weigh more than two pounds, and both species travel in large schools that are easy to spot.

Rock bass are stout and heavy compared with sunfish and crappies, measuring 10 inches on average and weighing around a pound. With red eyes and brassy-colored, black-spotted flanks, a rock bass is easy to identify when caught. Rock bass live in many streams and lakes in the Metro, generally preferring well-oxygenated, hard-water walleye lakes with boulder and sand bottoms.

The season for most of Minnesota's panfish runs year-round, with varying bag limits. Contact the DNR for more details.

Walleye, Sauger, and Perch

Walleye is the most sought-after fish in Minnesota, and anglers and restaurant patrons alike go crazy over the thick-filleted perch. Each year anglers in Minnesota catch and keep almost four million pounds of walleye, keeping the DNR's hands full stocking Minnesota lakes and rivers with the elusive fish.

The average walleye weighs one to two pounds, although some specimens caught have weighed in at as much as 10 pounds. The fish is torpedo shaped, with opaque, pearly eyes (for which the fish is named), and its color ranges from dark olive-brown to yellowish gold. Unlike its near cousin, the sauger, the walleye lacks spots on its dorsal fin, except for a dark patch on the rear base of the fin, which the sauger does not have. Also, the lower tip of the walleye's tail is white, while the lower lobe of the sauger's tail is all dark.

Both the walleye and the sauger are native fish, although walleye is much more commonly found in Minnesota's waterways than the sauger. Because of its popularity as a game and food fish, the walleye has been introduced to waterways all over the state and now occupies more than 1,600 lakes and 100 warmwater streams throughout the Midwest, including most of the lakes in the Metro. The walleye's low-level vision and sensitivity to light keep it hidden in the deep parts of lakes until dawn and dusk, at which point walleyes come to the shallows to feed. Their diet consists almost solely of other fish, and their biggest prey is yellow perch, which can't see well in the dark and are easily caught by the night-feeding walleye. Because of their sensitivity to light, walleyes are best caught at dawn or dusk, or when the skies are overcast.

Sauger are similar to walleye in appearance and habits, although their distribution throughout Minnesota is more limited. In the Metro, you are unlikely to catch one in most of the area's lakes, but there is a sauger presence in the Minnesota River, particularly around Fort Snelling State Park. Saugers seldom exceed three pounds and are generally much slimmer than walleye.

Yellow perch, cousin to both walleye and sauger as well as a shared common prey, are also found throughout the lakes and streams of the Twin Cities. They're often infected with parasites, and even the healthy ones are usually too small to reasonably consider eating. Walleye and yellow perch populations often coincide with each other, and lakes where the yellow population is strong are also home to big, healthy walleye—who may not be hungry enough to be interested in bait.

The season for walleye and sauger generally runs mid-May through mid-February of the following year, with a limit of six fish. The opening of walleye season is an annual event in Minnesota, opened with much fanfare by the governor casting a line in a chosen outstate lake with cameras clicking and TV cameras rolling. Perch season is year-round, with a limit of 10 fish per day. Contact the DNR for more details.

i Don't know what you've caught? The DNR can send you free information describing in detail how to tell which fish is which, describing species' markings to the minutest detail to avoid confusion. Similar information is available on their Web site, www.dnr.state.mn.us.

Harmful Aquatic Species

Several plant and animal species introduced to Minnesota waters over the past century have caused severe damage to native species populations. Among these are zebra mussels, Eurasian watermilfoil, ruffe, and round goby.

Eurasian watermilfoil is a water plant similar in appearance to duckweed that reproduces quickly in shallow water and can interfere with water recreation as well as harm oxygen levels in lakes and ponds. Even the tiniest of fragments clinging to boats and trailers can spread the prolific plant from one body of water to another. Zebra mussels, originally from Asia, can quickly displace native mussels, disrupt lake ecosystems, and clog industrial equipment. Their microscopic larvae can accidentally be transported in bait buckets or by moving a boat from one confined body of water to another. The best way to prevent the spread of Eurasian watermilfoil and Zebra mussels is to make sure you drain or pump all water from your boat before moving it from one body of water to another, and dump bait buckets on land and dry them thoroughly before putting them back in water. If you leave your boat in the water for more than a day in areas with zebra mussels (including the St. Croix River in the eastern Metro), you must wash your boat with a high-pressure hose and hot water and remove any attached mussels.

Ruffe is a small, perchlike fish from Europe that has taken over parts of Duluth harbor, displacing many native fish. Also from Europe is the bottom-dwelling round goby, which has displaced many fish in Minnesota lakes and is a serious threat to the fisheries in the Great Lakes, which it has already entered. The spread of both fish can be attributed to being transported from one body of water to another in bait buckets and livewells.

Ice Fishing

Ice fishing is a longtime tradition in Minnesota. The basic principle of ice fishing is to walk out on a deep lake with enough ice cover to safely support your weight (ice should be a minimum of 6 inches thick for walking, a foot or more for vehicles), cut a hole in the ice with an ice auger, and sink a hook through it with hopes of luring the few fish that aren't in a state of torpor to take your bait. Over the years this simple idea has expanded to include portable ice fishing houses for anglers to sit in comfort while waiting for fish to bite, equipped with televisions, suspended heating elements, radios, furniture, and the requisite cooler stuffed with beer.

Your best bet in ice fishing is to stake out lakes and rivers known for having good muskie populations, as these fish actually get more energetic as the weather grows cooler.

Some Metro-area parks with lakes deep enough (and enough lively coldwater fish) for ice fishing include Baker Park Preserve, Bald Eagle–

Otter Lakes, Bryant Lake, Carver Park Preserve, Como, Coon Rapids Dam, Fish Lake, French, Hidden Falls–Crosby Farm, Lake Byllesby, Lake George, Lake Minnewashta, Lake Rebecca Park Reserve, Lebanon Hills, Long Lake Regional Park, Martin-Island-Linwood Lakes, Minneapolis Chain of Lakes, Nokomis Hiawatha, Phalen, Rice Creek/Chain of Lakes, Snail Lake, and Theodore Wirth (see the Parks chapter for individual park listings).

Metro Fishing

Both Minneapolis and St. Paul have a surprising number of good fishing lakes within city limits, as do their nearby suburbs. More than 100 lakes and rivers in the Metro area are regularly stocked and monitored by the Minnesota DNR, with the purpose of providing safe, fun fishing lakes for urbanites, children, and those with limited mobility.

Some of the best fishing lakes in Minneapolis are Lake Calhoun, Lake of the Isles, Cedar Lake, Lake Harriet, and Lake Nokomis. Lake Calhoun, located about 3 blocks west of Lake Street and Hennepin Avenue South, is a deep (82 feet deep in spots) fishing and boating lake with largemouth bass, northern pike, crappie, sunfish, tiger muskie, walleye, perch, catfish, and carp swimming in its waters. Rental canoes are available at the concession stand, which also sells fast food but no bait. Calhoun has a couple of great fishing piers and three swimming beaches.

Connected to Lake Calhoun by a canoe-navigable channel is Lake of the Isles, located by land just south of Franklin Avenue and 1 mile west of Hennepin Avenue. Many of the same types of fish as in Lake Calhoun are in these waters, with a huge population of sunfish and crappies, much to the delight of the many species of waterfowl that also frequent the lakes.

Cedar Lake, located just south of I-394 and east of MN 100 and connected to Lake of the Isles by a winding channel, is stocked with largemouth bass, northern pike, crappie, sunfish, tiger muskies, perch, carp, and catfish and is a great shore fishing spot due to the deep water right next to shore. Anyone willing to bushwhack along the brushy banks can usually find some good-size largemouth bass hanging out along the lake's north shore.

Lake Harriet, another great Minneapolis fishing and boating lake with waters as deep as 87 feet in places, is located 1 mile west of Lyndale Avenue just north of 50th Street and just south of Lake Calhoun. Shore fishing at Lake Harriet is surprisingly good, considering that most of the really deep water is near the middle of the lake. Muskies, bass, sunfish, perch, catfish, and walleye can be caught here. The lake has a fishing pier and a boat rental facility nearby as well as a swimming beach and playground.

Lake Nokomis, located south of Minnehaha Parkway between Cedar and Hiawatha Avenues, is one of the best crappie lakes in the Twin Cities. Because it gets more sun and warms up quickly, the north shore fishing pier is the best spot to stake out in the spring. Also found in Lake Nokomis are northern pike, sunfish, tiger muskie, carp, bullhead, perch, and walleye.

St. Paul has a couple of excellent fishing spots for more serious anglers—meaning no picnic area, no playground, and little or no paved paths leading down to the water. Hidden Falls Regional Park, located just south of Ford Pkwy., is an excellent summer fishing spot for walleye, catfish, crappie, sunfish, white bass, smallmouth and largemouth bass, northern pike, and carp. If the water level is high, anglers can fish from the grassy picnic area, but if it's low you must descend a steep bank to reach the water.

Pike Island and Snelling Lake, both located in St. Paul's Fort Snelling State Park, are two rustic yet excellent fishing holes. Pike Island is good for early-season walleye fishing, as the fish pass here while moving upstream to spawn below Ford Dam. The best fishing is where the channel north of Pike Island meets the Mississippi River, where you can catch carp, catfish, smallmouth bass, walleye, sauger, white bass, and crappie. Snelling Lake has some nice paved paths leading to the shoreline, although to get to the best fishing areas, you have to stand in the marsh. There's also a good fishing pier here, from which you can catch largemouth bass, crappie, sunfish, northern pike, carp, and bullhead.

Other metro area parks that have areas set aside for fishing include Anoka County Riverfront, Baker Park Preserve, Bald Eagle–Otter Lakes, Baylor, Bryant Lake, Carver Park Preserve, Central Mississippi Riverfront, Cleary Lake, Como, Coon Rapids Dam, Fish Lake, French, Lake Byllesby, Lake Elmo Park Reserve, Lake George, Lake Minnetonka Regional Park, Lake Minnewashta, Lake Rebecca Park Reserve, Lebanon Hills, Lilydale–Harriet Island, Long Lake Regional Park, Rice Creek/Chain of Lakes, Rice Creek–West Regional Trail, Rum River Central, Snail Lake, and Theodore Wirth.

Becoming an Outdoors-Woman in Minnesota (888-646-6367), based in the DNR at 500 Lafayette Rd. in St. Paul, and **Women Anglers of Minnesota** (www.womenanglersmn.com) offer angling, ice fishing, and shore fishing classes for women interested in either taking up the sport or finding other women to fish with.

SPECTATOR SPORTS

People in the Twin Cities love sports. It is, however, a love tempered by regional priorities and perspectives on life. There are sports fanatics in the cities, men and women whose hearts bleed the purple of the Minnesota Vikings football team or have not missed a Twins game in decades, but most Twin Citians practice a little more restraint. They love the local teams but also value a summer trip "up north" to the cabin at the lake or a night at the other entertainment options the Cities offer.

AUTO RACING

ELKO SPEEDWAY
26350 France Ave., Elko New Market
(952) 461-7223
www.elkospeedway.com
For nearly 25 years, Elko Speedway has been affiliated with NASCAR. Elko Speedway is one of only 60 short racetracks in the nation sanctioned by NASCAR, and it is a member of the Whelan All-American Series and the Weekly Racing Series Presented by Dodge. The 3/8-mile track has an asphalt and granite aggregate surface and high banking. Elko Speedway usually has races from April through October, with races beginning in the evening on Friday and Saturday (most races are on Saturday).

RACEWAY PARK
1 Checkered Flag Blvd., Shakopee
(952) 445-2257
www.goracewaypark.com
Raceway Park also offers NASCAR racing in the Whelan All-American Series. This track has had racing for more than 50 years. The most talented local drivers race at Raceway Park. There are also racing events at the track geared toward children, including such oddball events as school-bus races and figure-8 trailer races. Racing is usually on Sunday, but the track also races on select Fridays and Saturdays, and on major holidays during the summer. The track stays open late April to the end of September.

BASEBALL

MINNESOTA TWINS
34 Kirby Puckett Place,
Minneapolis
(612) 375-7454 or (800) 33-TWINS
http://twins.mlb.com
Though its climate might indicate that Minnesota should be at heart a hockey state, the state also has a rich baseball heritage, from pickup stickball games in St. Paul parking lots to the community baseball teams that long gave farm towns something to do on weekends. The Minnesota Twins (for the Twin Cities), the state's major league team since the Washington Senators came to town and changed their name in 1961, have in recent decades been Minnesota's most successful pro team. Having won the World Series in 1987 and 1991 with a team including legends like Kent Hrbek and the late Kirby Puckett, the Twins are the only current Minnesota pro team to have won a national championship. Though they haven't made it to the World Series since '91, the team has consistently been among the best in the majors over the past several years, regularly making postseason appearances. The current face of the team is St. Paul native Joe Mauer, hot-test batter in the American League. After starting their Minnesota career in a long-gone outdoor park, the Twins moved to the Hubert H. Humphrey Metrodome in 1982. The Teflon-topped Dome was a relative novelty in the early '80s and became a local icon, thundering with noise as the

Twins rose to glory in its vast indoor expanse. The Twins gave the Dome one last immortal game as they wrested the Central Division championship from the Detroit Tigers in a 12-inning heartstopper, then quickly dropped the succeeding series to the New York Yankees and prepared to move across downtown to Target Field, their newly built outdoor stadium.

Though it's going to get chilly late in the season, excitement for outdoor baseball is high, and the new stadium looks great. Single-game tickets for the 2010 season will start at just $11 (many packages and deals are available; see the Twins' Web site for details), and catching a game at least once a season is a Minnesota must.

i Ever wonder why the L.A. Lakers are called the Lakers? It's because they came from the Land o' Lakes: They were the Minneapolis Lakers from 1947 to 1959, winning three straight national championships in the early '50s, before moving out west. It wouldn't be sporting of Minnesotans to nurse a grudge about the team's move, though—before coming to Minneapolis, the Lakers were the Detroit Gems.

ST. PAUL SAINTS
Midway Stadium, 1771 Energy Park Dr., St. Paul
(651) 644-6659
www.saintsbaseball.com
The Saints create an ambience reminiscent of the glory days of baseball. Each of the 6,329 seats at Midway Stadium has a great view of the game. There are also good concessions and the omnipresent tailgating. Because of long and harsh winters, Twin Citians love outdoor baseball—a beer, a hot dog, summer sun, and baseball.

The St. Paul Saints are a hot ticket in the Twin Cities. Tickets may be purchased at the stadium ticket office, by phone, or on the team's Web site. Keep in mind that games can and frequently do sell out.

Ticket prices are reasonable, considering there is not a bad seat at Midway Stadium, and are generally in the range of $5 to $15, with special discounts for seniors and children ages 14 and younger.

Parking is readily available for a small fee in the large parking lot abutting Midway Stadium. Feel free to bring some food and your favorite beverage for tailgating. The parking lot opens three hours before gametime.

i The St. Paul Saints offer outdoor baseball at its best, but there's a lot besides baseball going on at the ballpark—get a massage by a nun, watch the between-game antics, or rent the hot tub seating in left field.

BASKETBALL

MINNESOTA GOLDEN GOPHERS MEN'S BASKETBALL
Williams Arena, 1925 University Ave. SE, Minneapolis
(612) 624-8080 or (800) U-GOPHER
www.gophersports.com
The Twin Cities are a great place to be if you're a basketball fan. The area boasts both men's and women's professional teams as well as the collegiate Big Ten men's and women's teams, the University of Minnesota Golden Gophers.

Since the 1895–96 season the Minnesota Golden Gophers men's basketball team has played in one of the most august and competitive conferences in collegiate sports, the Big Ten. Current and former NBA stars, such as Joel Przybilla, Mychal Thompson, and Kevin McHale, wore the Gophers' maroon and gold. Today coach Tubby Smith, lured north from the fabled University of Kentucky program, brings new hope to the Golden Gophers.

The Gophers play at Williams Arena, a great place to watch basketball. It is a beautifully renovated brick building that feels comfortable yet electric because of the U of M students and alumni who attend games at "the barn."

You may purchase Gophers tickets by phone, online, or in person at Williams Arena. There is plenty of parking for Gophers basketball in lots on Oak Street Southeast and Fifth Street Southeast—but the U of M campus is among the diciest parking spots in the Twin Cities, so be sure to leave plenty of time to get to the game.

MINNESOTA GOLDEN GOPHERS WOMEN'S BASKETBALL
Williams Arena, 1925 University Ave. SE, Minneapolis
(612) 624-8080 or (800) U-GOPHER
www.gophersports.com

Under coach Pam Borton, who took over the Minnesota Golden Gophers women's basketball team in 2002, the future of Golden Gophers women's basketball looks bright. Each year under Coach Borton, the team has had a winning record, something that was quite rare under previous coaches.

Golden Gophers women's basketball has been in action since 1973 and has competed as part of the Big Ten since 1982. The intense games of the grueling Big Ten season bring numerous hard-fought battles to Williams Arena. Tickets are available by phone, online, or in person at Williams Arena.

i In 1997 the Saints made sandlot history when they signed Ila Borders, the first woman to pitch in an all-men's professional baseball league. She was traded to Northern League rival Duluth-Superior after seven games. Today a baseball signed by her is on display at the Baseball Hall of Fame.

MINNESOTA LYNX
Target Center, 600 First Ave. North
Minneapolis
(612) 673-8400
www.wnba.com/lynx

The Lynx share the Target Center with the Timberwolves; the season begins in late May and ends in early August. Though the WNBA is still very much up-and-coming compared to the NBA—you will never have difficulty getting tickets to any Lynx game—the women of the Minnesota Lynx have won a strong local following. The big excitement of the 2010 season is the Lynx's acquisition of Lindsay Whalen, a national

star when she played for one of the Gophers' best teams in recent memory. Tickets start at $10, and parking is convenient at Target Center's adjacent ramp.

i When Minnesota was awarded an NBA franchise in 1987, the name-the-team contest turned up possibilities such as the Flakes, the Purple Cows, and the Fighting Norsemen. "Timberwolves" was chosen because Minnesota has more of the animal than any state in the Lower 48.

MINNESOTA TIMBERWOLVES
Target Center, 600 First Ave. North
Minneapolis
(612) 673-8373
www.nba.com/timberwolves

Professional basketball has a long history in Minnesota, going back long before Timberwolves. From 1947 to 1960, the Twin Cities were home to the Minneapolis Lakers, a team that won six league championships during its time in Minnesota, including the first NBA championship after that league formed for the 1949–50 season. The team has been called the "forgotten dynasty," as it would go on to greater fame and success when the owners moved the team to Los Angeles after the 1959–60 season.

Minnesota remained without an NBA franchise for nearly 30 years. But the expansion Minnesota Timberwolves appeared on the scene for the 1989–90 season, finally returning NBA basketball to the Twin Cities. Target Center was constructed for the Wolves and opened in October 1990 as a single-sport arena. Target Center was the first Twin Cities facility for one major-league franchise. Today the Wolves share Target Center with the Minnesota Lynx WNBA team. In recent years, the Wolves were synonymous with Kevin Garnett, one of the best players in the NBA; after several frustrating seasons, in 2007 Garnett departed Minnesota for Boston, which proceeded to immediately win a national championship. Timberwolves are currently in what is known as a "rebuilding phase."

The Target Center is ideally located on the edges of the Warehouse District and the Hennepin Theater District in downtown Minneapolis. The structure fits tightly on its lot and almost spills out onto the street. It is comfortable on the inside, despite its size. Target Center has a capacity of nearly 20,000 for basketball.

Individual tickets for Wolves games range from $10 to $1,700 (the latter is for courtside seating next to the bench). There is ample parking in the municipal ramps behind the arena.

FOOTBALL

MINNESOTA GOLDEN GOPHERS FOOTBALL
Metrodome, 34 Kirby Puckett Place
Minneapolis
(612) 624-8080 or (800) U-GOPHER
www.gophersports.com
Long before the Minnesota Vikings arrived as an NFL expansion team, the Gophers were the Twin Cities' principal football team. They play in one of the premier NCAA conferences, the Big Ten, which has presented a significant hurdle for the team. The football team, like their basketball counterparts, lacks the recruiting base of many other Big Ten schools. Nevertheless, in recent years the Gophers football squad has improved—though it has a ways to go to reach the upper tier of the Big Ten.

After decades playing at the Metrodome, the Gophers returned to outdoor football in 2009 when the team's new TCF Bank Stadium opened on campus. Win or not, there's general agreement across the campus and across the Twin Cities that attending a Gophers game is a much more fun and exciting experience now. Single-game tickets start in the $10 range, a bargain compared to the Vikings.

MINNESOTA VIKINGS
Metrodome, 34 Kirby Puckett Place
Minneapolis
(612) 338-4537
www.vikings.com
The Minnesota Vikings, founded in 1961, have long been one of the most underachieving teams in the National Football League. They've been to four Super Bowls, the first team to reach that mark—and they've lost all four, the most recent being in 1977. Since then they've made five appearances in the NFC championship game that would take them back to the Super Bowl—and they've lost all five. All eyes were on the Vikings in 2009–10 when, in a bizarre twist of fate, they acquired 40-year-old quarterback Brett Favre, longtime staple of their archrival Green Bay Packers, and under Favre's leadership rode to an NFC championship game that they lost in a torturous overtime battle with the New Orleans Saints. The loss was greeted with a shrug: For all their devotion, Vikings fans have learned not to get their hopes up.

The Vikings play at the Hubert H. Humphrey Metrodome, of which they are left in (grudging) sole possession after the recent departures of the Minnesota Twins and the U of M Golden Gophers football team. The Vikings have a tremendous home-field advantage at the Dome, where Vikings fans cheer loud enough to create a near-deafening din. The Vikings' "Dome field advantage" acts as the 12th man on the field at Vikings home games.

Vikings tickets are pricey, but nonetheless their home games regularly sell out. See the team's Web site for details on availability and packages. Parking near the Dome is relatively convenient, but plan on doing some walking and paying $5 to $20 for parking, depending on how close to the action you want to be.

HORSE RACING

CANTERBURY PARK RACETRACK
AND CARD CLUB
1100 Canterbury Rd., Shakopee
(952) 445-7223 or (800) 340-6361
www.canterburypark.com
Canterbury Park has been the state's only horse track since 1985. Canterbury Park's horse racing is

⊙ Close-up

Dome Souvenir Plus & the Original Baseball Hall of Fame Museum of Minnesota

When you walk down Third Street en route to the **Hubert Humphrey Metrodome**, it's just about impossible to miss the building. A loudspeaker mounted on the outside of Ray Crump's deceptively small establishment invites passersby in, warning them that they'll be paying twice as much for the same souvenirs inside the Metrodome.

Few people passing by the brick storefront would confuse the building with the National Baseball Hall of Fame in Cooperstown, New York, but on entering the store, they'll be amazed by the wealth of local and national baseball history. The museum houses an impressive Wall of Celebrities, featuring a rotating display of the store's 10,260 signed photos, baseballs, and bats. The museum is free, and the adjoining **Dome Souvenir Plus** stocks extensive sports souvenirs and team-related merchandise for all the Twin Cities sports teams at reasonable prices.

Ray Crump arrived in Minnesota after the Twins relocated from Washington, D.C., for the 1961 season. Crump's career in Major League Baseball began as a batboy for the Washington Senators, where he would later assume the position of equipment manager. His career spanned 36 years with the Senators and then the Twins, where he was able to acquire the unique sports memorabilia found at the museum. An affable and insightful man, Ray Crump has written and published a book detailing his professional baseball experiences, *Beneath the Grandstands*.

Vintage Minnesota Twins collectibles are prominently displayed at the **Original Baseball Museum,** including the complete uniforms of retired Twins stars Harmon Killebrew, Tony Oliva, and Rod Carew. There is a special section dedicated to former Twins great Kirby Puckett, as well as plenty of Twins 1965, 1987, and 1991 World Series memorabilia. Included is a prominent display focusing on the Washington Senators' relocation to Minnesota. Unique displays include baseballs autographed not only by baseball stars but also by a wide array of nonsports stars: e.g., Jerry Lewis, Hubert Humphrey, and Louis Armstrong. The Elvis Corner displays personal items from the King of Rock 'n' Roll.

Crump's Wall of Celebrities includes autographed photos of such stars as Muhammad Ali, Hulk Hogan, Liberace, and Bill Cosby shown posing with a younger Ray Crump. Many of the

also the only sport in the Metro where gambling is legal. Live racing from Thursday through Sunday (plus major holidays) begins in mid-May and runs through the beginning of September. The track is open year-round for simulcast racing with pari-mutuel betting.

Admission is $5 for adults. Anyone under age 18 must be accompanied by an adult and is admitted free of charge. Seniors (60+) can get in for $3. Besides horse racing, the track also has a card club (see the Attractions chapter for more information). Parking at the track is free.

Canterbury Park is approximately 25 minutes from downtown Minneapolis and 15 minutes from the Mall of America.

HOCKEY

Minnesota Golden Gophers

MEN'S HOCKEY
Mariucci Arena, 1901 Fourth St. SE, Minneapolis
(612) 624-8080 or (800) U-GOPHER
www.gophersports.com

The Golden Gophers men's hockey team has a rich tradition at the University of Minnesota. It is the only Western Collegiate Hockey Association (WCHA) team in the Twin Cities and the largest university team in the area. In a state with so many sports entertainment options, Gophers photos were autographed long before the personalities became stars. "When I got the photo taken with Bill Cosby, no one knew who he was," says Crump. "He was some guy who had done a Jell-O commercial. I also have a baseball signed by Frank Sinatra, except he signed it 'Francis Sinatra.' Years later this woman who worked for him told me he never signed anything except business papers 'Francis,' and that he never signed autographs with anything but 'Frank.'"

When Ray Crump opened the museum and store, there was no Wall of Celebrities. These autographed photos of the stars were considered personal and cherished by the Crump family. Crump decided to display the autographs after making an observation: Many women seemed bored at the museum while their husbands refused to leave. He quickly realized displaying the celebrity photos made the museum more fun for the entire family.

And the focus of the museum is on family fun. "This is a family business," explains Crump. "My wife's right back there behind the counter most days, and my two sons frequently help me up front or in the snack bar. I like working at the snack counter better than the front of the store because it gives me a chance to talk to people more. I really enjoy talking to customers about the museum and all the souvenirs we've got here." When the museum/store is open, at least one Crump family member is available to serve the needs of Minnesota sports fans.

The amiable Crump gushes with interesting stories and minutiae about memorabilia and Major League Baseball. How many people can give you a detailed explanation of the differences between the National and American Leagues' methods for taking attendance, or know that the Vikings' lease at the Dome does not expire until 2011? If you have any questions about sports at all, Crump probably knows the answer or can tell you who does. As far as souvenir shopping goes, Dome Souvenir Plus has a huge selection of items at reasonable prices. Whether you are looking for a Twins hat, Vikings barbecue sauce, or a collectible bobblehead doll, Dome Souvenir Plus has it.

Dome Souvenir Plus & the Original Baseball Hall of Fame Museum of Minnesota is conveniently located 1 block directly north of the Dome, across from gate A (910 South Third St., Minneapolis). For further information call (612) 375-9707 or, to order merchandise, (888) 375-9707. They also can be visited at www.domeplus.com.

fans are diehards. They have been rewarded with a team that has consistently played high-caliber hockey in one of college hockey's toughest conferences, the WCHA.

The year 2002 brought glory back to Golden Gophers hockey, when, for the first time since 1979, the Golden Gophers reigned as NCAA National Champions. The team, amazingly, was able to repeat as champions in 2003.

The Gophers play at beautiful Mariucci Arena, a facility built specifically for the team. Here they have a significant home advantage behind the enormous enthusiasm of students and alumni.

Regular-season ticket prices were $35 in 2010. Tickets can be purchased by phone, online, or in person at Mariucci Arena. Plenty of parking for Gophers hockey is available in the lots across from Mariucci Arena on Oak Street Southeast.

WOMEN'S HOCKEY
Ridder Arena, 1815 Fourth St. SE, Minneapolis
(612) 624-8080 or (800) U-GOPHER
www.gophersports.com

The Golden Gophers men's hockey team is not the only hockey team on the U of M campus, nor is it the only team with a recent national championship. Women's hockey is blossoming in Minnesota, from young kids all the way to Division I athletics. Wildly successful, the Gophers women's hockey team won the NCAA National Championship in 2000, 2004, and 2005.

The Golden Gophers women's hockey team is the only women's hockey team in the country with an arena built specifically for it. Ridder Arena, a gorgeous 3,400-seat arena next door to Mariucci Arena, opened for the 2002–03 season and is considered by many to be the finest women's collegiate hockey arena in the country.

Tickets are available by phone, online, or in person at the Mariucci Arena ticket office. Tickets are a relative bargain, ranging from $8 to $10 for the 2009-10 season. Parking is widely available at lots and ramps near Ridder Arena.

i When the Minnesota Vikings beat the Green Bay Packers in 2009, Vikings quarterback Brett Favre (formerly of Green Bay) became the only player in NFL history to have defeated all 32 active teams.

MINNESOTA WILD
Xcel Energy Center, 175 West Kellogg Blvd., St. Paul
(651) 222-WILD
www.wild.com
The Minnesota Wild was an expansion team for the 2000–01 NHL season. However, a lot of work went into luring professional hockey back to Minnesota after losing the North Stars to Dallas in 1993. In fact, the NHL decision to come to St. Paul was incumbent on a new hockey-only facility. Efforts by city officials and fans led to the state-of-the-art Xcel Energy Center.

The Xcel Energy Center is located in downtown St. Paul. It is equipped with four 9-foot by 16-foot, high-definition scoreboards as well as two 16-foot by 24-foot, high-definition marquees outside the arena. A truly spectacular ribbon board circles the entire arena at the suite level, showing statistics and ads in 16.7 million shades of color. When the Wild score a goal, the lighthouse in the northeast corner of the arena sounds its foghorn, and the Wild fans go nuts.

Seating in the facility is comfortable and all seats have an excellent view of the action. There are 18,600 seats in the arena, with ticket prices ranging from $18 to $118 for the 2009–10 season. Wild tickets are a hot commodity in the Twin Cities, and you may have difficulty finding tickets at any price level after the season begins. There are many readily available parking options in downtown St. Paul within walking distance of the arena. The arena is connected to the extensive downtown skyway system

SOCCER

MINNESOTA STARS
National Sports Center, 1700 105th Ave. NE, Blaine
(763) 785-5601
www.nscminnesota.org
Professional soccer in Minnesota has a spotty history that begins in 1976 with the Minnesota Kicks (six seasons), continues in 1984 with the Minnesota Strikers (four seasons, the last three as members of an indoor league), and climaxes with the Minnesota Thunder, who started on a shoestring in 1990 and ultimately joined the USL First Division. The Thunder continually struggled to win fans, and from 2004 to 2007 moved their home field to the James Griffin Stadium in St. Paul in hopes of attracting fans among young urban soccer fans, particularly members of ethnic communities from soccer-obsessed countries. It didn't quite pan out that way, and the Thunder retreated to the sprawling National Sports Center in Blaine. With dreams of founding a new North American Soccer League, the team withdrew from the USL in 2009 but has apparently hit the financial rocks and all players have been released from their contracts. (Their associated women's team, the Minnesota Lightning, have simultaneously folded.)

The Thunder's replacements are the Minnesota Stars, a new second-tier pro team who played their first game on April 11, 2010. Based at the National Sports Center and coached by Manny Lagos, a former Thunder coach who has a lock on the title of greatest soccer coach in Minnesota history, the team have high hopes. Will they be shattered like those of the teams that went before them? You'll have to go to a game to find out. Most tickets are $13 general admission, with a few reserved seats going for $20–$30.

LACROSSE

MINNESOTA SWARM
Xcel Energy Center, 175 West Kellogg Blvd.,
St. Paul
(651) 602-6600
www.mnswarm.com
Playing their first regular-season game in 2005, the Minnesota Swarm have met unexpected success playing a sport—lacrosse—that's decidedly under the radar in the Minnesota sports galaxy. The Swarm's approach emphasizes fun and fan value, and at the pro level lacrosse can be a very exciting game to watch. It also helps that the Swarm play at the Xcel Energy Center, well known to sports fans as the home of the Minnesota Wild. Single-game tickets run $24–$82, and if you enjoy yourself, you might want to consider buying a relatively affordable season-ticket package for the following year.

DAY TRIPS AND WEEKEND GETAWAYS

Although there are more than enough attractions and sights in the Twin Cities to fill up your time, there's nothing like a good, long road trip through the countryside to clear one's mind of the hustle and bustle of the Metro.

The best time to hit the road is early spring, the last two weeks of April and the first two weeks of May, or when autumn is in full swing, the last two weeks of September and the first two weeks of October. Here is a sampling of the road trips well worth taking from the Twin Cities.

DULUTH

Located on the shore of Lake Superior and a major shipping port, Duluth was once the fastest-growing city in the country and was expected to surpass Chicago in size by 1870. When Jay Cooke, the wealthy Philadelphia land speculator, picked Duluth as the terminus of the Northern Pacific, Lake Superior, and Mississippi Railroads, Duluth's future appeared prosperous. Unfortunately, Jay Cooke's empire crumbled when the stock market crashed in 1873, and Duluth almost disappeared from the map. By the late 1800s, with the continued boom in lumber and iron mining and with the railroads completed, this shipping port again bloomed. By the turn of the 20th century, there were almost 100,000 inhabitants, and it was again a thriving community. At its economic height, Duluth had more millionaires per capita than anywhere else in the world.

With mining and shipping in decline, Duluth went through some hard decades in the late 20th century; today Duluth is betting on tourism to gird its economy. It's not a bad bet—Duluth is a beautiful town with a fascinating history. Most of the old warehouses by the Maritime Center and along the harbor have been converted into picturesque shopping centers and family-owned restaurants, many with the original facades left intact. Uphill from busy Canal Park Drive, the streets are lined with row houses and redbrick churches, many of which have been closed up

but left intact. While driving up the steep roads in Duluth is a little nerve-racking (especially in winter, despite the fact that the steepest roads are heated to keep ice from forming), the harbor looks absolutely stunning from the heights. An incredible stretch of blue water dotted with white sailboats and gigantic ore boats greets you, while the far, far North Shore of Lake Superior is barely visible even on the clearest days.

For more information on the sights and attractions of Duluth, call the **Duluth Convention & Visitor Bureau** at (800) 4-DULUTH, or check out its extensive Web site at www.visit duluth.com.

Getting There

Getting to Duluth from the Twin Cities is easy. Just take I-35E or I-35W north, and keep going until you hit Lake Superior

Attractions

Most of Duluth's attractions are located around the Duluth Harbor, so it's easy to walk from one to the next to make a full day of sightseeing. The **Great Lakes Aquarium** (GLA) at 353 Harbor Dr. (218-740-FISH; www.glaquarium.org) houses the largest freshwater aquarium in America. While the main focus of the GLA is the gigantic aquarium that is home to every known species of fish from Lake Superior (including several giant sturgeons), there are also many hands-on exhibits geared toward children—including a model of a lock and dam that they can navigate toy boats through. Right next door to the aquarium at 301 Harbor Dr. is the **S.S. *William A. Irvin*** (218-727-0022; www.williamairvin.com), a giant ore ship turned museum. The ship is open for tours Memorial Day through mid-October, with a special "Ship of Ghouls" exhibit around Halloween. For maritime buffs there's also the **Lake Superior Maritime Visitor Center,** 600 Lake Ave. South (218-727-2497; www.lsmma.com), owned and operated by the U.S. Army Corps of Engineers. Movies, model ships, and rotating exhibits are housed both inside and outside the free museum year-round. The museum also hosts a boat watchers' hotline (218-722-6489) and has a Web cam trained on the harbor.

At 506 West Michigan St. inside the depot is the **Lake Superior Railroad Museum** (218-727-8025; www.lsrm.org), which houses a rotating exhibit of historic railway cars, locomotives, and engines, most of which can be boarded for a close-up view of turn-of-the-20th-century machinery. On permanent display is a dining car china exhibit, the *William Crooks* (Minnesota's oldest engine), and the oldest known rotary snowplow in existence. The depot is also home to the **Duluth Children's Museum** (218-733-7543). The depot is full of hands-on exhibits for kids as well as education programs and tours, the Duluth Art Institute, the St. Louis Historical Society, and a performing arts wing where community and touring ballet companies, plays, and concerts take place throughout the year.

At 72nd Avenue West and Grand Avenue is the **Lake Superior Zoo** (218-730-4900; www.lszoo.org), home to more than two dozen endangered and threatened species from around the world. Admittedly on the small side, the zoo is a preservation project and educational tool as well as a tourist attraction.

For a little highbrow entertainment, check out the **Karpeles Manuscript Library Museum** at 902 East First St. (www.rain.org/~karpeles/dulfrm.html). This museum displays a rotating selection of original manuscripts from all over the world, including the original draft of the Bill

of Rights and Einstein's description of his general theory of relativity. The **Tweed Museum of Art,** located on the University of Minnesota–Duluth campus at 1201 Ordean Court (218-726-7823; www.d.umn.edu/tma), features nine separate galleries and exhibits with artwork dating from the 15th century. For a glimpse of what life was like for the well-to-do during the Iron Range boom, the historic **Glensheen Estate** at 3300 London Rd. (888-454-GLEN; www.glensheen.org) holds tours of its seven-acre grounds throughout the year (call for times and reservations).

For wintertime fun head to **Spirit Mountain** (800-642-6377; www.spiritmt.com), just outside Duluth, for cross-country and downhill skiing and, of course, snowboarding. Spirit Mountain has five chairlifts (including a covered one for skiers wanting to take a little break from the cold), and the 175-acre site has 23 separate downhill runs geared for all levels of skiers and two huge freestyle parks, one for skiers and one for snowboarders. Spirit Mountain has all sorts of package plans for extended stays in the area, including discounts on lodging, meals, and lift tickets. Call area hotels and motels directly for package information.

Accommodations and Camping

Right on the waterfront and steps away from Canal Park Drive, the following hotels are relatively new buildings designed with easy access to the hot spots of Duluth in mind. The **Canal Park Lodge**, at 250 Canal Park Dr. (800-777-8560; www.canalparklodge.com), features an indoor heated pool and hot tub, and all guests receive a complimentary breakfast each morning. The **Hampton Inn** at 310 Canal Park Dr. (218-720-3000 or www.hamptoninn.com) offers the same amenities with a full hot breakfast, while the **Inn on Lake Superior** at 350 Canal Park Dr. (218-726-1111 or 888-668-4352; www.innonlakesuperior.com) offers a lakefront view with its balcony suites. Downtown lodging is more affordable than the lakefront hotels. At 131 West Second St. is the **Best Western Downtown** (218-727-6851; www.bestwestern.com), located close to the skyway system that connects downtown Duluth. Two blocks away at 200 West First St. is the **Holiday Inn** (218-722-1202 or 800-477-7089; www.hiduluth.com), which has two pools and a sauna on the premises. Also downtown is the **Radisson Hotel** at 505 West Superior St. (218-727-8981 or 888-201-1718; www.duluthhotelrestaurant.com), **Fitger's Inn** at 600 East Superior St. (218-722-8826 or 888-FITGERS; www.fitgers.com), and the **Voyageur Lakewalk Inn** at 333 East Superior St. (218-722-3911 or 800-258-3911; www.voyageur lakewalkinn.com).

Duluth has many beautiful bed-and-breakfasts designed to make guests feel right at home. In town is the **Mathew S. Burrows 1890 Inn** at 1632 East First St. (218-724-4991 or 800-789-1890; www.1890inn.com), the **Ellery House** at 28 South 21st Ave. East (218-724-7639 or 800-355-3794; www.elleryhouse.com), and the **Firelight Inn** on Oregon Creek at 2211 East Third St. (218-724-0272 or 888-724-0273; www.firelightinn .com). All of these establishments are historic landmarks built around the turn of the 20th century and furnished with period antiques.

While there aren't any campsites in Duluth proper, there are several notable ones right outside the city limits. Ten miles south of Duluth is **Buffalo Valley Camping,** located at 2590 Guss Road, Proctor (218-628-7019; www.buffalohouse duluth.com), which has a full bar and restaurant at the campground as well as showers and electrical, sewer, and water hookups. Take exit 239 off I-35 and you'll find the **Knife Island Campground** at 234 MN 61, Esko (218-879-6063), right in the middle of the ghost town of Slateville and the adjacent abandoned logging camp. Water and electrical hookups are available at almost all of the 30 available sites, and firewood is provided by the campground.

Shopping

Unless you're just out for groceries, most of your Duluth shopping is going to take place around the museums and walkways in the Canal Park Drive and Lake Avenue area. Here original warehouse structures from Duluth's manufacturing past have been converted into shopping malls

and restaurants, while new structures have been built to integrate perfectly with the brickwork of the older buildings.

If you're into antiquing, the **Canal Park Antique Mall** at 310 Lake Ave. South (218-720-3940) is your best bet. The largest antiques and collectibles mall in Duluth is where you're sure to find that perfect knickknack for yourself or souvenir to take home to family and friends. If you prefer collecting old literature, **Old Town Antiques & Books** at 102 East Superior St. (218-722-5426) is a good place to stop.

And while you're on Superior Street, try out **Torke Weihnachten Christmas & Chocolates** at 600 East Superior St. (218-723-1225) for both specialty candies and European Christmas ornaments. Check out the northern branch of the Minneapolis-based **Electric Fetus** at 12 East Superior St. (218-722-9970) for the best selection of records, CDs, and tapes in this part of the state.

Along the Canal Park area is the **DeWitt-Seitz Marketplace** at 394 Lake Ave. South (www .dewitt-seitz.com), home to both **Hepzibah's Sweet Shoppe** (218-722-5049), with its wonderful homemade and imported candies, and toy and gift store **J. Skylark Company** (218-722-3794). Outside the mall and along Lake Avenue are even more gift shops—this is a great place to catch up on your window-shopping in the summer.

Restaurants

Traditional American fare dominates the restaurant scene in Duluth, with steakhouses on the high end of the scale and hamburger and french-fry joints at the low end. For many Minnesotans the historic **Pickwick** (218-727-8901; www .pickwickrestaurant.com) at 508 East Superior St. is *the* Duluth restaurant, a de rigueur stop for outdoorsmen and -women on their way up north. In the **Fitger's Brewhouse** complex at 600 East Superior St. is **Fitger's Brewhouse Brewery and Grill** (218-279-BREW; www.brewhouse.net). The casual brewpub offers live music entertainment most nights, homebrewed beer, and gourmet sandwiches. For something a little more exotic, try **Taste of Saigon** in the Dewitt-Seitz Marketplace at 394 Lake Ave. South (218-727-1598)—its food and selection are as good as the portions are large and generous. For late-night dining and carousing, the **Top of the Harbor** at the Radisson Hotel on 505 West Superior St. (218-727-8981) is a rotating restaurant—one of the few still in operation in the United States—that gives you a full view of the city every 72 minutes. The Radisson also has the **Fifth Avenue Lounge** at street level.

NEW ULM

Founded in 1857 by two German immigration societies, New Ulm is where you'll get the strongest flavor of Minnesota's most populous ethnic group. The town is *so* German, in fact, that composer Richard Wagner regarded the town as being more German than Germany itself and seriously considered moving to town to build the legendary opera house he ended up constructing at Bayreuth. The shadow of the **Hermann Monument,** set high on a hill just outside the business district, rises in the distance and is visible from just about anywhere in town. Accurately referring to itself as the "City of Charm and Tradition," New Ulm has a colorful history that is reflected in its attractions and many seasonal festivals.

Getting There

New Ulm is easily accessible by taking US 169 south from the Twin Cities to MN 99 west. From there, go west on US 14 (the Laura Ingalls Wilder Highway), which will take you into downtown New Ulm. The town is about 100 miles from the Metro.

For further information, brochures, or directions, be sure to visit the **New Ulm Area Chamber of Commerce/Visitors Information Center** at 1 North Minnesota St. (507-233-4300; www.newulm.com), located a short walking distance from most of the area attractions, shopping, and restaurants.

Attractions

At the forefront of New Ulm's attractions is the **Hermann Monument.** Representing the Teu-

tonic hero Hermann Arminius of Cherusci, the monument overlooks the city from the bluff on Center and Monument Streets. Dedicated in 1897, the monument stands 102 feet tall in Hermann Heights Park—a beautiful park with a panoramic view of the city below—and has been designated the national monument to German-American immigrants. The Hermann Monument is open Memorial Day through Labor Day and costs a nominal fee of $1, but you may visit the adjoining Hermann Heights Park year-round for free.

Another attraction is the **Glockenspiel/ Schonlau Park** at Fourth and Minnesota Streets. The New Ulm Glockenspiel is the only freestanding carillon clock tower on the continent. The glockenspiel chimes at noon, 3, and 5 p.m. daily and features a revolving stage of 3-foot-high characters that depict the city's history. (That description may give you the impression that kids will be thrilled by the Glockenspiel, but don't count on it.)

Brown County Historical Society and Museum at Center and Broadway Streets (507-233-2616; www.browncountyhistorymnusa.org) provides an excellent overview of the history of the New Ulm area. The building was once the New Ulm Post Office, and it was placed on the National Register of Historic Places in 1976. The Brown County Historical Society houses three floors of regional history: a Dakota Indians exhibit, a Brown County settlers area called "Made in Brown County," seasonal displays, and much more. All of the information is insightfully presented with great detail.

New Ulm is filled with beautiful historic homes, but the **John Lind House,** at the intersection of Center and State Streets (507-354-8802; www.thelindhouse.com), is especially aesthetically pleasing and historically significant. This lovely structure is an excellent example of Queen Anne–style architecture and was the home of the 14th governor of Minnesota and the first Swedish member of the U.S. Congress, Minnesota representative John Lind. Afternoon tours are held daily in summer, Friday through Sunday in spring and fall, and by appointment in winter.

Beer brewing was New Ulm's first industry. The **August Schell Brewing Company,** 1860 Schell Rd. (507-354-5528 or 800-770-5020; www .schellsbrewery.com), was founded in 1860, and since its inception Schell's has produced premium-quality crafted and specialty beers. Tours of the brewery, gardens, and park are available daily Memorial Day through Labor Day, and on weekends the rest of the year. Schell's is now home to the Grain Belt brand of beer, a well-known Minnesota brew of American lager formerly made in the Twin Cities.

New Ulm has a wealth of additional attractions. For lovers of the classic children's book *Millions of Cats,* author Wanda Gag's childhood home, the **Wanda Gag House,** 226 North Washington St. (507-359-2632; www.wandagaghouse .org), is open weekends in June, July, August, and December and during the rest of the year by appointment.

Yet another attraction of historical significance is the **Turner Hall,** at the intersection of First Street South and State Street (507-354-4916; www.newulmturnerhall.org). The New Turnverein opened in 1856 and was dedicated to improving the health of New Ulmers through gymnastics and exercise. Parts of the Turner Hall building date from 1865, including 70 feet of murals in the Ratskeller, a bar and restaurant. The Turner Hall is free and open daily, and there's no better place to get some hot polka action.

New Ulm has a full slate of annual festivals and events. New Ulm celebrates Christmas with traditional German hoopla. Included are the **Christmas Parade of Lights,** which celebrates the arrival of Santa Claus on the Friday evening after Thanksgiving, and the traditional German St. Nicholas Day, December 6; **Fasching,** a German version of Mardi Gras, occurs annually in late February or early March concurrent with Schell's **Bock Beer Fest.** Summer has an active festival schedule with both **Bavarian Blast and Polka Days** at the end of July, plus **River Blast** in Riverside Park over Labor Day weekend, which features a floating parade. **Oktoberfest** in October features traditional German food, music, and, of course, beer.

Accommodations

New Ulm has ample accommodations, including bed-and-breakfasts as well as hotels. As with all other aspects of New Ulm, most of the accommodations have a German flavor.

The **Holiday Inn,** at 2101 South Broadway St. (507-359-2941 or 877-863-4780; www.holidayinn .com), is the largest hotel in New Ulm. It hosts Oktoberfest for two weekends each fall and has a swimming pool, restaurant, and cocktail lounge. The **Budget Holiday Motel,** 1316 North Broadway St. (507-354-4145), was renovated in 2002. Another New Ulm hotel is the **Colonial Inn** at 1315 North Broadway St. (507-354-3128), a relatively small, 24-unit hotel.

The New Ulm area has many bed-and-breakfasts. The **W. W. Smith Inn** at 101 Linden St. SW in nearby Sleepy Eye (507-794-5661; www .wwsmithinn.com), for example, is located 14 miles from New Ulm. The W. W. Smith Inn has much to offer lovers of bed-and-breakfasts. Listed on the National Register of Historic Places, this elegant Queen Anne structure was constructed in 1901 for a wealthy area banker. In New Ulm, **Deutsche Strasse B&B** at 404 South German St. (507-354-2005; www.deutschestrasse.com) offers five rooms, two with queen-size beds and three with full-size beds, and all with private baths. Also included is a full breakfast.

Shopping

If you're looking for specialty shops with a German flair, you'll find them in New Ulm. New Ulm boasts businesses devoted to antiques, crafts, sweets, dolls, and sausages. The vast majority of shops are conveniently located on Minnesota and Broadway Streets, in the heart of beautiful old downtown. **Edelweiss Flower Haus,** 209 North Minnesota St. (800-831-8898), offers a variety of flowers and gifts. In addition, there's **NadelKunst Ltd.,** 212 North Minnesota St. (507-354-8708), specializing in knitting, crocheting, beading, and cross-stitch.

Of course, New Ulm has stores that specialize in German merchandise: the **Guten Tag Haus,** 127 North Minnesota St. (507-233-4287;

www.gutentaghaus.com), and **Domeier's New Ulm German Store,** 1020 South Minnesota St. (507-354-4231). Unlike the aforementioned businesses, Domeier's is located 10 blocks south of the downtown business district.

The **Christmas Haus,** 203 North Minnesota St., and **Lambrecht's,** 119 North Minnesota St., share an owner, a phone, and a Web site (507-233-4350; www.lambrechtsgifts.net). The former specializes in German and seasonal goodies, and the latter has two entire floors of flowers and gift items, from greeting cards and framed prints to lace, lamps, and shirts. At **August Schell's Brewing Company,** 1860 Schell Rd. (507-354-5528; www.schellsbrewery.com), there is something for every shopper. Naturally, there are many Schell and Grain Belt clothing items and collectibles, plus gourmet food and novelty gifts.

Restaurants

Surprisingly, German food does not dominate New Ulm's restaurant options. German food is often included with traditional American fare. Certainly the place to start when discussing New Ulm's restaurants is **Veigel's Kaiserhoff,** 221 North Minnesota St. (507-359-2071). The Kaiserhoff's most popular dish is the barbecue ribs. The menu also includes many German favorites such as bratwursts, schnitzels, landjaeger, and German chocolate cake. Eating at the Kaiserhoff probably won't convert you to being a lover of German food if you weren't already, but it's certainly an authentic southern Minnesota experience. Another restaurant with heavy German influences is **Otto's Feierhaus and Bier Stube** at 2101 South Broadway Ave. (507-359-5300). Otto's is conveniently located for travelers in the New Ulm Holiday Inn and serves American food and German specialties.

Traditional American food is popular in New Ulm. The **Ulmer Cafe,** 115 North Minnesota St. (507-354-8122), is right in the middle of New Ulm's shopping area and features breakfast and lunch in a hometown cafe.

For families, **Happy Joe's,** 1700 North Broadway (507-359-9811), specializes in food kids and adults love, such as pizza and chicken. There is also a smorgasbord at Happy Joe's, which outside Minnesota is called an all-you-can-eat buffet. **DJ's,** 1200 North Broadway (507-354-3843), is another family diner featuring lunch and dinner specials daily.

Main Jiang House is a Chinese restaurant at 400 North Minnesota St. (507-354-1228). New Ulm also has several sandwich, burger, pizza, and taco chain restaurants.

> **i** New Ulm is deep enough into farm country that you may need to pick up a little lingo. For example, lunch is often called "dinner," and the evening meal, "supper." For further reference, see Howard Mohr's indispensable reference tome *How to Talk Minnesotan.*

NORTH SHORE SCENIC DRIVE

The North Shore Scenic Drive, officially US 61, is lined with rental cottages, bed-and-breakfasts, RV parks, and motels, while the shore is dotted with rent-by-the-day boat docks and marinas. The first town outside Duluth is Two Harbors, a mecca of restaurants and gift shops, while the residences themselves are relatively new and tucked away some distance from the downtown area. Two Harbors is a good place to sit down and get a bite to eat or rest for the night before heading on to the beautiful parks that make up the attractions in this area, or to pick up a bag of regionally grown wild rice, fresh honey, fruit preserves, or a lighthouse-shaped refrigerator magnet.

Getting There

The North Shore Scenic Drive begins in Duluth and stretches 154 miles to Grand Portage, near the Canadian border. To reach the drive from the Twin Cities, take either I-35W or I-35E north to I-35 all the way to Duluth. I-35 ends at MN 61 (yes, the same one revisited by Minnesota native Bob Dylan on his classic 1965 album), which is the North Shore Scenic Drive. The beginning of the drive is about 150 miles from the Twin Cities.

Attractions

Thirteen miles northeast of Two Harbors on US 61 is **Gooseberry Falls State Park** (888-MINN-DNR; www.dnr.state.mn.us), which holds an amazing series of relatively untouched waterfalls that are open to the public to walk out on—literally. This is not recommended for those struggling with a fear of heights, as it's possible to climb to the very top of the waterfalls via hiking trails and walkways and walk right to the edge of the rocky face to peer over the edge—without the presence of handrails or safety mesh. A visitor center features exhibits on Lake Superior and the history of the park itself.

Split Rock Lighthouse State Park (218-226-6377; www.dnr.state.mn.us/state_parks), also on US 61 about 20 miles northeast of Two Harbors, surrounds the lighthouse that has been a landmark on the Lake Superior shore since 1910. Now a state-run historic site, it and the neighboring lighthouse keeper's houses and fog signal building have been restored to 1920s appearance and opened to visitors and tour groups. Call the lighthouse directly for tours. The attached History Center shows films and exhibits on the lighthouse, commercial fishing, and shipwrecks through most of the summer.

For more energetic travelers, the **Superior Hiking Trail** winds through the forested ridgeline of the coast for 200 miles. There are many small and midsize fishing lakes and tiny craft shops to be found all along the drive that parallels the trail—for more information, contact the Superior Hiking Trail Association in Two Harbors: (218) 834-2700; www.shta.org.

Accommodations and Camping

The **Lighthouse Bed & Breakfast,** at the harbor in Two Harbors (218-834-4814 or 888-832-5606; www.lighthousebb.org), is one of the few B&Bs on the Great Lakes housed inside a working lighthouse, built in 1892. The B&B has four rooms decorated with period antiques, and all have a view of Lake Superior. For more pedestrian comforts, **AmericInn Lodge and Suites,** 1088 US 61 West, Two Harbors (218-834-3000; www.americ

inn.com), offers guests an indoor pool, hot tub, and sauna, while just outside Two Harbors on the shoreline is the **Grand Superior Lodge,** 2826 US 61 (218-834-3796 or 800-627-9565; www.grandsuperior.com), a beautiful resort with individual log homes, an on-site restaurant and cocktail lounge, and an indoor pool and spa.

Shopping

Many metro residents make the trek up to the North Shore every summer for one reason—wild rice. The tiny one-quarter pound bags of wild rice you get at the supermarket in the Cities usually cost you a couple of dollars, while just about every store in Two Harbors on up sells four-pound bags for around $8. Wild rice is much richer than your typical white variety rice and adds a wonderful, hearty dimension to soups, poultry stuffing, and anything else that calls for rice.

All along the North Shore Drive can be found tiny houses converted into shops where you can buy anything from jars of wild clover honey to homemade preserves to lighthouse-shaped refrigerator magnets and, of course, fish bait. One is **Beaver Bay Agate Shop and Museum,** 1003 Main St. in Beaver Bay (218-226-4847), which is exactly what it sounds like, with jewelry and key chains made from agates found along the Lake Superior shoreline as well as permanent displays of man-made artifacts and geological marvels found in the area.

The remote shops in the small towns dotting the North Shore Highway all the way to the Canadian border often sell unique and memorable items and are worth a browsing stop. In particular, the beautiful town of Grand Marais, about 110 miles northeast of Duluth on US 61, is a haven for many artists, and the downtown region is alive with galleries and studios.

Restaurants

If you're more comfortable dining at familiar restaurant chains, then Two Harbors is the place to stop before heading on up the Lake Superior coast. Pretty much every fast-food chain in America is represented here, including Dairy Queen, Pizza Hut, and Culvers. If you're more interested in sticking to family owned-and-run establishments, there are plenty of those to choose from, too, either in Two Harbors or along the North Shore Drive. For burgers and sandwiches, and breakfast all day long, try **Judy's Cafe** at 623 Seventh Ave., Two Harbors (218-834-4802), or for traditional North Shore smoked fish as well as pickled herring, salmon spread, and cheese, head to **Lou's Fish House,** 1319 US 61, Two Harbors (218-834-5254; www.lousfish.com). For a north woods dining experience, try the **Northern Lights Restaurant** on US 61 in Beaver Bay (218-226-3012), with wild game and Scandinavian dishes, and for informal, family-style meals, there's **Our Place** on MN 1, Finland (218-353-7343). **Vanilla Bean Bakery and Cafe,** 812 Seventh Ave., Two Harbors (218-834-3714; www.thevanillabean.com), is a cozy bistro for designer coffees or meals.

RED WING

Perhaps best known as the home of the Red Wing Shoe Company, Red Wing is a charming Mississippi River town with a beautiful downtown composed of refurbished old warehouse buildings and historic churches that date from 1855. Set deep in the river valley surrounded by beautiful fishing lakes, scenic hilltop views, streams, picturesque farms, and apple orchards, Red Wing is well worth a visit—particularly when the fall colors are at their peak.

i No tickets are sold at the Red Wing Amtrak station, so make sure you buy a round-trip ticket at the Twin Cities station.

Getting There

There are several ways to get to Red Wing. The principal ways are via US 61 from St. Paul, which is quite scenic south of Hastings, or via train from the Amtrak station in St. Paul (730 Transfer Rd.; 651-644-6012) all the way to the historic **Old Milwaukee Depot** at 420 Levee St. in Red Wing. You may want to stop by the depot while in Red Wing anyway, since it doubles as the visitor center and

there are lots of maps, brochures, and free local newspapers with restaurant coupons and information on events and happenings around town. The depot, established in 1904, is located next to downtown Red Wing and all its sights, too, so there's no need to worry about transportation unless you have plans outside of town.

If you opt to drive, a nice alternative to US 61 is to cross the river just before Hastings and jump on Wisconsin Highway 35 south at Prescott. Follow WI 35 to Bay City, and then turn on to US 63 west to cross the Mississippi to Red Wing between Hager City and Bay City. WI 35 is a two-lane highway that passes through beautiful old hardwood forests and gently sloping farmlands dotted with old farmhouses, stone silos, and shallow creeks. It also roughly follows the Mississippi River here, providing spectacular views of the waterway and the bluffs across the river on the Minnesota side.

For more information about the area, contact the **Red Wing Visitors and Convention Bureau,** 420 Levee St.; (651) 385-5934 or (800) 498-3444; www.redwing.org.

Attractions

A good place to start exploring Red Wing is **Bay Point Park** on Levee Street. Located right on the Mississippi River, this is also the home of **Boathouse Village,** one of the only remaining "gin pole" boathouse installations in the country. The village looks just like a bunch of little houses floating in the water, with floating walkways connecting the "neighborhood." Close by is **Levee Park,** located just behind the historic 1904 Milwaukee Depot. Both parks have picnic tables and play areas for kids.

At the corner of Third Street and East Avenue at 443 West Third St. is the historic **Sheldon Theatre** (651-388-8700 or 800-899-5759; www.sheldontheatre.org). First opened in 1904, the theater was such an unabashed collection of sculpture, arches, marble columns, and gilded plaster detail, it was once described as a jewel box. Nowadays the 466-seat theater is used for everything, including children's plays, concerts, acrobats, and films. If you just want to walk in and look at the inside of this beautiful building, the helpful men and women at the ticket counter will gladly let you in to take a peek. Guided tours are offered on Saturday. Call ahead for tour times.

Red Wing has its share of museums, including the somewhat unconventional **Red Wing Shoe Museum,** 314 Main St. (651-388-8211; www.RedWingshoes.com). Owned and operated by Red Wing Shoes, the museum treats visitors to exhibits imparting the history of the company as well as an interactive display that helps you learn the process of making a pair of shoes. There are other displays, too, including a kiosk in which you can match occupation to shoe. About 9 blocks away at 1166 Oak St. is the **Goodhue County Historical Museum** (651-388-6024; www.good-huehistory.mus.mn.us), which contains more than 150,000 paintings, photographs, geological and natural history displays, and artifacts concerning Goodhue County from prehistory to the present. Culture vultures will want to be sure to stop by Red Wing Framing, a frame shop that also serves as a gallery displaying fine art; in recent years, it's been particularly notable for its displays of eye-popping vintage illustration art.

At the end of East Fifth Street is majestic **Barn Bluff,** immortalized by Henry David Thoreau in 1861 after he hiked to the top. The bluff is listed on the National Register of Historic Places, and a marked stairwell is available to hikers. An even easier climb (or drive) to the top of the bluffs is in **Memorial Park,** located at the end of East Seventh Street. On your way to the top of **Sorin's Bluff,** you'll find hiking trails, bike paths, and caves that may or may not be wise to explore. From either bluff, you get a great view of Red Wing and the Mississippi River, as well as the beautiful valley and tree-covered bluffs that stretch around the town. For another view of the valley, multiple companies offer boat rides along the rugged bluffs of the Mississippi River. Be sure to bring your binoculars, as everything from deer, beavers, bald eagles, and wild turkeys have been seen on these rides. Passengers are encouraged to pack a picnic lunch to take with them for the trip.

ℹ Bald eagles on their annual migration congregate in Red Wing's Colvill Park from November through the end of March. Often multiple eagles can be spotted in a single tree, looking for abundant shad in the Mississippi River.

In wintertime Red Wing and its neighbor, Welch, become ski country. Twelve miles northwest of town, just off US 61, is the **Welch Village Resort** (651-258-4567; www.welchvillage .com), which features some of the best downhill skiing in the state. Right next door, **Welch Mill,** at 14818 264th St. Path (651-388-9857; www .welchmillcanoeandtube.com), offers canoe and inner tube rentals and shuttle service to and from the Cannon River in spring, summer, and fall. For cross-country skiers, there's the **Cannon Valley Trail** (507-263-0508; www.cannonvalleytrail .com) in Cannon Falls, stretching through nearly 20 miles of countryside, following the original Chicago Great Western Railroad line that once connected Cannon Falls and Red Wing. A Wheel Pass is required to bike, inline skate, or skateboard on the trail April through November. Passes are available by calling the trail office or at trailside pay stations.

Ten miles north of Red Wing and just off US 61 is the glamorous **Treasure Island Resort and Casino** (651-388-6300 or 800-222-7077; www .treasureislandcasino.com), a tropical-themed casino and hotel that features 44 games tables, 2,500 slot machines, a 10-table poker room, and a 40-foot waterfall, and smoking and nonsmoking gambling areas. The casino is decorated with palm trees, and the slot machines and gambling tables are spread far enough apart that the casino never feels too crowded. The attached hotel has an indoor pool with another waterfall, a fitness room, and a child care facility, while outside is a RV park with 95 pull-through sites and a 137-slip marina.

Accommodations and Camping

If you plan to spend the night in Red Wing, you have many options. The most elegant of the hotels in the area is downtown Red Wing's historic **St. James Hotel** at 406 Main St. (800-252-1875; www.st-james-hotel.com), established in 1875 and a member of the National Trust's Historic Hotels of America. The elegant hotel has only 61 guest rooms, so you'll want to call ahead of time to make reservations.

Many beautiful old houses in Red Wing have been converted to bed-and-breakfasts and inns. Most of them are on the National Register of Historic Places, and many were former residences of Red Wing Shoe Company tycoons. The **Golden Lantern Inn** at 721 East Ave. (888-288-3315; www.goldenlantern.com) was home to three former presidents of the Red Wing Shoe Company. The Golden Lantern has since added whirlpools and fireplaces to some of the rooms and offers a full breakfast each morning to visitors. At 1105 West Fourth St. is the **Moondance Inn** (866-388-8145; www.moondanceinn.com), which offers a five-course gourmet brunch to weekend guests and rooms with private bathrooms and double whirlpools.

For more conventional lodging, there's an **AmericInn Motel** at 1819 Old West Main (651-385-9060; www.americinn.com), which offers guests a free continental breakfast and has a pool and sauna on the premises; and the **Parkway Motel** at 3425 US 61 West (651-388-8231; www.parkwaymotelmn.com), which features snowmobile trails, hiking trails, fishing lakes, and a golf course within walking distance.

If you're more happy "roughing it" while on vacation, there's the **Hay Creek Valley Campground** (651-388-3998 or 888-388-3998; www.haycreeekvalley.com), located 6 miles south of Red Wing on MN 58. The campground has a heated swimming pool and a restaurant, the Old Western Saloon, on the premises and borders a stocked trout stream. Right next to the campground is the **Hardwood State Forest** with trails laid out for horseback riding, hiking, snowmobiling, and areas set aside for in-season hunting.

Shopping

Red Wing has some amazingly good deals on antique furniture, toys, jewelry, and collectibles in general. The two main shopping areas in town are situated near each other, too. There's the Downtown District, which is composed of beautiful old warehouse buildings and storefronts that have been refurbished and turned into antiques stores, thrift stores, and restaurants, while about 12 blocks away, down Old West Main Street, is the Historic Pottery District, where you can buy antiques from **Al's Antique Mall** at 512 Plum St. (651-388-0572) or shop at antiques and outlet stores in what was once a pottery factory at the **Historic Pottery Place Mall** at 2001 Old West Main St. (651-388-1428).

The Downtown District has the widest variety of shops to choose from. At **Memory Maker Antiques** in the Boxrud Building at 415 Main St. (651-385-5914), you can find everything from 50-cent postcards to vintage dishes to antique wardrobes. At Main and Bush Streets is the **Uffda Shop** (651-388-8436; www.uffdashoponline.com) selling all things Scandinavian, such as gnomes, Norwegian sweaters, lefse grills, porcelain, solje jewelry, and, of course, Ole and Lena joke books.

Restaurants

While the majority of Red Wing's restaurants can be categorized as traditional American fare, quite a few add a unique twist to those traditional dishes. The **Staghead Restaurant** at 219 Bush St. (651-388-6581) offers a changing and eclectic menu of steak, Italian dinners, and specialty sandwiches; the restaurant has a huge wine list and more than 30 imported and domestic beers on tap. Former Staghead chef and Hüsker Dü bassist Greg Norton now owns and cooks at the **Norton's** (651-388-2711; www.thenortonsrestaurant.com) with his wife, at 307 Main St. The upscale menu has a little something for everyone. **Fiesta Mexicana,** 2555 Old West Main St. (651-385-8939), serves authentic Mexican food for the lunch and dinner crowd and is quite possibly the only nonchain Mexican restaurant you'll find within a 50-mile radius. **Bev's Cafe** at 221 Bush St. (651-388-5227) offers classic home-style meals from hash to roast beef dinners and a fish fry on Friday. For a very elegant evening, the historic St. James Hotel's restaurant, the **Port** (800-252-1875; www.port-restaurant.com) serves a limited but tantalizing dinner menu. Call ahead for reservations.

If you just want a cup of coffee and something to munch on while you read the paper, you're in luck. Red Wing has several cozy little nooks to grab a cup of java, including **Lily's Coffee House & Flowers** at 419 West Third St. (651-388-8797), which serves soups, sandwiches, pastries, coffee, and espresso drinks; **Tale of Two Sisters Tea Room and Gift Shoppe** at 204 West Seventh St. (651-388-2250) offers a full English tea or just a cup of coffee to patrons.

For the sports bar fan, **Andy's Bar** at 529 Plum St. (651-388-4471), has 10 TVs with satellite hookups to accompany its menu of beer, appetizers, burgers, and chicken dinners, while in downtown proper, the **Barrel House,** at 223 Main St. (651-388-9967), serves light food, pizza, and beer, with daily happy hour specials.

IN THE AREA

Twenty-three miles south of Red Wing across the Mississippi River on WI 35 is the historic town of Pepin, Wisconsin. Named after the Pepin brothers, who were two of the first French trappers in the area, the village was settled in 1846 and was known for years as a steamboat boomtown and a vacation spot for wealthy Chicago socialites who summered on Lake Pepin. This is the place to visit if you're interested in fishing, boating, or bird-watching—the 13,000-acre **Tiffany Wildlife Area,** right next to Lake Pepin, is a regular roosting spot for bald eagles and hawks, while Lake Pepin itself has several beautiful marinas with public docking ramps.

Perhaps the most famous of Pepin's residents was Laura Ingalls Wilder, immortalized in *Little House on the Prairie*. Every September, Pepin celebrates **Laura Ingalls Wilder Days** with events including a Laura knowledge contest, a parade, demonstrations of traditional crafts and industries, and bus tours of Wilder's birth site. For more information, see www.pepinwisconsin.com.

Stillwater

Stillwater is technically considered a Twin Cities outer-ring suburb, but it's a good half hour's drive from St. Paul. Long in competition with the Twin Cities for everything from being the state's logging and industry capital to making a bid for the state capital itself, Stillwater is a beautiful riverside city with much to offer antiques shoppers, architecture connoisseurs, book collectors, and nature lovers. There's more than enough to do in the Stillwater area to make it at least a day trip, if not a relaxing weekend getaway.

Gentrification is steamrolling through Stillwater like a (renovated) freight train—everywhere you go, brick-and-wood storefronts have been restored and repainted, and specialty stores, wineries, and espresso bars have set up shop where there were once just thrift shops and diners. With all of its parks and bicycle trails, Stillwater is sure to offer something that appeals to you and your family.

For more information about Stillwater, check out www.ilovestillwater.com, or call the Stillwater Chamber of Commerce at (651) 439-4001.

Getting There

Take MN 36 east until you reach Stillwater.

Accommodations and Camping

Stillwater boasts bed-and-breakfasts housed in Victorian mansions and quaint old hotels listed on the National Register of Historic Places as well as modern hotels with the expected amenities. The **Water Street Inn** at 101 South Water St. (651-439-6000; www.waterstreetinn.us) is a beautiful redbrick building that's located right next to the St. Croix and is furnished with turn-of-the-20th-century period pieces. Another fine choice is the **Elephant Walk** at 801 West Pine St. (651-430-0359 or 888-430-0359; www.elephantwalkbb.com), where each room is decorated with exotic finds from around the world. You're welcomed with a complimentary bottle of wine, cheese, fruit, and homemade crackers in your room.

The newer hotels and motels are clustered along MN 36 southwest of downtown. Options include the **Holiday Inn Express** at 2000 Washington Ave. (651-275-1401; www.hiexpress.com); **Days Inn Stillwater,** 1750 West Frontage Rd. (651-430-1300; www.americasbestvalueinn.com); and the **Super 8 Motel** at 2190 West Frontage Rd. (651-430-3990; www.super8.com).

For RV campers, there's the **Golden Acres RV Park & Picnic Area** at 15150 North Square Lake Trail (651-439-1147), which has 54 campsites with water, electrical, and sewer hookups available (no tent camping allowed). The campground, located on the shore of Square Lake, has a nice swimming beach and good fishing.

Shopping

Stillwater is antiques central, with shops that sell everything from collector's dolls and teddy bears to handmade Amish quilts and furniture. In Main Street Square at 124 South Main Street, you can buy pottery, jewelry, and vintage clothing at **Country Charm Antiques** (651-439-8202; www.countrycharmantiques.net). **Seasons Tique** at 229 South Main St. (651-430-1240) carries beautiful Christmas tree ornaments and decorations from around the world all year long. For the larger budget, **Enigma** at 213 South Main St. (651-439-2206) carries new and antique furnishings from Europe and Asia, and the **J. P. Laskin Company** at 306 East Chestnut St. (651-439-5712) carries handmade American goods made by Amish people and Native Americans, as well as hand-blown glass artifacts.

Stillwater has several independent bookstores to choose from. **St. Croix Antiquarian Booksellers** at 232 South Main St. (651-430-0732; www.booktown.com/stcroixbooks), carries more than 50,000 books on history, art, philosophy, Americana, and everything in between, while **Loome Theological Booksellers** in the Old Swedish Covenant Church at 320 North Fourth St. (651-430-1092; www.loomebooks.com) specializes in secondhand and out-of-print books on theology, religion, and philosophy. The **Valley Bookseller,** 217 North Main St. (651-430-3385; www.valleybookseller.com), is an independent bookstore selling new titles. The beautiful store is bright and sunny and features a strong children's section, a large selection of fiction and local his-

tory titles, and an exotic bird aviary in the middle of the store.

Restaurants

Stillwater has no shortage of coffeehouses and espresso bars. At the **Dreamcoat Cafe,** 215 South Main St. (651-430-0615), you can order sandwiches or ice cream to go with your coffee—on weekend nights, local acoustic acts perform at this neighborhood cafe. At the other end of Main, **Supreme Bean Espresso Cafe** at 402 North Main St. (651-439-4314) serves delicious sandwiches and pastries that you can take outside to eat on the patio.

There are just as many places to go for dinner in Stillwater, too. Featuring a beautiful view of the St. Croix as well as traditional American fare is the **Dock Cafe** at 425 East Nelson St. (651-430-3770; www.dockcafe.com). **Brine's** at 219 South Main St. (651-439-7556; www.brines-stillwater.com) serves hot deli sandwiches, soups and salads, and the famous "Brine Burger," which is a heck of a lot better than it sounds. (Brine's is also known, for no reason other than sheer novelty, for its beef stick Bloody Mary.) For German food, try the **Gasthaus Bavarian Hunter** at 8390 Lofton Ave. North (651-439-7128; www.gasthausbavarianhunter.com), which features live accordion music Friday and Sunday evenings.

For more refined dining, the historic **Lowell Inn** at 102 North Second St. (651-439-1100; www.lowellinn.com) serves elegant dinners in a variety of themed rooms.

Stillwater is also the home to two wineries with on-site tasting rooms, including **Saint Croix Vineyards** at 6428 Manning Ave. (651-430-3310; www.scvwines.com) and **Northern Vineyards Winery** at 223 North Main St. (651-430-1032; www.northernvineyards.com). Call ahead for an appointment at either place, just in case they're already booked.

IN THE AREA

Just south of Stillwater and across the St. Croix River is the city of **Hudson, Wisconsin,** which is basically a little Stillwater. There are plenty of antiques stores, jewelry stores, and coffee shops, as well as beautiful storefronts and turn-of-the-20th-century architecture throughout the downtown area. On the west end of Coulee Road is the turnoff to **Birkmose Park,** which, if you take the drive to the top, gives you a great view of the harbor as well as a few imposing-looking Native American burial mounds. Hudson is also the home of the **San Pedro Cafe** at 426 Second St. (715-386-4003; www.sanpedrocafe.com), which features excellent dishes with a Caribbean flair, such as jerk chicken and rubbed, slow-roasted BBQ pork.

North of Stillwater on MN 95 is the **Boomsite,** a large body of water where fresh-cut trees once poured in through the river mouth and were then collected by the hardworking men of Stillwater's logging past. Now the Boomsite is a wonderful park surrounded by forest with an easily accessible path down to the beach. This is a beautiful, well-maintained park, a fun place to stop and relax and let the kids run around before getting back on the road.

i In 1994 Stillwater was declared America's first "Book Town," an international designation sponsored by Welshman Richard Booth to honor notable book-friendly towns worldwide. Stillwater's multiple antiquarian and new booksellers line Main Street downtown. For more information about Stillwater's bookstores, visit www.booktown.com.

Taylors Falls

In order to properly appreciate autumn in Minnesota, a drive to Taylors Falls on the St. Croix River in the last two weeks of September or the first two weeks of October is absolutely necessary. During autumn, the leaves of the trees growing in the mineral-rich soil turn fluorescent shades of scarlet, gold, and yellow, looking more like bright springtime flower petals than dying tree leaves.

But don't just visit in the fall. Taylors Falls is just as beautiful in springtime, with millions of

tiny purple, white, and blue wildflowers springing up between even the smallest of sidewalk cracks. In the warm months, bird-watching is a popular pastime all along the

St. Croix River, and canoes can be rented at Interstate State Park for those who want to get a closer look at the cliffs that line the river. For more information, you can call the Taylors Falls Chamber of Commerce at (800) 447-4958 or visit its Web page at www.taylorsfallschamber.org.

Getting There

If you take I-94 east to MN 95 north to Taylors Falls, you'll be treated to scenes of beautiful old hardwood forests and the St. Croix River all the way. If you just want to get to Taylors Falls, the quickest route is to take either I-35E north or I-35W north (depending on where in the Twin Cities you are) to I-35, then take I-35 north to US 8 east and follow US 8 all the way to Taylors Falls. It's a little less scenic, but you'll travel through the nice towns of Chisago City, Lindstrom, and Center City, and you can still get a glimpse of the beautiful St. Croix Valley along the last few miles.

Attractions

Taylors Falls attractions run the gamut of breathtaking, cliffside views of a landscape carved out by Ice Age glaciers to wild water park rides to self-guided tours through a historic neighborhood with houses dating from the 1850s. You can take a trip down the St. Croix on your own in a rented canoe or get on a steamboat for a relaxing luncheon tour.

The centerpiece of the Taylors Falls, Minnesota, and the St. Croix Falls, Wisconsin, border is **Interstate State Park** (651-465-5711; www.dnr.state.mn.us/state_parks), just off US 8 in Taylors Falls, known for its rare flora and fauna. Perhaps the most distinguishing features of the park, however, are the dark gray basalt formations scattered throughout the region. Believed to once be full-size mountains, the dense stone was slowly eroded by glaciers into solitary pillars, winding towers, and the deepest glacial potholes in the world.

Aside from the unique geological formations, Interstate State Park is crisscrossed with nature trails that lead visitors through thick forests (breathtaking in the height of autumn), up into the greenstone cliffs and Precambrian basalt flows that encircle the Minnesota side of the park, and then into open fields of tiny purple trilliums and other native wildflowers. Bird-watching is another popular pastime in the park. Eagles and their hatchlings can be seen almost every summer. For another view of the park and its wildlife, catch a ride on the riverboat Taylors Falls Princess. The boat dock is located right next to the entrance to Interstate State Park, and you can buy tickets at the dock. For more information, call (651) 465-6315 or visit www.taylorsfallsboat.com.

For human-made entertainment, head over to **Wild Mountain** (651-465-6315 or 800-447-4958; www.wildmountain.com). To get there, follow MN 95 north to County Road 16, go right onto CR 16 to Wild Mountain. Park visitors can play on one of the giant waterslides, float down an 800-foot lazy river in an inner tube, splash around Wild Adventure Island (an interactive water playground), slide down one of the two 1,700-foot-high alpine slides, or race around on the park's go-kart track. In winter Wild Mountain becomes a ski and snowboard park.

While most of the historic houses in Taylors Falls are private residences and not open to tourists, you can stop by the **Folsom House Museum** at 272 West Government St. (651-465-3125). Listed on the National Register of Historic Places, along with the rest of the Angel Hill neighborhood, the Folsom House is a five-bedroom Greek revival home furnished with the original furniture, books, family pictures, and memorabilia belonging to Minnesota state senator W. H. C. Folsom and his family in the 1800s. The home is open to tour groups Wednesday through Monday from Memorial Day weekend to mid-October each year.

Accommodations and Camping

A few of the historic houses in Taylors Falls have been converted to bed-and-breakfasts. The **Cottage Bed & Breakfast,** 950 Fox Glen Drive (651-465-3595), was designed in the style of an 18th-century English country house and offers

guests a spectacular view of the St. Croix River. The house is furnished with English and French country period pieces and is minutes away from several state parks and Wild Mountain. Even more interesting—especially from a historical perspective—is the **Old Jail Bed & Breakfast** at 349 Government St. (651-465-3112; www.oldjail .com). Exactly what it sounds like, the Old Jail has three furnished suites available to rent, each with its own private bathroom, kitchen, sitting room, and entrance. The Old Jail is located a short walk from the St. Croix River, Interstate State Park, and downtown Taylors Falls. For modern hotel/motel options, search across the river in St. Croix Falls, Wisconsin, which has several chain motels.

For campers, Interstate State Park (651-465-5711; www.dnr.state.mn.us/state_parks) offers woodsy camping with some sites along the St. Croix River. There are sites for both tents and RVs, and some of the sites have electric hookups. The campground also has showers and flush toilets. The brave and well-insulated can camp here in the winter, but you'll have to snowshoe or ski into the campground as the road is not plowed. **Wildwood RV Park & Campground,** 1 mile west of Taylors Falls off US 8 (800-447-4958; www.wildwoodcamping.com), offers sunny or shaded campsites for both tents and RVs, with immediate access to hiking and bicycle trails, a swimming pool, and a miniature golf course. The campground also has well-maintained showers and flush toilets, as well as water, electrical, and sewer hookups.

Restaurants

The Drive In Restaurant at 572 Bench St. (651-465-7831) is a quaint, 1950s-style drive-in with wonderful burgers, shakes, and homemade root beer served by waitresses in hoop skirts wearing roller skates. Patrons of the Drive In also get to enjoy a great view of the St. Croix and the steamboats passing by while they eat either in their cars or at one of the picnic tables set up outside the restaurant.

For indoor dining, stop by **Romayne's on Main,** a sports bar and grill at 391 Bench St. (651-465-4405).

If you're just looking for a cup of coffee, stop by **Coffee Talk,** 479 Bench St. (651-465-6700). The cafe is in a beautifully renovated Victorian house with a small front porch and a gigantic, beautiful flower garden with lots of comfortable, quaint wicker furniture and chairs spread around in the back. The menu includes espresso and coffee drinks and fresh pastries.

IN THE AREA

While driving up to Taylors Falls on MN 95, a stop at the little village of **Marine on St. Croix** is a must. The community, composed of stately old houses surrounded by fantastic flower gardens and ancient hardwood and conifer forests, is so still and quiet and beautiful it feels completely apart from the rest of the world. Established in 1838 as a lumber town, Marine has kept the look of a 19th-century settlement while becoming less an industrial town and more an out-of-the-way retreat for artists and writers. Inspired by the forests, ancient stone silos, and farmhouses that pepper the landscape and, of course, by the St. Croix River, they create their art. Writer Garrison Keillor once compared Marine to his mythical hometown of Lake Wobegon, while the directors of such films as Grumpier Old Men, Beautiful Girls (which was also shot in nearby Stillwater), and The Cure all chose to film on location here.

Marine on St. Croix is mostly made up of residences, but there are several places worth stopping by. The 2-block downtown district on Judd Street, now on the National Register of Historic Places, has a gas station and general store, perfect for making pit stops, and the **Village Scoop** ice-cream parlor. The **Brookside Bar and Grill,** 140 Judd (651-433-2440), has a natural spring-fed stream that runs through its basement and keeps the beer cool. There are also plenty of cross-country skiing and hiking trails that start in town and head out into the forests.

If you take US 8 across the river to Wisconsin, you'll come to **St. Croix Falls, Wisconsin** (715-483-3580; www.scfwi.com). Located on the east side of the St. Croix River, the historic downtown area has many antiques shops and farm stores that sell knickknacks and produce. The countryside around the town is dotted with llama and ginseng farms, ancient farmhouses, and about a dozen abandoned one-room schoolhouses that date from the time when wealthy landowners built schools on their land for their own as well as their employees' children.

If you take US 8 all the way to US 63, you'll reach the town of **Turtle Lake, Wisconsin,** home of the St. Croix Casino & Hotel, 777 US 8 and US 63 (800-U-GO-U-WIN; www.stcroixcasino.com). An easy-paced, almost neighborly feeling casino decorated like a north woods lodge, the St. Croix has live entertainment every weekend.

LIVING HERE

In this section we feature specific information for residents or those planning to relocate here. Topics include real estate, education, health care, and much more.

RELOCATION

Minneapolis–St. Paul has always been an attractive place for relocation, given the region's consistently strong economy, the high quality of life, access to world-class educational resources, the numerous corporations based in the Metro, the lower crime rates than comparable metropolitan areas, and its vibrant cultural scene. Not surprisingly, many persons relocating to Minneapolis and St. Paul come from neighboring states, new Twin Citians accustomed to the cold. In recent years, however, thousands of Hispanic, Hmong, Somali, and Russian immigrants have chosen to come to Minnesota, adding new faces and languages to the Twin Cities community.

This chapter is designed to aid newcomers to the Twin Cities, with details about looking for work, buying real estate, renting, and choosing neighborhoods. We then give you listings for useful resources such as libraries, motor vehicle departments, and tourism bureaus (which can send you relocation packets in addition to comprehensive area info). If you don't find what you are looking for here, ask a native; 9 times out of 10, the famous quality of "Minnesota Nice" will come through and he or she will steer you in the right direction.

FINDING A JOB

The Twin Cities have jobs in manufacturing, banking, retail, airlines, information technology, medicine, law, publishing, state government, insurance, and many other fields. The following are a few sources to consult as you look for your perfect job.

Temp Agencies

Temp agencies can often provide short- or long-term employment in a variety of fields. They can be very useful for newcomers to an area who have not yet secured a full-time job. All the national temp agency chains have offices in the Twin Cities, as do many local agencies and specialized businesses that hire temp workers only in certain industries. The following are a few places to get you started.

ADECCO: THE EMPLOYMENT PEOPLE
www.adeccousa.com
Multiple locations in the Twin Cities
Adecco specializes in clerical, financial, technical, engineering, administrative, and light industrial jobs.

ALLIED PROFESSIONALS
3209 West 76th St., Edina
(952) 832-5101
www.alliedprofessionals.com
Allied focuses on medical and dental temporary positions, including jobs for nurses, X-ray technicians, dentists, medical secretaries, and home care assistance.

CELARITY: STAFFING
CREATIVE PROFESSIONALS
7835 Telegraph Rd., Bloomington
(952) 941-0022
www.freelancecreative.com
Celarity matches workers with jobs in creative fields, including graphic design, marketing, technical writing, editing, proofreading, and Web design.

PRO STAFF
Multiple locations in the Twin Cities
www.prostaff.com
Pro Staff is a national company specializing in hiring temps for companies looking for workers in the fields of accounting, creative services, office support, finance, and light industrial.

STROM ENGINEERING
10505 Wayzata Blvd., Minnetonka
(952) 544-8644 or (800) 205-8732
www.stromengineering.com
Strom Engineering finds temporary and permanent positions in engineering, technical, industrial, personnel, consulting, support services, and more.

TEACHERS ON CALL
3001 Metro Dr., Suite 480, Bloomington
(952) 703-3719
www.teachersoncall.com
Educational professionals can get their foot in the door with the help of Teachers on Call.

Employment Agencies

Of the many employment agencies in the Twin Cities, some specialize in certain fields, while others place candidates in nearly every kind of job. Some employment agencies charge a substantial fee to help you find a job; others charge their fee to the employer that hires you. Ask questions before you sign anything.

ROBERT HALF LEGAL
800 Nicollet Mall, Suite 2700, Minneapolis
(800) 870-8367
www.roberthalflegal.com
Robert Half Legal specializes in helping workers in the legal field find jobs, including lawyers, legal secretaries, and support staff.

CAREER PROFESSIONALS
7301 Ohms Lane, Suite 200, Edina
(952) 835-9922
www.gocpi.com
Career Professionals focuses on recent college graduates, finding entry-level positions in customer service, marketing, financial industries, sales, retail, and administrative settings.

CREATIVE GROUP
800 Nicollet Mall, Suite 2700, Minneapolis
(888) 846-1668
www.creativegroup.com
Creative Group serves clients looking for work in marketing or advertising, including art directors, copywriters, graphic designers, Web site developers, marketing managers, and similar positions.

THOMAS MOORE INC.
(612) 338-4884
www.thomasmooreinc.com
Thomas Moore matches accountants, financial professionals, and information technology specialists with jobs at Twin Cities companies.

State Agencies

MINNESOTA WORKFORCE CENTER
Multiple locations in the Twin Cities
www.MNWorkForceCenter.org
The Minnesota WorkForce Center is operated by the state. It offers free or inexpensive services, including access to its huge database of available jobs, help with resumes and interviewing skills, free local faxing, and free computer usage. After registering with the agency, you can have descriptions of available jobs of interest e-mailed directly to you. Positions run the full spectrum of the Twin Cities economy, including education, human services, state government, and executive management.

Classified Ads

The two major dailies in the Twin Cities, the *Pioneer Press* and the *Star Tribune,* have exhaustive classified job listings, particularly in their Sunday editions. The listings in the *Star Tribune* are generally more extensive, although the *Pioneer Press* is stronger in listings for jobs in the East Metro. Both newspapers allow you to search the classifieds on their Web sites for free (visit www.startribune.com or www.twincities.com). MinnPost, a nonprofit news site, is also getting into the act—see http://jobs.minnpost.com.

Several national Web sites allow you to search for jobs in the Twin Cities based on specific criteria. Some allow you to post your resume to the site for free, and some will e-mail you job openings that match your criteria.

BUYING A NEW HOME

The following are a few places to get you started on your search for a new home in the Cities.

Real Estate Agencies

Here are some of the major, national agencies that work through franchised operations in the Twin Cities metro area, as well as the larger independent agencies that are based here. Many allow you to search for houses through their Web sites.

CENTURY 21–LUGER REALTY
4536 France Ave. South, Edina
(952) 925-3901
www.century21luger.com
Century 21 is one of the largest residential real estate franchisers in the world, with more than 100,000 independently owned and operated franchised broker offices. Its local, independently owned branch, Century 21–Luger Realty, has achieved the highest honor conferred by Century 21, the Centurion Award, ranking it among the top 3 percent of all Century 21 offices worldwide. Luger Century 21 represents the entire Twin Cities metro area, including the outlying suburbs.

COLDWELL BANKER BURNET
(952) 820-4663
Several Twin Cities locations
www.cbburnet.com
The Minnesota division of Coldwell Banker national, Coldwell Banker Burnet makes an effort to make buying and selling homes as convenient as possible for clients, connecting potential buyers with local, accredited mortgage companies and payment plans specifically suited to each individual. More than 25 Coldwell Banker Burnet offices serve the Twin Cities metro area, both the Cities and the surrounding suburbs.

The Minneapolis Lakes office is Coldwell Banker's No. 1 office nationally and is equipped to handle relocation needs, set up mortgages, and refinance existing properties in the entire Twin Cities metro area, with an emphasis on properties in Minneapolis and St. Paul proper. In St. Paul the Highland Park office deals with properties in St. Paul, Mendota Heights, Highland Park, Lilydale, Inver Grove Heights, and Eagan.

COUNSELOR REALTY
7250 France Ave. South, Suite 300, Edina
(952) 921-0911
Several additional Twin Cities locations
www.counselorrealty.com
Established in 1964, Counselor Realty is a local Minnesota company with strong ties to the community and nine branches throughout the metro area. Counselor Realty prides itself on providing superior service tailored to each client's individual needs, as well as total integrity and honesty with clients. The agency has built its reputation through word-of-mouth referrals from satisfied customers and has firmly established itself with the local community by involvement in local charities and causes.

EDINA REALTY
Several Twin Cities locations
(952) 928-5563 or (877) 270-1289
www.edinarealty.com
Founded in 1955 by Emma Rovick, a Minnesota homemaker with three kids and a $2,000 loan, Edina Realty Home Services was built on a strict standard of quality and service that persists today. Now part of a company that is one of the largest real estate companies in the nation with a mortgage division (Edina Realty Mortgage), a title division (Edina Realty Title), and a relocation division (Edina Realty Relocation), Edina has independently run offices throughout the Metro. Edina realtors pride themselves in being able to match customers with their first-choice, affordable dream house as quickly and efficiently as possible without pressuring customers to settle for anything. The company Web site has many tools available for home buyers to use, including a mortgage calculator and full listings of all of the homes Edina represents.

RE/MAX RESULTS
11200 West 78th St., Eden Prairie
(952) 829-2900 or (800) 878-2901
Numerous additional Twin Cities locations
www.results.net
RE/MAX Results specializes in corporate reloca-tions, and, as such, has many highly trained Corporate Relocation Specialists (CRPs) on staff. RE/MAX Results has strategically located offices to service the Metro area's strongest and fastest-growing markets, including Eden Prairie, Plym-outh, and Woodbury.

ROGER FAZENDIN REALTORS
15550 Wayzata Blvd., Wayzata
(952) 473-7000
www.rogerfazendin.com
Founded in 1965, Roger Fazendin Realtors is the largest family-owned and operated residential real estate company in Minnesota. The company has more than 30 professional real estate agents to serve you. The company's agents practice broker reciprocity and have good connections within the local financial community. All of their listings are available on their Web site, including color photos and basic floor plans.

Other Sources for Finding Homes
Both Twin Cities newspapers carry extensive list-ings of homes for sale in the Metro, particularly in their Sunday editions. Pick up a paper, or check out their Web sites: the *Star Tribune* at www.startribune.com or the *Pioneer Press* at www.twincities.com.

There are general sites on the Internet that can be used to find homes in the Cities. The fol-lowing sites allow you to search by city and other specifics, with additional information about find-ing movers, financing, contacts, and more. Visit www.realestate.com, or www.realtor.com

Renting
The Twin Cities offer rental properties from his-toric apartments with hardwood floors, beauti-ful woodwork, and lots of character to modern apartments in complexes with many amenities.

In Minneapolis, one-bedroom apartments aver-age $900–$1,000 per month, and rent is around $700–$800 per month on average for a similar unit in St. Paul.

There are several ways to find an apartment in the Cities. One easy option is to consult with an agency. Two agencies in the Twin Cities with excellent reputations are **Relocation Cen-tral** (2756 Hennepin Ave. South, Minneapolis and other Twin Cities locations, 612-870-0525 or 800-832-7436; www.relocationcentral.com) and **Apartment Mart** (612-927-4591 or 888-254-5899; www.apartmentmartmn.com). Neither business charges a fee to the renter to locate an apartment.

Both Twin Cities newspapers carry extensive listings of apartments and houses for rent in the Metro, particularly in their Sunday editions. Pick up a paper, or check out their Web sites: the *Star Tribune* at www.startribune.com or the *Pioneer Press* at www.twincities.com. The Twin Cities' free weekly newspaper *City Pages* (www.citypages.com) also carries extensive rental ads. The newspaper can be found at most businesses throughout the Metro.

Several national Web sites allow you to search for apartments in the Twin Cities. The following sites should provide some good leads.
- www.craigslist.org
- www.rent.com
- www.rentnet.com
- www.apartments.com

If you are looking for a roommate, one option is to contact **Roommate Referrals,** 4104 Portland Ave. South, Minneapolis; (612) 827-5565; www.tcroommates.com. For a fee this company can match you up with persons looking to share their apartments or, if you've already found a place, with persons looking to move in with someone else. You get a list of matches, allowing you to screen potential roommates by telephone.

NEIGHBORHOODS

Each neighborhood in the Twin Cities has a dis-tinct personality, its own churches; often its own religious, ethnic, or social groups; city parks and schools specific to the neighborhood; and independently owned markets and delis, particularly in Minneapolis and St. Paul. Moving from one neighborhood to another is almost like moving to another town at times, with benefits and drawbacks to each location. With over 100 distinct neighborhoods in the two core cities alone, new residents have the opportunity to choose exactly what kind of place they'd like to live in, whether it's in buzzing Uptown Minneapolis; the family-oriented community of Highland in St. Paul; or one of the pleasant suburbs north, south, east, or west of the Cities. Listed here is just a selection of the major residential neighborhoods in the Twin Cities.

Minneapolis

Como

The Como community of Minneapolis is named after Como Avenue. The thoroughfare continues into St. Paul, where the similarly named Como Park neighborhood is located. The Minneapolis Como neighborhood is filled with middle-income homes. Van Cleve Park is a matter of pride for the community and includes baseball fields, a pool, and a community center. Housing prices tend to be lower than the city's averages.

Downtown

Downtown Minneapolis is one of the Twin Cities' fastest growing neighborhoods. The area is expanding rapidly as high-rises and renovations replace once vacant or dilapidated properties. Living options in downtown Minneapolis include apartments, condominiums, and lofts. In the past few years all three types of properties have been developed next to the old milling district and in the Warehouse District along the Mississippi riverfront. So you're in luck if you're looking to live downtown. However, most properties garner a premium price—seemingly contrary to the laws of economics, the overabundant supply of empty new condos has not dramatically driven down their average price.

The benefits of living downtown are many. There are numerous employment opportunities without the headache of commuting; don't underestimate the convenience of avoiding rush-hour freeway traffic. The cultural and shopping opportunities abound—though active nightlife spreads into northeast, southeast, and south Minneapolis, downtown is at the heart of things. And when the weather becomes inclement, most buildings downtown are connected by skyways, so a downtown resident often doesn't necessarily have to experience the unpleasant elements.

Linden Hills

Linden Hills is nestled between Lake Calhoun and Lake Harriet, two of the City of Lakes' most breathtaking bodies of water. Its location isolates the area from the bustle of Uptown and downtown but allows easy access to the lakes, which offer everything from bicycling and walking to riding a sailboat on a sunny summer day.

Linden Hills' appearance is reminiscent of a small town. Specialty shops and restaurants are located on Linden Avenue. The restaurants offer choices ranging from barbecue to Hmong cuisine. The idyllic shopping district is one of the many selling points of one of Minneapolis's loveliest neighborhoods. Housing prices tend to be considerably higher than Minneapolis averages in this desirable area.

Longfellow

Longfellow may be the Twin Cities' most idealistic neighborhood. The area is lined with beautiful old homes, and many have lovely gardens. The neighborhood has many schools and diverse shopping options. Ethiopian restaurants and diners coexist in this neighborhood, where community is emphasized. Churches of various faiths as well as New Age and wellness businesses can be found in this charming community. Housing prices in this neighborhood are slightly less than the city average.

Marcy-Holmes

Marcy-Holmes is named after the two neighborhood parks located within the community. The neighborhood is a healthy mix of students, senior citizens, college professors, and young families. Beautiful Victorian houses sit side by side with apartments in this neighboorhood next to the University of Minnesota.

Marcy-Holmes is also near many of Minneapolis's attractions. The historic St. Anthony neighborhood borders Marcy-Holmes, and the James J. Hill Stone Arch Bridge, now a pedestrian bridge, offers one of the best views and shortcuts to downtown. Home prices are a little higher compared with the rest of the city.

Northeast

A matter of ongoing debate in the Twin Cities is whether it's acceptable to refer to northeast Minneapolis by its longstanding nickname, "Nordeast"—a formulation playing on the accents of the Polish immigrants who made the neighborhood their home in the early 20th century. The tension over "Nordeast" illuminates the many layers of society in the big chunk of Minneapolis located northeast of the Mississippi River. Historically a working-class, industrial neighborhood, in recent decades it's become a hotbed of artistic activity. The converted Northrup King Building, a behemoth housing dozens upon dozens of art studios, looks like the Death Star to Northeasters looking to save their neighborhood from gentrification—where dwell today's abstract painters may dwell tomorrow's luxury condos. At the moment, though, Northeast is very safe from becoming Edina: With many homes for sale at relatively affordable prices, it's popular with young familes, particularly those who enjoy a little gallerygoing every now and again.

Northside

When one local news source published an article about the possible threat of gentrification in north Minneapolis, a resident of that neighborhood responded with a tart comment: "Gentrification? I wish! I have two vacant homes across the street from me." In recent years the section of Minneapolis north of downtown and west of the Mississippi River has become best known as ground zero in the foreclosure crisis, which added to the challenges of one of the Cities' least well-off neighborhoods. What's less often discussed are the neighborhood's strengths: a strong community, a developing arts scene, and, yes, a location near downtown, the river, and parks that give it the potential for (if not quite yet the reality of) significant gentrification. If you're a new transplant, the Northside probably won't be at the tip of people's tongues when they're listing potential places for you to take root, but the neighborhood has some real treasures if you take the time to look for them.

Powderhorn

The Powderhorn neighborhood takes its name from a lake shaped like a colonial-era gunpowder vessel; that lake sits in an eponymous park located just south of Lake Street in south-central Minneapolis. Powderhorn and the Phillips neighborhood just to its north are the crossroads of south Minneapolis, home to a busy and dense community in which recent immigrants—particularly Latinos—are highly visible. Familes who have called the neighborhood home for generations live in compact houses and small apartment buildings next to new arrivals from other countries and other neighborhoods, including an increasing stream of hipsters and artists looking for something more affordable than Uptown. To see Powderhorn at its proudest, make your way to the annual MayDay parade organized by In the Heart of the Beast, when giant puppets troop gaily through Powderhorn Park, followed by what seems like just about everyone in the city.

Prospect Park

The Prospect Park neighborhood is recognizable because of its historic water tower, which overlooks the Minneapolis community. The water tower, no longer in use, sits atop the highest point in Minneapolis and is one of the most scenic vistas in the area. The neighborhood is composed mainly of classic, expensive homes that sit on the many winding roads surrounding the water tower. The homes in Prospect Park are some of the most attractive in the Twin Cities. Prospect Park has easy access to all of the Twin Cities major thoroughfares and is centrally located between downtown Minneapolis and downtown St. Paul.

South Minneapolis

Technically, the term "south Minneapolis" can be applied to anything south of downtown—that is, the southern geographical half of the city—but it's most often used to describe the environs south of Lake Street, a quiet and attractive expanse with many stunning homes. Rather than a crossroads, this section of the city feels like a cocoon, where residents who can afford the relatively high housing prices (there are some relatively affordable pockets) enjoy access to Lake Nokomis, the business hub on I-494 immediately south of the city, and cherished neighborhood establishments like Kings Wine Bar and Java Jack's.

i The Minneapolis Neighborhood Revitalization Program (NRP) was founded in 1987 to distribute revenues from downtown real estate taxes to the city's residential neighborhoods. The funds were approximately evenly distributed among the city's neighborhoods, a policy that was criticized because some neighborhoods had substantially more pressing infrastructure needs than others. The classic example of a questionable use of NRP funds was a gorgeous but small bridge crossing Minnehaha Creek that became known as the "million-dollar bridge."

Uptown

Cherished by some as the Twin Cities' most creative neighborhood while disparaged by others as a "Yuptown" overrun by chain stores, Uptown is the inescapable home base for urban adventurers of all stripes. The sheer density of restaurants, bars, galleries, and affordable (not to say run-down) housing options makes Uptown the default destination for the Cities' most social

residents—as well as the undisputed capital of the local singles scene.

A favorite spot for summer recreation and relaxation, Uptown borders Lake of the Isles and Lake Calhoun, each a short walk from the neighborhood's commercial center. Housing prices vary by proximity to the lakes: The farther west you go, the more you pay. The fact that you can start in the pricey East Isles neighborhood and, crossing first Hennepin and then Lyndale in a matter of blocks, find yourself in the funky, sometimes sketchy Whittier neighborhood is part of what gives Uptown its distinctly diverse character.

St. Paul

Como Park

Not to be confused with the Como neighborhood in Minneapolis, St. Paul's Como Park neighborhood centers on Como Park, Como Zoo, and Como Lake. Residents here enjoy many pleasant neighborhood coffee shops and restaurants, and many of the bungalows and smaller two-story homes are reasonably priced.

Downtown

Downtown St. Paul is the Rodney Dangerfield of Twin Cities neighborhoods—it gets no respect. It's often compared derisively to downtown Minneapolis as a place where after 5 p.m. you can pretty much set up a board and play Scrabble in the street. There's some truth to that stereotype—the city has indeed struggled for generations to give its downtown a sense of bustling vitality—but it's not entirely fair either. From the old-school cultural hub of Rice Park on its west side to the up-and-coming Lowertown area on its east side (a zone that's now branding itself as an entertainment district and "the new Uptown"), there's quite a bit to do in downtown St. Paul, and some quite affordable housing options alongside the expected high-end condos.

East Side

St. Paul's East Side is not a destination neighborhood: It's a place where people live. Home to a long succession of ethnic and immigrant communities from Scandinavians to Latinos, the East Side is perhaps best known as home to 3M, whose water tower has become a neighborhood landmark. The East Side is relatively affordable, which means that there are some great bargains to be had among the area's classic housing stock.

Frogtown

Arguably St. Paul's most ethnically diverse community, the Frogtown neighborhood has been a magnet for immigrants for many years. With some of the lowest housing prices in the city, who could blame them? Property values for these same houses are on the rise (with the rest of St. Paul), as are the small storefronts and restaurants owned by the Thai, African-American, Vietnamese, Cambodian, and Hmong residents who populate this area.

Highland Park

Baby Boomers remember Highland Park as St. Paul's "sirloin section"—its carefully plotted streets and brand-new colonial-style homes were considered the height of urban luxury in the postwar years. Today those homes' very newness is a liability, as wealthier residents choose to renovate the vintage housing stock farther north. Still, Highland Park remains St. Paul's most genteel community, a very attractive destination particularly for families with children.

The area surrounds the shops and restaurants centered at the intersection of Ford Parkway and Cleveland Avenue South, with numerous specialty retailers, bookstores, ethnic restaurants (as well as fast-food fare), and a major grocery store within a short drive from home. Housing prices tend to be significantly higher than St. Paul averages.

Macalester-Groveland

Macalester-Groveland (Mac-Groveland to locals) has always been one of the Twin Cities' premier urban neighborhoods and in recent years has become white-hot as creative professionals have sought the neighborhood for its charming historic homes, its livability (parking is never a problem), and especially for its proximity to insti-

tutions of higher learning like Macalester College, the University of St. Thomas, and St. Catherine University. The neighborhood has several excellent schools and is filled with a growing number of diverse local businesses. The neighborhood borders the Mississippi River to the west. Home prices tend to be much higher than St. Paul averages but some reasonably priced rental units in historic buildings can be found here.

i There's no auto plant in America occupying such lucrative real estate as that occupied by the St. Paul Ford Plant, which sits in Highland Park between the neighborhood's central shopping district and the Mississippi River. The plant remains in operation as this guide goes to press, but Ford has announced plans to close the plant and redevelop the land—likely as housing. The status of that project is being watched with great interest by people across the Twin Cities—particularly by the plant's neighbors in St. Paul.

Midway

The Midway neighborhood is named for its location: midway between downtown St. Paul to its east and the Minneapolis border to its west. The neighborhood, which runs along and to the north of University Avenue, is representative of the people who call inner-city St. Paul home: a large portion of the local Hmong population and other recent immigrant groups as well as the old-school German Catholics who display shrines to the Virgin Mary in their front yards. The neighborhood is relatively affordable now, but that is apt to change relatively quickly in coming years as the Central Corridor light-rail line is installed down the length of University. Small-business owners are sensing the end of an era—and, indeed, it just may be. What comes next for Midway is anyone's guess.

Union Park

Every neighborhood has its partisans, but Union Park residents can make an unusually precise case for why their neighborhood is the best in the metro area. It sits right at the geographic center of the Twin Cities, it's located alongside the Mississippi River, central highways I-94 and I-35E cut right through it—as does Summit Avenue, the Twin Cities' most beautiful boulevard—and housing options are diverse and attractive. (Almost no one actually calls it "Union Park," though that's its official name—people will say they live in "Merriam Park," "Summit-University," or "Lex-Ham," depending on their location within Union Park's wide zone.) Housing prices in Union Park tend to be significantly higher than city averages.

West Side

Newcomers to the Twin Cities have their work cut out for them trying to make sense of the west side of St. Paul. For one thing, "the west side" is not the same as "West St. Paul," a separate city located contiguous to "the west side" of the city of St. Paul. Further, neither the west side nor West St. Paul are really west of the rest of St. Paul: They're south, qualifying as "west" only in a fantasy world where "north" is defined not by the earth's geographic pole but by the direction of the Mississippi River's flow. Got that? If not, that's okay: All you need to know is that the west side is home to a large population of families who enjoy its affordable housing, convenient location, and oft-spectacular views of downtown St. Paul. It's also notable as the historic center of the Twin Cities' Latino population, who make the District del Sol a festive and bustling desination for residents of all ethnicities.

North
Forest Lake

Founded in 1855 by Louis Scheil, a German immigrant, this area has long been a summer haven for tourists from Chicago and beyond and is now known as one of the most popular resort towns in the area. The city retains some of its small-town charm, but you'll have to run an astonishing gamut of fast food and traffic to get to it. Activities in Forest Lake center on Lakeside Memorial Park, where outdoor concerts and other cultural events take place at the gazebo in

summer. Ice-skating and ice fishing are popular in winter. Housing prices are on par with St. Paul city averages.

New Brighton

The land around New Brighton was originally inhabited by the Dakota and Ojibwe tribes. They were drawn to the area for its rich farmland and abundant wetlands, which were perfect for growing wild rice. French and English settlers first came to the area in the mid-1800s, looking for land to homestead and farm. By 1858 the settlement was named Mounds View Township, which was later broken up into the communities of New Brighton and Mounds View. Today New Brighton has a population just over 22,000, and many of the residents work within the city limits at the industries that have been established here. Housing prices tend to be somewhat higher than Twin Cities averages.

Roseville

Rose Township was originally named for Isaac Rose, one of the first white settlers in the area. Rose and his family settled on a claim near what is now St. Anthony Road and Fairview Avenue—look for the historical marker if you happen to pass by.

Today Roseville is a residential community and thriving commercial district of pleasant houses with expansive gardens, specialty shops, a major mall, many big box retailers, and restaurants. The city of Roseville has 23 park sites, ranging in size from 2 to 220 acres, including a large concert amphitheater in Central Park. The Guidant John Rose Minnesota Oval & Roseville Ice Arena have outdoor and indoor rinks available for hockey, figure skating, open skating, and speed skating.

Most of the residential areas are filled with split-level ramblers and bungalows in this suburb, with housing prices a little higher than those in the Twin Cities.

Shoreview

Socrates A. Thompson, the first white settler on the land that makes up present-day Shoreview, came to the area from St. Paul looking for a good place to farm. He decided on the east shores of Turtle Lake and was soon joined by other settlers from as far away as Germany and Switzerland.

In 1941 the U.S. government opened the Army Arsenal plant on the west side of Shoreview, bringing many new workers into the area. This expanse of residential property turned Shoreview from a small, lakeside, rural community into a Twin Cities suburb, and the township was officially made a city on January 1, 1974.

Today Shoreview is surrounded by expanses of farmland, lakes, and woods. Residents enjoy proximity to the Twin Cities as well as a strong sense of community, and housing prices are similar to averages in Minneapolis.

Vadnais Heights

Since its humble roots as a small rural farming community, Vadnais Heights has grown into the successful, thriving residential suburb and business community it is today. Within the city limits can be found many open, protected wetlands, lakes, and ponds, around which have sprung idyllic neighborhoods with relatively expensive houses. A solid industrial core and many service manufacturing jobs employ more than 5,000 residents, while many others make the easy commute into the Twin Cities. Housing prices are a little above St. Paul averages.

South
Apple Valley

Originally a small farming community named Lebanon, Apple Valley and its low-cost farmland first started drawing city developers as early as 1960. When the city was incorporated in 1968, the area was renamed Apple Valley for developer Orrin Thompson Homes's habit of putting an apple tree on every residential lot. Located a dozen or so miles south of Minneapolis and St. Paul off MN 38, Apple Valley today is a small business and residential community. Apple Valley is also home to the Minnesota Zoo, one of the state's best-known attractions. Housing prices tend to be a little lower than Minneapolis averages.

Bloomington

With its proximity to the Minneapolis–St. Paul International Airport and more than 30 hotels, Bloomington is often the first and last stop of visitors to the Twin Cities. Home of the Mall of America and several prestigious golf courses and country clubs, as well as more than 85,000 residents, Bloomington is a city in the middle of an economic boom. Because of Bloomington's proximity to Minneapolis and St. Paul, this is a choice community for those who don't want to live in the Cities but have to commute there for work. The city is surrounded by open country and maintained parklands. Housing prices tend to be a little higher than Twin Cities averages.

i Irwin Norling was an accomplished amateur photographer who captured Bloomington's dramatic midcentury transition from cozy small town to suburban strip. His fascinating photos are collected in the book *Suburban World*, edited by Brad Zellar.

Eagan

Aside from its rich agricultural history, Eagan has a thriving business community. Major employers in the area include Cray Research, Blue Cross–Blue Shield, Northwest Airlines, Thomson West Publishing, and Coca-Cola. Eagan features several beautiful, large parks, including Lebanon Hills Regional Park and the Caponi Art Park, which features an outdoor sculpture garden. Housing prices are near Twin Cities averages.

Eden Prairie

Eden Prairie is a refuge for commuters who want a quiet, beautiful town to escape to after a busy day at work. It's surrounded by parklands, including Bryant Lake Regional Park and its boating and fishing lake. Housing prices are far above Twin Cities averages.

Edina

No, it doesn't actually stand for "Every Day I Need Attention." Edina has long been one of the Twin Cities' wealthiest suburbs, and as such is the butt of everyone else's jokes about rich suburbanites.

Edina is what it is: the Cadillac of suburbs. Look to Edina if you can afford the costly housing and if you're seeking a location convenient to the business hub on I-494 (home to Best Buy and other large companies). Unsurprisingly, Edina's public schools are among the very best in the state.

Prior Lake

Located in the southwestern Metro area, Prior Lake centers on the 16-square-mile lake that shares its name. Of Prior Lake's attractions, perhaps the best known is Mystic Lake Casino, Minnesota's largest gaming and entertainment establishment. Prior Lake is also home to the world-class Wilds Golf Club. With its many swimming beaches and boating marinas, Prior Lake is a favorite recreation spot for watersport enthusiasts. Lakeside living, however, is linked with expensive homes; the farther you get away from the waterfront, the more reasonably priced the houses get. On average, housing prices in Prior Lake are well above Twin Cities averages.

Savage

The city of Savage is a dynamic community offering many housing options, all with easy access to the surrounding urban areas. An interesting mix of older homes and new construction, Savage is the fastest-growing and most populated community in Scott County. Housing prices are somewhat higher than Twin Cities averages.

East

Afton

Nestled between wooded river bluffs and the St. Croix River, the historic town of Afton is a rural community of approximately 3,000. Located on the eastern edge of Washington County along the St. Croix River, the quiet residential community has a small business district composed of restaurants, marinas, unique shops, and services. The village is surrounded by parks, farms, and nature preserves, and the residential area is made up of mostly upper-bracket houses. This highly desirable community has housing prices more than double Twin Cities averages.

Bayport

Settled more than 150 years ago, Bayport, known as South Stillwater until 1922, was known as a bootlegger's paradise during Prohibition. Today the small community on the St. Croix River boasts a charming downtown area, including a park, several marinas, and quaint little shops and restaurants in a downtown made up of turn-of-the-20th-century brick-and-wood buildings. Formerly a center of the lumber industry, today Bayport's main employer is Andersen Windows, one of the country's largest producer of windows and patio doors. Housing prices are somewhat higher than Twin Cities averages.

Lake Elmo

With the growth of the Twin Cities metro area, city dwellers seeking the quiet life have found Lake Elmo. Located on the old mail trail between Stillwater and St. Paul, the city boasts a big blue lake of the same name and eight other smaller lakes as well. Lake Elmo is a historic town that has kept its quaint, turn-of-the-20th-century feel. Because it has resisted growth as its neighbors have expanded, it has retained its small-town feel. Downtown Lake Elmo is made up of old brick-and-wood buildings and an old grain elevator, which have been turned into restaurants, antiques shops, and other businesses. Lake Elmo is also home to the Washington County Fairgrounds and an annual August county fair. The town's population is around 7,000 residents. Housing prices in Lake Elmo tend to be far higher than averages for the Twin Cities.

Mahtomedi/Grant

Founded in the mid-1800s as a Methodist summer colony, Mahtomedi soon became a desirable location for summer homes and resorts due to its proximity to beautiful White Bear Lake. Both Mahtomedi and the nearby former township of Grant, one of Minnesota's newest cities, are dotted with hobby farms and working farms as well as natural areas set aside for parkland. White Bear Lake is deep enough for waterskiing and boating in the summertime and is a popular ice fishing spot in the winter.

Many of the homes in Grant are located on the rolling acres of hobby, horse, or agricultural farms, while Mahtomedi offers more variety, including town houses, condominiums, and newer residential developments centered around small parks.

Housing prices in both areas tend to be considerably higher than Twin Cities averages.

Maplewood

Maplewood's three most distinct features are the Maplewood Community Center—containing a fully appointed fitness center with a pool, a senior lounge, and a craft center—the Maplewood Mall, and the worldwide corporate headquarters of the 3M company, a major employer in the area.

Like many other Twin Cities suburbs, Maplewood is rich in parks and recreation areas. The city-funded Maplewood Nature Center offers environmental programs for children and adults, with interactive displays and marked trails for seasonal use.

Maplewood housing prices are generally on par with Twin Cities averages.

North St. Paul

North St. Paul manages to combine the benefits of a bustling commercial and industrial district with the feel of a quiet residential area, with tree-lined neighborhoods, a historic downtown area, and many community events along the shores of Silver Lake. Housing prices tend to be somewhat lower than Twin Cities averages.

Stillwater

Stillwater on the St. Croix River is home to some of the finest examples of 19th-century residential architecture in the state. A short drive from the downtown area are homes built in the Queen Anne, second empire, and stick styles of the 1800s as well as the prairie style of the 1900s. Many of the older homes have been restored and reopened as bed-and-breakfasts.

Given the beautiful setting and vibrant community, Stillwater properties are some of the most expensive in the region, particularly if you have your heart set on a Victorian masterpiece with a turret and big front porch.

White Bear Lake

Set along the clear waters of White Bear Lake and located just 20 minutes from St. Paul, the city of White Bear Lake has a beautiful, turn-of-the-20th-century downtown area with modern residential areas situated around parks and wetlands. Golf courses, beaches, lakes, and nature trails can be found within the city limits, and White Bear Lake itself is the largest lake within the metropolitan area, making it a great place for boating and fishing in the summer and cross-country skiing and ice fishing during the winter.

Housing prices tend to be slightly higher than Twin Cities averages.

Woodbury

With both beautiful residential neighborhoods and a thriving business community, Woodbury has enjoyed a population explosion over the past 15 years. Commercial development has helped create a strong community with a high quality of life, making Woodbury a great place to live and do business. Although most of Woodbury is strictly residential, the city is also home to businesses from large corporations to small businesses and retail outlets.

Citizens of Woodbury enjoy four community parks: the Bielenberg Sports Center, Carver Lake, Ojibway, and Tamarack Nature Preserve, the latter three offering more than 120 acres of parkland connected by paved and turf trails. Woodbury has many neighborhood parks, too, with amenities such as basketball courts and ballfields.

Housing prices in Woodbury tend to be considerably higher than Twin Cities averages.

West

Deephaven

A small city surrounded by protected bays and woodlands, Deephaven is located on the south shore of Lake Minnetonka. The city is so close to the water, in fact, that few of its residents live more than 1 mile from the beaches of this beautiful lake. Deephaven has more than 76 acres of parkland, with Thorpe Park being the largest, offering picnic areas, a lighted hockey rink, basketball courts, and many flower gardens.

Housing prices tend to be considerably higher than Twin Cities averages.

Excelsior

The historic town of Excelsior is a perfect blend of the old and the new, combining a villagelike atmosphere of antiques shops and inns with modern hotels and restaurants. First settled in 1853, downtown Excelsior is full of old buildings and houses that date from the turn of the 20th century. Excelsior borders Carver Park Reserve and its 3,500 acres of parkland, campgrounds, and horseback and snowmobile trails, as well as Minnewashta Regional Park and its public swimming beach.

Housing prices in Excelsior are far higher than Twin Cities averages.

Minnetonka

Residents of this Twin Cities metro suburb may just have the best of both worlds—a thriving, competitive business community set in a beautiful residential area along the shores of Lake Minnetonka. Minnetonka has more than 40 city parks and is set close to the shores of Lake Minnetonka. Careful city planning over the years has allowed its beautiful woodlands, wetlands, and creeks to survive intact inside the city itself.

A highly desirable area, Minnetonka housing prices are far above Twin Cities averages.

i Tonka trucks were created by Mound Metalcraft of Mound, Minnesota. (The line is now produced by Hasbro.) The trucks' name is the Dakota word for "big," and in part honors nearby Lake Minnetonka.

Orono

This picturesque residential community is surrounded by many neighborhood and city parks, including Noerenberg Memorial Park, and five public marinas. City ordinances require minimum sizes for residential lots, so each home owner has at least two acres of land, and many home owners own five acres of land.

Housing prices tend to be far higher than Twin Cities averages.

Wayzata

Pronounced "why-ZEH-tah," Wayzata is a small city located on the north shore of Lake Minnetonka. The name comes from the Dakotas' god of the north, a giant who blew cold winds from his mouth. Today this area is a beautiful spot for a weekend retreat as well as a luxurious residential area with access to many downtown specialty shops, restaurants, and boutiques. The town has the only free trolley service in the Twin Cities, which takes visitors and residents around town spring through fall.

Housing prices are well above Twin Cities averages.

LIBRARIES

MINNEAPOLIS CENTRAL LIBRARY
300 Nicollet Mall, Minneapolis
(952) 847-8000
Fourteen additional locations in Minneapolis
www.hclib.org
The new central Minneapolis Public Library opened to the public on May 20, 2006, and the Cesar Pelli–designed masterpiece is a spectacular building worth a visit even if you're not looking for a book. For casual browsers, the new library has nearly 100 percent of its collection accessible to the public, a noticeable improvement from the 15 percent that was available in the old library. The transparent building is extremely energy efficient and allows readers to page through their finds under natural lighting. The windows are specially designed to avoid damage to fragile books from ultraviolet light. The building includes numerous meeting rooms, an auditorium, areas specifically for young children and teens, a New Americans Center for non–English-speaking immigrants, a cafe, a bookstore, vast computer services, and a connection to the Minneapolis Skyway System. The library will also be home to the Minnesota Planetarium and Space Discovery Center, scheduled for completion in 2010. As of a recent merger between the Hennepin County Library system and the Minneapolis Public Libraries, the Minneapolis Central Library is now the hub of all public libraries in the county.

RAMSEY COUNTY LIBRARY
4570 North Victoria St., Shoreview
(651) 486-2300
Six additional locations in Ramsey County suburbs
www.ramsey.lib.mn.us

The Ramsey County Library allows residents of the St. Paul suburbs of Arden Hills, Maplewood, Mounds View, North St. Paul, Roseville, Shoreview, and White Bear Lake convenient access to books and other materials. The seven libraries house more than one million items, and patrons can also access the Internet from library terminals, use Microsoft Word at all branches, and enjoy such amenities as a Dunn Bros. cafe in the Roseville branch library. Any resident of the seven-country metropolitan area can get a library card.

ST. PAUL PUBLIC LIBRARY
90 West Fourth St., St. Paul
(651) 266-7073
Twelve additional locations in St. Paul
www.sppl.org

The elegant St. Paul Public Library building in downtown St. Paul dates from 1917. Having reopened in 2002 after a $15.9 million renovation, the beautiful Italian Renaissance revival building brashly shows off its historical and artistic interior. The renovation included restoration of the building's detailed hand-painted ceilings, Mankato stone and plaster details, and compressed cork floors, as well as updating the library's telecommunications connections to allow high-speed Internet access. The library building is connected to downtown St. Paul's skyway system via a tunnel between the St. Paul Hotel and RiverCentre. Other features include an enlarged children's room, larger public browsing areas, a cafe on the first floor, and a new entrance from Kellogg Boulevard. St. Paul Public Library cards are available to residents of St. Paul, but nearly all residents of Minnesota can borrow books from the library using their home library card.

UNIVERSITY OF MINNESOTA LIBRARIES
Wilson Library, 309 19th Ave. South, West Bank Campus, Minneapolis
(612) 624-4520
www.lib.umn.edu

The University of Minnesota–Twin Cities Libraries contain the largest collection of materials in the state, including some 6 million books, 37,000 periodical subscriptions, 2.6 million government documents, and 400,000 maps. The library system's extensive holdings are housed in five major libraries and 14 branch locations on the U of M's campuses in Minneapolis and St. Paul. In addition to the main Wilson Library general collection, the system includes such specialized collections as the Veterinary Medical Library on the St. Paul campus, the Science and Engineering Library within Walter Library on the East Bank of the Minneapolis campus, and the Eric Sevareid Journalism Library in Murphy Hall on the East Bank. The U of M Library is also the regional depository for Minnesota and South Dakota of all publications produced by the U.S. Government Printing Office, and the library boasts more than one million full-text journal articles stored in electronic databases.

University students, faculty, staff, and research assistants enjoy free borrowing privileges to the library's collections. The general public can borrow books and other materials from the library by joining the Friends of the Libraries, with a minimum donation of $80 annually, or by requesting an interlibrary loan at a public library. The hours of Wilson Library and the other libraries and collections on campus vary widely, depending on the individual library's policies and the academic schedule of the university. Call Wilson Library for more information.

MOTOR VEHICLE REGISTRATION AND DRIVER'S LICENSES

MINNESOTA DEPARTMENT OF PUBLIC SAFETY DRIVER AND VEHICLE SERVICES
445 Minnesota St., Suite 168, St. Paul
(651) 297-2005
Numerous locations throughout the Twin Cities metro area
www.dps.state.mn.us/dvs

As a new resident of Minnesota, you have 60 days after moving to the Twin Cities to register your vehicle and obtain a driver's license if your vehicle is registered in another state and/or you have a driver's license from another state. Commercial vehicle drivers have 30 days to obtain a commercial driver's license.

To obtain Minnesota plates and register your vehicle, you will need the current vehicle registration card or certificate of title, your insurance information, the odometer reading from your vehicle, a driver's license (or other valid form of identification) and, if you are leasing your vehicle, a copy of the leasing agreement. The cost to register your vehicle is based on set fees for plates, filing, public safety tax, and title, as well as on the value of your vehicle for the registration tax. The registration tax for first-time registration of a vehicle in Minnesota is based on the value of the vehicle and can run into the neighborhood of $200, with annual renewals about half the cost of initial registration.

If you have a valid driver's license from another state, you will need to pass a knowledge test and vision check to obtain a Minnesota driver's license. If your license from another state has been expired for more than a year or you move to Minnesota from another country, you will also need to pass a skill (road) test. You will need to present your current driver's license when applying for a Minnesota license. A regular driver's license for adults over 21 costs $43; for those under 21, it's $23.

You don't need to be a resident of the town or county in which the Motor Vehicle Registrar Office is located to obtain a driver's license or vehicle plates there, and it is often a much shorter waiting time at suburban offices than at the main offices in Minneapolis and St. Paul. For a full list of Twin Cities registrar offices, contact the Minnesota Department of Public Safety at (651) 297-2005 or www.dps.state.mn.us.

TOURISM BUREAUS

Both Minneapolis and St. Paul have convention and visitor bureaus with a wealth of information about the Cities, on such topics as relocation, current arts and sporting events, restaurants, real estate agents, neighborhoods, and many other resources.

The Greater Minneapolis Convention and Visitors Association, 250 Marquette Ave. South, Minneapolis (888-676-MPLS; www.minneapolis .org), offers a visitor guide, a complete listing of visitor and resident resources, travel/hotel reservations, events calendars, and discounted tickets to certain events.

The St. Paul Convention and Visitors Authority, 175 West Kellogg Blvd., Suite 502, St. Paul (651-265-4900 or 800-627-6101; www.stpaulcvb .org), offers detailed information about the city's attractions, restaurants, hotels, neighborhoods, and more. A free visitor kit, with much information useful to new Twin Citians, is available through the bureau.

RETIREMENT

The Twin Cities and its suburbs are home to more than 100 retirement communities and nursing homes, many of which are located on scenic lakefronts or surrounded by parklike grounds. This chapter covers just a few of the residences senior citizens have to choose from in the greater Twin Cities metro area and is in no way meant to be all-inclusive. For more information about nursing homes, contact the Minnesota Department of Health (651-201-5000; www .health.state.mn.us), Care Providers of Minnesota (952-854-2844; www.careproviders.org), the Minnesota Health and Housing Alliance (651-645-4545; www.mhha.com), or the AARP (866-554-5381; www.aarp.org/states/mn).

Senior citizens are a vital force in the Twin Cities, as evidenced in many successful political campaigns that have run primarily on senior concerns and issues. This is in no small part because of the Twin Cities being home to some of the most dynamic senior rights advocacy groups, including the Gray Panthers, the AARP, the Minnesota Senior Federation, and many of the other lesser-known organizations that are listed in this chapter.

Retirement Communities

BETHANY COVENANT VILLAGE
2309 Hayes St. NE, Minneapolis
(612) 781-2691
www.bethanycovenantvillage.org
Located in northeastern Minneapolis, Bethany Covenant Village is a 16-room Christian facility that provides care to senior citizens who need assistance in their day-to-day living. Their supportive and sensitive staff provides assistance with such activities as dressing, bathing, medication management, and anything else that may be needed to help residents retain their independence. A licensed nurse supervises medical management; rehabilitation services include physical, occupational, speech, and intravenous therapy.

Studios and one-bedroom apartments are furnished and decorated by the residents. Each unit has a private bathroom, carpeting, drapes, individual climate control, master TV antenna, telephone outlets, and an emergency call system.

BROOKDALE SENIOR LIVING
17 locations across Minnesota
www.brookdaleliving.com
Brookdale Senior Living offers assisted living to older adults who want to retain their independence while receiving the personal services they need. The communities emphasize freestanding residences specifically designed for individuals with memory impairments such as Alzheimer's disease. Residents live in their own private apartments, complete with kitchens and private bathrooms, receiving individual care and personal assistance in a cheerful, homelike atmosphere. This allows residents to enjoy privacy yet still have access to a full-time professional staff that caters to their personal needs.

THE COMMONS ON MARICE
1380 Marice Dr., Eagan
(651) 688-9999
www.thecommonsonmarice.com
The Commons on Marice is an elegant senior living community offering independent and assisted living, a progressive memory center, and intergenerational learning opportunities. The luxurious apartments include a full kitchen and a private bathroom with a walk-in shower equipped with grab bars. The residents' common grounds feature a two-story atrium where resi-

dents can tend a garden, enjoy entertainment, or simply gather for conversation with neighbors. The library, fireplace, lounge, and billiards room provide residents with additional opportunities to gather.

The Commons' main claim to fame is fine dining—meals are prepared from scratch by an executive chef using only the finest ingredients. All meals are chosen by residents from a changing and extensive menu, and meals are taken when the resident chooses to do so and not on any predetermined schedule. There's also an ice-cream parlor, a chapel, and a Wellness Center offering everything from massage to aromatherapy. The Commons offers around-the-clock staffing, a 24-hour emergency call system, and programs aimed at three levels of living, from independent residences to assisted living to a Memory Center for residents with Alzheimer's.

i For up-to-date information about retirement communities in the Twin Cities, *New Lifestyle* magazine has a great Web site at www.NewLifeStyles.com listing regularly updated community overviews.

COVENANT VILLAGE
5800 St. Croix Ave. North, Golden Valley
(763) 546-6125 or (800) 296-4114
www.covenantretirement.com
Covenant Village is the first accredited continuing-care retirement community in Minnesota. Loving care is the essence of Covenant Retirement Communities, from assistance with daily activities to rehabilitative care following injury or illness to long-term skilled nursing care. Established in 1886, Covenant Village provides homes to more than 5,000 senior adults in 14 retirement communities found throughout the country.

Apartments of various sizes include a full kitchen and balcony, and some are equipped with dens and fireplaces. Housekeeping, maintenance, dining services, and amenities such as recreational facilities all contribute to residents' comfort, and regular group activities are scheduled. Residents enjoy the comforts of a community that cares for them physically, socially,

emotionally, and spiritually. Wellness programs, exercise facilities and programs, dietary services, and residential and nursing services are all a part of the Covenant facilities, and everything from assisted living to rehabilitative care is available from a licensed skilled nursing facility located on the grounds.

LAKE RIDGE CARE CENTER AND LAKE RIDGE MANOR
310 Lake Blvd. South, Buffalo
(763) 682-1434
www.elimcare.org/lrcc.htm
Located just 30 minutes west of Minneapolis in a quiet rural community, Lake Ridge Care Center (short- or long-term nursing care) and Lake Ridge Manor (assisted living) combine exceptional professional health care with personal attention to help residents achieve their highest level of ability and independence. Providing a family-like, Christian community, the care center and manor's gracious common grounds overlook beautiful Lake Buffalo. A licensed nurse supervises medical management; rehabilitation services include physical, occupational, and speech.

Residents are in charge of personally furnishing their single or double (private or semiprivate) residences. Each apartment has a private bathroom, carpeting, draperies, individual climate control, a master TV antenna, telephone outlets, and an emergency call system.

RIDGEPOINTE
12600 Marion Lane West
Minnetonka
(952) 540-6200
www.ridgepointeseniorliving.com
RidgePointe offers one- and two-bedroom apartments surrounded by gardens to active, independent seniors and adults. The complex is located conveniently near shopping centers, restaurants, medical facilities, theaters, and cultural centers. The complex itself has a group dining room, a fitness center, a hair salon, a convenience store, and hobby rooms on-site. There's also daily scheduled transportation to shopping, medical appointments, and church services for resi-

dents; and amenities figured into the apartment rent include weekly housekeeping, a complimentary continental breakfast, all utilities except telephone and electric, basic cable television, individual climate control, and centrally located elevators in each apartment building. For recreation, there's a card room, a complete library, a billiards room, and a tropical atrium and art gallery connecting the resident buildings.

TWIN LAKE NORTH
4539 58th Ave. North, Brooklyn Center
(763) 533-1168
http://langnelson.com/twinlakenorth.html
Twin Lake North's independent living six-apartment townhouses are surrounded by beautiful grounds that allow residents countrylike comfort with city convenience. One- and two-bedroom apartments are available, and rent includes utilities plus an attached garage. Many apartments have private balconies. Additional amenities include daily activities, garden plots, a fitness center, a clubhouse, a heated pool, and free van service.

SERVICES AND PROGRAMS IN THE METRO AREA

Many organizations in the Twin Cities are concerned with protecting the welfare of our senior community. These organizations deal with everything from helping senior citizens and their families choose a suitable retirement community to matching grandparentless children with volunteer senior citizens. For more information about senior advocacy groups in the Twin Cities, contact the AARP at (866) 554-5381 or www.aarp .org/states/mn.

ALZHEIMER'S ASSOCIATION, MINNESOTA/ NORTH DAKOTA CHAPTER
4550 West 77th St., Suite 200, Edina
(952) 830-0512
www.alzmndak.org
Formed by family caregivers who sought support and help, the nonprofit Alzheimer's Association is available to answer questions about Alzheimer's disease and to direct you to services, educational workshops, support groups, and information in the Twin Cities.

i For informed referrals to medical programs, specially trained personnel, or special housing arrangements, contact the Minnesota Home Care Association at (651) 635-0607 or www.mnhomecare.org.

CARELINK
(952) 854-2844
www.carelinkusa.com
CARELINK is an interactive resource to connect families with long-term care facilities throughout Minnesota. Up-to-the-minute information gives caregivers current resources to better define individual plans of care for senior citizens.

DARTS
1645 Marthaler Lane, West St. Paul
(651) 455-1560
www.darts1.org
DARTS (Dakota Area Resources and Transportation for Seniors) provides professionally coordinated transportation and in-home services for Dakota County seniors and their families. As a volunteer-based, nonprofit organization, DARTS offers services that support the full participation of seniors in community life, seeking out group activities and volunteer opportunities for seniors in the metro area and providing transportation to those functions.

ELDERHOSTEL
(800) 454-5768
www.elderhostel.org
Elderhostel is dedicated to providing learning adventures for people age 55 and older. About 3,000 programs are offered in sites around the world, including some in Minnesota. Elderhostel's learning vacations provide opportunities for older adults to take noncredit courses in many subjects—history, culture, food and wine, the outdoors, and more—while enjoying extracurricular activities with others who share similar interests. This is learning just for the pleasure of

learning. Visit Elderhostel's Web site or call them to be put on Elderhostel's mailing lists.

ESTATES IN TRANSITION INC.
5427 Pompano Dr., Minnetonka
(952) 938-5253
Estates in Transition Inc. has been helping individuals with household organization, financial management, and personal and care management since 1982. It is particularly concerned with senior advocacy in all the aforementioned cases.

GENTLE TRANSITIONS
7346 Ohms Lane, Edina
(952) 944-1028
www.gentletransitions.com
Gentle Transitions is a fully insured moving company that provides moving services for relocating senior citizens, offering premove planning, sorting, and packing, through to unpacking and settling into a new home.

TWIN CITIES GRAY PANTHERS
3255 Hennepin Ave. South, Minneapolis
(612) 822-1011
www.graypantherstwincities.org
The long-established Gray Panthers have worked on local, state, and national levels to fight ageism, press for legislation that promotes age equality, and to advocate social justice issues of concern to seniors such as health care and family security. Call to find out about what's going on in your local network.

HANDYWORKS
Greater Minneapolis Council of Churches,
1001 East Lake St., Minneapolis
(612) 721-8687
www.gmcc.org/handyworks
HandyWorks provides assistance to older adults and people with disabilities with household chores and minor home repairs to help people continue to live independently in their own homes. For some, HandyWorks is a solution to a temporary situation—an illness or recovery from an injury. For others, HandyWorks becomes an essential service to help them to remain in their

homes by providing assistance with such things as routine cleaning, yard work, and snow removal.

HOME INSTEAD SENIOR CARE
2580 White Bear Ave., #104, St. Paul
(651) 747-8722
6 additional Twin Cities locations
www.homeinstead.com
Home Instead Senior Care is the world's largest provider of comprehensive companionship and home care services for seniors. From a few hours a day, up to 24 hours' care, seven days a week, Home Instead helps with everyday tasks to enable older adults to live independently.

JEWISH FAMILY AND CHILDREN'S SERVICES (JFCS) OF MINNEAPOLIS
13100 Wayzata Blvd., Suite 400
Minnetonka
(952) 546-0616
www.jfcsmpls.org
Jewish Family and Children's Services of Minneapolis is dedicated to helping older adults maintain their autonomy, independence, and safety. The Older Adult Services staff includes social service and nurse case managers who are specialists in the field of aging and are knowledgeable about community resources— the staff also includes professionals who speak Yiddish and Russian. One phone call to JFCS puts you in touch with a case manager who will answer your questions and schedule a time for an in-home visit. Some of the services offered include housecleaning, personal grooming, Kosher Meals on Wheels, in-home health services, transportation to medical and dental appointments, grocery shopping, consultation with family and caregivers, household financial management, volunteer visitors, and individual and family counseling. Fees are based on income and ability to pay.

KEYSTONE COMMUNITY SERVICES
2000 St. Anthony Ave., St. Paul
(651) 645-0349
www.keystonecommunityservices.org
Keystone Community Services provides activities for mind and body, Meals on Wheels, jobs and

training, and supportive services that help seniors overcome obstacles to independence.

LUTHERAN SOCIAL SERVICE OF MINNESOTA
2485 Como Ave., St. Paul
(651) 642-5990 or (800) 582-5260
www.lssmn.org
Senior programs through Lutheran Social Service, one of Minnesota's largest statewide nonprofit charitable organizations, include assisted living, nonmedical in-home respite, counseling, debt counseling, foster grandparenting, grandparents raising grandchildren support, conservatorship, senior companions, Meals on Wheels, and healthy living workshops.

METROPOLITAN AREA AGENCY ON AGING INC.
2365 North McKnight Rd., Suite 3
North St. Paul
(651) 641-8612
www.tcaging.org
This state-designated agency advocates and educates on issues of aging, as well as plans, coordinates, and offers services that help older adults remain in their homes. This is a great resource that offers a range of help or links to help for a range of things: teaching seniors how to use the Internet, home-delivered meals, senior employment, and in-home assistance and care to counseling, prescription, and community service hotlines.

THE MINNESOTA BOARD ON AGING
540 Cedar St., St. Paul
(651) 431-2500
www.mnaging.org
The Minnesota Board on Aging is committed to providing leadership to ensure that the needs of the state's older citizens are met. The board provides many opportunities and programs to enhance quality of life. Programs include the Senior LinkAge Line (800-333-2433) that provides information about and assistance with a variety of senior issues, Eldercare projects, legal advocacy, coordinated health insurance, counseling, congregate housing services, nutrition programs, and services as an ombudsman for older Minnesotans.

MINNESOTA DEPARTMENT OF VETERANS AFFAIRS (MDVA)
20 West 12th St., Room 206C, St. Paul
(651) 296-2562
www.mdva.state.mn.us
The Minnesota Department of Veterans Affairs provides information to seniors on benefits for former armed forces personnel in Minnesota. The MDVA also operates LinkVet (888-LINKVET), which provides referrals, immediate crisis intervention, and psychological counseling 24 hours a day.

THE MINNESOTA RELAY SERVICE
(800) 627-3529 (both TTY or Voice)
The Minnesota Relay Service connects those who are deaf, hard of hearing, deaf-blind, or speech impaired to hearing people via the telephone, 24 hours a day, 365 days a year. Either party can initiate the call. One service is CapTel, where specially trained operators type the telephone users' verbal responses, relaying conversations to the CapTel user almost simultaneously with the spoken word. All calls are confidential.

MINNESOTA SENIOR FEDERATION (MNSF)
1885 University Ave., St. Paul
(651) 645-0261 or (877) 645-0261
www.mnseniors.org
The Minnesota Senior Federation is dedicated to maintaining a democratic, grassroots organization that trusts in the common sense of its members. Uniting seniors and their own organizations, the MnSF acts as a body of peers, leaders, and decision makers, influencing state policies regarding seniors and providing community information and services to benefit people of all ages with an emphasis on health, housing, retirement planning, and legal issues. The MnSF publishes a monthly newspaper for members.

OSHER LIFELONG LEARNING INSTITUTE
250 McNamara Alumni Center
200 Oak St. SE, Minneapolis
(612) 624-7847
www.cce.umn.edu/olli
OLLI is a voluntary, noncredit education and service program for older adults. It is an affiliated

program of University College at the University of Minnesota College of Continuing Education. The organization offers courses, luncheon programs, informal summer programs, educational tours, service opportunities, and special events. Courses are offered for an eight-week session each fall and spring and a six-week session each winter that meet weekly for one-and-a-half- to two-hour sessions. Courses focus on a wide range of interests—literature, psychology, world cultures, history, politics, economics, science, wellness, and the arts.

OUTFRONT MINNESOTA
Sabathani Center
310 East 38th St., Suite 204, Minneapolis
(612) 822-0127 or (800) 800-0350
www.outfront.org
Visit Outfront Minnesota's Web site for information on resources for older gays and lesbians for yourself, family, or friends. Information available includes several social groups, family and individual support, medical and mental health, housing, employment (volunteer, stipended, and paid), job search help, and many other services.

i Children of Aging Parents (CAPS) offers advice on all aspects of senior care, as well as support for those facing difficult decisions. Call (800) 227-7294 or visit them on the Web at www.caps4caregivers.org.

RECOVERY INC.
(612) 824-5773
Recovery Inc. organizes and sponsors free self-help groups throughout the Twin Cities to help people regain and maintain mental health when dealing with mood and personality disorders such as depression, anger, frustration, fear, and anxiety.

RSVP
2021 East Hennepin Ave., Suite 200
Minneapolis
(612) 617-7830

The Retired and Senior Volunteer Program invites persons 55 and older to make volunteering a part of their lives. RSVP provides free assistance in locating volunteer opportunities, along with supplemental insurance and limited reimbursement of travel expenses. Volunteer opportunities are available throughout the eleven counties.

ST. PAUL PARKS AND RECREATION
300 City Hall Annex, 25 West Fourth St.,
St. Paul
(651) 266-6447
www.stpaul.gov
St. Paul Parks and Recreation's Senior Citizen Recreation Program invites adults at least 50 years of age to spring into new activities. Bimonthly, the program publishes The Pioneer Spirit, a newsletter listing upcoming activities and registration materials—call the above phone number to get a copy mailed to you. There are special events and weekly groups with activities such as craftmaking, bowling, cards, movies, senior choir, and senior exercise.

ST. LOUIS PARK SENIOR PROGRAM
6715 Minnetonka Blvd., St. Louis Park
(952) 928-6444
www.slpcommunityed.com/senior.html
The St. Louis Park Senior Program organizes dozens of outings, guest speakers, and special events. Events include such things as trips to the Minnesota History Center, State Capitol, Chanhassen Dinner Theater, Lunch and Learn sessions with speakers discussing issues of interest to seniors, holiday concerts, and flu shot clinics. Their Web site lists the latest happenings.

SENIOR COMMUNITY SERVICES
10709 Wayzata Blvd., Suite 111,
Minnetonka
(952) 541-1019
www.seniorcommunity.org
Senior Community Services provides in-home counseling and case management to frail seniors and their families throughout suburban Hennepin County to help older adults remain inde-

pendent as long as possible. Its services include transportation, homemaking, medical care, and assistance with health insurance. The staff meets with seniors in their own homes to identify and connect with the combination of services that will fit their specific needs.

VOLUNTEERS OF AMERICA
2021 East Hennepin Ave., Minneapolis
(612) 331-4063
www.voamn.org
Volunteers of America has several programs under Senior Services. Options include meals at various locations and home-delivered meals; mental health services for seniors; the Park Elder Center with numerous programs and classes; legal services; Experience Corps, which involves seniors in tutoring and mentoring roles with kids in Kindergarten through third grade; assistance to caregivers of seniors; assisted living programs; and much more. The Wellness Initiative provides strength and flexibility classes, grocery shopping assistance, and one-on-one nutritional counseling by a registered dietitian. And the new Nutrition Education Web site helps seniors access nutrition education through current articles, links, and activities.

CHILD CARE

There are hundreds of child care providers and preschools in the Twin Cities metro area, ranging from small, home-based day care centers that cater to infants and toddlers to public schools that have specialized programs for children as young as two years old. Minnesota law has specific guidelines for child care providers. Minnesota's licensing procedure for potential child care providers is a strict one, too, requiring thorough background checks, drug testing, proof of completion of a child development course and a family day care training program, and unannounced site inspections that continue long after the license is granted. Minnesota law dictates that each day care must adhere to specific adult-to-child/infant ratios, usually of no more than six preschool-aged children per adult or two infants per adult.

The upside of this is that parents are able to rest much easier knowing their children are placed in such rigidly monitored day care facilities. Most day care centers in the Twin Cities have large, fenced-in play areas attached; serve one or two hot, homemade meals that meet USDA guidelines; and are run by people willing to go through rigorous screening procedures to become day care providers. The downside is that child care expenses in the Twin Cities are easily above the national standard, costing parents between $4,000 and $22,000 per year per child, with an average monthly bill of about $700. The following listings are by no means exhaustive but should give you a good foundation for your search for child care.

AFTER-SCHOOL CARE

Almost every school in Minneapolis and St. Paul offers some sort of after-school program for children, continuing education classes for adults, or weekend activities open to both children and adults as part of their continuing effort to both get parents involved in school and to keep public schools an important focus of their community. For information regarding after-school activities in your neighborhood, contact Minneapolis Public Schools at (612) 668-0000 or www.mpls.k12.mn.us, or the St. Paul Public Schools at (651) 767-8100 or www.stpaul.k12.mn.us.

Montessori Schools

Founded by Dr. Maria Montessori in 1907, Montessori education has gained favor with the public over the past two decades. In Minneapolis, Montessori schools that have specifically pre-K (from one year old on up) and kindergarten classes are Bernie's Montessori School (612-333-5460) at 115 Second Ave. South and Children's Village Montessori (612-378-7730) at 2929 University Ave. SE. In St. Paul there is Children's House Montessori (651-690-3403) at 1194 Randolph Ave. and Oak Hill Montessori School (651-484-8242) at 4665 Hodgson Road.

GROUP DAY CARE CENTERS

NEW HORIZON CHILD CARE
Numerous Twin Cities locations
www.newhorizonacademy.com

One of the largest child care providers in the Twin Cities with more than 50 branches in the metro area alone, New Horizon Child Care aims to give children under their care a safe place to play as well as a head start on their future academic careers. New Horizon has a curriculum for children, based on their age and developmental levels, which includes art, drama, computer, music, reading classes, field trips, lots of storytelling, and indoor and outdoor exercise (depending on weather).

Infants as young as six weeks old are accepted into the program, as well as children as old as 12.

KINDERCARE LEARNING CENTER
www.kindercare.com
With some 72 locations in the Twin Cities metro, this all-purpose day care is extended to children as young as six weeks old to kids as old as 12. The facilities offer transportation to and from home, and meals are provided three times a day.

ℹ️ The Greater Minneapolis Day Care Association (612-341-1177) connects parents to day care centers and child care providers in the Twin Cities metro area.

NANNIES

The state-required screening process for nannies and the potential hiring parents, as well as the extra screening completed by the individual agencies themselves, ensures a roster of child care professionals. Nanny care is not just for infants—the agencies listed below have nannies qualified to take care of infants and children up to age 14.

NANNIES FROM THE HEARTLAND
5490 Balsam Lane North, Minneapolis
(763) 550-0219
www.nanniesheartland.com

NANNY PROFESSIONALS
2456 Arkwright St., St. Paul
(651) 221-0587
www.nannyprofessionals.com

CHURCH-BASED CARE

Many of the hundreds of churches in the Twin Cities metro area offer weekday and/or weekend day care for young children. It would be difficult to list every church that offers day care, just because these programs are sometimes offered only in the summer or are even canceled due to lack of community support. Your best bet is to call the churches directly to find out if they are offering day care—church-based care generally costs about $150 per week for full-time care.

SPECIAL NEEDS

RONALD MCDONALD HOUSE
818 Fulton St. SE, Minneapolis
(612) 331-5752
www.rmhtwincities.org
The Ronald McDonald House of the Twin Cities is a home away from home for families who have children with cancer or other life-threatening illnesses and are accessing a local medical treatment facility. The purpose of the Ronald McDonald House of the Twin Cities is to support and strengthen families during times of medical crisis for children.

CRISIS NURSERY OF ANOKA COUNTY—CHILDREN'S HOME
1400 131st Ave. NE, Blaine
(763) 785-9222
www.chsfs.org
Crisis Nursery offers emergency care family services, including help for battered women, teen parents, and abused or neglected children. Families are encouraged to call ahead to set up a meeting, in either home or at Crisis Nursery's office, to see what action would be most beneficial. Referrals are available, so call with any problem and the staff will do their best to direct you to the most appropriate organization.

SUPPORT GROUPS

TUBMAN
3111 First Ave. S, Minneapolis
(612) 825-3333
www.tubman.org
Tubman holds classes and workshops for women, with a special emphasis on helping couples with children deal with divorce or separation—these meet the county requirements that divorcing families must attend. Child care is available during counseling and classes (Tubman has a child care program as well), and counseling is extended to children whose parents are separating or divorcing.

PREVENT CHILD ABUSE MINNESOTA
**1821 University Ave. West, Suite 202-S,
St. Paul
(651) 523-0099 or (800) 621-6322
www.preventchildabusemn.org**
Prevent Child Abuse Minnesota provides support groups for children and parents—adults talk about challenges and ideas while, in a different room, children learn new coping skills. Weekly meetings are offered around the metro. The organization also provides materials on preventing and coping with abuse, advocates strength-based family services and policies, and gives guidance to families in crisis.

RESOURCE CENTER FOR FATHERS AND FAMILIES
**1201 89th Ave. NE, Blaine
(763) 783-4938
www.resourcesforfathers.org**
With locations in Minneapolis, St. Paul, and Blaine, the Resource Center for Fathers and Families has programs aimed at single, married, or divorced fathers who want to improve their relationship with their children, including anger management groups, parent education classes, and support groups. The center also has information for fathers on legal issues, including referrals and up-to-date information on public policy and child support issues.

SOUTHSIDE FAMILY NURTURING CENTER
**2448 18th Ave. South, Minneapolis
(612) 721-2762
www.ssfnc.org**
Southside Family Nurturing Center offers parenting classes to men, women, and couples alike. The program features classes on the prevention of abuse and neglect, parent and child activity nights, anger management, and therapeutic group discussions and individual counseling.

EDUCATION

Education is a matter of considerable civic pride in the Twin Cities and is viewed as essential to the area's continued success. The area's school districts strive to incorporate the entire community in improving the quality of learning, and the influence of K–12 education is felt beyond the confines of the students in the classroom in important areas such as parent involvement, athletics, and local school boards. The State of Minnesota places a premium on education, and therefore an astounding number of local residents are directly or indirectly involved in the school system. The end result is one of the best educational environments in the nation.

This section's focus is on metro area public education, particularly Minneapolis and St. Paul. In addition, there are profiles of a few of the area's private preparatory schools, both nonsectarian and parochial, and profiles of institutions of higher education.

PUBLIC SCHOOLS

Organization

The organization of Minnesota public education (K–12) is based on a stable and efficient school board government. A significant issue with state school districts is consolidation, especially in rural areas. As Minnesota's population has swelled, the number of school districts has shrunk. Many suburban school districts have rapidly expanded to immense megadistricts, but they have shrewdly avoided the political difficulty of dividing districts. Today the state of Minnesota has over 500 school districts, from traditional K–12 districts to charter districts. All the different types of school districts have missions and objectives specified by the State of Minnesota.

All districts are subject to review and are granted powers by the state legislature and government. When school districts are negligent, their powers may be rescinded and inspected by the Minnesota School Board Association (MSBA). The MSBA frequently serves as a surrogate for direct state intervention in the school districts.

Minnesota school boards' size and lengths of elected terms differ, and they are frequently authorized to make personnel, curriculum, and budget decisions. The Minneapolis school dis-

trict is the largest in the state, with over 35,000 students, and is governed by seven "at large" elected school board members, who serve four-year terms. School District 623, the Roseville Area School District, in contrast, elects six members every odd year.

Both state and local government make enormous financial appropriations to Minnesota public education. The state serves approximately 800,000 K–12 students annually. The Twin Cities have an important organization dedicated to improving Twin Cities K–12 public education, the Association of Metropolitan School Districts (AMSD), which represents over 250,000 students from Minneapolis, St. Paul, and many of the Twin Cities' suburbs. AMSD's mission is to advocate for state education policy that enables metropolitan school districts to improve student learning. Organization is an essential component of Minnesota and Twin Cities K–12 public education, and efforts are continually made to better serve the area's children.

Grade Level

Most area school districts are divided into elementary (K–6 or K–5), junior high (7–8 or 7–9) or middle school (6–8), and high school (9–12). The state's two largest school districts, Minneapolis and St. Paul, differ in matters of grade level. Minneapolis has a standardized districtwide system of elementary (K–5 or K–8), middle school (6–8), and high school (9–12). St. Paul's demarcation of grades includes elementary (K–8 or 1–8), middle school (6–8), junior high (7–8), high school (9–12), as well as innovative 4–6, K–12, and 4-year-old programs. Twin Cities suburban public schools frequently use a system similar to Minneapolis for grade levels, and although junior highs continue to persist, middle schools have become much more prevalent over the past couple of decades.

Standards

Minnesota, unlike many other states, did not develop statewide graduation standards until 1993. Because Minnesota consistently has had a 90 percent graduation rate (18- to 24-year-olds), many argued against the trend toward state graduation standards. At the beginning of the 1990s, the legislature and what is now the Minnesota Department of Education jointly initiated a statewide graduation standards program. The resulting Minnesota State Graduation Standards, approved in 1993, had two distinct components: basic skills tests and the profile of learning. These standards were replaced in 2006.

Under the new standards students have to pass basic skills tests and Minnesota Comprehensive Assessments, and complete a certain number of credits in various subjects, in order to graduate. The Minnesota Comprehensive Assessments (MCA-IIs) were developed to help schools and districts measure student progress in mastering the state's new reading, writing, and mathematics standards. They are gradually replacing the basic skills tests. Students begin taking the MCA-IIs in grade 3 and their performance on these statewide assessments can be used as one of multiple criteria to determine grade promotion or retention. To graduate, students will have to pass the MCA-II written composition test given in grade 9, the MCA-II reading test given in grade 10, and the MCA-II math test given in grade 11. All public schools and charter schools must administer the tests.

Teachers

Minnesota has one of the nation's premier public education systems. Central to the state and the Twin Cities success are the 50,000-plus teachers statewide. Funding and class size are important, but nothing can overshadow passionate, well-educated, committed, student-centered teachers. Education Minnesota, the state's teachers' union, espouses and promotes only the highest caliber of members in its ranks. The strength of teaching in Minnesota can be attributed to a number of factors, from the Department of Children, Families, and Learning to individual school districts.

Requirements for teaching in Minnesota are more rigorous than in many other states. First, in order to receive a license, prospective teachers must attend an institution accredited by the state. Then they must successfully complete classes in a specific area of study; e.g., English, social studies, mathematics, or science. In addition, the state has designated requirements for teachers, which vary depending on the grade levels in which the license can be used. All licensed teachers in the state must pass a course in human relations. Since 1973 each teacher's education institution has been required to provide a course addressing race, culture, socioeconomic status, and general interpersonal communication. Specific licenses have additional requirements. For example, in social studies, and most prospective grade 6–12 disciplines, teachers must take a number of state-specified courses in teaching technology, assessment, kinesiology, special education, and drug and alcohol abuse. Beyond academic requirements, passing a relatively simple test of general knowledge, the Praxis I, is required. Finding employment as a teacher in the Twin Cities is highly competitive, especially in liberal arts subject areas such as social studies and English. Math, science, and special education teachers, in contrast, are in high demand.

Education Minnesota represents the teachers of the state. Education Minnesota developed after the first merger at the state level of the nation's two largest unions of the Minnesota

Federation of Teachers (affiliate of the American Federation of Teachers) and the Minnesota Education Association (affiliate of the National Education Association). The 1998 merger was completed to improve the bargaining position of Minnesota's teachers.

Special and Gifted/Talented

Over the past couple decades local educators have moved toward integrating special education students in the classroom to reflect society at large. The largest school district in the state, Minneapolis, has developed an approach to special education that is followed by most school districts statewide.

Both St. Paul and Minneapolis emphasize diagnosing and beginning special education students as early as possible. Both schools have early-childhood special education programs, which follow the proscriptions of state law: Students who are assessed to require additional educational enrichment prior to K–12 education receive it. St. Paul addresses these students with the Early Childhood Special Education program (ECSE). Minneapolis has a similar pre-K–12 program and promotes job seeking and job retention skills for high school special education students. Twin Cities special education integrates these students in the classroom so that they can fully participate in the community as adults.

Minnesota special education is among the best in the nation because of the stringent requirements of its teachers. Statewide, master's degrees or greater are required for all special education teachers. The University of Minnesota sponsors special education outreach programs, such as the Institute on Community Education, which provides social support to individuals with developmental problems.

Gifted and talented students in the Twin Cities also have access to specialized programs to meet their educational needs. St. Paul addresses gifted education at the elementary level with DISCOVER, where students are assessed and identified for enriched education. Most elementary districts have Schoolwide Enrichment Models

(SEMs), with programs for gifted students and teachers to meet their needs. At the senior high level, the International Baccalaureate program provides a challenging liberal arts curriculum. For Minneapolis talented students there is the Gifted Catalyst Program, which develops the strengths and talents of this important student group. Another essential part of gifted education statewide is a postsecondary option, where Minnesota high school students enroll in college and university classes and earn coursework toward graduation.

Alternative Education

Alternative education programs lead to degrees for nontraditional students who have dropped out of school or require a more flexible learning experience. The state features 145 area learning centers (ALCs), with many other options available within the Twin Cities. From night school GED programs to charter schools, the state has always been an innovator in education for every student.

School Choice

The Twin Cities have without great commotion implemented school choice programs. Integration in the Twin Cities has been relatively civil over the past few decades; compliance has occurred largely through districtwide magnet programs in both St. Paul and Minneapolis, which provide all area students with extensive choices in public education.

Minnesota state statute allows students to attend the public school of their choice, regardless of the community they live in and where their parents pay taxes. If the student is of low socioeconomic status, in some cases transportation may be provided free of charge. As long as there is space in the school, and the student completes registration before individual district's deadlines, then he or she is ensured admittance. Because of the success of open enrollment, the idea of vouchers has only been bandied about but not considered a serious public education option. The success of Minnesota school choice can in part be attributed to the relative parity in funding between Twin Cities school districts. If this condition did not exist, local public education expert Joe Nathan of the nationally recognized Center for School Change argues that school choice would surely fail. Minnesota is proud of the equitable school choice system developed by the state, which offers educational opportunity to every child.

Magnet schools are a major component of Twin Cities school choice. Minneapolis has a combination of magnet and community schools, where specific magnet programs and comprehensive options are available. Comprehensive takes a general, wide-breadth approach to curriculum, whereas the magnets feature a wide array of options. Some of the programs included at the high school level are travel and tourism, aviation and aerospace, communication and technology, education, international baccalaureate, automotive and liberal arts, and several more specific areas of study. There are also magnets available beginning in kindergarten, as well as community schools, which make it easier for families to participate in their particular elementary school's education policies. Minneapolis school choice provides almost infinite options for Minneapolis's children.

The St. Paul district's magnet system is similar to Minneapolis's, with some minor differences. In the jargon of St. Paul public education, there are magnet/citywide and neighborhood schools. Again, the system is developed as a voluntary form of desegregation and offers numerous educational opportunities in specific and broad areas of study.

In both districts magnet programs admission is competitive; however, the majority of students get into the program they desire during their first application. Magnet programs are an important part of the Twin Cities' school choice program, which offers specialized education for every area student.

Charter Schools

Minnesota passed the nation's first charter school law in 1991, and since then, both locally and nationally, there has been an exponential growth of charter schools.

As a laboratory for innovation in education, Twin Cities charter schools have distinguished themselves. Charter schools are independent educational entities, where experiments are permitted in the classroom. Minneapolis alone sponsors 37 charter schools. The charter schools vary widely in curriculum and environment. The Cyber Village Academy is a school dedicated to serving students with "a serious challenge to learning." Annually, approximately 150 homebound students participate in this program for students who may otherwise fall behind or drop out of school. The Oh Day Aki (Heart of the Earth) Charter School serves Twin Cities American Indians in a K–12 school. St. Paul has 31 charter schools to meet the needs of specific student groups, including Hmong Academy, which is a school that emphasizes Hmong culture for students whose first language is Hmong , and City Academy, where "hard to teach learners" receive an education. City Academy, founded in 1992, was the first charter school in the United States.

Homeschooling

Homeschooling is another sector of Minnesota education to experience significant growth in the past couple decades. Numerous organizations have developed to meet the requirements of homeschoolers and the complex labyrinth of local, state, and federal laws with which they must comply.

Minnesota has several laws that protect students from being denied a compulsory education, which also set minimum curriculum requirements for schools across the state, including homeschools. Other statutes ensure that homeschool teachers are competent and address other issues relevant to quality of education. Homeschool students are required annually to successfully complete a state exam to prove that they are being provided with a sufficient education. For the most part, homeschool students have scored well academically compared with their peers. Homeschooling is yet another option for Twin Cities students, requiring substantial planning and hard work by parents and teachers.

i Extensive homeschooling information is available from the Minnesota Home-schoolers Alliance: www.homeschoolers.org, (612) 288-9662

Athletics

Athletics play a significant role in Twin Cities education. The number of sports available for both boys and girls varies greatly across school district boundaries. Most schools have boys' baseball, soccer, football, basketball, and hockey. For young women sports include soccer, softball, basketball, gymnastics, and hockey. Girls' hockey is by far the fastest-growing sport in the state, the result of the sport becoming available in the last decade at most large Minnesota high schools. Over the years, the Twin Cities have produced a number of outstanding athletes of both genders.

Local residents support their area athletic teams with an outpouring of enthusiasm. March in Minnesota is tournament time, when high school sports fans become captivated with state championships over three successive weeks. Minnesotans love high school hockey. The Minnesota High School Hockey Tournament draws sellout crowds, and enormous television ratings, as the Twin Cities and greater Minnesota schools engage in annual rivalries. The men's and women's basketball tournaments are also well received throughout the state, as is the annual state football championship the day after Thanksgiving, the Prep Bowl.

The Minnesota State High School League (MSHSL) is the organization that oversees the state's interscholastic athletics and fine arts programs. As a nonprofit, the MSHSL promotes fairness and good sportsmanship by standardizing rules and acts as a bureaucratic force protecting the integrity of statewide athletics. Each year more than 200,000 students participate in MSHSL-sanctioned events.

Parent Involvement

Parents are encouraged to actively participate in their child's education, whether it's in the classroom or in local school board elections. In fact, Minneapolis has one of the nation's most proactive programs for parent involvement.

The first place parents can involve themselves is at the local polling place. There they can support school board members who espouse an agenda most closely resembling their own. In addition, school districts periodically have levies or referenda regarding funding. Twin Citians are usually willing to support more taxes if they believe it will markedly improve K–12 public education.

The Twin Cities school districts have specific initiatives for parent involvement. In 1996 the Minneapolis school district adopted family involvement standards. The program bridges the gap between students, parents, and the community to promote learning. Training and access to resources help families enrich their student's educational experience. Parent involvement creates an important link between Twin Cities children and the community.

English Language Learners (ELL)

In the past decade the Twin Cities have undergone a transformation in student composition, particularly in the two largest urban districts, Minneapolis and St. Paul. English Language Learners have always been a significant part of student demographics. In the late 19th and early 20th centuries, large groups of Czech, German, Swedish, Norwegian, Polish, Jewish, and other immigrant children entered Twin Cities public schools. Today ELL programs have been established to make the transition easier for Hmong, Somali, Tibetan, Bosnian, Hispanic, Amharic (Ethiopian), Russian, and other students whose first language is not English. The Minneapolis K–12 school guide is an excellent example of the school's commitment to ELL education; on the very first page, seven languages ask, "Do you speak a language other than English?"

In Minneapolis an ELL student must meet two requirements: The student's first language is not English, and he/she scores poorly on an English reading or language proficiency test. Throughout the district specific ELL programs are available at most schools. For example, the Ericcson Community School has Hmong and Spanish ELL programs.

PRIVATE SCHOOLS

The Twin Cities are home to nationally respected private schools. Many of the schools are denominational parochial institutions, but in most cases they include children of diverse faiths in their student body.

The area also features schools with innovative academic programs, which mirror charter schools with one exception—tuition. Many of these schools are quite expensive; however, many do offer scholarships for children with low socioeconomic status. Admission is another difficult matter, since some of the schools have fairly rigid admission requirements for K–12 education.

Minneapolis

DELASALLE HIGH SCHOOL
1 DeLaSalle Dr., Minneapolis
(612) 676-7675
www.delasalle.com
DeLaSalle was founded in 1900 by Archbishop John Ireland, who stipulated that it be run by the Brothers of the Christian Schools, a Roman Catholic congregation of religious laymen founded in 1680 by St. John Baptist de La Salle. Because of this Lasaillian underpinning, DeLaSalle emphasizes education for students from a variety of economic levels, academic abilities, racial communities, and ethnic backgrounds. Ninety percent of DeLaSalle graduates go on to college.

MINNEHAHA ACADEMY
3100 West River Pkwy., Minneapolis
(612) 729-8321
www.minnehahaacademy.net
Minnehaha Academy offers a pre-K–12 education with a distinctly Christian orientation. The school's approach to teaching and curriculum does not endorse a particular Christian denominational outlook but does emphasize "challenging minds and nurturing souls."

Minnehaha Academy has three campuses: one in suburban Bloomington and two Minneapolis campuses, idyllically located on West River Parkway overlooking the Mississippi River. Founded in 1913, Minnehaha Academy continues its mission of providing an excellent education rooted in faith.

St. Paul

CRETIN-DERHAM HALL
550 South Albert St., St. Paul
(651) 690-2443
www.cretin-derhamhall.org
Cretin-Derham Hall (CDH) is one of the premier private high schools in the Twin Cities area. The school is recognized throughout the area for providing a disciplined Catholic education. CDH is also respected statewide as an athletic powerhouse, especially in football and baseball, where students almost annually compete in state championships. (Cretin is the alma mater of Hall of Famer Paul Molitor and current Minnesota Twins star Joe Mauer.)

Cretin-Derham Hall's roots date from 1871. The Brothers of the Christian Schools founded Cretin High School exclusively for young men, and in 1905 the Sisters of St. Joseph Carondelet founded Derham Hall. The schools did not merge until 1987, creating a much larger coeducational Catholic high school. After all these years Catholic values remain central to the school's academic experience. CDH inculcates in its students such values as leadership, service, diversity, and equity.

FRIENDS SCHOOL OF MINNESOTA
1365 Englewood Ave., St. Paul
(651) 917-0636
www.fsmn.org
A school developed by parents, educators, and members of the Quaker community, the Friends School of Minnesota is in the tradition of Quaker education. The Friends School prepares children

with a specific Quaker curriculum in grades K–8.

The curriculum at the Friends School is characterized by several teaching techniques. One important aspect of the school's academic experience is a weekly silent meeting, where students and staff reflect on the events of the day. As a part of the Quaker tradition, students also have daily moments of reflection. The curriculum emphasizes hands-on education, especially with young children. The school has a community focus in the classroom, and group gatherings are a regular component of the curriculum, where students discuss group dynamic problems.

ST. PAUL ACADEMY AND SUMMIT SCHOOL
1150 Goodrich Ave.,
Goodrich Campus, St. Paul

1712 Randolph Ave.,
Randolph Campus, St. Paul
(651) 698-2451
www.spa.edu

St. Paul Academy and Summit School provides a private education on two beautiful campuses in St. Paul. The school's mission is to prepare students for life by providing academically challenging programs.

Another area private school that developed as the result of a merger, St. Paul Academy and Summit School are the result of consolidation to create a coeducational school. St. Paul Academy was founded in 1900 to educate young men (among its former students is F. Scott Fitzgerald), and Summit School first opened its doors in 1917. The two schools have been one since 1969 and have provided an excellent college preparatory education in beautiful, historic facilities.

North

TOTINO-GRACE
1350 Gardena Ave. NE, Fridley
(763) 571-9116
www.totinograce.com

Totino-Grace, a private Catholic high school, serves the northern Twin Cities suburbs. The school's mission centers on learning, faith, service, and community. As the second largest of the 13 Catholic high schools in the Archdiocese of St. Paul and Minneapolis, the school has an annual enrollment of more than 1,000. Totino-Grace was founded in 1965 to meet the needs of the rapidly expanding Twin Cities north suburban area.

> **i** Totino-Grace High School is named in part for Jim and Rose Totino, owners of Totino's frozen pizzas, who made a large donation to the private Catholic school.

South

ACADEMY OF HOLY ANGELS
6600 Nicollet Ave. South, Richfield
(612) 798-2600
www.ahastars.org

The Academy of Holy Angels, one of the Twin Cities' most picturesque campuses, sits on 26 acres in suburban Richfield, where the school actively pursues a diverse student population. The 850 students in grades 9–12 have ample academic resources available. Amenities include a theater, computer labs, and a library with more than 12,000 books. The school has excellent athletic facilities, which include a domed football stadium, two gyms, and a weight room with modern exercise equipment. The Academy of Holy Angels specializes in a Catholic education with state-of-the-art education facilities.

THE INTERNATIONAL SCHOOL OF MINNESOTA
6385 Beach Rd., Eden Prairie
(952) 918-1800
www.ism-sabis.net

The International School of Minnesota (ISM) is a private preparatory school for pre-K–12. The school is a member of the SABIS School Network that includes 50 schools worldwide and traces its history back to 1886 in Lebanon.

Located in Eden Prairie, a southern suburb of Minneapolis, ISM has an impressive 55-acre campus beside Bryant Lake. The school was founded in 1986 with an enrollment of only 24 students; since then the school has rapidly expanded to over

500 students. High school students at ISM have advanced placement programs in many academic fields, such as art, biology, history, French, English, and several more college-level courses.

East

HILL-MURRAY SCHOOL
2625 Larpenteur Ave. East, Maplewood
(651) 777-1376
www.hill-murray.org
Hill-Murray is a respected Catholic private school for the east metropolitan Twin Cities. The school enrollment is just under 1,000 students for grades 7–12, and it has an impressive 14:1 student/teacher ratio. Academics with a moral perspective are emphasized at Hill-Murray, and the results show in student standardized test performance. On average, 94 percent of the school's graduates attend college.

Athletics are another important aspect of a Hill-Murray education. There are 23 varsity sports teams, and the Pioneers excel in many, especially hockey, where they have regularly competed in state high school tournaments. Hill-Murray has provided an excellent Catholic education for 50 years.

West

BLAKE SCHOOL
Blake Campus, 110 Blake Rd., Hopkins

Highcroft Campus, 301 Peavey Lane, Wayzata

Northrop Campus, 511 Kenwood Pkwy., Minneapolis
(952) 988-3420
www.blakeschool.org
Blake School is one of the area's elite private preparatory schools and provides a nonsectarian, coeducational experience. The school features two campuses in the western Twin Cities metropolitan area and one next to the Walker Art Center in Minneapolis.

The Blake School's academic programs are challenging and intensive. All students participate in artistic, academic, and athletic activities

designed to prepare Blake students for higher education.

BRECK SCHOOL
123 Ottawa Ave. North, Golden Valley
(763) 381-8100
www.breckschool.org
The Breck School offers Episcopalian values in the curriculum and is coeducational. Breck has a campus just outside Minneapolis and features 37 acres for school activities.

HIGHER EDUCATION

The area's higher education institutions have long, storied histories. The University of Minnesota was founded in 1851, and throughout its history the school has shaped the quality of public education in the state and has provided a relatively inexpensive undergraduate education through significant state subsidies. The area's community colleges are evenly distributed throughout the Twin Cities to serve as a feeder system for the University of Minnesota and the Minnesota state colleges and universities. Another feature of Twin Cities' higher education is the many nationally recognized private colleges located in the area.

Minneapolis

AUGSBURG COLLEGE
2211 Riverside Ave. South, Minneapolis
(612) 330-1000
www.augsburg.edu
Located just east of downtown Minneapolis, near the University of Minnesota, Augsburg College is the Twin Cities' Evangelical Lutheran institution of higher learning. The college provides a largely secular education, though it retains its affiliation. The college, founded in Marshall, Wisconsin, in 1869, relocated to Minneapolis in 1872. Since then Augsburg has grown in scope and enrollment, with annual enrollments of nearly 4,000 students.

Professors at Augsburg concentrate on teaching rather than research, and the average class size is only 15. Another asset is the plentiful multicultural support programs, ranging from Pan-African and Pan-Asian to Hispanic/Latino student services.

Augsburg offers programs in most disciplines. Augsburg also offers majors not found at some other institutions of higher learning, e.g., Nordic Area Studies, which reflects the heritage of the region and the continuing influence of Scandinavian Lutheran culture.

Activities abound at Augsburg and enrich students' educational experience. With nine male and eight female intercollegiate sports, the "Auggies" are members of Division III of the NCAA in the MIAC (Minnesota Intercollegiate Athletic Association). More than 50 clubs and organizations are on campus, including forensics, cheerleading, and the student newspaper.

CAPELLA UNIVERSITY
225 South Sixth St., Minneapolis
(612) 339-8560
www.capella.edu
Capella University was the Twin Cities' first "distance learning" undergraduate and graduate school, primarily offering courses online but also offering directed studies programs. About 20,000 students are enrolled at the school in more than 20 nations worldwide.

Since receiving accreditation in 1997, the school has received significant media attention for its high-tech version of higher education. The university has five primary schools: Undergraduate Studies, Technology, Psychology, Human Services, and Education, plus 116 specialized areas of study. Conferred degrees at Capella University include B.S., Ed.S., M.S., MBA, Ph.D., and Psy.D. Adult students are the most common group in the student body.

DUNWOODY COLLEGE OF TECHNOLOGY
818 Dunwoody Blvd., Minneapolis
(612) 374-5800
www.dunwoody.edu
Dunwoody College of Technology is an excellent Twin Cities unified trade school. The institute is a nonprofit that offers more than 20 technical programs. Founded in 1914, Dunwoody has trained

more than 250,000 students for technical careers. The school sits on the edge of downtown Minneapolis and has one of the most panoramic views of the city, where many of its students move on to successful careers in various trades.

Among the programs offered at Dunwoody are construction, accounting, electronics, technology, auto collision repair, heating and cooling systems, and welding. There are continuing education and Web-based technical classes, such as night classes offered for construction industry trades.

i At 25th and Nicollet, the Spyhouse coffee shop is a favorite hangout for students at the nearby MCAD, and also frequently serves as a venue for the display and sale of their work.

MINNEAPOLIS COLLEGE OF ART AND DESIGN
2501 Stevens Ave. South, Minneapolis
(612) 874-3700 or (800) 874-MCAD
www.mcad.edu
Minneapolis College of Art and Design (MCAD) is the leading art educator in the Twin Cities. Since 1886 MCAD has served area art students. Today the art college shares a large portion of the state-of-the-art Minneapolis Institute of Arts (MIA) building. MIA is one of three excellent art museums in Minneapolis, all within a few miles of MCAD.

MCAD programs are available in more than 20 fields, which include comic art, advertising, and photography, plus business-friendly areas of art, such as furniture design and advertising design. Besides the rigorous studio art portion of most majors, important foundation and liberal arts courses are required.

MCAD confers many specialized graduate degrees. Offered are masters of fine arts programs as well as one-year postbaccalaureate and certificate programs in design, fine arts, and media arts. MCAD's continuing education courses are open to the general public, and include distance learning and design programs.

MINNEAPOLIS COMMUNITY AND TECHNICAL COLLEGE
1501 Hennepin Ave., Minneapolis
(612) 659-6290
www.minneapolis.edu

The focus at Minneapolis Community and Technical College (MCTC) is on creating an environment where recent high school graduates, working adults, and continuing education students are comfortable and excel together in various educational fields. The college has 12,000 students with an average age of 29.

Diversity is a major commitment at MCTC. As the state's most ethnically diverse school of higher education, MCTC has an important mission: providing a quality education to students who speak more than 80 languages and dialects. In part this is accomplished by the English as a Second Language program, which serves these frequently skilled students, who may need to improve their English language proficiency. MCTC offers programs that lead students into successful careers. A few of the most popular programs are liberal arts disciplines, law enforcement, nursing, and computer support. Associate in arts (AA) and Associate in science (AS) degrees are popular at MCTC, as are technical certificate programs.

> **i** Bob Dylan attended the University of Minnesota and lived and performed in the adjoining Dinkytown neighborhood from 1959 to 1960 (his apartment was upstairs from the drugstore that is now the Loring Pasta Bar). Some of the musicians he played with are still active on the local scene.

THE UNIVERSITY OF MINNESOTA– TWIN CITIES
231 Pillsbury Dr. SE, 240 Williamson Hall, Minneapolis
(612) 625-2008
www1.umn.edu/twincities

The University of Minnesota–Twin Cities pervades all aspects of the area's culture from sports, education, research and development to medicine, law, politics, and business. Known in the Twin Cities as the U, the institution is the flagship of Minnesota public higher education and a matter of tremendous civic pride. The University of Minnesota–Twin Cities has an undergraduate, graduate, and nondegree student enrollment of more than 50,000, making it the largest single university campus in the country.

The University of Minnesota public education system includes five campuses. Outstate campuses are located in Crookston, Duluth, Morris, and Rochester. The University of Minnesota–Twin Cities has two campuses. The vast majority of programs are on the Minneapolis campus, where the administration is housed. The St. Paul campus is devoted to agriculture and natural resources programs.

The academic options at the U of M are seemingly endless. From architecture to zoology, the university offers fields of study for just about any academic or professional interest. The two largest colleges are the College of Liberal Arts (CLA) and the Institute of Technology (IT). Eleven U programs are ranked in the top 10 in the nation, including Chemical Engineering, Psychology, Geography, Economics, and Forestry. In addition to the 16 distinct colleges of the U, there is University College, the continuing education program, which is important in serving Twin Cities nontraditional students.

University of Minnesota alumni appear in almost every imaginable field. Two vice presidents and Democratic Party nominees for president of the United States, Hubert H. Humphrey and Walter Mondale, attended the U. The school counts five alumni in the Pro Football Hall of Fame: Bud Grant, Leo Nomellini, Alan Page, Bobby Bell, and Bronko Nagurski. The list of alumni includes Seymour Cray, the founder of Cray Research and an important figure in the development of the supercomputer; Earl Bakken, who created the first battery-operated pacemaker and founded Medtronic; and 1998 Nobel Prize winner Dr. Louis Ignarro, who was instrumental in the development of Viagra. Another U Nobel Prize winner is Norman Borlaug, who received the award in 1970 for engineering the "green revolution," which resulted in unprecedented food yields for feeding the third world. University of Minnesota alumni have had enormous impact on the Twin Cities by creating 1,500 technological companies, which contribute $30 billion annually to the state economy.

The U's newspaper, the Minnesota Daily, has operated for more than a century and is regarded as one of the nation's best college newspapers. The university's radio station, KUOM, better known as Radio K, provides student radio programming from dawn to dusk daily. The U plays intercollegiate sports in the Big Ten conference and has been particularly successful in recent years in men's hockey, women's hockey, and men's wrestling, with the university's teams hauling in eight national championships since 2000. The Golden Gopher football team hasn't had as much success lately (the maroon-and-gold last won a national championship and went to the Rose Bowl in 1960), but they are looking forward to a new home. In the fall of 2009, the Gophers will move back outdoors onto their own field, TCF Bank Stadium, ending a long association with the climate-controlled Metrodome that never felt quite right for the pageantry and tradition of college football Saturdays.

St. Paul

ST. CATHERINE UNIVERSITY
2004 Randolph Ave., St. Paul
(651) 690-6000 or (800) 945-4599

601 Second Ave. South, Minneapolis
(612) 690-7700 or (800) 945-4599
www.stkate.edu

The largest Catholic college for women in the country is also the Twin Cities' newest university, having officially changed its name from the College of St. Catherine in 2009.

St. Catherine, or St. Kate's, has a notable history. The college was founded in 1905 by the Sisters of St. Joseph Carondelet, whose mission is improving women's educational opportunities. That said, St. Kate's does offer limited programs for men at its much smaller campus in Minneapolis as well as at the graduate school.

St. Kate's emphasizes a distinctly Roman Catholic spiritual and ethical approach to education. St. Kate's curriculum emphasizes depth and breadth and is reflected in critical inquiry, multicultural studies, and interdisciplinary teaching in the classroom. Offered at the college are nearly 50 different majors, from art and biology to theater and theology. Nursing is the most popular area of study, although there are many liberal arts programs. St. Catherine is the Twin Cities' oldest and largest health care educator and includes highly regarded programs in nursing, occupational therapy, and pre-med.

One of St. Kate's greatest educational innovations was the creation of "Weekend College" in 1979. Weekend College is designed to meet working women's needs for a college education. Classes meet every other weekend on Friday evening, Saturday, and Sunday. Fifteen practical, career-oriented majors are offered in the Weekend College program, including elementary education, accounting, communication, healthcare management, and nursing.

CONCORDIA UNIVERSITY—ST. PAUL
275 Syndicate St. North, St. Paul
(651) 641-8278 or (800) 333-4705
www.csp.edu

Concordia University (not to be confused with Concordia College in Moorhead, Minnesota) provides higher education in a Christian environment. The origins of Concordia date from 1893, when the Lutheran Church–Missouri Synod created a high school to prepare students for its ministry. The school became coeducational in 1950 and began granting bachelor's degrees in elementary education in 1962 for the first time as a college.

Today educational opportunities are available in numerous fields. Liberal arts, business, and health care are popular areas of study, including dozens of undergraduate degree programs and M.A. programs. The college continues to offer many specialized career majors in the ministry, such as directors of church, parish music, Christian outreach and Christian education, as well as preseminary studies. Concordia's School of Continuing Study offers many classes in the evenings, on weekends, and online.

HAMLINE UNIVERSITY
1536 Hewitt Ave., St. Paul
(651) 523-2800
www.hamline.edu
Hamline University is Minnesota's oldest university. The United Methodist Church organized the school in 1854 in Red Wing. Shortly thereafter, it relocated 50 miles north to its present site in St. Paul. Hamline was the third coeducational college in the United States. The cornerstone of Hamline's curriculum is liberal arts.

Hamline offers degrees and majors in numerous areas of study. Undergraduate bachelor's degrees in liberal arts disciplines are the most popular certificates granted. Also conferred are master's, doctoral, and law degrees. The campus is composed of approximately 4,900 undergrad and graduate students in areas of study ranging from art history to women's studies. The university offers over 40 undergraduate majors. Besides the Hamline Law School, there are several additional graduate programs: the Graduate School of Education and the Graduate School of Liberal Studies, including M.A.s in Teaching English as a Second Language and M.F.A.s in Writing .

LUTHER SEMINARY
2481 Como Ave., St. Paul
(651) 641-3456
www.luthersem.edu
Luther Seminary educates ministers for the Evangelical Lutheran Church in America (ELCA). It is the largest of eight ELCA seminaries in the United States. The seminary expanded and merged with other seminaries over nearly 150 years to its present size after the consolidation of six area institutions serving a similar function. The campus is located on a pastoral bluff in St. Paul, where they provide graduate degree programs in several religious areas of study and confer Master of Divinity for those wishing to become pastors. Luther also offers D.Min. (Doctorate of Ministry) and Ph.D. degrees, the latter in select fields of study related to the Lutheran Church.

MACALESTER COLLEGE
1600 Grand Ave., St. Paul
(651) 696-6000
www.macalester.edu
Macalester College is a preeminent private liberal arts college conferring undergraduate degrees on some of the world's brightest students. The college is respected locally, nationally, and internationally for maintaining high academic standards and championing internationalism and multiculturalism. Macalester is the recipient of enormous endowment monies, particularly from the DeWitt-Wallace fund, which helps underwrite the costs of tuition, through scholarships and other awards, for students of low socioeconomic status.

Macalester was founded in 1874 by the Reverend Dr. Edward Duffield Neill. A former superintendent for Minnesota Territory Schools, Neill did not move the college to its present site until 1885. In its early years the college received significant financial support from philanthropist Charles Macalester, for whom the college was named.

Macalester College's diversity is reflected in the exceptional students it attracts from the nation and abroad. Macalester is the alma mater of both former Vice President Walter Mondale and former Secretary General of the United Nations Kofi Annan, and the school is highly selective. Nestled on a leafy campus in the exquisite Macalester-Groveland neighborhood, the college creates an excellent learning environment. Macalester's demographics consistently have represented one of the most diverse schools of higher education in the nation. The roughly 1,900 full-time undergraduates come from 48 states, D.C., and around the world. There are 36 majors offered at Macalester, including geography, Russian, and classics, as well as African-American studies, women's and gender studies, urban studies, and several interdepartmental fields. A major area of focus at Macalester is the arts, particularly music and theater. Macalester hosts four or five theater productions a year. In addition, the college features numerous organized music groups, which include: Symphony Orchestra, Mac

Jazz, New Music Ensemble, Festival Chorale, Flying Fingers (a traditional bluegrass group), the Electric Guitar, and several other diverse music organizations.

METROPOLITAN STATE UNIVERSITY
700 East Seventh St., St. Paul
1450 Energy Park Dr., St. Paul
1501 Hennepin Ave., Minneapolis
(651) 793-1300
www.metrostate.edu
Metropolitan State University provides flexible and affordable education to nontraditional students in the Twin Cities. Convenience is emphasized in offering the chance to earn bachelor's and graduate degrees.

Metro State has served the Twin Cities since 1971. The university's original objective was to offer a program for working adults. This has remained Metro State's focus, though the university has broadened its objectives. In 1983 the first graduate program, master of management and administration, was launched. Today Metro State's enrollment is approximately 8,900 and the school continues to support education of diverse and underserved student populations.

Metro State offers more than 60 majors. Most majors are training toward occupations, such as accounting, social work, law enforcement, and nursing, although students can also study liberal arts areas such as English, sociology, ethnic studies, and anthropology. Metro State accounting students frequently distinguish themselves by annually placing in the top 10 percent on the CPA exam.

Metro State campuses are conveniently located to facilitate greater academic success. The Dayton's Bluff neighborhood, just outside downtown St. Paul, is the largest campus. Two additional campuses are in the heart of downtown Minneapolis and in St. Paul's Midway area. In addition, Metro State offers classes at other colleges and at businesses throughout the Twin Cities, which minimizes the time students spend getting to school and brings classes closer to their homes.

NORTHWESTERN COLLEGE
3003 Snelling Ave. North, St. Paul
(651) 631-5100
www.nwc.edu
Northwestern College is a nondenominational, conservative, private Christian college. The college has nearly 3,000 students studying nearly 50 different majors, and the college serves many nontraditional students with its adult degree completion program, Focus, and the Center for Distance Learning.

Northwestern College began as the Northwestern Bible and Missionary School in Minneapolis in 1902. Over time educational and vocational opportunities have been greatly expanded, with the creation of the Northwest Theological Seminary in 1935 and the College of Liberal Arts founded in 1944. Then the college acquired a former Roman Catholic seminary in 1970; the large, wooded, gated campus was renovated and reopened as Northwestern College in 1972.

Christian doctrine is central to the educational mission at Northwestern College. Unlike with many of the Twin Cities commuter campuses, most students live on campus. Northwestern College offers a distinctly conservative Christian education option.

ST. PAUL COLLEGE
235 Marshall Ave., St. Paul
(651) 846-1600 or (800) 227-6029
www.saintpaul.edu
Formerly St. Paul Technical College, St. Paul College is a remarkable educational institution. Foremost among its accomplishments is its astounding job placement statistics; since 2000, 84 to 92 percent of its students annually find positions in their field of study. Technically trained employees are highly sought by Twin Cities employers. St. Paul College provides education in more than 70 occupational fields, which include formal trades such as cabinetmaking, carpentry, and auto body repair, as well as numerous medical and computer service occupations, e.g., medical laboratory technician and computer programmer. Deaf education is another prominent field of study. St. Paul College offers an affordable education in numerous fields

and places graduates in frequently high-paying and rewarding trades.

UNIVERSITY OF ST. THOMAS
2115 Summit Ave., St. Paul
(651) 962-5000
www.stthomas.edu

In 1885 Archbishop John Ireland founded St. Thomas Aquinas Seminary. This higher education institution quickly grew beyond the bounds of its original purpose, as a high school, college, and seminary, with only two departments, Theology and Classics. However, the Twin Cities' largest Catholic university—the first Minnesota institution after the University of Minnesota to be ranked as a "national university" by *U.S. News & World Report*—was prepared to gradually expand into numerous other areas of study.

The first four-year baccalaureate degrees were conferred by then St. Thomas College in 1910. The college increased its liberal arts emphasis and broadened its demographic in 1977 when it became coeducational and accepted women for the first time.

St. Thomas has evolved into a private Catholic university with a liberal arts emphasis. The school offers 96 majors ranging from theology, Latin, and classical languages to history, English, and geography. The annual enrollment at St. Thomas is approximately 11,000 students. St. Thomas offers graduate education in numerous areas, including engineering, education, social work, business, psychology, and law.

Continuing education is another important focus at St. Thomas. Since New College opened in 1975, the needs of part-time, adult, and non-traditional students have been readily met with innovative methods, such as off-campus classes to make convening easier.

St. Thomas boasts several campuses. The main campus is 78 acres approximately halfway between downtown Minneapolis and St. Paul, on the western edge of historic Summit Avenue. In addition, the downtown Minneapolis campus is home to the Graduate School of Professional Psychology, the School of Education, the Opus College of Business, and the School of Law. St. Thomas also owns smaller campuses in out-state Owatonna and Rome, Italy.

Student activities abound at St. Thomas. Students can choose from a large slate of intercollegiate sports, such as basketball, swimming, cross-country running, and men's and women's hockey. The seminary also publishes Catholic Digest, a world-renowned Catholic magazine.

WILLIAM MITCHELL COLLEGE OF LAW
875 Summit Ave., St. Paul
(651) 227-9171 or (888) 962-5529
www.wmitchell.edu

Founded in 1900, what is today known as the William Mitchell College of Law has had many different names, but the goal has remained the same: providing a quality legal education for recent college graduates or, more frequently, students returning to school after a multi-year absence. William Mitchell began as a night school, and it was prescient in creating flexible schedules where nontraditional students could succeed.

Alumni of William Mitchell are an important group in Twin Cities government and law. The school's most famous graduate was Supreme Court Chief Justice Warren E. Burger of St. Paul, who attended one of the four predecessor law schools of William Mitchell. The Warren E. Burger Library was built in 1990 in his honor and is one of the finest law-school libraries in the nation.

The school is small (approximately 1,200 students) and moderately selective. The J.D. program emphasizes what it calls "practical wisdom," to train lawyers to not only to practice law, but to work constructively with other people, to think about the law with breadth and depth, and to learn from legal experiences.

North

ANOKA-RAMSEY COMMUNITY COLLEGE
11200 Mississippi Boulevard NW, Coon Rapids

300 Spirit River Dr. South, Cambridge
(763) 433-1100
www.anokaramsey.edu

Anoka-Ramsey Community College (ARCC) has served the north metropolitan Twin Cities since

1965. As the suburbs of Minneapolis and St. Paul have expanded, Anoka-Ramsey has grown to meet the area's needs.

After opening the first campus in Coon Rapids, presently one of the Twin Cities' fastest growing suburbs, the college added the Cambridge Campus in 1978 and shrewdly anticipated an area that would undergo significant urbanization.

Numerous programs can be started, and in some cases completed, at Anoka–Ramsey. They range from accounting, art, astronomy, music, and law enforcement, to Spanish, sociology, mathematics, and zoology. The community college offers associate in arts (A.A.) and associate in science (A.S.) degrees. Anoka-Ramsey was developed as a feeder school for students to begin their educations and then move on to a four-year college to complete their degrees, but it also offers many programs to train for practical careers in physical therapy, business, computer networking and telecommunications, nursing, and other specific trades.

BETHEL UNIVERSITY
3900 Bethel Dr., Arden Hills
(651) 638-6400
www.bethel.edu
Bethel College offers a four-year liberal arts education with an evangelical Christian perspective. The Baptist General Conference created Bethel Seminary in 1871. Preceding Bethel College was a secondary academy and a junior college, before the liberal arts college was formed in 1948. Today Bethel University offers programs in more than 100 different fields, from art to youth ministry. It also offers graduate programs in many fields, including divinity, business administration, counseling psychology, education, nursing, and more. The Baptist seminary offers graduate degrees with various concentrations from M.A. and M.Div. (Master of Divinity) to D.Min. (Doctorate of Ministry).

NORTH HENNEPIN COMMUNITY COLLEGE
7411 85th Ave. North, Brooklyn Park
(763) 488-0391 or (800) 818-0395
www.nhcc.edu

North Hennepin Community College (NHCC) serves the northern Twin Cities. The 80-acre campus has an annual enrollment of more than 9,000 students. NHCC has many liberal arts programs, which earn credit toward bachelor degrees. Associate in arts (A.A.) and associate in science (A.S.) are transferable to all Minnesota State Colleges and Universities (MnSCU) schools as well as the University of Minnesota. Also offered at NHCC are career-oriented programs, such as nursing and accounting, and professional development and enhancement classes. Continuing education is another important part of NHCC's mission; it is reflected in the 6,600 students enrolled in continuing education programs there.

UNITED THEOLOGICAL SEMINARY
3000 Fifth St. NW, New Brighton
(651) 633-4311
www.unitedseminary.edu
United Theological Seminary (UTS) is the Twin Cities' ecumenical theological school. Although chartered by the United Church of Christ, more than 20 denominations are represented at UTS—just about everything from Unitarian Universalist to Muslim. The school focuses on tolerance, empathy, and diversity in its educational program. Also of paramount importance to UTS is supporting students of diverse racial, ethnic, sexual orientation, and denominational traditions.

UTS's history is fairly brief in the Twin Cities, but its antecedents are rooted in the Evangelical and Reformed Church Seminary of Plymouth, Wisconsin (founded in 1862), and the Yankton School of Theology, which began serving the German Congregational churches in South Dakota in 1869. Not until 1960 did the seminaries merge and form UTS.

A progressive theological education is provided at UTS. Instruction reflects recent developments in curriculum, and the educational experience at UTS includes both field learning and classroom study.

UTS offers programs in ordained ministry, lay ministry, and some academic vocations, as well as continuing education programs. Degrees include conferred master's degrees in divinity, arts in religion and theology, religious leadership, and women's studies. Doctorate in ministry is also offered. There are specialized programs, which are available at few other seminaries, including Indian ministries, rural ministries, and religion and arts.

East

CENTURY COLLEGE
3300 Century Ave. North, White Bear Lake
(651) 779-3200 or (800) 228-1978
www.century.mnscu.edu
Students of all ages attend Century College based on their needs, whether to build a foundation for a four-year degree, solely for the joy of learning as a continuing-education student, or to learn a trade. There are classes to satisfy almost everyone's interest. With more than 12,000 students, Century is the largest two-year community college in Minnesota.

More than 80 technical, academic, and occupational programs are offered at Century College, as well as more than 100 degrees, certificates, and diplomas. Students with limited financial means may begin a four-year degree program in numerous subject areas, such as English, geography, and biology by earning associate of arts (A.A.) and associate of science (A.S.) degrees. When students complete their A.A. or A.S. and transfer to the University of Minnesota system or the Minnesota State Colleges and Universities (MnSCU), all credits are accepted toward a B.A. or B.S.

Another important function of Century College is continuing education. Century College serves more continuing-education students than any other college in Minnesota, making up 55 percent of the student body.

MINNESOTA SCHOOL OF BUSINESS AND GLOBE UNIVERSITY
11 campuses across Minnesota
www.msbcollege.edu
At all locations Globe University offers a quick track to many careers in business as well as technical fields. Degree programs include account-

ing, software development, e-commerce design, nursing, digital video and media production, massage therapy, and many more. In addition to regular classroom instruction, Globe University also offers distance education, which allows students to take classes online.

South

ARGOSY UNIVERSITY
1515 Central Pkwy., Eagan
(651) 846-2882 or (888) 293-1903
www.argosy.edu
Medicine is an important part of the Twin Cities economy, and Argosy University has the most comprehensive allied health care associate programs in the area. Students can pick from numerous health care programs. Here are a few of the associate degree programs available: histotechnology, radiologic technology, dental hygiene, medical laboratory technician, veterinary technology, and radiation therapy. Argosy also offers programs in psychology, education, and business.

BROWN COLLEGE
1440 Northland Dr., Mendota Heights
(888) 574-3777
www.browncollege.edu
Brown College is an important local technical and trade school. The school boasts many graduates from its programs in local television and radio positions. Brown provides an education that employs its students in their fields of study. Since it opened in 1954, the range of programs at Brown has rapidly expanded. The school has a second campus in Brooklyn Center.

Today Brown College has 14 programs in fields as varied as culinary arts and criminal justice. The culinary arts program is a member of Le Cordon Bleu French cooking school. Another important program is the Department of Visual Communications, where students train for such careers as graphic design and Web site design. Also of note at Brown is the radio and television broadcasting program, where students can train to become camera operators, producers, video editors, newscasters, and more. In addition, Brown has digital electronics and computer technology, telecommunications, PC/LAN, and e-commerce programs.

INVER HILLS COMMUNITY COLLEGE
2500 East 80th St., Inver Grove Heights
(651) 450-8500
www.inverhills.edu
Inver Hills Community College fulfills the needs of students working toward a four-year degree, to improve job skills, or simply to explore subjects of personal interest. The community college serves the south and east suburbs of St. Paul.

It offers numerous programs for degrees and certification. The associate in arts, or A.A. degree, is a popular stepping-stone toward four-year degrees in more than 50 academic areas, which include sociology, economics, and nursing, as well as more uncommon major fields, such as fish, game, and wildlife, and public health education. Another important two-year degree is the associate in science, or A.S., which is more career oriented (e.g., accounting, criminal justice, aviation, and construction management). The associate in applied science is a two-year degree aimed at immediate employment upon completion, and includes medical secretary, building inspection, and management/marketing. Finally, Inver Hills offers several vocational certificates. The certificates qualify students for various vocations or can be used to improve jobs already held. Many high-demand technical degrees are available, including desktop publishing, medical-office systems, computer applications, and many others.

NORMANDALE COMMUNITY COLLEGE
9700 France Ave. South, Bloomington
(952) 487-8200 or (866) 880-8740
www.normandale.edu
Normandale Community College serves the needs of the southern Twin Cities by offering associate degrees, certification programs, and classes for personal enrichment. The community college is easily accessible from I-494 and is located on a 90-acre site, complete with the beautiful Normandale Japanese Garden.

Founded in 1968, the school has an enrollment of 10,000 students. Normandale offers programs in occupational fields, including law enforcement, radiologic technology, hospitality management, dental hygiene, and computers/information management. Other popular programs include two-year liberal arts degrees.

NORTHWESTERN HEALTH SCIENCES UNIVERSITY
2501 West 84th St., Bloomington
(952) 888-4777
www.nwhealth.edu
Northwestern Health Sciences University offers classes in a frequently overlooked portion of medicine: natural approaches to health and health care. There are programs in acupuncture and herbal studies, professional massage, integrative health and wellness, and chiropractics. The university also offers master's programs in Oriental medicine and professional acupuncture.

The university's undergraduate programs are approximately two years in duration. Programs are also offered for nontraditional and/or adult learners. As medical technology increases, Northwestern Health Sciences University's programs have experienced growing importance.

RASMUSSEN COLLEGE
Five Twin Cities campuses
(888) 572-7687
www.rasmussen.edu
Mention Rasmussen to a Twin Cities resident, and you'll probably hear them ask, "Isn't that a business college?" Yes, Rasmussen was founded in St. Paul in 1900 as an institution to teach practical business skills, but it's come a long way since then. Exemplifying the good business sense it teaches its students, the for-profit college has expanded dramatically since then, acquiring other schools and founding new campuses across the Upper Midwest, in Florida, and online. Currently Rasmussen offers associate's degrees in a range of health, business, education, criminal justice, and technology fields as well as a growing number of bachelor's degrees.

HEALTH CARE

Minnesota has been a medical industry hub and site of health care innovation for decades, even before the founding of such illustrious facilities and companies as the Mayo Clinic, Medtronic, and Hazelden. Ironically, a good deal of this reputation came from rumors started by PR agents in territorial times, who were horrified to find that the rest of the country likened Minnesota to an American Siberia. With the hordes of health-challenged immigrants who moved to the state in the 1850s to 1870s to follow these claims of rejuvenation came doctors and scientists who were just as willing to test the healing powers of Minnesota's climate, including Dr. William W. Mayo, whose sons founded the Mayo Clinic in Rochester, and Dr. Brewer Mattocks, who wrote the highly partisan book *Minnesota as a Home for Invalids*.

Minnesota's health care system has been at the top of the field for many years. A strong emphasis on research ensures that hospitals and treatment facilities in the Twin Cities and throughout Minnesota will remain far ahead of the times.

HOSPITALS AND HOSPITAL COOPERATIVES

ABBOTT NORTHWESTERN HOSPITAL
800 East 28th St., Minneapolis
(612) 863-4000
www.abbottnorthwestern.com
Abbott Northwestern Hospital has grown to become the Twin Cities' largest nonprofit health care provider, with a tradition of compassionate care, outstanding service, and leadership in education and clinical research. The huge facility treats a wide range of health-related issues, from family practice to cosmetic medicine and surgery, cancer treatment, neuroscience, and behavioral studies.

CHILDREN'S HOSPITALS AND CLINICS

CHILDREN'S HOSPITALS AND CLINICS
2525 Chicago Ave. South, Minneapolis
(612) 813-6000

345 North Smith Ave., St. Paul
(651) 220-6000
www.childrenshc.org
Four additional Twin Cities locations

Children's Hospitals and Clinics was created by the merger of the children's hospitals in St. Paul and Minneapolis. With 268 staffed hospital beds at their main Minneapolis and St. Paul campuses, they are the largest children's health care organization in the upper Midwest, offering services in all major pediatric specialties.

Comfort is an important facet of each Children's Hospitals facility, with such amenities as videos available for checkout, computers with games, built-in beds in hospital rooms for a parent to sleep in, and a wheelchair-accessible garden. Playrooms full of toys, colorful play structures, art supplies, and games are on each floor of the hospitals. Special efforts are made to accommodate children who need to stay in their rooms.

FAIRVIEW HEALTH SERVICES
University of Minnesota Medical Center,
Fairview, Riverside Campus,
2450 Riverside Ave., Minneapolis

University of Minnesota Medical Center,
Fairview, University Campus,
500 Harvard St., Minneapolis
(612) 273-3000
www.fairview.org
Eight additional Twin Cities locations

University of Minnesota Medical Center, Fairview, is among the most respected teaching institutions in the nation. The medical center balances responsiveness to patients' needs and wishes with access to innovative treatments and technology. Located on two campuses on the east and west banks of the Mississippi River in Minneapolis, the medical center provides comprehensive services from primary care, emergency care, and the delivery of thousands of babies each year to care of patients with the most complex conditions, including organ and blood and marrow transplantation, heart disease, cancer, neurosciences, and behavioral illnesses.

University of Minnesota Children's Hospital, Fairview, is a renowned pediatric teaching and research hospital for children. The hospital is located in the Riverside and University campuses of the University of Minnesota Medical Center, Fairview; it is the primary pediatric teaching hospital for the University of Minnesota Medical School. University of Minnesota Children's Hospital provides a broad range of pediatric programs and services—including mental health, general surgery, imaging, neonatal, and intensive care; plus cardiac, cancer, and cystic fibrosis services; as well as blood, bone marrow, and organ transplantation.

i MinnesotaCare (651-297-3862 or 800-657-3772; www.dhs.state.mn.us) provides health care insurance to residents who cannot afford private insurance. Premiums are based on family income and size.

HENNEPIN COUNTY MEDICAL CENTER
701 Park Ave. North, Minneapolis
(612) 873-3000
www.hcmc.org
Four additional Twin Cities locations
Hennepin County Medical Center (HCMC) is a public teaching hospital in downtown Minneapolis affiliated with the University of Minnesota Medical School. HCMC is the centerpiece of Hennepin County's health services system. HCMC provides specialized and general medical care, often through hospital referrals.

MAYO CLINIC ROCHESTER
200 First St. SW, Rochester
(507) 284-2511
www.mayoclinic.org/rochester
The world-famous Mayo Clinic has been a pioneer in medical research and disease treatment for more than a century. While it is located almost 90 miles south of the Twin Cities, the very existence of the hospital is one of the reasons there is such a strong medical community in Minnesota. More than 2,000 physicians and 35,000 allied health staff work in the Mayo system, treating nearly half a million patients annually. Their specialties include (but are far from being limited to) cancer treatment, dermatology, diagnostic radiology, Native American studies and medicine, internal medicine, cardiovascular disease treatment, allergy studies and treatment, plastic surgery, HIV study, and general practice/family medicine.

MERCY HOSPITAL
4050 Coon Rapids Blvd., Coon Rapids
(763) 236-6000
www.allinamercy.org

UNITY HOSPITAL
550 Osborne Rd., Fridley
(763) 236-5000
www.allinamercy.org
Mercy and Unity Hospitals are nonprofit hospitals that have been serving the northern Minneapolis–St. Paul metropolitan area for more than 40 years. The two hospitals function as virtually one entity, with shared resources to help ensure quality, cost-effective care. Mercy and Unity specialty services include behavioral health, cardiac, emergency, family centered care, oncology, and bariatrics. The hospitals offer medical transportation, health education, and support groups. In addition, Mercy Hospital provides specialized services for senior citizens.

NORTH MEMORIAL MEDICAL CENTER
3300 Oakdale Ave. North, Robbinsdale
(763) 520-5200
www.northmemorial.com

The independently owned North Memorial Medical Center's history of responding to the health care needs of its communities has lasted for more than five decades and continues to be the main ingredient in its success. North Memorial was an early leader in emergency care and is home to the first totally integrated hospital-based medical transportation system in Minnesota. North Memorial also founded the I Can Cope cancer education program that is now used by the American Cancer Society and in hospitals throughout the country.

i Guided tours of the historic Plummer Building at the Mayo Clinic can be arranged through the hospital, or self-guided tours may be taken during public hours. Call (507) 284-2511 for more information.

ST. FRANCIS REGIONAL MEDICAL CENTER
1455 St. Francis Ave., Shakopee
(952) 428-2540
www.stfrancis-shakopee.com
St. Francis Regional Medical Centerspecialties including orthopedics, spine surgery, cardiology, and oncology. Hospital services include the St. Francis Cancer Center, emergency department, St. Francis Sleep Diagnostics Center, St. Francis Family Birth Place, St. Francis Breast Center, St. Francis Children's Pediatric Unit, St. Francis Rehabilitation and Sports Medicine, St. Francis Health Services, and several primary and specialty clinics. St. Francis is jointly owned and sponsored by the Benedictine Health System, Allina Hospitals & Clinics, and Park Nicollet Health Services.

ST. JOSEPH'S HOSPITAL
69 West Exchange St., St. Paul
(651) 232-3000
www.healtheast.org/st-joes.html
The first hospital in Minnesota, St. Joseph's was founded by the Sisters of St. Joseph of Carondelet in 1853. Today the downtown St. Paul Catholic hospital serves patients in the eastern Metro, with specialties in heart care, cancer care, mental health and chemical dependency treatment, and maternity care. St. Joseph's operates a 24-hour emergency room and comprehensive services for inpatient care. The hospital has been a member of the HealthEast Care System since 1987, which operates several hospitals, clinics, and rehabilitation centers throughout the eastern Metro.

UNITED HOSPITAL
333 North Smith Ave., St. Paul
(651) 241-8000
www.unitedhospital.com
United Hospital is a premier acute care medical facility. A part of the Allina Health System, United's facilities include a birth center, a pain center, the John Nasseff Heart Hospital, and a center for breast care; the hospital specializes in behavioral health studies and treatment, emergency care, heart/lung medicine, oncology, rehabilitation services, and surgery.

REHABILITATION CENTERS

HAZELDEN FOUNDATION AND RENEWAL CENTER
15251 Pleasant Valley Rd., Center City
(651) 213-4200 or (800) 257-7810
www.hazelden.org
Hazelden has a history spanning nearly 50 years of pioneering leadership in the care of chemically dependent people and their families. It is internationally recognized for its broad spectrum of interrelated services and continuum of care, which includes assessment and rehabilitation for adolescents and adults, aftercare and family services, renewal services, extended care and continuing care, professional development, counselor training, and clergy training and counseling. A nonprofit organization dedicated to helping people recover from alcoholism and other drug addiction by providing residential and outpatient treatment for adults and young people, Hazelden offers programs for families affected by chemical dependency as well as training for a variety of professionals. Hazelden is also the world's premier publisher of information on chemical addiction and related areas.

NEW BEGINNINGS
109 Northshore Dr., Waverly
(800) 487-8758
www.newbeginningsatwaverly.com
New Beginnings is nationally recognized for its treatment of alcohol, cocaine, methamphetamine, and other drug dependencies, providing intensive and individualized treatment programs for adults and adolescents. New Beginnings' program components are designed to help men and women overcome the physical, emotional, spiritual, behavioral, and social aspects of addiction. New Beginnings at Waverly offers intensive individualized treatment programs that include residential and outpatient levels of care. All dimensions of addiction are addressed under the principle that successful treatment demands the efforts of an interdisciplinary team that includes the patient, family, clinicians, and other professionals.

i Earl E. Bakken invented the first wearable cardiac pacemaker in Minneapolis. The company he cofounded, Minneapolis-based Medtronic, continues to be a world leader in medical technology.

HMOS

HEALTHPARTNERS
8100 33th Ave. South, Bloomington
(952) 883-5000
www.healthpartners.com
HealthPartners is a nonprofit, consumer-governed family of health care organizations focused on improving the health of its members, its patients, and the community. HealthPartners provides health care coverage at numerous HealthPartners Clinic sites across the Twin Cities and at Regions Hospital in St. Paul. Additionally, HealthPartners has a contracted network of thousands of providers in the Twin Cities and throughout the nation.

SPECIALTY CLINICS

PHILLIPS EYE INSTITUTE
2215 Park Ave., Minneapolis
(612) 775-8866
www.phillipseyeinstitute.com
Phillips Eye Institute is a premier specialty center devoted exclusively to the diagnosis, treatment, and care of eye disorders and diseases. The institute integrates the latest technologies in eye care with unprecedented staff expertise. Nearly 8,000 patients a year visit the institute for refractive surgery (LASIK), vision rehabilitation, and other inpatient services. The institute also has an established pediatric ophthalmology department.

HEALTH ASSOCIATIONS

ALZHEIMER'S ASSOCIATION
(800) 232-0851
www.alzmndak.org

AMERICAN CANCER SOCIETY OF MINNEAPOLIS
(612) 379-6352
www.cancer.org

AMERICAN DIABETES ASSOCIATION
(763) 593-5333
www.diabetes.org

AMERICAN HEART ASSOCIATION
(952) 835-3300
www.americanheart.org

AMERICAN LUNG ASSOCIATION OF MINNESOTA
(651) 227-8014
www.lungmn.org

AMERICAN PARKINSON'S DISEASE ASSOCIATION
(612) 863-5850 or (888) 302-7762
www.apdaparkinson.org

AMERICAN RED CROSS
(612) 871-7676
www.redcrosstc.org

ARTHRITIS FOUNDATION OF ST. PAUL
(651) 644-4108
www.arthritis.org

UNITED WAY
(612) 340-7400
www.unitedwaytwincities.org

COUNSELING

CATHOLIC CHARITIES OF ST. PAUL AND
MINNEAPOLIS
(612) 664-8500
www.ccspm.org

JEWISH FAMILY AND CHILDREN'S SERVICE
(952) 546-0616
www.jfcsmpls.org

LUTHERAN SOCIAL SERVICES OF MINNE-
SOTA
(651) 642-5990 or (800) 582-5260
www.lssmn.org

MEDIA

The Twin Cities have a strong tradition of engaged citizens, and that's reflected in the breadth and diversity of the local media. Though media in the Twin Cities are in just as much turmoil as anywhere else—with more and more content switching online, and everyone finding it harder and harder to sell the advertisements that have traditionally been the life-blood of journalism—in St. Paul and Minneapolis you have many ways to find out what's going on, and increasingly to contribute to the discussion.

DAILY NEWS

MINNPOST
900 6th Ave. SE, Minneapolis
(612) 455-6953
www.minnpost.com
Founded in 2007, *MinnPost* is—along with the *Twin Cities Daily Planet*—one of two daily online local news publications operating on a nonprofit basis. Whereas the *Daily Planet* operates on the model of citizen journalism, though, *MinnPost* bears the standard for a traditional model of journalism, employing experienced pros (many of whom formerly wrote for one or both of the area's print dailies). Each day *MinnPost* publishes a range of original articles and blog entries on topics of local interest, ranging from politics to business to the arts. Led by Joel Kramer—who was formerly the publisher of the *Star Tribune*—*MinnPost* has quickly become an essential source of local news.

PIONEER PRESS
345 Cedar St., St. Paul
(800) 950-9080
www.twincities.com
The *Pioneer Press*, based in St. Paul and commonly referred to as "the St. Paul paper," is Minnesota's oldest newspaper, founded as the *Minnesota Pioneer* in 1849. Today the paper is one of the Twin Cities' two dailies, providing especially strong coverage of St. Paul but also reporting news from Minneapolis and across the metro area. While

newsroom cuts have (as at the competing *Star Tribune*) reduced the extent of the paper's coverage, it's still the St. Paul paper, a morning ritual for thousands of Minnesotans.

STAR TRIBUNE
425 Portland Ave., Minneapolis
(612) 673-4000
www.startribune.com
Since 1867 the *Star Tribune* (a.k.a. "the Minneapolis paper" or "the Strib") has been a part of the Twin Cities community with a print newspaper that's read by over 300,000 people each day and an online network of services that has become the region's most-consulted online news source. With strong daily coverage of headline news, sports, and entertainment, the *Star Tribune* is Minnesota's biggest newspaper, and you're likely to frequently encounter it whether or not you're one of its tens of thousands of subscribers.

TWIN CITIES DAILY PLANET
2600 East Franklin Ave., Minneapolis
(612) 436-9196
www.tcdailyplanet.net
The *Twin Cities Daily Planet* is an online publication that produces multiple original news articles each day along with articles republished from its 100+ media partners—neighborhood papers, ethnic press, top bloggers. A project of the nonprofit Twin Cities Media Alliance, the *Daily Planet* is built on a citizen-journalism model in which all readers are potential contributors. Hyperlocal in

focus, the *Daily Planet* normally doesn't aspire to cover breaking news or national stories, preferring instead to be the place you'll find stories about local events that often aren't covered anywhere else.

MONTHLY MAGAZINES

METRO
900 South Third St., Minneapolis
(612) 548-3180
www.metromag.com
Just a few years old, *METRO* is a much-needed shot in the arm for local newsstands; it covers about the same mix of lifestyle topics (food, fashion, fun) covered by *Mpls/St. Paul* and *Minnesota Monthly*, but with a tone and focus aimed squarely at urban residents—especially members of Generations X and Y—who listen to The Current instead of KS95.

MINNESOTA MONTHLY
600 U.S. Trust Building,
730 Second Ave. South, Minneapolis
(612) 371-5800 or (800) 933-4398
www.minnesotamonthly.com
Now published by Greenspring Media Group, *Minnesota Monthly* originated as a member premium for Minnesota Public Radio members, and it still leans to the erudite side of glossy monthlies, with long articles about local history and culture in addition to the entertainment and dining coverage that's the staple of its breed.

MPLS/ST. PAUL MAGAZINE
MSP Communications
220 South Sixth St., Suite 500
Minneapolis
(612) 339-7571 or (800) 999-5589
www.mspmag.com
Mpls/St. Paul is the glossiest of local lifestyle magazines, its coverage heavy on shopping, style, travel, and juicy scoops on local celebrities. It's the kind of magazine you'll inevitably find on magazine racks at spas and supermarkets, with cover stories about best neighborhoods, best doctors, best bargains, best schools, and other lifestyle topics.

UTNE READER
12 North 12th St., Suite 400, Minneapolis
(612) 338-5040
www.utne.com
The *Utne Reader* is a nationally distributed monthly magazine that reprints articles from thousands of alternative media sources, providing interesting perspectives on current events, environmental issues, lifestyles, politics, books, and the arts. The magazine hosts a popular online discussion room, Cafe Utne (accessible through the magazine's Web site), with postings about many of the topics the magazine covers.

OTHER PUBLICATIONS

Business

MINNESOTA BUSINESS
900 South 3rd St., Minneapolis
(612) 548-3180
www.minnesotabusiness.com
Published by Tiger Oak Publications—the lifestyle and specialty publisher also responsible for *METRO*—*Minnesota Business* is a monthly magazine profiling local business leaders and reporting on stories of interest to the business community.

TWIN CITIES BUSINESS
MSP Communications
220 South Sixth St., Suite 500, Minneapolis
(612) 339-7571
www.tcbmag.com
Twin Cities Business, published by the same company that publishes *Mpls/St. Paul Magazine,* includes profiles of successful businesspeople and companies in the metropolitan area and information about business education, technology, and other topics of interest to business-oriented readers.

Ethnic and Special Interest Press

ASIAN AMERICAN PRESS
417 University Ave., St. Paul
(651) 224-6570
www.aapress.com
Asian American Press provides coverage of international and local news geared to Asian populations, from local business profiles to politics to festival information to the struggles recent immigrants have adjusting to life in a new country.

BEST OF TIMES
St. Louis Park
(952) 922-6186
www.familytimesinc.com
The sister publication of *Family Times,* the award-winning *Best of Times* (formerly known as *Senior Times*) is geared to the senior community. The paper is full of news about independent living and adjusting to retirement, as well as about senior events and activities around the Twin Cities and surrounding communities.

THE CIRCLE
Minneapolis
(612) 722-3686
www.thecirclenews.org
Approximately 25,000 Native Americans from various tribes live in the Twin Cities, and *The Circle* monthly newspaper is dedicated to publishing news, arts information, community calendars, and resource information for Native Americans in the region.

GENTE DE MINNESOTA
Latino Communications Network
1516 East Lake St., Suite 200, Minneapolis
(612) 729-5900
www.gentedeminnesota.com
Published in Spanish, *Gente de Minnesota* is a weekly newspaper that serves the Hispanic population of the Twin Cities with local, national, and international news, as well as sports, entertainment, and Spanish-language TV program listings.

GOOD AGE
1115 Hennepin Ave. South, Minneapolis
(612) 825-9205
www.mngoodage.com
This senior-oriented monthly publication contains pages of information on health care issues and developments dealing with medical expenses, support groups, and nursing homes, as well as lots of advice and tips on how to stay at your peak physical and mental shape for as long as possible. There's also information on less age-specific things like filing taxes and shopping for a new house.

HMONG TIMES
St. Paul
(651) 224-9395
www.hmongtimes.com
With some 70,000 Hmong residents, the Twin Cities have the largest population of Hmong of any urban area in the world. The community is served by the English-language *Hmong Times,* with news, community information, religion, sports, and agriculture coverage. Published twice a month, the newspaper reaches a wide audience among the community, which began settling in Minnesota after the Vietnam War.

LAVENDER
3715 Chicago Ave. South, Minneapolis
(612) 436-4660
www.lavendermagazine.com
The Twin Cities are home to the third largest gay, lesbian, bisexual, and transgender (GLBT) community in the United States. The best known of the local GLBT publications, *Lavender* contains interviews, features, events calendars, and book and music reviews of interest to GLBT Twin Citians and visitors. Published biweekly, it's carried in record stores, coffee shops, bars, and many other venues throughout the Twin Cities.

i E-Democracy is a nonprofit organization based in the Twin Cities that facilitates online community discussion in neighborhoods from New Zealand to England. E-Democracy runs e-mail listservs for the discussion of issues in St. Paul, Minneapolis, and many individual neighborhoods. The forums sometimes serve as soapboxes for cranky residents, but they're also a good way to take the pulse of your community and connect with your neighborhoods. You'll read about many breaking neighborhood news stories on E-Democracy long before you see them in the papers.

MINNESOTA INDEPENDENT
www.minnesotaindependent.com
A publication of the American Independent News Network, the *Minnesota Independent* is unapologetically left-leaning—but it employs skilled reporters who have broken some big local stories. If you're a liberal, you'll definitely want to read "the Indy." If you're not, you may want to keep an eye on it anyway.

MINNESOTA SPOKESMAN-RECORDER
3744 4th Ave. South, Minneapolis
(612) 827-4021
www.spokesman-recorder.com
For over 75 years, the *Spokesman-Recorder* has been a publication by and for the Twin Cities' African-American community—which also makes it Minnesota's oldest minority-owned business. The weekly paper covers local news and events from a proudly, distinctly, black perspective.

MINNESOTA WOMEN'S PRESS
771 Raymond Ave., St. Paul
(651) 646-3968
www.womenspress.com
When Norma Smith Olson and Kathy Magnuson decided to start a women's publication in the Twin Cities in 1984, they made a deliberate choice to make it a for-profit publication—just to prove their point that women's issues make for important news that will attract readers and advertisers. Still run by Olson and Magnuson today, the monthly *Minnesota Women's Press* continues to provide a fair and open-minded view of women in politics and feminist issues that affect women and men alike, as well as profiles and interviews with political personalities and prominent women in the Twin Cities.

Family Papers
FAMILY TIMES
St. Louis Park
(952) 922-6186
www.familytimesinc.com
Family Times is geared toward the entire family. News about children and senior events alike is listed here, as well as wellness information for everyone in the family. There's an extensive theater section in the back and a decent calendar of events for all members of the family. The people who produce *Family Times* also publish *Baby Times* and, for grandparents, *Grand Times*.

MINNESOTA PARENT
1115 Hennepin Ave. South, Minneapolis
(612) 825-9205
www.mnparent.com
Presenting itself both as a support group and a how-to guide to parenting, *Minnesota Parent* contains information on essentials like enrolling your children in school or helping them survive a divorce. The best part of this magazine, however, is the exhaustive calendar of events in the back, containing times, prices, and contact info for just about every museum and park in town.

Food and Entertainment
CAKEIN15
www.cakein15.com
CakeIn15 (the title is an inside joke) is the project of writer/artist/performer Carl Atiya Swanson and writer/photographer Stacy Schwartz. Swanson and Schwartz publish regular dispatches on the local arts and music scene, typically featuring Schwartz's fantastic photos and Swanson's wry prose. Besides previews and reviews (the latter filed under the heading "What You Missed"), the site features an

event calendar that can be integrated with your Google calendar to keep you up to date on the hippest happenings across the Cities.

CITY PAGES
401 North Third St., Suite 550, Minneapolis
(612) 375-1015
www.citypages.com
Since the 1970s, when it was called Sweet Potato, *City Pages* has been consistently providing great coverage of local politics, music events, and Twin Cities culture in general. The weekly calendar and A-List deliver information on what to do with your spare time, whether it be catching a lecture at the university or seeing a show at your neighborhood coffeehouse, while the interviews with notable Minnesotan artists and musicians are both entertaining and informative. The restaurant reviews are also worth noting, serving up the good and not-so-good news about area eateries. You can find this free weekly—now part of the Village Voice empire of alt-weeklies—all over the Twin Cities, especially in restaurants and bars. The publication also hosts a bursting portfolio of online content; its Gimme Noise blog, run by music editor Andrea Swensson, is an essential source of local music news.

HOWWASTHESHOW.COM
2751 Hennepin Ave. South, Minneapolis
www.howwastheshow.com
HowWasTheShow.com is a labor of love by David de Young, a veteran scenester who, when he's not at his beloved Kings Wine Bar, is everywhere else. The online publication has become one of the top alternative sources for news and reviews of musical and, increasingly, theatrical performances.

L'ETOILE MAGAZINE
http://letoilemagazine.blogspot.com
L'etoile magazine (all lowercase, please) is technically a blog, but *what* a blog! Kate Iverson and a team of conspirators publish a weekly event guide that's a must-read for the out-and-about crowd as well as occasional special features on shopping, parties, and other bodacious subjects.

i The people behind *l'etoile magazine* are also responsible for LOL OMG! (http://lol-omg-blog.blogspot.com), a blog that advertises "gossip from the seedy underbelly of the Twin Cities social media circuit," but actually traffics in nice gossip of the most affectionate, most amusing kind. If you are on Twitter and Facebook daily, you'll enjoy LOL OMG!

MNARTISTS.ORG
1750 Hennepin Ave., Minneapolis
(612) 375-7611
www.mnartists.org
Funded by the McKnight Foundation and hosted by the Walker Art Center, mnartists.org is a hub of information and connection for artists in all disciplines across the state. Thousands of artists have created pages on the site with portfolios of their work for you to explore; editor Susannah Schouweiler (formerly of the *Hungry Mind Review*) also publishes some of the best arts writing in the state by top local critics and artists. The site's event calendar is also invaluable for arthounds.

MPLSART.COM
www.mplsart.com
If your question is, "what shows are opening in galleries this weekend?" the quickest way to get an answer is to visit this site, maintained by designer/curator Emma Berg and ROBOTlove proprietor Kristoffer Knutson.

MORE COWBELL
www.morecowbell.net
More Cowbell is one of several local music blogs keeping the rabid community of music fans up to the moment on what's happening, to or with whom, and when. Follow @cowbell on Twitter to get near-instantaneous announcements about upcoming shows and late-breaking music news. To further sate your appetite for music news, also see: Gimme Noise (http://blogs.citypages.com/gimmenoise; mentioned above as part of *City Pages*), CakeIn15 (www.cakein15.com; see listing on p. 302), Switchblade Comb (www.switchbladecomb.com), Reviler (www.reviler.org), MFR

(search for "MFR blog," because the blog's full URL is not suitable for publication in this guide), We Heart Music (http://weheartmusic.vox.com), Perfect Porridge (www.perfectporridge.com), and Brit Rock at the Top (http://britishrockisalwaystop.blogspot.com).

RAIN TAXI REVIEW OF BOOKS
P.O. Box 3840, Minneapolis 55403
www.raintaxi.com
Noted national poetry blogger Ron Silliman has written that "there is more in the way of good material in a single issue of *Rain Taxi* than you will find in a year's worth of the *New York Times Book Review*." Distributed nationally, this free quarterly publication contains tons of book reviews (all genres) as well as interviews with established and up-and-coming authors from around the world.

SECRETS OF THE CITY
P.O. Box 3690, Minneapolis, 55403
(651) 356-8714
www.secretsofthecity.com
Secrets of the City is what's emerged from the dust settling in the wake of *The Rake*, a gloriously erudite free monthly that ceased publication in 2008. The publication takes its name from *The Rake*'s popular event-recommendation guide, which continues to be updated daily, and now also includes MNspeak, a blog of local news tidbits that inevitably spark lengthy discussions among commenters.

THE ONION
www.theonion.com
www.theavclub.com/twincities
You get a lot when you pick up a free copy of *The Onion*. There are the news parodies, which are the same in *Onions* across the country. Then, inside, you get an arts and entertainment section called "The A.V. Club," which contains both national entertainment news (also the same across the country) and local coverage produced in Minneapolis. The publication's listings are excellent, its editorial coverage sharp and humorous. The local Web site (see second URL above) is a good place to go when you're trying to figure out what to do with your night—or, possibly, with your life.

VITA.MN
www.vita.mn
Vita.mn is a free weekly publication and Web site published by the *Star Tribune*, highlighting local events and developments in entertainment and the arts. Online visitors are invited to actively contribute to the publication, scoring "karma points" for contributing comments and entries to lists that often end up in the print publication. Along with *City Pages*, *Vita.mn* is one of the two top sources for news and reviews about goings-on in the local entertainment scene and beyond.

Health, Religion, and Support Publications

THE EDGE MAGAZINE
(763) 433-9291
www.soulofthecities.net
Falling somewhere between a New Age and Christian publication, *The Edge* contains articles about miracles and biblical prophesies and articles about how they've been fulfilled—reincarnation, faith healing, and archaeological excavations that may or may not prove the existence of God. The magazine is carried at most bookstores in the Twin Cities.

ESSENTIAL WELLNESS
4270 Honey Tree Pass, Danbury, WI
(715) 259-3047
www.esswellness.com
This monthly paper (oddly, edited in Danbury, Wisconsin, otherwise best known as home of the Hole in the Wall Casino) is an excellent source of information about alternative healing techniques, breakthroughs in homeopathic and alternative medicines, and features written by practitioners of alternative medicine. There's information on where to find alternative and homeopathic doctors and treatment centers in the Twin Cities area, from massage therapy to herbal vendors.

FATE MAGAZINE
P.O. Box 460, Lakeville 55044
(952) 431-2050
www.fatemag.com

FATE is a monthly magazine that features accounts of the strange and unknown, from psychics, spiritualists, and "fringe science" to authoritative UFO and paranormal investigations.

NEIGHBORHOOD FREE PUBLICATIONS

Almost every neighborhood in the Twin Cities has a free paper that can be found in neighborhood convenience stores or appears on your doorstep. These papers cover local news, school district announcements, flea market schedules, city council efforts on the part of the district in question, and sometimes news that affects the entire city. Here are just a few of the neighborhood papers and the areas they cover:

Downtown Journal—downtown Minneapolis

Northeaster—northeast Minneapolis

Southwest Journal—southwest Minneapolis

Southeast Angle—southeast Minneapolis

The Villager—St. Paul, Highland Park area

The Riverview Times—Harriet Island; St. Paul riverside community

Midway/Como Monitor—St. Paul Como Park and Midway areas

Grand Gazette—St. Paul Summit Hill/Grand Avenue area

Seward Profile—Minneapolis, Seward/Cedar-Riverside/Cooper/North Longfellow neighborhoods

RADIO STATIONS

AM Stations

KFAN–1130 AM
1600 Utica Ave. South, Suite 400,
St. Louis Park
(651) 989-1130
www.kfan.com

KFAN is the Twin Cities sports radio leader. The Fan features interesting sports talk and occasional discussions about current affairs. The talk personalities on KFAN are the station's strength. Morning drive host Dan Cole, "the Common Man," is a seasoned veteran of local talk, who offers an offbeat look at various topics. The Fan is also the radio home of the Minnesota Timberwolves basketball games.

i Stations showcasing the Twin Cities' local music scene include the University of Minnesota's Radio K (770 AM and 106.5/100.7 FM) and MPR's The Current (89.3 FM).

KKMS–980 AM
2110 Cliff Rd., Eagan
(651) 405-8800
www.kkms.com

KKMS is a Christian talk radio station owned by Salem Communications. It features the *Salem Radio Network* and *Family News in Focus*.

KSTP–1500 AM
3415 University Ave., St. Paul
(651) 646-TALK
www.am1500.com

KSTP is one of many Hubbard Broadcasting Inc. media stations in the Twin Cities. KSTP specializes in sports and political talk radio. The station emphasizes local personalities such as Joe Soucheray, Bob Davis, and Matt Thomas but also carries some national shows such as Paul Harvey's.

KTIS–900 AM/98.5 FM
3003 Snelling Ave. North, Roseville
(651) 631-5000
http://ktis.nwc.edu

KTIS is a Christian music and talk station, with frequencies on the AM (900) and FM (98.5) dials.

KUOM–770 AM/106.5 AND 100.7 FM
University of Minnesota, 610 Rarig Center,
330 21st Ave. South, Minneapolis
(612) 625-3500
www.radiok.org

The Twin Cities' largest and most popular college radio station is KUOM or, as it is known locally,

Radio K. Radio K plays alternative, techno, ska, hip-hop, and much more. It features music from independent labels and local music as well as major label music. Radio K has the most diverse playlist in the Twin Cities. AM radio broadcasts stop at sundown, but the FM stations broadcast 24 hours a day on weekends. Radio K is also available 24/7 online.

KYCR–1570 AM
2110 Cliff Rd., Eagan
(651) 405-8800
www.kycr.com
KYCR features talk shows with a focus on business and the economy.

WCCO–830 AM
625 Second Ave. South, Minneapolis
(612) 370-0611
www.wccoradio.com
WCCO Radio was, until the 1990s, the undisputed leader in news and talk. In the past decade, ratings have slid as younger listeners turn their dials elsewhere, yet WCCO remains a vital force on Twin Cities radio. The station continues as the broadcast home of Minnesota Twins baseball as well as University of Minnesota Golden Gophers football and basketball.

FM Stations

KBEM–88.5 FM
1555 James Ave. North, Minneapolis
(612) 668-1735
www.jazz88fm.com
Jazz 88 focuses on light jazz, fusion, classic jazz, and cool jazz but also programs that include exotica, Latin, and bluegrass music. The station is operated by students attending Minneapolis Public Schools.

KCMP–89.3 FM
480 Cedar St., St. Paul
(651) 290-1212
http://minnesota.publicradio.org
KCMP, more popularly known as The Current, debuted in 2005, driving up the number of Twin

Cities Minnesota Public Radio stations to three. The Current plays largely indie rock, blessedly commercial-free and with a welcome emphasis on local artists. Nitpicking about The Current's playlists is a favorite pastime among local music geeks, but nonetheless the station has become a pillar of the music scene and a reliably good pick on the radio dial—not many cities have such forward-thinking public radio programmers.

KDWB–101.3 FM
1600 Utica Ave. South, St. Louis Park
(651) 989-KDWB
www.kdwb.com
Since the days of sock hops, KDWB has been the Twin Cities' leading (and sometimes only) top-40 station. It's the station of choice for most teens who actually bother listening to the radio, and a guilty pleasure for everyone else. The station sponsors many events, including a December "Jingle Ball" that packs the Xcel Energy Center with top hitmakers and reliably sells out.

KHTC–96.3 FM
5300 Edina Industrial Blvd., Edina
(952) 842-7200
www.b96online.com
KHTC was "Jammin' B96," a hip-hop station, until all of a sudden in early 2010 Miley Cyrus's "Party in the U.S.A." announced that a change had come and that KDWB was no longer the only game in town for mainstream top-40 radio. What's special about the station that's become "96.3 NOW"? It plays "the most hit music." Okay, then.

KFAI–90.3/106.7 FM
1808 Riverside Ave., Minneapolis
(612) 341-3144
www.kfai.org
Since 1978 the nonprofit KFAI has served the Twin Cities' many communities with an extremely wide array of programming. KFAI programming is remarkably diverse. Prominent features of the program schedule are arts, public affairs, world music, community affairs, jazz, and rock. In addition, KFAI hosts several weekly bilingual programs to serve the local immigrant communities.

KFAI features Khmer, Hmong, Somali, Eritrean, and Ethiopian programs. The station broadcasts on 90.3 in Minneapolis and the western suburbs and on 106.7 in St. Paul and the eastern suburbs.

ℹ️ KFAI offers many volunteer opportunities for locals looking to get their feet wet in radio, and the training the station offers is no joke: Several DJs and producers have made the jump from KFAI to Minnesota Public Radio stations.

KMOJ–89.9 FM
1422 West Lake St., Minneapolis
(612) 377-0594
www.kmojfm.com
KMOJ calls itself "the people's station," and that moniker is hard to argue with. The nonprofit community station, founded in north Minneapolis and now based in Uptown, is largely run and staffed by African-Americans, and showcases a range of black music (R&B, soul, jazz, blues, reggae) spanning several decades. The station also serves as an important information source and discussion forum for the metro area's black community.

KNOW–91.1 FM
45 East 7th St., St. Paul
(651) 290-1212
www.mpr.org
KNOW is the Twin Cities' Minnesota Public Radio news, information, and talk station. The programming consists of a mix of local, nationally syndicated, NPR, and BBC broadcasts.

KQQL–107.9 FM
1600 Utica Ave. South, St. Louis Park
(651) 989-2020
www.kool108.com
KOOL 108 has been the Twin Cities' "oldies" station for years, though its programming has changed many times as a result of both changes in its ownership and an evolving idea of what exactly counts as an "oldie." Currently the station showcases the pop music of the '60s, '70s, and '80s.

KQRS–92.5 FM
2000 SE Elm St., Minneapolis
(612) 989-7625
www.kqrs.com
"KQ 92" is the Twin Cities' classic rock station. When you pass a construction site and hear Pink Floyd or Led Zep blasting from a boom box, chances are it's tuned to KQRS. The station has a number of outspoken on-air personalities, most notably morning show host Tom Barnard, who not infrequently get themselves into hot water with people who take offense at their red-meat views.

KSJN–99.5 FM
45 East Seventh St., St. Paul
(612) 290-1212
www.mpr.org
KSJN is Minnesota Public Radio's Twin Cities classical music station.

KSTP–94.5 FM
3415 University Ave., St. Paul
(651) 989-5795
www.ks95.com
KS95 advertises the station's variety, though they don't mean the kind of variety you'll find on KFAI (where a Hmong-language program might follow a bluegrass show), they mean the kind of variety that embraces both Huey Lewis and Lady Gaga. It's the station of choice at relatively hip dentists' offices across the metro area.

KTCZ–97.1 FM
1600 Utica Ave. South, St. Louis Park
(651) 989-9797
www.cities97.com
Cities 97 owns the market between WLTE's light rock and The Current's indie rock, playing adult contemporary music from artists such as John Mayer, Damien Rice, Wilco, and Death Cab for Cutie.

KXXR–93.7 FM
2000 SE Elm St., Minneapolis
(612) 617-4000
www.93X.com

93X is the station for fans of acts like Offspring, Korn, Metallica, and Megadeath. The station serves up nonstop new metal and industrial music. The station's attitude is epitomized by the very name of its "Half Assed Morning Show," which features discussions of news items like "manly toothpaste" and "man tries to buy urine."

MYTALK 107.1 FM
3415 University Ave., Minneapolis
(651) 642-4107
www.mytalk1071.com

107.1 seeks to create the on-air equivalent of a gossipy beauty salon, with hosts dishing the dirt about everything from their lazy husbands to Tiger Woods to the new musical opening at the Orpheum. The faces of drivetime hosts Lori and Julia are unavoidable fixtures on purple billboards across the Twin Cities, and they dote on a range of colorful on-air guests, from *METRO's* rakish Scott Schneweis to Fox 9's smooth Jason Matheson to *Vita.mn's* droll Christian-Philipe Quilici.

WLKX–95.9 FM/KBGY–107.5 FM
15226 West Freeway Dr., Forest Lake
(651) 464-6796
www.spirit.fm

WLKX/KBGY is a Twin Cities adult contemporary Christian channel. WLKX reaches the Metro, northern suburbs, and western Wisconsin; KBGY reaches the Metro, southern suburbs, and a wide area of southeastern Minnesota.

WLTE–102.9 FM
625 Second Ave. South, Suite 300,
Minneapolis
(612) 370-0611
www.wlte.com

NSFW? Not WLTE, a light-rock station that calls itself "your station at work" and advertises "the most music for your workday." (They broadcast after hours too, in case you're bringing work home with you—or want to pretend you and your lover are having a forbidden copy-room fling.)

Television Stations

TPT2–CHANNEL 2
172 East Fourth St., St. Paul
(651) 222-1717
www.tpt.org

TPT is the Twin Cities' public television affiliate, where you'll find national programs like *Sesame Street* and *Frontline* as well as locally produced shows like the Friday-night news program *Almanac*.

WCCO–CHANNEL 4
90 South 11th St., Minneapolis
(612) 339-4444
www.wcco.com

The Twin Cities' CBS affiliate WCCO has a long history in television and radio in the Twin Cities. In fact, the acronym, WCCO, stands for Washburn and Crosby Company, the former name of the Twin Cities–based international corporation, General Mills.

WCCO promotes its newscasters as "the Home Town Team," and emphasizes several other programs and initiatives for the community.

KSTP–CHANNEL 5
3415 University Ave., St. Paul
(651) 646-5555
www.kstp.com

ABC-affiliated KSTP is recognized locally and nationally as an innovator in the television industry. KSTP was the first television station in the Twin Cities, signing on the air on April 27, 1948. It also was the first color television station and the first in the nation to broadcast daily newscasts.

News is important to KSTP and its "Eyewitness News Team." KSTP was a local pioneer in investigative journalism and weather reporting. It is also the only affiliated station in the Twin Cities that remains under local ownership, which is reflected in the station's news and programming.

FOX 9
11358 Viking Dr., Eden Prairie
(952) 944-9999
www.myfoxtwincities.com

FOX 9 is the Twin Cities' Fox affiliate. *Fox News Sunday* is the network's competition against such Sunday news institutions as NBC's *Meet the Press* and CBS's *Face the Nation*. The station carries plenty of Twin Cities sports. NFL football and Major League Baseball are featured prominently on the station. In addition, the Twin Cities NHL team, the Wild, is broadcast locally on Fox and also UPN's WFTC.

KARE-CHANNEL 11
8811 Olson Memorial Hwy., Minneapolis
(763) 546-1111
www.kare11.com
KARE is the Twin Cities home of NBC. Besides NBC programming, it consistently has the highest-rated news broadcasts at 6 p.m. and 10 p.m. KARE has created local initiatives such as "11 Who KARE," which recognizes citizens who have made significant contributions for the betterment of the Twin Cities.

WUCW-CHANNEL 23
1640 Como Ave., St. Paul
(651) 646-2300
www.thecwtc.com
WUCW, which changed its call letters from KMWB in 2006, is the Twin Cities CW network affiliate. WUCW airs CW programs, such as America's Next Top Model and Smallville, plus syndicated programming, movies, and infomercials. The *Jerry Springer Show* calls WUCW its Twin Cities home. There are also plenty of reruns of recent sitcoms to sate the viewing appetite of Twin Citians.

MY29 WFTC
11358 Viking Dr., Eden Prairie
(952) 944-9999
www.my29tv.com
After many years as an independent, WFTC is now the local affiliate of MyNetworkTV, a syndication service owned by Fox. The station primarily runs movies and sitcom reruns, with a few original programs.

KPXM-CHANNEL 41
601 Clearwater Park Rd.,
West Palm Beach, FL
(561) 682-4206
www.ionline.tv
KPXM is part of the Ion Television Network, with a steady diet of reruns and infomercials. The Florida-owned affiliate currently broadcasts from a tower in St. Cloud, though it's due to move to a tower in Shoreview that will improve metro-area reception.

KSTC-CHANNEL 45
3415 University Ave., St. Paul
(651) 645-4500
www.kstc45.com
KSTC, a sister station to KSTP but not an ABC affiliate, primarily shows rerun sitcoms and dramas, such as *Scrubs, The Shield,* and *24.*

MTN-CHANNELS 16, 17, 75
(MINNEAPOLIS)
125 SE Main St., Minneapolis
(612) 331-8575
MTN (Minneapolis Television Network) is Minneapolis's beloved community-access network, programming a riotously diverse lineup including children's programming (*Toad and Turtle: I Love to Read*), ethnic news (*Somali Voice TV*), and variety shows like *Drinking With Ian. MPLS.TV* has become the Twin Cities' *Saturday Night Live,* and the indescribable *Freaky Deeky* has earned a cult following. MTN also offers extensive classes and other opportunities to get involved.

SPNN-CHANNELS 14, 15, 16, 19 (ST. PAUL)
375 Jackson St., St. Paul
(651) 224-5153
SPNN stands for "St. Paul Neighborhood Network": it's the Capital City's community-access network, broadcasting everything from religious programming to senior-oriented cooking shows to technical-college basketball games. The non-profit organization has a great deal of youth involvement and runs a wide range of training programs for local residents who want to learn the ropes of broadcast media.

INDEX

INSIDERS' GUIDE®

The acclaimed travel series that has sold more than 2 million copies!

Pointing You in the Right Direction

Santa Barbara
Including Channel Islands
National Park

Glacier National Park

Columbus

INSIDERS'
guide®

Columbus

North Carolina's Outer Banks

The Twin Cities

Pittsburgh

Savannah and Hilton Head

Now with a fresh new look!

Written by locals and true insiders, each guide is packed with information about places to stay, restaurants, shopping, attractions, fun things for the kids, day trips, relocation tips, and local history. For over twenty years, travelers have relied on *Insiders' Guides* for practical and personal travel and relocation information.

To order call **800-243-0495**
or visit www.InsidersGuides.com